QUICKBOOKS® ONLINE 2023
Complete

QUICKBOOKS® ONLINE
2023
Complete

Unlock Your Bookkeeping Potential

COMPREHENSIVE • REAL-WORLD EXAMPLES • HANDS-ON EXERCISES

Alicia Katz Pollock, MAT

Copyrighted Material

QuickBooks Online Complete 2023

Copyright © 2023 by Questiva Consultants. All Rights Reserved.
Published by Questiva Consultants

No part of this publication may be reproduced, stored in a retrieval system or transmitted, in any form or by any means—electronic, mechanical, photocopying, recording or otherwise—without prior written permission from the publisher, except for the inclusion of brief quotations in a review.

For information about this title, or to order this and related other books and/or electronic media, contact the publisher:

Questiva Consultants
1501 Dry Creek Road, San Jose, CA 95125
Phone: 408 440 4182
Fax: 408 351 0473
www.questivaconsultants.com
info@questivaconsultants.com

ISBN: 978-1-942417-33-0

Printed in the United States of America

Author & editor of this edition: Alicia Katz Pollock
Contributing editor: Ellen Orr
Cover and Interior design: Kathryn Lloyd
Original concept: Douglas Sleeter

Disclaimer: This material is intended as a learning aid for QuickBooks Online software users. Under no circumstances shall the author or publisher be liable for any damages, including any lost profits, lost data or other indirect damages arising out of anything written in this document or expressed directly or indirectly by the author or publisher.

Questiva Consultants is the publisher and supplier of QuickBooks Accounting Textbooks to students, community colleges, business/trade schools and universities. The structural elements of this textbook were originally developed by The Sleeter Group.

Questiva Consultants also publishes a companion book to QuickBooks Online Complete 2023, titled Instructor's Manual for QuickBooks Online Complete 2023; ISBN: 978-1-942417-34-7. The Instructor's Manual is available only to the qualified instructors of QuickBooks. To obtain a complimentary PDF version of the Instructor's Manual, please visit www.questivaconsultants.com.

Trademarks: Intuit, the Intuit logo, QuickBooks, QuickBooks Pro, QuickBase, Quicken, TurboTax, ProSeries, ProConnect Tax Online, Lacerte, EasyStep, and QuickZoom, among others, are registered trademarks and/or registered service marks of Intuit Inc. in the United States and other countries. QuickBooks ProAdvisor is a trademark and/or service mark of Intuit Inc. in the United States and other countries. Other parties' trademarks or service marks are the property of their respective owners and should be treated as such.

TABLE OF CONTENTS

PREFACE xix
   Acknowledgments xix
   Using This Book xix
   About the Exercises xx
      Chapter Lessons: Craig's Design and Landscaping Services xx
      Apply Your Knowledge end-of-chapter exercises: Imagine Photography xx
      Case Study Scenario: YinYang Graphic Design xxi
   QuickBooks Online Student Trial Accounts xxi
   If You Aren't In a Classroom Setting xxi
      Option 1: A 30-day QBO Plus Trial xxii
      Option 2: A Practice QBOA Profile xxii
   Supplemental Files xxii
   Instructor Resources xxiii
   Certification xxiii
   Why Doesn't This Book Exactly Match My File? xxiv

CHAPTER 1 INTRODUCING QUICKBOOKS ONLINE 1
   Topics 1
   The QuickBooks Online Ecosystem 1
      QuickBooks Online vs. QuickBooks Desktop 1
      Third-party Apps 2
      QuickBooks Online Versions 2
      QuickBooks Online for Accountants 3
   Accounting 101 3
      Accounting's Focus 3
      The General Ledger 4
      Account Types and Financial Reports 4
      Double-Entry Accounting 5
      Accounting Behind the Scenes 5
      Accounting Basis: Cash or Accrual? 6
   Using a Browser to Access QBO 7
      Setting Up Your Chrome Browser 7
      Working in Multiple Tabs 9
      Opening Multiple Files 10
   Working with QuickBooks Online Files 10
      Opening the QuickBooks Online Sample File, Craig's Landscaping 10
      Switching Between Other QuickBooks Online Data Files 11

  Creating New Company Files 12
  Logging Out of QuickBooks Online Files 12
  QuickBooks Online Updates and New Features 12
  Backing Up QBO Files 12
 QuickBooks Online's Interface 13
  Dashboard 14
  The Left Navigation Bar 17
  Centers 17
  The Money Bar 18
  The Bottom Bar 19
  Dynamic Save Buttons 19
  Using the Search 20
  The Gear 20
  Shortcuts 21
 Entering Transactions in QuickBooks Online 22
  The +New Button for Forms 22
  Lists 24
  Accounts 25
  Registers 26
  Products and Services 27
 QuickBooks Online Help 29
  Support Resources 29
  Certified QuickBooks Online ProAdvisors 29
 Review Questions 30
  Comprehension Questions 30
  Multiple Choice 30
  Completion Statements 31
 Introduction—Apply Your Knowledge 31
 Prepare for Chapter 2: Set Up Your Practice Company 32
  Creating your Student User Account 32
  Setting up Imagine Photography 32
  Setting up the Chart of Accounts 33

CHAPTER 2   CUSTOMIZING QUICKBOOKS ONLINE 35

 Topics 35
 Starting a New QuickBooks Online Company 35
  Converting a QuickBooks Desktop File 35
  Starting From Scratch 36
 Configuring Account and Settings 38
  Company Settings 38
  Advanced Settings 41
 Setting Up the Chart of Accounts 45
  Account Types 46
  Activating Account Numbers 46

Adding Accounts	46
Modifying Accounts	48
Adding Sub-accounts	49
Removing Accounts from the Chart of Accounts	51
Seeing All Accounts	54
Sorting the Account List	55
Printing the Chart of Accounts	56
Setting Up Products and Services	56
Product and Service Categories	57
Products and Services Types	57
Collecting Sales Tax on Products and Services	67
Customizing Lists	67
The Terms List	67
Payment Methods	69
Implementing Custom Fields	70
Activating Class Tracking	71
Tagging	72
Setting Up Sales Tax	73
Collecting Sales Tax	73
Setting up Sales Tax Defaults	76
Applying Sales Tax on Forms	76
Customizing Sales Forms	78
Adding Users and Passwords	83
Setting Up Users in the Company File	84
Accountant Users	87
Review Questions	87
Comprehension Questions	87
Multiple Choice	87
Completion Statements	89
Customizing QuickBooks Online—Apply Your Knowledge	90

CHAPTER 3   THE SALES PROCESS 97

Topics	97
Configuring the Sales Settings	97
Tracking Company Sales	100
Cash vs. Credit Customers	100
Sales Receipts	101
Estimates	102
Invoices	102
Payments	103
Deposits	104
Setting Up Customers	104
Sub-customers	108
Inactivating Customers	109

Merging Customers 110
Recording Sales 111
   Entering Sales Receipts 111
   Creating Invoices 115
   Open Invoices Report 121
Receiving Payments from Customers 122
   Receiving Payments by Check 122
   Receiving Payments by Credit Card or ACH 123
   Handling Partial Payments 125
   Handling Payments Against Multiple Invoices 126
   What if the Payment Doesn't Match the Invoice? 127
Making Bank Deposits 128
   Undeposited Funds and Payments to Deposit 129
   Depositing Checks and Cash 130
   Depositing Credit Card Payments 135
   Viewing Deposits in the Register 137
Running Accounts Receivable Reports 138
   Using the Invoices Center 138
   Viewing the Invoice History 139
   The Accounts Receivable Aging Summary 140
Review Questions 141
   Comprehension Questions 141
   Multiple Choice 141
   Completion Statements 143
The Sales Process—Apply Your Knowledge 144

CHAPTER 4 MANAGING EXPENSES 151
Topics 151
Configuring the Expenses Settings 152
Tracking Company Expenses 153
   The Expenses Center 153
   Using the Vendors Center 154
   Cash and Credit Vendors 155
   Recording Transactions 156
Setting up Vendors 157
   Adding New Vendors 157
   Inactivating Vendors 159
   Merging Vendors 161
Tracking Job Costs 161
Entering Bills 162
   Vendor Invoices 163
   Bills with Products and Job Costing 164
   Attaching Documents 167
   The Unpaid Bills Detail Report 167

Paying Bills . . . 168
   Mark as Paid . . . 168
   Schedule Payments Online . . . 172
Using Credit Cards . . . 172
   Entering Credit Card Charges . . . 172
   Paying the Credit Card Balance . . . 174
Writing Checks . . . 176
   Applying a Check to an Unpaid Bill . . . 178
   Printing Checks . . . 178
Tracking Petty Cash . . . 182
The Contractors Center . . . 183
   Paying Contractors . . . 183
   Managing Contractors . . . 184
Running Accounts Payable Reports . . . 185
   The A/P Aging Summary Report . . . 185
   Bills and Applied Payments Report . . . 186
   Vendor Balance Detail . . . 187
   Transaction List by Vendor . . . 187
Review Questions . . . 188
   Comprehension Questions . . . 188
   Multiple Choice . . . 188
   Completion Statements . . . 190
Managing Expenses—Apply Your Knowledge . . . 190

CHAPTER 5 ADVANCED TRANSACTIONS . . . 197

Topics . . . 197
Controlling the Automation . . . 198
Managing Transactions . . . 199
   Editing Transactions . . . 199
   Copying Transactions . . . 199
   Voiding and Deleting Transactions . . . 200
   The Audit Log . . . 202
   Creating Recurring Transactions . . . 203
Using Journal Entries . . . 206
Advanced Accounts Receivable Workflows . . . 207
   Recording and Applying Credit Memos . . . 207
   Creating Customer Refunds . . . 211
   Handling Bounced Checks . . . 214
   Writing Off Bad Debts . . . 220
   Customer Tools . . . 224
Advanced Accounts Payable Workflows . . . 232
   Recording and Applying Vendor Credits . . . 232
   Creating Vendor Refunds . . . 236
   What To Do If Your Check Bounces . . . 238

Managing Loans 239
Paying Sales Tax 243
Review Questions 247
Comprehension Questions 247
Multiple Choice 247
Completion Statements 249
Advanced Transactions—Apply Your Knowledge 250

CHAPTER 6   BANKING AND RECONCILIATION 255
Topics 255
Transfer Funds Between Accounts 255
The Banking Feed 256
Opening the Sample File 257
Toggling Between Banking Feed Views 257
Connecting Your Bank and Credit Cards 258
The Banking Feed Interface 259
Using the Banking Feed for Data Entry 260
Matched and Partially-matched Transactions 261
Recognized Matches 262
Uncategorized Transactions 263
Entering Transfers 264
Entering Refunds 264
Batch Actions 265
Splitting a Transaction 266
Using Find Match 267
Excluding Transactions 269
Matching Credit Card Payments 269
Creating Rules 270
Viewing the Bank Register 272
When NOT to use the Banking Feed 272
Duplicating Sales Transactions 272
Purchasing Products and Services 273
The Receipts Center 273
Importing Transactions Downloaded from Your Bank 274
Reconciling Bank Accounts 276
How to Reconcile 276
Finding Errors During Bank Reconciliation 283
Bank Reconciliation Reports 286
Reconciling Credit Card Accounts 287
Review Questions 288
Comprehension Questions 288
Multiple Choice 288
Completion Statements 290
Banking and Reconciliations—Apply Your Knowledge 290

Chapter 7 Reports 295
Topics 295
Finding Transactions 296
Filtering the Register 296
Using Advanced Search 297
Cash vs. Accrual Reporting 299
Types of Reports 299
The Reports Center 300
Accounting Reports 301
Profit & Loss Statement 301
Balance Sheet 308
Statement of Cash Flows 309
General Ledger 310
Trial Balance 311
Business Management Reports 313
QuickReports 313
Customer Contact List 314
Vendor Contact List 314
Product/Service List 315
The Business Snapshot 317
Tag Reports 318
Accounts Receivable and Accounts Payable Reports 320
Collections Report 320
Invoices and Received Payments Report 321
Deposit Detail Report 322
Vendor Balance Detail Report 322
Creating Sales Reports 323
Transaction List by Customer Report 323
Income by Customer Summary Report 323
Sales by Product/Service Summary Report 324
Customizing Reports 325
The Report Header 325
The Customize Button 326
Saving Reports 330
Viewing Custom Reports 331
Emailing Customized Reports on a Schedule 331
Printing Reports 332
Exporting Reports to Spreadsheets 334
Review Questions 335
Comprehension Questions 335
Multiple Choice 336
Completion Statements 338
Reports—Apply Your Knowledge 338

Chapter 8 CASE STUDY: YINYANG GRAPHIC DESIGN ... 341
Description of Company ... 341
Goals ... 341
Create the Company File ... 341
Overview ... 342
YinYang Graphic Design Case Study ... 343
1. Account and Settings ... 343
2. Sales Tax ... 345
3. Chart of Accounts ... 345
4. Classes and Tags ... 346
5. Products and Services ... 346
6. Custom Form Styles ... 347
7. Business Transactions ... 348
8. Import the Banking Feed ... 353
9. Reconcile the Checking Account ... 354
10. Prepare the Reports ... 355
11. Complete the Analysis Questions ... 356

Chapter 9 PROJECTS AND JOB COSTING ... 357
Topics ... 357
Creating and Using Estimates ... 358
Creating Invoices from Estimates ... 359
Using Progress Invoicing ... 361
Creating Purchase Orders from Estimates ... 365
Tracking Estimates ... 366
Taking Customer Deposits on Work to Be Performed ... 368
Setting Up Prepayments and Deposits ... 368
Receiving the Customer Prepayment ... 370
Applying the Deposit to the Customer's Invoice ... 371
Managing Vendor Deposits ... 373
Vendor Refunds When You Used Accounts Payable ... 374
Passing Through Billable Expenses ... 376
The Billable Expense Workflow ... 377
Troubleshooting Billable Expenses ... 380
Using Two-Sided Items ... 381
Tracking Custom Orders ... 381
Using Services to Track Subcontracted Labor ... 382
Entering Time on a Project ... 384
Using the Projects Center ... 387
Creating a Project ... 387
Adding Transactions ... 390
Labor Costing ... 390
Creating Project Reports ... 394
Running Job Costing Reports ... 395

Customer Profitability 395
Unbilled Charges Report 395
Unbilled Time Report 395
Time Activities by Employee Detail Report 396
Estimate vs. Actuals 397
Additional Job Costing Features 397
Tracking Vehicle Mileage 397
Applying Price Rules 401
Review Questions 405
Comprehension Questions 405
Multiple Choice 405
Completion Statements 407
Projects and Job Costing—Apply Your Knowledge 407

CHAPTER 10 INVENTORY 413

Topics 413
Do You REALLY Need to Track Inventory? 413
Managing Inventory 414
Tracking Inventory with QuickBooks Online 415
Activating the Inventory Function 416
Setting up Inventory Products 417
Calculating FIFO Inventory 417
Buying and Selling Inventory Products 418
Using Purchase Orders 418
Selling Inventory Products 423
Handling Inventory Issues 425
Vendor Refunds for Inventory Items 425
Handling Overshipments 425
Handling Vendor Overcharges 426
Adjusting Inventory 427
Adjusting the Quantity of Inventory on Hand 428
Adjusting the Value of Inventory 429
Inventory Reports 429
Inventory Product QuickReport 430
Purchases by Product/Service Detail Report 430
Inventory Stock Status Report 431
Physical Inventory Worksheet 432
Inventory Valuation Summary 433
Inventory Valuation Detail Report 434
Profit and Loss Report by Product/Service 434
Review Questions 435
Comprehension Questions 435
Multiple Choice 435
Completion Statements 438
Inventory—Apply Your Knowledge 438

Chapter 11 Adjustments and Year-End Procedures 441
Topics 441
Creating Adjustments 441
  Making Journal Entries 441
  Zero-Dollar Checks and Sales Receipts 444
Tracking Depreciation of Fixed Assets 448
  Setting Up the Fixed Asset Accounts 448
  Calculating and Recording Depreciation 449
Processing 1099s 451
  Documenting Vendor Eligibility 452
  The Print/E-file 1099 Forms Wizard 453
Managing Equity 456
  Equity for Sole Proprietorships 457
  Equity for LLCs and Partnerships 459
  Equity for S-Corps 459
Closing the Books 460
  Closing the Accounting Period 460
  Closing Equity Accounts at the End of the Fiscal Year 461
Setting the Closing Date 463
Review Questions 465
  Comprehension Questions 465
  Multiple Choice 465
  Completion Statements 467
Adjustments and Year-End Procedures—Apply Your Knowledge 467

Chapter 12 Advanced Company Setup 471
Topics 471
Migrating an Existing QuickBooks Desktop file to QuickBooks Online 471
Starting a New QuickBooks Online File From Scratch for an Existing Company . . 472
  Step 1: Choosing a Start Date 473
  Step 2: Create the Company Subscription and Customize the Settings 473
  Step 3: Setting Up the Chart of Accounts and Other Lists 474
  Step 4: Entering Opening Balances 474
  Step 5: Entering Open Transactions 479
  Step 6: Entering Year-to-Date Income and Expenses 481
  Step 7: Adjusting Sales Tax Payable 481
  Step 8: Adjusting Inventory and Setting Up Fixed Assets 482
  Step 9: Set Up Payroll with YTD Payroll Information 483
  Step 10: Verifying Your Trial Balance 483
  Step 11: Closing Opening Balance Equity 483
  Step 12: Setting the Closing Date 484
Review Questions 484
  Comprehension Questions 484
  Multiple Choice 484
  Completion Statements 485

CHAPTER 13 PAYROLL SETUP 487

- Topics 487
- Intuit's Payroll Subscriptions 488
- Getting Help With Payroll 488
- Checklist for Setting Up Payroll 489
- The Accounting Behind the Scenes 489
  - *Payroll Tax Tables* 490
  - *Payroll Accounts* 490
  - *Payroll Items* 491
- The Payroll Setup Wizard 493
- Setting Up a Payroll Subscription 493
- Adding Employees 495
  - *Employee Self-setup Through QuickBooks Workforce* 495
  - *Setting Up Employees* 496
  - *Entering Tax Withholding Information* 497
  - *Setting Up Direct Deposit* 497
- Developing Company Pay Policies 498
  - *Creating Pay Schedules* 499
  - *Defining Pay Types* 500
  - *Assigning Paid Time Off Policies* 501
  - *Additional Compensation and Pay Types* 502
- Specifying Benefit Deductions & Contributions 502
  - *Health Insurance* 503
  - *Retirement Plans* 504
- Customizing the Payroll Settings 504
  - *General Tax Info* 505
  - *Scheduling Federal Tax Payments* 506
  - *Scheduling State Tax Payments* 506
  - *Setting Up Auto Payroll* 507
  - *Automating Tax Payments and Forms* 508
  - *Designating a Third-Party Preparer* 508
  - *Activating Email Notifications* 509
  - *Employee Workforce Profile Management* 510
  - *Authorizing Shared Data* 510
  - *Connecting Bank Accounts* 510
  - *Check Printing Options* 511
  - *Editing Payroll Account Mapping* 512
- The Payroll Overview 515
- Review Questions 516
  - *Comprehension Questions* 516
  - *Multiple Choice* 516
  - *Completion Statements* 518
- Payroll Setup—Apply Your Knowledge 518

Chapter 14 PAYROLL PROCESSING 523
Topics 523
Using the Payroll Center 523
The Employees Center 524
Time Sheets 525
Built-in Time Sheets 525
Using QuickBooks Time 528
Payroll Processing Checklists 528
Every Payday 528
Every Tax Deposit Due Date (monthly or semi-weekly) 528
Every Quarter (after the end of the quarter) 528
Every January 529
Paying Employees 529
Creating Paychecks 529
Printing Paychecks 534
Printing Pay Stubs 536
Supplemental Payroll Runs 536
Correcting Errors 537
Editing Paychecks 537
Voiding or Deleting Paychecks 540
Replacing Lost or Stolen Checks 540
Paying Taxes and Liabilities 541
The Payroll Tax Center 541
Payroll Compliance 542
Paying Taxes 542
Tax Payment Errors 544
Paying Deduction Liabilities 545
Viewing Payroll Tax History and Resources 546
Running Payroll Reports 548
Payroll Details Report 548
Payroll Summary Report 548
Payroll Tax Liability Report 548
Total Payroll Cost Report 549
Vacation and Sick Leave Report 550
Sales Rep Commissions 550
Managing Employees 551
Terminating Employees 551
Reactivating Employees 552
Review Questions 552
Comprehension Questions 552
Multiple Choice 553
Completion Statements 555
Payroll Processing—Apply Your Knowledge 555

CHAPTER 15 CAPSTONE PROJECT: YINYANG GRAPHIC DESIGN 559
- Our Story Continues 559
- Instructions 559
- YinYang Graphic Design Capstone Project 560
  - 1. Set Up Payroll 560
  - 2. Set Up a Project 563
  - 3. Add a Contractor 564
  - 4. Set Up Mileage 564
  - 5. Set Up Price Rules 564
  - 6. Enter Business Transactions 564
  - 7. Prepare Reports 584
  - 8. Analysis Questions 584

ANSWER KEY FOR END OF CHAPTER QUESTIONS 585
- Chapter 1: Introducing QuickBooks Online 585
- Chapter 2: Customizing QuickBooks Online 586
- Chapter 3: The Sales Process 590
- Chapter 4: Managing Expenses 591
- Chapter 5: Advanced Transactions 592
- Chapter 6: Banking & Reconciliation 593
- Chapter 7: Reports 594
- Chapter 8: YinYang Graphic Design Business Scenario 595
- Chapter 9: Projects and Job Costing 595
- Chapter 10: Inventory 596
- Chapter 11: Adjustments and Year-End Procedures 597
- Chapter 12: Advanced Company Setup 598
- Chapter 13: Payroll Setup 600
- Chapter 14: Payroll Processing 601
- Chapter 15: YinYang Graphic Design Business Scenarios 602

CERTIPORT MAPPING 603

INDEX 607

PREFACE

People are made of passion, skills, and brilliant ideas. Every time a person gets inspired to bring their ideas to life, a new business is born. For that business to succeed, it must operate at a profit and pay taxes. And to do THAT, it is crucial to track all its activity accurately. Every business needs a bookkeeper or at least an employee who truly understands how to keep books!

This guide introduces you to QuickBooks Online® Plus—Intuit's easy-to-use, powerful accounting system for small businesses.

This guide does not cover how to use the features in QuickBooks® Desktop or QuickBooks® for Mac.

While this textbook does not specifically address the additional features in QuickBooks Online Advanced or QBO® for Accountants, all of the techniques in this course will work with those editions as well.

ACKNOWLEDGMENTS

Standing on the shoulders of giants . . . while the last thing I want to do is start a book with a cliché, it's important for me to acknowledge Douglas Sleeter, Deborah Pembrook, Ellen Orr, and the additional authors and editors who created the bones of this book.

I also want to give a shoutout to the Intuit Trainer/Writer network and the dozens of other QuickBooks Online ProAdvisors who taught me (almost) everything I know. Instead of fighting over slices of the pie, we are baking a bigger pie so there is enough for everyone.

I would also like to express my heartfelt gratitude and adoration to Jamie Pollock, my husband and business partner, for his unconditional love and support, and my kids for understanding that mom is always going to work too hard. Please turn out like me in only the best ways.

USING THIS BOOK

Throughout this book, you will find tips on how to set up and use QuickBooks® Online (QBO®) so that you and your company have the information you need to make business decisions.

Each chapter covers how to manage a general workflow in your business. As you step through the lessons and exercises, you will build a complete company file from scratch. It will be important to do the lessons in order so that your file matches future exercises.

Each chapter is designed to aid understanding by providing an explanation of topics, key terms, the "accounting behind the scenes," and many extra notes.

The illustrated text includes step-by-step instructions with hands-on exercises to provide you with practical experience. These are identified throughout the book with the words HANDS-ON PRACTICE.

The end-of-chapter assessments include comprehension questions, multiple choice questions, and completion sentences. These quizzes reinforce your retention of key concepts.

At the end of each chapter is a self-paced practice exercise mirroring real-world situations. These APPLY YOUR KNOWLEDGE sections tell you what to do. If you are not sure how to do it, turn back to the lessons and follow the step-by-step instructions.

Two chapters of this book are case studies. They consist of summary problems covering topics from all the lessons.

From using this book, you will gain confidence in every aspect of QuickBooks Online by trying out each feature in the context of a "real" business. You will want to keep this book as a reference for years to come.

ABOUT THE EXERCISES

The chapter lessons, end-of-chapter exercises, and case studies all use separate QuickBooks Online accounts with real-world scenarios.

Chapter Lessons: Craig's Design and Landscaping Services

> Throughout the chapters of this book, the **HANDS-ON PRACTICE** lessons use a sample company provided by Intuit for free at **http://qbo.intuit.com/redir/testdrive**. This sandbox file will completely reset every time you use it, so be sure to capture any screenshots you need or print your reports at the time you create them.

This fictitious company, ***Craig's Design and Landscaping, Inc.***, provides routine landscaping maintenance, as well as garden design. Craig Carlson uses QuickBooks Online for his accounting and business management. Craig's Landscaping may not be exactly like your business; however, the examples in this text are representative enough to guide you on your own use of QBO.

As you think through the examples with Craig's Landscaping, ask yourself what parallels you see to your own organization. Certainly, areas such as sales, expenses, salaries, supplies, equipment, and others will be appropriate for your setup, but the names and specifics of the accounts, items, lists, and forms will probably be different.

Apply Your Knowledge end-of-chapter exercises: Imagine Photography

> Your homework assignments in **APPLY YOUR KNOWLEDGE** at the end of each chapter are based on a second company called **Imagine Photography, Inc.** You will build an entire company file starting from scratch through an account provided by your instructor or using a free trial of QBO Plus (page xxi).
>
> This file does not reset each time. In fact, the content in each chapter builds on the steps that came before, increasing in complexity as your skills develop. It is important to work through the end-of-chapter Apply Your Knowledge exercises sequentially to ensure that your screen will match the book's screenshots.
>
> Be sure to fix your mistakes as you go. For example, your reports in Chapter 7 won't be accurate if your transactions were created incorrectly in earlier lessons.

Imagine Photography is a photography studio that also sells camera equipment. Ernest Withers, the owner, uses QuickBooks Online for its accounting and business management, and has hired you as his bookkeeper. As with Craig's Landscaping, Imagine Photography's workflows are universal and will help you understand QBO.

Imagine Photography has two locations, one in San Jose and another in Walnut Creek, CA. They have two revenue streams, store sales and photography services. In order for management to separately track revenue and expenses for each income source, Imagine Photography uses **Classes** in QuickBooks Online.

As you proceed through the book, you'll see how each transaction (bill, check, invoice, etc.) is tagged with what class it belongs to, so that later you can create reports like the *Profit and Loss by Class*, or filter reports by store.

Imagine Photography also needs to separately track revenue and expenses for each job it performs. When a customer orders a photo shoot, Imagine Photography needs to track all of the revenue and expenses specifically related to that project so it can look back and see how profitable the job was. This concept is called **Job Costing**, and many different businesses need to track jobs in similar ways.

As you think through the examples with Imagine Photography, imagine how you would use these tools with a variety of companies in different industries.

Case Study Scenario: YinYang Graphic Design

> There are two Case Studies in the book, one halfway through the content, and another at the end. Your instructor will send you an invitation to a fresh Student Trial Account to use for these projects, or you can use a copy of QuickBooks Online for Accountants (page xxii).

This real-life scenario allows you to work through setting up and using QuickBooks Online as if you were the bookkeeper responsible for the subscription. You will practice setting up a second company from scratch. This graphic design and marketing agency has an e-commerce webstore so that you can practice entering daily transactions, using the banking feed, reconciling, and running reports.

The case study continues at the end of the book, allowing you to manage inventory, create job costing reports, run payroll, and close out the year.

QUICKBOOKS ONLINE STUDENT TRIAL ACCOUNTS

This school textbook guides you through learning QuickBooks Online using Student Trial accounts.

These are full-featured subscriptions to QuickBooks Online Plus provided by Intuit Education to academic programs. Your instructor will create two company files for you, one for Imagine Photography and one for YinYang Graphic Design.

You will receive an invitation from your instructor via email. Click on the link in the email, log in, create a password, select the company, and use the two files to complete the Apply Your Knowledge exercises and the Case Study projects.

These practice companies are valid for one year and cannot be used for real-life businesses.

The steps to gain access to your QuickBooks Online Plus accounts are outlined at the end of Chapter 1 and on the inside back cover of this book.

IF YOU AREN'T IN A CLASSROOM SETTING

This textbook was designed for instructor-led academic courses. Independent learners will be able to perform the steps in the chapters using Intuit's free Craig's Design and Landscaping practice account but will not have access to the two Student Trial accounts needed for the end-of-chapter exercises and case studies.

Instead, we suggest two options. Use either or both to create two subscriptions for the Imagine Photography Apply Your Knowledge exercises and the YinYang Graphic Design case study.

Option 1: A 30-day QBO Plus Trial

We can help you create two **free 30-day QuickBooks Online Plus trial accounts.** If you need more than 30 days to complete the material, enter your credit card number before the trial expires and receive a 50% discount on your QBO Plus subscriptions for up to three months. Be sure to cancel the billing when you are done!

To create QBO Plus subscriptions for Imagine Photography and YinYang Graphic Design, please fill in the form at http://royl.ws/questiva-get-qbo.

Option 2: A Practice QBOA Profile

To avoid any unexpected subscription fees, we recommend creating a free QuickBooks Online for Accountants (QBOA) profile by visiting https://quickbooks.intuit.com/accountants. It includes a free QuickBooks Online Advanced account including Payroll. The interface will have additional options not covered in this book – enjoy exploring the enhanced features!

> Because these are temporary accounts only for use with this curriculum, do not use an email address associated with your bookkeeping business. In the future you will want to create a real QBOA subscription for professional use under your company's username. Instead, register with a personal email address or create a gmail account specifically for this purpose.

If neither of these solutions are satisfactory for your Apply Your Knowledge exercises and Case Study, you can adapt the steps using the data in the Craig's Landscaping sample company. The steps and answers will not match the book, but you can at least practice the concepts.

SUPPLEMENTAL FILES

In addition to the QuickBooks Online accounts, there are also additional files that go along with the lessons, including logos and import files.

To install the files on your hard drive, follow these steps:

STEP 1.   Go to www.questivaconsultants.com/downloads/

STEP 2.   Find this book's title and click the link. You will be taken to the support page for this book.

STEP 3.   Click the *Product Support Download* tab and click the link to download **QuickBooks_Online_Classroom_Files.zip**. Save the files to the desired location on your local system. If you are using a computer in a classroom or lab environment, ask your instructor for the proper location to store your exercise files.

STEP 4.   Once you have saved the file to the proper location, you will need to "unzip" it. Select the zip file in Windows Explorer. You should see an option at the top of the window to *Extract*. Click the **Extract** option and choose **Extract All**.

If you're on a Mac, simply double-click the zip folder to view and use the contents.

INSTRUCTOR RESOURCES

Instructor resources, including the Instructor's Manual, test banks, solution files, and PowerPoints are available at www.questivaconsultants.com/downloads. You must be a verified instructor with an accredited school to access these files. If you do not already have an instructor login, please contact info@questivaconsultants.com.

CERTIFICATION

This book is excellent preparation for the Certiport QuickBooks Online User Certification Exam. This certification validates your QuickBooks Online knowledge. After successfully completing the exam, you will become an *Intuit QuickBooks Online Certified User*.

Turn to the Appendix on page 603 for a mapping of the Certiport exam objectives to the topics in this book. For more information and for locations of testing centers, visit http://www.certiport.com/QuickBooksOnline.

Note that there is a separate Intuit QuickBooks Online certification available through the *QuickBooks ProAdvisor Program*. This book will also prepare you for that exam as well (see page 29).

WHY DOESN'T THIS BOOK EXACTLY MATCH MY FILE?

As you use this book, you will notice that some of the instructions or figures don't exactly match what you see on your screen. Think of QBO as a "live" environment. Expect the unexpected, look around, don't panic. Enjoy the opportunity to grow your expertise by becoming comfortable with change!

You are welcome to visit our website at https://www.questivaconsultants.com/product/qbo-complete-2023/#tab-product_updates for a list of updates to the content.

New Features and Improvements

It's important to understand that QuickBooks Online is an ever-evolving software platform.

Intuit is always listening to customer feedback, so the interface is constantly shifting. Button names and locations occasionally change as they improve the user experience. Terminology is updated as they test names to see what makes the most sense to beginners.

They are also always innovating, and rolling out new features. You'll see alerts pointing you to what's new. Don't be afraid to explore!

Because Intuit does real-time beta testing, what you see in the sample file may not be the same as what you see in your student file . . . or in real company files. In fact, if you switch between several companies, they all may look just a little different!

Accountant View vs. Business View

QuickBooks Online has two user experiences, the **Accountant View** and the **Business View**. The *Business View*, shown on the right, is the default interface when a business owner creates their own QBO subscription. It uses a navigational structure that focuses on business management instead of financial workflows, and allows you to create your own bookmarks to favorite centers.

Because the *Accountant View* is favored by bookkeepers, it is what we use in this book's step-by-step instructions.

To toggle between these views, click on the *Gear* in the upper right corner of your screen, and look at the bottom of the menu. QuickBooks Online will tell you if *You're Viewing QuickBooks in Accountant View* or in *Business View*, as shown below. Use the blue "**Switch to . . .**" link on the right to choose **Accountant View**.

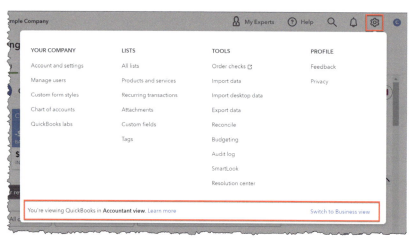

CHAPTER 1

INTRODUCING QUICKBOOKS ONLINE

TOPICS

In this chapter, you will learn about the following topics:

- The QuickBooks Online Ecosystem (page 1)
- Accounting 101 (page 3)
- Using a Browser to Access QBO (page 7)
- Working with QuickBooks Online Files (page 10)
- QuickBooks Online's Interface (page 13)
- Entering Transactions in QuickBooks Online (page 22)
- QuickBooks Online Help (page 29)

QuickBooks® Online, also known as **QBO**®, is one of the most powerful tools you will use in running your business. QuickBooks Online isn't just a robust bookkeeping program; it's a management tool. When set up and used properly, QBO allows you to track and manage income, expenses, bank accounts, receivables, inventory, job costs, fixed assets, payables, loans, payroll, billable time, and equity in your company. It also provides you with detailed reports that are essential to making good business decisions.

QuickBooks Online helps small business owners track their transactions efficiently without worrying about the debits and credits of accounting entries. However, to use QBO effectively, you still need to understand how the software is structured, how its files work, how to navigate in the system to do tasks, and how to retrieve information about your business. In this chapter you'll learn some of the basics of the QuickBooks Online ecosystem, as well as explore the world of accounting.

THE QUICKBOOKS ONLINE ECOSYSTEM

The QuickBooks Online family of products is designed to be easy to use, while providing a comprehensive set of accounting tools including a general ledger, inventory, accounts receivable, accounts payable, sales tax, and financial reporting. In addition, a variety of optional fee-based payroll services, merchant account services, and other third-party products integrate with the QBO software.

QuickBooks Online vs. QuickBooks Desktop

Intuit offers two distinctly different ways to use QuickBooks. The traditional version, **QuickBooks Desktop (QBDT)**, is software that you download and install on your local computer, company server, or host with a 3rd party service.

The newer version, **QuickBooks Online (QBO)**, isn't installed on your computer, but is instead accessed over the internet through a web browser, or using an app on your smartphone or tablet. This online subscription does bookkeeping similarly to QuickBooks Desktop, but the features and layout are entirely different. This textbook covers QuickBooks Online.

To keep your data safe, QBO uses the same security and encryption tools as online banking websites.

All editions of QuickBooks Online support multiple users. Since the software is web-based, anyone with a user account can log in from anywhere, even from a smartphone, and it doesn't matter whether they're on a Mac or a PC. There are no IT maintenance costs, nor cumbersome workarounds so that the bookkeeper and accountant can access the file.

QuickBooks Online is sold as a *subscription*. There are many benefits to subscribing:

- The software is always current, with new features and improvements appearing on a regular basis.
- You don't need to buy and install multiple copies to maintain a multi-user environment.
- You can upgrade or downgrade as your needs evolve.

While some people balk at the idea of recurring payments instead of one-time software purchases, the return on investment (ROI) of time and infrastructure costs saved while using QBO overcomes the expense.

Third-party Apps

Cloud computing also allows for automations that are not possible with QuickBooks Desktop. QuickBooks Online integrates with other cloud-based software you already use, including your bank, your customer management software (CRM), e-commerce webstore, gmail, and many others.

QBO is intentionally designed as a customizable experience. Instead of a complex computer program trying to be all things to all people, it integrates with hundreds of other web applications to synchronize information.

This makes it easy to customize a perfect workflow for each business, creating a streamlined experience that import and exports data with the rest of the company's tech stack.

The benefits of this approach include best-fit software solutions, preventing employee access to confidential information, and eliminating redundant data entry.

To review third-party apps that will address your company's needs, look for *Apps* at the bottom of your *Left Navigation Bar*, or visit the website **apps.com**. There you will find hundreds of third-party apps that have been vetted by Intuit.

These additional utilities and subscriptions can solve the pain points for every unique business, saving time and money.

QuickBooks Online Versions

The QuickBooks Online product line includes several separate versions: ***QuickBooks Online Self-Employed***, ***Simple Start***, ***Essentials, Plus, Advanced,*** **and *QuickBooks Online for Accountants***. Instead of being broken down into industry-specific versions as you see with the Desktop edition, the various subscriptions increase in additional features and user accounts.

- ***Simple Start*** is the version for small service-based businesses who don't have accounts payable.
- ***Essentials*** is the version for growing companies who have simple reporting needs.

- *Plus* introduces inventory, class tracking, and job costing.
- *Advanced* is used by larger companies who need bulk data entry and have complex reporting needs.
- *QBO for Accountants (QBOA®)* is a portal for QuickBooks Online ProAdvisors that allows bookkeepers to switch between multiple client files, and leverage additional professional tools.
- *Self-employed* is a standalone edition that does not upgrade. It is designed for gig workers and sole proprietors who run their businesses like a hobby, without a dedicated bank account. It should only be used by individuals with a side hustle who don't intend to grow their company, or W-2 employees who need to track work-related expenses.

For a comparison of all the products versions, visit http://www.quickbooks.com.

This book covers the features and usage of **QuickBooks Online Plus**, the most popular subscription level. Once you learn how to use this version, you'll be prepared to use the others.

QuickBooks Online for Accountants

If you are responsible for doing the books for several clients, create a free QuickBooks Online for Accountants (QBOA) portal. QBOA makes it easy to toggle between multiple files from a drop-down menu. It also includes additional tools for client management, file maintenance, and advisory.

QBOA also comes with a free QuickBooks Online Advanced file for your own use, including payroll. The best way to learn QBO is to use it yourself for your own company!

Bookkeepers who use QBOA also gain access to training materials, Intuit's certification exams, and a listing on findaproadvisor.com, Intuit's website connecting business owners to bookkeepers in their local area and same niche.

Please visit https://quickbooks.intuit.com/accountants/ for more information.

ACCOUNTING 101

This course focuses on teaching software that does accounting, rather than teaching you accounting through software.

Since you're going to learn QuickBooks Online to run your business, it is still important to understand the accounting process. In this section, we look at some basic accounting concepts and how they relate to QBO.

Accounting's Focus

Accounting's primary concern is the accurate recording and categorizing of transactions so that you can produce reports that accurately portray the financial health of your organization. Put another way, accounting's focus is on whether your business is succeeding, and how well it is doing.

Whether the company is a sole proprietorship, partnership, S-Corp, C-Corp, or Non-profit, the core accounting all works the same way.

The purpose of accounting is to serve management, investors, board members, creditors, and government agencies. Accounting reports allow any of these groups to assess the financial position of the organization relative to its debts (liabilities), its capabilities to satisfy those debts and continue operations (assets), and the difference between them (net worth or equity).

The fundamental equation (called the *Accounting Equation*) that governs all accounting is:

$$\text{Assets} = \text{Liabilities} + \text{Equity}$$
$$\text{or}$$
$$\text{Equity} = \text{Assets} - \text{Liabilities}$$

The General Ledger

Many factors go into making an organization work. Money and value are attached to everything that is associated with operating a company—cash, equipment, rent, utilities, wages, raw materials, merchandise, and so on. For an organization to understand its financial position, business transactions need to be recorded, summarized, balanced, and presented in reports according to the rules of accounting.

Business transactions (e.g., sales, purchases, operating expense payments) are recorded in several types of *ledgers*, called accounts or categories. The summary of all transactions in all ledgers for a company is called the *General Ledger*. This term goes back to the days before computers, when all accounting was done in ledger books... on paper... by hand.

A listing of every account in the General Ledger is called the *Chart of Accounts*. Each account summarizes transactions that increase or decrease the equity in your organization. The figure shows a general picture of the effect accounts have on the equity of your organization. Some accounts (those on the left) increase equity when they are increased, while others (such as those on the right) decrease equity when they are increased.

So, let's return to the accounting equation, **Assets = Liabilities + Equity**. To understand the accounting equation, consider the following statement: *Everything a company owns was purchased with funds from lenders, or funded by the owner's stake in the company.*

This means that the total of the assets (which represent what the company "owns") is always equal to the sum of the liabilities (representing what the company "owes") plus the equity (representing the owner's interest in the company).

Account Types and Financial Reports

Each account in the general ledger has a **Type**, which describes what kind of business transaction is stored in that account. There are five primary types of accounts: **Asset, Liability, Equity, Income, and Expense**.

Assets, liabilities, and equity accounts are associated with the *Balance Sheet* report, which is used to analyze the net worth of a business. The Balance Sheet demonstrates the fundamental accounting equation: *Total assets always equal the total liabilities plus equity.*

Operating income and expense accounts are associated with the *Profit & Loss* report (also called an *Income Statement*), which is used to analyze the profit or loss for a business over a specific time range (month, quarter, year, etc.).

Although income and expense accounts are not directly shown in the accounting equation, they do affect this equation via an equity account called **Net Income**. Income and expenses are tracked throughout the year as business transactions occur, and are totaled at the end of the year to calculate Net Income (or Loss).

Net Income = total revenues minus total expenses.

If the Net Income is positive at the end of the fiscal year, the company earned a profit for the year and *increased the owner's equity in the business*. If Net Income is negative because expenses exceeded revenues, the company took a loss for the year, *decreasing the owner's equity in the business.*

At the end of the year, the balance of each income and expense account is reset to zero so these accounts can track the next year's transactions.

Double-Entry Accounting

Double-entry accounting is a technique that goes back to the days of paper calculations. It divides each transaction into two sides: the left side is for debits, and the right side is for credits.

Matching the accounting equation of Assets = Liabilities + Equity, Asset accounts naturally carry a debit balance. Liabilities and Equity accounts carry credit balances.

In every transaction, an amount always goes *to* somewhere, *from* somewhere. One account is debited and the other is credited.

Therefore, debits do not always make an account go down, and credits do not always make an account go up. Debits are not "bad" and credits are not "good." They are just part of the system of accounting, as shown in Table 1-1:

ACCOUNT	INCREASED BY:	DECREASED BY:
ASSETS	Debit	Credit
EXPENSES	Debit	Credit
LIABILITIES	Credit	Debit
EQUITY	Credit	Debit
REVENUE	Credit	Debit

TABLE 1-1: *The Debits and Credits behind every transaction*

The rule of double-entry accounting is that *total debits must always equal total credits.* Every transaction creates a debit in one or more accounts and a credit in one or more accounts. If the debits and credits for any transaction are not equal, the transaction has an error or is incomplete.

Accounting Behind the Scenes

Recording and categorizing all of your business transactions into the proper accounts, summarizing and adjusting them, and then preparing financial statements can be an enormous, labor-intensive task without the help of a computer and software. This is where QuickBooks Online comes in. QBO handles this double-entry accounting so that you don't have to!

To make all this possible, QuickBooks Online uses familiar-looking forms for data entry such as checks, invoices, and bills. As you enter transactions using these forms, QBO handles the behind-the-scenes accounting for you. Every transaction you enter in the software automatically becomes a debit to one or more accounts and a credit to one or more other accounts. QBO won't even let you record the transaction until the total of the debits equals the total of the credits.

Letting QuickBooks Online create the accounting entries allows business owners to use QBO to efficiently run their company without getting bogged down with the debits and credits. You can always create reports that show the transactions in the General Ledger in the full double-entry accounting format whenever you need them.

As this book introduces new transaction types (e.g., Invoices, Bills, or Checks), the text will include a section called "**Accounting Behind the Scenes**," explaining the debits and credits.

While it's still important that you understand the bookkeeping terminology, letting QuickBooks Online handle the accounting behind the scenes means you can focus on the business transaction workflow rather than the debits and credits.

This allows you to spend your time managing your operations instead of your bookkeeping.

Accounting Basis: Cash or Accrual?

Another critical aspect of accounting is managing for the future. Many times, your organization will have assets and liabilities that represent money owed to the company, or owed to others, but are not yet due. For example, you may have sold something to a customer and sent an invoice, but the payment has not been received. In this case, you have an outstanding *receivable*. Similarly, you may have a bill for insurance that hasn't been paid yet. In this case, you have an outstanding *payable*.

An accounting system that uses the **Accrual Basis** method of accounting tracks these receivables and payables and uses them to evaluate a company's financial position. The accrual basis method specifies that revenues and expenses are recognized when the activity occurs. This helps you accurately understand the true profitability of the business in each period. Assets, liabilities, income, and expenses are entered when you know about them, and they are used to identify what cash you need on hand to meet both current and known future obligations.

In the **Cash Basis** method, revenues and expenses are not recognized until cash changes hands. So, revenue is only recognized when the customer pays, and a cost isn't recognized until you pay for it. Cash-based accounting focuses on business activity that is complete.

Although certain types of companies can use the cash basis method of accounting, the accrual method provides the most accurate picture for managing your business. Some organizations are not allowed to operate as cash basis under IRS regulations. You should check with your tax accountant to determine which accounting method—cash or accrual—is best for you.

In QuickBooks Online, you can record transactions such as invoices and bills to facilitate accrual basis reporting, and still create cash basis reports that remove the receivables and payables. This gives you the flexibility of selecting one basis for taxes and another for operational reporting, if you wish. For more information about cash vs. accrual reports, see page 299.

USING A BROWSER TO ACCESS QBO

QuickBooks Online works best using a Chrome browser, available for free at http://www.chrome.com.

It makes no difference whether you are on a PC or a Mac. The website will work the same way.

The web address (URL) for QuickBooks Online is http://qbo.intuit.com. When you log in using your email address and password, you'll see a list with one or more files that have a User Account associated with your email address, like the example shown in Figure 1-1. You will then click on the desired file to open it.

FIGURE 1-1: *Logging in to QBO at qbo.intuit.com*

Setting Up Your Chrome Browser

Chrome has features you can utilize to be efficient with your QuickBooks Online experience (see Figure 1–2).

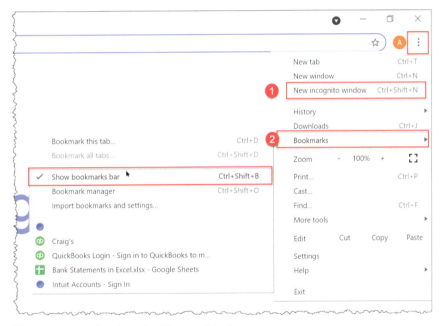

FIGURE 1-2: *Setting Up Chrome Tools*

Incognito Windows

One useful Chrome tool is an **Incognito window**. This special environment doesn't store cookies, a cache, or your browsing history. Open an Incognito window using the 3 dots in the upper right corner of your Chrome window, as shown in Figure 1-2.

If you're ever having trouble with your QBO, trying the same technique while logged in through Incognito tells you if the issue is with your computer or with Intuit's website.

If you can replicate the problem, the issue is with QBO—wait a few minutes and try again later . . . or contact Support.

If it works, then something on your computer is interfering with Chrome or the QuickBooks Online website.

Bookmarks

Be sure to turn on your **Bookmarks Bar**. That way you can create instant shortcuts to the sample company and your company file. Adding bookmarks for your favorite QBO tools like Banking, Search, and Reports makes navigation a snap.

HANDS-ON PRACTICE

For each tutorial, we will use Craig's Design and Landscaping, a sample QuickBooks Online company that allows you to explore the program. This way you can experiment without interfering with real data.

To set up Chrome so you can get to Craig's Landscaping easily throughout this course, follow this one-time setup:

STEP 1. Open up your **Chrome** browser.

STEP 2. Click the **three dots** in the upper right corner, as shown in Figure 1-2.

STEP 3. Highlight **Bookmarks**, then choose **Show Bookmarks Bar** if it doesn't have a checkmark next to it already. A new bar will show up below your URL address bar.

STEP 4. In the URL address bar at the top, type in **qbo.intuit.com/redir/testdrive**. Press **Enter** (or **Return** on a Mac).

FIGURE 1-3: Add a Bookmark for the Sample File

STEP 5. Drag the lock in the URL bar down to the Bookmark Bar. This will create a shortcut for future use (see Figure 1-3).

STEP 6. Right-click the **bookmark** and choose **Edit**... In the *Name* field type **Craig's** (see Figure 1-4).

STEP 7. Confirm that the URL still reads **qbo.intuit.com/redir/testdrive**. If it does not, triple-click in the box to highlight all the contents, delete the web address, and type in manually.

STEP 8. Click **Save**.

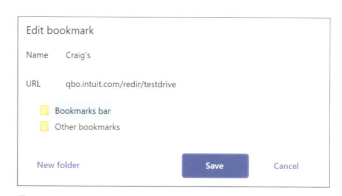

FIGURE 1-4: Rename the Bookmark

> **TIP:**
>
> You can add bookmarks to quickly jump to any center, report, or tool in QBO. When creating bookmarks, if the URL contains a prefix like "**c23.qbo**...", delete the "**c32.**" prefix so that the link begins with "**qbo**." This way all your bookmarks will be universal and work with any company file you have open.

Working in Multiple Tabs

You can open as many different windows in QuickBooks Online as you want by leveraging Chrome's *Tabs*. For example, while you're working in the *Banking Center*, you can open the *Customers Center* and the *Vendors Center* in additional tabs to reference all three at the same time.

There are several ways to create multiple tabs. Suggestions 1 and 2 are shown in Figure 1-5.

1. Click the **+ sign** on the right of the last tab to open a new tab, then use a bookmark to open the screen you want.

2. **Right-click** on buttons or action links in QBO and choose **Open Link In New Tab**.

FIGURE 1-5: *Open multiple browser tabs to see several screens at the same time*

3. Drag a *Center* from the *Left Navigation Bar* up to the tab bar to create a new tab.

4. **Right-click** on a tab itself and choose **Duplicate**.

IMPORTANT!

If you make a change in one window, be sure to **Refresh** the other tabs to retrieve the updated data from the server—the tabs don't update automatically. Refreshing a tab is also helpful if an action times out or a screen isn't behaving as expected.

Chrome's *Refresh* button is the round arrow to the left of the lock in Figure 1-5, or you can use the keyboard shortcut **Ctrl-R** (**Cmd-R** on a Mac).

HANDS-ON PRACTICE

Open more than one Center at the same time so that you can view both simultaneously.

STEP 1. Click on **Banking** in the *Left Navigation Bar* to open the *Banking Center*.

STEP 2. Right-click (Cmd-click on a Mac, two-finger press on a trackpad) on **Expenses** in the *Left Navigation Bar*, and choose **Open Link in New Tab** (if you're not in Chrome, your terminology may vary). A second browser tab opens. Click on it to view the *Expenses Center*.

STEP 3. Drag the **Sales** from the *Left Navigation Bar* up to the row of tabs at the top of the browser, to the right of the *Expenses* tab. Drop it. Click on the new tab to view it.

STEP 4. Toggle back and forth between the **first tab** with the *Banking Center*, the **second tab** with the *Expenses Center*, and the **third tab** with the *Sales Center*.

STEP 5. Return to the Dashboard.

STEP 6. **Close** Chrome.

Opening Multiple Files

It is possible to open two company files at the same time by opening one regular and one Incognito Chrome window. You can also leverage multiple browsers, like Firefox, Edge, or Safari.

A second approach is perfect for bookkeepers with multiple clients: utilize Chrome's **Profiles** to make dedicated environments for each of your clients, complete with their own sets of bookmarks.

To create multiple Profiles, click the circle just to the left of the 3 dots. Give each one a name and pick an image.

When you choose a Profile off this list, Chrome opens a new window with that client's settings and history. Each browser window is distinct, so you can open several company files at the same time.

WORKING WITH QUICKBOOKS ONLINE FILES

Before using QuickBooks Online, it is important for you to understand how to log in and access company files.

Opening the QuickBooks Online Sample File, Craig's Landscaping

Now that we have set up Chrome so you can get to the sample company easily, follow these steps to open it:

HANDS-ON PRACTICE

STEP 1. Open **Chrome**.

STEP 2. Click on the **Craig's** bookmark. If the window shown in Figure 1-6 does not open, delete the bookmark and repeat the steps above.

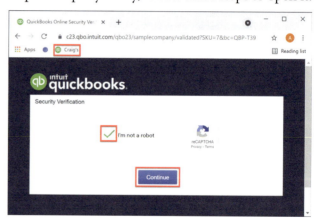

STEP 3. Check **I'm Not a Robot,** then click **Continue**.

FIGURE 1-6: *Log in to Sample File*

STEP 4. You may see a **ReCAPTCHA security window**, to confirm you're a real human being. Click the images it requests (you may see traffic lights, mountains, crosswalks, or vehicles), then click the **Verify** button (see Figure 1-7).

STEP 5. The *Craig's Design and Landscaping Services sample company* opens, as shown in Figure 1-8.

STEP 6. Click the **Hide** button on the upper right of the Setup Guide. We won't be using this guided tour (see Figure 1-8).

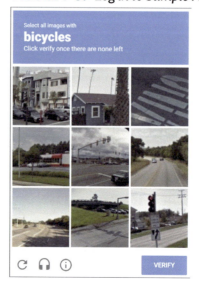

FIGURE 1-7: *ReCAPTCHA security verification*

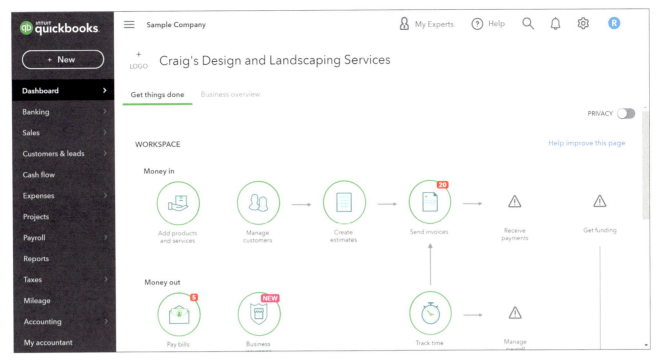

FIGURE 1-8: *The Sample Company used in lessons*

Switching Between Other QuickBooks Online Data Files

If you were a user of multiple company files, you can easily switch between files (see Figure 1-9). We will not complete these steps now.

1. Click on the Gear in the upper right corner and choose **Switch Company**. This takes you back to the list you see when you log in. Click on any file to open it.

2. If you are a bookkeeper using QuickBooks Online for Accountants (QBOA), you would be able to switch between multiple files from the drop-down menu at the top left.

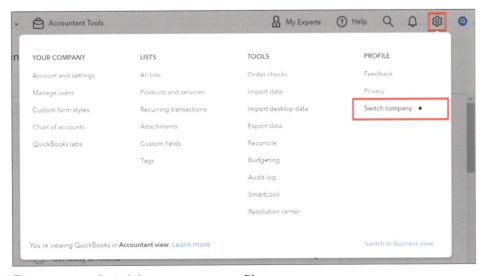

FIGURE 1-9: *Switch between company files*

Creating New Company Files

Unlike QuickBooks Desktop, where you can create as many files as you want, each company in QuickBooks Online is a distinct subscription with its own cost. If a business owner has several companies that all file separate tax forms, you will need a separate subscription for each. Use the same email address when creating each file so that you can access them all under the same login.

Visit http://www.quickbooks.com to create new QuickBooks Online files.

> **TIP:**
>
> QuickBooks Online ProAdvisors receive a discount on new files. This reduced pricing can be passed on to the client. For more information about the free ProAdvisor program, visit https://quickbooks.intuit.com/accountants/.

FIGURE 1-10: *Log out when done*

Logging Out of QuickBooks Online Files

Close the company data file by logging out. You could just close your Chrome window, but taking the time to log out ensures that no one can gain unauthorized access to your data. Click the **blue circle** in the upper right corner, then click the **Sign Out** button (see Figure 1-10).

QuickBooks Online Updates and New Features

Because QBO is subscription-based, there are never any new annual versions to buy or maintenance releases to install, as there are with QuickBooks Desktop. Instead, Intuit constantly updates the software, bringing you bug fixes and new features. This means QBO may have changed when you sit down to work that morning!

If you're someone who loves cutting-edge technology, you'll appreciate the innovations as they appear. If you're someone who doesn't like change, take it to heart that every update Intuit makes is due to customer feedback, and the improvements will save you time and money.

Intuit releases new features to a few companies at a time to make sure that they don't introduce any bugs. New features are commonly rolled out in waves, so sometimes two company files may not see the same options.

> **IMPORTANT!**
>
> Since QBO is ever-evolving, you will see some differences compared to the screenshots and instructions in this book.

Backing Up QBO Files

Because QuickBooks Online is server-based, there is no need to make **backups** to prevent data loss. Traditional backups are a safety net in case of hard drive failure or data corruption. Intuit's servers have redundant infrastructure to make sure they never lose company files.

That being said, there are times when you will want to make a backup:

1. Before you make big changes to your data, like a Chart of Accounts consolidation or a big data import, make a backup so that if it doesn't go as expected, you can roll back your file and try again.
2. At year end to create an archival copy of your data that matches your taxes. These can be exported and opened in a copy of QuickBooks Online for Desktop.

Only QBO Advanced has built-in tools for backups, but if you use other versions, there are 3rd party apps that can perform these functions for you. We talk about apps on page 2.

QUICKBOOKS ONLINE'S INTERFACE

The QuickBooks Online interface makes it easy to enter and locate transactions. There are four main areas to look for what you need: The *Left Navigation Bar*, the *+New button*, the *Top bar*, and the *Gear* (see Figure 1-11).

1. The *Left Navigation Bar* contains all the screens and **Centers** that organize your data. Note that each Center also has **Tabs** grouping the information (see page 17).
2. The *+New button* is where you add new transactions (see page 22).
3. The *Top bar* contains tools like **Help** and **Search** (see page 20).
4. The *Gear* holds all the settings and back-end tools to administer your QBO file (see page 20).

FIGURE 1-11: *The QuickBooks Online interface*

Dashboard

As soon as you open a company, QuickBooks Online displays the **Dashboard.** The Dashboard is broken up into two tabs, **Get Things Done** and the **Business Overview.**

Get Things Done

> **NOTE:**
>
> Your *Get Things Done* screen may vary. See two alternatives above and below.

The *Get Things Done* tab (Figure 1-11 and Figure 1-12) contains shortcuts to your frequent tasks. The *Workspace* variation also includes a diagram showing the interdependency between your workflow steps.

To start a task, just click on its icon.

FIGURE 1-12: *Your Get Things Done tab may show this Workspace*

Business Overview

The *Business Overview* shown in Figure 1-13 contains charts and bank account status so you can monitor your company's health at a glance.

Each chart is interactive—click on any colored segment to open up an instant report.

The *Privacy* button in the upper right is perfect when you're working in the coffee shop. It blanks out your sensitive information to prevent it from being seen by anyone looking over your shoulder.

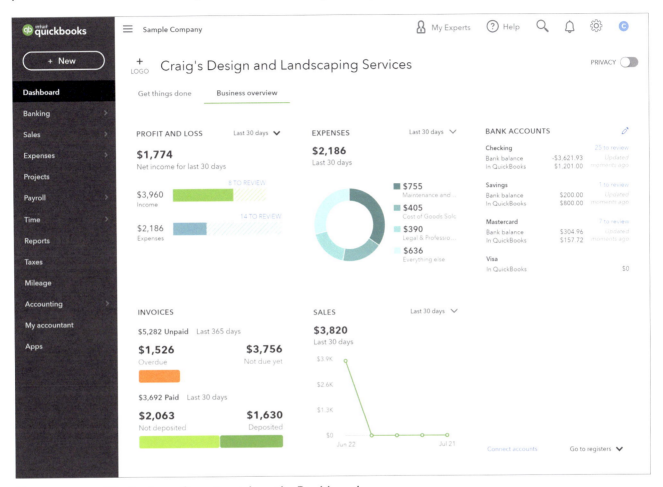

FIGURE 1-13: *The Business Overview tab on the Dashboard*

HANDS-ON PRACTICE
Try out the *Business Overview's* interactive features:

- **STEP 1.** In the *Profit and Loss* box, click on the **solid green bar**. These are income transactions already in QBO. A **Profit and Loss report** opens.

- **STEP 2.** Go back to the *Dashboard* by clicking your browser's **Back button,** or on **Dashboard** in the *Left Navigation Bar.*

- **STEP 3.** In the *Profit and Loss* box, click on the **hatched blue bar**. These are expense transactions waiting in the Banking Center to be entered. Go back to the *Dashboard*.

- **STEP 4.** In the *Expenses* box, click on the **Last 30 Days arrow**. Choose **This Fiscal Year**. You'll notice the segments and labels shift to reflect the new date range.

- **STEP 5.** Click on the **Miscellaneous** circle segment. A **Transaction Report** opens, showing what all those "miscellaneous" expenses really were.

STEP 6.   Click on **Hicks Hardware** to open and view the bill.

STEP 7.   To close the bill, either click the **Cancel button** in the lower left, or the **X** in the upper right.

STEP 8.   Go back to the *Dashboard* by **holding down** your browser's **Back button** and choosing **QuickBooks**. Because we have opened a report and drilled in to a bill, this is faster than clicking the Back button several times (see Figure 1-14).

STEP 9.   In the *Invoices* box, click the orange **Overdue** box. This takes you to the *Invoices* tab in the *Sales Center*. Scroll down to see all your customers' overdue unpaid invoices.

STEP 10. Click on the invoice for **Weiskopf Consulting** to see its details in a sidebar. Review the information shown.

STEP 11. Click the **X** in the upper right corner to close the *Invoice Details*.

STEP 12. Return to the *Dashboard's Business Overview* either using the **Back button** or clicking **Dashboard** in the *Left Navigation Bar*.

STEP 13. In the *Bank Accounts* box, click on the **Pencil**. Drag the 9-dot square next to **Mastercard** and drop it above **Savings** (see Figure 1-15). We'll use the credit card more often than the savings account.

STEP 14. Click the blue **Save** in the upper right of the box.

STEP 15. Click **Mastercard** to jump to the *Banking Center*. Note that the accounts are now in the same order. Go back to the *Business Overview*.

STEP 16. At the very bottom of the *Bank Accounts* box, click **Go To Registers** and choose **Checking**. If the *Register Basics* box opens, you can take the tour, or close it.

STEP 17. Go back to the *Dashboard*.

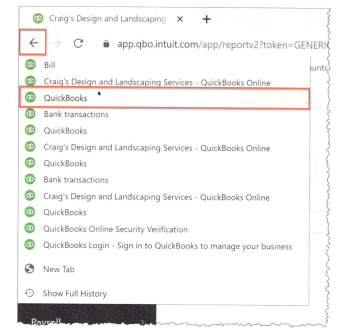

FIGURE 1-14: *Hold down the Back button to skip pages*

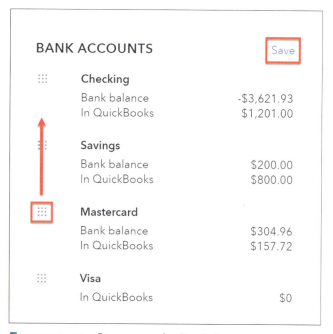

FIGURE 1-15: *Rearrange the Bank Accounts*

The Left Navigation Bar

QuickBooks Online's **Left Navigation Bar** allows you to visit Centers and available services (see Figure 1-16). You can open any Center by clicking its name in the black bar.

Click the **three lines** (the "**Hamburger**") at the right of the black bar to collapse it, giving you more workspace area.

> **IMPORTANT!**
>
> If your Left Navigation Bar looks nothing like the one in Figure 1-16, you may be in *Business View.* Follow the instructions in *Why Doesn't This Book Exactly Match My File?* on page xxiv to switch to *Accountant View,* which will match the layout in this textbook.

Centers

QuickBooks Online's **Centers** summarize pertinent information and transactions in one place. Many Centers are organized into **Tabs.** Your most-used Centers and tabs can be bookmarked in Chrome for easy access using the instructions on page 8.

FIGURE 1-16: *The Left Navigation Bar*

The Sales, Expenses, and Payroll Centers are very important since they provide the only way to access a list of your customers, vendors, and employees. These three lists are referred to as the **Center-based Lists**. For example, when you click on **Sales** in the *Left Navigation Bar* and then on **Customers**, the **Customers Center** opens to show each customer's balance, their contact information, and actions you can take (see Figure 1-17).

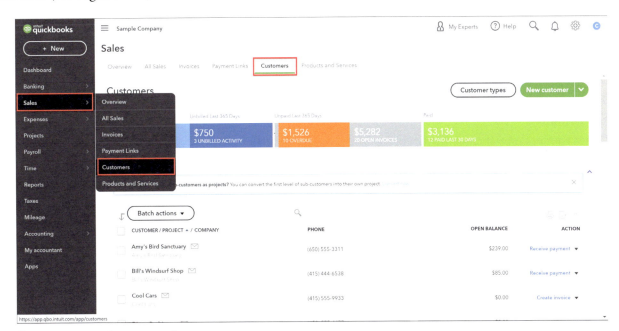

FIGURE 1-17: *Customers Center*

> **NOTE:**
>
> Your **Sales Center** may be called "**Invoicing**," depending on the business type chosen when setting up a new QBO file.

You can then click on any customer to drill into see their contact information, notes, and a list of their transactions (see Figure 1-18). From here you can **Edit** their information and create new **Transactions**. Note that almost everything is clickable! We'll learn more about managing your customers in Chapter 3, The Sales Process.

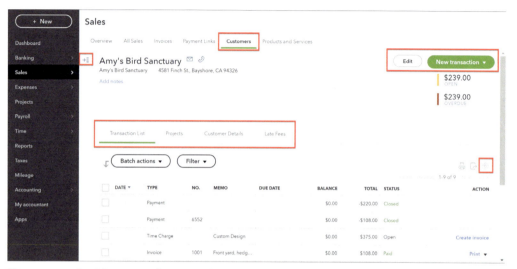

FIGURE 1-18: *Viewing a Customer's transaction list and details*

Click on the **Hamburger** next to *Amy's Bird Sanctuary*. A panel opens with a list of customers (see Figure 1-19). Now you can easily switch between customers without having to navigate in and out of the customer list. The buttons at the top allow you to return to the Customers list, add a new customer, collapse the panel, filter the list, sort alphabetically, and sort by open balance.

Other Centers may include the **Banking Center**, the **Projects Center**, the **Report Center**, the **Time Center**, and the **Mileage Center**.

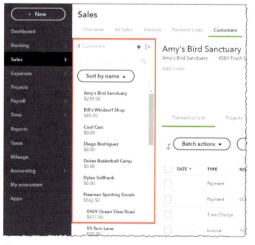

FIGURE 1-19: *The Customer panel*

The Money Bar

The **Money Bars** at the top of many of the Centers provide a fast way to see the status of your sales and expense transactions. Click on the colored boxes to filter the lists (see Figure 1-20).

For example, in the Customers Center, you can filter the list to just see Customers with open Estimates, Unbilled Activity, Open and Overdue Invoices, and recent Payments.

To view the full list of customers again, click the blue **Clear Filter/View All** link.

INTRODUCING QUICKBOOKS ONLINE | 19

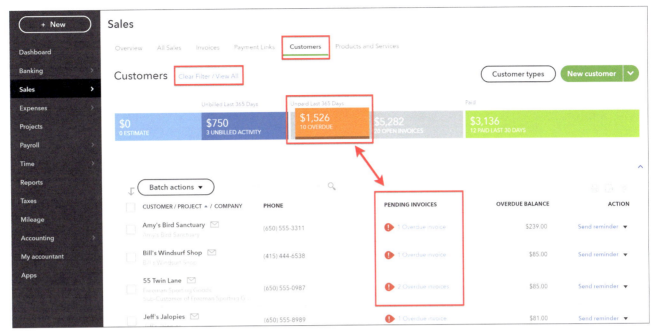

Figure 1-20: *The Money Bar filters your list-based Centers*

The Bottom Bar

At the bottom of many transaction windows is a black bar with several actions (see Figure 1-21). The options you see depend on what kind of transaction you are in.

Print or Preview shows you what the transaction will look like when you send it to the customer or vendor.

Make Recurring allows you to memorize a transaction to duplicate it later (see page 203).

Customize allows you to choose between your Custom Form Styles (see page 78).

Save maintains your progress while keeping the window open.

You may also see a *Revert* button used when you start making edits but need to discard the changes.

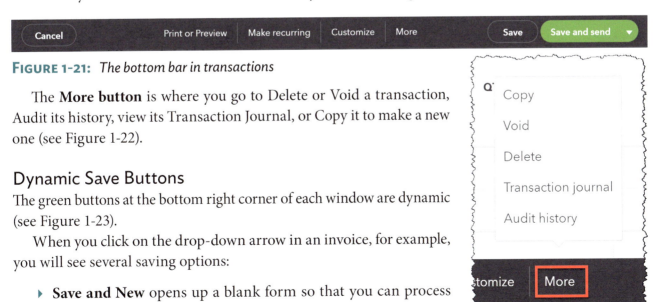

Figure 1-21: *The bottom bar in transactions*

The **More button** is where you go to Delete or Void a transaction, Audit its history, view its Transaction Journal, or Copy it to make a new one (see Figure 1-22).

Dynamic Save Buttons

The green buttons at the bottom right corner of each window are dynamic (see Figure 1-23).

When you click on the drop-down arrow in an invoice, for example, you will see several saving options:

▸ *Save and New* opens up a blank form so that you can process several similar transactions quickly.

Figure 1-22: *The More button*

- **Save and Close** closes a transaction and returns you to the screen you were on.
- **Save and Share Link** creates a URL web address that you can email or text to customers.
- **Save and Send** will email a copy directly to the customer or vendor.

This button is sticky. Once you change the action, it will stay that way until you change it again.

FIGURE 1-23: *Dynamic Save buttons*

Using the Search

To look for a transaction that you just entered recently, a transaction for a specific dollar amount, an invoice by number, or all transactions that meet a specific criteria, use the **Search** magnifying glass (see Figure 1-24).

> **TIP:**
>
> You can even use the *Search* field to run a report or jump to a customer! Be sure to read the **Search Tips** at the top of the box. Experiment!

We will learn more about using the **Advanced Search** tool on page 297.

HANDS-ON PRACTICE

You want to review a credit card expense to Hicks Hardware that your co-worker created a few minutes ago.

STEP 1. Click on the **Magnifying Glass** in the upper right corner, as shown in Figure 1-24.

STEP 2. Click on **Credit Card Expense | Hicks Hardware | $42.40**.

STEP 3. The expense opens. Review it, then **Cancel** the window so you don't save any changes.

The Gear

The big **Gear** in the upper right corner is the control center for all the back-end administrative tasks to manage your company file and QuickBooks Online experience (see Figure 1-25).

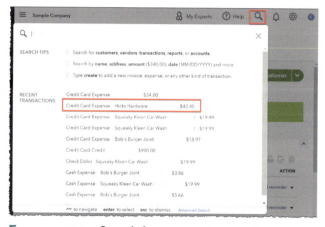

FIGURE 1-24: *Search for a recent transaction*

FIGURE 1-25: *The Gear is where you'll find administrative tools*

This is where you control your settings, lists, data, and support tools including feedback. We will talk about many of the features on the Gear throughout this course.

Feedback

Intuit, the company that makes QuickBooks Online, strives to "design for delight." If you find bugs in the software, or a feature doesn't work the way you need it to, be sure to click on **Feedback**. Tell the developers what isn't working, or what ideas you have.

The more people who let Intuit know about an issue, the higher a priority it will become on their feature roadmap. Many of the innovations in QBO were suggested by people like you!

Shortcuts

Autofill

When you're entering data in forms, Autofill saves you time from having to scroll up and down a long list scanning for the item you need, or from having to type the entire entry.

QuickBooks Online saves you time by filtering available options as you type. For example, instead of scrolling down through customer names looking for someone whose name starts with W, just type any of the letters from their name into the box. It doesn't even have to be the first word—any unique string of characters will do. QBO limits the list of options to only those that match. If a list contains headers and sub-accounts, some of the options on the list will appear indented but may not be related to the category directly above them.

If you type faster than QBO searches its list, you may override the match and trigger the software to **Add New**. If you suddenly find yourself creating a new entry that you know already exists, immediately stop, cancel the window, and try again a bit more slowly.

Keyboard Shortcuts

If you're a fan of **keyboard shortcuts**, you're in luck! Even though QBO is browser-based, you can still get around without taking your fingers off the keyboard. To see the list of shortcuts shown in Figure 1-26, press **Ctrl-Alt-?** (**Cmd-Option-?** on a Mac).

This is also one of the places to go to find your **Company ID** if you need to contact Support.

Date Shortcuts

When entering dates, you don't need to type in the leading 0s or the current year. For example, typing **2/1** then pressing the **Tab** key on your keyboard (to the left of the Q) will resolve the date to 02/01/2023 (using your current year).

The **Date fields** also have their own set of shortcuts, as shown in Table 1-2. Click in any *Date* field and tap these letters to jump to a date without typing.

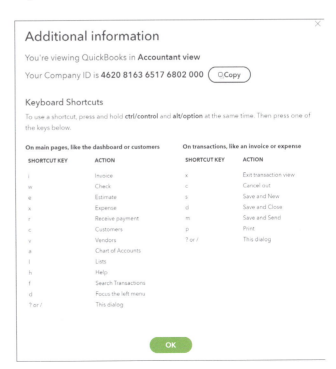

FIGURE 1-26: *Keyboard Shortcuts*

You can press them in any combination to reach any date. For example, to get to the last day of the year three years ago, you could type **YYYR**.

TODAY	T
TOMORROW, NEXT DAY	+ (plus)
YESTERDAY, PREVIOUS DAY	- (minus)
FIRST DAY OF THE YEAR (1/1)	Y
LAST DAY OF THE YEAR (12/31)	R

FIRST DAY OF THE MONTH (1ST)	M
LAST DAY OF THE MONTH (28TH, 30TH, 31ST)	H
FIRST DAY OF THE WEEK (LAST SUN)	W
LAST DAY OF THE WEEK (NEXT SAT)	K

TABLE 1-2: *These date shortcuts move you quickly through time*

Built-in Calculators
There is no need to pull out your calculator to do your math! In every **Quantity, Rate,** and **Amount** field, you can use +, -, *, /, and () to do instant math. Press **Tab** to calculate the result.

Currency
When entering dollar amounts, skip the dollar sign ($), the commas (,), and the ending decimals on whole dollar amounts. QuickBooks Online will autofill these when you press **Tab** on your keyboard. For example, if you type in **1000** then press **Tab**, it will resolve to **$1,000.00** automatically.

Search for text on a page
This trick uses a feature of your browser, not QuickBooks Online. The browser's Search, **Ctrl-F (Cmd-F** on a Mac), searches all the content of the screen you're looking at. Use it to find anything on a page instantly, without wasting time scrolling around scanning for it. Use the *Find* field's < > arrows to jump from instance to instance of matching text.

ENTERING TRANSACTIONS IN QUICKBOOKS ONLINE

Each time you buy or sell products or services, pay a bill, make a deposit at the bank, or transfer money, you enter a corresponding transaction into QuickBooks Online.

Each real-world activity will have one corresponding action in QBO. For example, a customer paying off several invoices with ONE check will have ONE Receive Payment form (more about that on page 126).

The +New Button for Forms
In QuickBooks Online, transactions are created by filling out familiar-looking **Forms** such as invoices, bills, and checks. Most forms in QuickBooks Online have drop-down lists to allow you to pick from a list instead of spelling out the name of a customer, vendor, product, or account. When you finish filling out a form, QuickBooks Online automatically records the accounting entries behind the scenes.

The **+New button** at the top of the *Left Navigation Bar* opens new blank forms for customers, vendors, employees, and general business transactions (see Figure 1-27). By using these forms to enter business activity, you provide QBO with all of the details of each transaction.

INTRODUCING QUICKBOOKS ONLINE | 23

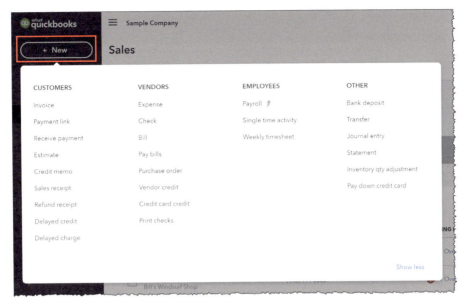

FIGURE 1-27: *The +New button to add new transactions through forms*

For example, by using the **Bill** form, QuickBooks Online tracks the vendor balance, the due date of the bill, the payment terms, and the debits and credits in the General Ledger. This is a good example of how QBO handles the accounting behind the scenes.

Before QuickBooks Online, many bookkeepers used **Journal Entries** to manually enter accounting transactions. Relying on journal entries limits QuickBooks Online from providing management information and analysis beyond just the debits and credits on simple reports. If a form is available that achieves your goal, use it so that you can capture business intelligence!

HANDS-ON PRACTICE

STEP 1. Click **Bill** in the *Vendors* column of the *+New Button* (see Figure 1-28).

STEP 2. Click the **Recent** button in the upper left corner of the *Bill* window, and choose the **most recent bill** at the top of the list (see Figure 1-29).

STEP 3. Look around the *Norton Lumber bill* shown in Figure 1-30. Click the **down arrow** next to the *Vendor* field to see the drop-down list of vendors.

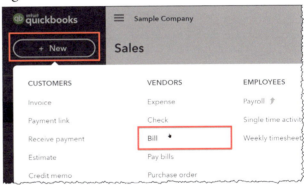

FIGURE 1-28: *Bills on the +New button*

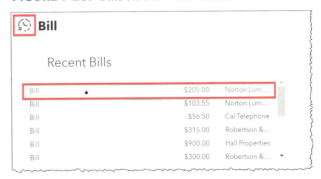

FIGURE 1-29: *Open a recent bill*

> **TIP:**
>
> You don't have to scroll up and down to choose items on lists. You can type in any letters from its name to limit the list of choices. They don't even have to be the first letters of the name! Try unique character strings that won't match any other names.

- **STEP 4.** Click the **Calendar icon** next to the date to see the **Date Picker**. Try out the date shortcuts you learned on page 22.
- **STEP 5.** Click in the **Amount** field. Try a math calculation using +, -, *, or /. Press **Tab** to calculate the answer.
- **STEP 6.** When finished exploring, click the **Cancel** button on the bottom left, then select **Yes** to close the bill without saving any changes you made.

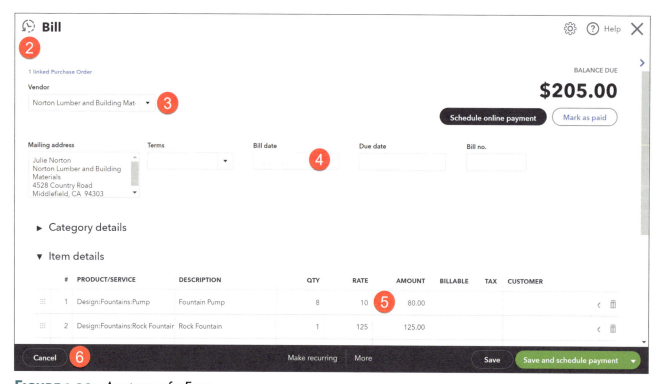

FIGURE 1-30: *Anatomy of a Form*

Lists

Lists are one of the most important building blocks of QuickBooks Online. Lists store information that is used again and again to fill out forms. For example, when you set up a customer including their name, address and other details, **QBO** will use the information to populate an invoice. Similarly, when you select a ***Product or Service***, QBO automatically fills in its description, price, and associated information. This helps speed up data entry and reduce errors.

> **NOTE:**
>
> There are two kinds of lists—**menu-based** and **center-based**. Menu-based lists are accessible through *All Lists* under the *Gear* and populate the fields on forms. Center-based lists include the **Customers Center** and **Vendors Center**, discussed on page 17.

To see all the menu-based lists you can customize, click on the **Gear** in the upper right corner, then **All Lists** (see Figure 1-31).

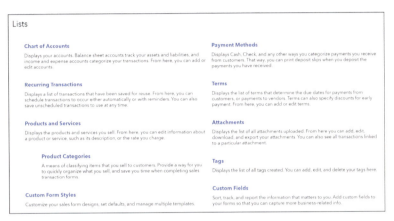

FIGURE 1-31: *The list of Lists*

Accounts

QuickBooks Online efficiently tracks all of your business transactions by categorizing them into *Accounts* in your *General Ledger*. The *Chart of Accounts* is the list of these accounts.

HANDS-ON PRACTICE

STEP 1. To display the Chart of Accounts, hold your cursor over *Accounting* in the *Left Navigation Bar*, then click on **Chart of Accounts**. Alternatively, you could select **Chart of Accounts** from the *Gear*, or press **Ctrl-Alt-A** (**Cmd-Option-A** on a Mac).

STEP 2. If you see the message *"Take a Peek Under the Hood,"* click **See Your Chart of Accounts**.

STEP 3. Scroll through the list. Leave the *Chart of Accounts* open for the next exercise.

By default, the Chart of Accounts is sorted alphabetically within each account type (see Figure 1-32). If you are using **Account Numbers**, the categories are sorted by account number.

Use the **Filter by Name box** at the top to quickly find the account you need.

The **Name** column shows the account names that you will use in transactions and reports. The **Type** column shows their account type. The **yellow arrows** indicate **Banking Feed** connectivity. The **Detail Type** indicates the tax form section mapping. The **QuickBooks Balance** column shows the balances for asset, liability, and equity accounts (except Retained Earnings). The **Bank Balance** column shows the balance according to the bank, for accounts that are connected. The **Action** column offers common activities you might need.

FIGURE 1-32: *Chart of Accounts List*

Registers

Each asset, liability, and equity account (except Retained Earnings) has a **Register**. Income and expense accounts do not have registers; rather, their transactions must be viewed in a report.

Registers allow you to view transactions in a single window. While you can enter new transactions into QuickBooks Online from the register, this is not a good idea because of the limited information available. Instead use **Forms**, as we discussed on page 22.

HANDS-ON PRACTICE

STEP 1. To open the **Checking** account register, click on **View Register** on the right of the *Checking account* in the *Chart of Accounts* list.

STEP 2. The **Checking** register opens (see Figure 1-33). Scroll through the register.

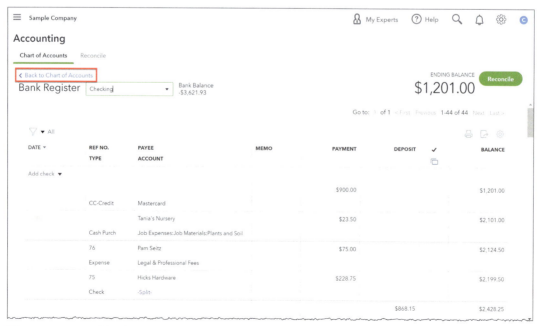

FIGURE 1-33: *Checking account register*

STEP 3. Return to the Chart of Accounts by clicking the **Back to Chart of Accounts** link in the upper left corner.

STEP 4. Scroll down to the **Sales of Product Income** account and click **Run Report**.

STEP 5. Instead of opening a register, QuickBooks Online opens an *Account QuickReport* (see Figure 1-34).

STEP 6. Change the *Date Range* to **All Dates** and click **Run Report**.

STEP 7. Go back to the *Chart of Accounts* again using the blue link.

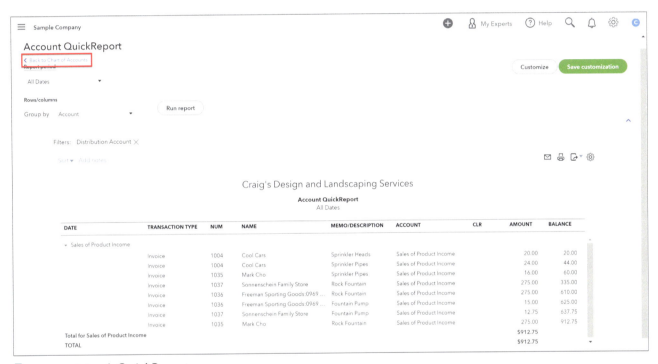

FIGURE 1-34: *A QuickReport*

Products and Services

Products and Services are used to track a company's sales items. Since every business has its own unique set of products and services, QuickBooks Online needs to be customized by creating items for everything you buy and sell.

Products and Services are necessary in order to use sales forms in QBO (e.g., *Invoices* and *Sales Receipts*). On an invoice, for example, each line has an item representing what people are paying for.

When you define items, you associate them with accounts in the Chart of Accounts. This connection between item names and accounts is the "magic" that allows QBO to automatically create the accounting entries behind each transaction.

QuickBooks Online uses the Products and Services items to manage all the accounting entries so that you don't have to. By setting up the item and then using it in forms, all the accounting happens behind the scenes, populating the reports so that you see the results without having to micromanage the activity.

HANDS-ON PRACTICE

STEP 1. To see what items the company buys and sells, hold your cursor over **Sales** in the *Left Navigation Bar*, then click **Products and Services** (see Figure 1-35).

Alternatively, you could select **Products and Services** from the *Gear*, or click the **Products and Services tab** from anywhere in the *Sales Center*.

STEP 2. Figure 1-36 shows the *Products and Services List*.

STEP 3. Click on the blue **Edit** button on the right of the **Rock Fountain** row.

STEP 4. The Rock Fountain's *Product/Service Information* window opens (see Figure 1-37). Rock Fountains are an **Inventory Item**, meaning that QuickBooks Online tracks the quantity and value in stock. Inventory-type items are associated with an **Inventory Asset account**, an **Income account**, and an **Expense account** in the Chart of Accounts.

STEP 5. Click the green **Save and Close** button to close the *Product/Service information* pane.

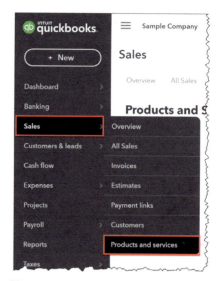

FIGURE 1-35: Products & Services

FIGURE 1-36: The Products and Services List

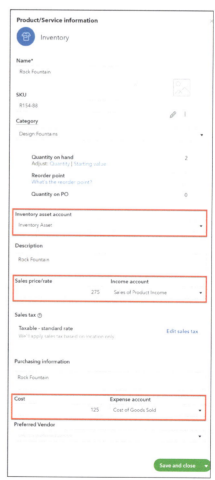

FIGURE 1-37: Rock Fountain product setup

ACCOUNTING BEHIND THE SCENES:

This is why using products and forms is so important! Bookkeepers used to have to track all this manually ... QuickBooks Online does the work for you.

QBO uses the Inventory Asset, Income, and Cost accounts from the product to track the revenue and expense associated with all inventory activity.

Every time a Rock Fountain product is purchased on an expense or bill, its cost is added to (debits) **Inventory Asset** on the Balance Sheet. Every time a Rock Fountain is sold by adding it to an invoice or sales receipt, the **Sales Price/Rate** increases (credits) the **Sales of Product Income** account, and QBO automatically moves its original cost out of (credits) **Inventory Asset** and into (debits) **Cost of Goods Sold**.

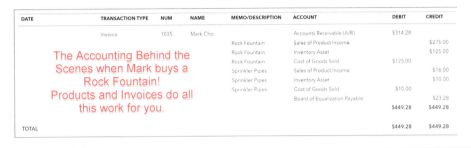

The Accounting Behind the Scenes when Mark buys a Rock Fountain! Products and Invoices do all this work for you.

QUICKBOOKS ONLINE HELP

Support Resources

QuickBooks Online provides a variety of support resources that assist in using the program. To access the support resources, click the **Help** button in the top bar, and the *Assistant* will open. QBO displays context-sensitive answers to problems you might be having, based on the window you have open. You can also search for keywords or ask a question, and QuickBooks Online will search its Help content and the **Online Community** for related answers.

Click **Contact Us** in the Help's *Search tab* to access live Support representatives through chat and call-back options. There is no need to call in and wait on hold! Note that the support specialists are intended for product help, and cannot answer bookkeeping questions.

Certified QuickBooks Online ProAdvisors

Certified QuickBooks Online ProAdvisors are independent consultants, accountants, bookkeepers, and educators with demonstrated proficiency in QuickBooks Online, who can offer guidance to small businesses in various areas of business accounting and bookkeeping. To find a Certified ProAdvisor, visit **www.findaproadvisor.com**.

If you will be developing a career using QuickBooks Online, consider signing up for the ProAdvisor Program at **quickbooks.intuit.com/accountants/proadvisor**. Passing Intuit's Certification exams does more than just prove your expertise. It also gives you access to a higher level of support, discounted pricing on products, free training and software, practice management, accountant-only tools, and a listing on www.findaproadvisor.com.

REVIEW QUESTIONS

Comprehension Questions

1. Explain the difference between the QuickBooks Online sample company in the tutorials, and this book's practice file at the end of the chapters.
2. Explain the difference between QuickBooks Desktop and QuickBooks Online. What are the different versions of QuickBooks Online?
3. Explain the importance of QuickBooks Online's Dashboard.
4. Explain why it is important to enter transactions in QuickBooks Online using Forms rather than accounting entries.
5. Describe the primary purpose of accounting in business.

Multiple Choice

Select the best answer(s) for each of the following:

1. The fundamental accounting equation that governs all accounting is:
    a. Net income = Revenue – expenses.
    b. Assets + Liabilities = Equity.
    c. Assets = Liabilities + Equity.
    d. Assets = Liabilities – Equity.

2. Which of the following statements is true?
    a. Debits are bad because they reduce income.
    b. Equity is increased by a net loss.
    c. Total debits equal total credits in every transaction.
    d. Assets are increased with a credit entry.

3. Under accrual accounting:
    a. A sale is not recorded until the customer pays the invoice.
    b. Income and expenses are recognized when transactions occur.
    c. An expense is not recorded until you write the check.
    d. You must maintain two separate accounting systems.

4. QuickBooks Online is:
    a. A job costing system.
    b. A payroll system.
    c. A double-entry accounting system.
    d. All of the above.

5. Which is not a method of accessing the data entry screens?
    a. +New button
    b. Dashboard
    c. Keyboard shortcuts
    d. The Gear

Completion Statements

1. As you enter data in familiar-looking _____, QuickBooks Online handles the _____ entries for you.

2. You do not need to _____ your data file regularly because it is stored on Intuit's servers.

3. When you open your working data file, QuickBooks Online displays the _____. This page is broken into two sections—one for navigation and one with charts.

4. _____ _____ _____ are used in QuickBooks Online Sales forms to represent what the company buys and sells.

5. A list which shows all the accounts in your working data file is called the _____ _____ _____.

INTRODUCTION—APPLY YOUR KNOWLEDGE

1. Open the Craig's Landscaping sample company file.

2. Select **Sales** and then **Customers** from the Left Navigation Bar to display the Customers Center.
    a. What is the first customer listed on the left of the *Customers Center*?
    b. In the *Customers Center*, single click on **Bill's Windsurf Shop**. What is Bill's balance?
    c. Click the *Filter button* at the top of Bill's transaction listing and make sure it says **All Dates**. How many transactions do you see, and of what type?

3. Select **Expenses** and then **Vendors** from the Left Navigation Bar to display the Vendors Center.
    a. Click the orange **Overdue Bills** button in the *Money Bar*. What is the name of the first vendor displayed on this list?
    b. What is the *overdue balance* on this bill?

4. From the Left Navigation Bar, select **Accounting** and then the **Chart of Accounts**.
    a. What type of account is the **Checking** account?
    b. How many total accounts are there of this same type?
    c. What is the *QuickBooks Online Balance* for the **Savings** account? What does the *Bank* say it should be?

5. **Sign out** of Craig's Landscaping.

PREPARE FOR CHAPTER 2: SET UP YOUR PRACTICE COMPANY

To get ready for Chapter 2, it's time to get your own student company, Imagine Photography, from your instructor. This free student trial subscription is good for one year.

There are two steps: First, your instructor will invite you to create an account with Intuit. Immediately after you create your account and password, the wizard will start setting up your student file.

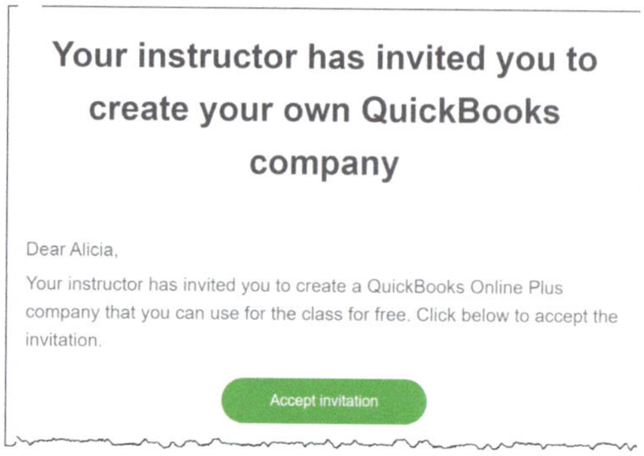

Creating your Student User Account

Your instructor will create your account using your school email address. If you already have an Intuit ID, ask your instructor if it would be OK to use that username.

You will receive an email with a link to click to create your account.

FIGURE 1-38: *Look for the email from your instructor*

HANDS-ON PRACTICE

- **STEP 1.** Find the email you received from your instructor. Click the **Accept Invitation** button as shown in Figure 1–38.
- **STEP 2.** On the Intuit account sign up screen shown in Figure 1–39, enter your information and choose a password. If you are using an existing account instead of creating a new one, click **Sign in**.
- **STEP 3.** Intuit may send you a verification code in a separate email. Enter it to continue.
- **STEP 4.** Save your password in a safe place!

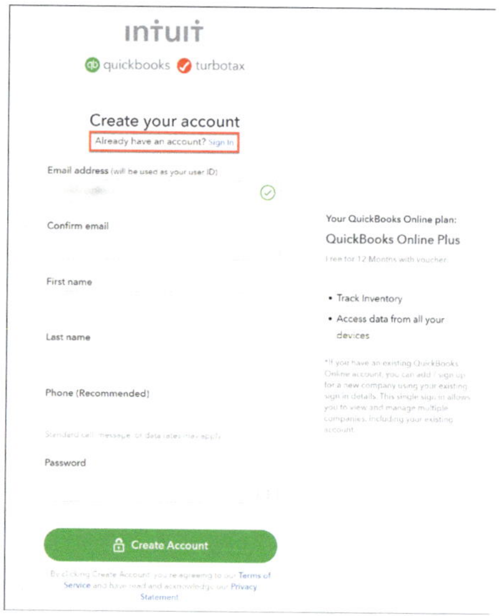

FIGURE 1-39: *Create Your Student Account*

Setting up Imagine Photography

After you create your user account, QuickBooks Online will continue right into setting up your classroom file. The first time you log in, QuickBooks Online will ask you a series of questions.

Be sure to use the answers below so that your screens will match the homework exercises.

Note that some of these questions will vary. When in doubt, choose the least specific option because we will set up the files manually in Chapter 2.

HAND-ON PRACTICE

- **STEP 5.** When QuickBooks Online asks, "*What do you call your business?*" enter the company name using this format **[Your first and last name]'s Imagine Photography**. Be sure to use your full name so that your instructor can easily identify you on their class list. Make sure *This Is My Legal Business Name* is **checked**. Click **Next**.

STEP 6. For *How have you been managing your finances?* click **Nothing, I'm Just Getting Started**.

STEP 7. For *What's your industry?* click the **Skip For Now** button.

STEP 8. For *What kind of business is this?* click the **I'm Not Sure** button. Click **Next**.

STEP 9. For *How does your business make money?* click both **Provides Services** and **Sells Products**. Click **Next**.

STEP 10. If you get the question, *What would you like to do in QuickBooks?* click all the boxes.

STEP 11. For *What's your main role at the business?* select **Bookkeeper or Accountant**. Click **Next**.

STEP 12. If you get the question, *What do you want to do today?* click **Skip For Now**.

STEP 13. For *Who works at this business?* select **everything** except **Only the Owner**. Click **Next**.

STEP 14. For *Want to add QuickBooks Online Payroll Premium?* select **No, I Don't Want to Add Payroll**. Click **Next**.

STEP 15. For *What apps do you use for your business?* click **Skip For Now**.

STEP 16. For *Link your accounts and see everything in one place*, click **Skip For Now**.

STEP 17. For *What is everything you want to set up?* click **Skip For Now**.

STEP 18. For *We're almost ready to dive in!* click on **Let's Go**. If prompted to *Take a Quick Tour*, click the **X** to close the window.

STEP 19. **Sign out** when done by clicking on **your initial** in the circle in the upper right corner and selecting **Sign Out**.

STEP 20. **Drag the URL** to your *Bookmarks Bar* for easy access.

STEP 21. Log in again to make sure you know the password.

Setting up the Chart of Accounts

STEP 22. Click on **Accounting** near the bottom of the *Left Navigation Bar*, and view your *Chart of Accounts*.

As of this writing, Intuit is experimenting with different Charts of Accounts in new QuickBooks Online subscriptions. This book was written using an accounts list that looks like Figure 1-40. Compare yours; if it matches, you can skip the rest of these instructions and simply **Sign Out**.

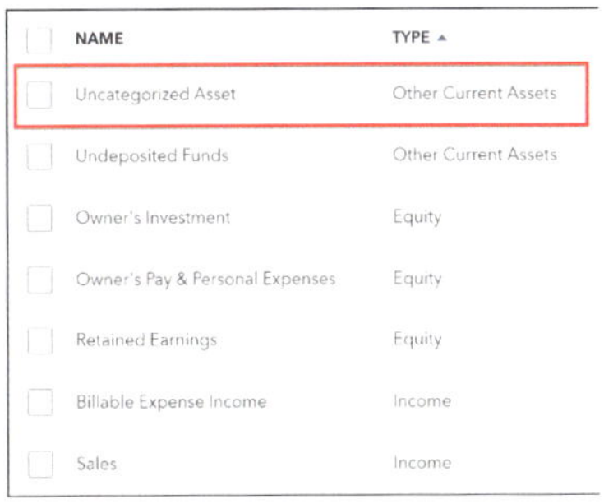

STEP 23. If your *Chart of Accounts* looks like Figure 1-41 instead, with *Uncategorized Asset* at the top of your list instead of *Cash*, follow the rest of the instructions on this page to set up your file to match the book.

FIGURE 1-40: The Chart of Accounts used in this book

FIGURE 1-41: If your Accounts look like this, follow the steps below

STEP 24. Edit Chrome's website URL by deleting **homepage** at the end and replacing it with **purgecompany**, as shown in Figure 1-42.

FIGURE 1-42: *Change the end of the URL to purgecompany*

STEP 25. QBO wants to make sure that we want to proceed. Type **YES** into the box on the lower right, then click **OK** (see Figure 1-43).

STEP 26. In the *What type of business is this?* box, choose **All Other Miscellaneous Services**.

STEP 27. Under *Create accounts based on my industry?* choose **Create an empty chart of accounts (select only with the advice of an accountant)**, as shown in Figure 1-44.

FIGURE 1-43: *Type YES and click OK to continue*

STEP 28. Click the **Wipe Data** button. QuickBooks will erase most of the accounts but leave a handful of default accounts that it needs in order to work properly.

FIGURE 1-44: *Select the business type and the option to empty the list*

STEP 29. Now we will import the Chart of Accounts that matches this book. Click the drop-down arrow next to the green **New** button on the upper right and select **Import**, as shown in Figure 1-45.

STEP 30. Click the **Browse** button, as shown in Figure 1-46. Navigate to your **QuickBooks Online Classroom Files** folder and open **ChartofAccounts.xlsx**. Click **Next**.

FIGURE 1-45: *Drop down New and click Import*

STEP 31. Accept all default mappings and click **Next** again.

STEP 32. Click **Import**.

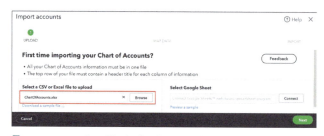

STEP 33. Your *Chart of Accounts* will now match Figure 1-40.

FIGURE 1-46: *Click the Browse button*

STEP 34. Your **Imagine Photography** file is now ready to be used in the *Apply Your Knowledge* end-of-chapter exercises. You can use these same steps if needed for the *YinYang Graphic Design Case Study*.

STEP 35. Don't forget to **Sign Out** when you're done for the day!

CHAPTER 2

CUSTOMIZING QUICKBOOKS ONLINE

TOPICS

In this chapter, you will learn about the following topics:

- Starting a New QuickBooks Online Company (page 35)
- Configuring Account and Settings (page 38)
- Setting Up the Chart of Accounts (page 45)
- Setting Up Products and Services (page 56)
- Customizing Lists (page 67)
- Implementing Custom Fields (page 70)
- Activating Class Tracking (page 71)
- Setting Up Sales Tax (page 73)
- Customizing Sales Forms (page 78)
- Adding Users and Passwords (page 83)

QuickBooks Online has many customizable options that allow you to configure the program to meet your own needs and preferences. This chapter introduces you to many of the ways you can make these configurations in QuickBooks Online by *importing data,* using **Account and Settings**, setting up your **Products and Services**, and creating templates for forms. This chapter also introduces some new lists including **Terms**, **Classes**, and **Custom Fields**.

OPEN THIS FILE:

Open the *Craig's Landscaping sample company* using the bookmark you created on page 8, or go to http://qbo.intuit.com/redir/testdrive.

STARTING A NEW QUICKBOOKS ONLINE COMPANY

Converting a QuickBooks Desktop File

If a company has been using QuickBooks Desktop and wants to convert to QuickBooks Online, they have the choice of starting over from scratch, or importing their existing file. There is an option on the *Company menu* in QuickBooks Desktop to import the file into QuickBooks Online.

Importing data is a good option if a file's reports are accurate, the lists are current, and the file is not overly large. Create the QBO subscription first, and then do the import. Once the data has been transferred, you would review the steps in this chapter to confirm that the file imported correctly, and then do a little fine-tuning.

Starting From Scratch

On the other hand, if the QuickBooks Desktop file's reports are inaccurate, or the lists are full of customers, vendors, and products/services that are no longer needed, starting over again in QuickBooks Online is a welcome opportunity for a fresh start. Many of the lists in QuickBooks Desktop or in Point of Sale systems can be exported into Excel or .csv data files, and then imported into QuickBooks Online. When setting up a brand new QBO file, uploading lists of current customers, vendors, products, and even a Chart of Accounts saves a lot of time from having to build all the lists from scratch as you go.

> *Do not perform these steps now. They are for reference only.*

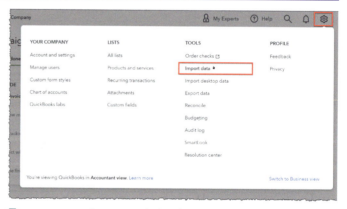

STEP 1. Click on the *Gear* and choose **Import Data**, as shown in Figure 2-1.

STEP 2. The screen in Figure 2-2 gives you the opportunity to import Customers, Vendors, a Chart of Accounts, Products and Services, and historic Invoices. There is also a button for importing Banking Feeds, which we will discuss on page 258.

FIGURE 2-1: *Import existing lists into your new QBO file*

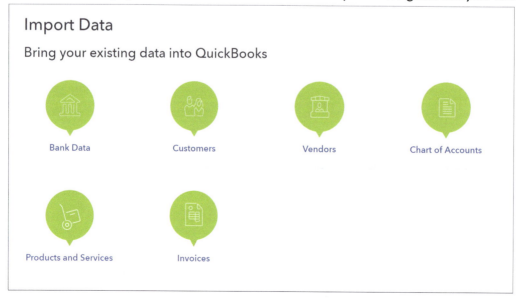

FIGURE 2-2: *Import these lists so that you don't have to start from scratch*

STEP 3. On the next screen shown in Figure 2-3, you'll choose the file you want to import. It's a good idea to **Download a Sample File** to see the fields QuickBooks Online needs, then use it as a template. Click **Browse** to locate the file on your computer, then click **Next**.

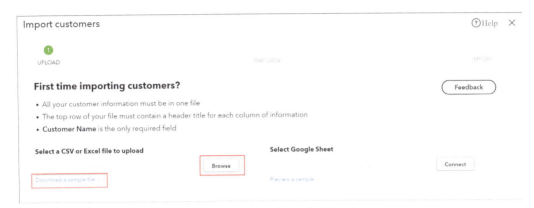

FIGURE 2-3: *Download a template and upload your data*

STEP 4. On the next screen shown in Figure 2-4, map the headings in your spreadsheet to the fields QuickBooks stores for customers. The only required field is *Name*. If you don't use one of the fields, leave **No Match** in the *Your Field* column.

If you don't like the results you see, click **Back** to return to the upload screen. Open your spreadsheet to fix any errors. Click **Browse** again to upload the corrected file.

FIGURE 2-4: *Map the headings in the spreadsheet to the fields in QBO*

STEP 5. Click **Next** when ready.

STEP 6. In the preview screen, verify your data is correct. In this example, none of the *Phone* numbers should say "**Phone:**" in front of the number. In the *Street* field, the city is also displayed. If you see errors, click the **Back** button, fix your original data file, and then start the import again from scratch.

STEP 7. Click the green **Import** button. QBO will tell you how many records were successfully imported.

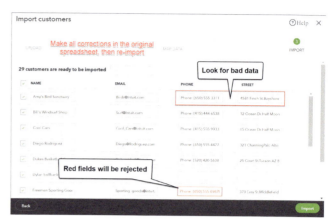

FIGURE 2-5: *Preview your data and look for errors*

DID YOU KNOW?

Sometimes QBO's import tools are not flexible enough for your needs. Third party apps such as **Transaction Pro Importer** and **Saasant** not only allow you to import additional data like bills and payments, but they even allow you undo an import if you don't like your results.

It may also be a good idea to use an app like **Rewind** to back up your QuickBooks Online file before you import, so that you can roll back the changes if the import does not go smoothly.

CONFIGURING ACCOUNT AND SETTINGS

At the end of Chapter 1, we created your company file for Imagine Photography. During the file setup process, the wizard walked you through questions about the company. In this chapter we will continue the setup process so that both *Craig's Landscaping* and *Imagine Photography* are ready to do business!

The first thing you need to do in a new QuickBooks Online company file is set up your preferences using **Account and Settings.**

It is important to go through your settings when you first set up your file in order to turn on and off the features needed for your company's workflow. In this chapter we will start with two of the company settings tabs and will later talk about the Sales and Expenses sections.

Company Settings

Open the *Craig's Landscaping sample company* using the bookmark you created on page 8, then click on the **Gear** in the upper right corner. Choose the first option, **Account and Settings** (see Figure 2-6).

Account and Settings contains all the preferences for your QBO file. It is broken up into five or more tabs; we will customize all these settings later in this course.

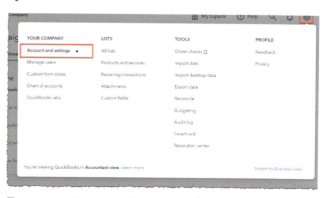

FIGURE 2-6: *Open Account and Settings*

When creating a new file, start with the *Company* settings (see Figure 2-7).

> **TIP:**
>
> Spelling and punctuation matter! The information you enter here will show up on all your customer forms and your tax reports, so be sure your entries are accurate.

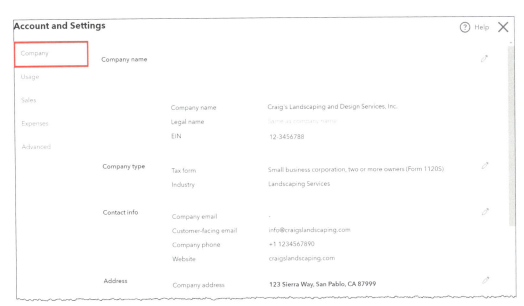

FIGURE 2-7: *Company Settings*

HANDS-ON PRACTICE

STEP 1. Click on the **Pencil** on the right in the *Company Name* section (see Figure 2-8).

FIGURE 2-8: *Enter in the Company Name and EIN*

STEP 2. Click on the **Company Logo.** Import the **CraigsLogo.jpg**, included in the folder of files that came with your textbook (*Note: Your sample company may not permit you to upload the logo. If that's the case, skip this step*).

STEP 3. Enter the *Company Name*, **Craig's Design and Landscaping, Inc.**.

STEP 4. If the company is a subsidiary of a parent company or you are a sole proprietor operating as a DBA ("Doing Business As," a fictitious name registered with your state), you would uncheck **Same as Company Name** and enter the **Legal Name**. We will not do this now.

STEP 5. Click the **dot** to the left of the *EIN (Employer Identification Number)* and enter **12-3456788**.

STEP 6. Click the **Save** button.

STEP 7. Click in the **Company Type** area (note that you don't actually need to click the *Pencil*). See Figure 2-9.

FIGURE 2-9: Enter the company's Tax Form and Industry

STEP 8. Choose the *Tax Form* **Small Business Corporation, Two Or More Owners (Form 1120S)**.

STEP 9. In the *Industry* box, start typing the word **Landscaping**. As you type, the list will filter to types of landscaping services. Choose **Landscaping Services**.

STEP 10. Click **Save**.

STEP 11. Click on the **Contact info** section (see Figure 2-10).

FIGURE 2-10: Enter the company's contact info

STEP 12. In the *Company email* field, enter the email address where QuickBooks Online can send you messages, **bookkeeping@craigslandscaping.com**.

STEP 13. Since we would like customers to contact the company at a different email address, uncheck **Same As Company Email**.

STEP 14. Enter the email address **info@craigslandscaping.com**.

STEP 15. Enter your company's customer service phone number, **123-456-7890**. Note that you don't need to type the () or hyphen. This is the phone number that will appear on sales forms.

STEP 16. Enter the company's website, **craigslandscaping.com**.

STEP 17. Click **Save**.

STEP 18. Note that there are three different address fields. The *Company Address* is the one Intuit will use for billing. The *Customer-facing Address* is the street address or mailing address that will be shown to customers. The *Legal Address* is the address used on tax forms. Because Craig uses just one address for all three, we don't need to change these fields.

STEP 19. In *Communications with Intuit*, you have the option to opt out of marketing email lists. We won't change these settings for now.

STEP 20. Double-check all the information for accuracy. Remember, typos here will cause your customers, vendors, and Intuit to be unable to reach you!

STEP 21. Leave this window open to get ready for the next step.

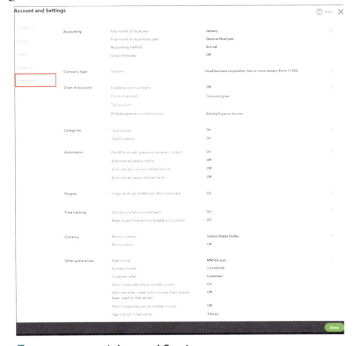

FIGURE 2-11: *Advanced Settings*

Advanced Settings

The next step in setting up a new company is to fine tune the **Advanced Settings**. These control the behavior and tools available in your file (see Figure 2-11).

Normally, you will set these preferences once for each company, and only change them as your needs evolve.

IMPORTANT!

Every time we use *Craig's Landscaping*, we may need to reset the settings required for the lesson. The settings in this section which we will frequently turn on include:

▸ Classes and Locations (page 71)

▸ Automations (page 44)

▸ Sign me out if inactive for 3 hours (page 45)

HANDS-ON PRACTICE

STEP 1. If you are not already in *Account and Settings*, click the **Gear** to open them.

STEP 2. Click the **Advanced** tab, the last on the list at left.

STEP 3. Click on the **Accounting** section (see Figure 2-12).

STEP 4. Leave your *First Month of Fiscal Year* on **January**. This field indicates the beginning of the year for year-to-date reports, such as the *Profit & Loss* report.

Some companies may have a July-June or October-Sept fiscal year. Most companies' *First Month of Income Tax Year* is the same as their fiscal year, but others will still file taxes for the calendar year.

> ### NOTE FOR NEW BUSINESSES:
>
> The **first month of your fiscal or income tax year** is NOT the month you started your business. It is the first month of your financial reporting period.
>
> Setting the first month in your fiscal year correctly is important as it specifies the default date range for accounting reports such as the *Profit & Loss Statement* and *Balance Sheet*. The first month in your tax year specifies the default date range for *Income Tax Summary* and *Detail* reports.

STEP 5. Leave the *Accounting Method* on **Accrual**. Craig's customers pay on account, and he likes to track his revenue based on when services are provided, not just on the payments he has already received. His state also calculates **Sales Tax** based on open invoices, even if he has not received the money yet.

STEP 6. Also leave the *Close the Books* slider **Off**. Closing the books is a way to prevent changes in historic data, so you may want to update this setting at the end of a fiscal period.

STEP 7. Click **Save**.

FIGURE 2-12: *Leave the Accounting section on the default settings*

CUSTOMIZING QUICKBOOKS ONLINE | 43

> **TIP:**
>
> If you are unsure how to answer the options in the *Account and Settings*, consider contacting a QuickBooks Online expert. **QuickBooks Online ProAdvisors** are bookkeepers, accountants, software consultants, and CPAs who offer QuickBooks Online-related consulting services. In addition, **QuickBooks Online Certified ProAdvisors** are those ProAdvisors who have completed a comprehensive training and testing program. For more information on QuickBooks Online ProAdvisors and Certified ProAdvisors, see page 29.

STEP 8. The *Company Type* section contains the same **S Corporation** form we selected on the previous screen. There is nothing to change here.

STEP 9. Click on the **Chart of Accounts** section to open it (see Figure 2-13).

STEP 10. If you wanted to turn on **Account Numbers**, you would turn on the **slider** next to *Enable account numbers*, and then put a **checkmark** in front of *Show Account Numbers*. See page 46 for more information. Do not do this now.

STEP 11. Leave all the defaults, including *Discount Account*, *Tips Account*, and *Billable Expense Income Account*.

STEP 12. Click **Save**.

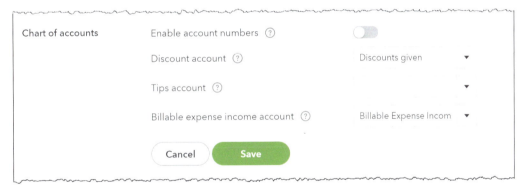

FIGURE 2-13: *This is where you would Enable Account Numbers*

STEP 13. The *Categories* section is where you'll turn on **Classes** and **Locations** (see Figure 2-14). We will discuss class tracking on page 71.

STEP 14. Turn on the **slider** for *Track Classes*. Place a **checkmark** in front of *Warn Me When A Transaction Isn't Assigned a Class*. When you use classes, you need to use them consistently.

STEP 15. Leave the default on *Assign Classes:* **One to each row in transaction**.

STEP 16. Turn on the **slider** for *Track Locations*. Note that you can change the label to use this feature for Departments, Divisions, Properties, Stores, and Territories. Only one location can be assigned per transaction.

STEP 17. Click **Save**.

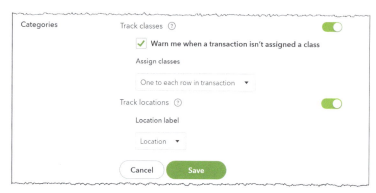

Figure 2-14: *Turn on Classes and Locations*

Step 18. The *Automation* section controls whether QuickBooks Online will help you out with Accounts Receivable and Accounts Payable transactions (see Figure 2-15).

Step 19. *Pre-Fill Forms With Previously Entered Content* is useful when you create a new invoice or bill. When you add a customer or vendor name, QBO will fill in the form using the same line items as the most recent transaction for that payee. This may help you save time, but if you find you constantly have to delete the products and services to start fresh, turn this slider off. We will leave it **On**.

Step 20. *Automatically Apply Credits* will apply credit memos to the oldest invoices without alerting you. For small businesses with forgetful owners this can be helpful, but in large companies it's important that you monitor Accounts Receivable. Click the **slider** to turn this **Off**. We will learn about credit memos on page 208, and see a demonstration of this automation on page 223.

Step 21. Leave the default **Off** for *Automatically Invoice Unbilled Activity*.

Step 22. *Automatically Apply Bill Payments* will apply your payments and vendor credits to your oldest bills without alerting you. In large companies it's important that you track Accounts Payable carefully. Click the **slider** to turn this **Off**.

Step 23. Click **Save**.

Figure 2-15: *Automation settings for Accounts Receivable and Accounts Payable*

Step 24. The next two sections in the Advanced settings turn on and off the features for **Projects** and **Currency**. We will leave these defaults.

Step 25. The *Other Preferences* section (see Figure 2-16) is where you can change your date formats and *Customer Label.* Do you call your customers **Clients, Donors, Members, Patients,** or **Tenants**? Renaming them here will change the terminology across your entire QuickBooks Online file. Do not change this now.

Step 26. Don't miss the option to lengthen the time you can stay signed in to QBO! By changing *Sign Me Out If Inactive For* to **3 Hours**, QBO's security is less likely to time out your file while you are working in it. Select **3 Hours** from the dropdown menu now.

Step 27. Click **Save**.

Step 28. Click the green **Done** button at the bottom right to return to the Dashboard.

> **TIP:**
>
> If you are working in multiple tabs and haven't touched one of them for more than three hours, that tab may time out even though you're still active in another one. When that happens, you don't need to sign again—just refresh your browser window and it should return to its previous state.

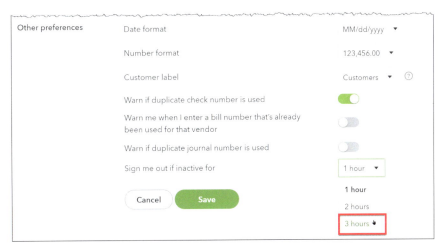

Figure 2-16: Other Preferences, where you can change the sign out time and Customer Label

SETTING UP THE CHART OF ACCOUNTS

The **Chart of Accounts** (COA) is one of the most important lists in QuickBooks Online. It is a list of all the accounts in the General Ledger, and it populates the categories in many of your reports including the Profit and Loss Statement and the Balance Sheet. If you are not sure how to design your Chart of Accounts, ask your accountant or QuickBooks ProAdvisor for help.

In QBO Simple Start through Plus, you can have a maximum of 250 categories on your COA. This is enough for most businesses. If you need more than that because your company is complex, upgrade to QuickBooks Online Advanced, which has unlimited accounts. You'll notice alerts in the system about actions that add to or reduce your count (such as the message in Figure 2-25 that says "won't reduce usage") to help you keep an eye out when you get close to the limit.

Account Types

There are five basic account types in accounting: *assets*, *liabilities*, *equity*, *income*, and *expenses*. QuickBooks Online breaks these basic account types into subtypes:

- Accounting uses five types of asset accounts: **Bank**, **Accounts Receivable**, **Other Current Assets**, **Fixed Assets**, and **Other Assets**.

- There are four types of liability accounts: **Accounts Payable**, **Credit Card**, **Other Current Liabilities**, and **Long Term Liabilities**.

- Income accounts can be divided into **Income** or **Other Income** types.

- Expenses can be classified as **Cost of Goods Sold**, **Expenses**, or **Other Expenses**.

- Equity doesn't have subtypes, but it does have specific required accounts including **Opening Balance Equity** and **Retained Earnings**.

Activating Account Numbers

QuickBooks Online does not require *account numbers*. If you prefer, you can use just the account *name* to differentiate between accounts.

In traditional accounting, the Chart of Accounts uses account numbers to identify the categories. The numbering system allows accounting professionals to instantly distinguish between different types of accounts by ID number across different company files. For example, 1000-1999 accounts are always asset accounts, and 4000–4999 accounts are always revenue.

Account numbers allow you to rearrange the categories in any order instead of the default, alphabetically by type. For example, if you want the **Savings** account to be above the **Money Market** account, assign account numbers accordingly.

Be sure to leave gaps between the numbers so there is room to add new accounts in the future.

Using account numbers also encourages consistency if you are working in multiple company files. For example, numbering the main operating checking account as 1000 means you don't have to remember the exact bank name in each QBO file.

If you prefer to use account numbers, you can activate them in the **Advanced section** of **Account and Settings**, following the instructions on page 43.

Adding Accounts

While QBO comes with a default Chart of Accounts, you will inevitably want to add categories of your own to represent your company's unique needs. On page 36 we saw that you can import your own Chart of Accounts.

HANDS-ON PRACTICE

Craig's Landscaping needs to track **Software** separately in its Profit and Loss report.

- **STEP 1.** Select the **Chart of Accounts** under the *Accounting* section of the *Left Navigation Bar*. If you get a *Take A Peek Under The Hood* screen, click **See your Chart of Accounts** (see Figure 2-17).

- **STEP 2.** Click on the **New** button at the top right of the *Chart of Accounts* window (be sure to click on the main button itself and not the drop-down arrow on its right side).

CUSTOMIZING QUICKBOOKS ONLINE | 47

FIGURE 2-17: The Chart of Accounts

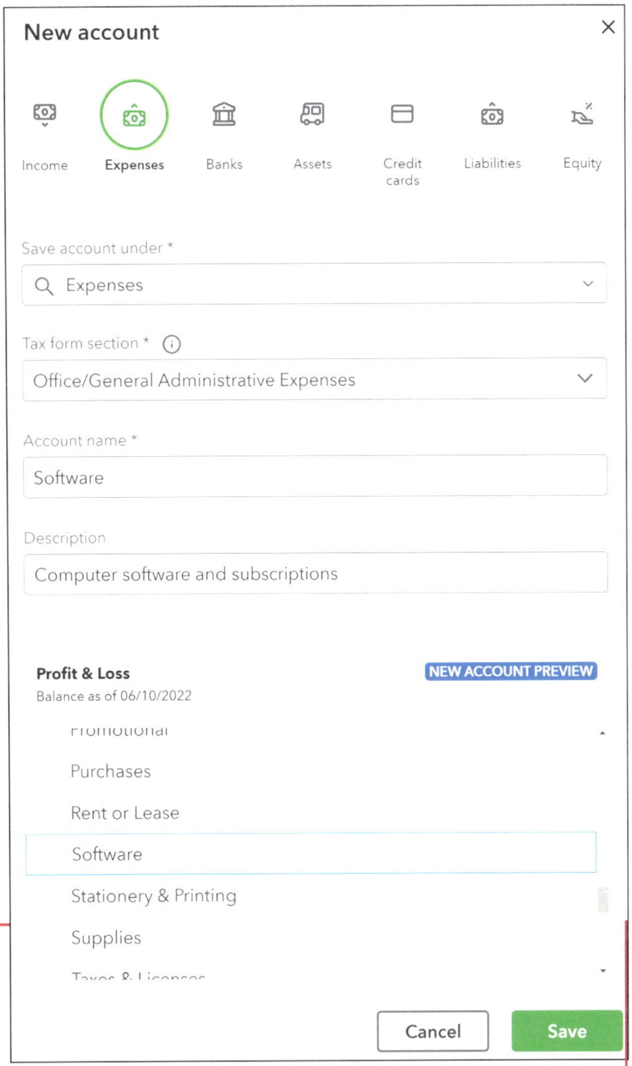

FIGURE 2-18: Add a new Expense account

> **ANOTHER WAY:**
>
> To open the *Chart of Accounts*, you may also select **Chart of Accounts** from the *Gear*, or press **Ctrl-Alt-A** (**Cmd-Option-A** on a Mac).

STEP 3. At the top of the pane that opens up on the right, select the **Expenses** circle (see Figure 2-18).

STEP 4. In the *Save Account Under** field, choose **Expenses**.

STEP 5. In the *Tax Form Section** field, choose **Office/General Administrative Expenses**.

> **DID YOU KNOW?**
>
> If you or your accountant uses TurboTax, ProSeries, Lacerte, ProConnect Tax, or other QuickBooks Online-compatible tax software to prepare your tax return, the *Tax Form Section* may help the software map your QBO accounts to the correct lines on your tax return. This allows the tax software to fill out your tax return automatically, based on the data in QuickBooks Online.

STEP 6. Enter **Software** in the *Account Name* field and press **Tab**. This is the name that will appear on your reports. Choose names that will help you or the business owner understand what type of transactions belong in this category.

STEP 7. Enter **Computer Software and Subscriptions** in the *Description* field. The *Description* field is not required, but it helps users understand the purpose of each category.

STEP 8. Scroll down to the *New Account Preview* to see how your new account will look in the Chart of Accounts and on your Profit and Loss Statement. Your screen should look like Figure 2-18 above. Click **Save** at the bottom of the window to save the account.

Modifying Accounts

Many business owners find it helpful when category names reflect the terminology used in their company or industry. You are welcome to rename categories, as long as you don't alter the original purpose of the account.

HANDS-ON PRACTICE

Craig finds the category **Supplies** too vague, so he asks you to edit the existing account name and function.

STEP 9. Click the drop-down arrow to the right of the *Supplies* row and choose **Edit** (see Figure 2-19).

FIGURE 2-19: *Edit the Supplies category*

STEP 10. Change the *Tax Form Section* to **Office/General Administrative Expenses** and the *Account Name* to **Office Supplies** as shown in Figure 2-20, then click **Save**.

STEP 11. When you get the confirmation alert, click **Yes**.

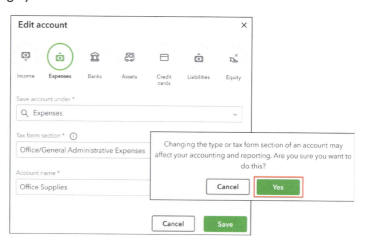

FIGURE 2-20: *Change the Tax Form Section and Account Name to Office Supplies*

Adding Sub-accounts

If you want additional detail in your Chart of Accounts, you can add **sub-accounts**. Account types for the main account and its sub-accounts must be same. You can add up to five levels of sub-accounts.

The main header account now totals the sub-accounts, so you will only use sub-accounts in transactions. In reports, whenever you see a total on the main account as well as under the sub-accounts, it means someone categorized a transaction into the header instead of the sub-account. To avoid this error, be sure to create all the sub-accounts you'll need for each contingency, or add an extra called **Other**.

When using a subaccount on a check, bill or other transaction, the account will appear with the main account followed by a colon and then the subaccount, in the format *Utilities:Garbage*.

DID YOU KNOW?

In *Reports* that include sub-accounts (e.g., *Balance Sheet* and *Profit & Loss Reports*), clicking the **Collapse** button removes the subaccount detail from the report. The balance of each primary account on the collapsed report is the total of its subaccount balances.

HANDS-ON PRACTICE

Craig's Landscaping determines that it would be useful to break out utility expenses on the *Profit & Loss Statement*. Their file already has utilities for **Gas & Electric** and **Telephone**, but also needs sub-accounts for **Garbage** and an **Other** category for any miscellaneous utility costs.

STEP 12. Display the **Chart of Accounts** using any method shown previously, if it is not already displayed.

STEP 13. Select the **New** button at the top right of the *Chart of Accounts* window.

STEP 14. Select the **Expenses** circle at the top (see Figure 2-21).

STEP 15. Choose **Utilities** for the *Save Account Under* field. Confirm the *Tax Form Section* also reads **Utilities**.

STEP 16. Type **Garbage** in the *Account Name* field, and enter **Trash and recycling** in the *Description* field.

STEP 17. Scroll down and confirm that **Garbage** appears indented under **Utilities** in the *New Account Preview*.

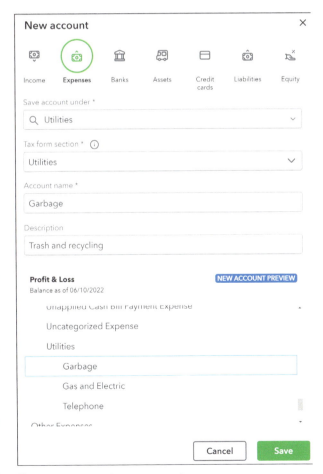

FIGURE 2-21: *Creating a sub-account*

STEP 18. Click the **Save** button.

STEP 19. Click the **New** button again.

STEP 20. Repeat the steps above to create a new **Other Utilities** sub-account under Utilities.

STEP 21. Enter **Other Utilities** in the *Description* field.

STEP 22. Click the green **Save** button.

STEP 23. Scroll down to the bottom of the list. Now the *Chart of Accounts* shows your new Utilities sub-accounts slightly indented under their main account, in alphabetical order (see Figure 2-22).

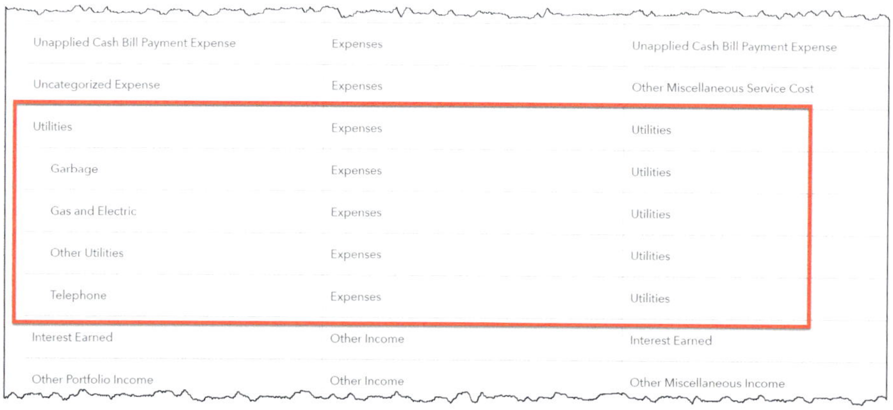

FIGURE 2-22: *Sub-accounts in the Chart of Accounts*

While sub-accounts provide granular detail, it is a best practice to keep your Chart of Accounts (COA) as tight as possible, while still providing sufficient operational data.

Notice that in the Income section of the Craig's Landscaping file COA in Figure 2-23, *Landscaping Services* are broken down into *Job Materials* and *Labor*, and then further into types of materials. This is usually too much detail for a Chart of Accounts.

Separating *Job Materials* and *Labor Income* is a useful distinction on a P&L report. The *Decks and Patios*, *Fountains*, *Plants*, *Sprinklers*, *Installation*, and *Maintenance* categories should all be tracked with **Products and Services** instead.

That way, you'll also be able to run a variety of Products and Services reports to see a detailed analysis of what the company buys and sells.

If you find yourself in this situation, you can simplify your Chart of Accounts either by *inactivating* or *merging* the accounts, as discussed in the next section.

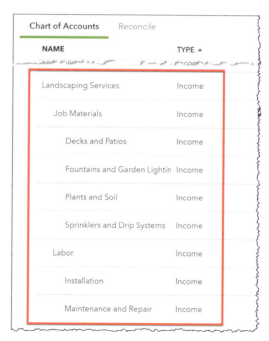

FIGURE 2-23: *A Chart of Accounts with too much detail*

Removing Accounts from the Chart of Accounts

When you no longer need an account, it is best to remove it from the Chart of Accounts list. Removing unnecessary accounts helps avoid data entry errors by ensuring that no transactions are accidentally posted to these accounts. There are two ways to remove an account from the Chart of Accounts: ***inactivating*** the account or ***merging*** the account with another account.

Note that some accounts are generated automatically for use by QuickBooks Online and cannot be edited or inactivated.

Inactivating Accounts

Most list items in QuickBooks Online cannot be completely deleted, only ***inactivated***. Inactivating an account category causes it to be hidden in the Chart of Accounts.

This is also true for lists, products and services, customers, and vendors. Inactivating unused items reduces the clutter in your lists while preserving your ability to see its history. Even after an account, product, customer, or vendor is made inactive, all transactions using that entry will still show on reports with **(deleted)** after the name.

> **IMPORTANT!**
>
> Asset, liability, and equity accounts cannot be inactivated if their balances are not zero. If you inactivate a Balance Sheet account, its balance will be automatically transferred to ***Opening Balance Equity***, causing an error in the company's equity.
>
> Before inactivating one of these categories, find out what happened to the remaining balance, and create the transfer or other transaction to move it to the correct account.

HANDS-ON PRACTICE

Craig notices that there's a **Purchases** expense account, but he doesn't use it. He would like to make it inactive. Before you inactivate it, do your due diligence to make sure that it's not important. Follow these steps to verify that it is not needed, then inactivate it:

STEP 1. Locate the **Purchases** expense in the *Chart of Accounts* list.

STEP 2. Click the blue **Run Report** action link on the far right to open a QuickReport.

STEP 3. In the *Report period* box in the top left, change the date range to **All Dates.**

STEP 4. Click the **Run Report** button.

FIGURE 2-24: *A QuickReport to confirm this account isn't important*

STEP 5. Notice that there are no transactions on the list. This account has never been used, so there's no reason to keep it.

STEP 6. Click the tiny blue **Back to Chart of Accounts** link in the upper left.

STEP 7. Click the **drop-down arrow** on the right of *Purchases*, and then choose **Make Inactive** from the menu (see Figure 2-25). Note the **(won't reduce usage)** message letting you know that inactivating this account won't affect your 250 category limit discussed on page 45.

FIGURE 2-25: *Making an account inactive in the Chart of Accounts*

Merging Accounts

If you find that two categories both contain similar transactions and you no longer need that level of detail, you can combine them. When you *merge* two accounts, QuickBooks Online updates each transaction from the merging account so that it posts to the remaining (combined) account instead. Then QuickBooks Online removes the account from the *Chart of Accounts* list.

You can only merge accounts of the same Account Type and Detail Type. In this example, both accounts are Legal and Professional Fees accounts.

> **IMPORTANT:**
>
> Merging cannot be undone. Once you merge accounts together, there is no way to find out which transactions were in the old account, except by reviewing a backup file. If you are about to do a Chart of Accounts cleanup, consider a third-party app like **Rewind** to backup and restore the file in case you have unexpected results.

HANDS-ON PRACTICE

Craig's Landscaping originally separated the **Accounting** and **Bookkeeper** categories, but now Craig has decided that the two accounts can be combined.

STEP 1. Display the **Chart of Accounts** list and scroll down to *Legal & Professional Fees*.

STEP 2. Click **Run Report** on the right of *Legal & Professional Fees*. In the *Report period* box in the top left, change the date range to **All Dates**, then click on **Run Report**.

In Figure 2-26, notice that the top transaction to *Pam Seitz* was accidentally coded to the main account instead of the subaccount (you would need to fix this later!), and that the two transactions to *Books by Bessie* are split between *Accounting* and *Bookkeeping*.

STEP 3. Click the blue **Back to Chart of Accounts** link in the upper left corner.

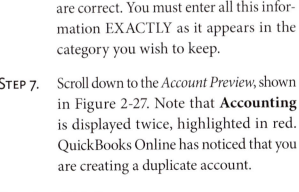

FIGURE 2-26: *Report with all Legal & Professional Fees*

STEP 4. Note the *Name, Type, and Detail Type* of the account you want to keep, **Accounting**. One way of ensuring that the name is exactly the same is to copy the name from the account you want to keep, and paste it into the name field of the one you want to inactivate.

STEP 5. Select the account whose name you *do not* want to keep. Click on the **drop-down arrow** to the right of **Bookkeeper**, then choose **Edit**.

STEP 6. Enter or paste **Accounting** in the *Account Name* field (see Figure 2-27). If there is an *Account Number*, delete it. Confirm the **Expenses** *Type, Save Account Under*, and *Tax Form Section* are correct. You must enter all this information EXACTLY as it appears in the category you wish to keep.

STEP 7. Scroll down to the *Account Preview*, shown in Figure 2-27. Note that **Accounting** is displayed twice, highlighted in red. QuickBooks Online has noticed that you are creating a duplicate account.

STEP 8. Click **Save**.

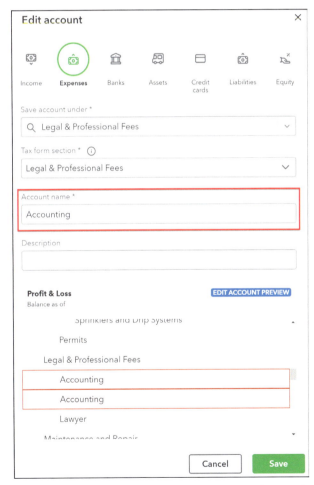

FIGURE 2-27: *Modify the account to exactly match the account you will keep*

STEP 9. Now that this account has the same name as the other account, QuickBooks Online asks if you want to merge the two accounts (see Figure 2-28). Click **Yes, Merge Accounts**.

STEP 10. Click **Save**.

Now that the **Bookkeeper** account has been merged into the **Accounting** account, running the QuickReport again shows that QBO has updated all the transactions that were categorized to **Bookkeeper** and moved them to **Accounting** instead, as shown in Figure 2-29.

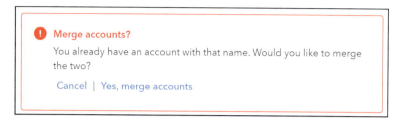

FIGURE 2-28: *Click Yes to merge the accounts*

Craig's Design and Landscaping Services

Account QuickReport

Since

DATE	TRANSACTION TYPE	NUM	NAME	MEMO/DESCRIPTION	ACCOUNT	CLR	AMOUNT	BALANCE
▾ Legal & Professional Fees								
	Expense	76	Pam Seitz	Counsel	Legal & Professional Fees		75.00	75.00
Total for Legal & Professional Fees							$75.00	
▾ Accounting								
	Check	12	Books by Bessie		Legal & Professional Fees:Accou...		55.00	55.00
	Bill		Books by Bessie		Legal & Professional Fees:Accou...		75.00	130.00
	Bill		Robertson & Associates		Legal & Professional Fees:Accou...		315.00	445.00
Total for Accounting							$445.00	
▾ Lawyer								
	Check		Tony Rondonuwu	Consulting	Legal & Professional Fees:Lawyer		100.00	100.00
Total for Lawyer							$100.00	
Total for Legal & Professional Fees with sub-accounts							$620.00	
TOTAL							$620.00	

FIGURE 2-29: *The Merged report shows the two Books By Bessie transactions together*

DID YOU KNOW?

Inactivating and merging is not limited to just the Chart of Accounts list. You can clean up most lists within QuickBooks Online, including Customers, Vendors, and Products and Services.

Seeing All Accounts

To view all accounts in the Chart of Accounts, including the inactive accounts, click the ***Grid Gear*** to drop down additional settings for the list. Select **Include Inactive**, and change the number of *Rows* to 300 (see Figure 2-30).

From this Grid Gear you can also show and hide columns.

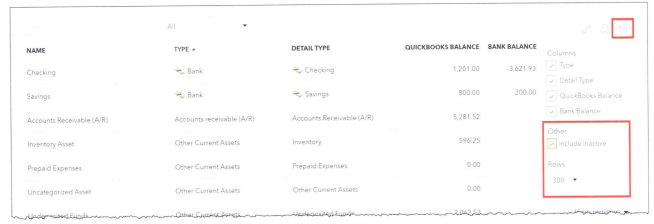

FIGURE 2-30: When Include Inactive is checked, all accounts appear in the list

The word **(deleted)** next to an account name indicates that it has been inactivated or merged. To reactivate the account, click on the blue **Make Active** link on the right. The account name will be restored to the Active list. Note that if two categories were merged, the action was permanent and you will not see the original transactions in the reactivated account.

FIGURE 2-31: Click Make Active to bring back an inactivated account

Sorting the Account List

The account types in the Chart of Accounts are arranged in the order in which they appear on financial statements. For example, all of the Bank accounts come first, followed by Accounts Receivable, Other Current Assets, and so on.

There are several ways to reorder the Chart of Accounts. Lists can be sorted by any column header. By default, the Chart of Accounts list sorts first by account type, and then alphabetically by account name within the account type.

If account numbers are in use, the Chart of Accounts will sort numerically by account number, instead of alphabetically.

> **NOTE:**
>
> When account numbers are active and you click the **Number** header, QuickBooks Online sorts the list only by account number and not by account name or type. Therefore, if you assign an account number of 7000 to a Bank account, QuickBooks Online will place that account near the bottom of the Chart of Accounts, instead of the top.

Sorting by Header

When account numbers are inactive and you click the **Name** header, QuickBooks Online sorts the account list alphabetically by account name. Click the **Name** header again to sort it from Z to A.

You may also sort the table by **QuickBooks Balance** or **Bank Balance**.
Click the **Type** header to return the list to its original order.

Printing the Chart of Accounts

To print the Chart of Accounts, click the **Printer** on the top right of the list, next to the *Grid Gear*. A new tab opens with a printable list, ready to be saved to a PDF or printed (see Figure 2-32). Close the tab when you're done.

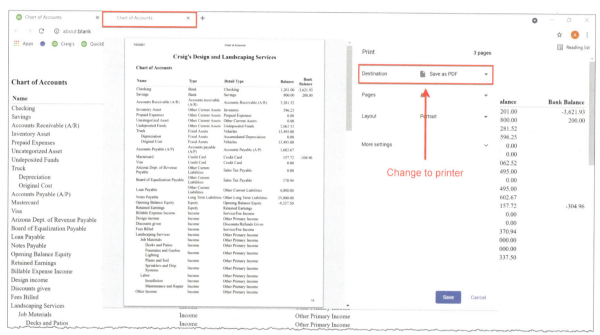

FIGURE 2-32: *The Chart of Accounts, ready to print*

SETTING UP PRODUCTS AND SERVICES

The **Products and Services List** is used to identify the goods and services your business sells and/or purchases.

In this section, you will learn more about QuickBooks Online's ***Products and Services*** items and how they affect the "accounting behind the scenes" as you create transactions. Every time you use a product or service in your transactions, its value flows into the linked accounts. In this way, Products and Services affect the financial statements for a company.

Products and Services in the *Products and Services List* are also used as part of the sales tax tracking process, as a means of generating subtotals, and as a method of calculating discounts.

Open the *Products and Services List* in one of four ways:

- Hover over **Sales** (or **Invoicing**) in the *Left Navigation Bar*, then click **Products and Services**.

- From anywhere the in the *Sales Center*, click the **Products and Services tab** at the top.

- Click **Products and Services** from the *Gear* in the upper right corner.

- Click **All Lists** from the *Gear* in the upper right corner and then click **Products and Services**.

The first time you view the Products and Services list, you will see default items suggested by QuickBooks Online based on the business entity type and industry you selected during the setup process (see page 40). Before you start using the file, be sure to update this list to reflect your company's offerings.

If you have a list of Products and Services from another system, you can import it using the instructions on page 36. Be sure to download the sample template because items and inventory have specific requirements.

In the Craig's Landscaping sample company, the list has already been created for you (see Figure 2-33).

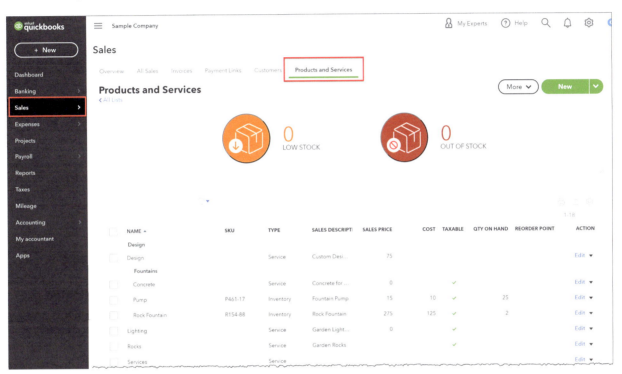

Figure 2-33: *The Products and Services List*

Product and Service Categories

Categories allow you to create groups of items. This is helpful when you have long lists of products, and for stores using a point-of-sale system that tracks departments.

When you use item categories, the *Sales by Product* reports will show totals for all inventory items by group. Categories are also handy when using Price Rules.

It is common to create a *Category* called **Admin** to contain fees and other non-commerce related items needed on sales forms.

The category list can be created by clicking on the **More** button in the upper right of the *Product and Services Center*, as seen in Figure 2-33. We will create our item categories on the fly as needed during these exercises.

Products and Services Types

There are four different types of Products and Services items in QuickBooks Online as shown in Figure 2-34. When you create a new product or service, you indicate the **Type** along with the **Name** of the item and the **Account** with which the item is associated.

- **Inventory items** track the quantity and value of your stock on hand.
- **Non-inventory items** are products you buy and/or sell but don't track quantity.
- **Service items** track services you provide to customers. They can also be used for administrative charges such as shipping and finance charges.
- **Bundle items** allow you to group several separate products and services together as a package and easily enter them on sales forms. Sales information for each item in the bundle is still tracked individually.

Service Items

Service items are used for all items on invoices and sales receipts that are not tangible goods.

FIGURE 2-34: *The New Product/Service Information window*

HANDS-ON PRACTICE

Craig's Landscaping sells mowing services by the hour. To track the sales of this **Service**, create a new service called **Mowing**, and associate the item with the **Services Income** account

- **STEP 1.** Go to the **Products and Services List** if you are not already there.
- **STEP 2.** Click the green **New** button in the upper right.
- **STEP 3.** Choose **Service** from the *Product/Service Information* pane shown in Figure 2-34.
- **STEP 4.** Fill in the detail of the **Mowing** service as shown in Figure 2-35.

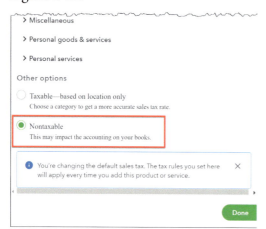

FIGURE 2-36: *Specify the service as Nontaxable*

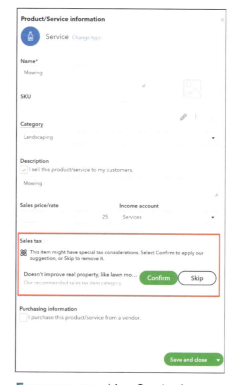

FIGURE 2-35: *New Service Item*

Step 5. If you see a suggestion for the *Sales Tax*, click **Confirm**. Even though this service is now marked as taxable, QBO will only charge sales tax if required by your state.

If you don't see a suggested tax as show in Figure 2-35, click **Edit Sales Tax** and select **Nontaxable**, as shown in Figure 2-36, then click **Done** to return to the *Product/Service Information* pane. Services are usually not taxable.

Step 6. When your Service looks like Figure 2-35, click **Save and Close**.

TIP:

You will be able to edit the *Description* each time you use the **Mowing** service on an invoice or sales receipt. When setting up the item, you can enter a default description as placeholder text, or leave it blank.

If the price for this service varies, you can override this amount when you use it on a sales form. Therefore, when you set up the item, enter the rate you most frequently charge. Leave it blank if the price is always different.

Subcontracted Services

To track your **subcontracted services** in QuickBooks Online Plus and Advanced, you can set up a special **Two-sided Service item** to track both the sale to the customer and the cost of the subcontractor. By using a single item to track both the income and expense for the subcontracted service, you can track the profitability of your subcontractors.

HANDS-ON PRACTICE

Craig subcontracts a tree trimming service instead of providing the service through his employees. Match these steps to Figure 2-37.

Step 1. With the *Products and Services* list displayed, click the **New** button.

Step 2. Select **Service** from the *Product/Service Information* pane.

Step 3. Enter **Tree Trimming** in the *Name** field. The asterisk indicates that this name will be used as the identifier for this item in QuickBooks Online, and must be unique.

Step 4. Drop down the *Category* field, and then choose **Landscaping** from the list.

KEY TERM:

Categories help to organize the *Products and Services List*. Use categories to group and subtotal information about similar products or service categories in sales reports.

Step 5. Enter the *Description* **Tree Trimming**. You may choose to copy the service *Name* and paste it here.

Step 6. Enter **120** in the *Sales Price/Rate* field.

Step 7. Choose **Landscaping Services:Labor:Maintenance and Repair** for the *Income Account*. Note that the colon separates indented sub-accounts.

Step 8. This service is not taxable in CA, so update the *Sales Tax* by clicking **Edit Sales Tax**. Change it to **Nontaxable**. If the suggestion appears, click **Skip**.

Step 9. Check the box **I purchase this product/service from a vendor** in the *Purchasing information* area at the bottom.

Selecting this box allows you to use the same item on sales transactions to "sell" the service to a customer, and on purchase transactions to "buy" the service from a vendor. Both types of transactions will flow through to the correct accounts on financial statements, and allow you to run item profitability reports.

Step 10. The *Description on Purchase Forms* is the same, **Tree Trimming**.

Step 11. The *Cost* that Craig pays the vendor for each tree is **$75**.

Step 12. The *Expense Account* is **Cost of Goods Sold**, since this is a direct expense that Craig must incur in order to resell the service.

Step 13. In the *Preferred Vendor* box, type in **Tony** to quickly filter the list, then choose **Tony Rondonuwu**.

Step 14. Use the *drop-down arrow* next to the *Save* button, and then click **Save and New** to save this service and open another *New Item* window.

Figure 2-37: *Subcontracted Service Item*

Non-Inventory Products

To track physical products that you buy and/or sell but don't monitor as inventory, set up **Non-Inventory Products**.

HANDS-ON PRACTICE

Craig's Landscaping doesn't track grass seed in inventory, so they use a **Non-inventory** item to calculate how many cubic feet they sell.

Grass seed is a special tax category in the State of California, so you will need to specify its tax code.

If you were starting from scratch, you would select **Non-inventory** from the *Product/Service Information* pane. This time, because we are creating several products and services in a row, our sequence starts a little differently. Fill in the detail of the item as shown in Figure 2-38:

STEP 1. Click the blue **Change type** link next to *Service* at the top of the pane. Choose **Non-inventory**.

STEP 2. Enter **Grass Seed** in the *Name* field.

STEP 3. Choose **Landscaping** in the *Category* field.

STEP 4. In the *Description*, enter **Grass Seed**.

STEP 5. The *Sales Price/Rate* is **3** dollars.

STEP 6. Enter **Sales of Product Income** in the *Income Account*. Sales of Product Income is typically used for tangible goods.

STEP 7. Click the blue **Edit Sales Tax** link. Because Grass Seed has a special tax rate in this state, select it from the *Suggested* list, as shown in Figure 2-39.

You could also use the *Search* to quickly find the tax category by typing in **Grass Seed**, or **Browse All** to find it under *Professional Goods & Services*, then *Landscaping*, then *Grass Seed*.

STEP 8. Click the **Done** button to return to the product.

STEP 9. When your *Grass Seed* looks like Figure 2-38, click **Save and New** to save the item and start the next one.

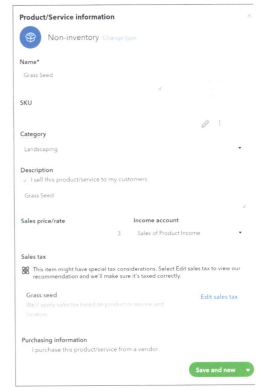

FIGURE 2-38: *A Non-inventory product item*

Non-inventory Products—Passed Through

You can also track the profitability for each Non-inventory product. In this case, you should create a **Two-sided Non-inventory item** to track the purchase costs in a Cost of Goods Sold account, and the sales amounts in an Income account.

Two-sided non-inventory products are particularly useful for special orders. For example, Craig's Landscaping tracks all sculpture orders with one Non-inventory product, since each piece is unique. It doesn't make sense to create a new product for a one-time use.

HANDS-ON PRACTICE

STEP 1. If you are continuing from the previous step, you are ready to create a new Non-inventory product. If not, start a new **Non-inventory product**.

STEP 2. Fill in the detail of the item as shown in Figure 2-40.

FIGURE 2-39: *Select the special sales tax category*

STEP 3.   This time we will leave the *Sales Price/Rate* and *Cost* fields empty, since the price changes with every order.

STEP 4.   Click **Edit Sales Tax**. Search for **Retail**, then select **General taxable retail products (use this if nothing else fits)**. Click **Done**.

STEP 5.   When your Non-inventory product matches the Custom Statue in Figure 2-40, drop down the arrow next to the **Save** button and choose **Save and Close** to save the item and go back to the *Products and Services list*.

Inventory Products

Sometimes a company not only purchases merchandise for resale, but also tracks the quantity and value of the stock on hand. **Inventory products** are common in retail businesses, and are two-sided by nature.

Inventory items are only available in QBO Plus and Advanced.

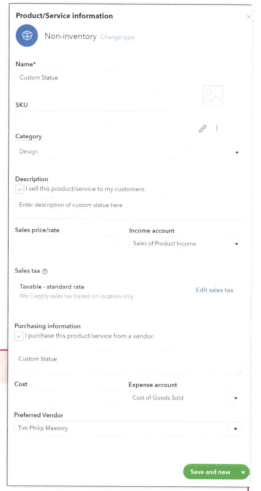

FIGURE 2-40: A Two-Sided Non-inventory product

> **TIP:**
>
> Before setting up inventory, think about what products should be tracked as **Inventory products**. It may not be necessary to separately track every product you sell as inventory. If you do not buy items for resale, run detailed valuation reports, or require at-a-glance stock status information about the products, instead use **Non-Inventory Products** to track them.
>
> Also, if you are syncing your QuickBooks Online to an ecommerce website, point of sale system, or other third-party app that tracks your wares, you may not need to set up inventory in QBO. Some apps sync to QBO. Even if yours does not, there is no need to maintain inventory in two independent systems. Instead, use the other software for stock management and limit your accounting in QuickBooks Online to the daily sales totals.

HANDS-ON PRACTICE

Craig's Landscaping sells and installs birdbaths when they do landscape design, as backyard sanctuaries have become popular! Craig would like to be able to look up how many he has in stock instead of having to go out to the warehouse to look, and he wants to make sure he never runs out so that he doesn't have to delay any installations.

STEP 1.   Go to the *Products and Services List* if you are not already there.

STEP 2.   Click the green **New** button in the upper right.

Step 3. Choose **Inventory** from the *Product/Service Information* pane (see Figure 2-41).

Step 4. Enter **Bird Bath** in the *Name* field and press **Tab**.

Step 5. You may optionally assign each item in your inventory a SKU number, a code used in inventory management for internal barcoding or for manufacturer's part numbers. This enables you to reference the same number on purchase orders and bills to eliminate confusion.

We will skip this field for now. Press **Tab** to move to the next field.

Step 6. Enter **Fountains** in the *Category* field.

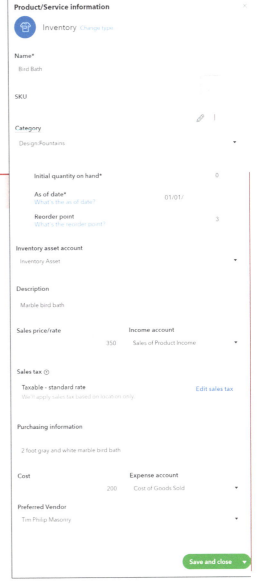

Figure 2-41: An Inventory Item

> **IMPORTANT!**
>
> The next three fields, **Initial quantity on hand***, **As of Date***, and **Reorder point** are used to set the starting points for your inventory tracking. It's crucial that you NOT use today's date and quantity in these fields! If you do, you will be unable to enter any transactions involving the inventory product if they occurred before this date.
>
> Instead, use a **0** quantity and a date long before your first transaction involving the product (for example, **January 1**).
>
> After you're done setting up the products, create the actual expenses or bills to buy the product and record sales.
>
> Alternatively, use a single **Inventory Qty Adjustment** transaction to set up the quantity and value on hand for *all* the inventory items. This feature is found on the *+New* button.

Step 7. In the *Initial Quantity on Hand** box, enter **0**.

Step 8. In the *As of Date** field, use the calendar to select **January 1**.

Step 9. Enter **3** in the *Reorder Point*. When you dip below this threshold, QuickBooks Online will show a **Low Stock Indicator** at the top of the *Products and Services list*, alerting you that it is time to place an order.

Step 10. The *Inventory Asset Account* should default to **Inventory Asset** from your Chart of Accounts. This holds your purchase costs as an asset on your Balance Sheet until the products are sold.

Step 11. Enter **Marble bird bath** in the *Description* field and press **Tab**.

The description you enter here appears as the default description when you use this item on purchase orders and bills.

STEP 12. Enter **350** in the *Sales Price/Rate* field. The sales price is the rate normally charged to customers for the item. You can enter a default here and later override it on sales forms if you need to.

STEP 13. Select **Sales of Product Income** from the *Income Account* drop-down list. This is the income account to which you want to post sales of this item.

STEP 14. Click *Edit Sales Tax*. Search for **Retail**, then select **General taxable retail products (use this if nothing else fits)**. Click **Done**.

Sales *Tax Codes* determine the default taxable status of the item. QuickBooks Online will calculate sales tax on this item when it appears on sales forms. If the item is sometimes taxable and other times nontaxable, create two separate items and use the appropriate item as needed. For more information on Sales Tax see page 73.

STEP 15. In the *Purchasing Information* box, enter **2 foot gray and white marble bird bath**.

QuickBooks Online allows you to have two descriptions for this item: one for purchase forms and one for sales forms. If you'd like, you can use your vendor's description when purchasing the item and a more customer-oriented description on your sales forms.

STEP 16. Enter **200** in the *Cost* field.

Use this field to track the amount you pay to your vendor (supplier) for the item. QuickBooks Online uses this amount as the default when you enter this item on *Purchase Orders, Bills, Checks,* and *Credit Card Charges*. You can override the amount on any current transaction, but if the price changes, you should come back and edit the default amount here.

STEP 17. In the *Expense Account* field, select **Cost of Goods Sold** if it is not already there.

QuickBooks Online uses the Cost of Goods Sold account to record the FIFO ("First In, First Out") cost of this item when you sell it.

KEY TERM:

FIFO stands for "First In, First Out." It is a method for calculating inventory costs, meaning that when a product sells, you sell the oldest one on hand and its COGS is its actual original purchase price. QuickBooks Desktop uses *Average Cost*, meaning that when a product sells, its cost is calculated using the average purchase price of all items on hand. For this reason, QuickBooks Online's inventory calculation is technically more accurate than QuickBooks Desktop.

STEP 18. Select **Tim Philip Masonry** from the *Preferred Vendor* drop-down list.

The *Preferred Vendor* field is used to associate an item with the vendor from whom you normally purchase this part. It allows you to create a Purchase Order from an Estimate. It is an optional field that you can leave blank without compromising the integrity of the system.

STEP 19. Compare your inventory product to Figure 2-41. Click **Save and Close** to save the new item.

> ### THE ACCOUNTING BEHIND THE SCENES:
>
> When you purchase inventory, QuickBooks Online increases (debits) the **Inventory Asset** account by the amount of the purchase price, and credits the **payment method** used.
>
> | TRANSACTION TYPE | NUM | NAME | MEMO/DESCRIPTION | ACCOUNT | DEBIT | CREDIT |
> |---|---|---|---|---|---|---|
> | Expense | | Tim Philip Masonry | | Checking | | $125.00 |
> | | | | Rock Fountain | Inventory Asset | $125.00 | |
> | | | | | | $125.00 | $125.00 |
>
> When you sell inventory, QuickBooks Online decreases (credits) the **Inventory Asset** account and increases (debits) the **Cost of Goods Sold** account for the FIFO cost of that item at the time it is sold. We saw an example of this on page 29.

Bundles

Bundles allow you to use one item to group several separate products and services together as a package on sales forms. Instead of having to add individual line items every time, a bundle adds multiple lines all at once. You have the option of displaying the full list, or just the summary bundle. Quantities are tracked behind the scenes for each product or service within the bundle.

HANDS-ON PRACTICE

Every time Craig's Landscaping sells a rock fountain, it comes with a pump, requires concrete, and takes two hours to install. Instead of repeating these entries for every sale, Craig would like to be able to sell the products, materials, and service as one unit.

STEP 1. Open the *Products and Services list* if it is not already open.

STEP 2. Click the green **New button** in the upper right corner.

STEP 3. Select **Bundle** (see Figure 2-42).

STEP 4. Enter **Rock Fountain Installation** in the *Name** field. Press **Ctrl-A** to highlight all the text, then **Ctrl-C** to copy it (on a Mac, hold down **Cmd** instead).

STEP 5. Press **Tab** three times to move to the *Description* field, then press **Ctrl-V** (**Cmd-V**) to paste **Rock Fountain Installation** in the box.

STEP 6. Place a **checkmark** in front of *Display Bundle Components When Printing or Sending Transactions*. Craig wants to save time in typing, but he still wants his customers to see everything that goes into installing a fountain.

STEP 7. In the *Product/Service* grid, click in the first row and type **Rock**. Choose **Rock Fountain** from the list.

STEP 8. In the second row, add a **Pump**.

> **TIP:**
>
> If you type too quickly and you override the autofill, QBO may pop up a window asking you to create a new product. If this ever happens, just click **Cancel** and try again, a little more slowly.

STEP 9.   On line three, enter **Concrete**.

STEP 10. On the fourth line, add **Installation**. In the *Qty* box, enter **2**. It takes two billable hours to install a fountain.

STEP 11. When your Bundle matches Figure 2-42, click **Save and Close** to save the item and return to the *Products and Services* list.

STEP 12. Try out the bundle! Click the **+New button** at the top of the black *Left Navigation Bar*. Choose **Invoice**.

STEP 13. Enter **Weiskopf Consulting** in the *Customer* field.

STEP 14. In line 1 of the *Product/Service grid*, enter **Rock Fountain Installation** and press **Tab** or click away. The bundle will burst into five lines, a header and four line items.

STEP 15. Change the *Qty* of the *Rock Fountain Installation* on the first row to **2**. Press **Tab** or click away.

All quantities and prices will recalculate according to the number of bundles sold. The prices and descriptions for each of the four line items may

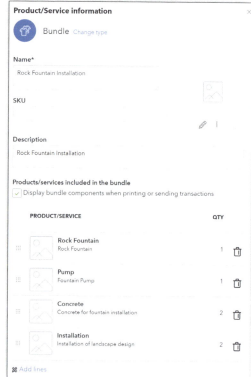

FIGURE 2-42: *Create a Bundle to turn multiple items into one*

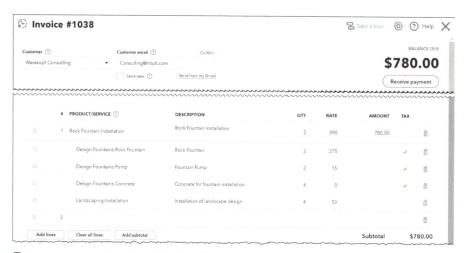

FIGURE 2-43: *Invoice with Bundle*

be customized. Behind the scenes, the inventory accounting will update automatically (see page 65).

STEP 16. Change the green button in the lower left corner to **Save and Close** the invoice. If you are prompted about missing *Class* fields, click **Yes**.

Collecting Sales Tax on Products and Services

It's important to understand how QuickBooks Online calculates sales tax. Every product and service is assigned to be *Taxable* or *Non-taxable* when created. As you add these items to invoices and sales receipts, a checkmark allows you to toggle whether or not sales tax will be calculated for that particular transaction.

But don't get fooled! If a product is sometimes taxable and other time non-taxable, create **two products**, one with each tax status. On your forms, be careful to choose the correct taxable or nontaxable item.

While checking or unchecking the taxable status on a sales form will change whether or not you collect tax in that single transaction, the Sales Liability Report calculates based on *the product sold, regardless of whether or not you actually collected the tax*.

IMPORTANT!

Using the checkmark to toggle sales tax on and off will create a discrepancy between the tax you collect and the tax you remit to your state agencies. Avoid overpaying sales tax by creating separate items for taxable and non-taxable sales.

CUSTOMIZING LISTS

QuickBooks Online provides many *Lists* that allow you to add information to each transaction and help you track more details. If you go to the *Gear* and click on **All Lists**, you'll see a list of lists. Some of these lists are fundamental building blocks of your company file, like the *Chart of Accounts* and *Products and Services*. Some of these populate the drop-down menus on the forms, like *Payment Methods* and *Terms*. And some are collections of items you create, like *Recurring Transactions*, *Attachments*, and *Custom Form Styles*.

In this section, you will learn how to modify the **Terms List** and **Payment Methods List**.

The Terms List

The *Terms List* is the place where you define the payment terms for invoices and bills. QuickBooks Online uses terms to calculate when an invoice or bill is due.

QuickBooks Online allows you to define two types of terms:

- **Standard Terms** calculate based on how many days from the invoice or bill date the payment is due.

- **Date-Driven Terms** calculate based on the day of the month that an invoice or bill is due. Date-driven terms are not applicable in all businesses. They are typically used when invoices are generated at the same time each month, such as invoicing for monthly dues or services. Businesses will often prorate the first month's charges in order to get the customer into the regular billing cycle.

Customers and vendors can be assigned default terms. You can override the default terms on each sale or purchase as necessary. When you create reports for Accounts Receivable or Accounts Payable, QuickBooks Online takes into account the due date calculated by the terms on each invoice or bill.

Due on Receipt means that the payment is due immediately. Unpaid invoices and bills are marked **Overdue** the very next day.

Net 30 means that payments must be received within 30 days before being considered late. It's a common practice to add **late fees** to overdue invoices and bills, as discussed on page 231.

HANDS-ON PRACTICE

STEP 1. Select the *Gear* menu, and then choose **All Lists**. From there, click on **Terms** (see Figure 2-44).

STEP 2. If there are terms on this list you will never use, you can remove them. Craig's Landscaping never uses *Net 10* (meaning that the invoice or bill is due 10 days after its date). Click the **drop-down arrow** on its right and choose **Make Inactive**. Click **Yes** to confirm.

STEP 3. To set up additional terms, select the **New** button in the upper right.

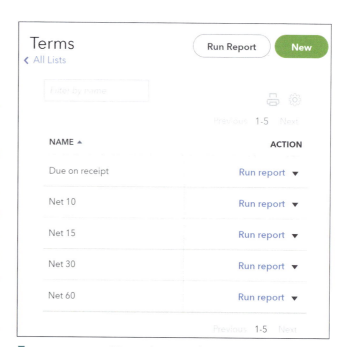

FIGURE 2-44: *Terms List window*

STEP 4. Craig prefers to have all his clients pay him by the first day of the month, unless he does the work in the last week (in that case, they can pay the following month). Fill in the fields as shown in Figure 2-45, then click **OK**.

STEP 5. **Save** the *New Terms* window.

STEP 6. Take a look at how these date-driven terms play out on an invoice. Click the **+New button**, then on **Invoice** (see Figure 2-46).

STEP 7. Click on the **drop-down arrow** to the right of the *Terms* field. Choose the new **First of the month** option you just created. Change the *Invoice Date* to a day in the last week of the month. You'll see that the *Due Date* updates to the first of the following month.

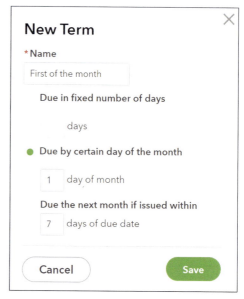

FIGURE 2-45: *The New Terms window with date-driven terms*

STEP 8. Click the **X** in the upper right corner, and click **Yes** to leave without saving the invoice.

FIGURE 2-46: *Change the Terms on an invoice, and the Due Date will update accordingly*

Payment Methods

QuickBooks Online creates common **Payment Methods** by default, but you will want to customize this list to the ones you accept. Payment methods refer to both how you receive payments and how you make payments.

This list integrates with **QuickBooks Payments**, QBO's built-in merchant services. When you have QB Payments turned on, any of the payment methods marked **Credit Card** will allow you to run a credit card right inside the interface. The payment method **Check** is used not just for paper checks, but for ACH (e-checks) as well.

We will see these payment methods in use when we receive invoice payments on page 122.

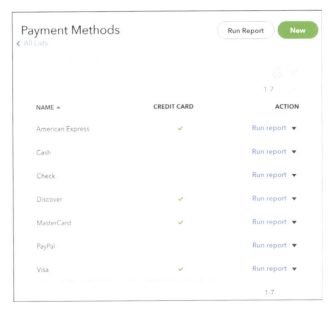

FIGURE 2-47: *The list of Payment Methods*

HANDS-ON PRACTICE

Craig's Landscaping doesn't take Diner's Club, but they do take PayPal, so you decide to edit the list.

STEP 1. Select the *Gear* menu, and then choose **All Lists**. From there, click on **Payment Methods** (see Figure 2-47).

STEP 2. If there are terms on this list you will never use, you can remove them. Craig's Landscaping does not accept *Diner's Club,* so there's no reason to keep it as an option. Click the **drop-down arrow** on its right and choose **Make Inactive**. Click **Yes** to confirm.

STEP 3. To create a new payment method, select the **New** button in the upper right.

STEP 4. Enter **PayPal** in the *Name* field.

STEP 5. Leave *This Is a Credit Card* unchecked. Only select that option when you will use the payment method to run credit cards inside QBO.

STEP 6. **Save** the *New Payment Method* window.

FIGURE 2-48: *Add a Payment Method*

IMPLEMENTING CUSTOM FIELDS

When you create transactions, you can define **Custom Fields** for tracking additional information. Custom fields are available as columns or filters on most reports.

Some common uses for Custom Fields include tracking Sales Reps, PO Numbers, and crews or vehicles assigned to a job. In some cases, your vendors or clients may require you to include specific information on your forms, like PO Numbers.

QuickBooks Online has three basic built-in fields. Upgrading to QuickBooks Online Advanced extends this limit:

- Up to 12 custom fields for each type of form.
- Attach custom fields to vendors, customers, and employees.
- Implement data types including drop-down lists, text, number, and date formats.

HANDS-ON PRACTICE

Craig's Landscaping tracks each customer and vendor transaction by **Sales Rep**. This information allows the company to track employee productivity and customer satisfaction.

STEP 1. Access **Custom Fields** from the *All Lists* window under the *Gear*.

STEP 2. The first time you go to *Custom Fields*, click the green **Add Custom Field button**.

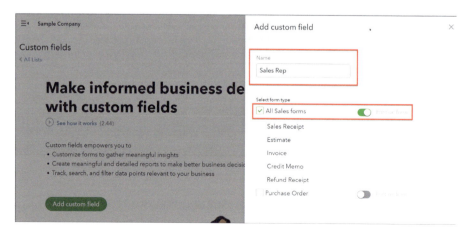

FIGURE 2-49: *Add Custom Fields*

STEP 3.   Enter **Sales Rep** in the *Name box* (see Figure 2-49).

STEP 4.   Click the **checkmark** next to *All Sales Forms*. Turn the *slider* to **On** so that the Sales Rep field appears when you print and email forms.

STEP 5.   Click **Save**.

FIGURE 2-50: *The Custom Fields list*

In the *Custom Fields* list shown in Figure 2-50, you can edit existing custom fields, inactivate those you no longer need, view inactive fields, and add up to three in total. If you need more than three fields or would like enhanced features, upgrade to QuickBooks Online Advanced.

ACTIVATING CLASS TRACKING

In QuickBooks Online Plus and Advanced, the **Class** and **Location** fields give you additional ways to segregate your transactions. You can use classes to separate your income and expenses by revenue stream, profit center, or any other meaningful breakdown of your business activity. You can use locations to track income and spending by department or branch. Alternatively, if your business is a not-for-profit organization, you could use classes to separately track transactions for each program or activity within the organization.

When you use classes and/or locations on each transaction (checks, bills, invoices, etc.), you'll be able to create separate reports for each class or location of the business, either by filtering reports for a specific class, or breaking up the report into multiple columns for each class. An example of a Profit and Loss by Class report can be found on page 306.

For example, a landlord might classify all income and expenses by property and be able to create separate Profit & Loss reports for each building or unit. A law firm might wish to view income and expenses by partner.

Classes can be nested seven levels deep.

Since you will have income or expenses that apply to all or none of your classes and locations, always include an additional entry called **Overhead** and assign such transactions there.

IMPORTANT!

Because the *Craig's Landscaping sample company* resets itself each time you use it, we will only turn on classes in some of the lessons. In your *Imagine Photography company file*, we will use classes to track each store branch throughout the exercises.

HANDS-ON PRACTICE

Craig's Landscaping provides services for both residential and commercial customers. Craig would like to be able to view his reports separated by these income and expense streams.

Follow these steps to create the **Classes List**:

STEP 1. Click on the **Gear**, and then choose **All Lists**.

STEP 2. Click on **Classes** (if you don't see an option for *Classes*, turn to page 44 to them on again).

STEP 3. Click the green **New** button.

STEP 4. Enter **Residential** in the *Name* box (see Figure 2-51).

STEP 5. Click **Save**.

STEP 6. Repeat steps 3–5 to add **Commercial** to the *Class List*.

STEP 7. Add a third class for **Overhead**.

STEP 8. The *Classes* list now looks like Figure 2 52.

FIGURE 2-51: *Creating a Class*

FIGURE 2-52: *Craig's Landscaping's Classes list*

Tagging

If you are not using QuickBooks Online Plus or Advanced and do not have access to classes, the **Tags** feature under the Gear is a great replacement. In fact, in some ways it is more flexible.

Tags are similar to classes in that they label income and expense transactions, and can be used as filters and columns in reports.

The difference is that tags can be color-coded into groups, and you can apply as many tags as you want to any transaction (although you can only apply one tag from each group).

Tags are a creative way to track events, employee activity, marketing sources, and other dimensions that don't fit into other QuickBooks Online fields.

HANDS-ON PRACTICE

Craig decides that he would like an easy way to analyze his jobs according to whether they are maintenance or new installations.

CUSTOMIZING QUICKBOOKS ONLINE | 73

Step 1. Click on the **Gear**, and then choose **Tags**.

Step 2. From the green **New** button, select **Tag Group**

Step 3. In the *Group Name* box, enter **Job Type**.

Step 4. Change the *color* to **Green** (top row, third circle). Click **Save**.

Step 5. In the *Tag Name* box, type **Maintenance**. Click **Add**.

Step 6. In the *Tag Name* box, type **New Install**. Click **Add**.

Step 7. Click **Done**.

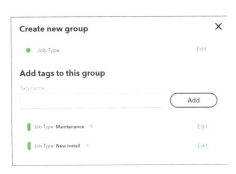

Figure 2-53: *Creating Tag Groups and Tags*

SETTING UP SALES TAX

If you sell products and certain types of services, chances are you will need to collect and remit **Sales Tax** to your state. In many states, each county or city may impose additional local taxes that businesses are also required to collect and report.

If you sell non-taxable goods and services, or if you sell to customers that are exempt from paying sales tax, your state will probably require a breakdown of non-taxable sales and the reason sales tax was not assessed.

These differing conditions may not apply in all jurisdictions, but QuickBooks Online allows you to track sales tax for all of these different situations.

> **DID YOU KNOW?**
>
> Sales tax is complicated! Some states are **home rule** states, meaning that your company address matters more than the location of your customers. Other states are **location-based**, and your taxes are calculated according to your customers' addresses.
>
> Also consider **nexus**. If you only have a few transactions or low total sales in particular jurisdictions, you may not owe any sales tax there.
>
> If you are not familiar with the sales tax rates or reporting requirements in your area, consult your state agency, your local QuickBooks Online ProAdvisor, or an accountant for guidance.

Collecting Sales Tax

You must set up your **Sales Tax Agencies** before using the Sales Tax feature in QuickBooks Online.

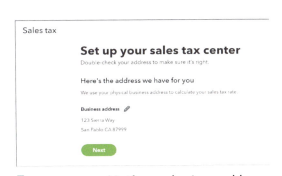

Figure 2-54: *Verify your business address*

HANDS-ON PRACTICE

Step 1. Click **Taxes** on the *Left Navigation Bar*.

Step 2. The *Let's Set Up Your Sales Tax Center* dialog box appears. Click **Get Started**.

Step 3. Verify that your *Business Address* is correct. If you need to make changes, click the **Pencil**. Otherwise, click **Next** (see Figure 2-54).

Step 4. The next step is to set up the states where you do business. If you have already been using your QBO file, QuickBooks Online may suggest some tax rates for you (see Figure 2-55).

In the *Official Agency Name* column, assign the tax agencies. Some states just have one flat rate for all cities and counties. For other states, you may need to set up individual rates for every county where your customers reside.

If you have a lot of local taxes, use the **Bulk Matching** tool at the top.

Step 5. On the *California* row, select **California Department of Tax and Fee Administration**.

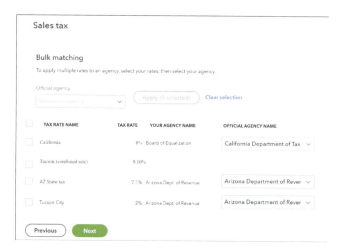

Figure 2-55: *Assign Sales Tax agencies*

Step 6. On both the *AZ State Tax* and *Tucson City* rows, choose **Arizona Department of Revenue**.

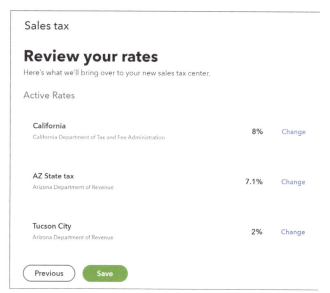

Figure 2-56: *Sales Tax agency rates*

Step 7. Click **Next**.

Step 8. QBO asks you to review your states, agencies, and tax rates. If you need to make any changes, click the blue **Change** link (see Figure 2-56). These are correct for Craig's Landscaping, so click **Save**.

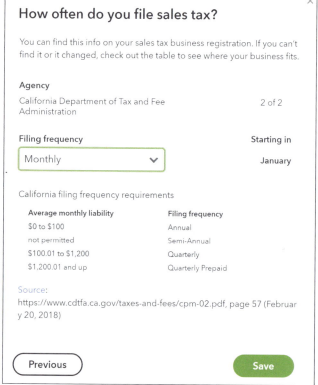

Figure 2-57: *Assign each agency's filing frequency*

STEP 9. Click **Continue**, then click through any additional informational screens.

STEP 10. Next QuickBooks Online will ask you *How Often Do You File Sales Tax?* Choose your *Filing Frequency* for each agency (see Figure 2-57). Be sure to get this information directly from your state's Department of Revenue.

For *Arizona*, select **Yearly**, then click **Next Agency**.

STEP 11. For *California*, choose **Monthly**, then click **Save**.

THE ACCOUNTING BEHIND THE SCENES:

Sales Tax automatically calculates on each sales form by applying the sales tax rate to all taxable items on that sale. QuickBooks Online increases (credits) the **Sales Tax Payable** for the amount of sales tax on the sale.

Also, QuickBooks Online tracks the amount due (debits) by *Tax Agency* in the *Sales Tax Liability* report on page 245 and in the *Pay Sales Tax* window shown below.

Craig's Landscaping is now set up to track sales tax for Arizona and California. Your *Sales Tax Center* will look similar to Figure 2-58. Dates and amounts will vary. Click on each state. Expand the *Tax Period Date* field as far back as you can to see past taxes.

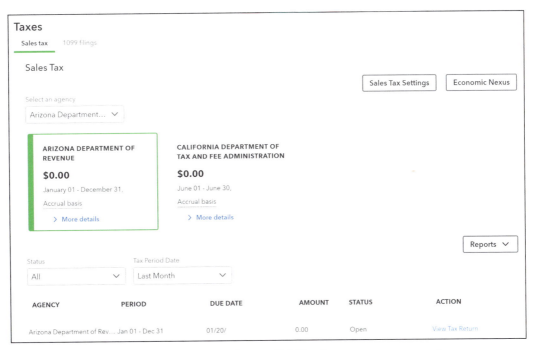

FIGURE 2-58: *The Sales Tax Center tracks your liability (your screen may vary)*

> **IMPORTANT!**
>
> When you pay your sales taxes every month, be sure to use this *Sales Tax Center* to determine how much you owe. **More importantly, be sure to use this center to mark your sales taxes as paid!** The Sales Tax Center will apply the payment to decrease (debit) your **Sales Tax Payable liability account** to clear the balance owed. If you simply write a check or create a credit card payment without using the Sales Tax Center, you will overstate your expenses and the liability will remain on your Balance Sheet.
>
> For more on paying the collected sales tax, see page 243.

If you look in your *Chart of Accounts*, you'll see new **Other Current Liabilities** collecting your unpaid sales tax until you remit it to your state agencies (see Figure 2-59).

FIGURE 2-59: *Sales Tax Liability categories in the Chart of Accounts*

Setting up Sales Tax Defaults

After setting up your sales tax agencies, the next step is to assign a default ***sales tax status*** to each product or service item, as well as to each customer. The Sales Tax defaults indicate whether a specific product or service, and this particular customer, are taxable or non-taxable.

For example, if you sell products to a reseller, they are typically exempt from paying sales tax, since their customers will pay the sales tax when they purchase the items.

> **IMPORTANT!**
>
> If you have products and services that are sometimes taxable and other times non-taxable, create two products, one with each tax status. While checking or unchecking the taxable status on a sales form will change whether you collect tax or not, the Sales Liability Report calculates based on the product sold, regardless of whether or not you actually collected the tax.

We will set up these defaults in your Imagine Photography exercises when we create new Products in Chapter 2 and Customers in Chapter 3.

Applying Sales Tax on Forms

After you properly set up your QuickBooks Online **Sales Tax Agencies**, **Products and Services**, and **Customers**, QuickBooks Online automatically calculates and tracks sales tax on each invoice or sales receipt (see Figure 2-60).

Each line on a sale is taxed according to the combination of how the item and customer are set up. Only taxable customers will be charged sales tax, and only on taxable products. If the customer is taxable, then the **sum of the taxable items is multiplied by the sales tax rate**.

▸ Either the *Billing Address* or the *Shipping From* fields will be used to identify the appropriate tax agency, based whether your state calculates sales tax based on your company's location or the client's billing and shipping address. Sometimes the *Shipping From* field may be labeled *Location of Sale*.

▸ The *Tax* column shows if each line item is taxable.

▸ *Select Tax Rate* at the bottom allows you to change the tax agency.

In the example below, the customer is taxable. All three products on the invoice are taxable, so the total on each line ($335.25) is multiplied by the rate for California (8%) for a resulting sales tax of $26.82, which is then added to the balance due.

The tiny blue *See the Math* link allows you to see how the tax was calculated, and override the amount if necessary.

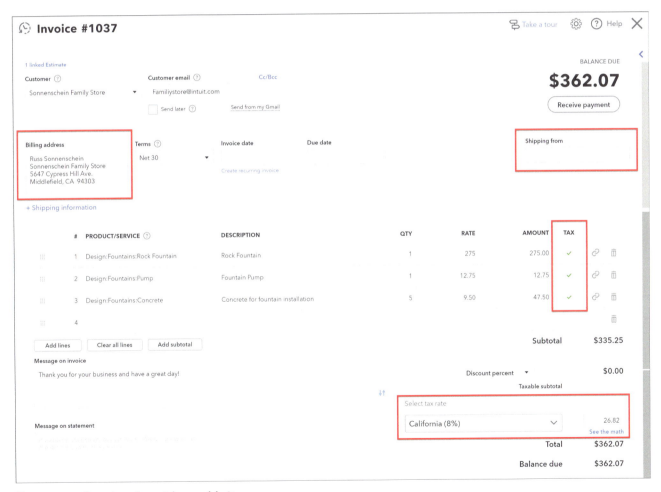

FIGURE 2-60: *Invoice with taxable items*

CUSTOMIZING SALES FORMS

QuickBooks Online provides **Custom Form Styles** so that you can personalize your sales forms and payment receipts. Customizing your invoices, sales receipts, estimates, and payment receipts with your logo and branding projects a professional image.

You can modify the standard form that QuickBooks Online provides, and you can create your own variations so that you can control the way your forms appear on both the screen and the printed page.

The *Custom Sales Forms list* can be found under the *Gear*, at the bottom of most forms in the black bar, or under *Account and Settings* on the *Sales tab*.

HANDS-ON PRACTICE

Craig would like his invoices and sales receipts to display his logo and company colors. He would like a layout that looks stylish, and is easy for customers to read.

STEP 1. Click the *Gear*, and then choose **Custom Form Styles** in the first column. This list shows the standard template that comes with QuickBooks Online, as well as any forms the user may have created. In this sample company, the list may appear empty.

STEP 2. Click the **New Style button**, then choose **Invoice** (see Figure 2-61).

STEP 3. Change the *Name* at the top to **Service Invoice**. Give your templates unique, descriptive names so that you will easily recognize them when selecting them on forms.

STEP 4. Note that there are three tabs up at the top. We will start with the **Design** options (see Figure 2-61).

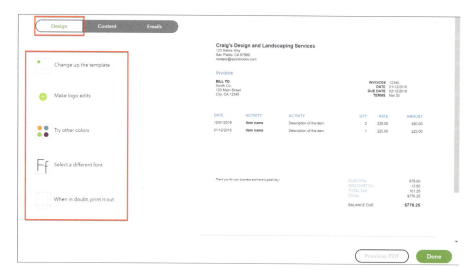

FIGURE 2-61: *The Custom Form Styles window*

TIP:

If you are using Locations in QuickBooks Online, you can create separate form styles with the contact information for office or store.

CUSTOMIZING QUICKBOOKS ONLINE | 79

STEP 5. In the *Dive in with a Template* or *Change Up the Template* section (the name changes), choose **Fresh**.

STEP 6. Click on **Make Logo Edits**, then click the **Add a Logo** box. A window will open (see Figure 2-62). Adding a business logo to your invoice helps customers identify your invoice, and familiarize themselves with your brand.

> **NOTE:**
>
> This step may not work in the Craig's Landscaping sample company unless you are in an Incognito window (see page 7). You can also add the logo in the **Company** tab in *Account and Settings*.

STEP 7. Click the blue **+ box**. Navigate on your computer to find the **CraigsLogo.jpg** in your student files, or substitute a logo of your choice. Click **Save**.

STEP 8. Next to the logo are three circles for the logo *Size*. Choose **L** for Large.

STEP 9. The next three circles align the logo on the left, center, or right of the header. Try all three to see the layouts, then select **right**.

FIGURE 2-62: *Upload the company logo*

STEP 10. If you add the logo through this window, QuickBooks Online will look at your logo and find a coordinating color. If you don't like the color chosen, or you have company-branded colors, click **Try Other Colors** (your window may say **Splash On Some Color**).

Craig wants the accent color to be green instead of brown. Click the **bright green** in the top row. The boxes and border lines on the invoice change to the selected color.

If the business had its own *Hex code* for the company colors, you could enter that in the box.

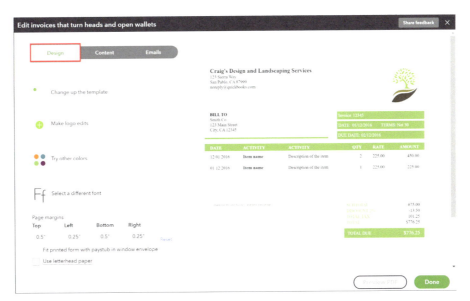

FIGURE 2-63: *Design options*

STEP 11. Click on **Get Choosy with Your Font** or **Select a Different Font** (the name changes), then choose **Arial Unicode MS**, and **12pt**.

STEP 12. If you see *Edit Print Settings*, you can adjust page margins, align the form with envelope windows, and print on letterhead.

STEP 13. Click the **Content tab** at the top, then click on the **top section** in the preview on the right.

STEP 14. Note that your **Header fields** may not match the default data in Figure 2-64.

> **TIP:**
>
> Each of the fields you see in the *Preview* are demonstration placeholders. If you don't use a field in your transaction, the box will be empty when your print or email the form.

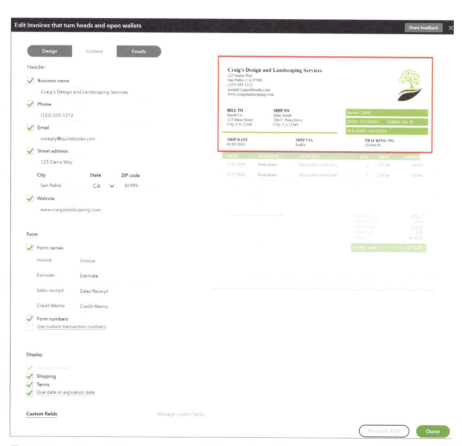

FIGURE 2-64: *Add your contact information, form numbers, and additional header fields to match this image*

STEP 15. Click the **middle section** of the *Preview* to modify how the columns display on the invoice (see Figure 2-65).

STEP 16. In *Account Summary*, place a checkmark in front of **Show on Invoice**. This adds an *Account Summary* with *Balance Forward* and *Total Amount Due* for customers on account.

STEP 17.   Notice the **Date** column. While every transaction will always have a date in the header, this option also adds an extra date field to every row. This is useful for businesses that want to show the specific date each line item was performed. We will leave this option **On**.

STEP 18.   If you want to change the width of the columns to make them wider or narrower, click the blue **Edit Labels and Widths** link. We will leave these on the defaults.

STEP 19.   At the bottom, view the **Show More Activity Options** by clicking the blue link. Turn these options on or off to add additional rows to each sales form for progress invoicing, displaying all markup, and showing billable time. We will leave all of these on the defaults.

STEP 20.   Compare your screen to Figure 2-65 and make sure it matches.

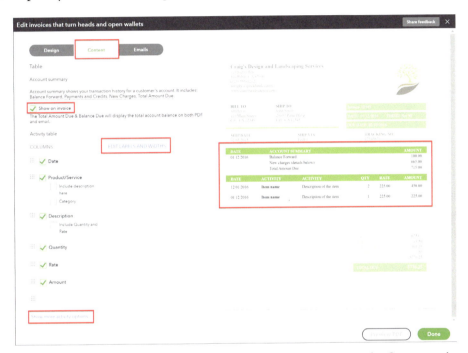

FIGURE 2-65: *Customize the appearance of the line items on the Content tab*

STEP 21.   Click the **bottom section** of the *Preview* to modify the messages on the invoice (see Figure 2-66).

STEP 22.   Display the **Discount** and **Estimate Summary**. These add a dedicated Discount field and a Progress Invoicing summary below the invoice total.

STEP 23.   The *middle box* that says "Thank you for your business . . ." is typically used for terms and conditions, or a thank you message. We will leave the default. Change the font size to **12pt**.

STEP 24.   The *Footer text* is commonly used for mottos, slogans, and licensing numbers (such as a contractor's CCB number). Enter **Mowing your lawn so that you don't have to, since 1991.** Change the font size to **12pt Centered**.

STEP 25.   Click the **Emails** tab at the top to set the defaults for your *Email messages* (see Figure 2-67).

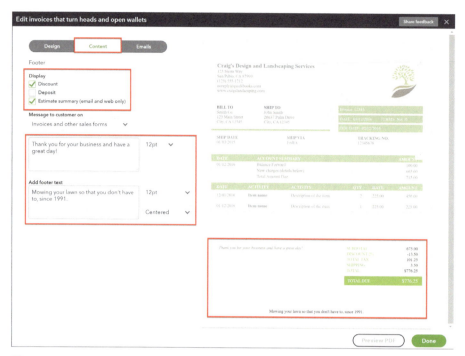

FIGURE 2-66: *Add a message and footer text*

STEP 26. In the *How Your Invoice Appears in Emails* section, **Full Details** will include all your form's line items right in the email message. **Summarized Details** only include the due date and balance. The customer can click **Print or Save** to view the sales form online. If you have **QuickBooks Payments merchant services** turned on, the button becomes **Preview and Pay**, and the customer can pay the invoice immediately with a credit card or ACH payment.

If you leave **PDF Attached** on, the email message will include a PDF of the form for easy download. If you turn it off, the customer can still click the **Print** button and download it that way. Intuit's research demonstrates that if you prefer customers to pay electronically, turn **off** the *PDF Attached* option, or they might not notice the streamlined payment option.

STEP 27. In the *Standard Email* section, use the *drop-down box* to create default email messages for invoices, sales receipts, and estimates. Edit the **Subject line**, **Greeting**, and **Message to Customer** to reflect your company's terminology and communication style.

We will not change the default email messages at this time.

STEP 28. Click **Preview PDF** at the bottom right to view a sample of your finished form in a separate tab. Close the window when done.

STEP 29. If you have changes to make, go back and edit any of the segments. When you are satisfied with the appearance, click the green **Done** button.

STEP 30. The **Standard** form is the default form used on all transactions. If you have more than one custom form style, you'll be able to choose which one is the default.

CUSTOMIZING QUICKBOOKS ONLINE | 83

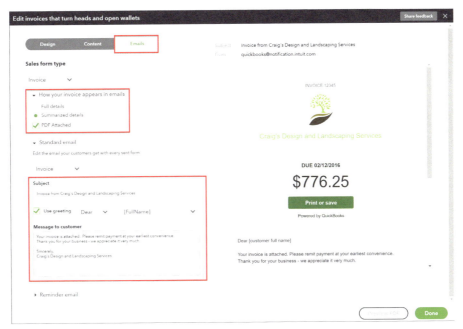

FIGURE 2-67: *Edit the default email messages so they reflect your communication style*

In every invoice or sales receipt, you'll be able to click **Customize** in the *black bar* at the bottom of the window to choose which form to use. Click **Print or Preview** to see what the customer's copy will look like, and to print out your own copy if necessary.

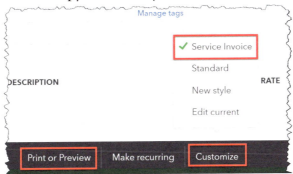

FIGURE 2-68: *Switch form styles, and preview before sending*

ADDING USERS AND PASSWORDS

QuickBooks Online is multi-user by nature. The number of user accounts available depends on your subscription:

- *Simple Start* gets only **1** user login.
- *Essentials* subscriptions include **3** users.
- *Plus* subscriptions can have **5** users, and unlimited **Reports Only** users.
- *Advanced* files can have up to **25** users.

Every account has one **Primary Admin** who is the owner of the file with full access. This Primary Admin can add additional users and set privileges for each.

Optional modules like Payroll and QuickBooks Payments also allow for unlimited **Time Tracking** and **Payments Only** users so that employees can use the features without having any access to QBO itself.

Setting Up Users in the Company File

Each user should have a separate **username** and **password** to log into the file. That way you can see who made what changes when you look at the *Audit Log* (see *page 202*). The privileges granted to each user by the administrator determine what functions of QuickBooks Online they can access. For example, a user might have access to Accounts Receivable or Accounts Payable, but not payroll.

QuickBooks Online Advanced has additional granular control for user permissions.

> **NOTE:**
>
> To protect and secure your QuickBooks Online data file, always use a complex password. Complex passwords use at least eight characters, including a capital and lowercase letter, a number, and a special character. It is a good practice to use passwords that cannot be easily guessed.

HANDS-ON PRACTICE

Craig's Landscaping needs a user account for employee John Johnson to be able to make sales receipts when he is out on a job. By logging in to the mobile app, John can create sales forms when he is onsite, instead of waiting until he's back in the office. He will also be able to swipe credit cards to take payments in the field. Craig does not want John to be able to create expense transactions, or view payroll.

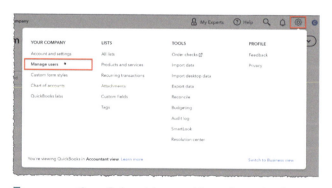

FIGURE 2-69: *Select Manage Users from the Gear*

STEP 1.   On the *Gear* in the upper right corner, select **Manage Users** (see Figure 2-69).

Note that there are two tabs, one for *Users* and a second for *Accounting Firms*, as shown in Figure 2-70.

> **NOTE:**
>
> Because Craig's Landscaping is a sample company, it will have no users and we will not be able to send invitations.

STEP 2.   To create an additional user, click **Add User**.

STEP 3.   QuickBooks Online walks you through a setup wizard where you specify user types (see Figure 2-71). Choose **Standard User**, then click **Next**.

CUSTOMIZING QUICKBOOKS ONLINE | 85

FIGURE 2-70: The Manage Users list for a company file

- A *Standard User* has customizable options.

- A *Company Admin* has full access.

- *Reports Only* users appear in QuickBooks Online Plus and Advanced. Users with this permission level can view all reports but not make any changes to the data.

- *Time Tracking Only* are unlimited accounts for employees to log in and use QuickBooks Online's time sheets to populate payroll as well as job costing reports in the Projects Center.

- *Payments Only Users* appear when you are connected to QuickBooks Payments Merchant Services, to allow staff to log in through the mobile app to swipe credit card payments.

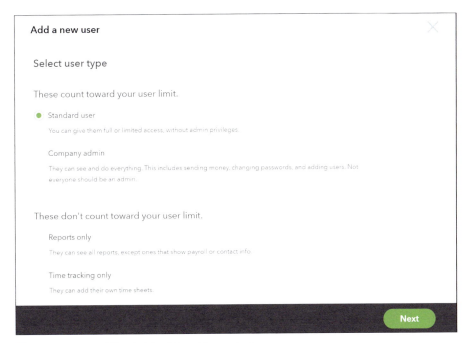

FIGURE 2-71: The Add a New User window

STEP 4. In the *Select Access Rights* window, choose **Limited**, and check off **Customers** (see Figure 2-72). The list on the right shows what John will and won't be able to do when he logs in. Click **Next**.

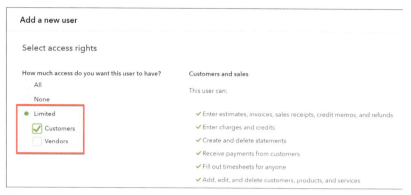

FIGURE 2-72: *You can restrict a user's access*

IMPORTANT!

If the QuickBooks Online file has an active payroll subscription, you will also see an option to prevent users from viewing confidential payroll data.

STEP 5. On the *Select User Settings* window, leave all the defaults. We don't want the employee to be able to manage users, edit company info, or see the billing. Click **Next** (see Figure 2-73).

STEP 6. Enter the user's **First Name**, **Last Name**, and **Email** address as shown in Figure 2-74. This will be their username when they log in.

By clicking **Save**, QuickBooks Online would send an invitation to the user to create a new account and password.

Because this is a sample company, we will not do this right now. Instead of clicking **Save**, click the **X** in the upper right to cancel the process.

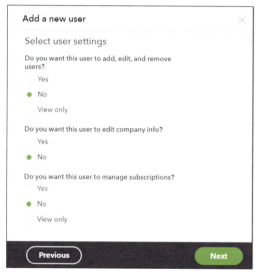

FIGURE 2-73: *Can the user modify the QBO subscription?*

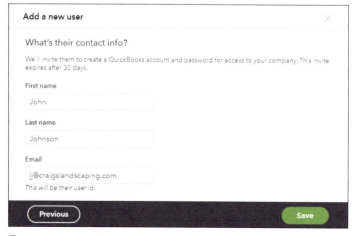

FIGURE 2-74: *Create the username and send the invitation*

Accountant Users

QuickBooks Online also provides two *Accounting Firms* users (QBO Advanced has three). These logins are to be used by ProAdvisors, bookkeepers, and tax preparers.

Accountant logins allow financial professionals instant access to the company file. Not only can the accountant log in any time, but they also have additional tools not available to company users, including the ability to undo reconciliations, reclassify transactions, write off bad debts, and make books-to-tax adjustments.

FIGURE 2-75: *Invite your accountant or bookkeeper*

To invite an accountant, simply enter their **email address**, and click **Invite**, as shown in Figure 2-75.

REVIEW QUESTIONS

Comprehension Questions

1. Why is it important to go through Account and Settings when you first set up a new company file in QuickBooks Online?
2. What is the purpose of the Chart of Accounts?
3. Describe the purpose of the Products and Services List.
4. Describe how Classes are used in QuickBooks Online. Give an example of how a business could use classes.
5. How does QuickBooks Online calculate Sales Tax?
6. What are some of the reasons you might use Custom Fields?

Multiple Choice

Select the best answer(s) for each of the following:

1. You can create Custom Fields for:
   a. Customers.
   b. Templates.
   c. Vendors.
   d. Both a and c.

2. You can customize your QBO company settings under:
   a. Gear > Account and Settings.
   b. Left Navigation Bar > Accounting.

c. Left Navigation Bar > Account and Settings.
d. Gear > Preferences.

3. The Chart of Accounts contains categories for:
   a. Products and Services.
   b. Customer names.
   c. Assets, Liabilities, Equity, Income, and Expenses.
   d. Payment methods.

4. Which of the following is not available as a Custom Sales Form?
   a. Invoice.
   b. Estimate.
   c. Check.
   d. Sales Receipt.

5. Which of the following is displayed vertically on the far left side of the screen?
   a. The Dashboard.
   b. The Left Navigation Bar.
   c. The Gear.
   d. None of the above

6. The types of Products and Services include:
   a. Invoices, Sales Receipts, and Estimates.
   b. Customers, Vendors, and Employees.
   c. Inventory Asset, Cost of Goods, and Income.
   d. Inventory, Non-inventory, Service, and Bundle

7. To add a new Sales Tax to the list:
   a. See if QBO suggests any based on your company information.
   b. Specify the states where you do business.
   c. Add a new service item for each sales tax rate.
   d. Either a or b.

8. Where can you find Custom Form Styles to manually design the layout of an Invoice?
   a. The Gear.
   b. Account and Settings > Sales.
   c. Click Customize at the bottom of sales forms.
   d. All of the above.

9. Which list creates the payment due dates for sales and expense forms?
   a. Terms.
   b. Payment Methods.
   c. Classes.
   d. Tags.

10. You would like your customers to pay you within 15 days. What List would you open to start creating this option?
    a. Customers.
    b. Products and Services
    c. Payment Methods.
    d. Terms.

11. What is the benefit to using Bundles on a sales form?
    a. Save time in data entry.
    b. Calculate quantities on several items at once.
    c. Combine several Products and Services into one.
    d. All of the above.

12. Where should you go to pay your Sales Taxes?
    a. Write a check or enter a credit card expense.
    b. The Sales Tax Center.
    c. Pay a bill.
    d. The Banking Feed.

13. You can rearrange the width of columns on a sales form using:
    a. Columns.
    b. Design.
    c. Edit Labels And Widths.
    d. Emails.

14. The Payment Methods list:
    a. Contains the forms of payment you accept from customers.
    b. Contains the forms of payments you use for vendors.
    c. Should be customized to reflect your business's needs.
    d. All of the above.

15. The setting to change the time limit for your browser before you get logged out is found:
    a. You can't change this limit.
    b. Account and Settings > Company.
    c. Gear > Sign Out.
    d. Account and Settings > Advanced.

Completion Statements

1. Use _____ ____ _____ to enter your company's contact information for use across all of QuickBooks Online.

2. The ____ ____ _____ list defines the items you buy from vendors and sell to customers.

3. Use _____ _____ to create extra fields specific to your reporting needs.

4. _____ _____ terms calculate based on the day of the month that an invoice or bill is due.

5. Products and Services that you both buy and sell are called _____ _____.

CUSTOMIZING QUICKBOOKS ONLINE—APPLY YOUR KNOWLEDGE

It's time to set up Imagine Photography with the Account and Settings, Chart of Accounts, Products and Services, and Lists you will need throughout this course.

> **IMPORTANT!**
>
> As you enter set up information, proofread and review carefully to make sure you don't have any typos or spelling errors. Remember this information will be used for all transactions and reports going forward, so accuracy is important.
>
> As you work through the setup, confirm that the information on the screen matches the book. If a setting is not mentioned in the instructions, you don't need to make any changes.

1. Sign in to **Imagine Photography**, your student company.

2. Set up the following **Account and Settings** > **Company** settings as shown in Table 2-1. Some options are already set up and will not need to be changed.

COMPANY SETTINGS	
LOGO	ImagineLogo.png
COMPANY NAME	[Your Name]'s Imagine Photography
LEGAL NAME	Imagine Photography, Inc.
EIN	11-1234567
TAX FORM	Small Business Corporation, Two or More Owners (Form 1120S)
INDUSTRY	Miscellaneous Store Retailers
COMPANY EMAIL	[Your email address]
CUSTOMER-FACING E-MAIL	info@imaginephoto.biz
COMPANY PHONE	+1 925-555-1111
WEBSITE	http://www.imaginephoto.biz
ADDRESS	123 Main St. Pleasanton, CA 94566 (note: be sure QBO autofills the company address. After you type "St", start typing "Pleasanton" until the address shows up on the list, then click on it)

TABLE 2-1: *Company Settings*

3. Update and confirm the following **Account and Settings > Advanced** settings as shown in Table 2–2. Click **Save** between sections.

ADVANCED SETTINGS	
FIRST MONTH OF THE FISCAL YEAR	January
FIRST MONTH OF INCOME TAX YEAR	Same as fiscal year
ACCOUNTING METHOD	Accrual
CLOSE THE BOOKS	Off
ENABLE ACCOUNT NUMBERS	Off
TRACK CLASSES	**On**
WARN ME WHEN A TRANSACTION ISN'T ASSIGNED A CLASS	**Yes (check this box)**
TRACK LOCATIONS	Off
PRE-FILL FORMS WITH PREVIOUSLY ENTERED CONTENT	On
AUTOMATICALLY APPLY CREDITS	**Off**
AUTOMATICALLY INVOICE UNBILLED ACTIVITY	Off
AUTOMATICALLY APPLY BILL PAYMENTS	**Off**
ORGANIZE ALL JOB-RELATED ACTIVITY IN ONE PLACE (PROJECTS)	On
SIGN ME OUT IF INACTIVE FOR	3 Hours

TABLE 2-2: *Advanced Settings*

4. Update and confirm the following **Account and Settings > Time** settings as shown in Table 2–3. Click **Save** between sections.

TIME SETTINGS	
FIRST DAY OF WORK WEEK	**Monday**
SHOW SERVICE FIELD	On
ALLOW TIME TO BE BILLABLE	On

TABLE 2-3: *Advanced Time Settings*

5. Go to **Account and Settings > Sales** and turn on **Track Inventory Quantity on Hand** under the *Products and Services* section. Accept all dialog boxes. Click **Save**. Click **Done** to save the settings.

6. Go to **Taxes** in the *Left Navigation Bar* and turn on **Use Automatic Sales Tax**. You only collect tax for California customers. File sales taxes **Monthly**.

7. Set up your **Chart of Accounts.** Add the account categories shown in Table 2–4. You do not need to enter *Descriptions*.

ACCOUNTS TO ADD TO THE CHART OF ACCOUNTS

ACTION	ACCOUNT TYPE	SAVE ACCOUNT UNDER	TAX FORM SECTION	ACCOUNT NAME
Add	Banks	Bank Accounts	Checking	Business Checking (1025)
Add	Banks	Bank Accounts	Money Market	Money Market (7809)
Add	Credit Cards	Credit Cards	Credit Card	Business Visa (5678)
Add	Income	Income	Service/Fee Income	Photography Income
Add	Expenses	Office Expenses	Office/General Administrative Expenses	Computer Expense
Add	Expenses	Advertising & Marketing	Advertising/Promotional	Marketing

TABLE 2-4: *Add these accounts*

8. Continue to modify your **Chart of Accounts** using Table 2-5. Merge, edit, or inactivate these accounts:

CHANGES TO MAKE TO THE CHART OF ACCOUNTS

ACTION	ACCOUNT NAME	SAVE ACCOUNT UNDER	EDITS TO MAKE:
Merge	Sales	Income	*Tax Form Section*: **Sales of Product Income** *Account Name*: **Sales of Product Income**
Edit	Website ads	Advertising/Promotional	*Account Name*: **Website**
Inactivate	Land	Fixed Assets	Not needed
Inactivate	Supplies:Supplies & materials	*Note: Inactivate the Expense but keep the Cost of Goods subcategory.*	Not needed. Supplies & materials will be tracked under Cost of Goods Sold.

TABLE 2-5: *Edit or inactivate these accounts*

9. Click the **Run Report** button. Compare your Chart of Accounts to the *Imagine Photography Account List* in your student QuickBooks Online Classroom Files folder.

10. Set up your **Classes List**. Imagine Photography uses classes to track income and expenses for each of its two stores—**San Jose** and **Walnut Creek**. Set up these two classes, along with a third class for **Overhead**.

11. Set up your **Products and Services List** by importing the **ImaginePhotographyProductList.xls** spreadsheet in your classroom files folder.
    a. Use the **Import a File** link at the bottom of the *Products and Services* window. The fields are already mapped, so you can just click **Next** to accept the defaults.

b. In the confirmation window, update any fields the tool doesn't recognize. In the confirmation window, update any fields the tool doesn't recognize. For example, you may have to manually choose the **Cost of Goods Sold:Supplies & Materials—Cost of Goods Sold** account for the five *Inventory Type* items. Click in the three *Qty* of zero that are shown in red, as shown in Figure 2-76.

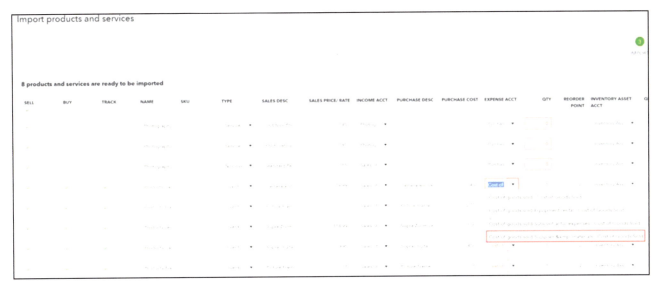

FIGURE 2-76: *Fix any import errors*

c. When your screen matches the figure, click on the green **Import** button in the lower right corner of the screen. If you don't see the button, adjust your browser settings.

d. After the import, close the window. This will import eight products and services, for a total of 10 including QBO's default items.

12. Create the rest of your **Products and Services List** by adding the three items shown in Table 2-6. Leave any other fields blank or accept the defaults if not shown in the table.

	SERVICE	SERVICE	NON-INVENTORY
NAME	Indoor Session	Videographer	Photo Paper
CATEGORY	Photography	Photography	Products
CLASS	San Jose	San Jose	Walnut Creek
DESCRIPTION	Indoor Studio Session	Videographer	Standard Photo Paper, Glossy, 8.5"x11", Pack of 100
SALES PRICE/RATE	225	125	25
INCOME ACCOUNT	Photography Income	Photography Income	Sales of Product Income
SALES TAX	Nontaxable	Nontaxable	Taxable—based on location only
CHECK "I PURCHASE THIS PRODUCT/ SERVICE FROM A VENDOR"		Subcontracted Videographer	Standard Photo Paper, Glossy, 8.5"x11", Pack of 100
COST		75	15
EXPENSE ACCOUNT		Cost of Goods Sold:Subcontractor Expenses	Supplies & Materials

TABLE 2-6: *Cost of Goods Sold:Supplies & Materials*

13. Create two **Bundles** as shown in Table 2-7 below. Check **Display Bundle Components When Printing or Sending Transactions**. The Qty is 1 for each line. When finished, compare your *Products and Services* list to the Answer Key on page 588.

NAME	DESCRIPTION	PRODUCT/SERVICE
Deluxe Shoot	Deluxe Photo Shoot	Indoor Session
		Outdoor Session
		Retouching
		Standard Package
Supra Package	Supra Camera Package	Camera SR32
		Lens
		Case

TABLE 2-7: *Create two Bundles*

14. Set up your **Terms List** according to Table 2-8.

TERM NAME	OPTIONS	
1st of the Month	Select *Due by certain day of the month* **1** *day of month*	*Due the next month if issued within* **5** *days of due date*
Due on Receipt	No change	
Net 30	No change	
Net 15	Inactivate	
Net 60	Inactivate	

TABLE 2-8: *Terms List*

15. Add two *Custom Fields* for **Sales Rep** and **PO Number**. Add both to **All Sales Forms** and set them to **Print on Forms**.

16. Edit the **Standard Custom Form Style**. Accept all defaults if not shown in the table. Click **Preview PDF**. Compare it to the Answer Key at the end of the book.

ELEMENT	OPTION
DESIGN TAB:	
Change up the template	**Airy New**
Make logo edits	Size = **Medium**, Placement = **Right**
Try other colors	**Aqua**, top row, second from right (#0e909a)
Select a different font	**Arial** Unicode MS, **10pt**
CONTENT TAB:	
Phone	Check box to turn on, reformat to **(925) 555-1111**
Address	Uncheck to turn **off** (note: we could make separate forms with each store location address if we were using QBO's Locations feature)
Display	Check to turn on **Shipping**
Account Summary	Click in the middle *Account Summary* section. Check **Show on invoice**
Message to Customer	Click in the bottom *Footer* section. Type **Satisfaction guaranteed! Come back within 30 days for a store credit.** Size = **12pt**
Footer text	**Give It Your Best Shot!** Size = **12pt**, **Centered**
EMAILS TAB:	
Email Greeting	Change [Fullname] to [First]

TABLE 2-9: *Use this data to edit the Standard form style.*

17. Add a *Tag Group* named **Type**. Change the color to **Light Blue** (2nd row, 1st circle). Add *Tag Names* for **Weddings, Portraits, Real Estate, Corporate,** and **Retail**.

CHAPTER 3

THE SALES PROCESS

TOPICS

In this chapter, you will learn about the following topics:

- Configuring the Sales Settings (page 97)
- Tracking Company Sales (page 100)
- Setting Up Customers (page 104)
- Recording Sales (page 111)
- Receiving Payments from Customers (page 122)
- Making Bank Deposits (page 128)
- Running Accounts Receivable Reports (page 138)

> **OPEN THIS FILE:**
>
> Open the *Craig's Landscaping sample company* using the bookmark you created on page 8, or go to http://qbo.intuit.com/redir/testdrive.

In this chapter, you will learn how QuickBooks Online can help you record and track revenue in your business.

Each time you sell products or services, you will record the transaction using one of QuickBooks Online's forms. When you fill out a QuickBooks Online **Invoice** or **Sales Receipt**, QuickBooks Online tracks the detail of each sale, allowing you to create reports about your income.

At the end of the day, you'll deposit the day's sales grouped by payment method.

CONFIGURING THE SALES SETTINGS

In Chapter 2, we learned how to set up the company and QBO file settings. In this chapter we will continue the process so that both *Craig's Landscaping* and *Imagine Photography* have the proper settings to receive money from their customers.

> **TIP:**
>
> Remember that your work isn't permanently saved in the Craig's test drive company. Every time you close the Craig's QBO window, the sample company is reset to the default settings and data. This is not the case for your Imagine Photography company, which will always remember your changes.

HANDS-ON PRACTICE

It is important to go through these settings before you start entering transactions, in order to turn on and off the features appropriate for Craig's Landscaping's workflow.

- **STEP 1.** Open the *Craig's Landscaping sample company* using the bookmark you created on page 8, then click on the **Gear** in the upper right corner. Choose the first option, **Account and Settings**, then on the **Sales** tab (see Figure 3-2).

- **STEP 2.** We already learned how to **Customize Look and Feel** of your forms on page 78, so we can skip this section.

- **STEP 3.** Click on the **Pencil** on the right in the *Sales Form Content* section (see Figure 3-2).

- **STEP 4.** Leave the *Preferred Invoice Terms* on the default, **Net 30**.

- **STEP 5.** Change the *Preferred Delivery Method* to **None**. If we printed or emailed all our invoices in one batch at the end of the day, we could choose **Print Later** or **Send Later**.

- **STEP 6.** Turn *Shipping* to **On** by clicking the slider. This will add shipping addresses and tracking number fields to all forms.

- **STEP 7.** Turn **Off** *Custom Transaction Numbers*. In most cases, it is most straightforward to leave this setting **Off** and let QuickBooks Online auto-increment the form numbers. Some companies use a manual numbering system that includes the date or service codes for enhanced tracking, so they would leave this setting on.

> **NOTE:**
>
> If you implement Custom Transaction Numbers, make sure that all employees use the numbering convention consistently, and that there is a tracing system to prevent multiple users from accidentally duplicating the numbering.

- **STEP 8.** *Service Date* adds an additional **Date field** on every line of the sale, separate from the sales form's date. This allows a company to see the dates a service was performed on multi-phase projects. We will turn this slider **On**.

- **STEP 9.** Craig's Landscaping does occasionally give discounts to their customers, so confirm that the *Discount* slider is set to **On**.

STEP 10. QuickBooks Online does have a built-in tool for taking deposits, but it doesn't treat the prepayment properly as a liability for unearned revenue. Instead, it treats the deposit as an initial payment. Leave this slider in the **Off** position.

STEP 11. Occasionally Craig's clients give him *Tips (Gratuities)*. When you turn this slider to **On**, QBO will ask you *Who's Receiving These Tips?* as shown in Figure 3-1.

FIGURE 3-1: *Who is receiving the tips?*

When you choose **Just Me**, QuickBooks Online creates a new *Tips Income* category in the Chart of Accounts. If you had chosen **My Team**, QBO would have created an *Undistributed Tips* liability category in the Chart of Accounts the first time you use it.

QBO will ask if you want to *Update Your Sales Receipt Template?* Choose **Update**.

STEP 12. Turn the *Tags* slider to the **Off** position.

STEP 13. Verify that your screen matches Figure 3-2, then click the **Save button**.

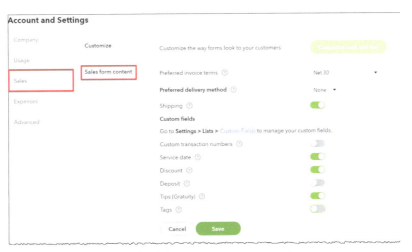

FIGURE 3-2: *Refine the Sales Form Content settings*

STEP 14. Click in the **Products and Services** area as shown in Figure 3-3. We will leave all of these settings on the defaults, but it's important to understand each option.

> ▸ The only time you would turn off *Show Product/Service Column on Sales Form* would be if your company only provides one single product or service with no variations, and you don't need any sales reports. Your forms will still show a description, but all sales will go to a single income category.

> ▸ *Show SKU Number* displays each item's manufacturer SKU code number on the sales forms.

> ▸ *Turn on Price Rules* allows you to build in pricing tiers for specific customers, products, or holiday specials.

- If all your products and services are bought and sold using one lump sum and NEVER need rates or quantities, you can turn off the quantity and rate fields completely by turning off *Track Quantity and Price/Rate*. Almost all companies leave this setting **On**.

- QuickBooks Online's entire inventory system is toggled on and off with the *Track Inventory Quantity on Hand* slider. Leave this **On**.

STEP 15. Click **Cancel** so that you don't update these settings.

FIGURE 3-3: *Settings for Products and Services*

STEP 16. The rest of the settings in this window will not affect the sales transactions covered in this chapter, so we will skip them for now.

STEP 17. Click on the **Advanced** tab on the left, and scroll to the bottom. Set *Sign Me Out If Inactive For* to **3 Hours**, then click **Save**.

It's a good idea to make this change every time you use the sample company, so that it doesn't time out in the middle of your practice session and erase all your work.

STEP 18. Click the green **Done** button at the bottom of the screen.

TRACKING COMPANY SALES

Cash vs. Credit Customers

Sales are recorded with two different workflows. When the customer pays at the time of sale or service (called a **cash customer**) use a **Sales Receipt**. When the customer pays after the sale or service (called a **credit customer**), create an **Invoice**.

In this case, the terms "cash" and "credit" are NOT referring to the payment methods used. Instead, they referring to the specific bookkeeping workflow needed to track the sale.

> **NOTE:**
>
> Payment with a credit card is received immediately; therefore, a customer who pays at the time of sale with a credit card is still a "cash" customer.

Table 3-1 provides more details about the cash and credit customer sales processes. In this table, you can see how to record business transactions for cash and credit customers, including the accounting behind the scenes of each transaction. As discussed on page 5, **the accounting behind the scenes** is critical to your understanding of how QuickBooks Online converts the information on forms (invoices, sales receipts, etc.) into double-sided accounting entries.

Each row in the table represents a business transaction you might enter as you proceed through the sales process.

BUSINESS TRANSACTION	CASH CUSTOMERS (PAY AT TIME OF SALE, SALES RECEIPT)		CREDIT CUSTOMERS (PAY AFTER THE SALE DATE, INVOICE)	
	QBO TRANSACTION	ACCOUNTING ENTRY	QBO TRANSACTION	ACCOUNTING ENTRY
ESTIMATE (OPTIONAL)	Not usually used		Create Estimates	Non-posting entry used to record estimates (bids) for customers or jobs
RECORDING A SALE	New Sale	Increase (debit) **Undeposited Funds**, increase (credit) **Income** account	New Invoice	Increase (debit) **Accounts Receivable**, increase (credit) **Income** account
RECEIVING MONEY TO PAY AN INVOICE	No additional action is required		Get Paid	Increase (debit) **Undeposited Funds**, decrease (credit) **Accounts Receivable**
DEPOSITING MONEY IN THE BANK	Bank deposit	Decrease (credit) **Undeposited Funds**, increase (debit) **Bank** account	Bank deposit	Decrease (credit) **Undeposited Funds**, increase (debit) **Bank** account

TABLE 3-1: *Steps in the sales process*

KEY TERM:

Non-Posting transactions are forms that store information for business operations, but don't affect the general ledger or any financial reports.

Sales Receipts

When payment is made at the time of sale, a **Sales Receipt** is issued, and then a **Deposit** is recorded. A sales receipt tracks both the items sold and the amount of money received, both on one form.

The sales receipt form records the details of what you sold to whom, and then holds the pending deposit in a special account called either **Undeposited Funds** or **Payments to Deposit**. This account is an *Other Current Asset* account that is created automatically by QuickBooks Online. Think of it as the drawer where you keep your checks and cash before depositing them in the bank. Then at the end of the day, the funds are deposited into the bank along with the rest of that day's sales. See page 128 for more information on making bank deposits.

> ### THE ACCOUNTING BEHIND THE SCENES:
>
> When you create a **Sales Receipt**, QuickBooks Online increases (with a debit) **a bank account or Undeposited Funds**, and increases (with a credit) the appropriate **Income** account. If applicable, **Sales Receipts** also increase (with a credit) the **Sales Tax Liability** account. If the sale includes an Inventory item, it also decreases (credits) the **Inventory Asset** and increases (debits) the **Cost of Goods Sold** account.
>
> | TRANSACTION TYPE | NUM | NAME | MEMO/DESCRIPTION | ACCOUNT | DEBIT | CREDIT |
> |---|---|---|---|---|---|---|
> | Sales Receipt | 1038 | Amy's Bird Sanctuary | | Undeposited Funds | $297.00 | |
> | | | | Rock Fountain | Sales of Product Income | | $275.00 |
> | | | | Rock Fountain | Inventory Asset | | $125.00 |
> | | | | Rock Fountain | Cost of Goods Sold | $125.00 | |
> | | | | | Board of Equalization Payable | | $22.00 |
> | | | | | | $422.00 | $422.00 |

Estimates

If you prepare *Estimates* (sometimes called bids) for customers or jobs, you can track the details of what the future sale will include. Estimates are provided to customers to help them decide to move forward with their purchase of a product or service. Estimates do not post to the General Ledger, but they help you track a project from bid to completion.

When it's time to receive payment to the customer, turn the estimate into an invoice with the click of a button. You can turn the entire estimate into one invoice, or use **Progress Invoicing** to create several invoices at different stages of a project.

If you don't win the contract, be sure to **reject** the estimate. Your *Estimates List* should always show only pending and current jobs.

QuickBooks Online Plus has an innovative **Projects Center** that provides reports that help you compare estimated vs. actual revenues and costs.

> ### THE ACCOUNTING BEHIND THE SCENES:
>
> When you create an **Estimate**, QuickBooks Online records the bid, but there is no accounting entry made. Estimates are "Non-Posting Entries" entries, which means they don't show up on your Profit & Loss Statement or Balance Sheet. They are only used to track business activity.

Invoices

When working with a credit customer who pays after the fact, the sales process has additional steps. Often, the first step is to create an *Invoice* recording the details of who you sold to and what you sold. The *Payment* is later received and applied to the invoice. Then a *Deposit* is recorded to put the money in the bank (see Figure 3-4).

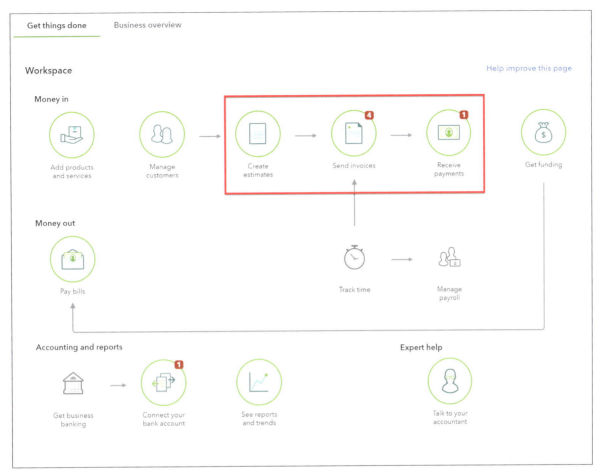

FIGURE 3-4: Invoicing workflow on the Dashboard displayed in some files (screen may vary)

THE ACCOUNTING BEHIND THE SCENES:

When you create an **Invoice**, QuickBooks Online increases (with a debit) **Accounts Receivable** and increases (with a credit) the appropriate **Income** account. If applicable, invoices also increase (with a credit) the **Sales Tax Liability** account. If the sale includes an Inventory item, it also decreases (credits) the **Inventory Asset** and increases (debits) the **Cost of Goods Sold** account.

TRANSACTION TYPE	NAME	MEMO/DESCRIPTION	ACCOUNT	DEBIT	CREDIT
Invoice	Freeman Sporting Goods:0969 ...		Accounts Receivable (A/R)	$387.00	
		Weekly Gardening Service	Landscaping Services		$90.00
		Rock Fountain	Landscaping Services:Job Materials:Fountains and Ga...		$275.00
			Board of Equalization Payable		$22.00
				$387.00	$387.00

Payments

When you receive money from customers with open invoices, use the **Receive Payment** form to record the receipt. If you have created an invoice for the sale, you must accept payment through this process to close the invoice.

You can also apply a single payment to more than one invoice, or apply multiple payments to one invoice.

THE ACCOUNTING BEHIND THE SCENES:

When you record a received **Payment**, QuickBooks Online increases (debits) **Undeposited Funds** or a **Bank** account, and decreases (credits) **Accounts Receivable**. When a customer's invoice is fully paid, their Accounts Receivable balance will be zero.

TRANSACTION TYPE	NAME	ACCOUNT	DEBIT	CREDIT
Payment	Freeman Sporting Goods:0969 ...	Undeposited Funds	$387.00	
		Accounts Receivable (A/R)		$387.00
			$387.00	$387.00

Deposits

After you post to **Undeposited Funds** (sometimes called **Payments to Deposit**) using a sales receipt or a payment, the last step in the process is always to make a **Deposit** to your bank account by using the **Bank Deposit** function. This step is the same for both cash and credit customers.

SETTING UP CUSTOMERS

The **Customers Center** is your central location to view contact information and transaction lists for each customer. Create a record in the Customers Center for each person or business who receives your services or buys your products. This makes it easy to view and manage the history of their activity with your company.

HANDS-ON PRACTICE

Craig's Landscaping has a new credit customer—Dr. Tim Feng. To add this new customer, follow these steps:

STEP 1. Hold your cursor over **Sales** in the *Left Navigation Bar*. Click **Customers** to go to the *Customers Center*.

STEP 2. To add a new customer, click the green **New Customer** button in the upper right (see Figure 3-5).

FIGURE 3-5: *Adding a new Customer record*

STEP 3. Fill in *Customer Information* window using the data in Table 3-2. You do not need to make changes to any fields not included below.

FIELD	DATA
TITLE	Dr.
FIRST NAME	Tim
MIDDLE NAME	S.
LAST NAME	Feng
COMPANY NAME	Because this customer is an individual, skip the Company field.
CUSTOMER DISPLAY NAME*	Tim Feng
EMAIL	drf@df.biz
PHONE NUMBER	408-555-8298
STREET ADDRESS 1	300 N. First St.
CITY/TOWN	San Jose
STATE/PROVINCE	CA
ZIP CODE	95136

TABLE 3-2: *Data to complete the Address tab*

> **NOTE:**
>
> In QuickBooks Online, you can turn on the settings to include a *Shipping Address*. This is useful when one customer requests that products be sent to, or work be performed at, a different address.

STEP 4. Figure 3-6 shows the finished *Name and Contact Info* and *Addresses* sections at the top of the customer record. Verify that your screen matches.

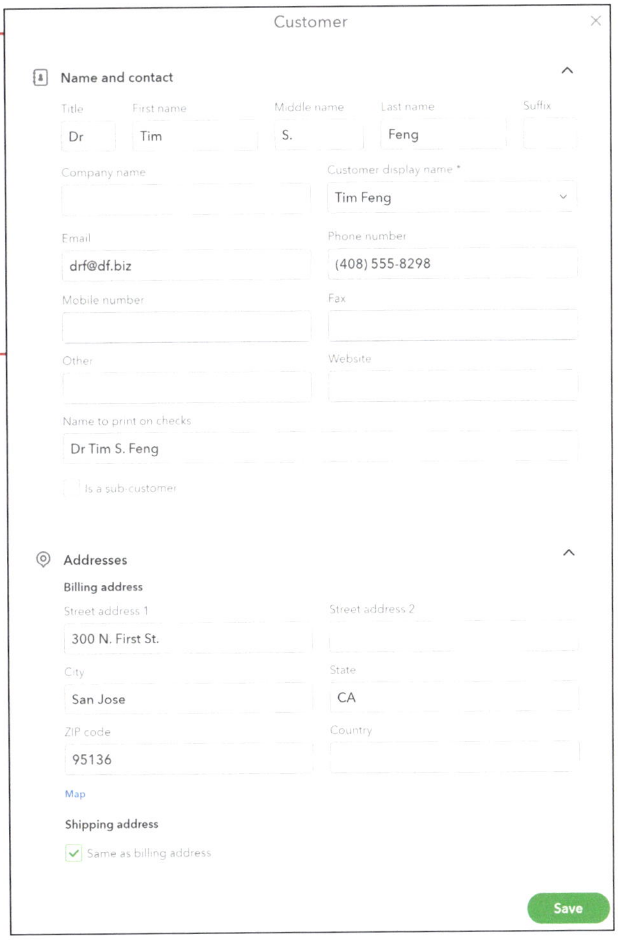

FIGURE 3-6: *Completed Customer Name and Address information*

> **TIP:**
>
> There are three name lists in QuickBooks Online: **Vendor**, **Customer**, and **Employee**. After you enter a name in the *Customer Display Name* field of the *Customer Information* window, you cannot use that same exact **Display Name** on either of the other two lists in QuickBooks Online.
>
> *When Customers are also Vendors:*
> When you sell to and make purchases from the same company, you'll need to create two records, one in the Vendor list and one in the Customer list. Make the two names slightly different. For example, you could include a middle initial or "Inc." after the company name in the Vendor list. Another strategy is to enter **Tim Feng-c** in the *Customer Information* window and **Tim Feng-v** in the *Vendor Information* window.
>
> The vendor and customer records for Tim Feng can contain the same contact information; it is just the name that needs to be different on each list.

We will complete the *Customer* window by scrolling down the rest of the panel. If you accidentally closed the customer record for Tim Feng, click on his name in the *Customer List* and then select **Edit** to continue.

- **Step 5.** The *Notes and Attachments* section contains a freeform field where you can save details including the customer's **Account Number**, **Credit Limit**, and any other information you'd like to capture about the customer. These notes will show under the name in their customer record.

    Enter **Account #3546, Credit Limit $8000**.

- **Step 6.** In the *Attachments* box, you can upload contracts and other documentation to store it with the customer's record. This does not apply to Tim, so we will leave it blank.

- **Step 7.** Scroll down to the *Payments* section. Select **Visa** from the *Primary Payment Method* drop-down list. When you run your first sales receipt or invoice payment using QuickBooks Payments Merchant Services, you will be prompted to add and save a credit card number.

- **Step 8.** Select **Net 30** from the *Terms* drop-down list. For more information about setting up your Terms list, page 67.

- **Step 9.** Make sure the *Sales Form Delivery Options* field is set to **Use Company Default**.

- **Step 10.** Click the *Language to Use When You Send Invoices* drop-down arrow. If your client base is multi-lingual, this option will print and email their forms in the customer's native language. Tim speaks English, so we will not change this default.

- **Step 11.** Scroll down to the next section, *Additional Info*. The *Customer Type* comes into play when you are using **Price Rules**. Leave this blank.

Step 12. Customers are considered taxable by default, but you can assign a default tax code. Since Tim is a regular retail customer, he is taxable and his default tax code is **California (8%)**.

If a customer is tax exempt for any reason (reseller, non-profit, church, etc.), check the *This Customer Is Tax Exempt* box, specify their *Reason for Exemption*, and use the *Exemption Details* box to enter their Resale Certificate ID or other applicable notes.

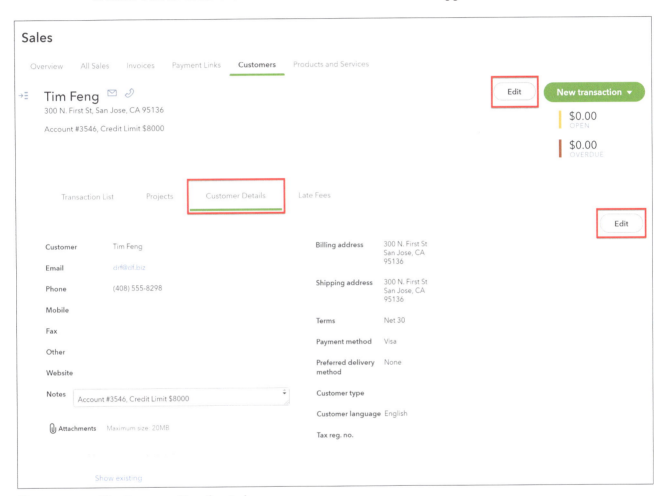

Figure 3-7: *The Customer Details window*

Step 13. Always leave the *Opening Balance* field blank. If this were a new company file and the customer had open invoices, you would instead enter those invoices as of their original dates, rather than filling in this field.

Step 14. **Save** the *Customer* window.

Step 15. Click on Tim's **Customer Details** tab to view the information you just entered. Compare your results to Figure 3-7. If you have any changes to make, click the **Edit** button either next to the *Customer Details* or at the top right near the green *New Transaction* button.

Sub-customers

Each customer listed in the *Customers Center* can have one or more **Sub-customers** representing *jobs* you do for a customer. Setting up sub-customers underneath the customers helps group income and expenses by project, allowing you to create separate reports showing detailed information about each one. This is particularly important for some industries such as construction.

> **DID YOU KNOW?**
>
> As an alternative to the traditional workflow of adding sub-customers under a customer record in QuickBooks Online, QBO also has a dedicated **Projects Center** with innovative tools to manage multiple projects including job costing and labor reports.

HANDS-ON PRACTICE

Craig's Landscaping's customer **Freeman Sporting Goods** has two locations on Ocean View Road and Twin Lane (see Figure 3-8). Let's take a look at how this is set up.

STEP 1. Click on **0969 Ocean View Road,** and then click **Edit** to open the *Customer Information* window (see Figure 3-9).

STEP 2. At the bottom of the *Name and Contact* section, look for the **Is a Sub-customer** checkbox. Pick the main customer from the drop-down list, then decide whether to **Bill Parent Customer**.

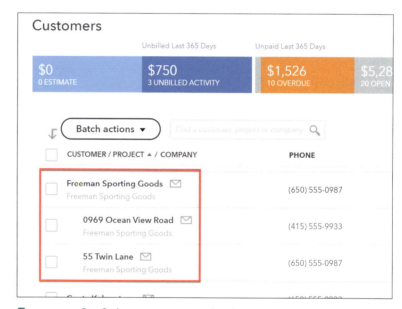

FIGURE 3-8: *Sub-customers on the Customers list*

If each sub-customer will receive and pay their own invoices independently, leave this box unchecked. If the parent account will pay all the bills for all of its jobs, perhaps even in the same payment, turn on **Bill Parent Customer**.

The *Bill Parent Customer* setting is common for subcontractors who do several jobs for a general contractor, and for food manufacturers who sell their products to a chain with multiple locations.

STEP 3. Sasha will pay invoices for both Freeman Sporting Goods locations with one payment, so choose **Bill With Parent**. Click **Save**.

FIGURE 3-9: *Adding a subcustomer to a customer record*

KEY TERM:

Tracking income and expenses separately for each sub-customer is known as **Job Costing**. If your company needs to track job costs, make sure you include the sub-customer name on each income and expense transaction using the *Customer* field. Job costing reports such as a *Profit & Loss by Job* provide useful insights into your business.

Inactivating Customers

When you will no longer be doing business with a customer, you can inactive them. QuickBooks Online maintains the customer history, but it hides the customer record so it no longer appears on your active list.

HANDS-ON PRACTICE

Craig's Landscaping has never done any business with Wedding Planning by Whitney, so there is no reason to keep them on the list.

- **STEP 1.** From the *Customers Center*, click on **Wedding Planning by Whitney**.
- **STEP 2.** Drop down the arrow on the **Edit** button on the upper right.

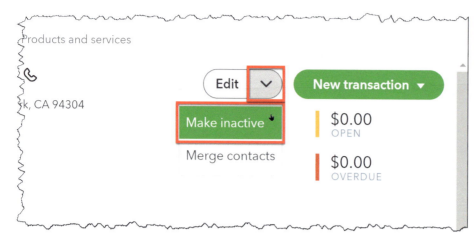

FIGURE 3-10: *Make a customer inactive*

FIGURE 3-11: *Show inactive customers*

- **STEP 3.** Choose **Make Inactive**, as shown in Figure 3-10.

- **STEP 4.** When you see a confirmation window that says *Are You Sure You Want To Make Wedding Planning by Whitney Inactive?*, click **Yes, Make Inactive**.

- **STEP 5.** The Customer Record now includes **(deleted)** after the name. Return to the *Customers Center*. Wedding Planning by Whitney no longer shows on the list.

- **STEP 6.** If the customer comes back in the future, use the *Grid Gear* at the top right of the *Customer List* to **Include Inactive**.

- **STEP 7.** Scroll down to the bottom of the *Customers Center*. You can now see Wedding Planning by Whitney (deleted) on the list. You could click the blue **Make Active** action on the right to reactivate her account. Do not do this now.

> **TIP:**
>
> You can also inactivate a customer right from the Customers Center by dropping down the arrow in the *Action* column and selecting **Make Inactive**.

Merging Customers

If you find you have two customer records for the same company or individual, you can merge them. All the transactions from both accounts will be automatically combined into one. Note that this action cannot be undone.

While we will not do this now, to merge two accounts you would:

1. Decide which one you would like to keep.

2. Click the **Edit** button on the customer you want to keep, and **copy** the *Customer Display Name* field. Click the **X** in the upper right corner to cancel the window.

3. **Edit** the customer you want to inactivate. **Paste** the copied name into the *Customer Display Name* field. Click **Save**.

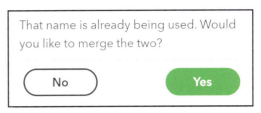

FIGURE 3-12: *Confirmation to merge two customers*

4. When you get the *That Name Is Already Being Used. Would You Like To Merge the Two?* warning as shown in Figure 3-12, click **Yes**.

5. The merged account will now show as *(deleted)*, and all the transactions will display on the list of the customer being saved.

RECORDING SALES

Now that you've set up your customers, you're ready to begin entering sales. We will look at the **Sales Receipts** form first. Use this form when you receive a cash, check, or credit card payment at the time of the sale or service. We will later look at **Invoices**, the way to record sales to customers on account who will be paying afterwards.

You can initiate sales receipts and invoices, and in fact almost any transaction, in several different places.

- The **+New** button is available any time you see the *Left Navigation Bar*.
- When you are looking at a *customer record*, use the green **New Transaction** button.
- Use the **Shortcuts** on the *Dashboard's Get Things Done* tab.
- The *Sales Center's Overview* tab has **Shortcuts** on the bottom right.
- Use keyboard commands (see page 21).

Entering Sales Receipts

When customers pay at the time of the sale by cash, check, or credit card, create a **Sales Receipt** transaction.

HANDS-ON PRACTICE

STEP 1. Use the **+New button** in the *Left Navigation Bar* (see Figure 3-13). This opens the *Sales Receipt* window (shown in Figure 3-16).

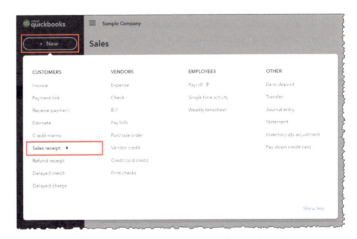

FIGURE 3-13: *Adding a Sales Receipt from the +New button*

STEP 2. Enter **Mariette Martinez** in the *Customer* field. Note that Mariette is not already in the system, so QuickBooks Online suggests adding her on the fly (see Figure 3-14). Click **Add New Mariette Martinez**.

DID YOU KNOW?

At the top of most drop-down lists is an **Add New** option. Whenever you type a new name into any field on any form, QuickBooks Online will prompt you to **Quick Add** or set up the entry details.

STEP 3. When the *Customer* popup appears (see Figure 3-15), you can either just save the name quickly, or take the time to add details to the *Customer* card.

Click **Save**. You can always edit the customer record later to add more details.

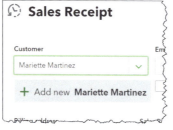

FIGURE 3-14: *Adding a new customer on the fly*

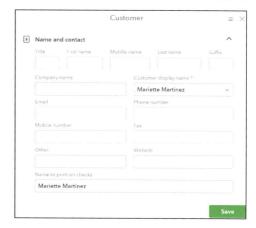

FIGURE 3-15: *Add information, or just Save for a quick add*

TIP:

If you have a large list of individual customers (i.e., not businesses), you may prefer to enter the customer's last name first. This way, your **Customer** list sorts by last name so it will be easier to find names when scanning the list.

STEP 4. Skip the *Billing address* box.

QuickBooks Online automatically fills in this field using the address information in the customer record. Since you used Quick Add to add this customer, there is no address information. You could enter an address in the *Billing address* field by entering it directly on the sales form, but it won't be saved to the customer's details for future use.

STEP 5. Leave today's date in the *Sales Receipt Date* field. Note that the date you use should always be the actual date of the sale, not the date you entered the transaction.

DID YOU KNOW?

Note that there is no field for *Sales Receipt No.* until after the transaction is saved. The number will be assigned automatically.

If we had turned on **Custom Transaction Numbers** when we personalized the Sales settings on page 98, there would be an additional box on the right, assigning a sequential number based on the company's numbering convention, and allowing employees to override it.

STEP 6.   Select **Check** for *Payment Method*.

STEP 7.   Enter the check number **3459** in the *Reference No.* field. The number you enter here shows up on your reports. If you were receiving a cash or credit card payment, you would leave this field blank.

STEP 8.   Leave **Undeposited Funds** in the *Deposit To* field. Note that in some companies, this option is called **Payments to Deposit** instead.

While you may be tempted to change this to the checking account, it's a best practice to save all payments to Undeposited Funds. The Banking Feed, which we'll learn about on page 256, looks first to Undeposited Funds to find matches, and it's the place you need to go to combine payments into one lump sum that matches your bank statement (we will create Deposits on page 130).

STEP 9.   In the *Service Date* field, type **T** to enter today's date. In this case, the *Service Date* and the *Sales Receipt Date* are the same, but that is not always true.

STEP 10. Select **Gardening** from the *Product/Service* drop-down list, and then press **Tab**.

As soon as you choose an item, QuickBooks Online fills in its description, rate, and sales tax defaults. Notice that QBO also includes the item's *Category* from the Products and Services list, separated with a colon (:).

STEP 11. Press **Tab** to accept the default description, **Weekly Gardening Service**, in the *Description* column. If you wanted, you could modify the description, which appears in reports.

STEP 12. Enter *3* in the *Qty* (quantity) column and then press **Tab**.

STEP 13. Enter *25* in the *Rate* column and then press **Tab**. Note that you don't need to enter a $ or .00, as QuickBooks Online will automatically format the number for you.

STEP 14. QuickBooks Online calculates the *Amount* by multiplying the quantity by the rate.

If you override the *Amount* field, QuickBooks Online recalculates the rate by dividing the amount by the quantity.

STEP 15. The *Tax* column is unchecked because gardening services are not taxable in California. This default was specified in the **Gardening** service on the Products and Services list.

Don't forget that you should not toggle this checkmark on and off. If you need a different taxable status on an item, duplicate the product or service and change the tax default. The *Sales Tax Liability* report calculates based on the item's status, not whether you actually collected the tax or not.

STEP 16. On the second line, skip the *Service Date*.

STEP 17. Select **Soil** from the *Product/Service* drop-down list. Press **Tab** until you're in the *Qty* field.

STEP 18. Enter *2* in the *Qty* column and press **Tab.**

STEP 19. Press **Tab** to accept the default of **10.00**.

You can override this amount on each sale if necessary. As with the line above, QuickBooks Online calculates the total in the *Amount* column, and applies the default sales tax status, which is set up as **Taxable** for the Soil product.

STEP 20. Notice that **Thank you for your business and have a great day!** has been autofilled in the *Message displayed on sales receipt* field.

You can enter a message in the **Customer Message** field that will show on the printed sales receipt. This is typically a thank you message or a place to enter return policies, but it can be whatever you want. If you replace this message, it will only be used in this sales receipt. If you want to permanently edit an existing customer message, set it up in **Custom Form Styles**, as we saw on page 78.

STEP 21. Confirm that the *Select Tax Rate* box in the *Subtotals* area displays **California**. The **8% Sales Tax** calculates to **$1.60**.

STEP 22. One of the soil bags ripped and spilled, so Craig decides to give Mariette a $5 discount. Switch the *Discount Percent* to **Discount Value**. Enter **5** in the box. This reduces the amount of taxable sales since the discount is split proportionally between the line items.

TIP:

You can switch the order of *Discount* and the *Sales Tax* calculations. If you want the discount to be taken off the total amount after sales tax, click the **blue arrows** shown in Figure 3-16.

STEP 23. Click **Save and Close** to record the sale. If Mariette would like a copy of her receipt, choose **Save and Send** instead.

QuickBooks Online does not record any of the information on any form, or create an ID number for the transaction, until you save it by choosing **Save, Save and Close, Save & Send**, or **Save & New**.

THE ACCOUNTING BEHIND THE SCENES:

This Sales Receipt increases (debits) **Undeposited Funds**, and increases (credits) **Income**. It also increases (credits) the **Sales Tax Liability** and increases (debits) **Discounts Given**, which in turn decreases **Income**.

TRANSACTION TYPE	NAME	MEMO/DESCRIPTION	ACCOUNT	DEBIT	CREDIT
Sales Receipt	Mariette Martinez		Undeposited Funds	$91.52	
		Weekly Gardening Service	Landscaping Services		$75.00
		2 cubic ft. bag	Landscaping Services:Job Mater...		$20.00
			Board of Equalization Payable		$1.52
		Discount	Discounts given	$5.00	
				$96.52	$96.52

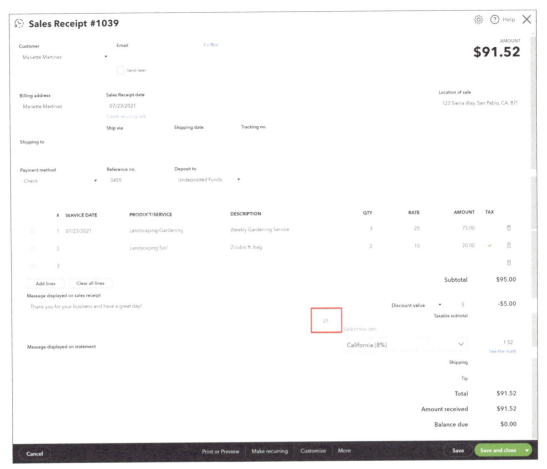

FIGURE 3-16: *Completed Sales Receipt*

Creating Invoices

Invoices are very similar to **Sales Receipts**. The only difference is that invoices increase ***Accounts Receivable*** while sales receipts directly increase Undeposited Funds (or Payments to Deposit). Use invoices to record sales to your customers who are not paying in full immediately, instead buying on credit.

HANDS-ON PRACTICE

To create an **Invoice**, follow these steps:

STEP 1. In the *Customers Center*, open **Video Games by Dan**.

FIGURE 3-17: *Use the Customer Search by typing in letters or a phone number*

Try using the *Find a Customer, Project, or Company* search field just above the list of customers as shown in Figure 3-17, or just scroll down to the bottom of the list and click on the name.

STEP 2. Click the green *New Transaction* button, then select **Invoice** (see Figure 3-18).

Alternatively, click the **Add Invoice** icon on the *Dashboard, or* **Invoice** from the *+New button*, then select **Video Games by Dan** from the *Customer* drop-down list.

> ### DID YOU KNOW?
>
> When you type characters into a field populated by a list, QuickBooks Online completes the field using a feature called **QuickFill**. QuickFill searches the list for the characters you type to find the names that contain those letters. You don't have to start with the first letters in the name; choosing unique letter combinations will suggest the shortest list of choices.

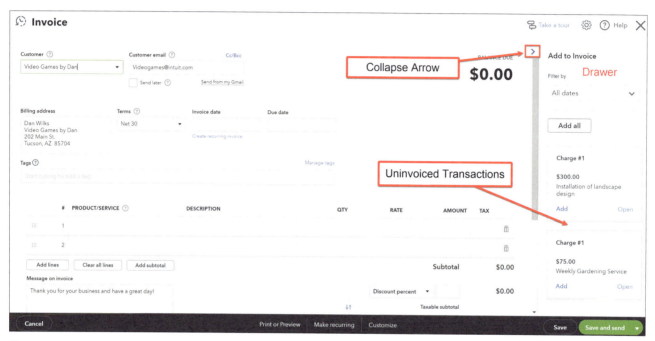

FIGURE 3-18: *Invoice after Customer selected, showing the Drawer, before remaining data entered*

STEP 3. Notice that Dan Wilks has two uninvoiced charges listed in the *Drawer* on the right.

The **Drawer** displays uninvoiced billable expenses and time charges (see page 167), and delayed charges (see page 224). These transactions are pending, waiting to be added to the customer's next invoice.

STEP 4. To hide the *Drawer* and save those transactions for later, click the blue **Collapse** arrow (see Figure 3-18). Note that the blue arrow now points to the left, reminding you not to forget these pending charges.

STEP 5. Note the default information already appears in the *Billing Address* and *Shipping To* fields.

QuickBooks Online automatically enters the addresses in these fields, using the information from the customer record. If necessary, modify the addresses in this one transaction by typing over the existing data. To change the information for future sales, edit the *Customer record* instead.

STEP 6. In the *Terms* field, **Net 30** is already selected.

The *Terms* field on the invoice indicates the due date for the invoice and how long your customer can take to pay you. The entry in this field determines how this invoice is reported on *Who Owes You* reports such as the *A/R Aging Summary* and the *Collections Report*.

STEP 7. Click inside the *Invoice Date* field and then press **– (minus)** to go to **yesterday's date**, or use the **Calendar icon**. The *Due Date* field will also update accordingly.

STEP 8. In the *Ship Via* field, enter **UPS**.

STEP 9. Type the letter **T** in the *Shipping Date* box to bring up today's date.

STEP 10. In the *Tracking No.* box, enter **1234567890**.

STEP 11. Enter **Pump** in the *Product/Service* field.

STEP 12. In the *Description* field, enter **Replace broken fountain pump**.

STEP 13. Because Dan lives in Arizona, select **Tucson** in the *Select a Sales Tax Rate* box.

Alternatively, you could update the *Tax Info tab* in Dan's customer record to update his default tax settings for future orders.

STEP 14. Scroll down to the bottom. On the right is a *Shipping* field. Enter **6.50**. This adds shipping charges to the invoice. The revenue will appear in a *Shipping Income* account on your Profit and Loss report.

STEP 15. Enter **Replace broken fountain pump** in the *Message on Statement* box at the bottom left of the form.

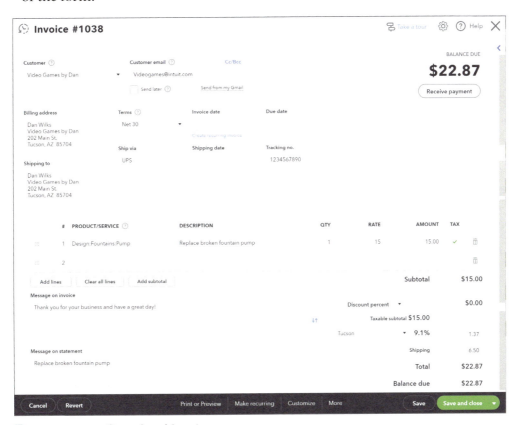

FIGURE 3-19: *Completed Invoice*

> **TIP:**
>
> When you frequently send statements to your customers, the **Message on Statement** field is important. Statements only show invoice summary information, but they do display this field. Therefore, if statements are part of your workflow, it may be useful to copy the information about the products or services you sold to the customer in this field. See page 226 to learn more.

STEP 16. Compare your screen with the invoice shown in Figure 3-19. If you see any errors, correct them. Otherwise, click **Save and Close** to record the invoice.

QuickBooks Online automatically tracks all of the accounting details behind this transaction so that your reports will immediately reflect the sale. For example, the *Open Invoices* report, the *Profit & Loss* report, and the *Balance Sheet* report will all change when you record this invoice.

Adding Calculating Items to an Invoice

On the next invoice, you'll learn how to include **Subtotals** and **Line-item Discounts** to an invoice.

On page 114 we added a **Discount** that applied to the entire sale, but there may be times when you want to apply a discount only to specific line items. By creating a **Discount service item**, we can add a row to manually multiply the line(s) above by the discount rate, and enter that number as a negative in the *Amount* column.

HANDS-ON PRACTICE

To create an invoice with a subtotal and a discount, follow these steps:

STEP 1. From the *Customer* list, select the Freeman Sporting Goods subaccount for **55 Twin Lane**.

STEP 2. Select **Invoice** from the *New Transaction* button.

STEP 3. Enter **today's date** in the *Invoice Date* field (press **T**).

STEP 4. Enter the two items shown in Table 3-3 in the body of the invoice.

PRODUCT/SERVICE	DESCRIPTION	QTY	RATE	AMOUNT
Gardening	Weekly Gardening Service	4	25	100
Pest Control	Pest Control Services	1	35	35

TABLE 3-3: *Data for use in the Invoice*

STEP 5. While you are still on the second line of the invoice, click the **Add Subtotal** button under the grid on the left.

Notice that on the next row, QuickBooks Online automatically calculates the sum of the first two lines on the invoice.

STEP 6. On line 4, click the *Product/Service drop-down arrow* and choose **+Add New** at the top of the list.

> **NOTE:**
>
> We are adding a new item to QuickBooks Online on the fly, but you could also make this addition from the Products and Services list. Once you've created the new service, you will be able to use it on all future transactions.

STEP 7. Click on **Service**.

STEP 8. Enter **Discount** in the *Name* box as shown in Figure 3-20.

STEP 9. Since this company uses Product and Service *Category* groupings, add a new category called **Admin** to hold bookkeeping items.

STEP 10. Enter **Discount applied** in the *Description*.

STEP 11. Leave the *Sales Price/Rate* blank since it only holds dollar values, not percentages.

STEP 12. In the *Income Account* box, choose **Discounts Given**. Because this income account was created to hold contra-income accounts (reductions to income that offset revenue), it will appear as a negative amount on your Profit and Loss report.

> **KEY TERM:**
>
> **Contra accounts** are categories on the Chart of Accounts that hold offset transactions. On a Profit & Loss report, they appear as a negative.
>
> For example, customer discounts reduce revenue. By tracking these discounts in a separate account instead of simply reducing the original income category, business owners can see the true revenue they would have earned had they not given the discounts.

STEP 13. Set the *Sales Tax* to **Nontaxable**.

STEP 14. Click **Save and Close**.

STEP 15. The **Admin:Discount** line item is added to row 4. In the *Description* field, enter **10% Discount applied to services**.

STEP 16. Click in the *Rate* field and type in **-135*.1**, then press **Tab** (if you see a warning message as you type, just ignore it).

STEP 17. The *Amount* will fill in with **-13.50**. A 10% discount has now been subtracted from the $135 subtotal.

STEP 18. On line 5, add **Soil**, with a *Qty* of **1**. This way Craig is separating his materials from his labor costs.

STEP 19. Enter **California** in the *Select a Sales Tax Rate* field.

STEP 20. Enter **Gardening, Pest Control, and Soil** in the *Message on Statement* field.

STEP 21. Verify that your screen matches Figure 3-21.

STEP 22. To save the invoice, click **Save** in the *black bar* at the bottom of the invoice. We will leave this invoice open for the next exercise.

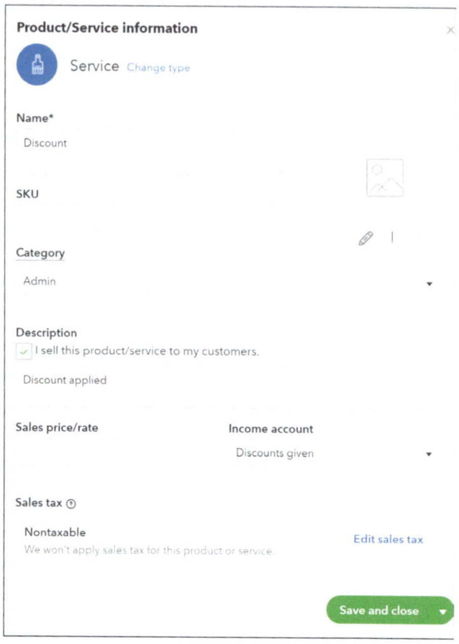

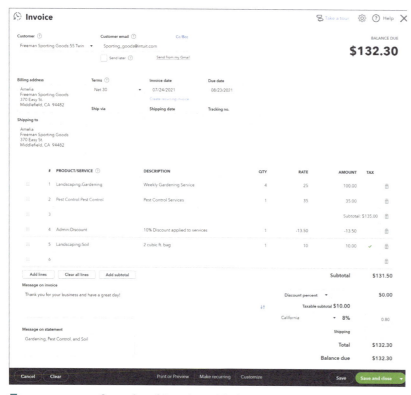

FIGURE 3-20: *Create a Discount service item*

FIGURE 3-21: *Completed Invoice with discount*

Adding Attachments to Invoices

It's important to maintain a paper trail, the documentation behind your transactions. You can add attachments to invoices, expenses, and most transaction types throughout QuickBooks Online.

When you have Word documents, Excel spreadsheet, pdfs, or images that you would like to associate with an invoice, they can be saved in QBO right along with the form for future access.

FIGURE 3-22: *Add Attachments to any QuickBooks Online form*

To attach a document to this invoice, such as a customer's original purchase order, scroll down to the bottom of the form. Either drag the file into the *Attachments* box in the bottom left corner, or click the **Attachments** paperclip above the box to navigate your computer to locate the file (see Figure 3-22).

When you email an invoice and want to include the attachment, check **Attach to Email**.

To view the attachment, click the **blue filename** and it will open in a new tab for viewing and downloading.

To see all the attachments stored in QuickBooks Online, go to the **Gear** > **Attachments** list.

STEP 23. Attach any file you have on your computer to the invoice.

STEP 24. Click **Save and Close** to close the invoice.

Open Invoices Report

Now that you've entered invoices for your customers, run QuickBooks Online's reports to monitor invoices and their status. The *Open Invoices* report, which is useful for seeing invoices that have not been matched up with customer payments, is shown in Figure 3-24.

HANDS-ON PRACTICE

STEP 1. In some companies, you can click in the **Search magnifying glass** to quickly open reports. Try typing in **Open Invoices**, as shown in Figure 3-23. Click on the report to open it as soon as you see it appear on the list; you don't have to finish typing the entire report name!

If that doesn't work, click in **Reports** in the *Left Navigation Bar*. Use the *Find Report by Name* search to choose **Open Invoices**.

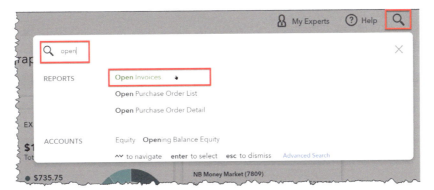

FIGURE 3-23: *Use the Search to find the Open Invoices report*

STEP 2. Verify that your *Open Invoices* report matches Figure 3-24.

Craig's Design and Landscaping Services

Open Invoices

As of

DATE	TRANSACTION TYPE	NUM	TERMS	DUE DATE	OPEN BALANCE
Amy's Bird Sanctuary					
	Invoice	1021	Net 30		239.00
Total for Amy's Bird Sanctuary					$239.00
Bill's Windsurf Shop					
	Invoice	1027	Net 30		85.00
Total for Bill's Windsurf Shop					$85.00
Freeman Sporting Goods					
0969 Ocean View Road					
	Invoice	1036	Net 30		477.50
Total for 0969 Ocean View Road					$477.50
55 Twin Lane					
	Invoice	1028	Net 30		81.00
	Invoice	1005	Net 30		4.00
	Invoice	1039	Net 30		132.30
Total for 55 Twin Lane					$217.30
Total for Freeman Sporting Goods					$694.80
Geeta Kalapatapu					
	Invoice	1033	Net 30		629.10

FIGURE 3-24: *Open Invoices report*

RECEIVING PAYMENTS FROM CUSTOMERS

Receiving Payments by Check

Now that you've recorded invoices for your customers, you're ready to begin receiving their payments for what they owe. To apply payments from your customers to specific invoices, follow these steps:

HANDS-ON PRACTICE

STEP 1. Click the **+New button** in the *Left Navigation Bar* and select **Receive Payment**.

STEP 2. In the *Customer* box, start typing **Travis** and click his name as soon as it appears, or scroll down to **Travis Waldron** and select it.

STEP 3. Travis's open invoice appears (see Figure 3-25).

Under *Outstanding Transactions* you can view the **Invoice Number**, **Invoice Date**, **Due Date**, the **Original Amount**, and the **Open Balance** (the amount still due).

STEP 4. Keep **today's date** in the *Payment Date* field.

STEP 5. Select **Check** as *Payment Method*.

STEP 6. Enter **4242** in the *Reference No.* field.

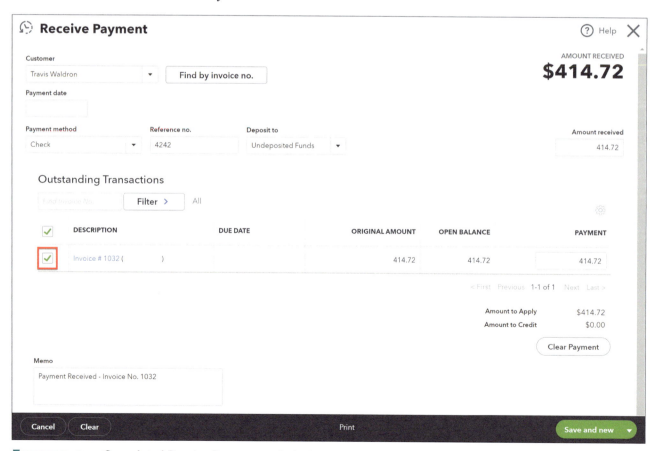

FIGURE 3-25: *Completed Receive Payments window*

STEP 7.   Confirm that the *Deposit To* field says **Undeposited Funds** (or **Payments to Deposit**).

STEP 8.   Place a **checkmark** in the box to the left of the invoice under the *Outstanding Transactions* section. The payment amount will autofill in the *Payment* box on the right and in the *Amount Received* field in the header (see Figure 3-25).

STEP 9.   Verify that the *Amount Received* field and the *Payment* column for the selected invoice both show **$414.72**.

STEP 10. Enter **Payment Received—Invoice No. 1032** in the *Memo* field.

When entering a memo, type **Payment Received** followed by the invoice number. Memos do not affect the application of payments to specific invoices, but they are helpful in two ways. First, if you send your customers statements, only the information in the *Reference No., Date,* and *Memo* fields will show on statements. Also, if you ever have to go back to the transaction and verify that you've applied the payment to the correct invoice(s), you'll be able to look at the *Memo* field to see the invoice(s) to which you should have applied the payments.

STEP 11. Verify that your screen matches Figure 3-25. If you see errors, correct them. Then click **Save and Close** to record the payment.

Receiving Payments by Credit Card or ACH

You can receive credit card payments or electronic checks (ACH) right in QuickBooks Online using **QuickBooks Payments**, or record payments received through other merchant services.

By signing up for QuickBooks Payments, you can:

- run credit card and ACH payments right inside your transactions
- email invoices with a Pay Now button that allows the customer to pay right on their phone or computer
- create recurring sales receipts that charge the card on the date you specify, and email the customer the receipt . . . without you lifting a finger!

The rates are comparable to PayPal and Square, and because the automation creates invoice payments, batches daily, and matches the Banking Feed automatically, you save hours of time. For example, you won't need to make the adjustment demonstrated on page 136.

To sign up for QuickBooks Payments, visit the **Payments** tab in the **Account and Settings** in your QuickBooks Online subscription.

> **TIP:**
>
> ProAdvisors get discounted rates for QuickBooks Payments. If you sign up through a **QuickBooks Solutions Provider (QSP)**, one of Intuit's resellers, you will pay lower merchant service fees.

HANDS-ON PRACTICE

Mark Cho paid off his invoice using a credit card.

STEP 1. In the *Customers Center,* click on **Mark Cho**. Select **Payment** from the *New Transactions* drop-down list.

STEP 2. Enter **$314.28** into the *Amount Received* field and press the **Tab** key (see Figure 3-27).

Notice that because the amount entered exactly matches the amount of the open invoice, QBO automatically checks off the transaction and fills in its *Payment* box.

STEP 3. Enter **Visa** in the *Payment Method* field.

STEP 4. If your QuickBooks Online file was connected to **QuickBooks Payments**, a button would appear allowing you to *Enter Credit Card Details* and *Process Credit Card,* as shown in Figure 3-26. Since this sample company is not connected to the built-in merchant services, we will not do this now.

The *Credit Card Information* window would open for you to fill in payment details. QuickBooks Online immediately masks all but the last 4 digits of the credit card number with x's for security purposes.

After filling in the information, QBO may also ask if you want to store this information for future use, and suggest you get verbal approval or written approval from the customer to run the charge.

Click the **Use This Info button** when finished entering the credit card information.

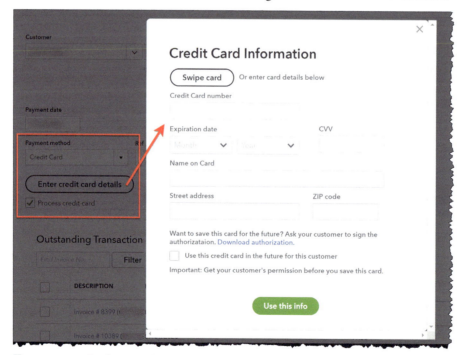

FIGURE 3-26: *Process Credit Cards and e-Checks right in QBO*

STEP 5. Leave the *Reference No.* field blank.

STEP 6. Enter **Inv. 1035** in the *Memo* field.

STEP 7. Verify that your screen matches Figure 3-27 and click **Save and Close.**

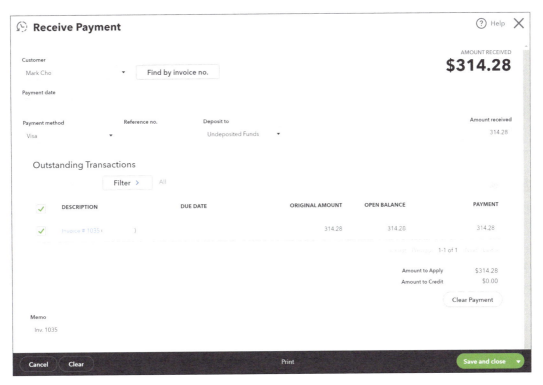

FIGURE 3-27: *Customer Payment by Visa*

> **NOTE:**
>
> If you want to save a customer's credit card information for future payments, you can also enter the credit card information into the *Payment and Billing* tab of the customer record before you process the payment through the *Receive Payment* window, as we saw in *Setting Up Customers* on page 106. When you initiate the credit card or ACH payment, QuickBooks Online will enter the credit card information automatically.

ACH Payments

If the customer were paying by ACH (electronic transfer) using QuickBooks Payments, you would select **Check** as the *Payment Method*. The rest of the instructions are the same, except that you would enter the customer's bank routing number and checking account number instead of their credit card information.

Many businesses prefer taking payments by electronic check because the fees are lower, and there's no expiration date as there is on a credit card.

Handling Partial Payments

In the last example, Mark Cho paid his invoice in full. However, if a customer pays only a portion of an invoice, you should record the payment just as you did in the last example, except that the amount would be less than the full amount due on any of the open invoices.

Apply the partial payment to the appropriate invoice. The next time you use the **Receive Payment** function for that customer, the invoice will indicate the remaining amount due. You can record additional payments to the invoice in the same way as before.

> **IMPORTANT!**
>
> If there is more than one open invoice on the list, be sure to choose carefully! If a customer pays an amount that does not exactly match one of the unpaid invoices, be sure to check off the correct transaction. A common error is to pay the invoices from oldest to newest, even when the customer is paying a recent invoice before paying off older ones.

Handling Payments Against Multiple Invoices

You can apply one payment from a customer to multiple invoices in one step. It is a common mistake to break a single payment into multiple payments and apply them to multiple invoices. Each real-life action should have one corresponding QuickBooks Online transaction.

When a customer pays more than one invoice by check or credit card, check off the appropriate invoices in the *Receive Payment* window until the *Amount Received* equals the amount of the payment.

You can also override the amounts in the *Payment* column to apply the total to invoices in whatever combination is necessary.

If you do not allocate the entire payment, QuickBooks Online will hold the remaining balance as a **Credit** for the customer.

HANDS-ON PRACTICE

STEP 1. Go to the *Customers Center* and click on the gray **Open Invoices** box in the *Money Bar*.

STEP 2. Scroll down to view the **Red Rock Diner**. Note that they have two open invoices.

STEP 3. Click the blue **Receive Payment** link in the *Action* column on the right (see Figure 3-25).

STEP 4. Select **Check** as *Payment Method*.

STEP 5. Enter **5256** in the *Reference No.* field.

STEP 6. Confirm that *Deposit To* says **Undeposited Funds** or **Payments to Deposit**.

STEP 7. Confirm that **226.00** appears in the *Amount Received* field.

STEP 8. Confirm that **both payments** are already checked.

STEP 9. Verify that the *Open Balance* and *Payment* columns for the selected invoices are the same, showing that each invoice is being paid in full.

The checkmarks to the left of the *Description* column indicates the invoice(s) to which QuickBooks Online will apply the payment. QuickBooks Online automatically selected both invoices because the amount of the customer's check is the same as the unpaid sum of the two invoices. If applicable, you can deselect an invoice by clicking on the checkmark and instead choose another invoice from the list.

STEP 10. Enter **Payment Received—Invoices 1024 & 1023** in the *Memo* field.

STEP 11. Verify that your screen matches Figure 3-28. If you see errors, correct them.

STEP 12. Click **Save and Close** to record the payment.

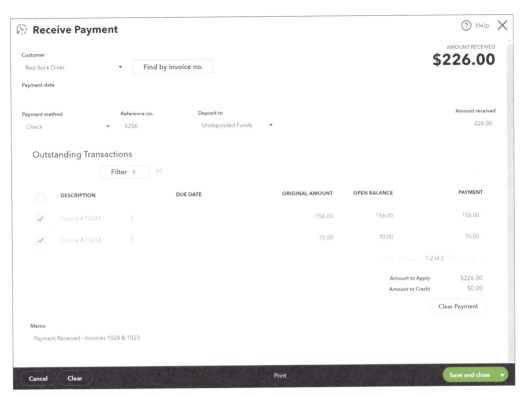

FIGURE 3-28: *Completed Receive Payment window with multiple invoices*

THE ACCOUNTING BEHIND THE SCENES:

Receiving payments increases (debits) **Undeposited Funds** and decreases (credits) **Accounts Receivable**.

TRANSACTION TYPE	NAME	MEMO/DESCRIPTION	ACCOUNT	DEBIT	CREDIT
Payment	Red Rock Diner	Payment Received - Invoices 102...	Undeposited Funds	$226.00	
			Accounts Receivable (A/R)		$226.00
				$226.00	$226.00

What if the Payment Doesn't Match the Invoice?

If the customer's payment amount doesn't exactly equal the invoice, you'll need to make a choice. Do you want to leave a remaining balance or credit and follow up with them? Or would you rather just close the invoice and finish the sale?

If the payment amount is significantly different, send the invoice back to the customer showing the remaining balance due (if the payment was too low), send a **Refund** to the customer (if the payment was too high), or leave the balance as a **Credit Memo** to apply to their next invoice. You may wish to send a **Statement** to the customer showing the history of the activity (see page 226).

If the discrepancy isn't worth bringing to your customer's attention and you choose to just complete the transaction, edit the invoice so that the payment exactly matches the balance. If the payment is too low, either enter the amount in the *Discount* field, or add a new line item with an explanation, subtracting the difference. If the payment is too high, add a new line item to increase the total on the sale, and note in the *Description* that there was an overpayment.

MAKING BANK DEPOSITS

You will receive payments from your customers in several different ways: cash, checks, and credit cards. Merchant service processors batch all the day's credit card payments together into one bank deposit. A business owner typically brings an envelope of cash and checks to the bank to deposit them.

Because daily transactions of each payment type are grouped together by the bank, you will also record their deposits separately in QuickBooks Online. Creating deposits in QuickBooks Online mirrors traditional deposit slips, making bank reconciliations much easier.

Figure 3-29 demonstrates the workflows used to receive payments and deposit the funds into the bank.

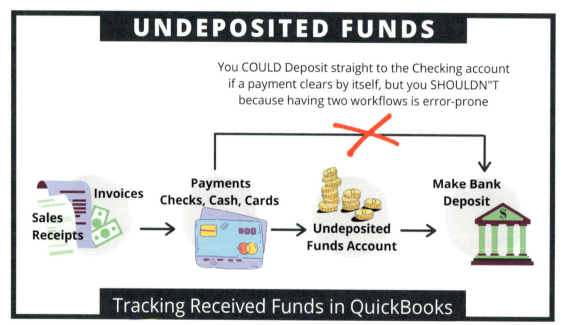

FIGURE 3-29: *All funds from sales transactions go through Undeposited Funds or directly to a bank account.*

You will make several deposits each day. Start with your checks and cash, followed by credit card receipts. Deposits into multiple bank accounts are created individually.

Different merchant service companies batch their transactions in a variety of ways:

▸ Most merchant services combine MasterCard and Visa receipts when they credit your bank account.

▸ American Express receipts may require a separate deposit.

▸ You may need to combine credit cards across dates. Some payment processors close their daily batches in the middle of the day. For example, charges after 6pm may get grouped with the following day's receipts.

▸ If service fees are deducted from the deposit, like those charged by PayPal and Square, they are subtracted during this workflow.

As you become familiar with your banks' processes, you will learn the best practices for your business.

Undeposited Funds and Payments to Deposit

Undeposited Funds is a special account that is automatically created by QuickBooks Online. In some QuickBooks Online company subscriptions, Undeposited Funds is instead called ***Payments to Deposit***. This new name makes it easy to understand the function of the asset account.

This category works as a temporary holding account where QuickBooks Online tracks money received from customers before the money is deposited into a bank account. Undeposited Funds is the equivalent of a cash box (or the owner's desk drawer), to hold cash and checks before driving them to the bank.

Figure 3-30: *The Deposit To field*

As illustrated in Figure 3-30, when you record payments and sales receipts, QuickBooks Online gives you a choice between grouping all receipts into the **Undeposited Funds** account, or immediately depositing the funds to one of your **Bank** accounts.

TIP:

This *Deposit To* field is sticky—it will repeat the most recent selection. If you leave it on **Undeposited Funds** or **Payments to Deposit**, you can implement one consistent workflow. If you change it to **Checking**, you create two different workflows depending on the situation. You also run the risk of forgetting to change it back, inadvertently depositing payments to the wrong account, introducing errors in your data.

Since it is most common to have multiple sales transactions deposited together, using Undeposited Funds gives you an opportunity to batch credit cards, or collect cash and checks together, so that the deposit total in the bank register matches the bank's activity. If you skip the Undeposited Funds account, each sales transaction creates a separate deposit in your bank account, which won't match what actually occurs in real life . . . or on your bank statement.

Unless you only make one sale each day and your deposits include only the funds from that single sale, it's a best practice in QuickBooks Online for all payments and sales receipts to go to the Undeposited Funds account. The benefits include:

▸ You know at a glance how much money is in transit.

▸ The Banking Feed looks at Undeposited Funds first to find matching transactions (see page 261).

▸ It is much easier to reconcile the bank account at the end of each month because the deposits on the bank statement will match the deposits in your QuickBooks Online bank account.

THE ACCOUNTING BEHIND THE SCENES:

Deposits decrease (credit) **Undeposited Funds,** and increase (debit) the **Bank** account.

Depositing Checks and Cash

In this age of electronic banking, fewer people are using cash and checks as their go-to payment method. In fact, when customers do pay by check, you may not even need to go to the bank—most financial institutions now have phone apps that allow you to take a picture of the front and back of the check to deposit it from home. This saves time and prevents checks from collecting in your wallet waiting for you to drive to the bank. A second benefit is that each check gets deposited singly, which makes it easy to match the Banking Feed.

HANDS-ON PRACTICE

To record a deposit of cash and checks at a bank, follow these steps:

Step 1. From the *+New* button above the *Left Navigation Bar*, select **Bank Deposit** on the far right at the top of the *Other* column.

Step 2. QuickBooks Online displays the *Bank Deposit* window (see Figure 3-31, your transaction list may vary).

Figure 3-31: *The Bank Deposits window with two payments selected (your screen may vary)*

Step 3. Since the checks and cash you deposit in your bank account will post to your account separately from credit card receipts, you may find it helpful to sort the window by *Payment Method* to group **cash, checks, and credit cards**.

You can click on each of the headers to sort the list however it is most convenient.

Step 4. The Cool Cars and Freeman Sporting Goods payments were both received on the same day, although the person who entered the payment didn't specify the payment method, so they're blank. Update the Cool Cars *Payment Method* to **Check** and the Freeman Sporting Goods *Payment Method* to **Cash**.

Step 5. Select these two customer payments by clicking the **checkmarks** on their left.

A checkmark in the column on the left indicates that QuickBooks Online will include the payment in the deposit.

Step 6. Scroll up to the top of the screen. Note the *Amount* in the upper right corner, **$2062.52**. This is the total amount that you would see on your bank statement.

STEP 7.   The **Checking** account is already displayed in the *Account* field. This field is sticky, and will repeat your previous deposit. Always confirm that the correct bank account is selected, based on the transactions you clicked.

STEP 8.   Enter the *Date* the deposit was made. Be sure to enter in the actual date of the transaction at the bank, not the day you are adding the entry in QBO.

In this case, enter the **same date** that you see on the Cool Cars and Freeman Sporting Goods payments.

Adding Additional Funds to the Deposit

On this deposit, we will also add a non-sales-related item. Occasionally, you will deposit money that is not from sales transactions, like a **Vendor Refund**, and these can be entered directly in the *Bank Deposit* window, as shown in Figure 3-34.

Today, Craig received a check in the mail from his insurance company, a partial refund because he had no claims this year. He adds it to that day's deposit.

STEP 9.   Scroll down to the *Add Funds to This Deposit* grid at the bottom of the *Bank Deposit* window.

STEP 10. On the first blank line, enter **Brosnahan Insurance Agency** in the *Received From* column and press **Tab**.

STEP 11. In the *Account* column, enter **Insurance**. Always code the refund to the same account as the original expense. This will credit (reduce) the expense on reports.

STEP 12. Enter **Insurance rebate** in the *Description* column and press **Tab**.

STEP 13. Choose **Check** as the *Payment Method*, and enter **13451** in the *Ref No.* column. Press **Tab**.

STEP 14. Enter **142** in the *Amount* column.

STEP 15. Compare your work in the *Add Funds to the Deposit* section in Figure 3-34. The total should deposit after this step should be $2,204.52. Leave this window open for the next step.

Holding Cash Back from Deposits

If you **hold back cash** when you make your bank deposits, fill in the bottom part of the deposit screen indicating the account to which you want to post the cash (see Figure 3-32).

FIGURE 3-32: *The bottom of the deposit slip deals with an Owner Draw*

There are two ways you might use the *Cash Back* section of the deposit:

1. If you routinely hold back cash from your deposits and use it as cash on hand, enter the **Cash** account in the *Cash Back Goes To* field. While this Cash account is not a true bank account, it is the equivalent of a cash box or envelope. Be sure to gather receipts for all cash expenditures and reconcile Petty Cash monthly (see page 182).

2. If the owner is keeping back cash for their own use, enter their **Owner Draws** account. In the *Cash Back Memo*, enter the owner's name. Enter the amount of the cash being withheld into *Cash Back Amount*.

> **TIP:**
>
> It's not a good idea to routinely hold cash back from deposits for the owner's "pocket money." If the business is a Sole Proprietorship or LLC, it's better to write a monthly check to the owner (or make a bank transfer) and code it to **Owner Draws**. Then encourage the owner to spend their own personal money instead of the business's money. Discuss this with your QuickBooks Online ProAdvisor, or with your accountant.

HANDS-ON PRACTICE

STEP 16. Create a new Petty Cash bank account on the fly. Click in the *Cash Back Goes to* list, then select **+Add New** at the top of the drop down list. In the *Account* window that opens, create a new **Bank** account called **Cash**, using the *Detail Type* **Cash on Hand**, as shown in Figure 3-33.

STEP 17. In the *Cash Back Memo*, enter **Cash on hand**.

STEP 18. In the *Cash Back Amount* field, enter **300** and press **Tab** or click away.

STEP 19. When you're done, the total in the *Bank Deposit* window, **$1904.52**, will equal the exact amount of money being deposited in the bank, and it will match the bank statement (see Figure 3-34).

STEP 20. Click **Save and New**.

STEP 21. Reopen the deposit by clicking the **Recent Deposits** button to the upper left of the *Bank Deposit* window

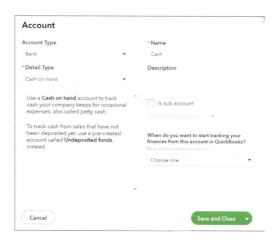

FIGURE 3-33: *Create a new Petty Cash account on the fly*

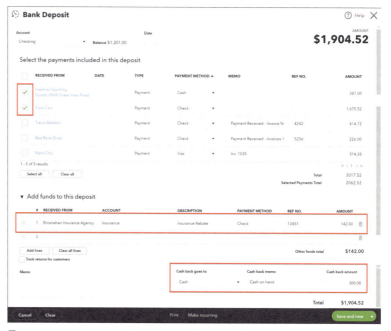

FIGURE 3-34: *Bank Deposit with a Vendor Refund and Cash Back (your screen may vary)*

title (the circular clock arrow). Click on the deposit you just made for **$1,904.52** to open it again.

Alternatively, you could press your browser's **Back button**.

STEP 22. Click on the **More** button in the *black bar* at the bottom of the screen (see Figure 3-35) and choose *Transaction Journal*. The report shows the double-entry accounting happening because of this deposit. Compare it to **The Accounting Behind the Scenes** below.

STEP 23. If QBO asks you if you want to save before continuing, click **Yes**.

FIGURE 3-35: *Show the Transaction Journal*

FIGURE 3-36: *The Transaction Journal for this complex Deposit*

THE ACCOUNTING BEHIND THE SCENES:

In today's Deposit, the **Checking** account increases (with a debit) by the total **Deposit** ($1904.52). The customer cash and checks decrease (credit) the balance in **Undeposited Funds**, the refund from the vendor decreases (credits) the **Insurance Expense**, and the cash back increases (debits) the balance in the **Cash** bank account.

Printing Deposit Slips

QuickBooks Online can print **Deposit Slips** on preprinted deposit slips or blank paper. Follow these steps:

HANDS-ON PRACTICE

STEP 24. Click on the **Search Magnifying Class** in the upper right corner and open the deposit again from the *Recent Transactions* list.

STEP 25. Click **Print** in the *black bar* at the bottom of the window, as shown in Figure 3-37.

Step 26. Choose **Print Deposit Slip and Summary**.

Step 27. The *Print Preview* appears as shown in Figure 3-38. Normally, you would load preprinted deposit slips into the printer before printing. However, if you do not have a deposit slip, print the deposit on blank paper. Click **Print**.

Figure 3-37: *Print a Deposit Slip if you wish*

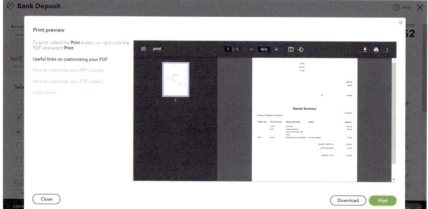

Figure 3-38: *Print a deposit slip or save as a PDF*

Step 28. The **Deposit Summary** opens in a new window. You'll see yet another preview that you can download, save, or print (its exact appearance will depend on your browser and computer settings).

Step 29. The final result will look like Figure 3-39. **Close** the *Print Preview* window.

Step 30. **Save and Close** the *Bank Deposit*.

Figure 3-39: *Deposit slip and deposit summary*

Depositing Credit Card Payments

As mentioned previously, to ensure that your bank reconciliations go smoothly, you should always deposit your checks and cash separately from your credit card payments.

Make sure you group transactions together in a way that matches the actual deposits made to your bank. Some merchant service companies batch payments during your business hours, so that nighttime sales get grouped with the following day. Confirming these totals is a critical step in making your bank reconciliation process go smoothly.

QuickBooks Payments

One of the benefits of using **QuickBooks Payments**, Intuit's built-in merchant services, is its automation when matching payments to deposits.

While we can't view this in our sample company, there is a tab for *Deposits* in the *Sales Center* of companies using QuickBooks Payments. It shows the status of merchant service payments including when you can expect each deposit and which transactions make up each batch (see Figure 3-40), including when you can expect each deposit and which transactions make up each batch, as shown in Figure 3-40.

Merchant service fees are deducted in a separate expense transaction, so your bank deposits work the same way as depositing cash and checks, as described on page 130.

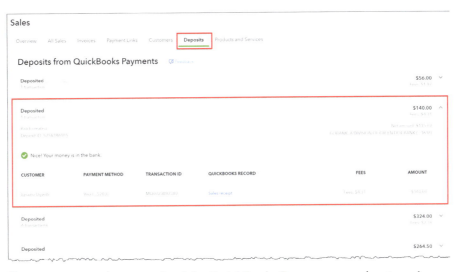

FIGURE 3-40: *An example of the QuickBooks Payments merchant services deposit status window*

PayPal and Square

Some merchant services providers (like PayPal or Square) deduct their fees from each transaction. You must either manually edit each sale to deduct the fees, or use a third-party app integration that does this for you.

If your merchant services provider deducts fees in a separate daily or monthly transaction, skip these steps; you would simply add the fees as a separate expense as they appear in the Banking Feed.

While we will not do this now, the process uses the *Add Funds to This Deposit* grid, as we saw with the vendor refund on page 131.

> *Do not perform these steps now. They are for reference only.*

Using PayPal as an example, here are the steps:

Step 1. Create a sales receipt for the individual PayPal sale. Use PayPal as the *Payment Method*.

Step 2. Create a new **Bank Deposit** from the *+New* button.

Step 3. Check off the PayPal or Square transaction.

Step 4. Scroll down the *Add Funds to This Deposit* grid.

Step 5. On the first blank line, choose the payment processor's vendor name in the *Received From* field (i.e., **PayPal**).

Step 6. Enter **Merchant Service Fees** in the *Account* column and then press **Tab**.

Step 7. Enter **PayPal** in the *Payment Method* column and then press **Tab**.

Step 8. In the *Amount* field, subtract the amount of the PayPal fee.

TIP:

If you don't know the merchant service fee offhand, you can use the QuickMath feature to calculate it directly in the *Amount* field, as shown in Figure 3-41. Type the amount that got deposited, minus the actual sale total. When you press tab to perform the calculation, the difference will be negative, subtracting the fees from the total sale. The remaining deposit total will match your bank statement.

Figure 3-41: *Calculate PayPal's deposit minus the original sale total*

Step 9. The PayPal deposit would look like Figure 3-42.

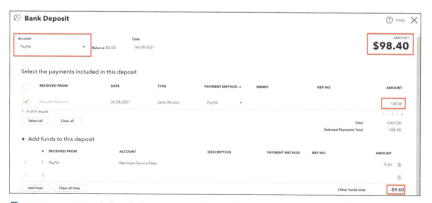

Figure 3-42: *A Bank Deposit window with merchant service fees deducted*

> **IMPORTANT!**
>
> QuickBooks Online has a direct bank connection to PayPal that automates this process so that you do not need to manually adjust every transaction. There is an entire ecosystem of third-party integrations that streamline your data entry. If you find any part of your bookkeeping tedious, be sure to visit **apps.com** to look for a solution!

Viewing Deposits in the Register

Now that you have entered your deposits, the checking account register shows each one, along with the updated balance in the account.

Open the *Checking Register* by clicking **Accounting** in the *Left Navigation Bar*, then **Chart of Accounts**. On the far right of the **Checking** account, click **View Register** (see Figure 3-43).

> **IMPORTANT!**
>
> Your screen will not match, although you will see some of these transactions. The illustration is for training purposes only.

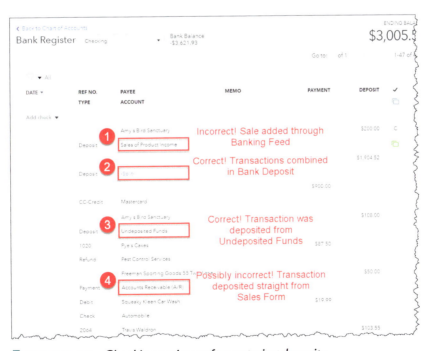

FIGURE 3-43: *Checking register after entering deposits*

There are four scenarios for how deposits wind up in the register. You can tell which workflow was used by the content of the *Account* field.

1. **This is incorrect.** If the account says **Sales, Sales of Product Income, or any of your customized Income** categories, this shows that the deposit was made improperly. Instead of matching to a Bank

Deposit containing sales receipts and invoice payments, someone clicked on a Received entry in the Banking Feed and typed in the customer name and income account manually. This results in duplicated income in QuickBooks Online. Delete the transaction and create a Bank Deposit that gathers the already-existing invoice payments and sales receipts to correctly match the Banking Feed. We'll look at the Banking Feed in detail on page 259.

2. **This is correct.** If the Account says **Split**, hover your cursor over the field to see the contents. This shows that the Bank Deposit window was used to combine several individual sales into one group to match the bank statement.

3. **This is correct.** If the Account says **Undeposited Funds** or **Payments to Deposit**, this is a single transaction that was deposited properly from Undeposited Funds.

4. **This may be fine, or it may indicate duplicated revenue, depending on your company's workflow.** If the Account says Accounts Receivable, this is an invoice payment that was deposited directly to the checking account instead of into Undeposited Funds, as we saw on page 129.

RUNNING ACCOUNTS RECEIVABLE REPORTS

Using the Invoices Center

The **Invoices Center** provides you with a fast way to see the status of your unpaid sales transactions all from one location. It also provides features to improve invoicing and collections, as well as create new invoices. You can access the *Invoices Center* under **Sales** in the *Left Navigation Bar* (see Figure 3-44), or by clicking the **Invoices** tab from anywhere in the *Sales Center*.

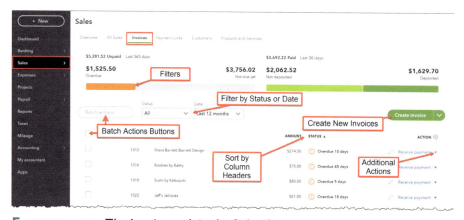

FIGURE 3-44: *The Invoices tab in the Sales Center*

The colored bar across the top is called the **Money Bar**. We looked at other Money Bars on page 18. From the Invoices Center you can:

▸ See all of your **Not Due Yet** (gray bar) and **Overdue** (orange bar) invoices.

▸ See your **Not Deposited** (light green) and **Recently deposited** payments (dark green).

▸ Filter using the **Status** drop-down.

▸ Use the **Date** filter to shorten the list.

THE SALES PROCESS | 139

- Click on any transaction to **view its activity**.
- Use the **Action** button to **Receive a payment**.
- Use the **Action** drop-down to **print or send a copy** (or a reminder) by email.
- Use the **Action** drop-down to **duplicate, void,** or **delete** an invoice.
- Sort the list by clicking on any **column heading**.
- Use the **Batch Action** button to print, email, or delete a group of invoices all at once.

HANDS-ON PRACTICE
To explore the **Invoices Center**,

STEP 1. Click the **Invoices** tab under **Sales** in the *Left Navigation Bar*, as shown in Figure 3-45.

STEP 2. Click the **Orange box.** The list filters to show only invoices past their date due.

STEP 3. Drop down the *Date* box and select **This Year**. How many invoices do you see?

FIGURE 3-45: *Invoices on the left*

STEP 4. Click the **Pencil** on the right of the top invoice. What happens? Cancel the window.

STEP 5. What happens when you click **Receive Payment** next to one of the open invoices? Cancel the window.

STEP 6. Change the *Status* to **All**.

STEP 7. Click on the *Amount* column header. What happens? What happens when you click it again?

STEP 8. Click the **drop-down arrow** on the far right of the first invoice. What options do you see there? Notice that all of these actions can also be performed in other places in QuickBooks Online, but in this window you have quick access to most functions.

As you can see, the flexibility of the Invoices Center means that you can use it with every company's unique workflow.

Viewing the Invoice History
To track activity on an invoice, click on the **Customer** name. A pane opens up on the right (see Figure 3-46). The **Invoice History** window includes detailed information and an *Activity History*. Open and collapse each section you want to view.

FIGURE 3-46: *Invoice History*

The *Status Bar* lets you know where the invoice is in its lifecycle. Green circles appear with a date when the invoice was **Sent**, when it was **Viewed** by the customer in their email, if they paid it electronically or you marked it as **Paid**, and when the money has been **Deposited** from Undeposited Funds.

Click on **Products and Services** at the bottom for a quick glimpse of the contents.

From here you can open and **Edit the Invoice**, or take other actions.

The Accounts Receivable Aging Summary

It is essential to keep track of whether your customers are paying promptly, and if any accounts are delinquent. The *Accounts Receivable Aging Summary* report lists each customer with a balance, and how long their account has been overdue.

HANDS-ON PRACTICE

STEP 1. Click the **Reports** button in the *Left Navigation Bar*. Click on the **Accounts Receivable Aging Summary** at the top, or you can scroll down to the *Who Owes You* section of the list to find it (see Figure 3-47).

The *Current* column contains all the invoices that are not past due. The remaining columns refer to the number of days after the due date assigned to each invoice. A **Net 30** invoice will move to the 1–30 column on the 31st day as it would be one day past due. Invoices with the term **Due on Receipt** will immediately move into the second column if left unpaid.

The *Days Per Aging Period* and *Number of Periods* fields at the top can be adjusted for longer time frames or shorter breakdowns.

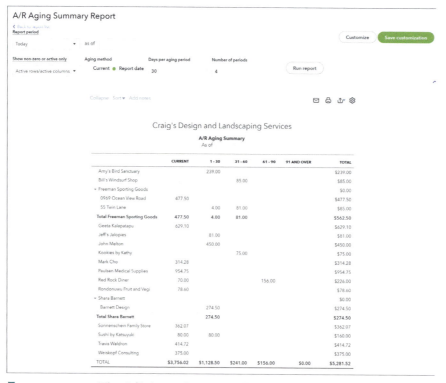

FIGURE 3-47: *The A/R Aging Summary Report*

Negative numbers represent customer **credits**.

If you see zeros, the customer has open invoices and an equivalent amount of credit memos. To fix this, create a Receive Payment form and apply the credit memo as a payment to the invoice (see page 209).

Click on any of the totals to drill into the detailed list of transactions that make up each number. To return to the report summary, click the blue **Back to Report Summary** link at the top left.

REVIEW QUESTIONS

Comprehension Questions

1. When you make a sale to a customer who pays at the time of the sale, which type of form should you use in QuickBooks Online to record the transaction?

2. Explain how the Undeposited Funds account works and why it is best to use Undeposited Funds as the default Deposit To account?

3. How does QuickBooks Online automatically apply payments?

4. QuickBooks Online allows you to attach documents to invoices and expenses. Why would you do this? What file types can you attach?

Multiple Choice

Select the best answer(s) for each of the following:

1. In the New Customer window, you find everything except:
    a. Customer Name.
    b. Customer Billing and Shipping addresses.
    c. Customer Tax Info.
    d. Year-to-date sales information.

2. You should record a Sales Receipt when the customer pays:
    a. By cash, check, or credit card at the time of sale.
    b. By cash, check, or credit card at the end of the month.
    c. Sales tax on the purchase.
    d. Their invoice.

3. Which statement is false?
    a. Invoices are very similar to the Sales Receipt form.
    b. Invoices decrease Accounts Receivable.
    c. Sales Receipts have no effect on Accounts Receivables.
    d. Invoices should be created when customers are going to pay after the date of the initial sale.

4. You may specify payment Terms on the New Customer window; however:
   a. The payment Terms will only show on sales receipt transactions.
   b. The Terms can only be changed once a year.
   c. The sales representative must be informed.
   d. You are also permitted to override the Terms on each sale.

5. Your company has just accepted a payment for an invoice. What should you do in QuickBooks Online to record this payment?
   a. Open the invoice by clicking the *Invoices* icon on the *Dashboard*.
   b. Create a sales receipt by clicking the *Sales Receipt* icon on the *Dashboard*.
   c. Make a deposit by clicking the *Record Deposits* icon on the *Dashboard*.
   d. Receive the payment by clicking the *Receive Payment* icon on the *Dashboard*.

6. Which statement is false?
   a. Your form date should be the date the transaction occurred.
   b. You can have a form date and a separate service date on sales forms.
   c. Your form date should be the date you created the transaction.
   d. You don't need to type in leading 0s and the full year when entering dates.

7. To record a deposit in QuickBooks Online:
   a. Make a separate deposit that includes both Checks and Cash receipts.
   b. Make a separate deposit that includes both VISA and MasterCard receipts.
   c. Make sure each deposit total matches the Banking Feed or bank statement.
   d. All of the above.

8. Your company has just received an order from a customer who will pay within 30 days. How should you record this transaction in QuickBooks Online?
   a. Create an invoice by clicking *Invoice* on the *+New* button.
   b. Create a sales receipt by clicking *Sales Receipt* on the *+New* button.
   c. Make a deposit by clicking *Bank Deposit* on the *+New* button.
   d. Receive the payment by clicking *Receive Payment* on the *+New* button.

9. When you make a deposit, all of the following are true except:
   a. You must print a deposit slip in order to process a deposit.
   b. A Bank Deposit transaction typically transfers money from Undeposited Funds into your bank account.
   c. You should separate your deposits by payment type.
   d. You should create deposits so that they match exactly with the deposits on your bank statement.

10. Which statement is true regarding subtotals on invoices?
    a. *Subtotals* do not need to be used on invoices because the total is calculated automatically.
    b. A *Subtotal* always calculates the amount of all the lines above it.
    c. You have to use a *Subtotal* on every invoice.
    d. A *Subtotal* uses the amount of the preceding line to calculate its amount.

11. When creating a customer record, which statement is false?
    a. After you enter a *Customer Display Name* in the *Customer* window, you cannot use that name in any of the other name lists in QuickBooks Online.
    b. You can set defaults for the customer's sales tax status and payment terms.
    c. A sales rep must be selected when creating a new customer.
    d. When you sell to and purchase from the same company, you should create two records with slightly different names, one in the Vendor list, and one in the Customer list.

12. When receiving payments from customers to whom you have sent invoices, you must:
    a. Receive the payment in full. Partial payments cannot be accepted in QuickBooks Online.
    b. Enter them directly into the checking account register.
    c. Enter the payment into the receive payments window and check off the appropriate invoice(s) to which the payment applies.
    d. Delete the invoice so it does not show on the customer's open records.

13. You need to calculate the amount of a bankcard fee by multiplying the amount of the received payments by -3%. What useful QuickBooks Online feature could you use?
    a. Calculating Items.
    b. QuickMath.
    c. Quick Add.
    d. The *Fees* button on the bottom of the *Make Deposit* window.

14. The Undeposited Funds account tracks:
    a. Bad debts.
    b. Funds that have been received but not deposited.
    c. Funds that have not been received or deposited.
    d. All company sales from the point an invoice is created until it is deposited in the bank.

15. When typing an existing customer name in a form, a dialog box opens to suggest that you need to create them. What should you do?
    a. Add the customer to the *Customer List* again.
    b. Try a *Vendor* name instead.
    c. Click *Cancel* to check the name you entered for typos . . . or just type slower.
    d. None of the above.

Completion Statements

1. A new customer can be added to the customer list without opening the New Customer window by clicking _____ _____ after entering a new customer name on a sales form.

2. When you create a sales receipt, QuickBooks Online increases (with a debit) a(n) _____ account or the _____ _____ account.

3. Discounts and Subtotals are called _____ Items.

4. Receiving payments reduces the balance in _____ _____ and increases the balance in Undeposited Funds or Payments to Deposit.

5. _____ _____ is the built-in merchant services in QuickBooks Online.

THE SALES PROCESS—APPLY YOUR KNOWLEDGE

> Log into your **Imagine Photography** class file at qbo.intuit.com.

1. Open **Account and Settings > Sales.** Confirm that your file is set up with these preferences. Change any that are different. Skip any that are not mentioned:

SALES SETTINGS	
PREFERRED INVOICE TERMS	Net 30
PREFERRED DELIVERY METHOD	None
SHIPPING	On
CUSTOM TRANSACTION NUMBERS	*Off*
CLASSIFICATION OF TAX AND RETAIL INVOICES	*Off*
SERVICE DATE	On
DISCOUNT	*On*
DEPOSIT	Off
ACCEPT TIPS	Off
TAGS	On
SHOW PRODUCT/SERVICE COLUMN ON FORMS	On
SHOW SKU COLUMN	Off
PRICE RULES	Off
TRACK QUANTITY AND PRICE/RATE	On
TRACK INVENTORY QUANTITY ON HAND	On
LATE FEES	Off
PROGRESS INVOICING	Off
STATEMENTS	On

TABLE 3-4: *Sales Settings*

2. Open the **ImagineCustomers.xls** spreadsheet in your classroom files folder. Enable editing. Enter **your email address** into all the records in **Column D** so that you'll be able to send yourself receipts as you complete the *Apply Your Knowledge* assignments (of course, in a real company you would enter the customer's email address, and not your own!). **Import** the spreadsheet into your *Customers* list. You don't need to make any changes to the field mapping. Seven customers will be imported. **Close** the *Import Customers* window when done.

3. Edit **Jaime Madeira** so the Display Name is **Madeira Builders**. Add **Madeira Builders** as the first line of the *Billing Address*, just above the street address, so that it appears on the sub-customers' forms, since they will pay the invoices for all their jobs.

4. Edit **Alison Satterley** so the *Display Name* is **Satterley Wedding Planners**.

5. Add the following **Sub-customers** to Madeira Builders and Satterley Wedding Planners. You will use your own email address so that you can email the receipts to yourself.

VENDOR INFORMATION	MADEIRA SUB-CUSTOMER 1	MADEIRA SUB-CUSTOMER 2	SATTERLEY SUB-CUSTOMER 1	SATTERLEY SUB-CUSTOMER 2
COMPANY NAME	Barnett Residence	Devoe Residence	Gregg and Andrew David	Robyn and Brad Tarnow
CUSTOMER DISPLAY NAME	Barnett Residence	Devoe Residence	Gregg and Andrew David	Robyn and Brad Tarnow
EMAIL	Your email address	Your email address	Your email address	Your email address
PHONE NUMBER	(925) 890-1234	(925) 901-2345	(925) 123-4567	(925) 664-7809
IS SUB-CUSTOMER	Yes	Yes	Yes	Yes
PARENT CUSTOMER	Madeira Builders	Madeira Builders	Satterley Wedding Planners	Satterley Wedding Planners
BILL PARENT CUSTOMER	Yes	Yes	No	No
SAME AS BILLING ADDRESS	No	No	No	No
SHIPPING STREET ADDRESS 1	1304 Shoreview Ct	100 Mary Way	4499 Deerberry Ct	3641 Citrus Ave
SHIPPING STREET ADDRESS 2	Leave Blank	Leave Blank	Leave Blank	Leave Blank
CITY	San Jose	Los Gatos	Concord	Walnut Creek
STATE	CA	CA	CA	CA
ZIP CODE	95122	95032	94521	94598

TABLE 3-5: *Customer List*

6. Click the **Grid Gear** on the right just above the *Customers List* and check the **Address** box to display the customer billing address. Note that the Satterley Wedding Planners still displays the main address even though her sub-customers are invoiced directly.

7. Create two **Sales Receipts** for today's store sales using the data in Table 3-6. **Print** each sales receipt on blank paper. **Save and send** each one to yourself. If you get an alert that you're missing a class, double-check that you assigned **Walnut Creek** to each product row, then dismiss the warning.

SALES	SALES RECEIPT 1	SALES RECEIPT 2
CUSTOMER NAME	Nayo Garcia	Veronica Vasquez
DATE	Today	Today
SALES REP	MM	MM
TAGS	Retail	Retail
PAYMENT METHOD	Cash	Credit Card
DEPOSIT TO:	Payments to Deposit	Payments to Deposit
PRODUCT/SERVICE	Frame 5x7 Metal, Qty 1	Supra Package
PRODUCT/SERVICE	Frame 6x8 Wood, Qty 2	
SALES TAX	$4.10 (auto calculates)	$98.40 (auto calculates)
CLASS	Walnut Creek (on both line items)	Walnut Creek (on all line items)
TOTAL	$44.10 (auto calculates)	$1,058.38 (auto calculates)

TABLE 3-6: *Use this data to create two Sales Receipts*

8. You find an old outstanding invoice for **Shonette Dymond** that was never entered into QuickBooks Online. Create and print the invoice in Table 3-7.

INVOICE	SALES
CUSTOMER NAME	Shonette Dymond
DATE	Two months ago
TERMS	Net 30
SALES REP	MM
TAGS	Retail
1—PRODUCT/SERVICE	Lens, Qty 2 (Shonette is purchasing two additional specialty lenses)
2—PRODUCT/SERVICE	Supra Package (bundle)
CLASS	Walnut Creek on all lines
SALES TAX	$136.32 (auto calculates)
TOTAL	$1,466.28 (auto calculates)

TABLE 3-7: *Use this data to create an Invoice*

9. Your employee, Kaydee Roppa, has been busy booking photo shoots. Create these four **Invoices** for upcoming sessions using the data in Table 3-8. **Print** each invoice on blank paper. **Save and Send** each one to yourself.

THE SALES PROCESS | 147

INVOICE	SALES
CUSTOMER NAME	Lynda Fulton
TERMS	Net 30
DATE	Today
SALES REP	KR
TAGS	Portraits
1—PRODUCT/SERVICE	1 week from today, Indoor Session, Qty 3, $225/hour
2—PRODUCT/SERVICE	The day after that, Retouching, Qty 4, $195/hour
CLASS	Walnut Creek on both lines
SALES TAX	$0, services are not taxable (auto calculates)
TOTAL	$1455.00 (auto calculates)

CUSTOMER NAME	Satterley Wedding Planners:Gregg and Andrew David
TERMS	Net 30
DATE	Today
SALES REP	KR
PO NUMBER	11042
TAGS	Weddings
PRODUCT/SERVICE	1 month from today, Deluxe Shoot
CLASS	San Jose on all lines
SALES TAX	15.11, only photo package is taxable (auto calculates)
TOTAL	$785.11 (auto calculates)

CUSTOMER NAME	Jaime Madeira:Barnett Residence
TERMS	Net 30
DATE	Today
SALES REP	KR
PO NUMBER	2468
TAGS	Real Estate
PRODUCT/SERVICE	3 weeks from today, Videographer, 4 hours
CLASS	San Jose
SALES TAX	$0, services are not taxable (auto calculates)
TOTAL	$500.00 (auto calculates)

CUSTOMER NAME	Jaime Madeira:Devoe Residence
TERMS	Net 30
DATE	Today

INVOICE	SALES
SALES REP	KR
PO NUMBER	2469
TAGS	Real Estate
PRODUCT/SERVICE	2 weeks from today, Videographer, 3 hours
CLASS	San Jose
SALES TAX	$0, services are not taxable (auto calculates)
TOTAL	$375 (auto calculates)

TABLE 3-8: *Use this data to create four invoices*

10. The next day, Kaydee receives a corporate order from **Liz Kildal** at First Community Bank for equipment that they would like you to ship to them. They would also like to hire Imagine Photography to send a videographer to their customer appreciation event next Friday. Create an invoice with the following requirements. Make sure the *Discount Percent* field is before the *Sales Tax* so that you don't pay taxes on money you did not collect.

INVOICE	SALES
CUSTOMER NAME	Liz Kildal
TERMS	Net 30
INVOICE DATE	Tomorrow
SALES REP	KR
PO NUMBER	90210
TAGS	Corporate
1—PRODUCT/SERVICE	Camera SR32
2—PRODUCT/SERVICE	Case
3—SUBTOTAL	Subtotal the equipment
4—PRODUCT/SERVICE	*Service Date:* Next Friday, *Service:* Videographer, *Description:* Videographer for customer appreciation event, *Qty:* 3
CLASS	Walnut Creek (on all lines)
DISCOUNT PERCENT	10% ($115)
SALES TAX	Auto calculates ($71.49)
SHIPPING	$32
TOTAL	$1,138.48 (auto calculates)

TABLE 3-9: *An invoice with a subtotal and additional fields*

11. Run an **Accounts Receivable Aging Summary** dated **Tomorrow** (be sure it includes the Kildal invoice). Print the report.

12. **Liz Kildal** at First Community Bank pays **$806.99** for the equipment and shipping at the time of her order, using her credit card. Create a partial payment using the same date as her invoice, deposited to **Payments to Deposit**.

13. Record a payment dated **two weeks from now** for the full amount from **Lynda Fulton**. Lynda paid by **Check** number **5309**. Deposit the payment into **Payments to Deposit**. Print a receipt. Open up the **original invoice now showing PAID with a $0 balance**, and email it to yourself.

14. **Jaime Madeira** sends you a check for **$875**, dated **the last day of the month**, to pay off the invoices for both **the Barnett and Devoe Residences**. The check number is **87501**. Deposit the check in **Payments to Deposit**. Print a receipt, and email a copy to yourself.

15. Make a **Bank Deposit** for the two credit card sales from Kildal and Vasquez batched together, with merchant fees deducted:
    a. Deposit to the **Business Checking (1025) account** using the date of the latest payment in that group (Liz Kildal's date).
    b. The *Selected Payments Total* for the top grid is **$1865.37**.
    c. Scroll down to *Add Funds to this Deposit* to subtract 3% merchant service fees.
    d. Create a new vendor named **National Bank** on the fly, as shown in Figure 3-48.
    e. Choose the *Account* **Merchant Account Fees**.
    f. In the *Amount* field, enter **-.03*1865.37**, then press **Tab**. You should get **-55.96**.
    g. Assign the Class as **Walnut Creek** (all the merchant processing runs through the Walnut Creek location).
    h. The total deposit is now **$1809.41**.
    i. Change the green Save and Close button to **Save and New**.

FIGURE 3-48: Add National Bank as a new vendor on the fly

16. Deposit **Nayo Garcia's** Cash, also to **Business Checking (1025)**
    a. Use the **same date** as her payment.
    b. Use the *Cash Back Goes To* box to hold back **$4.10**—Use **Owner Draws** since the owner, Ernest Withers, kept the change.
    c. The total deposit is now **$40.00**.
    d. Print a **Deposit Summary**.
    e. Click **Save and New**.

17. Deposit **Lynda Fulton** and **Jaime Madeira's** checks, also to **Business Checking (1025)**.

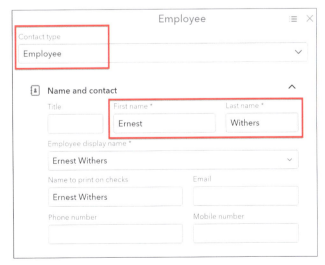

FIGURE 3-49: Add the owner, Ernest Withers, as a new Employee

Ernest is adding a check for **$1000** from his personal bank account, to cover some unexpected company expenses.
- a. Use the *later of the two dates* as the payment date.
- b. **Check off** both checks.
- c. Use **Add Funds to this Deposit** to add Ernest's check
- d. In the *Received From* list, add **Ernest Withers** as an **Employee** on the fly (see Figure 3-49).
- e. In the *Account* field, use **Owner Investments**.
- f. The *Payment Method* is **Check**, and the Ref No is **2001**.
- g. The *Amount* is **$1000**.
- h. The *Class* is **Overhead**.
- i. The total deposit is now **$3330.00**.
- j. Print a **Deposit Summary**.
- k. Change the green button to **Save and Close**.

CHAPTER 4

MANAGING EXPENSES

TOPICS

In this chapter, you will learn about the following topics:

- Configuring the Expenses Settings (page 152)
- Tracking Company Expenses (page 153)
- Setting up Vendors (page 157)
- Tracking Job Costs (page 161)
- Entering Bills (page 162)
- Paying Bills (page 168)
- Using Credit Cards (page 172)
- Writing Checks (page 176)
- Tracking Petty Cash (page 182)
- The Contractors Center (page 183)
- Running Accounts Payable Reports (page 185)

In this chapter, we will discuss several ways to track your company's expenditures and suppliers. We will start by adding vendors to your file, and then discuss several methods of paying them. In addition, this chapter shows you how to track expenses by job.

> **OPEN THIS FILE:**
>
> Open the *Craig's Landscaping sample company* using the bookmark you created on page 8, or go to http://qbo.intuit.com/redir/testdrive.

CONFIGURING THE EXPENSES SETTINGS

In Chapter 2, we learned how to customize QBO's company settings. Now we will continue the process so that both *Craig's Landscaping* and *Imagine Photography* have the proper settings to pay their vendors and track the flow of expenses.

HANDS-ON PRACTICE

It is important to go through these settings before you start entering transactions in order to turn on and off the features appropriate for Craig's Landscaping's workflow.

STEP 1. Open the *Craig's Landscaping sample company* using the bookmark you created on page 8, then click on the **Gear** in the upper right corner. Choose **Account and Settings** at the top left, then click on the **Expenses** tab. Click the **Pencil** icon to edit the *Bills and Expenses* section (see Figure 4-1).

STEP 2. The *Show Items Table on Expense and Purchase Forms* is important when you buy products for resale or hire subcontractors to provide your services. This option allows you to buy the things you sell. This setting should be **On**.

STEP 3. *Show Tags Field on Expense and Purchase Forms* allows you to use the **Tags** feature in QuickBooks Online. While we won't use it for these exercises, we will leave this setting **On**.

STEP 4. Since Craig is interested in **Job Costing** reports that allow him to see profitability by customer, make sure *Track Expenses and Items By Customer* is **On**.

STEP 5. When you purchase products and services on behalf of a customer and pass the expense on for reimbursement in their next invoice, the *Make Expenses and Items Billable* option turns on the passthrough and markup settings.

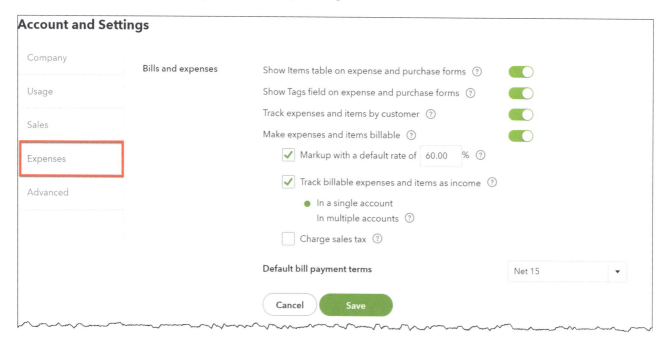

FIGURE 4-1: *Configure your Expenses defaults in Account and Settings*

MANAGING EXPENSES | 153

Step 6. Compare your screen to Figure 4-1. Click **Save**.

Step 7. Click on **Advanced** in the sidebar, and change *Sign Me Out If Inactive For* to **3 Hours**, then click **Save**.

Step 8. Set the *Default Bill Payment Terms* to **Net 15**.

Step 9. Click **Done** to close the *Account and Settings* window.

TRACKING COMPANY EXPENSES

With QuickBooks Online, you can pay your vendors in several ways. You can pay by check, credit card, electronic funds transfer, direct deposit, or (though not recommended) cash.

Most of the time, you'll pay your vendors from a checking account, using one of three workflows:

▸ Recording Accounts Payable through the *Bill* window and using the *Pay Bills* function to pay them later (page 162).

▸ Using the *Expense* function for credit card, debit card, and electronic payments (page 172).

▸ Using the *Check* function to write and print checks (page 176).

QuickBooks Online provides several tools to help you manage the expenses in your business. These tools allow you to track your expenses in detail so that you can create extensive reports that help you manage your vendor relationships and control the costs.

The Expenses Center

The **Expenses Center** under the *Expenses* section of the *Left Navigation Bar* provides you with a chronological list of all your **Expenses**, **Checks**, **Bills**, **Bill Payments**, **Purchase Orders**, and **Billable Expenses** (see Figure 4-2). It includes money-out transactions from all your funding sources, as indicated by the *Type* column. While many transaction types use the same **Expense form**, the payment method used becomes apparent in this view.

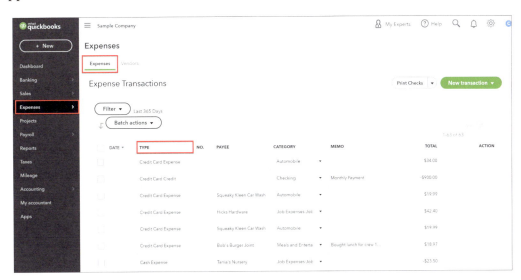

Figure 4-2: *The Expenses Center*

You can click on any transaction in the Expenses Center to open it.

The *Filter* tool allows you to zero in on exactly the transactions you want to view (see Figure 4-3).

If you see errors in the *Category* column, you can update them here, and also use the **Batch Actions** button to check off several transactions and update their *Categories* all at once by choosing **Categorize Selected**.

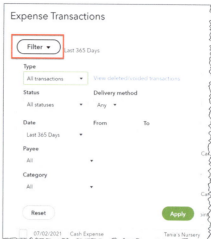

FIGURE 4-3: *Filter the Expenses list*

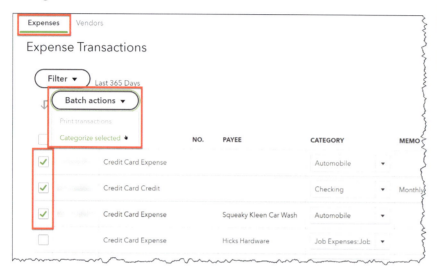

FIGURE 4-4: *Use Batch Actions to correct Category errors*

Using the Vendors Center

Clicking the **Vendors** tab above the *Expenses Center* or on the *Left Navigation Bar* brings up the **Vendors Center** (see Figure 4-5). The Vendors Center organizes information about the suppliers you pay and their transactions.

Managing purchase orders, bills, and payments can be complex. Sometimes, bills come in from your vendors before you receive the ordered items; however, it's important to wait to pay those bills until after the items are received. Also, it's a good idea to prioritize which bills to pay by date due.

The Vendors Center makes this task simple. It presents all of the information you need to manage your bills in one screen, presented in the same visual layout used in the Customer Center.

As you learned earlier while exploring the Customers Center, this window contains a number of tools to manage your bills and expenses.

▸ Clicking on the *Money Bars* at the top filters the list by status.

▸ The *Find a Vendor or Company* search box limits the list to a single vendor.

▸ You can sort the display by clicking on any column heading, such as *Open Balance*.

▸ Use the *Grid Gear* to add and remove columns, including **Address** and **Attachments**. There is also an option to *Include Inactive* vendors.

- The *Action* column's blue links and drop-down arrows let you perform activities for each vendor. You can create new bills, checks, expenses, purchase orders, make payments, or inactivate a vendor right from this screen.

- *Batch Actions* can be used to email or inactivate a number of vendors at the same time. Check the boxes to the left of each desired row, then click the **Batch Actions** button.

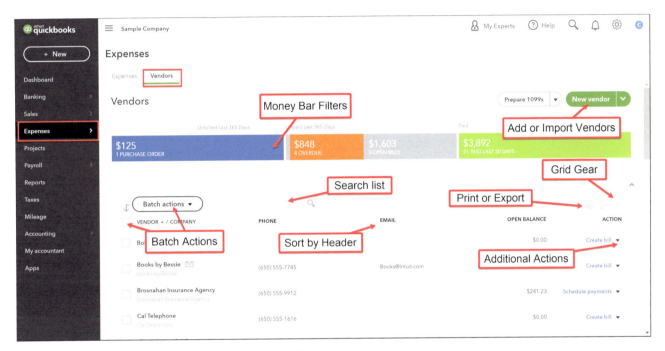

FIGURE 4-5: *Use the Vendors Center to track A/P at a glance*

Cash and Credit Vendors

For illustrative purposes, we have defined two major groups of vendors—cash vendors and credit vendors.

For some vendors, you will create **Bills** and make **Bill Payments**. The **Accounts Payable (A/P)** account will be used to show how much you owe these suppliers. We will refer to these as your **credit vendors**, and you will see their balances in Accounts Payable when you run an *Accrual-based Balance Sheet*.

With other vendors, you will skip the Accounts Payable workflow and pay them directly, coding the transactions to the appropriate expense accounts. We will refer to these as your **cash vendors**. Although you probably will not pay these vendors with actual cash, but more likely with checks, credit cards, or electronic payments, we use the term "cash" vendor because these expenses are reported on *Cash-based Profit and Loss Statements*.

Table 4-1 shows how to enter transactions for each of these two types of vendors. The table also shows what QuickBooks Online does behind the scenes to record these transactions.

BUSINESS TRANSACTION	CASH VENDORS		CREDIT VENDORS	
	QUICKBOOKS ONLINE TRANSACTION	ACCOUNTING ENTRY	QUICKBOOKS ONLINE TRANSACTION	ACCOUNTING ENTRY
RECORDING A PURCHASE ORDER	Not used		Purchase Orders	Non-posting entry used to track Orders
RECORDING A BILL FROM A VENDOR	Not used		Add bill	Increase (debit) **Expenses**, Increase (credit) **Accounts Payable**
PAYING BILLS	Not used		Pay bill	Decrease (debit) **Accounts Payable**, Decrease (credit) **Checking**
ENTERING EXPENSES	Check	Increase (debit) **Expenses**, Decrease (credit) **Checking**	Not usually used	
	Expense (Credit Card)	Increase (debit) **Expenses**, Increase (credit) **Credit Card**		

TABLE 4-1: *Options for entering expenses*

Recording Transactions

The first row in Table 4-1 references **Recording a Purchase Order**. Some vendors require *Purchase Orders* so they can properly process incoming orders. When a purchase order is recorded, no accounting transaction is entered into QuickBooks Online that affects the General Ledger. Instead, a "Non-Posting" entry is made to track the order until the products are received or the services are provided.

The second row references **Recording a Bill from a Vendor**. When you receive a bill from a vendor, you will record it using the *Bill* window, showing on your reports that you owe a supplier money.

Then, when it is time to pay your bills, you will use the **Pay Bill** window to select the bills you want to pay by check, credit card, or ACH. Similar to what we saw with our income transactions, you can initiate bill payments from the *+New button*, from the *Vendors Center*, or from within a bill itself.

The fourth row references **Entering Expenses**. Sometimes you will need to write a check to pay someone immediately, instead of paying a bill. In that case, you will use the *Check* window, accessible by clicking **Check** from the *+New button*, the **Check** option from the *New Transaction* buttons in the *Expense Center*, or by pressing **Ctrl-Alt-W** (**Cmd-Option-W** on a Mac).

If you are recording an expense paid by credit card or any other payment method, choose **Expense** from the *+New button*, the **Expense** option from the *New Transaction* buttons in the *Expense Center*, or by pressing **Ctrl-Alt-X** (**Cmd-Option-X** on a Mac).

MANAGING EXPENSES | 157

SETTING UP VENDORS

Adding New Vendors

Vendors include every person or supplier you pay, including product manufacturers, service providers, and 1099 contract workers. Before you record any transactions to a vendor in QuickBooks Online, you must set them up in the *Vendors Center*.

> **TIP:**
>
> When a vendor is also a customer, you will need to set up two separate records: a vendor record in the *Vendors Center* and a customer record in the *Customers Center*. The customer name must be slightly different from the vendor name, although the contact information for both can be identical.
>
> For example, you could enter **Boswell Consulting, Inc.** for the vendor name in the *Vendor Information* window, and **Boswell Consulting** for the customer name in the *Customer Information* window. Alternatively, some bookkeepers append -V and -C to the names.

HANDS-ON PRACTICE

To set up a **Vendor**, follow these steps:

- **STEP 1.** To display the *Vendors Center*, hold your cursor over **Expenses** in the *Left Navigation Bar*, and then choose **Vendors** (see Figure 4-6).

- **STEP 2.** Click the **New Vendor** button in the *Vendors Center* (see Figure 4-7).

- **STEP 3.** The *Vendor Information* window displays (see Figure 4-8).

- **STEP 4.** Enter **Bernard & Stretch Law** in the *Company Name* field.

- **STEP 5.** Enter **Ms. Janice Brechner** in the *Title*, *First Name*, and *Last Name* fields.

- **STEP 6.** Choose **Janice Brechner** in the *Vendor Display Name** field.

FIGURE 4-6: Opening the Vendors Center

FIGURE 4-7: Add a New Vendor to the Vendor list

> **TIP:**
>
> The **Vendor Display Name** must be unique. The *Vendor List* sorts alphabetically by **Vendor Display Name**, just like the *Customer List*. Therefore, if your vendor is an individual person, you can choose to alphabetize by first name, last name, or company name.

STEP 7. Continue entering the rest of the *Email, Phone, Mobile, Website,* and *Address* fields in the vendor record, as shown in Figure 4-8. Press **Tab** after each entry to move to the next one.

STEP 8. The *Notes* field can be used to store any information not otherwise included on this card, such as credit limit.

The *Attachments* box can hold contracts, photos, scans of business cards, or any other documentation associated with this supplier.

STEP 9. Enter *12-1234567* in the *Business ID No./Social Security No.* field.

The Taxes field is where you enter the social security or taxpayer identification number for your Contractors who receive Forms 1099-MISC and 1099-NEC.

1099s are issued to Sole Proprietors, LLCs, and LLPs who you pay over $600 a year for services via cash, check, ACH, or direct deposit. QuickBooks Online prints this number on the 1099 Forms at the end of the year.

STEP 10. Check the box next to **Track payments for 1099**. Select this box for all contractors who may become eligible to receive a 1099 Form.

STEP 11. Enter **250** in the *Billing Rate (/hr)* field.

STEP 12. Select **Net 30** from the *Terms* drop-down list.

This field sets the default for this vendor's new bills, although you can override the payment terms on each bill as necessary. When you create reports for Accounts Payable (A/P), QuickBooks Online considers the terms on each bill.

STEP 13. Enter **66-112** in the *Account No.* field.

In this field, enter the account number that your vendor uses to track you as a customer. If your vendor requires you to enter your account number on the checks you send, this is where you store it, although you will need to paste it into the Memo field if you want it to print on the check.

STEP 14. Select **Legal & Professional Fees:Lawyer** from the *Default Expense Category* field. This sets a default expense account for future transactions with this vendor. This account may be updated if needed when you create bills and expenses.

STEP 15. Leave the *Opening Balance* and *As Of* fields blank.

The *Opening Balance* field shows only when you create a new vendor record. You will not see this field when you edit an existing vendor. The date in the *As of* field defaults to the current date. Since you will not enter an amount in the *Opening Balance* field, there is no need to change this date..

STEP 16. Click **Save** to save and close the *Vendor* window.

MANAGING EXPENSES

> **IMPORTANT:**
>
> It is best *not* to use the *Opening Balance* field in the *Vendor Information* window. If you *do* enter an amount for a vendor in the *Opening Balance* field, QuickBooks Online creates a **Bill** that increases (credits) **Accounts Payable** and increases (debits) a **Miscellaneous Expense**. Instead, enter actual **unpaid bills** individually after you create the vendor record.

Inactivating Vendors

When you will no longer be doing business with a vendor, you can inactive them. QuickBooks Online maintains the history, but hides their record so it no longer appears on your list.

HANDS-ON PRACTICE

Craig's Landscaping has never done any business with Met Life Dental, so there is no reason to keep them on the Vendors list.

STEP 1. From the *Vendors Center*, click on **Met Life Dental**.

STEP 2. Click on the drop-down arrow on the **Edit** button on the upper right.

STEP 3. Choose **Make Inactive**, as shown in Figure 4-9.

STEP 4. When you see the confirmation window in Figure 4-10 that says *Are You Sure You Want To Make Met Life Dental Inactive?*, click **Yes, Make Inactive**.

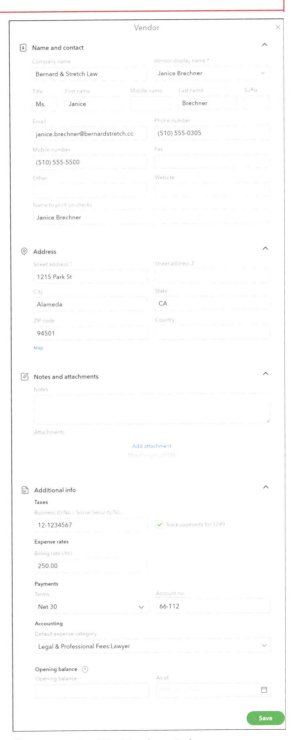

FIGURE 4-8: *The Vendor window*

FIGURE 4-9: *Make a vendor inactive*

STEP 5. The Vendor Record now includes **(deleted)** after the name. Return to the Vendors Center. Met Life Dental no longer shows on the list.

STEP 6. If you use the vendor again in the future, use the *Grid Gear* at the top right of the *Vendor List* to **Include Inactive**, as shown in Figure 4-11.

STEP 7. When you scroll down to the Vendors list. You can now see **Met Life Dental (deleted)** on the list, as shown in Figure 4-12. You could click the blue **Make Active** action on the right to reactivate the account.

FIGURE 4-10: *Confirm you want to inactivate the vendor*

FIGURE 4-11: *Show inactive vendors*

FIGURE 4-12: *A deleted/inactivated Vendor*

> **DID YOU KNOW?**
>
> You can also inactivate a vendor right from the *Vendors list* by dropping down the **arrow** in the *Action* column on the far right and choosing **Make Inactive**.

Merging Vendors

If you find you have two vendor records for the same company or individual, you can merge them. All the transactions from both accounts will be automatically combined into one. Note that this action cannot be undone.

Although we will not do this now, to merge two accounts, you would:

1. Decide which one you would like to keep.

2. Click the **Edit** button on the vendor you want to keep, and **copy** the *Vendor Display Name** field. Click the **X** in the upper right corner to cancel the window.

3. **Edit** the vendor you want to inactivate. **Paste** the copied name into the *Vendor Display Name** field. Click **Save**.

4. When you get the *That Name Is Already Being Used. Would You Like To Merge the Two?* warning as shown in Figure 4-13, click **Yes**.

5. The merged account will now show as *(deleted)*, and all the transactions will display under the vendor being saved.

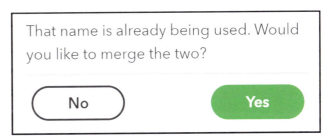

FIGURE 4-13: *Confirmation to merge two vendors*

TRACKING JOB COSTS

You can track the expenses related to each **Customer** or **Project** (i.e., track **Job Costs**) in QuickBooks Online Plus or Advanced. To turn on this feature, follow the setup instructions on page 152.

When you record an expense transaction, use the *Customer* field to associate each expense category or item with the customer, sub-customer, or project for whom it relates (see Figure 4-14).

The *Billable* checkmark indicates that you will later pass this expense on to the customer's next invoice for reimbursement, with or without markup. If you are not asking the customer to pay for time and materials, leave *Billable* unchecked.

FIGURE 4-14: *Linking expenses to Customers, Sub-customers, and Projects (i.e., job costing)*

When you track job costs, you can create reports such as the *Profit & Loss by Customer* report that displays income and expenses separately for each project (see Figure 4-15). This shows your profitability for each of your customers.

Craig's Design and Landscaping Services

Profit and Loss by Customer

	RED ROCK DINER	TRAVIS WALDRON	TOTAL
▼ Income			
▼ Landscaping Services		75.00	$75.00
▼ Job Materials			$0.00
Fountains and Garden Lighting	48.00	84.00	$132.00
Plants and Soil		300.00	$300.00
Sprinklers and Drip Systems	108.00		$108.00
Total Job Materials	156.00	384.00	$540.00
Total Landscaping Services	156.00	459.00	$615.00
Pest Control Services	70.00		$70.00
Services		103.55	$103.55
Total Income	$226.00	$562.55	$788.55
GROSS PROFIT	$226.00	$562.55	$788.55
▼ Expenses			
▼ Job Expenses			$0.00
▼ Job Materials			$0.00
Decks and Patios	88.09	103.55	$191.64
Total Job Materials	88.09	103.55	$191.64
Total Job Expenses	88.09	103.55	$191.64
Total Expenses	$88.09	$103.55	$191.64
NET OPERATING INCOME	$137.91	$459.00	$596.91
NET INCOME	$137.91	$459.00	$596.91

FIGURE 4-15: *Profit & Loss by Customer report*

ENTERING BILLS

You can use QuickBooks Online to track **Accounts Payable (A/P)**. Accounts Payable balances show on an *Accrual-based Balance Sheet,* allowing you to include how much a company owes for upcoming bills in your cashflow reporting.

When you receive a bill from a vendor that you are not paying immediately, enter it into QuickBooks Online using the **Bill** window. Recording a bill allows QuickBooks Online to track the amount you owe to the vendor along with the detail of what you purchased.

For a bill to be considered paid by QuickBooks Online, you must pay it using the **Pay Bills** window (see page 168) or **Schedule a Payment** to pay it right through QBO's bill payment system (see page 172).

MANAGING EXPENSES | 163

> ### DID YOU KNOW?
>
> Be sure to use the correct terminology. When you enter vendor transactions in QBO, you use a **Bill**, which represents money you owe. The actual vendor bills you receive, however, will be labeled **Invoice** at the top, because you are their customer.

Vendor Invoices

When an invoice arrives from your vendor, enter it into QuickBooks Online using the *Bill* window.

HANDS-ON PRACTICE

STEP 1. Click on the **Vendors** button from the *Expenses* tab on the *Left Navigation Bar* to display the *Vendors Center*.

FIGURE 4-16: *Selecting Bill from the New Transaction drop-down list*

STEP 2. Choose the vendor **Lee Advertising**, and then select **Bill** from the *New Transaction* drop-down list (see Figure 4-16). Alternatively, you can click **Bill** from the *+New* button and choose **Lee Advertising** from the *Vendor* drop-down field (see Figure 4-17).

STEP 3. If the defaults have been set up for the vendor as we saw on page 159, QuickBooks Online uses that information to complete the *Terms*, *Due Date*, and *Category* fields automatically when you enter the payee name. You can override this information if necessary.

If the *Terms* didn't autofill, enter **Net 15**.

STEP 4. Enter **today's date** in the *Bill Date* field. QuickBooks Online calculates the *Due Date* field by adding the *Terms* information to the date in the *Bill Date* field.

STEP 5. If **Custom Transactions Numbers** is turned on in *Account and Settings*, you'll see a *Bill No.* box. If it's turned on in your Craig's Landscaping sample company, enter **4210** in this field.

> ### TIP:
>
> When an A/P transaction increases what is owed, it is called a "**Bill**." However, vendors send "**Invoices**." Therefore, the *Bill No.* field on the *Bill* form should match the number on the invoice you received from the vendor. The *Bill No.* field is important for two reasons. First, it is the number used to identify this bill in the *Pay Bills* window, and second, it is the number that shows on the voucher of the bill payment check.

STEP 6. In the *Category* field in the *Category Details* section, enter **Advertising.**

STEP 7. In the *Description*, type **Monthly marketing budget**, and press **Tab**.

STEP 8. Enter **360** in the *Amount* field and press **Tab**.

STEP 9. Verify that your screen matches the bill shown in Figure 4-17. Use the drop-down arrow to change the green button to **Save and Close** to record the bill.

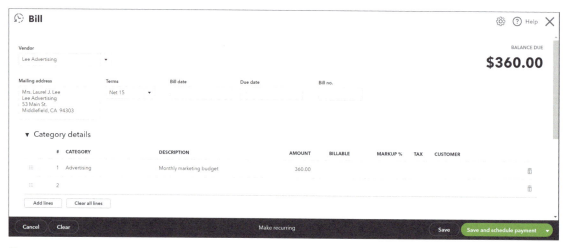

FIGURE 4-17: *Recording the Lee Advertising bill*

THE ACCOUNTING BEHIND THE SCENES:

When you create a Bill, it increases (credits) **Accounts Payable** and increases (debits) the **Expense** category.

TRANSACTION TYPE	NAME	MEMO/DESCRIPTION	ACCOUNT	DEBIT	CREDIT
Bill	Lee Advertising		Accounts Payable (A/P)		$360.00
		Monthly marketing budget	Advertising	$360.00	
				$360.00	$360.00
				$360.00	$360.00

Bills with Products and Job Costing

On page 156 we discussed creating a purchase order (PO) when you place an order for merchandise. When the products arrive, you can turn the PO into a bill, which brings the products into inventory and enters the liability into the general ledger.

HANDS-ON PRACTICE

A bill arrives from Tim Philip Masonry for a Rock Fountain you have on order. Turn the **Purchase Order** into a bill right from the *Bill* window.

STEP 1. Click on the **Vendors** button from the *Expenses* tab on the *Left Navigation Bar* to display the *Vendors Center*.

STEP 2. Open the vendor **Tim Philip Masonry**, and then select **Bill** from the green *New Transaction* button. Alternatively, you can choose **Bill** from the *+New* button and choose **Tim Philip Masonry** from the *Vendor* drop-down field.

> **TIP:**
>
> You can also open an existing purchase order and click the **Copy to Bill** button in the upper right. This will convert the PO into a bill, fill in the products, and close the PO.

STEP 3. Note that in the drawer on the right-hand side, Craig's Landscaping already has an open **Purchase Order** with Tim Philip Masonry (see Figure 4-18). Click the blue **Add** link to convert the existing PO to a new Bill. This indicates that you have received the Rock Fountain on order, closing the PO.

After adding the PO, you'll see the Rock Fountain in the *Item Details* in the bottom grid as shown in Figure 4-20. Note the tiny blue **1 linked Purchase Order** link in the upper left corner. Click on this any time to see the original PO from when you placed the order.

> **NOTE:**
>
> The **Product/Service** drop-down in the bottom *Item Details* grid pulls from the **Products and Services List** so that you can purchase inventory, or services from contractors. Items appear on this list when you create them as two-sided products or services, as you saw on page 59 and page 62. This way you can both buy and sell an item, and track its profit margin.

FIGURE 4-18: Add the Purchase Order to the Bill

STEP 4. Change the *Terms* field to **Net 30**.

STEP 5. Enter **today's date** in the *Bill Date* field. The *Due Date* will update automatically.

STEP 6. Enter **2085** in the *Bill No.* field. Many bookkeepers enter the vendor's *Invoice number* into this field for easy reference.

Step 7. Compare your *Bill* to Figure 4-20. When the bill arrived with the fountain delivery, it also included freight charges. Because the Craig's Landscaping sample company doesn't already have a Shipping category in its Chart of Accounts, create it now on the fly. In the top *Category Details* grid, click on the *Category* field's drop-down arrow, and select **+Add New** at the top of the list. Copy the data in Figure 4-19, then click **Save and Close**.

Shipping, Freight, and Delivery—COS is a frequently-used **Cost of Goods Sold** category for the shipping you pay when ordering products. It is separate from any **Postage** expense used in the back office.

> **IMPORTANT:**
>
> If your vendor requires you to enter your account number on the checks you send, store it in the *Account No.* field in the vendor record as shown on page 159, and enter it in the *Memo* field on the check. QuickBooks Online prints the contents of the *Memo* field on *Bill Payments* to the vendor.

Step 8. Enter **Rock Fountain shipping** in the *Description* box. Press **Tab**.

Step 9. In the *Amount* field, enter **35**, the cost of shipping for the Rock Fountain. When you press **Tab** or click anywhere in the form, the bill's *Balance Due* will update to **$160.00**, the cost of the fountain including shipping.

Step 10. To job cost the fountain and shipping, check the two **Billable** boxes in both the *Category Details* grid and the *Item Details* grid, and enter **Amy's Bird Sanctuary** in the *Customer* column on each.

FIGURE 4-19: *Add a Cost of Goods Sold category for Shipping*

Both the fountain and the shipping will later be passed on to Amy's Bird Sanctuary to be included (with markup) on her next invoice for reimbursement.

> **IMPORTANT!**
>
> If you ever get a popup that says *The transaction you are editing is linked to others. Are you sure you want to modify it?*, always take a moment to think. Make sure you're not taking an action that changes a past transaction.
>
> Most of the time this message just alerts you that the modification you are making involves a related transaction, and it's fine to say **Yes** and continue. But if you're not 100% sure, click **No** and double-check your work.
>
>

Step 11. Verify that your screen matches that shown in Figure 4-20. Use the drop-down arrow next to the green *Save and Schedule Payment* button, changing it to **Save and Close** to record the bill.

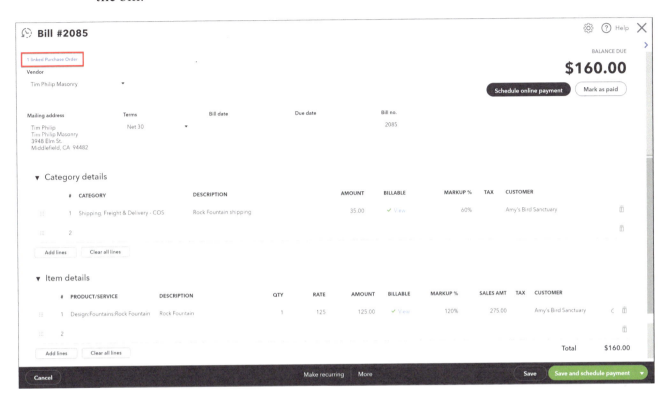

Figure 4-20: *Recording a Bill for a product with shipping*

Attaching Documents

There are many advantages to storing documents electronically. Going paperless increases efficiency and eliminates costly storage.

QuickBooks Online allows you to attach digital documents to bills, invoices, and other QuickBooks Online forms. To attach documentation directly to a QuickBooks Online transaction, look for the ***Attachments*** box at the bottom left of every transaction.

For example, you could attach a copy of the invoice that Tim Philips Masonry sent you for the Rock Fountain, so that it is always handy.

The Unpaid Bills Detail Report

To view a list of your unpaid bills, use the ***Unpaid Bills*** report.

Figure 4-21: *Attachments in the Bills window*

HANDS-ON PRACTICE

STEP 1. From the *Reports* menu in the *Left Navigation Bar*, scroll down to *What You Owe* and then choose **Unpaid Bills** (see Figure 4-22).

STEP 2. The report defaults to **All Dates** in the *Report Period* box at the top left.

STEP 3. Note the new bill at the bottom for **Tim Philip Masonry**. The *Past Due* column shows **-30**, indicating that it will be another 30 days until the bill is considered late.

Craig's Design and Landscaping Services
Unpaid Bills
All Dates

DATE	TRANSACTION TYPE	NUM	DUE DATE	PAST DUE	AMOUNT	OPEN BALANCE
▼ Brosnahan Insurance Agency (650) 555-9912						
	Bill			23	241.23	241.23
Total for Brosnahan Insurance Agency					$241.23	$241.23
▼ Diego's Road Warrior Bodyshop						
	Bill			-2	755.00	755.00
Total for Diego's Road Warrior Bodyshop					$755.00	$755.00
▼ Lee Advertising (650) 554-4622						
	Bill			-15	360.00	360.00
Total for Lee Advertising					$360.00	$360.00
▼ Norton Lumber and Building Materials (650) 363-6578						
	Bill			26	205.00	205.00
Total for Norton Lumber and Building Materials					$205.00	$205.00
▼ PG&E (888) 555-9465						
	Bill			41	86.44	86.44
Total for PG&E					$86.44	$86.44
▼ Robertson & Associates (650) 557-1111						
	Bill			26	315.00	315.00
Total for Robertson & Associates					$315.00	$315.00
▼ Tim Philip Masonry (800) 556-1254						
	Bill	2085		-30	160.00	160.00
Total for Tim Philip Masonry					$160.00	$160.00
TOTAL					$2,122.67	$2,122.67

FIGURE 4-22: *Unpaid Bills report*

PAYING BILLS

QuickBooks Online keeps track of all your bills in the Accounts Payable account. When you pay your bills, you will reduce the balance in Accounts Payable by creating electronic bill payments, checks, or credit card charges.

Mark as Paid

This is the workflow used when you are paying bills by check, credit card, or using any method outside of QuickBooks Online. While the *Hands-on Practice* below demonstrates how to perform this function using menus, note that you can also click **Mark as Paid** in several other locations including *Action* links and the drop-down arrow on the green *Save* button.

MANAGING EXPENSES | 169

HANDS-ON PRACTICE

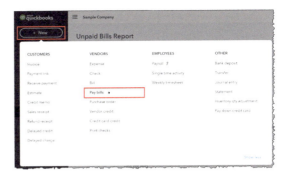

STEP 1. Select **Pay Bills** from the *+New* button (see Figure 4-23).

STEP 2. QuickBooks Online displays the *Pay Bills* window, as shown in Figure 4-24.

FIGURE 4-23: Select Pay Bills from the +New button

If you want to view one of the bills, simply click on it to open it. You can sort the list by clicking on any of the *column headers*. You can also click the **Filter** button to only view bills for a specific **Payee** (vendor), or those due on or before a given date (see Figure 4-25).

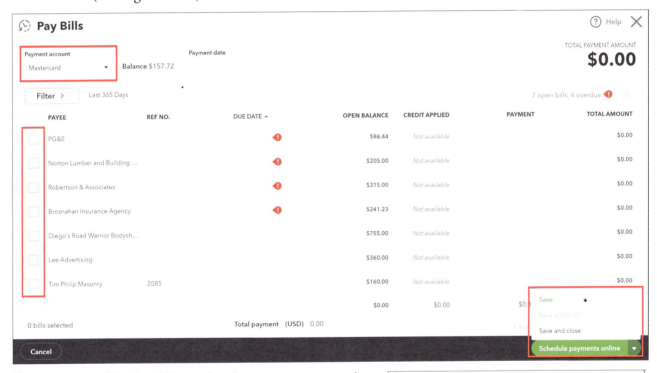

FIGURE 4-24: The Pay Bills window (your screen may vary)

Pay your bills in groups by ***payment method***. For example, if you are going to pay some bills by Visa and others through the built-in **Melio Bill Pay**, you'll process the credit card payments first, then do a second round to schedule the remaining payments online.

STEP 3. To pay **Diego's Road Warrior Body Shop** by Visa, change the *Payment Account* to **Visa**.

STEP 4. Confirm **today's date** in the *Payment Date* box.

FIGURE 4-25: Use the Filter to specify Due Dates and Payees

Step 5. Place a **checkmark** in the box to the left of **Diego's Road Warrior**. The *Payment* box will fill in with the open balance, **$755**.

Step 6. Drop down the arrow next to the green button and change it to **Save**. A **Bill Payment** transaction is added, and the open bill disappears from the list.

Step 7. Next you'll pay the PG&E electric bill by writing a check and mailing it to the utility company. Change the *Payment Account* to **Checking**.

Step 8. Click in the *Payment Date* field, and type + on your keyboard to advance the date to **tomorrow**.

Step 9. If you were handwriting the check, you would enter the **check number** in the box. Because we will be printing checks, check the **Print Later** box so that you can print all checks at once after you are finished creating all the payments.

Step 10. Place a checkmark in front of the **PG&E bill** for **$86.44**.

Note the *Current Account Balance, Total Payment, and New Account Balance* information at the bottom of the transaction. This will help prevent you from bouncing checks!

Step 11. Compare your screen to Figure 4-26. When it matches, click the green **Save** button. The PG&E bill is marked paid, a bill payment transaction has been created, the bill disappears from the list, and a check is now waiting in the **Print Checks** queue.

> **IMPORTANT!**
>
> If you select more than one bill for the same vendor, QuickBooks Online combines all of the individual bills into a single bill payment when marking them paid by check or credit card.

Figure 4-26: *Paying a Bill with a paper check*

> **TIP:**
>
> To make a partial payment on a bill, enter only the amount you want to pay in the *Payment* column. If you pay less than the full amount due, QuickBooks Online will continue to track the remaining amount due for that bill in Accounts Payable. The next time you go to the *Pay Bills* window, the partially-paid bills will display the balance due.

Figure 4-27 and Figure 4-28 show what these payments look like in the *Checking register* and the *Accounts Payable register*.

FIGURE 4-27: Checking account register after Pay Bills (your screen may vary)

FIGURE 4-28: Accounts Payable register after Pay Bills (your screen may vary)

THE ACCOUNTING BEHIND THE SCENES:

When you use a check or credit card to pay bills, the **Bill Payment** reduces (credits) the balance in the **Checking** account or increases (credits) the **Credit Card liability**, and reduces (debits) **Accounts Payable**.

TRANSACTION TYPE	NAME	MEMO/DESCRIPTION	ACCOUNT	DEBIT	CREDIT
Bill Payment (Check)	PG&E	00649587213	Checking		$86.44
			Accounts Payable (A/P)	$86.44	
				$86.44	$86.44

Schedule Payments Online

The rest of the bills could be paid electronically from right inside QuickBooks Online, without having to print checks, call the vendor to pay by credit card, or log into your bank to make the payment. This built-in app integration from *Melio Bill Pay* allows you to create a payment in QBO and push it out to Melio to pay each bill by direct deposit, or send a paper check on your behalf.

Figure 4-29: *An alert for Melio Bill Pay*

Keep an eye out for Melio Bill Pay alerts that look similar to the one shown in Figure 4-29!

There is no charge for unlimited ACH payments sent using your checking account, but if you use your credit card as the funding source, there is a 2.9% convenience fee. If you chose to send paper checks, the first two are mailed for free, and then there is a $1.50 charge per check after that. This is still cheaper than writing and mailing the check yourself once you include the costs for check stock, ink, stamps, and your time.

You will need the mailing address and/or banking information for each of your vendors, although you can also send an invitation to create their own account and set themselves up as a recipient.

- **Step 12.** Click the **Select All Bills** button at the top of the left column to select the remaining bills that are displayed.

- **Step 13.** Because we are in a sample company, we cannot demonstrate the **Schedule Payments Online** workflow. You need to be in an active QuickBooks Online file to continue paying bills electronically using the built-in *Melio Bill Pay* app.

Figure 4-30: *Sign up for Melio Bill Pay*

In an actual QBO company, you would be able to click the arrow to the right of the green button and choose **Schedule Payments Online** (do not click this now). The first time you schedule online payments, you'll see the popup shown in Figure 4-30.

USING CREDIT CARDS

To track charges and payments on your company credit cards, set up each card in your *Chart of Accounts*, using the *Detail Type* (or *Tax Form Section*) **Credit Card**. Credit card balances will appear on your Balance Sheet as Liabilities.

Enter each charge as it occurs, using an *Expense* form. Alternatively, almost all credit cards allow you to import your credit card charges into QuickBooks Online through the **Banking Feed**, eliminating the need to enter each charge manually. For more information, see page 260, Using the Banking Feed for Data Entry.

To pay the credit card balance, use QuickBooks Online's *Pay Down Credit Cards* feature.

Entering Credit Card Charges

Each time you use a business credit card, use the *Expenses* window to record the transaction.

HANDS-ON PRACTICE

Step 1. Click the **Expense** option on the *+New* menu. Alternatively, when you're looking at a Vendor record, you can click the *New Transaction* button and choose **Expense**.

Step 2. Choose **Computers by Jenni** in the *Payee* field.

> ### DID YOU KNOW?
>
> In QuickBooks Online, you will see both vendor and customer name fields labeled as **Payee**, since there are times when you do send money to a customer or receive money from a vendor.

Step 3. Change the *Payment Account* to **Visa**.

Step 4. Use **today's date** as the *Payment Date*.

Step 5. Enter **Visa** in the *Payment Method* field.

The *Payment Method* field is optional. In this case, the only kind of payment we would make with the Visa card is a Visa payment. But because this *Expense* window is multi-purpose, there are times when you'll use it for a charge to your checking account that could be a debit card, direct deposit, a check, or some other method of payment.

Step 6. The *Ref No.* field is optional. Its purpose is to tag each charge with the number on the charge slip. Because there is no ID number associated with a credit card charge, we will leave it blank.

Step 7. Enter **Supplies** in the *Category* field. Press **Tab**.

> ### TIP:
>
> Remember that if you are purchasing products or services, you should use the *Item Details* grid below instead. Note that it might be collapsed—click the ▶ to expand it.

Step 8. In the *Description* box, type **Printer ink**, then press **Tab**.

Step 9. Enter **86.48** in the *Amount* field.

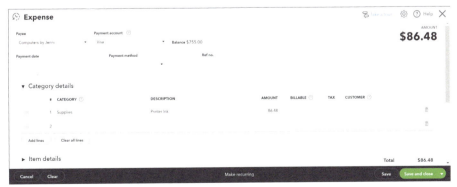

Figure 4-31: *Enter a Credit Card Expense for an Office Supplies purchase*

STEP 10.   Verify that your screen matches Figure 4-31. Change the button to **Save and New** to record the credit card charge and start another one.

STEP 11.   Create a second credit card expense on today's date to **Tania's Nursery** on the **Mastercard** that matches Figure 4-32. This time you are purchasing two bags of **Soil**, a product, and marking it as **Billable** to **Amy's Bird Sanctuary**, passing the cost on to her next invoice for reimbursement. Choose **Save and Close**.

> **TIP:**
>
> If your Tania's Nursery expense auto-filled with the previous purchase, use the **Trashcan** on the right of the line item, and click the triangle to the left of *Item Details* to open the bottom grid. If QBO's automation creates more work than it saves you time, you can turn it off using the *Advanced Automations settings* explained on page 44.

FIGURE 4-32: *Enter a Mastercard expense for products billable to a customer*

THE ACCOUNTING BEHIND THE SCENES:

When you record **credit card charges**, QuickBooks Online increases (credits) your **Credit Card Liability** account and increases (debits) the **Expense** account.

Paying the Credit Card Balance

Follow the steps below to record a ***payment made to your credit card bill***. Note that these steps record a payment you initiated through your bank's website or a payment by check, but it does not push an actual payment to the credit card company.

HANDS-ON PRACTICE

STEP 1. Choose **Pay Down Credit Card** on the *+New* button (see Figure 4-33).

STEP 2. Pick **Visa** from the *Which Credit Card Did You Pay?* field.

STEP 3. Because your credit card is with **Chance Bank**, which is not already in your QuickBooks Online vendor list, click **+Add New** in the *Payee (optional)* box and add **Chance Bank** on the fly (see Figure 4-34). Click **Save**.

STEP 4. Enter **150** in the *How Much Did You Pay?* field. Note that you can pay any amount, whether you are paying off your credit card's statement balance, current balance, or making a partial payment.

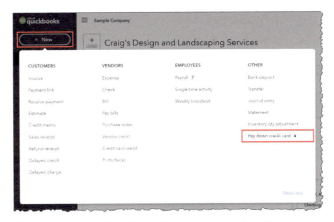

FIGURE 4-33: *Pay Down Credit Card on the +New menu*

FIGURE 4-34: *Add Chance Bank as a new Payee*

STEP 5. In the *What Did You Use To Make This Payment?* field, select the **Checking** account.

STEP 6. Most people today pay their credit card balance by making a transfer from the bank's website. If you were mailing a paper check, you could click *I Made a Payment With a Check*, which allows you to enter a check number or queue the check for printing later. We will leave this box **unchecked**.

STEP 7. Verify that your screen matches Figure 4-35, then click **Save and Close** to record the transaction.

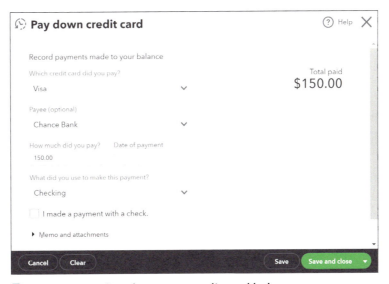

FIGURE 4-35: *Pay down your credit card balance*

> **NOTE:**
>
> **Classes** and **Locations** are not used when posting credit card payments.

To see the detail of your credit card charges and payments, look in the **Visa** account register as shown in Figure 4-36. This register can be accessed by pressing **Ctrl-Alt-A** to open the *Chart of Accounts* (or go to **Accounting** in the *Left Navigation Bar*), and then clicking on the **View Register** link on the right of the Visa credit card account.

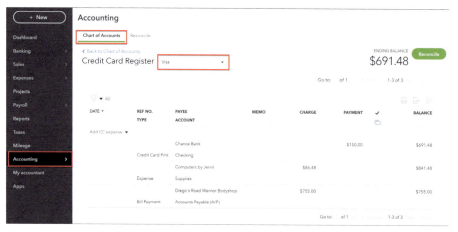

FIGURE 4-36: *The Visa account register—your screen may vary*

> **THE ACCOUNTING BEHIND THE SCENES:**
>
> When you record a **credit card payment**, QuickBooks Online reduces (credits) the **Checking** account and reduces (debits) the **Credit Card liability** account.
>
> | TRANSACTION TYPE | NUM | NAME | MEMO/DESCRIPTION | ACCOUNT | DEBIT | CREDIT |
> |---|---|---|---|---|---|---|
> | Credit Card Payment | | Chance Bank | | Checking | | $150.00 |
> | | | | | Visa | $150.00 | |
> | | | | | | $150.00 | $150.00 |

WRITING CHECKS

The world is moving towards the immediacy of electronic payments, and away from the workflow of mailing bills, handwriting or printing checks, and then sending them back through the mail. However, there are still times when you will want to write a check.

HANDS-ON PRACTICE

Craig's Landscaping still pays their rent by check because the landlord has not yet adopted an electronic payment system.

STEP 1. To display the *Checks* window, click on **Check** in the *+New* button, as shown in Figure 4-37. Alternatively, press **Ctrl-Alt-W** or **Cmd-Option-W** on a Mac. A new check will open (see Figure 4-38).

MANAGING EXPENSES | 177

STEP 2. Select **Hall Properties** from the *Payee* drop-down list. Notice that QuickBooks Online enters the name and address from the vendor record as soon as you choose the payee name from the list.

STEP 3. Make sure **Checking** is already selected in the *Bank Account* field.

STEP 4. Check the **Print Later** checkbox. The *Check No.* box will fill with **To Print**.

This indicates that you want QuickBooks Online to run this check through your printer. When you print the check, QuickBooks Online will assign the next check number in the sequence of your checks. To record a handwritten check, enter the **check number** instead of clicking **Print Later**.

STEP 5. Confirm **today's date** in the *Payment Date* field.

FIGURE 4-37: *Create a new Check*

STEP 6. Enter **Rent or Lease** in the *Category* column.

Note that if you had set the default expense category when setting up the Hall Properties Vendor details as we saw on page 158, and set the **Automations** under the *Advanced Account and Settings* as discussed on page 44, the *Category* might auto-fill, repeating the same account used in the most recent expense to that vendor.

DID YOU KNOW?

When you enter your own expenses, use multiple rows to split a transaction between several different accounts, customers, and classes.

STEP 7. In the *Description* field, enter **Monthly Rent**.

STEP 8. Enter **3200** in the *Amount* field and press **Tab**.

STEP 9. In the *Memo* field, enter **123 Sierra Way**. By entering the property's address in the *Memo*, it will print on the check so that the vendor knows which unit the payment is for.

TIP:

The **Memo** field is a perfect place to communicate with a vendor on checks. For example, when paying a bill, you can use the *Memo* box to indicate the invoice number(s) you are paying, and the information will print on the check's memo line. It's also a good location for recording details you need to remember about a transaction, because the Memo field can be searched and included on reports.

STEP 10. Verify that your screen matches Figure 4-38. Do not print the check now; we will print it later.

STEP 11.   Click **Save and Close** to record the transaction.

FIGURE 4-38: *Write a Check to Hall Properties for rent*

> **NOTE:**
>
> In the example above, you recorded the check with a **To Print** status, so that you can print it later in a batch with other checks. If you want to print the check immediately after entering it, click **Print Check** in the black bar at the bottom of the *Check* window.

Applying a Check to an Unpaid Bill

If you start writing a check for a vendor who has an unpaid bill, QuickBooks Online will show the bill in the drawer on the right side of the screen so that you can make sure you aren't duplicating the expense (see Figure 4-39).

Click the blue **Add** link to convert this check to a bill payment, or close the drawer by clicking the **blue** > to continue writing your check.

FIGURE 4-39: *Applying a Check to an open Bill*

Printing Checks

You can print each check or bill payment separately as you create it. You also have the option to record each check with a **Print Later** status, and print them all as one batch.

Setting Up the Printer

The first time you print checks in QuickBooks Online, you'll need to set up the printer alignment. After that one-time step, you'll be able to go straight to printing. QuickBooks-compatible check stock is available from many sources including Intuit, Costco, office supply stores, and online sites like checks-forless.com.

Most businesses prefer to use full-page Voucher style checks that have 3 parts—the check, a remittance stub to mail to the vendor, and a tear stub to keep for your files. Standard 3-up style checks are also available.

HANDS-ON PRACTICE

Follow these steps to print checks and bill payments that you have previously recorded as **Print Later**:

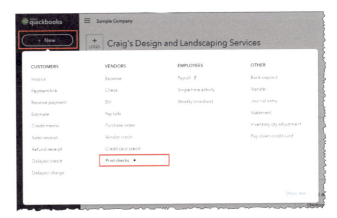

STEP 1.   From the *+New* menu, select **Print Checks** (see Figure 4-40).

STEP 2.   Because we have never printed checks before in QuickBooks Online, we have to set up the printer so that the check stock aligns properly. The window shown in Figure 4-41 appears.

FIGURE 4-40: *Click Print Checks on the +New button*

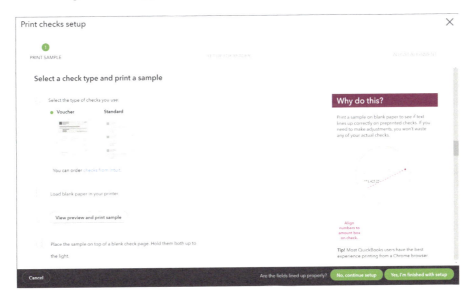

FIGURE 4-41: *Set up check printing*

STEP 3.   Choose whether you have **Voucher** checks (full page with stubs) or **Standard 3-up** checks. Craig's Landscaping uses voucher checks, so leave the default.

STEP 4.   Load blank paper in your printer, then click **View Preview and Print Sample**. Print a blank check on paper. Hold it up to the light, stacked together with a blank sheet of pre-printed check stock. Compare the alignment of the printout with the lines and boxes on the check stock.

If the two pages did not line up, you would click **No, Continue Setup**, and proceed to the *Fine-tune Alignment* page as shown in Figure 4-42. While we will not do this now, you would drag the **grid** up or down to tell QuickBooks Online where it appears on your printout, so that QBO can make the necessary adjustments. Follow the suggestions in the *Important* box on the right for best results.

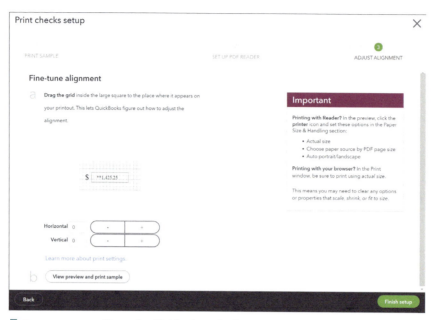

FIGURE 4-42: *Drag the Grid where it shows on your printout*

STEP 5. Click **View Preview and Print Sample** again. Repeat these steps until your printout on blank paper looks good when superimposed over your stock.

STEP 6. Once you are satisfied with the alignment, click the green **Finish Setup** button.

STEP 7. If the *Print Checks* window has closed, open it again from the +*New* menu.

Printing Checks

STEP 8. In the *Print Checks* window, confirm that **Checking** is selected in the *Bank Account* field (see Figure 4-43). This box is the bank account from which the checks are written.

STEP 9. Enter **77** in the *Starting Check No.* field.

This field is where you set the number of the first check you put in the printer.

> **NOTE:**
>
> QuickBooks Online assigns check numbers every time it prints checks starting with the next unused number. Verify the first check number just before you print the checks, and confirm the numbers after printing.

STEP 10. If you use standard 3-up checks, you'll be given an option to specify whether there are 1, 2, or 3 checks on the first sheet of your check stock. This way you never waste unprinted checks.

STEP 11. Select all the checks for printing by placing check marks to their left.

To prevent one or more checks from printing, you can click in the left column to remove the checkmark for each check you don't want to print. Since we did not print the rent check, it shows in Figure 4-43 along with any other checks from this lessons (your screen may vary).

FIGURE 4-43: Select checks to print in the Print Checks window, and set the starting number (your list may vary)

STEP 12. Load your printer's paper tray with QuickBooks-compatible checks. For this exercise, use plain paper so that you don't waste your check stock.

STEP 13. Click the green **Preview and Print** button.

STEP 14. When the *Print Preview* window displays, you can click **Print** to continue using your browser's print dialog box, or click the **Printer icon** in the upper right corner to open your computer's print box (see Figure 4-44).

Adobe PDF Reader is QBO's preferred print driver, but the dialog box also includes a link to print using your computer's dialog box, which has more settings.

Notice that you can also download the PDF to your computer using the down arrow to the left of the print icon.

FIGURE 4-44: The Print Preview window

STEP 15. When QuickBooks Online has finished printing the checks, you will return to the *Print Preview* window. Click **Close** when you're done.

STEP 16. A *Did Your Checks Print OK?* confirmation dialog box appears, as shown in Figure 4-45. If you have a paper jam or other printing issue, use this box to reprint as needed.

STEP 17. Click **Done**.

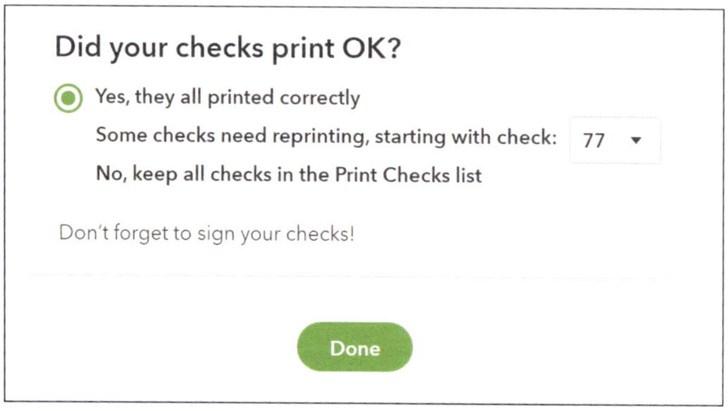

FIGURE 4-45: *Print Checks confirmation dialog box*

> **TIP:**
>
> If you are paying multiple bills with a single check and you want the vendor to be able to identify their invoice numbers, enter the invoice numbers in the **Memo** field of the *Bill Payment*.

Printing Problems

Not all print runs go smoothly. Here are common issues and solutions:

1. Make sure your checks are oriented correctly in the printer, as every printer feeds differently. Do you need to:
   a. Feed the top of the page in first, or the bottom?
   b. Insert the check stock face up or face down?
   c. Leave the checks in numerical order, or rearrange the pages so the last number is first?

2. Verify your check numbers. If the checks printed in a different sequence than intended, you can renumber them in the checking register.

3. If your printer damages your checks and you select checks for reprinting, it is a best practice to **Void** each damaged check and create a replacement (see page 201). This maintains a check number history for all checks so that you don't have any missing numbers.

TRACKING PETTY CASH

It is sometimes necessary to use cash for minor expenditures, such as supplies, postage, parking, or other small items. In order to track these expenditures, set up a separate bank account in QuickBooks Online called **Petty Cash**. Some QBO subscriptions come with a default bank account called **Cash on Hand** that you can use for this purpose.

The method to record the deposit of money into your petty cash account depends on how the money got there. If it was a withdrawal of cash from your checking account, like an ATM withdrawal, use a *Transfer* from Checking to Petty Cash (transfers are covered on page 255).

If the cash was withheld from a *Bank Deposit*, fill in the *Cash Back Goes To* field with **Petty Cash** and the dollar amount, as we saw on page 132.

When you use cash for a company expense, use an *Expense* form with **Petty Cash** as the *Payment Account*, and code it to the appropriate *Payee, Category, Class* and *Customer*. This reduces the balance in the petty cash account so that it always agrees with the actual amount of cash you have on hand.

Reconcile Petty Cash monthly as you would any other bank account.

> **TIP:**
>
> Don't forget to save your receipts! Keeping them in an envelope with your cash will help you track the money removed. Use QBO's Mobile app to snap a picture of the receipt, and attach it to the Expense transaction.

THE CONTRACTORS CENTER

The **Contractors Center** is an alternative workflow in QuickBooks Online specifically for managing your 1099 subcontractors.

QuickBooks Online's Contractor tools are found in QBO Essentials and above by clicking on **Payroll** in the *Left Navigation Bar* and then on **Contractors** (see Figure 4-46).

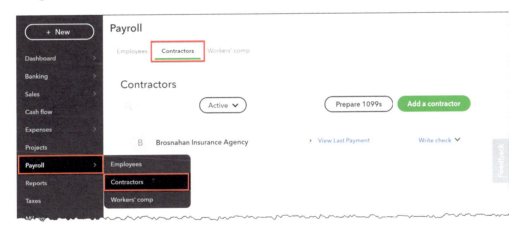

FIGURE 4-46: *QBO's Contractors Center*

Vendors appear on this list when you check the *Track Payments for 1099* box in the *Vendor Information* details window.

You can use the Contractors Center to invite new service vendors to fill out their W-9 forms electronically. At the end of the year, you can use the *Prepare 1099s* wizard to process 1099-NEC and 1099-Misc forms for your eligible contractors.

Paying Contractors

Instead of managing your Vendor transactions in the Vendor Center, use the tools here.

Click the blue **Write Check** link to pay contractors for their services, or click the drop-down arrow to create a credit card **Expense** or a **Bill**.

If you subscribe to QuickBooks's built-in Payroll, you can also pay your Contractors right in this interface using **Direct Deposit** for your same per-employee price.

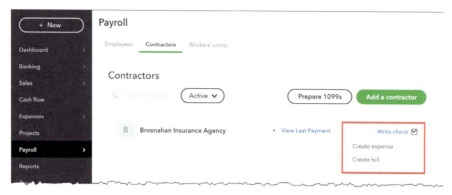

FIGURE 4-47: *Pay a 1099 Vendor through the Contractors Center*

Managing Contractors

Click on the Contractor's name to view their history.

The *Details* tab, shown in Figure 4-48, displays their contact information, and you can connect their bank account to pay them directly through this interface.

FIGURE 4-48: *View your Contractor's details*

The *Payments* tab allows you to filter your payments by Date, Type, and Payment method.

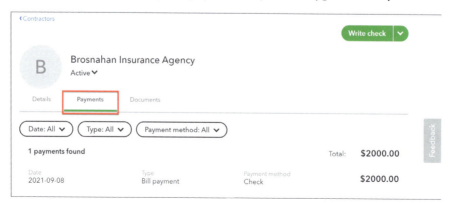

FIGURE 4-49: *View your Contractor's payments*

If you invite the contractor to fill in their W-9 form electronically, it will appear in the *Documents* tab.

MANAGING EXPENSES | 185

RUNNING ACCOUNTS PAYABLE REPORTS

QuickBooks Online has several reports that you can use to analyze and track your purchases and vendors. Following are two sample reports for you to create. See the *Reports* chapter for more information on creating and customizing reports.

> **TIP:**
> Close your browser window, and log into Craig's Landscaping again for a fresh start. This will make sure your reports match those below.

The A/P Aging Summary Report

It is essential to keep track of whether you are paying your vendors promptly, and if any of your bills are delinquent. The **Accounts Payable (A/P) Aging Summary** report lists each vendor balance, and how long your bills have been overdue.

HANDS-ON PRACTICE

STEP 1. From the **Reports** option in the *Left Navigation Bar*, scroll down to *What You Owe* and then choose **Accounts Payable Aging Summary** (see Figure 4-50).

The *Current* column contains all the current month's bills. The remaining columns refer to the number of days after the terms assigned to each bill. A **Net 30** bill will move to the *1–30* column on the 31st day. Bills with the Term **Due on Receipt** will immediately move into the next column if left unpaid.

The *Days Per Aging Period* and *Number of Periods* can be adjusted for longer time frames or shorter breakdowns.

Negative numbers represent **Vendor Credits**.

FIGURE 4-50: *The A/P Aging Summary—your screen may vary*

Click on any of the numbers to drill into the detailed list of transactions that make up each number. To return to the report summary, click the blue **Back to Report Summary** link at the top left.

> **TIP:**
>
> If you see **zeros** on this list, it means you have bills and payments or vendor credits, but the payments have not been applied directly to the bill. Be sure to complete the Payment step!

Bills and Applied Payments Report

QuickBooks Online has a **Bills and Applied Payments** report to help you monitor Accounts Payable activity. In the *Reports Center*, scroll down to *What You Owe* and choose **Bills and Applied Payments**, or use the *Search* field to find it quickly (see Figure 4-51).

This report groups vendor activity together so that you can look up a payment you made and see which bills and vendor credits it paid off.

FIGURE 4-51: *Bills and Applied Payments shows the activity for each bill, credit, and payment—your screen may vary*

Vendor Balance Detail

The *Vendor Balance Detail* shows the detail of each bill and bill payment to each vendor. However, this report only includes bills and bill payments because they are posted to Accounts Payable. When you write checks to your vendors directly or enter credit card charges, those transactions will not show in this report.

HANDS-ON PRACTICE

STEP 1. From **Reports** in the *Left Navigation Bar*, scroll down to *What You Owe* and then choose **Vendor Balance Detail** (see Figure 4-52).

Craig's Design and Landscaping Services

Vendor Balance Detail

All Dates

DATE	TRANSACTION TYPE	NUM	DUE DATE	AMOUNT	OPEN BALANCE	BALANCE
▾ Brosnahan Insurance Agency						
	Bill			241.23	241.23	241.23
Total for Brosnahan Insurance Agency				$241.23	$241.23	
▾ Diego's Road Warrior Bodyshop						
	Bill			755.00	755.00	755.00
Total for Diego's Road Warrior Bodyshop				$755.00	$755.00	
▾ Norton Lumber and Building Materials						
	Bill			205.00	205.00	205.00
Total for Norton Lumber and Building Materials				$205.00	$205.00	
▾ PG&E						
	Bill			86.44	86.44	86.44
Total for PG&E				$86.44	$86.44	
▾ Robertson & Associates						
	Bill			315.00	315.00	315.00
Total for Robertson & Associates				$315.00	$315.00	
TOTAL				$1,602.67	$1,602.67	

FIGURE 4-52: *Vendor Balance Detail Report—your screen may vary*

Transaction List by Vendor

The *Transaction List by Vendor* report shows all transactions associated with your vendors, including transactions that did not go through Accounts Payable (e.g., checks, expenses, cash, and credit card charges).

Craig's Design and Landscaping Services

Transaction List by Vendor

January - December 202

DATE	TRANSACTION TYPE	NUM	POSTING	MEMO/DESCRIPTION	ACCOUNT	AMOUNT
▾ Bob's Burger Joint						
	Cash Expense		Yes		Checking	-5.66
	Cash Expense		Yes		Checking	-3.86
	Credit Card Expense		Yes	Bought lunch for crew 102	Mastercard	18.97
▾ Books by Bessie						
	Check	12	Yes		Checking	-55.00
	Bill		Yes		Accounts Payable (A/P)	75.00
	Bill Payment (Check)	3	Yes		Checking	-75.00
▾ Brosnahan Insurance Agency						
	Bill		Yes	Opening Balance	Accounts Payable (A/P)	2,000.00
	Bill		Yes		Accounts Payable (A/P)	241.23
	Bill Payment (Check)	1	Yes		Checking	-2,000.00
▾ Cal Telephone						
	Bill		Yes		Accounts Payable (A/P)	56.50
	Bill		Yes		Accounts Payable (A/P)	74.36
	Bill Payment (Credit Card)	1	Yes		Mastercard	74.36

FIGURE 4-53: *The Transaction List by Vendor report*

HANDS-ON PRACTICE

STEP 1. From the **Reports** option in the *Left Navigation Bar*, scroll down to the *Expenses and Vendors* section and then choose **Transaction List by Vendor** (see Figure 4-53).

STEP 2. Set the *Report Period* on the top left to **This Year**. Click **Run Report** to refresh the report data.

REVIEW QUESTIONS

Comprehension Questions

1. Describe how to track expenses by customer in QuickBooks Online.
2. Describe the different types of Accounts Payable transactions you can perform in QuickBooks Online, and how to use the Forms to perform them.
3. What is the difference between a cash vendor and a credit vendor?
4. Describe the steps you must use to record Credit Card charges and payments.
5. What is the proper workflow for managing Petty Cash?

Multiple Choice

Select the best answer(s) for each of the following:

1. You may record payments to your vendors by:
   a. Paying by credit card using an *Expense*.
   b. Using *Check* to write and print a check.
   c. Using a *Bill* to record Accounts Payable and then using *Pay Bills* to pay open bills with either a check or credit card.
   d. All of the above.

2. To display the Vendors Center:
   a. Click *Vendors* on the *Dashboard*.
   b. Click the *+New* button and then on *Vendors*.
   c. Type *Vendor* into the *Search*.
   d. Hover over *Expenses* in the Left Navigation Bar and then click on Vendors.

3. You can add a vendor:
   a. Only at the beginning of the fiscal year.
   b. Only if you will purchase over $600 from that particular vendor and a Form 1099 will be issued.
   c. Only at the beginning of the month.
   d. At any time by selecting *New Vendor* in the *Vendors Center*.

4. Which statement is true?
   a. QuickBooks Online records each *Bill Payment* in a bank account register (or credit card account register) and the Accounts Payable register.
   b. *Pay Bills* increases the balance in both the Checking account and the Accounts Payable account.
   c. QuickBooks Online has built-in *Discount Terms*.
   d. You cannot make partial payments on a bill.

5. When you print checks, which of these is not true?
    a. You can print checks one at a time.
    b. You have to print checks in batches.
    c. You can enter handwritten checks.
    d. Checks can be written to customers.

6. If you pay a Bill by check, all of the following occur, except:
    a. QuickBooks Online increments the check number.
    b. The bill is marked Paid.
    c. The Checking account balance decreases.
    d. The Accounts Payable account increases.

7. If you want to track the expenses for each customer or project:
    a. Enter each expense in the job-cost section.
    b. Use the pay liabilities function.
    c. Link each expense with the customer, sub-customer, or project to which it applies.
    d. Create a separate expense account for each job.

8. To make a credit card payment, the best practice is to:
    a. Itemize the expenses when you enter the credit card payment in the Checking account.
    b. Choose *Pay Liability* from the *+New* button.
    c. Use *Pay Down Credit Card* on the *+New* button.
    d. None of the above.

9. If you create an expense instead of paying off a bill, which of these is NOT true:
    a. You can open the Expense and use the drawer to turn it into a bill payment.
    b. It doesn't matter, since on the expense only shows in Cash-based reports.
    c. The expense is doubled in Accrual-based accounting.
    d. The expense will match in the Banking Feed.

10. Which Account type should you use to track Petty Cash:
    a. Credit Card.
    b. Equity.
    c. Bank.
    d. Other Current Asset.

11. The Vendor Balance Detail Report:
    a. Shows the detail of each bill, vendor credit, and bill payment to each vendor.
    b. Shows the detail of each payment created using the *Check* window.
    c. Can be created by selecting *Vendor Balance Detail* report from the *Vendors Center*.
    d. None of the above.

12. What is the accounting behind the scenes for the Pay Bills window when payments are made from the Checking account?
    a. Increase (debit) Accounts Payable, Decrease (credit) the Checking account.
    b. Decrease (debit) Accounts Payable, Decrease (credit) the Checking account.

c. Decrease (debit) Accounts Payable, Increase (credit) the Checking account.
d. Decrease (credit) Accounts Payable, Decrease (debit) the Checking account.

13. It is best not to use which field in the new vendor setup window:
    a. Opening Balance.
    b. Vendor Name.
    c. Address.
    d. Terms.

14. In the Pay Bills window, you can sort the bills by:
    a. Due Date.
    b. Payee.
    c. Open Balance.
    d. All of the above.

15. Which statement is true regarding bill payments:
    a. Bill Payments increase the balance in the Accounts Payable account.
    b. When you pay bills by issuing a check using the *Pay Bills* window, QuickBooks Online records each Bill Payment in the Checking account register and in the Accounts Payable account register.
    c. If you select more than one bill for the same vendor, QuickBooks Online creates a separate bill payment for each bill.
    d. There is no way to send money to pay bills inside QuickBooks Online.

Completion Statements

1. The _____ _____ shows a list of the companies and individuals you pay for products and services.
2. Bills and Bill Payments are part of the workflow with _____ Vendors.
3. Credit cards appear on the Balance Sheet as a _____.
4. To track job costs in QuickBooks Online, link each expense with the _____ to whom it applies.
5. To manage Vendors who will need 1099 forms, use the _____ _____.

MANAGING EXPENSES—APPLY YOUR KNOWLEDGE

> Log into your **Imagine Photography** class file at qbo.intuit.com.

1. Set up **Account and Settings** > **Expenses** with these Account and Settings:

EXPENSES SETTINGS	
SHOW ITEMS TABLE ON EXPENSE AND PURCHASE FORMS	On
SHOW TAGS FIELD ON EXPENSE AND PURCHASE FORMS	On
TRACK EXPENSE AND ITEMS BY CUSTOMERS	On
MAKE EXPENSES AND ITEMS BILLABLE	On
MARKUP WITH A DEFAULT RATE	On, 50%
TRACK BILLABLE EXPENSES AND ITEMS AS INCOME, IN A SINGLE ACCOUNT	On
CHARGE SALES TAX	Off
DEFAULT BILL PAYMENT TERMS	Net 30
USE PURCHASE ORDERS	On

TABLE 4-2: *Expense Settings*

2. Open the **ImagineVendors.xls** spreadsheet. Enter **your email address** into all the records in **Column D** so that you'll be able to send yourself receipts. **Import** the spreadsheet into your Vendors list. You don't need to make any changes to the field mapping. Seven vendors will be imported. **Close** the Import Vendors window when done.

3. Update the following Vendor information in your *Vendors List*:

NAME	VENDOR DISPLAY NAME	TRACK PAYMENTS FOR 1099	BILLING RATE (/HR)	TERMS	ACCOUNT NO.	DEFAULT EXPENSE ACCOUNT
Esther Gandhi	Gandhi Video, LLC	Yes	95	Net 30		
Shannon Grosskurth	Donna Distributing			Net 30	3456	
Erin Long	Erin Long, CPA	Yes	250	Due on receipt		Accounting Fees
Kim Peterson	Peterson Office Supply			Due on receipt		Office Supplies
Vicki Barton	Barton Insurance, Inc.			Net 30		Business Insurance
Dan Kahn		Yes		1st of the Month		Building & Property Rent
Ogaga Photo Supply	Ogaga Photo Supply			Net 30	43-234	

TABLE 4-3: *Vendor List*

4. Click the **Grid Gear** above the *Vendors List* and turn off the **Email** column.

5. Run the **Vendor Contact List** (from *Reports* in the *Left Navigation Bar*, scroll down to **Expenses and Vendors** and then choose **Vendor Contact List**). Use the *Grid Gear* or the *Customize* button to turn on columns for **Vendor, Email, Full Name, Address, Account #, Phone, Track 1099, Company Name, Tax ID, Terms,** and **Billing Rate**. Turn off the **Phone Numbers** column. Print the report. **Save** the customized report as **Vendor Contact List with Details**.

6. Write a **Check** to **Dan Kahn** from the **Business Checking 1025** account dated **the first of this month** for **$1,500.00** for **Building & Property Rent**. Add the *Tag* **Retail**. Assign the *Class* to the **Walnut Creek** store. Make the check as **Print Later**, but don't print the check yet.

7. The monthly insurance **Bill** from Barton Insurance arrives for **$1210**. The cost is allocated on two rows, split 50/50% between the **San Jose** and **Walnut Creek** stores. **Save and Close** the bill without scheduling a payment.

BILL	FIELDS
VENDOR	Barton Insurance, Inc.
TERMS	Net 30
BILL DATE	The 1st day of this month
BILL NO.	None
CATEGORY, LINE 1	Business Insurance
AMOUNT	605
CLASS	San Jose
CATEGORY, LINE 2	Business Insurance
AMOUNT	605
CLASS	Walnut Creek

TABLE 4-4: *Insurance bill split between classes*

8. Today you buy a printer and ink for **$725.00** from **Peterson Office Supply**, paid with the **Visa** credit card. The **Office Supplies** are split on two rows between the two store locations. Enter the following **Expense**:

EXPENSE	FIELDS
PAYEE	Peterson Office Supply
PAYMENT ACCOUNT	Business Visa (5678)
PAYMENT DATE	Today
PAYMENT METHOD	Credit Card
CATEGORY, LINE 1	Office Supplies
DESCRIPTION	Printer and ink
AMOUNT	435
CLASS	San Jose
CATEGORY, LINE 2	Office Supplies
DESCRIPTION	Laser toner
AMOUNT	290
CLASS	Walnut Creek

TABLE 4-5: *Credit card expense for office supplies split between classes*

9. In Chapter 3, **Veronica Vasquez** purchased the Supra Camera Package at the **Walnut Creek** store. To bring the camera bundle into inventory, buy the items from **Ogaga Photo Supply** using an **Expense** totaling **$595**.

EXPENSE	FIELDS
VENDOR NAME	Ogaga Photo Supply
PAYMENT ACCOUNT	Business Visa (5678)
PAYMENT DATE	The 2nd day of this month
PAYMENT METHOD	Credit Card
REF NO.	4635
TAGS	Retail
PRODUCT/SERVICE 1	Camera SR32, Qty 1, $450
PRODUCT/SERVICE 2	Lens, Qty 1, $100
PRODUCT/SERVICE 3	Case, Qty 1, $45
BILLABLE/MARKUP %	No, since we already created her sales receipt
CUSTOMER	Veronica Vasquez on all 3 lines
CLASS	Walnut Creek on all 3 lines

TABLE 4-6: *Purchase of camera equipment paid by credit card*

10. You are hiring **Gandhi Video, LLC** as a 1099 Contractor to do the **Videography** for the two Madeira projects, the **Barnett Residence** and the **Devoe Residence**. Create the following **Bill** totaling **$665**:

BILL	FIELDS
VENDOR	Gandhi Video, LLC
TERMS	Net 30
BILL DATE	The 15th of this month
BILL NO.	None (Esther didn't provide one)
TAGS	Real Estate
PRODUCT/SERVICE 1	Videographer
DESCRIPTION	Subcontracted Videographer, Barnett Residence
QTY	4
RATE	95 (increase amount from 75)
CUSTOMER	Barnett Residence
CLASS	San Jose
SALES TAX	None
PRODUCT/SERVICE 2	Videographer
DESCRIPTION	Subcontracted Videographer, Devoe Residence
QTY	3
RATE	95 (increase amount from 75)
CUSTOMER	Devoe Residence
CLASS	San Jose

TABLE 4-7: *A bill for subcontracted services on two jobs*

11. Create and print an **Unpaid Bills** report for **All Dates**.

12. Select **Pay Bills** from the **+New** menu. Pay all of the unpaid bills from the Checking account on the **last day of this month**. Select **Print Later**. **Save and Close** the window.

13. Print the three checks that you recorded with a Print Later status on blank paper. When you get the *Set Up Printing* dialog box, accept all defaults. Use the **Business Checking (1025)** account starting with check number **1001** (Note: The checks numbers will not appear on the printout as these would be imprinted on check stock used for printing actual checks).

14. In Chapter 3, Nayo Garcia bought three picture frames. To bring these items into inventory, create the following **Bill** for **$192.15**:
    a. Use the table below to create the bill.

BILL	FIELDS
VENDOR	Donna Distributing
TERMS	Net 30
BILL DATE	The 2nd day of this month
BILL NO.	38-9904
TAGS	Retail
PRODUCT/SERVICE 1	Frame 5x7 Metal, Qty 1, Rate $2.15
PRODUCT/SERVICE 2	Frame 6x8 Wood, Qty 2, Rate $5
PRODUCT/SERVICE 3	Photo Paper, Qty 10, Rate $15
BILLABLE/MARKUP	No on all lines
CUSTOMER	Nayo Garcia on the top 2 lines for the frames
CLASS	Walnut Creek on all 3 lines

TABLE 4-8: *A purchase including products sold to a customer*

    b. The bill included **$30** for shipping. Using the *Category Details* grid at the top, add a new **Cost of Goods Sold** sub-account on the fly for **Shipping, Freight, & Delivery**—COS, as shown in Figure 4-54.

    c. Assign this shipping charge to the **Walnut Creek** *Class*. Because it is mostly because of the weight of the paper, we will not allocate it to Nayo.

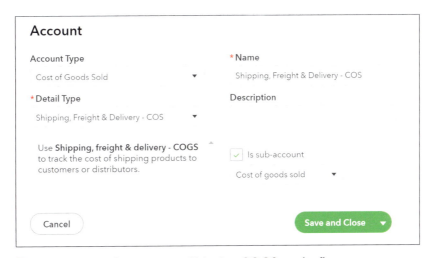

FIGURE 4-54: *Create a new Shipping COGS on the fly*

15. Print a **Transaction List by Vendor** report for **All Dates**.

CHAPTER 5

ADVANCED TRANSACTIONS

TOPICS

In this chapter, you will learn about the following topics:

- Controlling the Automation (page 198)
- Managing Transactions (page 199)
- Voiding and Deleting Transactions (page 200)
- The Audit Log (page 202)
- Creating Recurring Transactions (page 203)
- Using Journal Entries (page 206)
- Recording and Applying Credit Memos (page 207)
- Creating Customer Refunds (page 211)
- Handling Bounced Checks (page 214)
- Writing Off Bad Debts (page 220)
- Delayed Charges and Delayed Credits (page 224)
- Creating Customer Statements (page 226)
- Sending Payment Reminders (page 228)
- Adding Late Fees (page 231)
- Recording and Applying Vendor Credits (page 232)
- Creating Vendor Refunds (page 236)
- What To Do If Your Check Bounces (page 238)
- Managing Loans (page 239)
- Paying Sales Tax (page 243)

OPEN THIS FILE:

Open the *Craig's Landscaping sample company* using the bookmark you created on page 8, or go to http://qbo.intuit.com/redir/testdrive.

In the previous two chapters, you learned the fundamental workflows for sales and expenses. In this chapter, you will take it a step deeper, and see how QuickBooks Online records common but less-frequent transactions including **returns**, **refunds**, **bounced checks**, and **statements**.

We will also explore several additional Accounts Receivable and Accounts Payable transactions that you might implement for each company.

CONTROLLING THE AUTOMATION

In Chapter 2 we learned how to configure QuickBooks Online's company settings. In this chapter we need to update some additional settings so that you can see how they affect specific QBO features. If you work on this chapter over several sessions, you will need to reset these Account and Settings in the Craig's Landscaping sample company each time you log in.

HANDS-ON PRACTICE

STEP 1. Click on the **Gear** in the upper right corner. Choose **Account and Settings**, then click on the **Sales** tab. Click on the pencil icon to edit the *Sales Form Content*, turn on the **Service Date** option, then click **Save**. We discussed this option in *Configuring the Sales Settings* on page 98.

> **DID YOU KNOW?**
>
> When editing the *Account and Settings*, you don't actually need to click the pencils. You can click anywhere in the sections to open them, although you do need to click **Save** to close them and keep your changes.

STEP 2. Open the **Advanced** tab and click in the **Automation** area, as shown in Figure 5-1.

STEP 3. Slide *Automatically Apply Credits* and *Automatically Apply Bill Payments* to **Off**.

STEP 4. Click **Save**.

FIGURE 5-1: *Turn off Credit automations*

STEP 5. Scroll to the bottom and set *Sign Me Out If Inactive For* to **3 Hours**, then click **Save**.

STEP 6. Click **Done.**

ADVANCED TRANSACTIONS | 199

MANAGING TRANSACTIONS

QuickBooks Online allows you to change any transaction at any time. However, you should almost never change transactions dated in closed accounting periods, or transactions that have been reconciled with a bank statement.

> **KEY TERM:**
>
> For the purposes of this discussion, a **Closed Accounting Period** is a period for which you've already issued financial statements and/or filed tax returns.
>
> Depending on the business, a closed period may be the previous year, or it may be the previous month. Make sure you know how often your company closes periods before you make changes to transactions that might affect past history.

When you edit or delete a transaction, QuickBooks Online updates the General Ledger with your change, preserving the date of the transaction. Therefore, if you change transactions in a closed accounting period, your financial statements will change for that period, causing discrepancies between your QuickBooks Online file and your tax return.

> **TIP:**
>
> To prevent this from happening, use a **Closing Date** to "lock" your data file to prevent users from making changes on or before a specified date. You can set the closing date in *Account and Settings* under the **Advanced** tab. If you choose to require a password, be sure not to lose it!

Editing Transactions

From time to time, you may need to modify transactions to correct posting errors. To edit a transaction in QuickBooks Online, change the data directly on the form. For example, if you forgot to add a line item and *you have not already sent the invoice to your customer or vendor*, you can simply **Edit** the transaction and update the existing information.

> **NOTE:**
>
> Some companies cannot change transactions if they have already been sent to the vendor or customer. In that case, you would need to create a new invoice or bill with an adjusting charge.

Copying Transactions

If you would like to duplicate an existing transaction because it already has the information you need, you can **Copy** it.

The **Copy** option can be found on the *Action* drop-down on many transaction lists, or under the **More** button when you are viewing the desired transaction, as shown in Figure 5-2.

When you copy a transaction, look for the alert reminding you that this is not the original, as shown in Figure 5-3. Update the date, amount, and other details in the transaction, and then save the duplicate.

Figure 5-2: *Use the More button to Copy a transaction*

Figure 5-3: *Create a copy of any transaction and then modify it*

Voiding and Deleting Transactions

Voiding and *deleting* transactions both have the same effect on the General Ledger—the effect is to zero out the debits and the credits specified by the transaction.

There is one significant difference between voiding and deleting. When you **void** a transaction, QuickBooks Online keeps a record of the date, number, and detail of the transaction, but zeros out the amount. When you **delete** a transaction, QuickBooks Online removes it completely from your records.

To maintain a history of business activity, it is preferable to void transactions that are no longer relevant, instead of deleting them.

> **IMPORTANT!**
>
> Deleting or voiding a transaction may affect past reports and taxes. If the error is discovered in a past period after reports or taxes have been filed, you would have to make a compensating adjustment in the current period—see *Writing Off Bad Debts* on page 220, and *Vendor Credits* on page 232.

Deleting a Transaction

If you make a mistake while creating a transaction, an error that is not supposed to be in QuickBooks at all, you can simply delete the transaction right after you make it, and it will go away completely.

Deleting a transaction is permanent, and cannot be undone. You can view the original transaction in the Audit Log (see page 202) if you need to recreate it.

To **delete** a transaction:

1. Open the transaction you wish to delete.

2. Click the **More** button in the *black bar* at the bottom, then choose **Delete** (see Figure 5-4).

3. On the *Are You Sure You Want To Delete This?* window, click **Yes**.

Voiding a Transaction

Proper accounting procedures do not allow you to simply delete transactions at will. In some cases it is perfectly fine to use the **Delete** command, when the transactions are internal, in the current period,

FIGURE 5-4: *Deleting a transaction*

and true errors. However, if the transaction has business activity of any type associated with it, you can't just delete it. Because you need a continuous transaction history, you would instead *Void* the transaction.

For example, it is acceptable to delete a check that you have not printed. On the other hand, if you have already printed the check, you should **Void** it instead of deleting it so that you will have a record of the voided check and the numbering sequence remains intact in the register.

It is important to enter each check into your register even if the check is voided or unused, to prevent gaps in your check number sequence.

HANDS-ON PRACTICE

Craig's Landscaping printed a check for Tim Phillip Masonry, but at the last minute decided to pay by credit card instead. They need to remove the check from QuickBooks Online.

STEP 1. To open the **Checking register**, go to the **Chart of Accounts** from *Accounting* in the *Left Navigation Bar*. Click on the *Checking* account's blue **View Register** link on the right.

STEP 2. Scroll down and find **Bill Payment 45** to **Tim Philip Masonry**. Click once on the transaction to activate it.

STEP 3. Click the **Edit** button to open the payment.

STEP 4. Select **Void** from the **More** button in the *black bar* at the bottom of the window (see Figure 5-5).

FIGURE 5-5: *Voiding a check*

Since you are voiding a check that pays a bill, QuickBooks Online warns you that this change will affect the application of this check to the bills (see Figure 5-6). In other words, voiding a bill payment will make the bill open and payable again.

STEP 5. Click **Yes** (notice that it is NOT the green button, to make sure you've thought this through!), then click **OK** on the *Transaction Successfully Voided* confirmation box. The transaction closes.

STEP 6. Click the browser's **Refresh** button to update the register. You'll notice the *Memo* now says **Voided**.

> ### DID YOU KNOW?
>
> Because QuickBooks Online is web-based, you may have to refresh your window after making changes, to pull the updated information from the server. If you make a change but don't see it immediately reflected on the screen, use your browser's **Refresh** or **Reload** button. **Ctrl-R** is a handy keyboard shortcut to refresh the screen without having to stop what you're doing (**Cmd-R** on a Mac).

STEP 7. **Edit** the voided payment from the *Register* to open it again.

Notice that the *Payment Status* says **VOID**, the *Memo* includes **Voided**, QuickBooks Online changed the amount of the check to zero, and the original bill is back in the drawer waiting for a new payment (see Figure 5-7).

FIGURE 5-6: Warning about voiding the check

STEP 8. Cancel the voided bill payment to close the window.

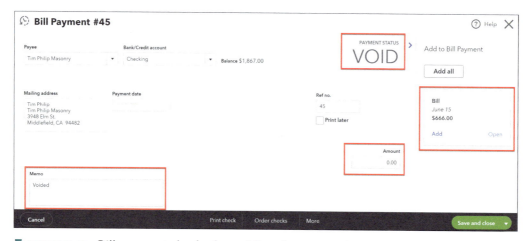

FIGURE 5-7: Bill payment check after voiding the transaction

The Audit Log

The ***Audit Log*** feature of QuickBooks Online records all transaction activity, including the date, time, and user who performed the action. It lists each accounting transaction and displays every addition, deletion, or modification. The Audit Log cannot be manually altered.

Open the **Audit Log** from the *Gear* in the upper right corner. You can also access the **Audit History** from inside any transaction by clicking on the **More** button in the black bar at the bottom of the screen.

You can filter the Audit Log by transaction type, date, or user. When you edit a transaction, the Audit History allows you to compare the before-and-after for each change made, highlighting the edits in yellow, as demonstrated in Figure 5-8.

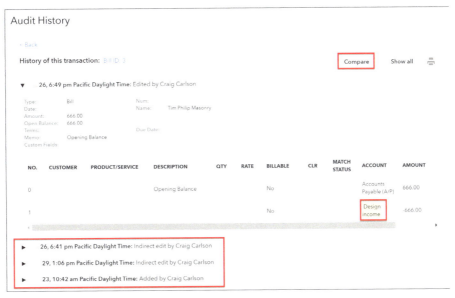

FIGURE 5-8: *The Audit History showing changes to an expense*

> **TIP:**
>
> Users of QuickBooks Online for Accountants (QBOA) have a *Voided/Deleted Transactions Report* that lists all voided and deleted transactions. This report, which is actually a filtered view of the Audit Log, is very useful when you have several users and transactions seem to change, since the report shows the time, date, and username associated with the edits or deletions.

Creating Recurring Transactions

If you frequently enter the same transaction (or similar ones), you can memorize and schedule the entry of the transaction.

There are three types of recurring transactions:

- **Scheduled** transactions run automatically. For example, if you use QuickBooks Payments Merchant Services, you can create a sales receipt that runs the customer's credit card or ACH, and emails them the receipt automatically. Their money just shows up in your bank account, without you having to lift a finger.

- **Reminder** transactions add an alert to the Dashboard when it is time to process them. That way you can update the date, dollar amount, or other details. For example, if you want QuickBooks Online to create a bill for your cell phone payment each month, you can memorize the transaction and update the amount when the bill arrives.

- **Unscheduled** transactions serve as templates for complex transactions that you can call on and use when needed. Examples include journal entries for payroll or job costing, and pre-built estimates that can be further customized for each job. This is preferable to opening and duplicating an existing transaction, so that you don't accidentally forget to save a copy, and mistakenly change the original.

> **NOTE:**
>
> You can memorize all first-stage transactions including *Journal Entries, Invoices, Sales Receipts, Bills,* and others. However, second-stage transactions such as *Bill Payment* and *Receive Payment* cannot be memorized, because QuickBooks Online doesn't know which bill or invoice to pay against.

Memorizing a Transaction

HANDS-ON PRACTICE

Craig's Landscaping performs pest control services for Pye's Cakes every month. To streamline the sales cycle, you decide to make a recurring transaction to save steps in the future.

STEP 1. Find and open **Sales Receipt #1011** from Pye's Cakes.

There are several routes to get there—through *All Sales*, through **Pye's** *Customer record*, or by using the *Search magnifying glass* (see Figure 5-9).

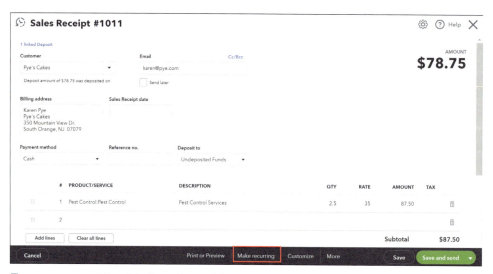

FIGURE 5-9: *Monthly Pest Control Payment*

STEP 2. Click **Make Recurring** on the *black bar* at the bottom. The window shown in Figure 5-10 opens.

STEP 3. Update the *Template Name* to **Pye's Cakes Pest Control**. Always use names that you will recognize easily on the *Recurring Transactions* list.

STEP 4. In the *Type* field, you could change the recurring transaction to Reminder or Unscheduled. We will leave it on **Scheduled** so that it runs automatically.

STEP 5. Select **Automatically Send Emails** in the *Options*.

STEP 6. Update the *Interval* to **Monthly on the Last Day of 1 Month** (**Monthly, Day, Last, 1**).

These date settings are completely flexible, allowing you to create daily, weekly, monthly, and annual transactions that can trigger either on a date or day of the week.

STEP 7. We do not need to enter a *Start Date* or *End*, but those options are available if you require a date range.

STEP 8. Change the *Payment Method* to **MasterCard**. If you were using QuickBooks Payments, you would enter the credit card number or bank account to be charged automatically every month (not shown).

IMPORTANT!

If you are not using QuickBooks Payments, QBO's built-in merchant services, be sure to replicate this workflow in your merchant services portal so that the dates and dollar amounts match . . . and that the payment gets processed! Otherwise, you will enter this sales receipt into QuickBooks but never actually receive the money.

STEP 9. When your screen matches Figure 5-10, click **Save Template**.

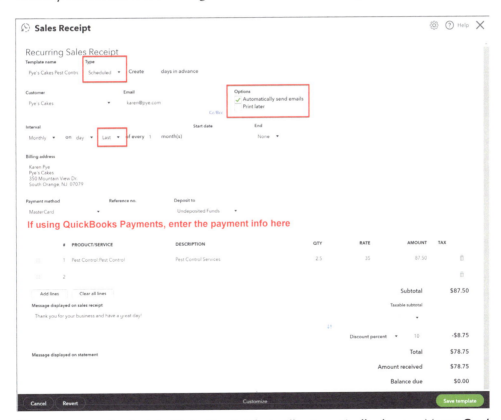

FIGURE 5-10: *A scheduled Sales Receipt that will automatically charge a MasterCard and email the receipt*

Using, Editing, and Managing Recurring Transactions

To work with the *Recurring Transactions* list, click on the *Gear* in the upper right corner, and choose **Recurring Transactions** (see Figure 5-12).

There are several options in the *Action* column, as shown in Figure 5-12:

- **Edit** a recurring transaction to update anything about it. For example, you might change the *Telephone Bill* to **Reminder** so that you can update the amount every month.

- Select **Use** to run any recurring transaction on demand, any time.

- **Duplicate** allows you to use an existing recurring transaction as the basis for a new one. For example, you could duplicate the **Pye's Cakes Pest Control** sales receipt, then change the customer name and payment method to create a new template for a different customer.

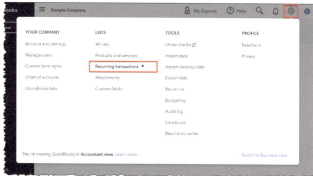

FIGURE 5-11: Open the Recurring Transactions list

- **Delete** is used when you no longer need the recurring transaction.

- **Skip** and **Pause** may also show up on the list, allowing you to temporarily prevent the transaction from triggering.

FIGURE 5-12: Recurring Transaction List

USING JOURNAL ENTRIES

Journal Entries (also called a **General Journal Entry**, or abbreviated as **GJE** or **JE**) are behind-the-scenes transactions that manually adjust the balance of two or more general ledger accounts.

Never use a journal entry if there is a QuickBooks Online form that serves that purpose. For example, if a vendor is giving you a credit, don't post a JE to Accounts Payable, create an actual bill credit instead.

Here are a few appropriate times a bookkeeper or accountant would use journal entries in QuickBooks Online:

- Allocate account balances across classes, customers, or jobs.
- Distribute prepaid expenses each month throughout the year.
- Record non-cash expenses.
- Close Owners Equity.
- Make adjustments at year end.

Journal entries use **Debits** and **Credits** to move funds between accounts. They are particularly useful for transferring funds between Balance Sheet and Profit & Loss accounts, because QBO's Transfer forms do not have this ability. The total of the *Debit* column must match the total of the *Credit* column (see *Double-Entry Accounting* on page 5).

When an accountant using QBOA creates a journal entry to fix mistakes in the data, there is an additional checkbox to mark these as **Adjusting Journal Entries**.

Figure 5-13 shows a sample journal entry for recording the ownership change on a truck title from personal to business.

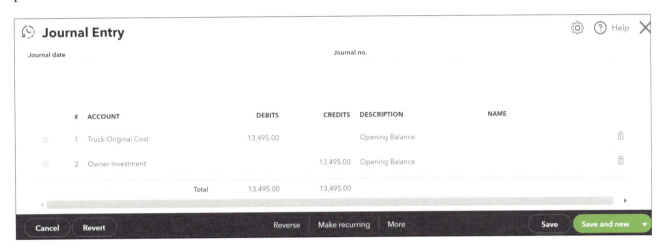

FIGURE 5-13: *A sample Journal Entry*

ADVANCED ACCOUNTS RECEIVABLE WORKFLOWS

In Chapter 3, we looked at the common workflows for recording customer sales. In this section we will explore additional income workflows in QuickBooks Online that you probably won't use every day, but are essential to know when you do need them.

We will also look at common but infrequent accounts receivable transactions including customer credits and refunds, bounced checks, and collection options.

Recording and Applying Credit Memos

Occasionally you may have a customer who isn't satisfied with a product or service, and needs a credit on their account to apply to a future sale. To record these credits in Accounts Receivable, use a **Credit Memo**. Credit memos can be used in the following situations:

- To record a return of merchandise from a customer.
- To record a credit-on-account for services.
- As a correction technique to clean up Accounts Receivable on an accrual basis.
- To reverse a sale that had been invoiced in a previous reporting period.

When you create a credit memo in QuickBooks Online, you must use a Receive Payment form to apply the credit to pay off one or more existing or future invoice*s*.

Creating a credit memo in the current period can be used to write off old uncollectible invoices from past periods. For more information, see *Writing Off Bad Debts* on page 220.

> ### KEY TERM:
>
> **Credit Memos** are sales forms that reduce the amount a customer owes your company.

QuickBooks Online gives you the option of automating the application of customer credits, as we saw on page 198. If a company is small and the business owner doesn't pay careful attention to details, it may be helpful to switch on QBO's automations. That way, when you create a credit memo, QBO will look for an existing open invoice and apply the credit as a payment. The customer's remaining invoice balance will decrease without having to take any extra steps.

On the other hand, if the company has a lot of Accounts Receivable, you may want more control. It may make better sense to turn the automations off, allowing you to manually choose which invoices to apply the credits.

> ### THE ACCOUNTING BEHIND THE SCENES:
>
> Credit Memos look similar to invoices, but they perform the opposite function. That is, a Credit Memo reduces (debits) **Sales Income** and also reduces (credits) **Accounts Receivable**. In some cases, they also reduce (debit) **Sales Tax Payable**.
>
> If the credit memo returns inventory into stock, a Credit Memo also increases (debits) the **Inventory asset** and reduces (credits) the **Cost of Goods Sold** account.
>
> | TRANSACTION TYPE | NAME | MEMO/DESCRIPTION | ACCOUNT | DEBIT | CREDIT |
> | --- | --- | --- | --- | --- | --- |
> | Credit Memo | Red Rock Diner | | Accounts Receivable (A/R) | | $12.96 |
> | | | Return unused Sprinkler Pipes | Sales of Product Income | $12.00 | |
> | | | Return unused Sprinkler Pipes | Inventory Asset | $7.50 | |
> | | | Return unused Sprinkler Pipes | Cost of Goods Sold | | $7.50 |
> | | | | Board of Equalization Payable | $0.96 | |
> | | | | | $20.46 | $20.46 |

Creating a Credit Memo

The first step in issuing a credit memo is to show the detail of the products returned and/or services rejected.

HANDS-ON PRACTICE

A few months ago, Red Rock Diner paid $156 for 12 sprinkler pipes but only used 9 of them. We can't just change the original invoice, because it would overwrite the business's historical activity and alter previous reports. Instead, create a credit memo to return 3 of the pipes and apply the credit to reduce what they still owe on the open invoice.

STEP 1. Click **Customers** from the *Sales* menu on the *Left Navigation Bar*.

STEP 2. Select **Red Rock Diner** from the *Customers Center* list. You can see they have an overdue invoice for $156.

STEP 3. Click the green **New Transaction** button, then choose **Credit Memo** (see Figure 5-14).

STEP 4. Set the *Credit Memo Date* to **today**.

STEP 5. Choose **Sprinkler Pipes** from the *Product/Service* field.

STEP 6. Update the *Description* so it says **Returned unused Sprinkler Pipes**.

STEP 7. Change the *Qty* to **3** and press **Tab**. The *Amount* will update to **12.00**.

STEP 8. Update the *Sales Tax* to **California**. It will add **.96** to the credit memo, also refunding the sales tax paid.

STEP 9. When your screen matches Figure 5-14, change the green button to **Save and Close**.

FIGURE 5-14: *Create a Credit Memo to return products on account*

Applying a Credit Memo to an Open Invoice

The second step of the process is to apply the credit memo against the invoice, using a **Receive Payment** form. On page 198 we turned off the Automations so that we could apply this payment manually. In the *Writing Off Bad Debts* section on page 220, you will see what it looks like when the automation is left on and QuickBooks Online creates the invoice payment for you.

STEP 10. On the Red Rock Diner's transaction list shown in Figure 5-15, you can see the **Unapplied Credit Memo** for $12.96 as well as an **Overdue Invoice** for $156 (Note: if the credit memo says **Closed** instead, your Automations are still turned on. See page 198 to turn them off).

When you look in the upper right corner, you can see that the Red Rock Diner has an *Open Balance* of **$213.04**. This balance is the sum of the two open invoices totaling $126, minus the $12.96 credit memo.

STEP 11. Click **Receive Payment** on the right side of the overdue *Invoice*. The window in Figure 5-16 opens.

STEP 12. Scroll down to the bottom. Notice the *Credit Memo* in the *Credits* grid is checked. In the *Outstanding Transactions* at the top, there are two open invoices. Confirm the older of the two invoices, the one with the original sale for $156, has a **checkmark** in the box on its left.

The benefit of turning off QuickBooks Online's *Automatically Apply Credits* automation is that you get to choose which invoice to pay down.

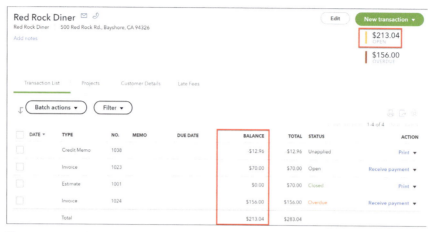

FIGURE 5-15: *An unapplied credit memo and two open invoices*

STEP 13. Change the *Payment* amount on the right of *Invoice #1024* to **12.96**, the amount of the credit. You are paying $12.96 of the $156 invoice using the credit memo.

STEP 14. Verify the *Amount Received* box at the top now says **0.00**, since we are not taking an additional payment at this time.

STEP 15. If the customer were paying off the rest of the invoice, you could leave the **$156** in the invoice row to pay off *Invoice #1024* in full, enter **$143.04** as the remaining *Amount Received* balance to be paid, then add the *Payment Method*.

Make sure your screen matches Figure 5-16. When done, choose **Save and Close** on the green button.

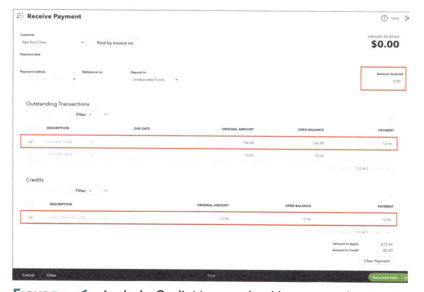

FIGURE 5-16: *Apply the Credit Memo to the oldest outstanding invoice*

Creating Customer Refunds

A *Refund* returns money to the customer. There are several situations when you may need to issue a refund:

1. When a customer pays for merchandise and then returns it.
2. When a customer requests a discount or refund on services for which they have already paid.
3. When a customer overpays an invoice and requests a refund.

If the customer paid with cash or check, you should issue their refund by check. If the customer paid with a credit card, you should return the funds to the customer's credit card.

Refunding Customers by Check

HANDS-ON PRACTICE

Last week when Craig's Landscaping did some gardening for Mark Cho, one of the crew accidentally pulled up one of his plants, thinking it was a weed. Craig decides to refund Mark for one hour of gardening by sending him a check.

STEP 1. Select **Refund Receipt** from the *+New* button, as shown in Figure 5-17.

STEP 2. Fill in the Refund Receipt as shown in Figure 5-18. The *Customer* is **Mark Cho**, and the *Product/Service* is **Gardening**.

STEP 3. In the *Description*, enter **Pulled up a plant**. Enter **25** as the *Rate*, then press **Tab** to autocalculate the *Amount* to **25**.

FIGURE 5-17: *Create a new Refund Receipt*

STEP 4. In the *Payment Method* field, choose **Check**. Choose the **Checking** account in the *Refund From* field. If you are handwriting the check, enter the check number. If you were printing checks, you would select **Print Later**.

Leave the *Check No.* on the default, **71**.

STEP 5. When your *Refund Receipt* looks like Figure 5-18, click **Save and New**.

STEP 6. When you get a confirmation message such as shown in Figure 5-19, click **OK**.

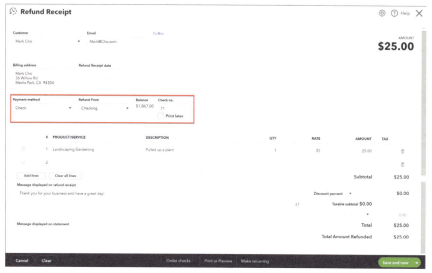

FIGURE 5-19: *Refund confirmation message*

FIGURE 5-18: *Refund Receipt paid by check—your screen may vary*

STEP 7. The check has been recorded in the register, and a new blank refund receipt is ready for the next step.

THE ACCOUNTING BEHIND THE SCENES:

Issuing a refund with a check decreases (or debits) the **Income** account associated with the product or service on the refund receipt and decreases (or credits) the **Checking** account.

TRANSACTION TYPE	NAME	MEMO/DESCRIPTION	ACCOUNT	DEBIT	CREDIT
Refund	Mark Cho		Checking		$25.00
		Pulled up a plant	Landscaping Services	$25.00	
				$25.00	$25.00

Refunding Credit Cards

The process for refunding a customer's credit card is similar to the last example, except that credit card refunds are held in the Undeposited Funds account and processed with that day's batch.

HANDS-ON PRACTICE

Craig's Landscaping did some design work for Kate Whelan, but she decided not to implement the plan. To maintain their good customer relationship, Craig agrees to refund her money back to the credit card she paid with.

STEP 8. You should see a new **Refunds Receipt** after the previous step. If not, open a new one from the *+New* button.

STEP 9. Fill in **Kate Whelan** in the *Customer* field (see Figure 5-20).

STEP 10. Choose **Design** in the *Product/Service* field, and enter the *Qty* **3**. Press **Tab** to calculate the total, **$225**.

STEP 11. In the *Payment Method* field, enter **MasterCard**, and *Refund From* the **Undeposited Funds** account (your company may display **Payments to Deposit** instead).

STEP 12. If you use QuickBooks Payments merchant services, you can refund the credit card used for the original charge by clicking **Process Credit Card** right on this form. If you use a third-party payment service, you would use your regular payment system to manually process the actual refund itself.

STEP 13. When your refund receipt matches Figure 5-20, click **Save and Close**.

STEP 14. Click **OK** in the *Refund Successfully Issued* dialog box.

FIGURE 5-20: *A Refund Receipt refunded to a credit card by batching in Undeposited Funds*

THE ACCOUNTING BEHIND THE SCENES:

Issuing a refund to a credit card decreases (debits) the **Income** account associated with the product or service on the refund receipt, and decreases (credits) the **Undeposited Funds** account.

TRANSACTION TYPE	NAME	MEMO/DESCRIPTION	ACCOUNT	DEBIT	CREDIT
Refund	Kate Whelan		Undeposited Funds		$225.00
		Custom Design	Design income	$225.00	
				$225.00	$225.00

STEP 15. To record the credit card refund into the bank account, select **Bank Deposit** from the *+New* button.

STEP 16. **Check off** all the three payments shown in Figure 5-21 (your transaction list may vary).

The merchant services deposit subtracts the refund from that day's batch.

STEP 17. Click **Save and Close**.

FIGURE 5-21: *The Credit card refund is subtracted from daily credit card batch*

Making Negative Deposits

If the refund is larger than the rest of the day's credit card payments, money is drawn from your checking account instead of deposited.

When this happens, create the **Bank Deposit** to the checking account as normal. Mark off all the day's charges and refunds. The selected transactions will total the amount deducted from the bank account.

> **DID YOU KNOW?**
>
> Merchant services companies normally charge two types of fees for processing credit cards: a **Transaction Fee** and a **Discount Fee**. A transaction fee is a flat fee for each credit card transaction, regardless of whether it is a sale or refund. A discount fee is a percentage charge based on the transaction amount.
>
> Some merchant services companies only charge a discount fee for credit card sales. Other companies, however, charge a discount fee for both credit card sales and refunds. **Intuit's QuickBooks Online Payments Merchant Services** charges a discount fee for both sales and refunds.

Handling Bounced Checks

Banks and accountants often refer to **Bounced Checks** as NSF (non-sufficient funds) transactions. This means there is not enough money in the account to cover the check.

When a check received from a customer bounces for non-sufficient funds, the money is deposited into your account, then withdrawn from the account. Your customer must then pay you a second time. You may even incur bank fees, and choose to pass them on to the customer for reimbursement.

The process for recording it in QuickBooks Online can be confusing. When these steps are not handled appropriately, common mistakes include miscategorizing bounced checks as bank charges, or duplicating the original sale.

Instead, when you invoice your customer the second time, they will pay you for the bounced check and any associated fees. Creating the invoice for the **Bounced Check** will pull the money out of the checking account, matching the activity on the Banking Feed and bank statement.

One-time Setup Steps
Creating the Bounced Check Item to Include on the Invoice

The first one-time setup step is to create a service item for the **Bounced Check** as shown in Figure 5-22.

STEP 1. Open up the **Products and Services** list under *Sales* in the *Left Navigation Bar*.

STEP 2. Create a new **Service**.

STEP 3. Give it the *Name* **Bounced Check**.

STEP 4. Add a new *Category* called **Admin** on the fly.

STEP 5. Enter **Bounced Check** in the *Description* field.

STEP 6. In the *Income Account*, select the **Checking** bank account.

STEP 7. Make sure the *Sales Tax* is **Nontaxable**.

STEP 8. When your screen matches the figure below, click **Save and Close**.

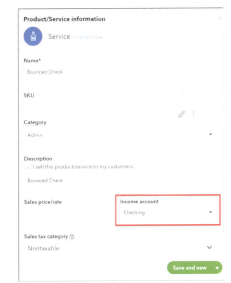

FIGURE 5-22: *Create a Bounced Check service item*

THE ACCOUNTING BEHIND THE SCENES:

This creative solution seems counter-intuitive. Why would you use the **Checking** account as the *Income Account*? Normally, this field **credits** a **Revenue** account, which increases it. By using it to **credit** an **Asset** account, it instead decreases the bank account.

Creating a customer invoice for this **Bounced Check** deducts the amount from the checking account register.

For more information about debits and credits and how they affect different account types, see page 4.

TRANSACTION TYPE	NAME	MEMO/DESCRIPTION	ACCOUNT	DEBIT	CREDIT
Invoice	Travis Waldron		Accounts Receivable (A/R)	$113.00	
		Bounced Check	Checking		$81.00
		NSF Fees	Fees Billed		$32.00
				$113.00	$113.00

If You Will Pass on NSF Fees to Customers

When the bank charges you an NSF fee, it is your choice whether you are going to pass it on to your customer for reimbursement. If you choose not to charge your customer a fee for bounced checks, you can skip to the next section.

There are two one-time setup steps for passing on bank fees:

1. Adding a category to the *Chart of Accounts* so that the reimbursement **Fees Billed Income** shows up on your Profit and Loss report.

2. Adding a service to the *Products and Services list* to create an **NSF Fee** line item to include on customer invoices.

HANDS-ON PRACTICE

To properly get reimbursed for NSF fees, you need an Income category for the **Fees Billed** on your Chart of Accounts. Some QuickBooks Online files contain one by default.

STEP 9. Open up the **Chart of Accounts** through *Accounting* on the *Left Navigation Bar*.

STEP 10. Scroll down to the *Income* section of the list. The Craig's Landscaping sample company already has a **Fees Billed** account, but if your company didn't have one, you would create the account as shown in Figure 5-23.

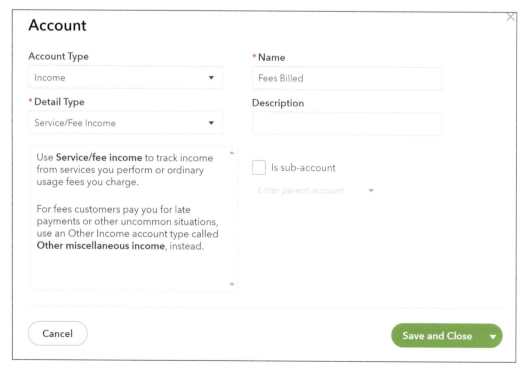

FIGURE 5-23: *Create an Income account category for Fees Billed*

STEP 11. Open the **Products and Services** list under *Sales* in the *Left Navigation Bar*.

STEP 12. Click the **New** button, and select **Service**.

STEP 13. Create a new **NSF Fees** item as shown in Figure 5-24. Enter **Admin** in the *Category* field, and **NSF Fees** in the *Description*.

STEP 14. Set the *Income Account* to **Fees Billed**.

STEP 15. Change the *Sales Tax* to **Nontaxable**.

STEP 16. Click **Save and Close**.

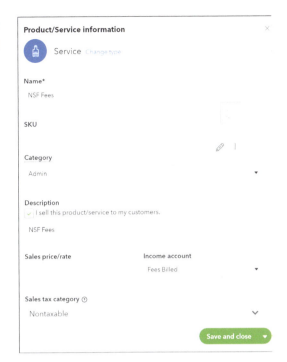

FIGURE 5-24: *Create a new NSF Fees service item*

TIP:

If you are using product *Categories*, group these bounced check items together in an **Admin** group, to distinguish them from your products and services for sale.

Invoicing and Receiving the Replacement Payment

Instead of sending another invoice for the original service, the customer now is charged for the bounced payment and any NSF fees you pass on for reimbursement.

HANDS-ON PRACTICE

Travis Waldron recently paid Invoice #1013 with a check for $81, but it bounced. The bank charged your company a $32 fee, which you are passing on to the customer for reimbursement. First you will record an expense for the fees you paid, then you'll create a replacement invoice to send to Travis.

STEP 1. From the *+New* button, create a new **Expense.**

STEP 2. In the *Payee* field, add **Chance Bank** as a new Vendor on the fly.

STEP 3. Fill in the *Expense* as shown in Figure 5-25. Use **Bank Charges** in the *Category Details*, **Bounced Check Fee** in the *Description*, **32** for the *Amount*, and choose **Travis Waldron** for the *Customer*.

STEP 4. When your screen matches the figure below, click **Save and Close**.

> **TIP:**
>
> If you are using *Billable Expenses* in your workflow in QuickBooks Online Plus or Advanced, instead of using the NSF item in the following steps, you could make this charge *Billable*, and pull it into Travis's next invoice from the drawer on the right.

Figure 5-25: *Create an Expense for the bank's NSF fees*

Step 5. Open **Travis Waldron's** *Customer record* to view his original $81.00 invoice payment.

Step 6. Create a new **Invoice** from the *New Transaction* button (see Figure 5-26).

Step 7. Add a *Product/Service* to the invoice for the **Bounced Check** with an *Amount* of **81**, the amount of the original receipt.

Step 8. Add a second row for the **NSF Fees** with an amount of **32** (or if you are using the Billable Expenses workflow, you could pull in the pass-through expense from the drawer on the right).

Step 9. The new invoice to Travis Waldron is now for **$113.00**. Normally you would click **Save and Send**, but we will click **Save and Close**.

Figure 5-26: *Create a replacement invoice for the Bounced Check and NSF fees*

> ### DID YOU KNOW?
>
> In Intuit's ProAdvisor Certification training, they recommend editing the original payment that bounced, and applying it to the new bounced check invoice instead of the original invoice. This re-opens the first invoice with its original date, indicating that it remains unpaid.

STEP 10. Fast-forward a week, and Travis has now sent you a new payment. Click the blue **Receive Payment** link, and change the date to **a week from today**.

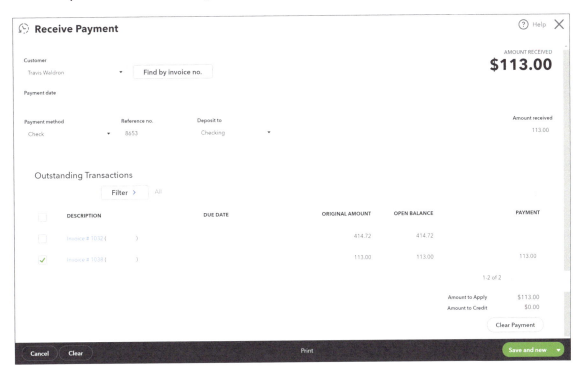

FIGURE 5-27: *Receive the replacement payment for the bounced check, including fees*

STEP 11. Make sure the invoice for **$113** is checked.

STEP 12. Their new *Payment Method* is **Check**, and its *Reference No.* is **8653**.

STEP 13. Normally all payments are deposited into **Undeposited Funds**, but for the sake of this exercise, update the *Deposit To* field to **Checking**.

STEP 14. When your screen matches Figure 5-27, click **Save and Close**.

Notice how the both the original invoice for *$81* and the rebilled invoice for *$113* are both marked **Paid**.

Now let's look at how these transactions affected the Checking register.

Open the **Checking** account by going to the *Left Navigation Bar* and selecting **Chart of Accounts** from the *Accounting* menu. Click **View Register** on the right of the *Checking* bank account to open the screen shown in Figure 5-28.

1. Travis's original $81 payment was part of the $868.15 deposit. When you hover your cursor over the blue *Split* link, you can see the individual payments that made up the total. This deposit remains unchanged, since it is still historically correct

2. The NSF charges from the bank, entered as an expense.

3. The replacement invoice with the **Bounced Check** pulls the funds out of the checking account, matching the Banking Feed and bank statement.

4. The replacement payment from Travis, including both the bounced check reimbursement and the fee income.

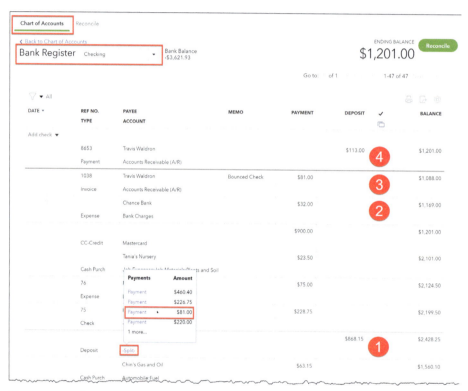

FIGURE 5-28: *The Checking register showing all the transactions related to the bounced payment*

Writing Off Bad Debts

If an invoice becomes uncollectible, you'll need to **write off the debt**. If you use cash-basis accounting, the uncollectible invoice has never been recognized as income on your *Profit & Loss* report, and therefore, you can simply void the invoice or discount it to zero, removing the balance from Accounts Receivable.

It's important to understand that accrual-based accounting practices differ. You have already included the income in your previous period's reporting, including sales tax and corporate taxes. Therefore, you can't just void, delete, or discount the original transaction. Instead, you'll enter a new transaction to credit the customer balance, reduce the income, and offset your upcoming sales tax payments.

To properly write off the bad debt for accrual-based companies, use a **Credit Memo** with a **Bad Debt** item. This converts the Accounts Receivable into a bad debts expense without changing the sales history.

ADVANCED TRANSACTIONS | 221

> **DID YOU KNOW?**
>
> QuickBooks Online for Accountants (QBOA) has a **Write Off Invoices** function, but it only works for cash-based businesses without sales tax, because it simply adds a discount to each open invoice, zeroing out the balance.

One-time Setup Steps

To properly write off old unpaid invoices, there is a one-time setup process. You will need to create a new **Bad Debts** expense category on the *Chart of Accounts*, and two new *Products and Services*, one **taxable** and one **nontaxable**.

HANDS-ON PRACTICE

Kookies by Kathy has an invoice for $75 that is only a few months old, but because she's a friend, Craig decides he's not going to collect on it. Craig's Landscaping has already run reports for previous months, so he can't just void the invoice. Instead, you will write it off to bad debt.

STEP 1. Open the **Chart of Accounts** from the *Accounting* option in the *Left Navigation Bar*.

STEP 2. Click the **New** button.

STEP 3. Create a new **Expenses** account called **Bad Debts**, as shown in Figure 5-29.

STEP 4. Click **Save**.

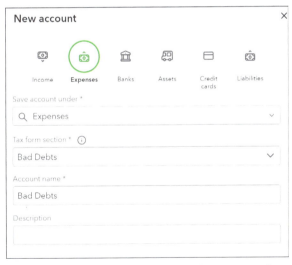

FIGURE 5-29: *Add a Bad Debts Expense to the Chart of Accounts*

FIGURE 5-30: *The Bad Debts Service item*

STEP 5. Open the **Products and Services** list under *Sales* in the *Left Navigation Bar*.

STEP 6. Click **New**.

STEP 7. Create a new **Service** called **Bad Debts** as shown in Figure 5-30. Note that the *Income Account* points to the **Bad Debts** expense. This item is **Nontaxable**.

STEP 8. If you also need a Bad Debts item for taxable sales, change the green button to **Save and New**, then repeat the previous step to create a second **Bad Debts—Taxable** item. Be sure to make the *Sales Tax Category* **Taxable**. We will not do this step now.

STEP 9. Click **Save and Close.**

Apply a Bad Debt Credit Memo

Once the initial setup is done, you can follow the below steps any time you need to zero out an uncollectible invoice.

STEP 10. Open **Kookies by Kathy's** Customer record, then choose **Credit Memo** from the *New Transaction* button. Alternatively, you could select **Credit Memo** from the *+New* button and enter **Kookies by Kathy** in the *Customer* field.

STEP 11. Use **today's date**.

> **TIP:**
>
> If you are cleaning up old Accounts Receivable from past years, it is a common practice to date these adjusting entries on the first day of the fiscal year (usually January 1 of the current year). That way it is easy to identify adjusting entries to correct past history.

STEP 12. Fill out the *Credit Memo* as shown in Figure 5-31.

STEP 13. Enter **Bad Debts** in the *Product/Service* field, and **75** for the *Rate*.

STEP 14. Click **Save and Close.**

STEP 15. Create a $0 payment to apply this bad debt credit memo to the open invoice using the steps in the section about *Recording and Applying Credit Memos* on page 207.

FIGURE 5-31: *Write off a bad debt with a Credit Memo*

> **NOTE:**
>
> If the original sale was taxable, you already paid sales tax on the sale. To compensate, you would use the **Bad Debts—Taxable** item in the credit memo.
>
> By making this Bad Debts line item taxable, QuickBooks Online adds the sales tax to the credit memo, and reduces your next sales tax payment by that amount.

Automatically Applying Credit Memos

On page 198, we configured the *Account and Settings* to turn off the feature that automatically applies credits to open invoices. Let's take a moment to see how QuickBooks Online behaves when that automation is left on.

When QuickBooks Online sees both a $75 open invoice and a $75 credit memo, it applies the credit and closes the invoice for you, as shown in Figure 5-32.

On Kookies by Kathy's transaction list, note the automatically-created **Payment** is marked *Created by QB Online to Link Credits to Charges*. If you open the payment you will see the credit memo applied as a payment to the invoice, as normal.

FIGURE 5-32: *An automatic payment applying a credit memo to close an invoice*

> **THE ACCOUNTING BEHIND THE SCENES:**
>
> When you use the Bad Debt item on a credit memo, it decreases (credits) **Accounts Receivable** and increases (debits) the **Bad Debts expense**. If sales tax is involved, it also decreases (debits) the **Sales Tax Liability**.
>
> | TRANSACTION TYPE | NAME | MEMO/DESCRIPTION | ACCOUNT | DEBIT | CREDIT |
> |---|---|---|---|---|---|
> | Credit Memo | Kookies by Kathy | | Accounts Receivable (A/R) | | $75.00 |
> | | | Bad Debts | Bad Debts | $75.00 | |
> | | | | | $75.00 | $75.00 |

Customer Tools

These features extend your ability to work with customers in QuickBooks Online.

Delayed Charges and Delayed Credits

Delayed Charges is a sales form used when you provide a service or product throughout the month, but only invoice the customer at the end of the period for all accumulated charges.

Delayed charges work best when the *Service Date* field is turned on, as discussed on page 98.

Delayed Credits work exactly the same way, but accumulate credit memos throughout the month to pay open invoices all at once.

HANDS-ON PRACTICE

Craig's Landscaping does weekly gardening maintenance for the Sonnenschein Family Store. Instead of paying at the time of service, they accumulate the weekly charges and invoice for all of them at the end of the month.

STEP 1. Using the *+New* button, open a **Delayed Charge** (see Figure 5-33).

STEP 2. Select **Sonnenschein Family Store** as the *Customer* (try typing **S-o-n** instead of scrolling).

STEP 3. Copy the **Delayed Charge Date** into the *Service Date* field (if your *Service Date* field is not showing, turn it on in the **Sales** settings in *Account and Settings*, as described on page 98).

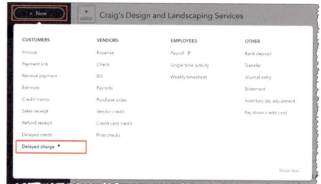

FIGURE 5-33: Create a new Delayed Charge

STEP 4. Fill in the form for **1** hour of **Gardening** at **$25** as shown in Figure 5-34.

> **TIP:**
>
> The *Delayed Charge Date* will show the date the service was provided when you view the charges on transaction lists. Copying the date into the *Service Date* field on the *Product/Service* row will display the service date on the monthly invoice so that it's easy to tell when each charge was accrued.

STEP 5. Click **Save and New** to open a second *Delayed Charge*.

STEP 6. Enter the **Sonnenschein Family Store** again.

STEP 7. Change the *Delayed Charge Date* to **one week from today**.

STEP 8. Repeat steps 3 and 4 to create an identical gardening charge, then click **Save and Close**.

STEP 9. Open the **Sonnenschein Family Store** Customer record, and view the two **Charge** rows at the top of their transaction list (see Figure 5-35).

Alternatively, the two delayed charges also can be seen in the *All Sales Center*, labeled **Charge**.

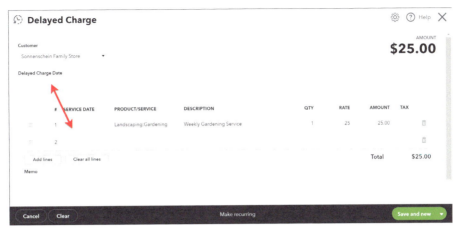

FIGURE 5-34: *Create two Delayed Charges, one week apart*

FIGURE 5-35: *Two Delayed Charges on the Customer transaction list*

STEP 10. On the right of either of the **Charge** line items, click the blue **Create Invoice** link.

You can also choose **Invoice** from the green *New Transaction* button.

STEP 11. When the *Invoice* opens, one of the two delayed charges will appear in the drawer on the right. Click **Add All** to add the rest of the charges, as shown in Figure 5-36.

STEP 12. Click in the *Invoice Date* field (but not on the calendar) and type the letter **H** to jump to the last day of the month (because "H" is the last letter of the word "montH").

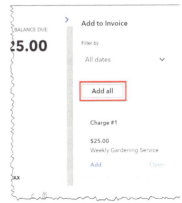

FIGURE 5-36: *Add all Delayed Charges to the invoice*

STEP 13. Look at the *Service Dates* of both line items. If you would like them in chronological order, click on the **9-dot "waffles"** on the left of the rows and drag the earliest date to the top.

STEP 14. When your invoice looks like Figure 5-37, click **Save and Close**.

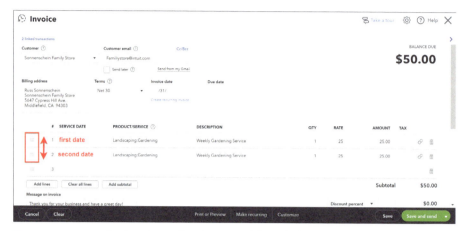

FIGURE 5-37: *An invoice collecting two delayed charges*

STEP 15. On the Sonnenschein Family Store's transaction list, the two *Charges* are now **Closed** and a new **Invoice** shows the sum of the two charges, as shown in Figure 5-38.

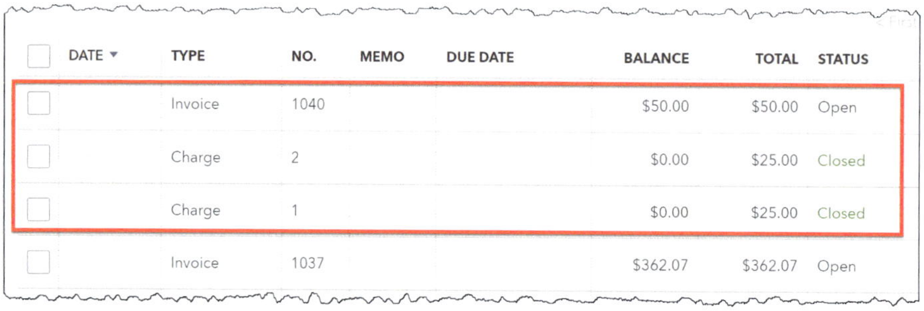

DATE	TYPE	NO.	MEMO	DUE DATE	BALANCE	TOTAL	STATUS
	Invoice	1040			$50.00	$50.00	Open
	Charge	2			$0.00	$25.00	Closed
	Charge	1			$0.00	$25.00	Closed
	Invoice	1037			$362.07	$362.07	Open

FIGURE 5-38: *The Delayed Charges are closed and a new monthly invoice combines all totals*

Creating Customer Statements

Customer Statements provide a summary of the activity for a credit customer during a specific period of time. There are three *Statement Types*:

- **Balance Forward** shows the customer balance as of the *Start Date*, and all transactions that occurred until the *End Date*.
- **Open Item** shows all unpaid invoices after the *Statement Date*.
- **Transaction Statement** lists invoices and credit memos, with the *Total Amount* invoiced and the *Total Received*.

The **Balance Forward** and **Transaction Statement** both give the option of including only open transactions, overdue transactions, or all transactions during the date range.

It's a good idea to preview and experiment with the statement types, the customer balance status, and the date ranges until you get the reports you prefer.

HANDS-ON PRACTICE

Craig's Landscaping only emails statements to customers who have open balances, but they do like to include the entire transaction history for the year.

STEP 1. From the *+New* button click **Statement** to open the *Create Statements* window, as shown in Figure 5-39.

STEP 2. Confirm that **Balance Forward** appears in the *Statement Type* (see Figure 5-40).

STEP 3. Use **today's date** in the *Statement Date* field.

STEP 4. Leave **Open** selected in the *Customer Balance Status*.

FIGURE 5-39: *Choose Statement on the +New menu*

STEP 5. Set the *Start Date* to **1/1** (press the letter **Y**, the first letter in "Year").

STEP 6. Set the *End Date* to **today** (press the letter **T**, the first letter in "Today").

You need to include a *Statement Date* and a *date range*, because the *Statement Date* is the "current" date on the *Statement*, while the date range filters the transactions shown.

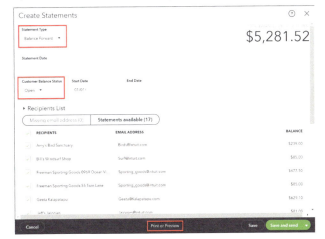

STEP 7. Click **Apply**.

STEP 8. The *Recipients List* shows all customers who qualify under the selected parameters.

FIGURE 5-40: *Create Statements window*

If any customers are missing email addresses, you can enter them here, but it is a best practice to edit the customer record so that you keep the information permanently on file.

STEP 9. Click **Print or Preview** in the *black bar* at the bottom of the window.

STEP 10. While you could **Print** the statements from here to snail-mail to customers, most companies elect to send them via email instead.

After previewing the statements in the *Print Preview* window (see Figure 5-41), click the **Close** button.

STEP 11. Normally, you would click **Save and Send** to send the statements by email. Because this is a sample company, change the green button to **Save and Close**.

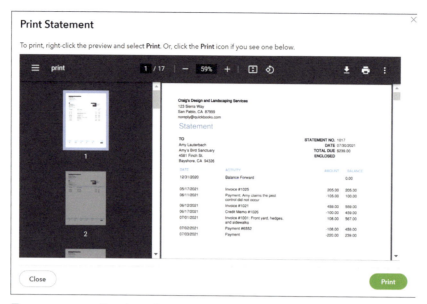

FIGURE 5-41: *Preview of statements that match the criteria*

STEP 12. To view the statements, go to *Sales* in the *Left Navigation Bar* and select **All Sales**. Use the *Filter* to view transactions of the *Type* **Statements**, then click **Apply.** Alternatively, you can also see the statements for a single customer by using the *Filter* inside each customer's transaction list.

Be sure to click the blue **Clear Filter/View All** link to return to the unfiltered list.

> **TIP:**
>
> If you make changes to any of the transactions on the statement, those updates will be reflected the next time you view it.

Sending Payment Reminders

Instead of manually sending Statements, consider sending a ***Payment Reminder***. You can manually initiate reminder emails, or turn on QuickBooks Online's feature to automatically notify customers about upcoming or late invoices.

A payment reminder can be initiated from the drop-down arrow to the right of any open invoice, as shown in Figure 5-42.

FIGURE 5-42: *Send an invoice reminder any time*

You can also **Batch Send Reminders** from any invoice list, such as the *Invoices Center* or a *Customer Transaction List*, as shown in Figure 5-43.

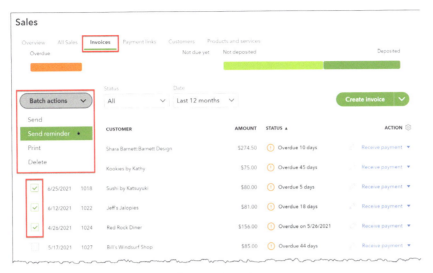

FIGURE 5-43: *Send Reminders in a batch*

HANDS-ON PRACTICE

Instead of manually sending **Payment Reminders** every month, Craig's Landscaping would like to automate the process.

STEP 1. Open *Account and Settings* from the *Gear*, and go to the **Sales** settings. Scroll down and click on **Reminders**.

STEP 2. Turn **On** the slider for **Automatic Invoice Reminders**.

STEP 3. Click on **Reminder 1**, then change the slider to **On**.

STEP 4. Note that you can change the number of days before or after the invoice's due date for the reminder to be sent.

STEP 5. You may further customize the subject line and the body of the email so that it reflects your company's branding and style. The content in brackets pulls in customer's company name, or invoice number. These fields should not be edited, although they can be removed.

STEP 6. Review Figure 5-44 to make sure it matches your screen.

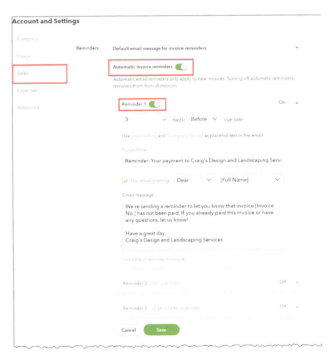

FIGURE 5-44: *Scheduling the Reminder Email*

STEP 7. Let's add a second reminder in case the customer doesn't pay the invoice. Click **Reminder 2**, and turn on the slider. Set the reminder to send **7 days After** the due date, as shown in Figure 5-45.

STEP 8. Consider using a third reminder 30 or 60 days after the due date, to follow up with overdue invoices.

> **TIP:**
>
> You can also type in your desired number instead of choosing from the drop-down list.

STEP 9. Click **Save** at the bottom of the *Reminders* section to accept the changes.

STEP 10. Click **Done** to close *Account and Settings*.

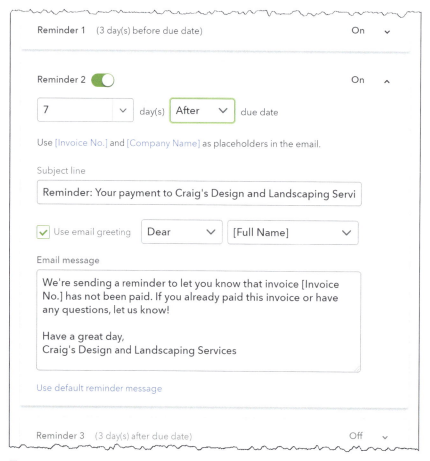

FIGURE 5-45: *Two automatic payment reminders*

> **IMPORTANT!**
>
> When you turn on automatic payment reminders, the settings apply to all invoices for every customer. There is no way to customize or exclude specific circumstances.

Adding Late Fees

You can also add **Late Fees** to your customers' overdue invoices automatically. Once this feature is turned on in *Account and Settings* under *Sales*, fees will calculate automatically, but you can turn off the option manually on a customer-by-customer basis.

As you can see in Figure 5-46, late fees are completely flexible. You can apply flat fees or a percentage of the open balance. You can also accrue them just once, every month, or every day.

If you automatically apply late fees, it is good courtesy to add that policy to your invoices using the *Message* box (see *Customizing Sales Forms* on page 78).

When you turn on late fees, it only applies to new invoices; it will not update existing overdue invoices.

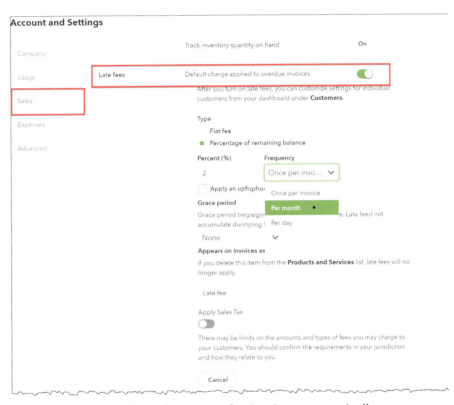

FIGURE 5-46: *Add Late Fees to overdue invoices automatically.*

To manage late fees for a specific customer, go to the *Late Fees tab* in their Customer record. There you can disable the automatic entry, or customize their terms, as shown in Figure 5-47.

If you would rather apply late fees manually on a case-by-case basis, create a new **Income** account in the *Chart of Accounts* called **Late Fee Income**, and a new **Service** on the *Products and Services List* called **Late Fees** that points to the new Income account. Then add an additional line on existing invoices, or create a new invoice for the fees.

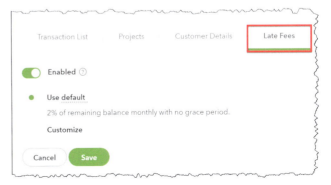

FIGURE 5-47: *Manage Late Fees customer by customer*

ADVANCED ACCOUNTS PAYABLE WORKFLOWS

In Chapter 4, we looked at the common workflows for recording vendor purchases. In this section we will also look at common but infrequent accounts payable transactions including vendor credits and refunds, bounced payments, and vendor deposits.

Recording and Applying Vendor Credits

This section covers how to handle money you receive back from your vendors. If you return a product or are not satisfied with a service, the vendor may *credit* your account.

When you receive a *Vendor Credit*, this reduces the amount you owe on your next bill.

Creating Vendor Credits

When a vendor credits your account for an unsatisfactory service or a returned product, record the transaction in the *Vendor Credit* window using the same expense account or item purchased, and then apply it as a payment to an open bill.

Another common use for vendor credits is when a vendor offers a *discount* for early payment. Some vendors utilize **Early Payment Discount Terms** such as **2% 10 Net 30**, which translates to "if you pay within 10 days instead of waiting until the bill is due 30 days from now, we'll give you a 2% discount in appreciation."

While QuickBooks Online doesn't have these terms built in, you can use a vendor credit for the early payment discount, and then pay the remaining bill. These credits typically appear on the Chart of Accounts as a *contra account* under Cost of Goods, reducing the cost of materials or services purchased.

> **TIP:**
>
> If a **Vendor Credit** is for the return of an item or because of dissatisfaction with a service, use the same item or service from the original bill. In your reports you would then see a reduction (credit) of that **Cost of Goods Sold, Inventory Asset,** or **Expense** account.

HANDS-ON PRACTICE

Craig has an open bill for $205 with Norton Lumber and Building Materials. Today he had to go in and return a broken pump, so the supplier gave him a credit towards his next bill. While he is there, the manager agrees to change his payment terms to 1% 10 Net 30, which means that while Craig has 30 days to pay, if he pays within 10 days, he'll get a 1% discount off his bill. Craig is happy ... it's not much of a savings, but every penny counts if he can pay early!

You will create two vendor credits and apply them to the unpaid Norton Lumber bill.

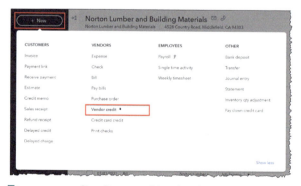

FIGURE 5-48: *Create a Vendor Credit*

STEP 1. From the *+New* button, choose **Vendor Credit** (see Figure 5-48).

STEP 2. Fill in the *Vendor Credit* information for **Norton Lumber and Building Materials** as shown in Figure 5-49. Note that you are using the bottom *Item Details* grid to credit a product;

you may need to click the *triangle* to expand the section. This will also reduce the inventory count on the item.

STEP 3. Enter **Return Broken Fountain Pump** in the *Description* field, so that you can remember the business activity.

STEP 4. Click **Save and New** to record the *Vendor Credit* and start a second one.

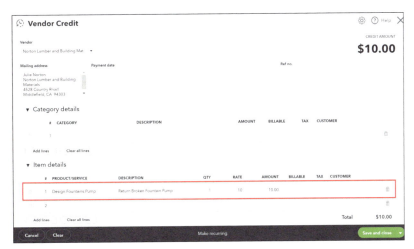

FIGURE 5-49: *Creating a Vendor Credit to return a product*

Next, we will create a vendor credit that includes a new **Purchase Discounts** account. This *Cost of Goods Sold* contra account will separate out vendor discounts on a separate line on your Profit and Loss Report, to distinguish the actual cost of your products and how much you saved by paying early.

STEP 5. Create a new **Vendor Credit** and select **Norton Lumber** in the *Vendor* field.

STEP 6. In the *Category* field, click **+Add New**. Create a new *Account* as shown in Figure 5-50. Click **Save and Close**.

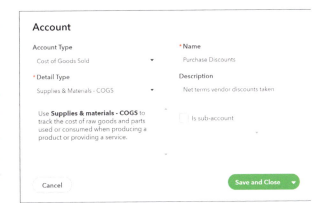

Note that the layout of this account setup window is different than the one we worked with in earlier chapters. This is the former design of the Chart of Accounts creation window, and an example of how QBO evolves over time.

FIGURE 5-50: *Create a new Cost of Goods Sold account for the Purchase Discount*

STEP 7. Back in the *Vendor Credit* form, click in the *Description* field and type **1% 10 Net 30 discount for $205 bill**, so that you remember the transaction.

STEP 8. Craig's unpaid bill is for $205. In the *Amount* field, type **205*.01**, then press **Tab**. The field will calculate to **$2.05**.

STEP 9. Compare your screen to Figure 5-51. Scroll down to review the *Item Details* section. Did QuickBooks Online automatically add a **Pump** in the *Item Details* grid below? If so, your automations to repeat a vendor's most recent transaction are turned on. QBO thought it would help you out by repeating your most recent vendor credit to Norton Lumber.

Click the **Trashcan** to remove the extra line for the pump in the *Item Details* grid.

STEP 10.   Click **Save and Close**.

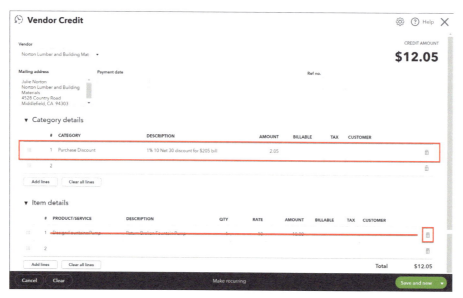

FIGURE 5-51:   *Create a Vendor Credit for the Purchase Discount*

THE ACCOUNTING BEHIND THE SCENES:

When you record a **Vendor Credit** for a discount, QuickBooks Online reduces (debits) **Accounts Payable** and reduces (credits) **Purchase Discounts**, a **Cost of Goods Sold** account.

TRANSACTION TYPE	NAME	MEMO/DESCRIPTION	ACCOUNT	DEBIT	CREDIT
Vendor Credit	Norton Lumber and Building Ma...		Accounts Payable (A/P)	$2.05	
		1% 10 Net 30 discount for $205 ...	Purchase Discount		$2.05
				$2.05	$2.05

Applying Vendor Credits

HANDS-ON PRACTICE

Now that we have two vendor credits, one for returning a product and another for a terms discount, we'll apply the two credits to the bill and pay the balance.

STEP 1.   Navigate to the *Vendors Center*, and open the transaction list for **Norton Lumber and Building Materials** (see Figure 5-52).

STEP 2.   Find the **Bill** for **$205** on the list. Click the drop-down arrow on the far right in the *Action* column, and choose **Mark As Paid**.

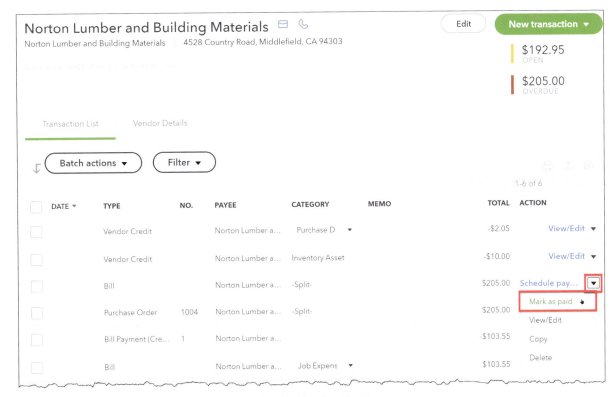

FIGURE 5-52: *Select Mark As Paid to apply the Vendor Credits*

STEP 3. The *Bill Payment* is created, as shown in Figure 5-53. Scroll down and check off the two credits.

STEP 4. The *Amount* field at the top shows the balance of the *Outstanding Transactions* ($205) minus the applied *Credits* ($10 and $2.05). This creates a bill payment for **$192.95**.

STEP 5. Update the *Bank/Credit Account* at the top to pay it with the **Mastercard**.

IMPORTANT!

You can also apply the credit without paying the bill, which will reduce the balance shown in the Vendors Center, mark the bill as partially paid, and keep the bill open to pay it later. To do this, update the *Amount* box at the top to **$0** (since you're not making a payment), and change the *Payment* on the right of the Bill from $205 (the bill balance) to the sum of the credits, **$12.05**.

In other words, you're reducing $12.05 of the bill using the available credits, but not making a payment at the moment.

STEP 6. When your transaction matches Figure 5-53, click **Save and Close**.

STEP 7. You may choose to run a *Bills and Applied Payments Report* as shown on page 186 to see how the vendor credits and payments were applied.

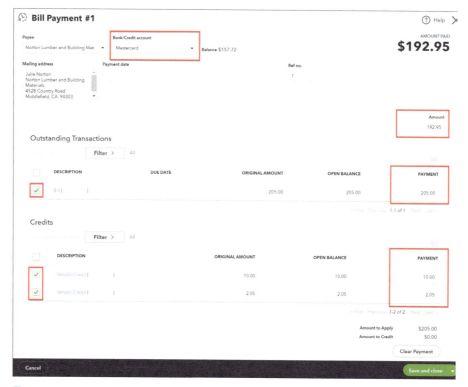

FIGURE 5-53: *Bill Payment window for Norton Lumber with vendor credits applied*

Creating Vendor Refunds

This section covers how to handle money you receive back from your vendors. If you return a product or are not satisfied with a service, the vendor may give you a **Refund**.

When you receive a Refund, the proper way to enter the transaction depends on whether they cut you a check or refunded your credit card, and whether inventory products were involved.

Refunds to a Credit Card

If a vendor refunds a purchase to your credit card, use the **Credit Card Credit** window found under the +*New* button, as shown in Figure 5-54. This window works the same way as the vendor credit, with separate sections for *Category Details* and *Item Details*. The difference is you will see money deposited back to your credit card when you look in the credit card's register.

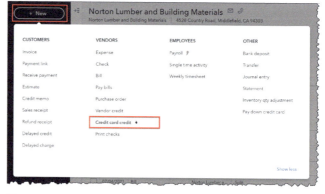

FIGURE 5-54: *Create a new Credit Card Credit*

Refunds by Check for Expenses

If you receive a Vendor refund by check or ACH transaction, record the refund using a **Bank Deposit** transaction. Use the same expense account you used on the original payment to the vendor (see Figure 5-55).

This is the same workflow we used when we added the insurance refund check to a daily bank deposit on page 131, by including it in the *Add Funds To This Deposit* section of the *Bank Deposit*.

Figure 5-55: *Bank Deposits window applying the refund to an expense account*

Refunds Created in the Banking Feed

Vendor refunds can sometimes be recorded when they appear in the Banking Feed. See *Entering Refunds* on page 264 for more information.

Refunds by Check for an Inventory Product

When you receive a refund in the form of a check for returned products, it's a little more complicated, because the Bank Deposit window only credits Chart of Accounts categories, not the Products and Services list. When you are tracking inventory, the method above doesn't take returned items out of stock.

The solution is to make use of a vendor credit, but with one extra step as shown in Figure 5-56. We're not crediting Accounts Payable to apply to a future bill; instead we need to add the transaction to Undeposited Funds to include in the next bank deposit.

After entering the returned product in the *Item Details* grid at the bottom of the *Vendor Credit* window, add an extra entry in the top *Category Details* grid to offset the product cost as a negative number. Use **Undeposited Funds** (Payments to Deposit) for the *Category*, which will put the refund in *Bank Deposit* window to make it available to be combined with any other deposits for the day, and match the Banking Feed.

The *Vendor Credit* itself equals **$0**, as shown in Figure 5-56.

Figure 5-56: *Use a Vendor Credit form for a refund on an inventory product, offset to Undeposited Funds*

When it is time to make the daily Bank Deposit, you'll see the refund in the list, as shown in Figure 5-57.

FIGURE 5-57: *Add the Vendor Refund to the daily Bank Deposit*

You can also see the Pump removed from inventory by looking at the *Products and Services list*, clicking the **drop-down arrow** on the far right of the *Pump*, and selecting **Run Report** (see Figure 5-58).

FIGURE 5-58: *A report showing the returned item deducted from inventory*

THE ACCOUNTING BEHIND THE SCENES

This creative use of a Vendor Credit bypasses Accounts Payable by decreasing (crediting) **Inventory Asset** and increasing (debiting) **Undeposited Funds**.

TRANSACTION TYPE	NAME	MEMO/DESCRIPTION	ACCOUNT	DEBIT	CREDIT
Vendor Credit	Tim Philip Masonry		Accounts Payable (A/P)	$0.00	
		refund for broken Fountain Pump	Inventory Asset		$10.00
		refund for broken pump	Undeposited Funds	$10.00	
				$10.00	$10.00

What To Do If Your Check Bounces

If you write a check to a vendor that overdraws your account and your bank returns the check, follow these steps:

1. If your balance is sufficient for the check to clear, tell the vendor to redeposit the check.

2. If your balance is not sufficient, consider other ways of paying the vendor, such as using a credit card. Alternatively, negotiate delayed payment terms with your vendor.

3. When the bank sends you the notice that your check was returned, there may be an NSF charge from your bank. Enter an expense in the bank account register for **Bank Charges** using the date the bank charged your account, similarly to the expense we created when your customer bounced a check on page 218.

4. If your vendor charges you a bounced check fee, you will need to replace the payment with a new one that includes the fees:
   a. First, **Void** the original check.
   b. If you are using accounts payable, create a new *Bill*, and code the extra charge to the **Bank Charges** expense account (alternatively, you can also add this line to the original bill). Make a replacement payment that applies to both the original bill and the additional bill with the fees.
   c. If you are not using bills, but simply writing checks or creating expenses, create the new payment that includes an additional line item for the fees.

Managing Loans

When you receive a loan from a financial institution, it is recorded as a liability on your Balance Sheet. Loans can be received in cash to increase your checking account, or they may be disbursed directly to purchase vehicles or equipment, increasing your Fixed Assets.

Every time you make a payment, the payment must be split into line items to pay off the loan principal, interest, and escrow as appropriate.

Setting up Loans

There are one-time steps to set up a loan in QuickBooks Online. You must add the **Loan Liability** account, the **Fixed Asset** account, and the **Interest Paid** accounts to the Chart of Accounts, then create a Journal Entry to set up the initial financial transaction.

For this example, Craig's Landscaping purchases a new trailer to haul their equipment for $20,000. They write a check for a $5,000 down payment, and take out a loan with National Bank for $15,000.00.

STEP 1. From the *Accounting* option in the *Left Navigation Bar*, open the **Chart of Accounts**.

STEP 2. Click the green **New** button in the upper right.

STEP 3. Click on **Liabilities**, then choose **Long Term Liabilities** in the *Save Account Under* field (see Figure 5-59).

STEP 4. The *Tax Form Section* is **Notes Payable**.

STEP 5. In the *Account Name* field, enter **Trailer Loan**. In the *Description* field, type **Loan for trailer**.

STEP 6. Click **Save**.

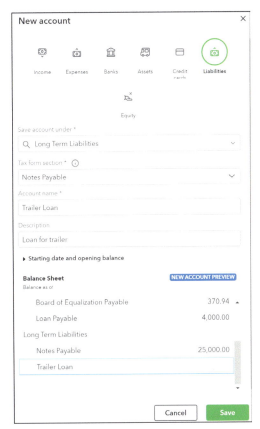

FIGURE 5-59: *Set up the Long Term Liability for the Trailer Loan*

Step 7. Click the **New** button to add another account.

Step 8. Change the *Account Type* to **Assets**. In the *Save Account Under* field, select **Fixed Assets**.

Step 9. Update the *Tax Form Section* to **Machinery & Equipment.**

Step 10. Change the *Account Name* field to **Trailer**. In the *Description* field, type **New equipment trailer**.

Step 11. When your *New Account* window looks like Figure 5-60, click **Save**.

Step 12. Many times there is already a default Interest Expense account in your file. Use the *Filter by Name* box at the top of the list to check to see whether your QuickBooks Online file already has an *Expense* account that you can use, such as **Interest Paid**, **Interest Expense**, or **Business Loan Interest**. If yours does not, create a new Expense account as shown in Figure 5-61.

Step 13. Your Chart of Accounts will now have new categories for the **Trailer** in Fixed Assets and the **Trailer Loan** in Long Term Liabilities (you will have to scroll to find them, or enter **Trailer** in the *Filter by Name* field at the top of the list). The new **Interest Expense** is further down.

Step 14. To enter the $5,000 check for the down payment, create a new **Check** from the *+New* button.

Step 15. Make out the check to **Diego's Road Warrior Bodyshop** in the *Payee* field.

Step 16. In the *Category* field, select **Trailer**.

Step 17. In the *Description*, type **Down payment for trailer**. Press **Tab**.

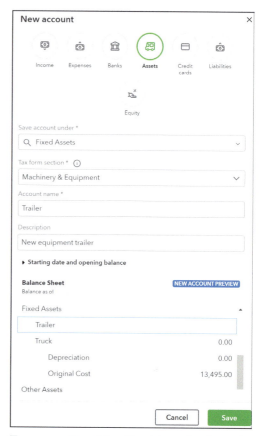

Figure 5-60: *New Fixed Asset for the trailer*

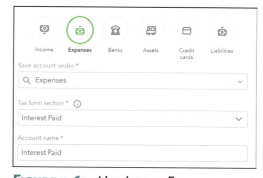

Figure 5-61: *New Interest Expense account*

DID YOU KNOW?

Many bookkeepers prefer to track the original cost and depreciation of each Fixed Asset separately using sub-accounts. For example, look at the Truck shown in Figure 5-60. The purchase transactions for the vehicle are categorized to Original Cost, and the accountant's year-end Depreciation entry has its own contra-account. This way, the Balance Sheet provides insight into the remaining **Net Book Value (NBV)** of your Fixed Asset at any point in time.

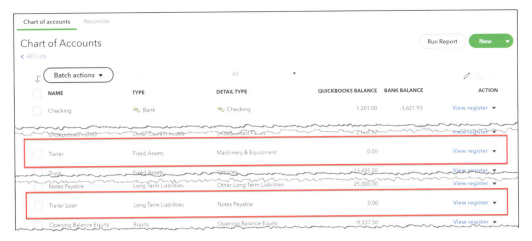

FIGURE 5-62: *The Chart of Accounts with new categories for the Trailer Fixed Asset and Loan Liability*

STEP 18. The *Amount* is **5000**. Press **Tab**.

STEP 19. When completed, your screen should look like Figure 5-63.

STEP 20. Click **Save and Close**.

FIGURE 5-63: *The down payment for the Trailer loan.*

STEP 21. To set up the loan, make a new **Journal Entry** using the *+New* button.

We will use a journal entry because the funding is coming from an external lender, and the money is moving between balance sheet accounts.

STEP 22. In the first line, enter **Trailer** in the *Account* field.

STEP 23. In the *Debits* column, enter **15000**, then press **Tab** twice.

STEP 24. Type **Trailer loan from bank** in the *Description* field.

STEP 25. In the *Name* box, enter **National Bank**. You may need to use the *+Add New* option at the top of the *Name list* set it up as a new **Vendor** on the fly (be sure to choose Vendor!).

STEP 26. On line 2, select **Trailer Loan**. The *Credits* and *Description* fields will autofill. Add **National Bank** as the *Name* on this row as well.

STEP 27. When your screen matches Figure 5-64, click **Save and Close**.

FIGURE 5-64: *Create a Journal Entry to set up the opening balances for the Fixed Asset and the Loan*

When you look at the *Chart of Accounts* or run a *Balance Sheet report*, you'll now see $20,000 in the Trailer's Fixed Asset account ($5,000 down payment from checking plus $15,000 from the loan), and $15,000 in the Trailer Loan.

THE ACCOUNTING BEHIND THE SCENES:

Setting up a loan increases (debits) the **Bank** account or **Fixed Asset** account, and increases (credits) the loan's **Long Term Liability** account.

TRANSACTION TYPE	NAME	MEMO/DESCRIPTION	ACCOUNT	DEBIT	CREDIT
Journal Entry		Trailer loan from bank	Trailer	$15,000.00	
		Trailer loan from bank	Trailer Loan		$15,000.00
				$15,000.00	$15,000.00
				$15,000.00	$15,000.00

Making Loan Payments

The monthly loan payment comes from the checking account, and is split between principal and interest. This split will vary every month. Traditional loans begin with a low principal payment and high interest. When you are close to paying the loan off, the payments will be almost all principal with low interest.

Most lenders provide monthly statements with the breakdown, or an amortization schedule. Be sure to look for the *previous* split, and not the *upcoming month's* split . . . some loan statements are tricky to read!

If you create a **Recurring Transaction** every month to remind you to create the payment, you will need to update each transaction with the proper breakdown. Reconcile your loan statement every month to confirm your accuracy.

HANDS-ON PRACTICE

Every month, Craig's Landscaping makes their $500 monthly payment as an automatic payment from their Checking account. National Bank considers this an ACH payment ("automated clearing house," or an e-check).

To enter the monthly payment in QuickBooks Online, create an *Expense* and split it into two lines, one for the principal and one for the interest.

STEP 1. From the *+New* button, select **Expense**. Create the transaction to **National Bank** as shown in Figure 5-65.

STEP 2. Add a new *Payment Method* for **ACH** on the fly.

STEP 3. Enter the **Trailer Loan** on the first line, and enter **Principal payment** in the *Description*.

STEP 4. Enter **450** in the *Amount*.

STEP 5. On the second line, use the **Interest Paid** *Category*, and type **Interest Payment** in the *Description*. Press **Tab** to move to the *Amount* field, and enter **50**.

STEP 6. When your *Expense* matches Figure 5-65, click **Save and Close**.

FIGURE 5-65: *An Expense for the monthly loan payment, split into Principal and Interest*

THE ACCOUNTING BEHIND THE SCENES:

Making loan payments decreases (credits) the **Bank** account, decreases (debits) the loan **Liability**, and increases (debits) the **Interest Expense**.

TRANSACTION TYPE	NAME	MEMO/DESCRIPTION	ACCOUNT	DEBIT	CREDIT
Expense	National Bank		Checking		$500.00
		Principal payment	Trailer Loan	$450.00	
		Interest payment	Interest Paid	$50.00	
				$500.00	$500.00

Paying Sales Tax

Many QuickBooks Online users need to collect sales tax each time they sell products and certain types of services. In Chapter 3, you learned how to collect sales tax as you make each sale. At the end of each month, quarter, or year (depending on your sales volume) **Sales Tax** needs to be paid to the appropriate state or local agencies.

To correctly pay your sales tax liability, be sure to use the **Sales Tax Center**. When you pay your sales tax, do not create a *Check* or *Expense*, or pull it in through the *Banking Feed*, because the payment may not affect the Sales Tax Liability or show properly on the *Sales Tax Liability* reports.

The *Sales Tax Center* also provides a place to make necessary adjustments for discounts, interest, penalties or rounding, to match QuickBooks Online's calculations to the amount your sales tax agency says you owe.

If you are not familiar with the sales tax rates or reporting requirements in your area, consult your state's Department of Revenue, your local QuickBooks Online ProAdvisor, or an accountant for guidance.

HANDS-ON PRACTICE

Craig's Landscaping files sales tax returns in two states, California and Arizona. In this example, we will view reports and process returns for the previous month.

STEP 1. Click on **Taxes** in the *Left Navigation Bar* to go to the *Sales Tax Center*. If it is not set up, turn back to *Setting Up Sales Tax* on page 73 and repeat the steps there before moving on to Step 2.

STEP 2. The *Sales Tax Center* displays boxes for each state including taxes currently due.

STEP 3. Click on the box for **California**. Underneath you can see the sales taxes currently due, as shown in Figure 5-66—your screen may vary.

STEP 4. To see past periods, expand the date range by changing *Tax Period Due* up to a year back.

STEP 5. Buttons in the Sales Tax Center allow you to update your **Sales Tax Settings**, explore **Economic Nexus**, and run sales tax reports.

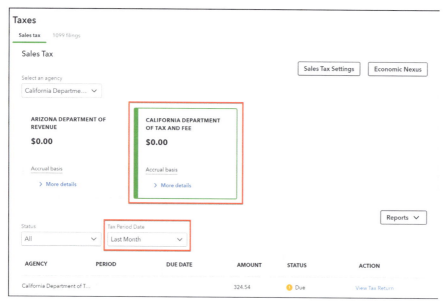

FIGURE 5-66: *The Sales Tax Center (your screen may vary)*

STEP 6. At the bottom you can view taxes currently due. Find the month with $324.54, and click the **View Tax Return** link in the *Action* column.

STEP 7. The *Review Your Sales Tax* window shown in Figure 5-67 contains instructions for filing your sales taxes on your state's website. There is also a blue link to **Add an Adjustment** if you need to change the amount because you made prepayments, have rounding errors, or need to accommodate other variances.

> **IMPORTANT!**
>
> If you **increase** the amount of the tax, you are paying more than you collected. The variance will go to an **Expense** account. If you **decrease** the amount of the tax, you are remitting less than you collected. The difference will go to an **Income** account.

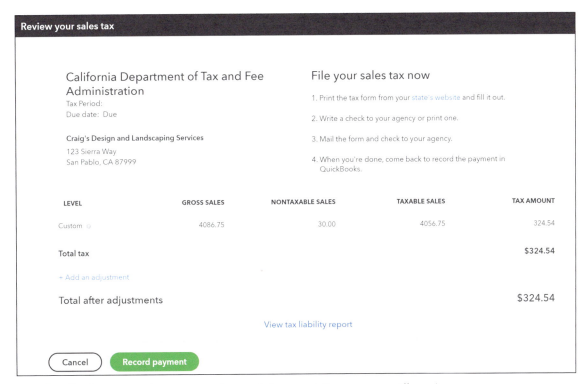

FIGURE 5-67: *Review your sales tax to make sure it is correct (your screen will vary)*

STEP 8. Click the **View Tax Liability Report** link to see how QuickBooks Online came up with the number. This summary report shows gross sales, divided into non-taxable and taxable sales. Drill into any of the numbers for a detailed breakdown.

Craig's Design and Landscaping Services
Sales Tax Liability Report

TAX NAME	GROSS TOTAL	NON-TAXABLE	TAXABLE AMOUNT	TAX AMOUNT
▼ California Department of Tax and Fee Administration				
California	4,086.75	30.00	4,056.75	324.54
Total for California Department of Tax and Fee Administration				$324.54

FIGURE 5-68: *The Sales Tax Liability Report (your report will vary)*

STEP 9. Click your browser's **Back button** to return to the *Review Your Sales Tax* window.

STEP 10. Click the green **Record Payment** button. The *Record Payment* window opens, as shown in Figure 5-69.

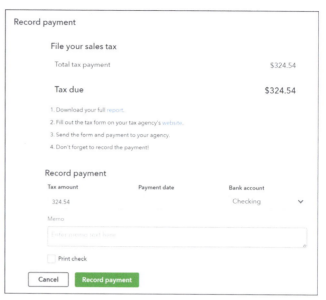

STEP 11. Use the **20th of the current month** in the *Payment Date* field. This field is the date of your actual sales tax payment.

STEP 12. Choose **Checking** for the *Bank Account*. If you were printing and mailing a check, you would click **Print Check**.

Remember that the *Sales Tax Center* does not make the payment for you. You still need to log in to your state's Department of Revenue website to submit your forms and payment.

FIGURE 5-69: *Pay Sales Tax window (your screen may vary)*

STEP 13. Click **Record Payment** to finish. A *Return Paid* window appears.

STEP 14. Click **Back to Sales Tax Center** to continue.

After you record the sales tax payment, QuickBooks Online will create a special type of check called a **Sales Tax Payment** in your checking account for the total tax due to each sales tax agency (vendor), as shown in Figure 5-70. This transaction cannot be edited, but you can delete it and start over.

When the transaction clears your bank, it will Match in the Banking Feed.

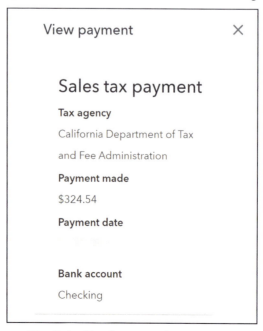

FIGURE 5-70: *The Sales Tax Payment (your screen may vary)*

> **THE ACCOUNTING BEHIND THE SCENES:**
>
> Paying Sales Tax decreases (credits) the **Bank** account and decreases (debits) the **Sales Tax Liability**.

REVIEW QUESTIONS

Comprehension Questions

1. When would you choose to give a customer a Refund Receipt? What form of payment should you use?
2. How can Credit Memos be used?
3. What are two types of transactions that CANNOT be made recurring? Why not?
4. Why is it important to use the Sales Tax Center to make Sales Tax Payments?

Multiple Choice

Select the best answer(s) for each of the following:

1. Customer Statements:
    a. Provide a summary of all accounts receivable activity for a Customer during the period you specify.
    b. Are not available in QuickBooks Online.
    c. Automatically assess and calculate finance charges for overdue accounts without any user action.
    d. Should only be created and mailed if the customer's balance is over $500.

2. When you purchase a vehicle, you should code the purchase to:
    a. An Expense account.
    b. A Liability account.
    c. A Current Asset account.
    d. A Fixed Asset account.

3. What is the best way to write off a bad debt?
    a. Delete the original invoice.
    b. Create a credit memo using a *Bad Debt* item and apply the credit to the past due invoice.
    c. Create a credit memo for the amount of the past due invoice and retain the available credit.
    d. Any of the above.

4. In which of the following situations would you create a Credit Memo?
    a. You need to record a cancelled order that has already been invoiced but not paid.
    b. A customer returns merchandise and wants the return credited to a future invoice.

c. An old invoice is on the books in a past period, and it will never be paid.
d. Any of the above.

5. The Audit Log:
   a. Can be turned on and off.
   b. Only shows the most recent changes to a transaction.
   c. Is found on the +New menu.
   d. Tracks all QuickBooks Online activity.

6. You need to issue a refund to a customer. The customer originally paid with a Visa card. How do you issue the credit?
   a. Pay the refund with your company's credit card.
   b. Pay the refund using any method of payment.
   c. Pay the refund by issuing a refund check.
   d. Pay the refund through the customer's credit card.

7. Your company policy is overdue invoices should incur a one-time $5 finance charge. Where is the best place to set this value in QuickBooks Online?
   a. Add $5 to each overdue invoice.
   b. Enter a $5 flat fee in the Late Fees section of Account and Settings.
   c. Create a $5 Service item for Late Fees.
   d. Go to each Customer's record and add a $5 custom Late Fee.

8. Voiding and Deleting transactions both do the following:
   a. Zero out the debits and credits specified by the transaction
   b. Keep a record of the date, number, and detail of the transaction
   c. Completely remove all details of the transaction
   d. Both b and c

9. When a vendor credits your account, you record it in:
   a. An *Expense* form.
   b. A *Bank Deposit* form.
   c. A *Vendor Credit* form.
   d. A *Credit Memo* form.

10. Which is NOT a common mistake people make when processing bounced checks?
    a. Creating a new invoice for the bounced check.
    b. Creating a second invoice for the original product or service.
    c. Categorizing the bounced check as a bank fee.
    d. Not invoicing the client a second time.

11. A past due invoice contains items that were taxed and items that were not taxed. How would you write off this invoice as a bad debt?
    a. Delete the original invoice.
    b. Delete the taxed items from the original invoice and then delete the entire invoice.

c. Create a credit memo with two *Bad Debt* items, the first set to non-taxable with the total of non-taxable items, the second set to taxable with the total of taxable items. Apply this credit memo to the original invoice.

d. Create a credit memo for the taxable amount from the original invoice. Apply the credit memo to the invoice, and then delete the invoice.

12. Which is true about Payment Reminders?
    a. You can only send Payment Reminders to one customer at a time.
    b. You can only send Payment Reminders for one invoice at a time.
    c. You can set up Payment Reminders for specific customers.
    d. Payment Reminders can be automated for all invoices.

13. After issuing a refund by credit card,
    a. The refund waits in undeposited funds until it is batched with the rest of the day's credit card sales in a deposit.
    b. The customer sees a credit on their account.
    c. The checking account is reduced by the amount.
    d. The *Total* field on the refund is 0.00.

14. Which of the following is true?
    a. You can only apply a credit memo to an invoice if the *Credit* amount is equal to the *Amount Due*.
    b. Credit memos must be automatically applied to open invoices.
    c. Credit memos look similar to invoices but perform the opposite function, reducing (debiting) Sales accounts and reducing (crediting) Accounts Receivable.
    d. You should not use a credit memo to write off a bad debt.

15. To make a loan payment, you:
    a. Select the loan liability account in the Chart of Accounts and enter the payment in the register.
    b. Choose Pay Loan from the +New menu.
    c. Use the *Loan Manager* to calculate the interest and principal amounts.
    d. Manually split the payment into principal and interest.

Completion Statements

1. Regarding Refunds: If the customer paid by _____ or _____, you will need to issue a refund check. If the customer paid with a(n) _____ _____, you will need to credit the customer's credit card account.

2. _____ _____ are used to write off bad debt or apply credits to existing invoices.

3. You can _____ _____ an uncollectible invoice as a bad debt.

4. When a customer is late paying an invoice, you can assess _____ _____.

5. A customer _____ is a summary of all activity on an account in a specified period.

ADVANCED TRANSACTIONS—APPLY YOUR KNOWLEDGE

> Log into your **Imagine Photography** class file at qbo.intuit.com.

1. Confirm that all four **Automation Settings** in the *Advanced* tab of *Account and Settings* are **Off**, so that you have to manually apply credit memos and bill payments.

2. **Liz Kildal at First Community Bank** only needed 2.5 of the 3 hours she paid for a Videographer. To reduce the balance on her Invoice, create a **Credit Memo** with **today's date** to write off the 30 minutes (**Qty 0.5**). The *Sales Rep* is **KR**, and the *Tag* is **Corporate**. The **Videographer** service is **not taxable**. The *Class* is **Walnut Creek**. Apply the credit to reduce the open invoice, but don't pay the balance. Print the credit memo.

3. **Shonette Dymond** stops in to the Walnut Creek store and picks up a pack of photo paper every Friday, but if it's busy she hates waiting in line. Because she's the best friend of the owner, Ernest always lets her get away with it. Create four **Delayed Charges**, one on **every Friday of this month**, for a pack of **Photo Paper** with a *Tag* for **Retail** and the **Walnut Creek** *Class*. The product is **Taxable**.

4. Create an **Invoice** dated **the last day of the month** and add all four charges for all the photo paper Shonette Dymond bought throughout the month. The Sales Rep is **MM**. Rearrange the **service dates** so they're in order from earliest to latest. The total should be **$110.25**, including tax. Print the invoice.

5. On the **last Monday of this month**, **Nayo Garcia** brings back one of the **Wood Frames** because it didn't match her sofa. Even though the Imagine Photography's policy is to give store credit on returns, the owner approves a refund. Create a **Refund Receipt** to her **credit card** from **Payments to Deposit**. In the *Description*, type **Refund approved by Ernest**. The *Sales Rep* is **MM**, the *Tag* is **Retail**, and use the **Walnut Creek** *Class*. The total, with tax, is **$16.54**. Print the refund receipt.

6. Jaime Madeira recently paid both of his open invoices with a check for $875, but it bounced. Your bank charged you $21 in NSF fees, and you want Jaime to reimburse you. Create the following new accounts and services, then issue a new Invoice for the bounced check.
    a. In the *Chart of Accounts*, create a new **Service/Fee Income** account.
    b. In the *Products and Services list*, create a new *Service* with the *Name* and *Description* **Bounced Check**. Create a new **Admin** *Category* on the fly. Assign the *Income Account* to **Business Checking (1025)**. The item's *Sales Tax Category* is **Nontaxable**.
    c. In the *Products and Services list*, create a new *Service* with the *Name* and *Description* **NSF Fees**. Add it to the **Admin** *Category*, and assign it to the **Service/Fee Income** *Income Account*. It is **Nontaxable**.
    d. Create a new *Invoice* for the bounced check and fees as shown below, totaling $896. Print the invoice.

INVOICE	FIELDS
CUSTOMER	Madeira Builders
TERMS	Due on Receipt
INVOICE DATE	The 1st day of next month
SALES REP	MM
PRODUCT/SERVICE 1	Bounced Check
AMOUNT	875
CLASS	San Jose
PRODUCT/SERVICE 2	NSF Fees
AMOUNT	21
CLASS	San Jose

TABLE 5-1: *Send an invoice for the bounced check*

7. Make a **Bank Deposit** on the last day of the month. Normally there are other credit card sales, but on that day the only transaction was Nayo's refund. As a result, that day the refunds are higher than the day's credit card sales, so the deposit will be negative, taking money out of the Business Checking (1025) account.

8. Create Customer Statements of the type **Balance Forward** with a *Statement Date* of **the first day of next month** for customers who have an **Open** *Customer Balance Status*. Use a date range of **January 1 of this year** through **the last day of this month**. Print statements for the three customers who have a balance due, and save the statements.

9. Donna Distributing realized they overcharged you on shipping, and is reducing your bill. Enter a **Vendor Credit** for **$10.00**, using the information in the table below.

VENDOR CREDIT	FIELDS
VENDOR NAME	Donna Distributing
PAYMENT DATE	The 3rd day of this month
REF NO.	38-9904c
TAGS	Retail
CATEGORY	Shipping, Freight, and Delivery—COS
DESCRIPTION	Overcharged shipping on paper
AMOUNT	10
CLASS	Walnut Creek

TABLE 5-2: *Add a Vendor Credit for Shipping*

10. Apply the Donna Distributing Vendor Credit to Bill number **38-9904**. Pay the remaining bill for **$182.15** on **the last day of the month** with the **Business Visa (5678)**.

11. You return one of the **San Jose** store's ink cartridges to **Peterson Office Supply**, and they refund **$25** to your **Visa** card, the original form of payment you used for the purchase. Create the following **Credit Card Credit**:

CREDIT CARD CREDIT	FIELDS
VENDOR NAME	Peterson Office Supply
BANK/CREDIT ACCOUNT	Business Visa (5678)
PAYMENT DATE	The 15th of this month
REF NO.	None
CATEGORY	Office Supplies
DESCRIPTION	Returned ink cartridge
AMOUNT	25
CLASS	San Jose

TABLE 5-3: *Credit Card Credit*

12. Now that you found Shonette Dymond's missing invoice from two months ago, you have overdue **sales tax**. Go to the *Taxes Center* and change the date range to **This Year**. Record a payment for **$136.32** as of the **20th of this month** from your **Business Checking (1025)** account.

13. The owner, Ernest Withers, buys a used cargo van for the business to carry gear for photo shoots. He takes out a loan for $25,000 from National Bank, and makes a $5,000 down payment using a cashier's check at the bank. He would like to track the original cost and the depreciation on the vehicle separately, similar to the way the Truck is set up in the Craig's Landscaping sample file in Figure 5-60.
    a. In the *Chart of Accounts*, add a new **Asset**, saved under **Fixed Assets**. The *Tax Form Section* is **Vehicles**. Name the new account **Cargo Van**.
    b. Create two additional Fixed Asset sub-accounts under the Cargo Van, one for **Original Cost** (*Tax Form Section* **Vehicles**) and one for **Depreciation** (*Tax Form Section* **Accumulated Depreciation**).
    c. In the *Chart of Accounts*, edit the *Long Term Liabilities* category called **Long-term Business Loans**. Change its *Tax Form Section* to **Notes Payable**. Rename it **National Bank Cargo Van Loan**.
    d. Record a **Check** for the down payment on the van using the information in Table 5-4:

CHECK	FIELDS
PAYEE	Weathers Auto (add vendor on the fly)
PAYMENT ACCOUNT	Business Checking (1025)
PAYMENT DATE	The 21st of this month
CHECK NO.	12340987
CATEGORY	Cargo Van:Original Cost
DESCRIPTION	2020 Ford Transit
AMOUNT	5000
CLASS	Overhead

TABLE 5-4: *The vehicle down payment*

e. Create a **Journal Entry** to add the Cargo Van Loan and apply it to the Fixed Asset:

JOURNAL ENTRY	FIELDS
JOURNAL DATE	The 21st of this month
JOURNAL NO.	1
LINE 1—ACCOUNT	Cargo Van:Original Cost
LINE 1—DEBITS	25000
LINE 1—DESCRIPTION	2020 Ford Transit Loan
LINE 1—NAME	National Bank
LINE 1—CLASS	Overhead
LINE 2—ACCOUNT	National Bank Cargo Van Loan
LINE 2—CREDITS	25000
LINE 2—DESCRIPTION	2020 Ford Transit Loan
LINE 2—NAME	National Bank
LINE 2—CLASS	Overhead

TABLE 5-5: *The Loan Journal Entry*

14. Create an **Expense** for your first loan payment for **$500** to **National Bank**. The loan is on autopay, so the money will come out of your bank account automatically every month. Save the expense before going on to the next step, but don't close it.

EXPENSE	FIELD
PAYEE	National Bank
PAYMENT ACCOUNT	Business Checking (1025)
PAYMENT DATE	The 21st of next month
PAYMENT METHOD	ACH (add on the fly)
LINE 1—CATEGORY	National Bank Cargo Van Loan
LINE 1—AMOUNT	437.50
LINE 1—CLASS	Overhead
LINE 2—CATEGORY	Interest Paid
LINE 2—AMOUNT	62.50
LINE 2—CLASS	Overhead

TABLE 5-6: *Create the first Loan Payment*

15. Turn the expense into a **Recurring Transaction** of the *Type* **Reminder**. Use the *Description* fields to provide instructions for determining future calculations. In the *Amount* fields, enter **0** as a placeholder. Since the amounts will change every month, keeping the original values may cause data entry errors later.

RECURRING EXPENSE	FIELD
TEMPLATE NAME	NB Cargo Van Loan Payment
TYPE	Reminder
REMIND	5 days before the transaction date
PAYEE	National Bank (should automatically display)
ACCOUNT	Business Checking (1025) (should automatically display)
INTERVAL	Monthly on day 21st of every 1 month
START DATE	The last day of next month (since we already created the first payment)
LINE 1—CATEGORY	National Bank Cargo Van Loan
LINE 1—DESCRIPTION	Total monthly payment is $500
LINE 1—AMOUNT	0
LINE 1—CLASS	Overhead
LINE 2—CATEGORY	Interest Paid
LINE 2—DESCRIPTION	3% Interest
LINE 2—AMOUNT	0
LINE 2—CLASS	Overhead

CHAPTER 6

BANKING AND RECONCILIATION

TOPICS

In this chapter, you will learn about the following topics:

- Transfer Funds Between Accounts (page 255)
- The Banking Feed (page 256)
- Using the Banking Feed for Data Entry (page 260)
- Creating Rules (page 270)
- When NOT to use the Banking Feed (page 272)
- The Receipts Center (page 273)
- Importing Transactions Downloaded from Your Bank (page 274)
- Reconciling Bank Accounts (page 276)
- Finding Errors During Bank Reconciliation (page 283)
- Bank Reconciliation Reports (page 286)
- Reconciling Credit Card Accounts (page 287)

> **OPEN THIS FILE:**
>
> Open the *Craig's Landscaping sample company* using the bookmark you created on page 8, or go to http://qbo.intuit.com/redir/testdrive.

In this chapter we will look at the relationship between QuickBooks Online and your banks. One of QBO's hallmarks is its deep integration with online banking. The direct connection allows you to match and confirm transactions for accuracy, and automate routine data entry.

TRANSFER FUNDS BETWEEN ACCOUNTS

A *Transfer* is a form that moves funds from one balance sheet account to another. Use transfers to record transactions such as moving money from a checking to a savings account.

HANDS-ON PRACTICE

Every week Craig transfers $100 from his checking account to his savings account.

STEP 1. Click on the *+New* button and choose **Transfer** (see Figure 6-1).

STEP 2. In *Transfer Funds From* select **Checking**. The account's current balance appears (see Figure 6-2).

STEP 3. In *Transfer Funds To* select **Savings**. The account's current balance appears.

STEP 4. In *Transfer Amount* enter **100**.

STEP 5. Enter **today's date** in the *Date* field.

STEP 6. In the *Memo* field type **Weekly Checking to Savings transfer**.

STEP 7. Click **Save and Close**.

FIGURE 6-1: Select Transfer on the +New menu

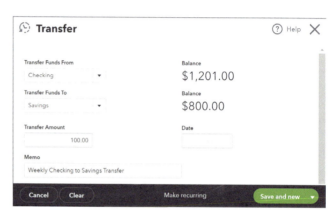

FIGURE 6-2: Transfer Funds between balance sheet accounts

Because this is a weekly transfer, consider clicking **Make Recurring**, so that QBO creates the transfer every week automatically. For more information about *Creating Recurring Transactions*, see page 203.

THE ACCOUNTING BEHIND THE SCENES:

When you transfer funds between balance sheet accounts, you decrease (credit) the **Transfer Funds From** account and increase (debit) the **Transfer Funds To** account.

TRANSACTION TYPE	MEMO/DESCRIPTION	ACCOUNT	DEBIT	CREDIT
Transfer	Weekly Checking to Savings Tra...	Checking		$100.00
	Weekly Checking to Savings Tra...	Savings	$100.00	
			$100.00	$100.00

THE BANKING FEED

The QuickBooks Online **Banking Feed** feature allows you to connect directly to financial institutions to import transactions directly into your QuickBooks Online company.

You must go through an initial setup process to connect your bank and credit card accounts before you can begin downloading transactions. Authorizing this connection saves you time by decreasing manual entry and increasing accuracy. It is important to review each downloaded transaction to avoid adding miscategorized data to your company file.

Online banking is secure, just like using your bank's website. QuickBooks Online uses state-of-the-art encryption when transferring information from your financial institution. Banks do not charge for this service, although you may have to turn on third-party access permissions on your bank's website.

Note that the Banking Feed is one-way. It imports data into QuickBooks Online, but does not push your QBO activity to the bank to initiate actual transactions.

Opening the Sample File

The Craig's Landscaping sample company at http://qbo.intuit.com/redir/testdrive already has a Banking Feed demo set up for you. Remember that this file resets every time you use it.

Toggling Between Banking Feed Views

Depending on your choices in your initial QuickBooks Online setup interview, you will see either **Banking** or **Transactions** in your *Left Navigation Bar*.

If your file says *Banking*, you are in **Accountant View**. If your file says *Transactions*, you are in **Business View**.

You are welcome to experiment with the two layouts to see which one you prefer. They have the same functionality, but a different appearance. We will use Accountant View in this book.

HANDS-ON PRACTICE

Follow these steps to view the Banking Feed in the sample company, and toggle between the Accountant and Business View:

STEP 1.   In the *Left Navigation Bar*, look at the option immediately below *Dashboard*. Click on either **Banking** or **Transactions**, as shown in Figure 6-3.

STEP 2.   Click on the *Gear* in the upper right corner of your screen, and look at the bottom of the menu. QuickBooks Online will tell you if *You're Viewing QuickBooks in Accountant View* or in *Business View*, as shown in Figure 6-4.

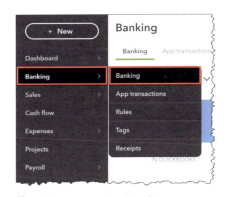

FIGURE 6-3: *The Banking menu*

STEP 3.   If you are in **Business View**, click **Switch to Accountant View**.

STEP 4.   In the Craig's Landscaping sample company, the *Banking Center* will look like Figure 6-5.

Note that the first time you go to Banking in a brand new QBO file, you won't see this view until after you connect your first account.

FIGURE 6-4: *Switch between Accountant View and Business View*

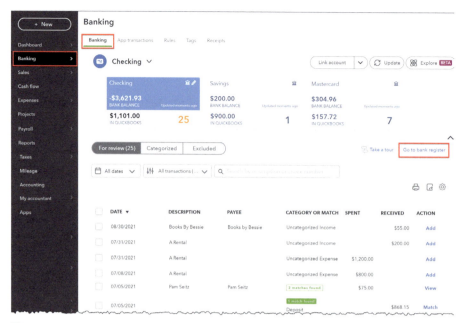

FIGURE 6-5: *The Banking Center in Accountant View*

Connecting Your Bank and Credit Cards

> *Do not perform these steps now. They are for reference only.*

One of the hallmarks of QuickBooks Online is its ability to automatically connect all of your business checking accounts, savings accounts, and credit cards. All you have to do is push a button and QBO will import your transactions for you.

The technology behind the scenes uses a ***token*** to establish a permanent connection. Even if you change your password on the financial institution's website, the link to QuickBooks Online will not be affected.

> **IMPORTANT!**
>
> We will not be able to use the Craig's Landscaping sample company to set up an actual online banking connection, since this would require a real account at a financial institution and cannot be simulated in an educational environment.
>
> If you are following along using a real QuickBooks Online account and not the sample company, you won't have access to the features in this chapter until you actually create a live connection. After you add at least one account, you can explore the interface, but your transaction list will not match the book.

To connect your QuickBooks Online file to your bank, click the **Link Account** button in the upper right. QuickBooks Online opens a *Connect an Account* window, as shown in Figure 6-6. Click on your bank from the list; if you do not see it, type your bank name in the *Enter Your Bank Name or URL* search box. The list will filter down to your bank. Click on it.

BANKING AND RECONCILIATION | 259

> **TIP:**
>
> If you are not sure which bank is correct, open up a separate browser window and visit your bank's login page. Copy the URL (web address), and then paste it into this box!

Next QBO will ask you to log into your bank. Enter the same username and password that you would use if you were logging directly into the bank's website. You may receive a phone call or text message with a security code, or be asked to answer security questions. Accept any requests to **share data**.

QuickBooks Online will display a list of all the bank or credit card accounts associated with that username, as shown in Figure 6-7.

- Map all business accounts to the existing accounts in your Chart of Accounts.

- If the account is not yet in QBO, you can click **Add New** to create the bank account or credit card on the fly.

- Include all open business credit card accounts and savings accounts, even if they have a $0 balance or are not used often.

- Ignore all personal accounts. Personal funds do not belong in a business's financial reports.

The Banking Feed Interface

Each account appears in a *Card* showing the account name, an account info button, an edit button, the actual balance at the bank, the balance in QuickBooks Online, the number of transactions waiting for review, and how recently the banking feed was updated (see Figure 6-8).

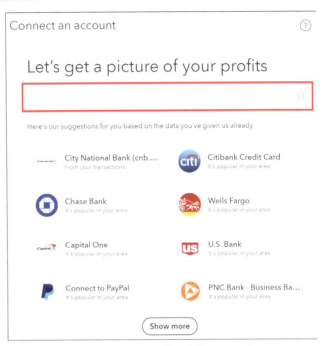

FIGURE 6-6: *Choose your bank from the list*

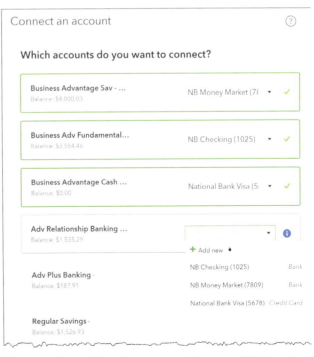

FIGURE 6-7: *Map the accounts between QBO and the bank*

FIGURE 6-8: *Cards for connected bank accounts*

The active account is highlighted in blue. To view the rest of your connected accounts, click on each card. When you have more accounts than fit across the top, use the scroll arrows that appear on the right and left.

You can also drop down the account label at the top to switch between each bank (see Figure 6-9).

Each day, refresh the accounts by clicking the **Update** button in the upper right. QuickBooks Online will download all the new transactions from each financial institution.

As the transactions are imported, QuickBooks Online searches for similar transactions that have already been entered. It looks for unreconciled transactions already in each register, or pending transactions in the Bank Deposit window.

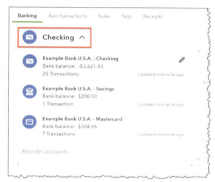

Figure 6-9: *Toggle between connected banks*

The **date** the transaction cleared the bank is listed in the first column. Note that the date the transaction actually occurred may be earlier than this date. For example, an ACH payment may take several days to be deposited, or a check you wrote may not be cashed for several months. If you would prefer an **Editable Date Field** so that you can correct the transaction date, click the *Grid Gear* on the right, just above the list.

There are three tabs in the interface: **For Review, Categorized, and Excluded** (see Figure 6-10). There are also date filters, a status filter, and a search field.

As you add or match each transaction on the **For Review** tab, it will move to the **Categorized** tab. If you make a mistake, you can **Undo** a transaction on the *Categorized* tab to move it back to *For Review*.

If a transaction on the Banking Feed is a duplicate (it is rare, but it happens), you can **Exclude** the entry, knowing that it has already been recorded.

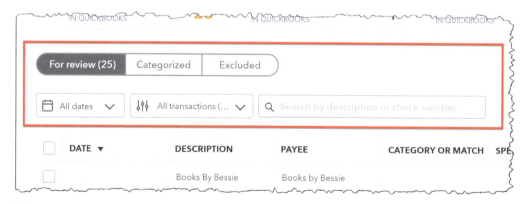

Figure 6-10: *The Banking Feed's tabs and filters*

USING THE BANKING FEED FOR DATA ENTRY

As part of your daily workflow, update the Banking Feed then clear out all the transactions from all the accounts. That way you will have the confidence that your QuickBooks Online file is completely current.

If your company creates most of your daily transactions as they occur, those existing entries will **match** in the Banking Feed, confirming your accuracy.

The Banking Feed can also be used to enter expenses, expediting and reducing your workload. It is excellent for entering after-the-fact expenses from credit cards and processing routine bank transactions.

> **IMPORTANT!**
>
> When your workflow includes making invoices and sales receipts to record customer income, verify that all Banking Feed deposits **match** existing transactions. If you find yourself manually typing in deposit details from the Banking Feed, you are duplicating your income.
>
> Be sure to prepare your customer payment bank deposits using the instructions on page 129 so that they equal the totals you see in the Banking Feed.

When you click on each transaction in the Banking Feed, you can see the **Bank Detail** at the bottom. This is the same information found on the bank statement, or when you view transactions on your bank's website. Not only can you use it to identify and categorize the transactions from the Banking Feed, but that detail is permanently attached to each transaction.

When you open a transaction that was entered or confirmed through the Banking Center, a blue link appears in the upper left corner that says **Online Banking Match**. Click on it to see the cleared date and Bank Detail, as shown in Figure 6-11. If you find that it is mis-matched, you can **Unmatch** it to put the entry back on the Banking Feed to be properly categorized.

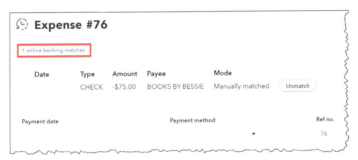

FIGURE 6-11: View the Online Banking Match in every confirmed transaction

Matched and Partially-matched Transactions

When you look at the transactions in the *For Review* tab, notice that QuickBooks Online uses its artificial intelligence to assist you. The transactions may be *matched*, *partially-matched*, *recognized*, or *left uncategorized*. Figure 6-12 demonstrates how QBO determines matches.

1. If a downloaded transaction and an already-existing unreconciled transaction have an identical amount in a similar date range, like Pye's Cakes in Figure 6-12, QuickBooks Online confirms the two with a green box that says **1 Match Found**. Once you have confirmed that the transaction is a true match, click **Match** to accept it. This removes it from the Banking Feed, and adds a green square and a C (for Cleared) in the account's register (see the register in Figure 6-28).

2. If there is more than unreconciled transaction with the same dollar amount, like Squeaky Kleen Car Wash in Figure 6-12, you'll see a white box that says **# Matches Found**. Click on the transaction and compare the dates. Choose the transaction that is most likely to be the match based on the date it occurred.

Figure 6-12: *Matched and Partially-matched transactions*

HANDS-ON PRACTICE

Step 1. If needed, click on **Banking** (or **Transactions**) in the *Left Navigation Bar*.

Step 2. Select the **Checking account**. Scroll down and click once on the **Deposit** for **$868.15**.

Step 3. Notice that the date and the dollar amount match. In some cases, the bank's date may be after the transaction date, since a deposit may take one or more days to clear the bank.

Step 4. To view the original transaction, click the blue **Deposit** link. The original *Bank Deposit* window opens. You can see the $868.15 deposit was created to combine five individual sales, and $200 was transferred to Savings through the *Cash Back* field. Click **Cancel** in the lower left (or the **X** in the upper right) so that you don't make any changes.

Step 5. Because this transaction is correct, click the green **Match** button. The transaction disappears from the list.

Step 6. Click on the **$19.99** transaction from **Squeeky Kleen Car Wash**.

Step 7. There are two potential matches, indicated by a white box that says **2 Matches Found**. They appear because neither existing transaction has been matched or reconciled yet. Compare the dates of the two options. Make sure the transaction with the same date has the green dot in it, then click **Match** (see Figure 6-12).

Recognized Matches

The Banking Feed will **repeat** past payees and account categories when QuickBooks Online notices that the bank description is identical to an already-existing transaction in the register. These transactions display the *Payee* and *Category* in green (see Figure 6-13). The artificial intelligence learns how to associate the bank detail to your history, and accuracy will improve over time.

> **IMPORTANT!**
>
> Not only does the artificial intelligence repeat your past categories, it also **suggests** possible payees and categories based on its database. These are frequently incorrect. Be sure to verify all these **Recognized** entries before adding them. If they are not correct, don't panic! Just click on them and categorize them as you normally would.

Transactions created using **Rules** will also appear as *Recognized* (see page 270).

FIGURE 6-13: *A transaction recognized by the artificial intelligence*

Uncategorized Transactions

Some transactions on the list may be labeled Uncategorized Asset, Uncategorized Income, or Uncategorized Expense. QBO doesn't know what they are. These transactions don't match anything already in your books, and no Rules could be applied (see page 270).

If you know the entry is already in your QuickBooks Online, figure out why it doesn't match. Is the date too far away? Is the dollar amount wrong? Is it in the wrong bank account? Did you forget to make the bank deposit properly? This may be a sign you need to correct a data entry error.

If the transaction is not already in your QuickBooks Online, you can use the Banking Feed to add the entry to your QuickBooks Online account register. Click on a transaction and categorize it manually, as shown in Figure 6-14. At a minimum, add a **Payee** (vendor or customer name) and choose a **Category**. You should also include a **Memo** so you remember what the transaction was for. Click **Add** when done.

If you are using QBO's features for job costing, billable expenses, classes, or locations, the Banking Feed will display fields to include this information as well.

HANDS-ON PRACTICE

STEP 8. Locate the two recent expenses for **A Rental**. Click on the one for **$1,200.00**. Notice the **A Rental** suggested *Description* is not identical to the *Bank Detail's* **A1 Rental**. That's because A1 Rental is not yet on your Vendor List, so QuickBooks Online was suggesting its best guess.

Click in the *Vendor/Customer* field and add **A1 Rental** as a new vendor on the fly.

STEP 9. In the *Category* box, change Uncategorized Expense to **Job Expenses:Equipment Rental**.

Don't forget that you can type part of the category name to filter the list, instead of scrolling up and down looking for it!

STEP 10. Add **Amy's Bird Sanctuary** to the *Customer/Project* field for job costing, and check **Billable** to prepare the expense to be included on Amy's next invoice.

STEP 11. Add **Backhoe Rental** to the *Memo*.

STEP 12. When your transaction matches Figure 6-14, click **Add**. The transaction is removed from the Banking Feed and is added to the Checking account register.

FIGURE 6-14: *Click on a transaction to manually categorize it*

Entering Transfers

If QBO recognizes the same dollar amount going in and out of two bank accounts, it suggests a green box that says **Paired to Another Transaction**. Clicking **Record Transfer** accepts the transaction in BOTH accounts.

If this match doesn't appear, it is usually easiest to create the transfer first using the instructions on page 256, then match the Banking Feed on both sides.

If you use the Banking Feed to manually create transfers, work from the "money-in" side. For example, when you transfer money from Checking to Savings, go to the card for the Savings account, click on the transaction, select **Record As Transfer**, then enter the *Transferred From* account (see Figure 6-15).

On the Checking side, be sure to **Match** the other side of the transaction. Be careful not to enter it a second time, creating a duplicate!

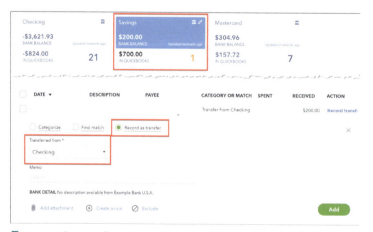

FIGURE 6-15: *Creating a Transfer. Be sure to Match the other side of the account!*

Entering Refunds

Vendor Refunds for expenses can be entered directly from the Banking Feed. Click on the entry, enter the Payee, and choose the same Category as the original expense.

HANDS-ON PRACTICE

STEP 13. **Books by Bessie** accidentally charged you twice for **Bookkeeping**. Click on the top entry that says **$55** in the *Received* column.

STEP 14. Make sure the green dot next to **Categorize** is selected.

STEP 15. Enter the information as shown in Figure 6-16. Change the *Category* to **Legal & Professional Fees:Bookkeeper**. Enter the *Memo* **Refunded extra charge**.

STEP 16. Click **Add**.

FIGURE 6-16: *Categorize a refund to reverse the original charge*

Batch Actions

Instead of entering transactions one at a time, you can process several at once.

While we will not do this now, you are able to check off the transactions you want to process using the boxes on the left side, as shown in Figure 6-17.

FIGURE 6-17: *Use Batch Actions to process several Banking Feed items at the same time*

- Use **Accept** to add multiple entries that are already correctly matched or recognized, instead of clicking **Add** one at a time on every line.

- **Update** assigns the same *Payee*, *Category*, and *Class* to several rows simultaneously, instead of editing each one individually, as shown in Figure 6-18. This works particularly well when the owner is commingling (using their business account for personal expenses)—you can add the **owner's name** and the **Owner Draws** account to many transactions all at once.

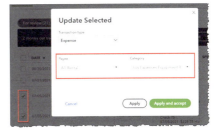

FIGURE 6-18: *Batch Update several transactions at the same time*

- **Exclude** removes items from the list. We will talk more about excluding transactions on page 269.

HANDS-ON PRACTICE

Step 17. If needed, click on **Banking** (or **Transactions**) in the *Left Navigation Bar*. Select **Checking**.

Step 18. Click on the *All Transactions* filter and change it to **Recognized**, as shown in Figure 6-19. The list now shows just matched transactions, including suggestions from the artificial intelligence.

Step 19. Select all the transactions by clicking on the **square** at the top of the list to the left of *Date*, as shown in Figure 6-20.

Step 20. Scroll up and down the list to confirm that all the transactions are ready to be added. If you see any that don't have a match, click on them to see if you agree with the artificial intelligence. If not, edit the *Payee* or *Category*.

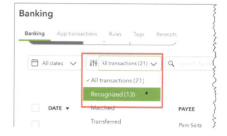

Figure 6-19: *Filter the Banking Feed for Recognized transactions*

Step 21. Click **Accept** in the *black bar* that appeared at the top of the list.

Step 22. If you get a **Suggested Rule** for **A Rental**, click the **X** in the top right corner to close it.

Adding Suggested Rules will introduce errors into your data if you don't click **Edit Rule** and look it over carefully before creating it. We will talk about *Rules* on page 270.

Step 23. Click the **X** next to the blue *Recognized* filter to return to the rest of the list.

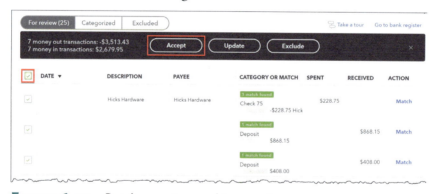

Figure 6-20: *Batch accept several transactions at once*

Splitting a Transaction

You can click the **Split** button to divide an expense into multiple lines, allocating it to several *Categories*, *Customers*, or *Classes*.

HANDS-ON PRACTICE

Craig's Landscaping had Lara's Lamination create an all-weather sign for Amy's Bird Sanctuary, but the company also included their business cards in the same order. When the charge came through the Banking Feed, the bill had not been entered in the system.

Step 24. Click on the **Mastercard** account at the top of the *Banking Feed*.

Step 25. Click on the transaction for **Lara's Lamination** for **$150.00**. Click the **Split** button in the lower right.

STEP 26. Fill in the *Split Transaction* as shown in Figure 6-21. You will need to add the new vendor on the fly. In the first row, enter **Cost of Goods Sold**, with the *Description* **All-weather sign**. Make it **Billable** to **Amy's Bird Sanctuary**. The *Amount* is **$100**.

STEP 27. On the second line, the *Category* is **Advertising**, and the *Description* is **Business Cards**. Enter **50** into the *Amount* field.

STEP 28. When your transaction matches Figure 6-21, click **Apply and Accept**.

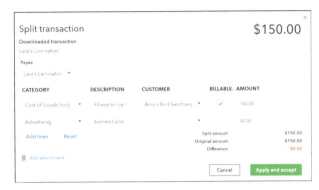

FIGURE 6-21: *The Split button allows you to allocate expenses across categories, customers, and classes*

Using Find Match

If QuickBooks Online doesn't recognize a match to transactions that you know are already in the register, use **Find Match** to identify multiple expenses or payments that can be combined to add up to the total (see Figure 6-22).

Be careful when using this tool. It frequently acts as a band-aid for incorrect procedures. For example, if one payment was made against three bills, but the owner created three separate payments instead, this tool will recognize that the three payments add up to the one bank transaction . . . but there really should have been one payment created, not three.

Another use is that Find Match will locate individual payments that were deposited directly to the checking account instead of using *Undeposited Funds* to create a combined Bank Deposit.

The benefit of Find Match in both these cases is the bank balance will be correct because the payments will be marked as cleared, but the drawback is that the register will not match the bank statement when it's time to reconcile.

FIGURE 6-22: *Use Find Match to group transactions and Resolve discrepancies*

Sometimes *Suggested Matches* offers several combinations of transactions that all equal the amount, as shown in Figure 6-23. If you see several boxes across the top with different calculations, click on each option to see which grouping is correct, then click **Save**.

FIGURE 6-23: *Sometimes Find Match shows suggested combinations*

If there is a discrepancy, you can use the **Resolve** tool at the bottom to make an adjusting entry, as shown in Figure 6-24. Using **Resolve** forces the balances to match, but you are better off correcting the original transactions than adding an error to the books.

In other words, while you CAN use Find Match, always question whether you SHOULD.

HANDS-ON PRACTICE

STEP 29. The **Hicks Hardware** expense for **$24.38** is already in QuickBooks Online, but for some reason it is not showing as a match. Click on it to expand the entry.

STEP 30. Click the **Find Match** circle. The *Match Transactions* window opens.

STEP 31. There is an Expense on the same date for Hick's Hardware, but the amount is .02 different. The best practice would be to cancel this window, fix the error, and then Match the transaction in the Banking Feed.

STEP 32. **Check** the expense on the *Select Transaction to Match* grid.

STEP 33. Scroll down to the bottom and click the slider for **Resolve**.

STEP 34. Under *Add Resolving Transactions*, add **Hick's Hardware** to the *Payee*, and choose **Landscaping Services:Job Materials:Plants and Soil** in the *Category*. This is the same account used in the original transaction.

STEP 35. In the *Memo*, enter **Data entry error**.

STEP 36. Click **Save**. QuickBooks Online marks the existing check in the register as a match to the Banking Feed.

FIGURE 6-24: *(Don't) Use Resolve to create adjusting entries*

Excluding Transactions

If you know for certain that a transaction is already in your register, but it's not matching the Banking Feed for some reason (perhaps it's already reconciled, or the import somehow occurred twice), use **Exclude** to remove the transaction from the list (see Figure 6-17).

If you later find you needed the entry, click on the *Excluded* tab, then **Undo** the transaction to put it back under *For Review*.

Matching Credit Card Payments

If you properly entered credit card payments, the payment will match on the feeds for both on the checking account and the credit card.

If you did not use the *Pay Down Credit Card* feature, you can create one right in the Banking Feed from either the checking or the credit card account by clicking on **Record as Credit Card Payment**.

Figure 6-25 demonstrates this step while looking at the Mastercard feed. Enter the **bank account** you paid from in the *Select Bank Account* field, and enter the **bank name** in the *Vendor* field. Click **Add**.

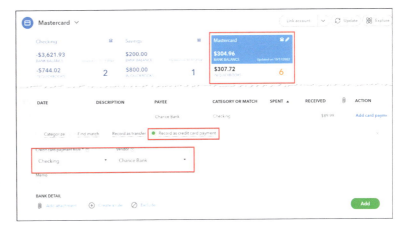

FIGURE 6-25: *Recording a Credit Card Payment*

As with transfers, you will **Match** the transaction on the other side. Be careful not to add the payment twice.

CREATING RULES

Automate data entry for routine transactions using **Rules**, found on the tab at the top of the *Banking Center*. The Rules look at the Bank Detail and/or the dollar amount that gets imported with each transaction, and use that information to automatically assign a payee, category, and class. Transactions can also be **Auto-added**, moving them directly to the *Categorized* tab in the Banking Feed and into the account register, skipping *For Review* completely.

A limitation is that Rules cannot be used to enter transactions involving products and services.

Rules will trigger in the order they were created, starting with the first and working their way down the list. Drag the 9-dot waffle on the left of each row up or down to re-order them by priority.

Rules have complete flexibility, and can be customized to automatically categorize and enter a wide variety of transactions, as shown in Figure 6-26.

FIGURE 6-26: *Create Rules to automate data entry*

1. Name the Rule something descriptive. Avoid punctuation.
2. Choose **Money In** or **Money Out**.
3. Select the *Bank Account* the transaction applies to. If it could be paid from any account, change this to **All Bank Accounts**. The best use for specifying an account is when a transaction would be categorized differently depending on which account it came from. For example, an Intuit charge from the checking account is a Merchant Services expense, but if it's on the credit card it would be a software subscription.
4. While most of the time you will choose just one criterion for your rule, it's also possible to use multiple tests to qualify a transaction. Click the blue *+Add a Condition* link to add up to five criteria.
   a. If you choose **Any**, the Bank Detail could match any one of several possibilities. For example, if the *Description* said **Any** of Chevron, Shell, Gulf, Amoco, or BP, then categorize the transaction as a Fuel Expense.
   b. If you choose **All**, the transaction must match **all** the conditions to trigger. For example, if the *Description* says Amazon **and** the *Amount* says 12.99, then categorize the transaction as an Amazon Prime subscription.
5. Choose between **Description**, **Bank Detail**, and **Amount** for the conditions. *Description* relies on the artificial intelligence to interpret the payee. *Bank Detail* looks for an exact match and is most accurate. *Amount* refers to the transaction total.
6. Choose **Contains**, **Doesn't Contain**, or **Is Exactly** for *Description* and *Bank Detail* comparisons. For *Amount*, choose from **Doesn't Equal**, **Equals**, **Is Greater Than**, or **Is Less Than**.
7. This is the most important box! Copy the **Bank Detail** and paste it here for greatest accuracy. Include just enough text to identify a unique match, but not so much that you override the possibilities. For example, erase branch numbers and transaction IDs.

8. Click the *Test Rule* button to confirm that your criteria above will trigger the Rule properly.

9. *Money In* transaction types include **Deposit/Credit Card Credit** and **Transfer**. *Money Out* options are **Expense**, **Transfer**, and **Check**.

10. In *Category*, choose an account from the **Chart of Accounts**. This selection is important as it controls the behind-the-scenes accounting.

11. You can **Split** a transaction by percentage or dollar amount across several categories or classes. This is ideal for situations such as the owner's cell phone bill. It's not uncommon that while 75% of the phone's use may be business, 25% may be personal and should be categorized as Owner Draws.

12. The *Payee* is who you are paying (usually a Vendor).

13. When the settings are turned on, fields appear to assign Customers, Classes, Locations, and Tags.

14. You can specify a *Memo* to be included on all transactions. This can replace the Bank Detail or be appended to it (recommended).

15. *Automatically Confirm Transactions This Rule Applies To* is the magic **Auto-add**. Use this when a transaction is routine, doesn't need a custom memo, there's no job costing, and you don't need to monitor it every month. When the transaction comes in from the bank, it will be entered straight into the register. This one option can save you hours of time every month.

HANDS-ON PRACTICE

Craig's Landscaping buys propane for their shop heater from Chin's Gas and Oil. It's a routine purchase, and Craig doesn't need to verify the transaction each time it happens. Create a Rule to automatically add these expenses directly to the register.

STEP 1. If needed, click on **Banking** (or **Transactions**) in the *Left Navigation Bar*, then on the *Rules* tab.

STEP 2. Click the **New Rule** button.

STEP 3. Enter **CHINS GAS AND OIL** into the *What Do You Want to Call This Rule?** field at the top. Omit the apostrophe in **CHINS**.

STEP 4. Change the *Description* dropdown to say **Bank Text**.

STEP 5. In the third box, enter **CHIN'S GAS AND OIL**.

A best practice is to copy the vendor name from the *Bank Detail* in the Banking Feed before making the Rule, and then **Paste** it into this box. This ensures an exact match.

STEP 6. Enter **Utilities:Gas and Electric** for the *Category*.

STEP 7. Choose **Chin's Gas and Oil** from the *Payee* list.

STEP 8. When your screen looks like Figure 6-27, click **Save**.

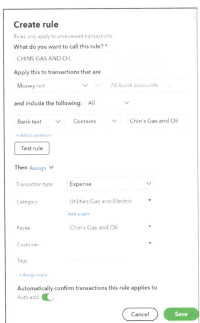

FIGURE 6-27: *Auto-add all future Chin's Gas and Oil expenses*

If you get an error message, remove the apostrophe from **CHIN'S** in the rule's name at the top so that it reads **CHINS** instead, then **Save** the rule again. This field does not like punctuation.

STEP 9. The Rule will trigger. The Chin's Gas transaction for $185, as well as all future matching expenses, will be categorized and added to the check register.

VIEWING THE BANK REGISTER

Any time you would like to view a list of bank account or credit card transactions, the Banking Feed has a link to jump directly to their registers. This is often faster than navigating to *Accounting > Chart of Accounts > View Register*.

Viewing the **Bank Register** provides clues about a transaction's origin inside QuickBooks Online.

While viewing any account in the *Banking Feed*, click on the blue **Go To Bank Register** link on the right side, below the cards but above the grid (refer to Figure 6-5 on page 258). This takes you to that account's *Register*, shown in Figure 6-28.

- In the right column, *the C and the green squares* indicate that the transaction has been Cleared (matched) by the Banking Feed.
- The *green square with the +* indicates that an *Auto-add Rule* was applied.
- A transaction with an *R* instead of a *C* has been reconciled (not shown).
- A transaction with no green square indicates that the transaction was manually created and has no match in the Banking Feed. This helps identify errors and transactions that never hit the bank.

FIGURE 6-28: *How Banking Feed transactions display in the register*

WHEN NOT TO USE THE BANKING FEED

There are some scenarios when using the Banking Feed is not the most effective way to enter your transactions.

Using the Banking Feed incorrectly can create bad data. Be sure to train the artificial intelligence instead of trusting it!

Duplicating Sales Transactions

If you routinely create sales receipts and take invoice payments for customer income, **DO NOT ENTER THE SALE THROUGH THE BANKING FEED!** All deposits in the Banking Feed must be MATCHED to existing sales transactions.

If you find yourself clicking on a deposit and typing in the customer name and the sales category, *YOU ARE DUPLICATING YOUR REVENUE*.

Instead, be sure to properly create Bank Deposits using the sales workflows on page 128, grouping the transactions so that the deposit totals match the bank statement and the Banking Feed.

Purchasing Products and Services

The Banking Feed only utilizes the *Chart of Accounts* categories. There is no way to add transactions using the *Product and Services* list. If you are purchasing inventory products or paying subcontractors, use the workflows found in Chapter 4, and MATCH those expenses instead of adding them through Banking.

THE RECEIPTS CENTER

It's important to maintain a paper trail of receipts to verify your business transactions. The IRS requires that receipts be saved for seven years in case of audit. Bank and credit card statements are not sufficient—you may need the itemized receipt to demonstrate to the IRS that your hardware purchase was for your office and not your home.

While you can still keep a filing cabinet full of paper receipts, these tend to fade, and many stores now send digital receipts instead of printing them out. QuickBooks Online has the ability to attach pdfs and jpgs of your receipts to most transactions. We looked at Attachments on page 120.

Not only you can import receipts in a variety of ways, the Banking Center has optical character recognition (OCR) to extract information from the receipts and use it to create the transactions.

Electronic storage of your receipts satisfies IRS requirements. Because each one is attached to its actual transaction, you have the copies at your fingertips.

The *Receipts* tab at the top of the *Banking Center* provides three ways of bringing receipts into QBO: **Upload from Computer**, **Upload from Google Drive**, and **Forward from Email** (see Figure 6-29).

FIGURE 6-29: *The Receipts Center in Banking*

There is also a fourth way! Using QBO's Mobile App on your smartphone, you can snap a picture of your paper receipt, and it imports immediately. Download the app for free from the App Store or Google Play, and log into your QuickBooks Online file with the same username and password you use in your browser.

To set up your company's receipt forwarding, click on **Forward from Email**. Create a custom email address, such as **craigslandscaping@qbodocs.com**. You can't change this address later, so make it something relevant to your company and easy to remember. Any employee with a QBO login can forward attachments to this email address as long as they send it from the email account that makes up their username.

Note that you will be unable to create a forwarding email from the Craig's Landscaping sample file.

Uploaded receipts take about 15 minutes to process. At that point, you can enter all the information about the transaction including the date, payee, category, and funding source, as shown in Figure 6-31.

If QuickBooks Online can identify an existing entry with matching information, it will append the receipt to the transaction.

If not, you can use Receipt Capture to create an *Expense* or a *Bill*. When the payment shows up in the Banking Feed, it will match this transaction.

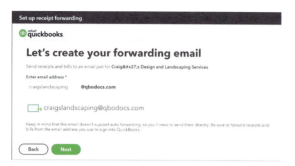

FIGURE 6-30: *Set up a custom email address to forward receipts*

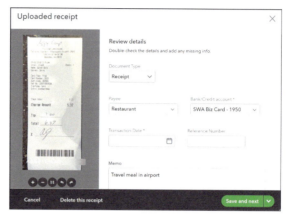

FIGURE 6-31: *Enter the information off the receipt image*

IMPORTING TRANSACTIONS DOWNLOADED FROM YOUR BANK

> *Do not perform these steps now. They are for reference only.*

If you need to add transactions to QuickBooks Online in a date range earlier than your bank is able to download when you first establish the connection, or if your bank is unable to sync at all, it is possible to import the Banking Feed using **Web Connect**.

Log into your bank's website and find their **Download** option. Search for the date range desired. Download the file in a QuickBooks .qbo file format, or try .csv, .qfx, .ofx, or .txt files.

Use the **Upload From File** option under the *Link Account* drop-down in the upper right to import the transactions, as shown in Figure 6-32.

In the *Manually Upload Your Transactions* window shown in Figure 6-33, either drag your downloaded file into the **Drag and drop** box, or click **Select Files** to browse for your file. Once you have located it, click **Continue.**

In the next window shown in Figure 6-34, tell QBO which bank account or credit card you are importing.

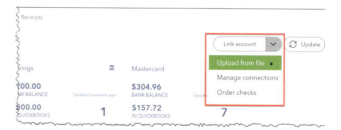

FIGURE 6-32: *Upload transactions manually*

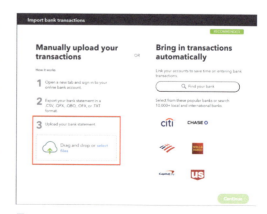

FIGURE 6-33: *Import a web connect bank export*

When you click **Next**, you will get one of two screens. If you see the message in Figure 6-35, click **Done**, and the imported transactions will appear, ready to be categorized.

If QuickBooks Online is not able to determine which of your data fields is which, instead you will see the window shown in Figure 6-36 asking you to map the columns in the file with the *Date*, *Description*, and *Amount* fields required by QBO. Drop down each field and choose the associated column header from the download.

You may need to open the downloaded file in Excel and edit it if you can't make the data line up.

When you are done with the import, your transactions will appear in the Banking Feed just like they would through the direct connection.

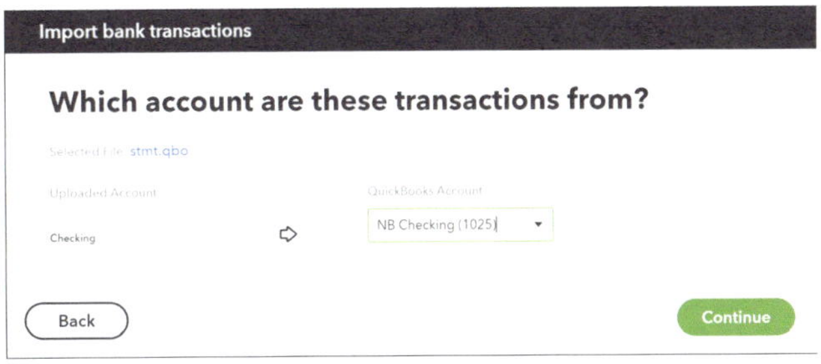

FIGURE 6-34: *Map your upload to your bank account*

FIGURE 6-35: *Import completed*

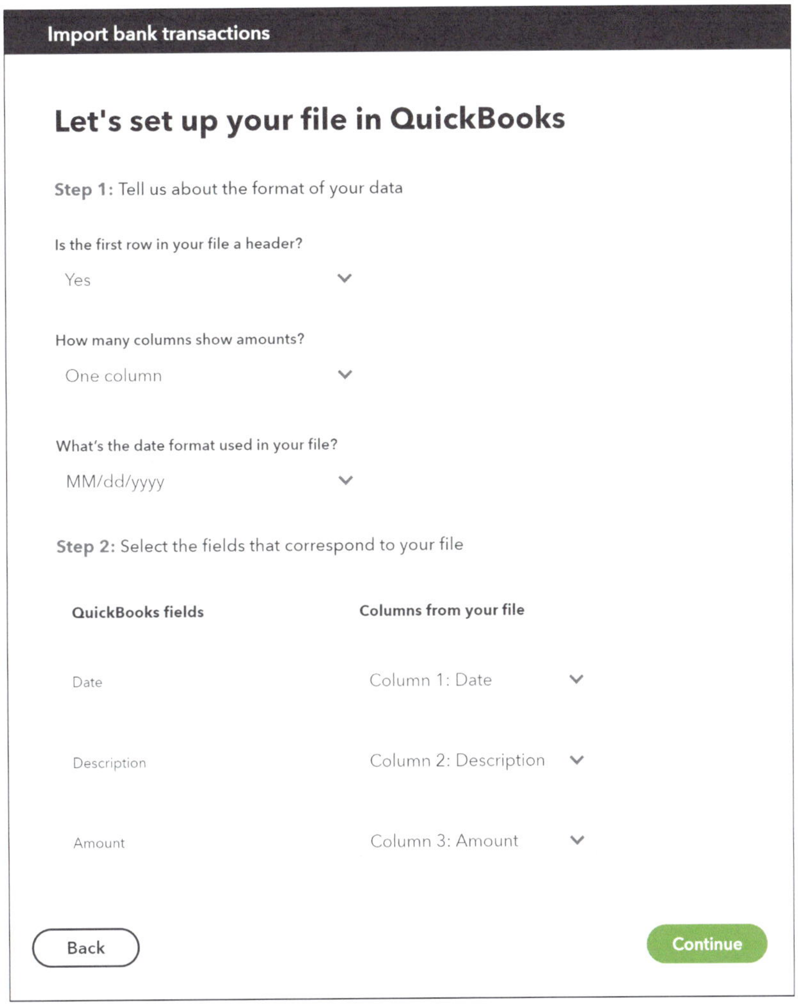

FIGURE 6-36: *Map the fields in the data file to the Date, Description, and Amount in QBO*

RECONCILING BANK ACCOUNTS

At the end of each month, you must compare the transactions you have entered into QuickBooks Online with your bank statements to confirm that QBO matches the bank's records. This process is called **Reconciliation**. It is a very important step in the overall accounting process, and ensures the accuracy of your accounting records.

Matching and creating transactions from the Banking Feed speeds up your reconciliation because those transactions are imported directly from the bank's monthly statement. In fact, when you begin a reconciliation, QuickBooks Online will recognize these transactions and mark them as cleared for you. But it's also important to look for other duplicated, missing, or miscoded transactions.

The first accounts you'll reconcile are your checking accounts, savings accounts, credit cards, and loans, since these types of accounts always have monthly statements.

In addition to reconciling the bank accounts, you can also reconcile all Balance Sheet accounts using the same process. In fact, you can reconcile almost any Other Current Asset, Fixed Asset, Credit Card, Other Current Liability, Long Term Liability, or Equity account using the same process presented in this chapter.

How to Reconcile

Before reconciling the account in QuickBooks Online, make sure you've entered all of the transactions for that account and that the Banking Feed is empty. For example, if you have direct deposit payments in your checking account (EFTs) or interest charges on your credit card, you will need to enter those transactions before you start the reconciliation.

Your goal is to get the *Difference* in the upper right corner to **0**. There are several steps:

1. Entering the information from the statement.

2. Getting the Difference to 0 by matching all the transactions on the bank statement.

3. If the Difference isn't zero, managing missing and mismatched transactions.

4. Analyzing the remaining transactions that are not on the statement. Are they pending, duplicates, or errors?

Figure 6-37 shows Craig's Landscaping's bank statement for the checking account as of today.

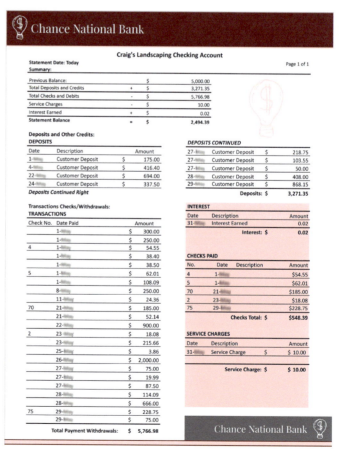

FIGURE 6-37: Sample bank statement. Note that your dates will not match. Use today's date when you reconcile.

> **NOTE:**
>
> Because we are using a sample company, the dates are dynamic. *The dates on your screen will not match the dates on the statement below.*

HANDS-ON PRACTICE

Before you begin, close and re-open the Craig's Landscaping sample data file to get a fresh start. Be sure that the Banking Feed is back to the default list, otherwise your transactions in this exercise won't match.

Follow these steps to reconcile the Craig's Landscaping Checking account with the bank statement shown in Figure 6-37.

Part 1: Setting Up the Statement

Step 1. If you haven't already, close and re-open the Craig's Landscaping sample data file.

Step 2. Click the **Reconcile** option under *Accounting* in the *Left Navigation Bar*. Alternatively, when you are looking at the *Checking Register*, you can click the green **Reconcile** button in the upper right corner.

Step 3. If you see a *Match the Books to the Bank Records* screen, click the green **Get Started** button, then click **Let's Get Reconciled**. Dismiss all additional training alerts (you should read them later!). Eventually you will see the window in Figure 6-38.

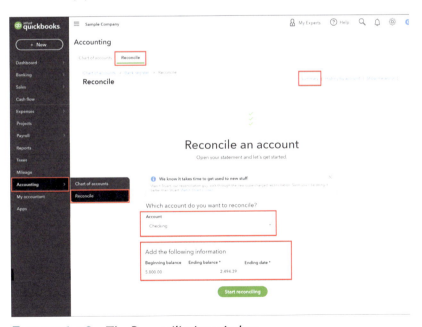

Figure 6-38: *The Reconciliation window*

Step 4. Select **Checking** from the *Account* drop-down list.

Notice that this list includes all the accounts on your Balance Sheet.

> **TIP:**
>
> QuickBooks Online has a new feature to download your bank and credit card statements right from this window. When you see an **Enroll** button, click it to initiate the connection. Then use the **Get Statements** button to access PDFs of your bank statements for each month. Note that we will not be able to see or use this tool in this exercise since we are using a sample company, and that the feature is not yet available for all financial institutions.

STEP 5. Look for the *Previous Balance* on the bank statement in Figure 6-37. Compare this amount with the **Beginning Balance** amount in the *Reconcile* window in Figure 6-38. Notice that they are the same.

QuickBooks Online calculates the *Beginning Balance* field in the *Reconcile* window by adding and subtracting all previously reconciled transactions. If the beginning balance does not match the bank statement, you probably made changes to previously cleared transactions. See page 283 for more information and how to fix this.

STEP 6. Enter *2,494.39* in the *Ending Balance* field. This amount is the *Statement Balance* shown on the bank statement in Figure 6-37.

For the *Ending* Date, enter **today's date**. Real bank statements usually (but not always) end on the last day of the month.

STEP 7. Click **Start Reconciling**. The window in Figure 6-39 opens.

> **TIP:**
>
> When reconciling some accounts, the QuickBooks Online *Reconcile* screen may display additional fields to enter service charges and interest. If the statement lists any finance charges or interest earned, enter those amounts in the appropriate fields. QuickBooks Online will add the corresponding transactions to your bank account register.
>
> If you already imported monthly bank charges and interest through the Banking Feed, skip those fields to avoid duplicate entry of the charges.

> **IMPORTANT!**
>
> In this exercise, we will reconcile this account manually. When you use the Banking Feed to import and confirm transactions, you will see green boxes in the column to the right of the *Memo*. Those transactions will be pre-selected with circles in the column on the far right, because QuickBooks Online already knows they are on the statement.
>
> Sometimes your reconciliation is 95% done as soon as you start! In the *Apply Your Knowledge* exercise at the end of this chapter, you will see this in action.

BANKING AND RECONCILIATION | 279

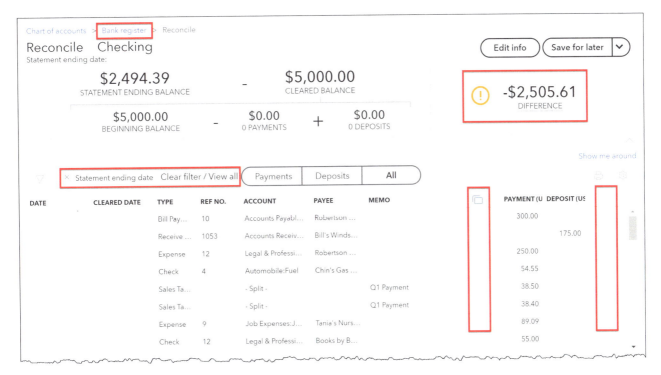

FIGURE 6-39: *Reconcile the Checking account*

Part 2: Getting the Difference to $0.00

Once you get to the Reconcile Checking window, your goal is to make sure that every transaction that appears on the bank statement is marked cleared in your *Reconcile Checking* screen. Once that happens, the *Difference* amount will be **$0.00**.

Compare the *Reconcile* window to the *Chance National Bank Statement* in Figure 6-37.

As you work, if you see a transaction on the statement that is not in QuickBooks Online's *Reconcile* screen, make a note of it.

STEP 8. Because the bank statement is organized by deposits and payments, it is usually easiest to start by matching the deposits shown at the top of the Chance bank statement first.

STEP 9. Click on the **Deposits** button in the center of your *Reconcile* screen to filter the list so it just focuses on these transactions.

STEP 10. Confirm each deposit transaction on the bank statement to those in the **Deposits** column by clicking the **circle** on the far right of each row.

You should find **8 deposits** that match those shown on the bank statement, totaling **$2854.95**.

STEP 11. There's a deposit for **$416.40** on the bank statement that's not in the *Deposit* column, but there are three unmarked deposits for **$86.40**, **$225.00**, and **$105.00**.

Click on any one of these unmatched deposits and choose **Edit** to open the transaction. You'll notice that the *Deposit To* field says **Checking** instead of **Undeposited Funds**. Click **Cancel** to close the transaction and return to the reconciliation.

STEP 12. These three payments were deposited directly to the checking account instead of **Undeposited Funds** to be grouped together to match the bank statement. Even though it's a best practice to batch them together in a *Bank Deposit* window to match the daily deposit, it is acceptable to check them off individually now.

Place checkmarks next to the three remaining deposit lines. You now have **11** cleared deposits totaling **$3,271.35**. This total matches the total shown on the bank statement.

STEP 13. Click on the **Payments** button in the center of the screen to filter the list for the money-out transactions. Using the Chance bank statement as your guide, start at the top of the Payments list shown on bank statement and check off each matching entry on the right side of the *Reconcile* screen.

If a transaction does not appear on the bank statement, do not check it off in the Reconcile window. When finished, the top of your QuickBooks Online Reconcile window should show **23** payments for **$5,766.98**.

STEP 14. The *Difference* is now -9.98. Note that on the statement there is an **Interest Deposit** of **.02**, and a **$10 Service Charge**. Most of the time these will come through the Banking Feed, and are a great opportunity to create rules. In this case, they weren't imported, and you need to create them manually:
   a. Using the *+New* button, create a new **Expense** for **$10** to **Chance Bank** using the *Category* **Bank Charges**. Add **Chance Bank** as a **Vendor** on the fly. Date it on the **last day of the previous month**. Click **Save and close** to return to the reconciliation.
   b. Using the *+New* button, create a new **Bank Deposit**. Date it the **last day of the previous month**. Use the *Add Funds to This Deposit* grid at the bottom. In the *Received From* field, enter **Chance Bank**. In the *Account*, enter **Interest Earned** with an *Amount* of **.02**. Click **Save and Close**.
   c. Click on the **All** filter button to view all the transactions. Check off both these transactions at the bottom of the list.

STEP 15. After you've marked all the cleared checks and deposits, look at the *Difference* field. It is now **0.00**, indicating that your bank account matches the bank statement.

> **TIP:**
>
> If you need to exit the *Reconcile* window to finish it another time, you can drop down the green button in the upper right corner and choose **Save for Later**. QuickBooks Online will save your progress so you can pick up where you left off and complete the reconciliation at another time.

Part 3: If the Difference Still Is Not Zero

It is very important that you do not click **Finish Now** unless the *Difference* field shows **0.00**. If you do, QuickBooks Online will create a transaction in the bank account for the difference, coded to a *Reconciliation Discrepancies* expense account.

While this may seem like an easy solution, the reality is that a balance in Reconciliation Discrepancies creates an over- or understatement in net income. Instead of writing off the error, you should research why it exists and fix it.

To find errors in your bank reconciliation, try the following steps:

Double-check the Ending Balance and Statement Date

Don't spend hours chasing down a typo! Click the **Edit** button in the upper right corner and compare these fields to your statement. Sometimes statements make it hard to distinguish the statement date from the due date. If either the date or the ending balance was incorrect, fix it.

Compare the Payments and Deposits Totals

At the top of the *Reconcile* window, QuickBooks Online calculates the sum of your marked **Payments** and **Deposits**. Compare the figures to your bank statement. If you find a discrepancy with these totals, that helps you know in which column to find your error. Search your statement for an item you forgot to mark, or for one that you marked in error.

> **TIP:**
>
> To help locate missing transactions, sort the columns in the *Reconcile* window by clicking the column headings. Sorting the grid by **Cleared Date**, **Payment**, or **Deposit** can help you locate transactions and look for duplicates.

Are There Post-Dated Transactions?

If you are missing a transaction that is dated *after* the statement's ending date but it cleared in the current period, click the **x Statement Ending Date** link at the top left of the transactions list. This temporarily removes the statement ending date filter and displays the rest of the transactions. **Check off** the missing transaction so that the *Difference* equals **$0**, then click **Reset Statement Ending Date** to reestablish the date range. If the *Difference* doesn't stick at $0, you may either adjust the transaction date to match the *Cleared Date*, or finish the reconciliation with the *Statement Ending Date* off.

Part 4: Analyzing the Remaining Transactions

Once the **Difference** is zero, next look at anything that was NOT checked off.

It's not enough to just mark off the transactions that ARE on the bank statement. It is essential to also take care of transactions that are NOT on the bank statement.

If a check wasn't cashed yet, decide if it's pending, it was issued in error, or perhaps it was lost. If you see other unmarked transactions you may have duplicates, data entry errors, or transactions categorized to the wrong account.

HANDS-ON PRACTICE

STEP 16. The **$55 check to Books by Bessie** and the **$100 Check to Tony Rondonuwu** are both more than a month old, so it would be a good idea to call them and make sure the checks are not lost. Leave them **unchecked** on the list.

STEP 17. **Expense 9 for $89.09 to Tania's Nursery** is an error. A week later there's another cleared charge for $108.09 on the statement. The fact that both end in **.09** is a sign they may be duplicates.

After you have confirmed that the $89.09 expense is not needed, it is fine to **Delete** this transaction, since this transaction was made in error during the current period. Click on the transaction, select **Edit**, click on **More**, then choose **Delete**. In the confirmation window, click **Yes**.

> **IMPORTANT!**
>
> If Craig's Landscaping closed its books every month, you would not want to delete the transaction. Instead you would create a **Bank Deposit** with the current statement date to reverse the expense, using the same vendor and expense categories. Reconcile both the erroneous charge and the deposit together, since they net to $0.

STEP 18. The **$19.99** cash expense to **Squeeky Kleen Car Wash** was really paid by credit card. Click on the transaction, select **Edit**, then change the *Bank/Credit Account* to **Mastercard**. **Save and Close** the expense.

STEP 19. The **$5.66** cash expense to **Bob's Burger Joint** was paid by with the owner's personal money, not from the business checking account. In addition, this was just Craig getting lunch between jobs, not a true Meals expense. He had paid for his lunch with his own money but imported the receipt out of habit; therefore, it's not really a business transaction.

Click on the transaction and **Edit** it. Click on **More** and then **Delete** the transaction.

FIGURE 6-40: *The finished checking account reconciliation*

STEP 20. The remaining transactions at the end of the month haven't had enough time to be processed, and will appear on next month's reconciliation. Leave them **unchecked**.

BANKING AND RECONCILIATION | 283

STEP 21. When your window matches Figure 6-40, click **Finish Now**.

STEP 22. A confirmation window appears (see Figure 6-41). Click **Done**. We will look at the *Reconciliation Report* shortly.

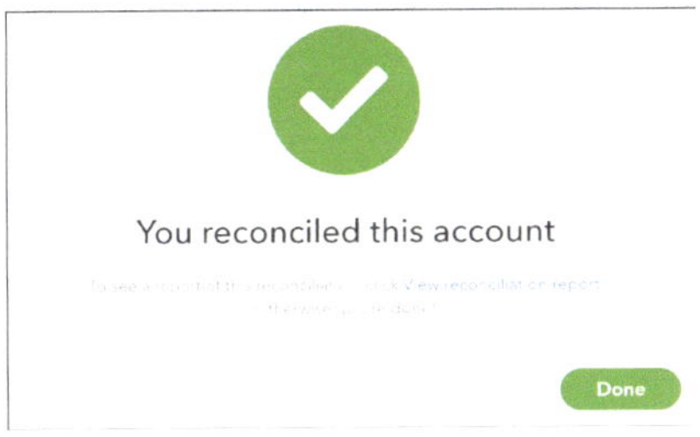

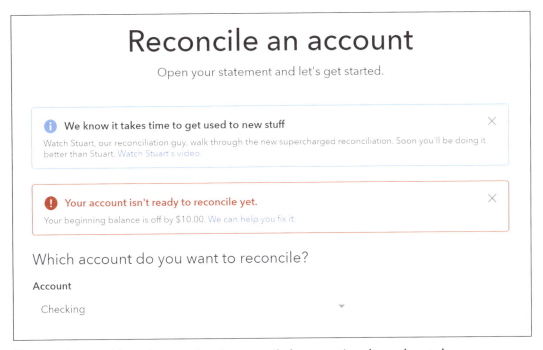

FIGURE 6-41: *The reconciliation confirmation message*

Finding Errors During Bank Reconciliation

Occasionally, errors are uncovered during the reconciliation process. Here are some common issues and what to do about them.

When the Beginning Balance is Incorrect

When you start a reconciliation, the *Beginning Balance* should match the statement, carried over from the previous month's *Ending Balance*. If it does not, you will see the error message shown in Figure 6-42:

FIGURE 6-42: *Alert when previously-reconciled transactions have changed*

There are two possibilities for why the beginning balance no longer matches the bank statement:

1. One or more reconciled transactions were voided, deleted, or edited since the last reconciliation. At the time you said **Yes** to the warning message shown in Figure 6-43.

   FIGURE 6-43: *A warning when editing a reconciled transaction*

   If you are just changing a payee or a category on an expense, it's fine to click through this warning, but changing dates or dollar amounts can create errors in the books.

2. The reconciliation status for one or more transactions in the account register was changed, as shown in Figure 6-44. When you click on the status, you can toggle between R (reconciled), C (cleared in the Banking Feed), or no status (manually entered). Never manually change a transaction status from this box as it is not the proper workflow!

FIGURE 6-44: *Never change the Reconcile status in the account register*

To correct the problem, there are two steps.

1. The first is to simply repeat the most recent reconciliation, duplicating the previous ending balance and date. Sometimes transactions are changed and then corrected. You may see the stray transactions there, ready to be selected. Marking them again may bring your *Difference* back to zero. If it does, click on **Finish Now**. You're ready to pick up where you left off reconciling the current month.

   If this doesn't work, choose **Close Without Saving** to return to the *Reconcile* window.

2. The second troubleshooting step is to use the blue **We Can Help You Fix It** link shown in Figure 6-42 above. When you click this link, a *Reconciliation Discrepancy Report* opens (see Figure 6-45).

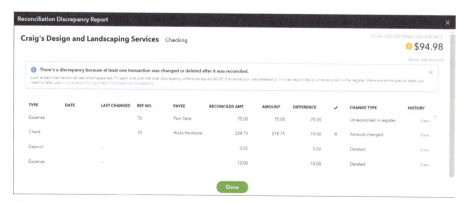

FIGURE 6-45: *A Reconciliation Discrepancy report (your screen will vary)*

   a. If the *Change Type* column reads **Unreconciled in Register** or **Reconciled in Register**, click on the transaction and toggle the **R/C** status back to the proper designation. You can fix this error right here without having to return to the register.

b. If the *Change Type* reads **Amount Changed**, click on the transaction, then change the amount back to the original total. You can **Edit** this transaction to fix the error without having to navigate to the register.
c. For each line of the report with **Deleted** in the *Change Type* column, click **View** to see the original transaction, then recreate it from scratch.

After returning all transactions to their original state as they were at the time of the last reconciliation, you can then proceed to reconcile the current month.

Undoing a Bank Reconciliation

If reconciliations have been done incorrectly going back in time (for example, only matching the transactions on the statement and ignoring all the incorrect transactions), it is possible to **Undo a Reconciliation**. This can only be done by a user with Accountant access.

This is another great reason to join Intuit's **ProAdvisor Program**, as we discussed on page 29.

Managing Incorrectly-Recorded Transactions

When you find a discrepancy between a transaction in QuickBooks Online and a transaction on the bank statement, you need to correct it. You will use different methods to correct the error, depending upon the date of the transaction.

Fixing Duplicated Deposits

If you see deposits that were coded directly to an income category instead of matching existing sales, that is a sign that the deposit was added through the Banking Feed but the transactions are still waiting unmatched in Undeposited Funds (or Payments to Deposit). Edit the deposit, check off the actual sales from the grid at the top, and use the **Trash can** to delete the extra deposit at the bottom in the *Add Funds to This Deposit* grid.

Correcting or Voiding Transactions in the Current Accounting Period

If you find that you need to correct a transaction in QuickBooks Online and the transaction is dated in the **current accounting period** (i.e., a period after your most recent financial statements and/or tax returns have not yet been issued), correct the error as described in the following paragraphs.

If You Made the Error

If you made an error in your records, you can make a correction in QuickBooks Online so that your records agree with the bank. For example, if you wrote a check for $400.00, but you recorded it in QuickBooks Online as $40.00, simply update the check amount in QBO. Edit the transaction right from the *Reconcile* window. Make the correction, and then click **Save and Close.** This will return you to the *Reconcile* window and you will see the updated amount.

When this happens, it's likely that you also see a second transaction for the correct amount that was imported from the Banking Feed. **Edit** the transaction from the Banking Feed and **Delete** it. Return to the Banking Feed, where the transaction will be waiting to be re-matched to the correction you just made.

If the Bank Made the Error

If the bank made an error, delete the transaction that came in from the Banking Feed, and **Exclude** it. Create an extra transaction in the bank account register to adjust your balance for the error, then continue reconciling the account, checking off the true transaction and the compensating adjustment.

Contact the bank and ask them to post an adjustment to correct your account balance. When you receive the bank statement showing the correction, enter a subsequent entry in the bank account register to record the bank's adjustment. This register entry will show on your next bank reconciliation, and you can clear it like any other transaction.

Voiding Checks and Stop Payments

When you find a check dated in the current accounting period that you know will not clear the bank (e.g., if you stop payment on a check), you need to void the check. Open the check from the *Reconcile* window. Select the *More* button and then choose **Void**. Click **Save and Close** to return to the *Reconcile* window.

Correcting Transactions in Closed Accounting Periods

A **closed accounting period** is the period prior to and including the date on which a company officially *closes* its books (for example, 12/31), creates its financial reports, and presents its finalized reports to external stakeholders such as the IRS and investors. Large companies close their books every month.

You do not want to change transactions dated in a closed accounting period because doing so will change financial reports during a period for which you have already issued financial statements or filed tax returns.

This is the most important reason why it is critical to reconcile every month. Not only do you have to account for the transactions that ARE on the statement, there needs to be a good reason for additional transactions NOT on the bank statement. If you have lingering transactions, manage or delete them as soon as you notice them, instead of waiting until you have to create reversing entries to compensate for them.

Removing Deposits

Create an **Expense** dated the first day of the current accounting period (the first day of this month or of this year) that reverses the original deposit. In the *Description*, note the date and transaction number of the original invoice payment, sales receipt, or other deposit. In the original transaction, note the date and transaction number of the reversing entry. Reconcile the two against each other.

Removing Expenses

Use a **Bank Deposit** dated the first day of the current accounting period (the first day of this month or of this year) that reverses the original expense. In the *Description*, note the date and transaction number of the original expense. In the original transaction, note the date and transaction number of the reversing entry. Reconcile the two against each other.

Bank Reconciliation Reports

Many companies will file a paper copy of the bank statement with a printout of the *Reconciliation Report*. With QuickBooks Online, both are available on-demand, but it never hurts to have a backup.

Two links in the upper right allow you to view **Summary** reports and a reconciliation **History by Account**.

As you complete each reconciliation, the confirmation window contains a link to the Reconciliation Summary report for quick access, or you can view them any time as shown below.

BANKING AND RECONCILIATION | 287

HANDS-ON PRACTICE

STEP 1. In the *Reconcile Center* (see Figure 6-38), click the **Summary** link in the upper right corner. The *Reconciliation Summary window* displays a list of all your reconciliations.

FIGURE 6-46: *The Reconciliation Summary window*

This list shows the statement ending dates, and the dates the reconciliations were performed, as shown in Figure 6-46.

STEP 2. Click on the **Checking reconciliation** you just completed.

STEP 3. The *Reconciliation Report* opens, as shown in Figure 6-47. The sections include a *Summary*, the *Checks and Payments Cleared*, and *Deposits and Other Credits Cleared*.

STEP 4. If changes have been made to reconciled transactions, you will also see a *Reconciliation Change Report* at the top.

STEP 5. At the bottom are two sections showing transactions that have not yet been reconciled. Depending on your company, this list may be very long. Click the **Hide Additional Information** box at the top to toggle these sections on and off.

STEP 6. Click the **Reconcile** link at the top right of the report to return to the *Reconciliation* screen.

FIGURE 6-47: *The Reconciliation Report (your screen will vary)*

Reconciling Credit Card Accounts

When you use a ***credit card liability*** account to track all of your credit card charges and payments, you also reconcile the account every month just as you do your bank accounts. The credit card reconciliation process is exactly like the bank account reconciliation, except that when you finish the reconciliation, QuickBooks Online asks you if you want to **Pay All or a Portion of the Bill Now** or **Enter A Bill To Pay Later**.

When this window appears, just click **Done**. Use the *Pay Down Credit Card* feature on page 175 instead.

FIGURE 6-48: *When this box appears, just click Done*

REVIEW QUESTIONS

Comprehension Questions

1. Explain how QuickBooks Online calculates the Beginning Balance field in the Reconciliation window. Why might the beginning balance calculated by QuickBooks Online differ from the beginning balance on your bank statement?

2. Explain why it's important not to change transactions in closed accounting periods.

3. What are the benefits of using the Banking Feeds?

Multiple Choice

Select the best answer(s) for each of the following:

1. When the Beginning Balance field in the Reconcile window doesn't match the beginning balance on the bank statement, you should:
   a. Call the bank.
   b. Repeat the most recent reconciliation to see if the missing transactions are waiting to be re-reconciled to $0.
   c. Click the **We Can Help You Fix It** link.
   d. Both b and c.

2. Which statement is false?
   a. You can enter bank service charges using *Enter Statement Charges*.
   b. You can sometimes enter bank service charges on the *Reconcile* window.
   c. Bank service charges may come in through the Banking Feed.
   d. You can enter bank service charges using an *Expense* before you start your reconciliation.

3. When you find an erroneous amount on a transaction while reconciling, correct the amount by:
   a. Changing the amount in the Banking Feed.
   b. Opening the original transaction and changing its amount.
   c. Editing the entry in the **Reconcile** window and changing the amount on the transaction.
   d. Performing either b or c.

4. To properly void an uncashed lost check from a closed accounting period:
   a. Void the check in the register.
   b. Delete the check.
   c. Make a deposit in the current period for the same amount, and code it to the same account as the original check you want to void. Then mark both transactions as cleared in the **Reconcile** window.
   d. Leave it in the register to remind you it was never cashed.

5. Which of the following columns cannot be displayed in the Reconcile window?

a. Ref No..
   b. Class.
   c. Date.
   d. Payee.

6. You know you have reconciled your bank account correctly when:
   a. You make a *Reconciliation Discrepancy* entry.
   b. The *Difference* field shows **0.00**.
   c. You have marked off all the transactions on the bank statement, even if there are others remaining.
   d. All of the above.

7. The Reconciliation Report shows:
   a. The Beginning Balance shown on the Bank Statement.
   b. All the transactions on the statement for the month.
   c. The actual Register Balance as of the reconciliation date.
   d. All of the above.

8. What accounts should be reconciled?
   a. Most Balance Sheet accounts.
   b. Any account that receives regular statements.
   c. Any bank, income or expense account.
   d. Only bank accounts can be reconciled.

9. You should connect which accounts to the Banking Feed?
   a. Business checking and savings accounts.
   b. Business credit cards.
   c. Personal accounts if the owner commingles funds.
   d. Both a and b.

10. All sales income in the Banking Feed should:
    a. Be entered by hand.
    b. Be Excluded, since the sales receipts and invoice payments are already in the system.
    c. Be ignored.
    d. Match with Bank Deposits.

11. When you finish reconciling a credit card account and the confirmation box appears, it is a best practice to:
    a. Click *Pay All or a Portion of the Bill Now*.
    b. Click *Enter a Bill to Pay Later*.
    c. Dismiss the confirmation box without taking further action.
    d. Click *Pay Down Credit Card* right from this box.

12. The two view options for the Banking Feed are the:
    a. Business View and the Bookkeeper View.
    b. Entry View and the Confirmation View.
    c. Accountant View and the Business View.

d. None of the above.

13. In what account is a transaction created if you complete a reconciliation and your difference is not 0.00?
    a. Opening Balance Equity.
    b. Uncategorized Income.
    c. Reconciliation Discrepancies.
    d. Other Expense.

14. Your Net Income is vastly overstated. What could be causing the problem?
    a. Deposits were added through the Banking Feed instead of matched to existing sales transactions.
    b. Transactions in the checking register were left unreconciled.
    c. Vendor checks still haven't been cashed.
    d. Both a and b.

15. If the Banking Feed shows an incorrect Payee or Category, you should:
    a. Click on the transaction and enter the correct information.
    b. Stop using it because something's wrong.
    c. Add it as is—QuickBooks Online must know what it's doing.
    d. Use Find Match to update the information.

Completion Statements

1. QuickBooks Online calculates the Beginning Balance in the Reconcile window by adding and subtracting all previously _____ transactions.

2. Using Banking _____ to automate data entry.

3. The _____ tab in the Banking Feed shows all transactions imported from the bank waiting for review.

4. You can attach copies of your _____ to your transactions to maintain a paper trail.

5. The banking feed uses state-of-the-art _____ to keep your data secure.

BANKING AND RECONCILIATIONS—APPLY YOUR KNOWLEDGE

*Log into your **Imagine Photography** class file at qbo.intuit.com.*

Because we can't connect a live bank account to Imagine Photography, we will import a .csv data file. Note that the dates may not match the transactions you created.

1. Create a bank file to upload.
    a. In Excel, open the **ImagineBankingImport.xls** file from the textbook's Classroom Files.

b. Click on **File** and choose **Save As**.
c. Change the *File type* to **.csv** as shown in Figure 6-49, then **Save** the new file.

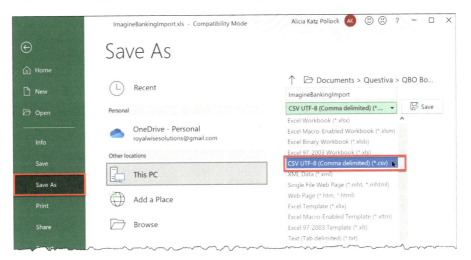

FIGURE 6-49: *Save the xls file as csv for import*

2. Upload transactions into the Banking Center downloaded from your bank
    a. From the *Banking Center*, click on **Upload Transactions**.
    b. **Browse** to your new **ImagineBankingImport.csv** file, then click **Continue**.
    c. In the *QuickBooks Account* field, choose **Business Checking (1025)**, then click **Continue**.
    d. Use the settings in Figure 6-50 to prepare your import.
    e. Click **Continue**.
    f. Click the **checkbox** at the top of the list (the square to left of the *Date* column header) to select all the transactions, then click **Continue** again.
    g. In the box that says *QuickBooks Will Import 19 Transaction(s) Using The Fields You Chose. Do You Want To Import Now?* Click **Yes**. In the next window, click **Done**.

FIGURE 6-50: *Use these settings to prepare your import*

3. The next step is to Match existing transactions. Nine of the transactions in the Banking Feed match the work you have done in the exercises. Note that some of the dates may be different.
    a. If transactions appear with **Matches** that say **1 Record Found**, click **Match** next to each one, or use the **Batch Accept** feature.
    b. If you don't have nine matches, your dates may too far away. Use **Find Match** on the transactions you recognize from lessons so far. If necessary, extend the *From Date* in the *Match Transactions* window to start with an earlier date. *If you are not sure of all of the matches, follow the steps below to eliminate the new transactions, and then return to this step.*

4. Click on the **$200** transaction with the Description **Transfer To 7809.** Change the *Dot* to **Record as Transfer**. Update *Transferred To* to **Money Market (7809)**, then **Add** the transaction.

5. Click on the **$10,000** received from **Owner Contribution**. This is the money the owner, Ernest Withers, deposited to open the bank account. If needed, change the *dot* to **Categorize**. Enter **Ernest Withers** as the *Vendor/Customer*. Change the *Category* to **Owner Investments** with the *Class* **Overhead**. Click **Add**.

6. Find the **Facebook** expense for **$15.67**. Add **Facebook** as a new **Vendor** on the fly. Update the *Category* to **Advertising & Marketing:Social Media**. In the *Class* field, choose **San Jose**. Choose the *Tag* **Weddings**. Click **Add**.

7. Notice a second **Facebook** expense for **$16.72** is now recognized with a *Payee* in green. Click on the transaction to review it and update the *Tags* to **Weddings**, then click **Add**.

8. Because this is the second Facebook transaction you've categorized, QuickBooks Online asks if you want to create a Rule. Turn **off** the **Auto-add** slider, because sometimes the ads may be for other services besides weddings. Click **Create Rule**.

9. There's a third **Facebook** transaction for **$5**, but it's a Deposit because Facebook gave you an advertising refund. Add Facebook in the *Vendor/Customer* field, and enter **Advertising & Marketing:Social Media** in the *Category* field. Update the *Class* to **San Jose**, and the *Tags* to **Weddings**. Update the *Memo* to read **Facebook Advertising Refund.** Click **Add**.

10. The Adobe expense is software for photo editing on the Satterley Wedding Planners jobs. Add **Adobe** as a new *Vendor* on the fly. Change the *Category* to **Office Expenses:Software & Apps**. In the *Customer/Project* field, choose **Gregg and Andrew David**, but do not make it Billable. The *Class* is **San Jose**. Add **Weddings** in the *Tags* field. In the *Memo*, type **Adobe Software for photo retouching.** **Add** the transaction.

11. Create a **Rule** for **Mailchimp Expenses** using the information below. You'll need to add a new Vendor on the fly. Click the *Test Rule* button—you should get 1 match. Set it to **Auto-add**.

RULE	FIELD
WHAT DO YOU WANT TO CALL THIS RULE?	Mailchimp
APPLY THIS TO TRANSACTIONS THAT ARE	Money Out
IN	All Bank Accounts
BANK TEXT—CONTAINS	Mailchimp
TRANSACTION TYPE	Expense
CATEGORY	Advertising & Marketing:Marketing
PAYEE	Mailchimp
CLASS	Overhead
AUTO-ADD	Yes

TABLE 6-1: *An Expense Rule*

12. Create a **Rule** to split the internet utilities 50/50 between the two Classes. Use the information in the table below. You'll need to add a new Vendor on the fly. Set it to Auto-add.

RULE	FIELD
WHAT DO YOU WANT TO CALL THIS RULE?	InternetLink
APPLY THIS TO TRANSACTIONS THAT ARE	Money Out
IN	All Bank Accounts
BANK TEXT—CONTAINS	InternetLink
TRANSACTION TYPE	Expense
ADD A SPLIT	Percentage
SPLIT DETAIL 1—PERCENTAGE	50
SPLIT DETAIL 1—CATEGORY	Utilities:Internet & TV Services
SPLIT DETAIL 1—CLASS	San Jose
SPLIT DETAIL 2—PERCENTAGE	50
SPLIT DETAIL 2—CATEGORY	Utilities:Internet & TV Services
SPLIT DETAIL 2—CLASS	Walnut Creek
PAYEE (ADD ON THE FLY)	InternetLink
AUTO-ADD	Yes

TABLE 6-2: *An Expense Rule with Split Classes*

13. Create a **Rule** called **Interest Earned** for the Interest transaction. Apply this to **Money In** transactions. Set the *Condition* to **Bank Text Contains Interest**. The *Category* is **Other Income:Interest Earned**. The *Payee* is **National Bank**. The *Class* is **Overhead**. Set it to **Auto-add**.

14. Create a **Rule** called **Bank Fees** for transactions where the **Bank Text Contains Service Charge**. The *Category* is **General Business Expenses:Bank Fees & Service Charges**. The *Payee* is **National Bank**. The *Class* is **Overhead**. Set it to **Auto-add**.

15. Using the sample bank statement shown below, reconcile the checking account for **the last day of the current month**, using an *Ending Balance* of **5455.51**.
    a. Include any **$0** transactions (you are welcome to **Edit** and review them for confirmation).
    b. Depending on the date of your reconciliation, Jaime Madeira's $875 bounced check invoice dated the *1st of next month* may not show because it was dated the first of the next month. If it is missing from your Reconciliation, refer to the *Are There Post-Dated Transactions?* instructions on page 281.
    c. Are there transactions in your register that aren't on the statement? These are payments that haven't cleared the bank yet.

IMPORTANT!

Reconciliations are typically done for past dates. Because we are in an exercise file and do not have historic transactions, we will reconcile this month's data, even though the month is not over yet.

National Bank

Imagine Photography's Checking Account 123409871025

Statement Date: The last day of this month
Page 1 of 1

Summary:

Previous Balance:		$	0.00
Total Deposits and Credits	+	$	15,184.41
Total Checks and Debits	-	$	9,718.91
Service Charges	-	$	10.00
Interest Earned	+	$	0.01
Statement Balance	=	$	5,455.51

Deposits and Other Credits:

DEPOSITS

Date	Description	Amount
31-	Customer Deposit	$ 10,000.00
19-	Customer Deposit	$ 5.00
21-	Customer Deposit	$ 3,330.00
21-	Customer Deposit	$ 40.00
30-	Customer Deposit	$ 1,809.41
	Deposits: $	15,184.41

Transactions Checks/Withdrawals:

TRANSACTIONS

Check No.	Date Paid	Amount
1001	1-	$ 1,500.00
	2-	$ 180.00
	8-	$ 29.99
	12-	$ 9.99
	12-	$ 15.67
	19-	$ 16.72
	20-	$ 16.54
	21-	$ 5,000.00
1002	30-	$ 665.00
1003	30-	$ 1,210.00
	30-	$ 200.00
1011	30-	$ 875.00
Total Payment Withdrawals: $		9,718.91

INTEREST

Date	Description	Amount
31-	Interest Earned	0.01
	Interest: $	0.01

CHECKS PAID

No.	Date	Description	Amount
1001	1-		$1,500.00
1002	30-		$665.00
1003	30-		$1,210.00
1011	30-		$875.00
		Checks Total: $	$4,250.00

SERVICE CHARGES

Date	Description		Amount
30-	Service Charge	$	$ 10.00
	Service Charge: $		$ 10.00

National Bank

FIGURE 6-51: Checking statement for the last day of the current month. Your dates will not match.

16. Print a Reconciliation Report.

CHAPTER 7

REPORTS

TOPICS

In this chapter, you will learn about the following topics:

- Finding Transactions (page 296)
- Cash vs. Accrual Reporting (page 299)
- Types of Reports (page 299)
- The Reports Center (page 300)
- Accounting Reports (page 301)
- Business Management Reports (page 313)
- Accounts Receivable and Accounts Payable Reports (page 320)
- Creating Sales Reports (page 323)
- Customizing Reports (page 325)
- Printing Reports (page 332)
- Exporting Reports to Spreadsheets (page 334)

> **OPEN THIS FILE:**
>
> Open the *Craig's Landscaping sample company* using the bookmark you created on page 8, or go to http://qbo.intuit.com/redir/testdrive.

This chapter starts with the different search features that allow you to locate transactions.
   Then we'll dive into QuickBooks Online reports to allow you to get the information you need to make critical business decisions. You'll learn how to create a variety of reports to help you manage your business. Every report in QuickBooks Online gives you immediate, up-to-date information about your company's performance.
   In addition to the built-in reports, you can customize reports to include or exclude whatever data you want. Once you get a report looking just the way you want, you can save the modifications so that you can quickly open it again later.
   Reports can also be exported into a spreadsheet program for further manipulation.

FINDING TRANSACTIONS

There are several ways to find transactions in QuickBooks Online depending on what you are looking for. Sometimes you only know the date of a transaction; other times you know only the customer, product, or amount. Some of the ways you can locate a transaction include *Filtering* the register, using the *Search* magnifying glass, and using the *Advanced Search*.

Filtering the Register

If you're looking for a particular transaction based on multiple criteria, or would like to see it with others created around the same time, *Filtering* the checking or credit card register allows you to view transactions in context.

This powerful filter allows you to search any register by any combination of **memo**, **reference number**, **dollar amount**, **reconciliation status**, **transaction type**, **payee**, and **date**.

HANDS-ON PRACTICE

Craig would like to see a list of all checks he has written that have not yet been cashed by his vendors.

STEP 1. Click on **Chart of Accounts** in the *Accounting* section of the *Left Navigation Bar*.

STEP 2. Click the **View Register** link to the right of the *Checking* account.

STEP 3. Click the **Funnel** at the top left of the transaction list as shown in Figure 7-1.

STEP 4. Change the *Reconcile Status* to **No Status**.

STEP 5. Change the *Transaction Type* to **Check**.

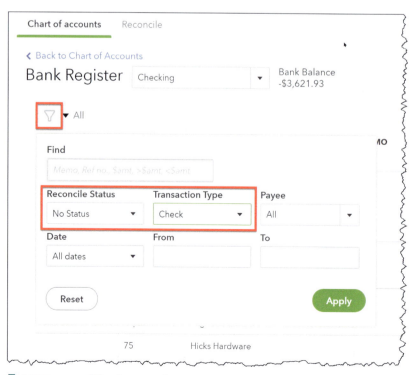

FIGURE 7-1: *Filtering a register*

Step 6. Click **Apply**. The *Checking Register* now only shows checks that have no Banking Feed match (see Figure 7-2).

Not only can you now view a list of checks that never cleared the bank, but you can also print the list or export it to Excel using the buttons on the top right.

Step 7. Click the blue **Clear Filter/View All** link to remove the filters. Filters can also be removed individually by clicking the **X** next to each.

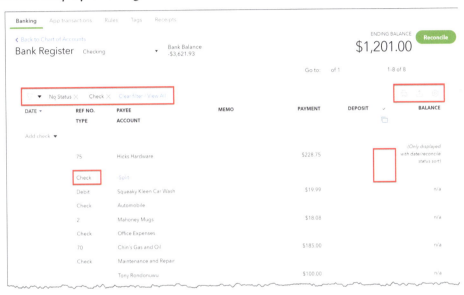

Figure 7-2: *The checking register with filters applied*

Using Advanced Search

We introduced the *Search Magnifying Glass* on page 20. It makes reopening your 10 most recent transactions a breeze, and you can jump to any transaction, customer, vendor, or report in a few keystrokes.

If the Search doesn't find an instant match, it will open the *Advanced Search* window. You can also open it any time using the link at the bottom of the Search results (see Figure 7-3).

The *Advanced Search* window, shown in Figure 7-4, allows you to search for a specific **Date**, **transaction Type**, **Reference Number**, **Contact**, and **Amount**. The *Additional Filters* button adds drop-down lists for **Products and Services** or **Accounts**. In addition, the *Search field* at the top helps refine the search by specifying **Description**, **Memo**, or even **dollar amounts on lines inside a transaction**. You can combine several filters together to refine the results.

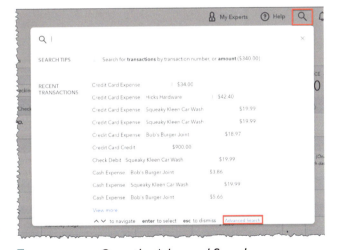

Figure 7-3: *Open the Advanced Search*

This is a great tool to add as a browser bookmark so you can get to it quickly! See page 8 for more information on creating bookmarks.

HANDS-ON PRACTICE

Craig's Landscaping knows that they wrote a $100 invoice to Amy's Bird Sanctuary, but they don't see it on her transactions list.

STEP 1. Open the *Advanced Search* window by clicking on the **magnifying glass** in the upper right of your screen, then on **Advanced Search** in the bottom right corner of the *Search* window (see Figure 7-3).

STEP 2. Enter **100** in the field at the top, then click the **Magnifying Glass**. You will see three results (see Figure 7-4).

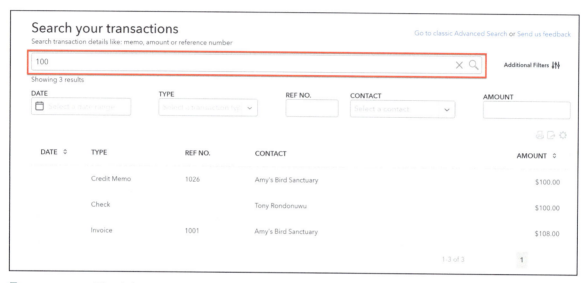

FIGURE 7-4: The Advanced Search window

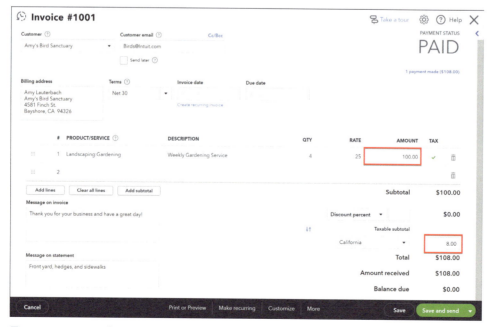

FIGURE 7-5: A $100 line item on a $108 invoice

Step 3. Amy's Bird Sanctuary has two results on the list, an invoice and a credit memo. The invoice is for **$108**, not $100. Click on it to open the transaction (see Figure 7-5).

Step 4. The invoice shows a sale of **$100** for Gardening Services, plus **$8** in sales tax. Click **Cancel** or the **X** in the upper right corner to close the form without saving.

CASH VS. ACCRUAL REPORTING

QuickBooks Online can automatically convert reports from accrual basis to cash basis.

If you use *Cash-basis accounting*, you regard income or expenses as occurring at the time you receive a payment from a customer or pay a bill to a vendor. Cash-basis accounting recognizes income or expenses only when cash is received or paid, no matter when the original business activity occurred.

If you use *Accrual-basis accounting*, income and expenses are recorded on the date of the business activity, when you ship a product, render a service, or are charged by a vendor. Under this method, the transaction is recognized on the date of the invoice or bill, even if the date you actually pay or receive payment is different.

Even though most small businesses in the US operate day-to-day on an accrual basis using Accounts Receivable and Accounts Payable, most small business owners think of themselves as cash-based and file their taxes that way.

Cash-based reports focus on transactions that are complete, whereas Accrual-based reports provide a big-picture look at all business activity.

Regardless of how taxes are filed (as you declared in the Advanced Settings on page 41), you can toggle QuickBooks Online's Reports back and forth between cash and accrual. Both views provide important information about your business.

> **DID YOU KNOW?**
>
> ProAdvisors using QuickBooks Online for Accountants (QBOA) have an option in their *Accountant Tools* briefcase called **Report Options**. This setting lets them apply a default date range and basis for all reports. See page 3 for more information about QBOA.

TYPES OF REPORTS

There are two major types of reports in QuickBooks Online: **accounting reports** and **business management** reports. In addition, many reports have both "**Summary**" and "**Detail**" styles. Summary reports show totals for categories of transactions, while Detail reports show lists of the individual transactions that make up these totals.

Accounting reports contain information about accounts and transactions. For example, the *Profit & Loss* report is a summary report of all transactions coded to income and expense accounts in the General Ledger for a specified period of time. Your accountant or tax preparer will need several accounting reports from QuickBooks Online in order to provide advisory and tax services for your company.

Business management reports provide critical information that you need to operate your business. These reports are used to generate lists, review and analyze transactions that have already occurred, and monitor business activity to help plan for the future.

REPORT TYPE	EXAMPLE REPORTS
ACCOUNTING	Profit & Loss, Balance Sheet, Trial Balance, Statement of Cash Flows, General Ledger
BUSINESS MANAGEMENT	Open Invoices, Unpaid Bills, Check Detail, Sales by Product/Service Detail, Income by Customer Summary, Customer Contact List, Product/Service List, Time Activities by Employee Detail, Physical Inventory Worksheet

TABLE 7-1: *Types of QuickBooks Online reports*

THE REPORTS CENTER

The **Reports Center** in the *Left Navigation Bar* brings all your reports together in one place.

Depending on the version of QuickBooks Online you have, you will see between 20 and 100+ reports. As you turn on additional features, their associated reports will appear as well. For example, you will only see inventory reports if you are using QuickBooks Online Plus or Advanced, and have *Inventory* turned on.

The *Reports Center*, shown in Figure 7-6, has three tabs across the top:

▸ *Standard* is the main list of built-in reports.

▸ *Custom Reports* contains the reports you customized and saved.

▸ *Management Reports* contain professionally-designed report layouts. You can compile several reports into one document, and email it to your company stakeholders or your clients automatically on a schedule.

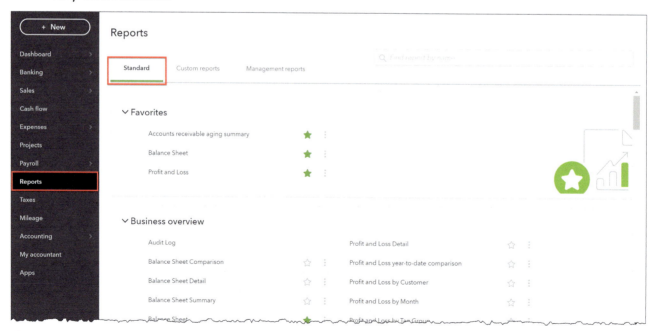

FIGURE 7-6: *The Reports Center*

As you scroll down the list of reports on the *Standard* tab, they are broken up into groups. You can click the arrow to the left of each group to collapse a set of reports if you don't need them.

- *Favorites* contains your frequently-run reports. Click the star next to any report to include it on this list.

- *Business Overview* contains variations of the most important operations reports including the Profit and Loss Statement, Balance Sheet, and Statement of Cash Flows.

- *Who Owes You* contains useful Accounts Receivable reports.

- *Sales and Customers* includes reports about your income based on what you sold, and who you sold it to.

- *What You Owe* features Accounts Payable reports.

- *Expenses and Vendors* analyzes your expenses based on what you paid for, and who you bought it from.

- *Sales Tax Reports* appear when you turn on the Sales Tax Center.

- *Employees* contains reports about your personnel and their time sheets.

- *For My Accountant* includes reports commonly used by bookkeepers and tax preparers.

- *Payroll* starts with basic reports. More appear when you subscribe to QuickBooks Payroll.

> **TIP:**
>
> If you're not sure which report you're looking for, use the **Find Reports By Name** search box. Type in the information you're looking for, and QuickBooks Online will make suggestions that include those words.

ACCOUNTING REPORTS

There are several built-in reports that summarize transactions. These reports are used for tax prep and also help you analyze the performance of your business.

Profit & Loss Statement

The **Profit & Loss** report (also referred to as an **Income Statement** or a **P&L**) is a company's operating results, showing all the income and expenses during a given period, normally 12 months or less.

As discussed earlier, the goal of accounting is to provide the financial information needed to measure the success (or failure) of your organization, as well as to file proper tax returns. The *Profit & Loss* report is one of the most valuable tools for this analysis.

The *Profit & Loss* report summarizes the totals of all your **Income** accounts, followed by **Cost of Goods Sold** accounts, then **Expenses**, **Other Income**, and finally **Other Expenses**. The total at the bottom of the report is the **Net Income** (or loss) during the period specified in the *Report Period* fields.

QUICKBOOKS COMPLETE

HANDS-ON PRACTICE

Step 1. Click on **Reports** in the *Left Navigation Bar.*

Step 2. Click on **Profit and Loss** in the *Favorites* section at the top (see Figure 7-7). Alternatively, this report is also found in the *Business Overview* section.

Step 3. Toggle the **Collapse/Expand** option to view and hide the sub-accounts.

Figure 7-7: *The Profit and Loss Statement*

Step 4. This report is accrual-based, meaning that it includes unpaid invoices and bills. In Figure 7-7 above, the *Total Income* is **$10,200.77** and *Total Expenses* is **$5,237.31**. The *Net Income* is **$1,642.46**, representing the profit on all the business Craig's Landscaping has done.

Step 5. At the top, change the *Accounting Method* to **Cash**, then click **Run Report**.

The numbers in *Total Income* and *Total Expenses* change, because now the report excludes open invoices and bills. It only shows money received and paid. If the *Net Income* is negative, this indicates that Craig's Landscaping has spent more money than it has received.

Step 6. Click on the *Total* to the right of the **Landscaping Services** income row. A *Transaction Report* opens, showing a detailed list of transactions that make up the P&L total (see Figure 7-8).

Step 7. When you're done reviewing the report, click the blue **<Back to Report Summary** link in the upper left. You will return to the Profit & Loss report.

Figure 7-8: *A Transaction Detail Report for the Landscaping Services category on the P&L*

Analyzing the Profit & Loss Report

To understand the P&L Statement, refer to the sections indicated in Figure 7-7 above.

1. *Income*—The total of each of your income categories for the period specified on the report. If you have sub-accounts, QuickBooks Online indents those accounts on the report and subtotals them. Notice on your screen that (when viewed on the Accrual basis) the **Labor** income category has two sub-accounts: **Installation** and **Maintenance and Repair**. To hide sub-accounts on this report (or any summary report), click the **Collapse** link at the top of the report, then click **Expand** to bring them back again.

2. *Cost of Goods Sold*—These accounts record the direct costs of the products and services sold in your business (e.g., inventory, cost of labor, etc.). If you use **Inventory Items**, QuickBooks Online increases **Cost of Goods Sold** as each product is sold, using the **"First In First Out" (FIFO) method** (discussed in the Inventory products section starting on page 63).

   Cost of Goods Sold is subtracted from your *Total Income*, calculating your *Gross Profit*, the total amount of money you earned from selling products and services.

3. *Expenses*—The cost of doing business. Use these accounts to record overhead costs associated with operations (e.g., rent, salaries, supplies, etc.). These are the costs you incur whether or not you have any sales.

   Expenses are recorded in QuickBooks Online as you write checks, enter credit card charges, and create bills, but can also be recorded directly into a register or as a journal entry.

4. *Other Expense* and *Other Income*—Use these accounts to record income and expenses that are generated outside the normal operation of your business. For example, if you provide bookkeeping services but sold an old business computer, the income generated from the disposal would be classified as **Other Income** because it did not result from your regular revenue streams.

5. *Net Income*—The total of your Gross Profit minus your operating expenses, offset by Other Income and Other Expenses.

HANDS-ON PRACTICE

You may want to view your expenses (such as rent, office supplies, employee salaries, etc.) as a ***percentage of total income*** to help you locate excessive expenses in your business.

STEP 8. Change your Profit & Loss *Report Period* to **Since 365 Days Ago** and **Accrual** basis.

STEP 9. Drop down the *Compare Another Period* box and click the **% of Income** box, then click **Run Report** (see Figure 7-9).

STEP 10. The *Profit & Loss* report now has a *% of Income* column (see Figure 7-10).

Monitoring these numbers allows you to quickly identify how much of your income came from specific revenue streams. It also allows you to notice when income and expenses deviate from the norm. Familiarize yourself with the

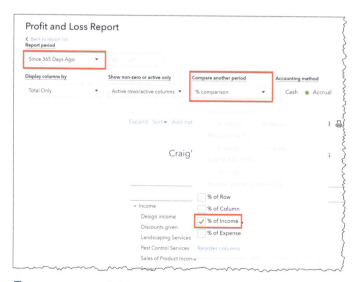

FIGURE 7-9: *Add % of Income to the P&L*

percentages of expenses in your business, and compare these allocations to benchmarks in your industry. Review this report periodically to make sure you allocate your spending appropriately.

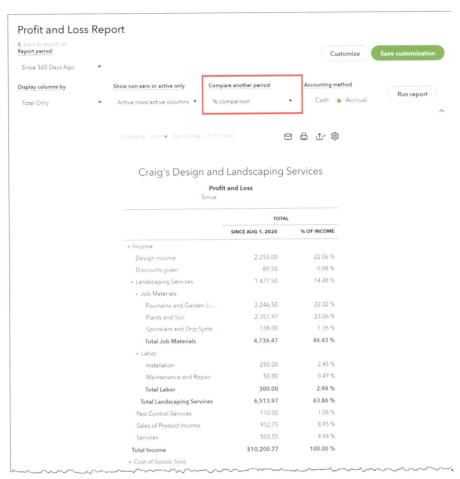

FIGURE 7-10: *Profit & Loss report modified with a % of Income column*

Profit & Loss by Class Report

Do not perform these steps now. They are for reference only.

Classes (discussed on page 71) must be turned on in your file to see this report in the *Business Overview* section of the *Report Center*.

To divide your *Profit & Loss* report into classes, use the *Profit & Loss by Class* report. Alternatively, you can also turn on columns for **Classes** from the *Display Columns By* drop-down at the top of many reports.

Figure 7-11 displays a sample Profit and Loss by Class report from the Imagine Photography exercise file. Notice that totals for *San Jose*, *Walnut Creek*, and *Overhead* are displayed in separate columns.

This report includes a *Not Specified* column, which means that some of the transactions were not assigned a class when they were created. When using *Classes*, be sure to always enter the class as you save each form to prevent any transactions from appearing as *Not Specified*. If a transaction does not fall within one of the classes in your company file, use a general class such as *Overhead*.

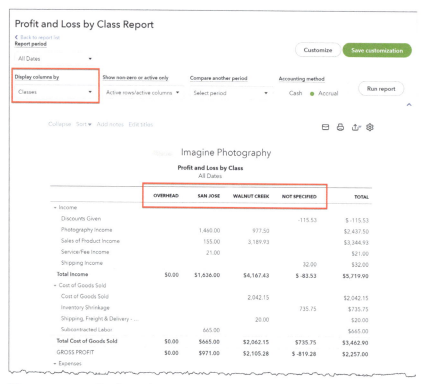

FIGURE 7-11: *Profit and Loss by Class report*

To ensure that transactions are always assigned to classes, configure the *Advanced Account and Settings* so that QuickBooks Online will prompt you to assign a class before saving each transaction. To review these settings, see page 44.

If the class was simply skipped during the entry process, you can fix them by drilling in to the *Not Specified* totals and editing the transactions to add the missing information.

Unfortunately, some transactions cannot be attributed to a class, including discounts on an invoice, or transfers. These can be manually distributed to classes using **Adjusting Journal Entries**.

At year end, an advanced business management technique is to reallocate all Overhead and Not Specified transactions across all of the classes, according to % of income in each class. The end result is a P&L that only has columns for the classes, allowing you to analyze your company's net income by class.

> ### DID YOU KNOW?
>
> In QBOA, the Accountant's version of QuickBooks Online, the **Reclassify Transactions** tool is used to add or change classes on each transaction. It is much faster than manually updating transactions, and more accurate than using journal entries to make adjustments.
>
> As a bonus, *Reclassify Transactions* can also be used to move transactions from one expense category to another, allowing you to quickly fix data entry errors.
>
> Sometimes regular users can access this tool using the URL **https://app.qbo.intuit.com/app/reclassify-transaction**. By replacing everything after "app/" in your QBO's web address with "reclassify-transaction," you may be able to gain access to this magical tool.

Profit & Loss by Customer Report

To divide your *Profit & Loss* into **customers** and **sub-customers**, use the *Profit & Loss by Customer* report. This report, also called a **Job Costing** report, allows you to see your profitability by each customer or job. This information helps you to spot pricing problems, as well as costs that are out of the ordinary. For example, if this report showed that Craig's Landscaping lost money on all the jobs where they installed sprinklers and drip systems, they would probably want to raise their prices for those jobs. Similarly, if the cost on a job for one customer is significantly higher or lower than other jobs of similar size, you might look closer at that job to see if intervention is needed to control costs.

HANDS-ON PRACTICE

To create a *Profit & Loss by Customer* report, follow these steps:

Step 1. In the *Reports Center*, click on **Profit and Loss by Customer** in the *Business Overview* section (see Figure 7-12).

This report can be quite wide, depending on your date range and number of active customers.

Step 2. Note there are header and subtotal columns for *customers* and *sub-customers*. For example, there are four columns for **Freeman Sporting Goods, 0969 Ocean View Road, 55 Twin Lane**, and **Total Freeman Sporting Goods**.

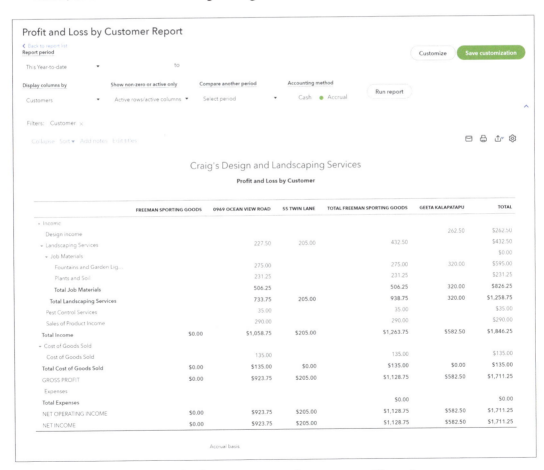

Figure 7-12: *Profit & Loss by Customer report (your screen will vary)*

> **DID YOU KNOW?**
>
> You can **adjust any column** on the report to make it wider or narrower. Hold your cursor over the thin lines between the column headers until you get a double-headed arrow, and drag to the left or to the right. It takes a very fine touch!

Balance Sheet

Another essential report for analyzing your business is the *Balance Sheet*. The Balance Sheet shows your financial position, as defined by the balances in each of your assets, liabilities, and equity accounts on a given date.

HANDS-ON PRACTICE

STEP 1. Click on **Reports** in the *Left Navigation Bar*.

STEP 2. Click on **Balance Sheet** in the *Favorites* section at the top (see Figure 7-13).

> **TIP:**
>
> Familiarize yourself with how your *Balance Sheet* changes throughout the year. Banks examine this report very closely before approving loans. Often, the bank will calculate the ratio of your current assets divided by your current liabilities. This ratio, known as the **Current Ratio**, measures your ability to satisfy your debts.

Analyzing the Balance Sheet

As we discussed at the beginning of the book on page 4, the *Balance Sheet* represents the accounting equation, Assets = Liabilities + Equity.

Assets

1. *Bank Accounts*—all the cash you have in the bank that can be used to pay expenses.
2. *Accounts Receivable*—the money customers owe you (viewed on accrual basis).
3. *Other Current Assets*—assets likely to be converted to cash or used up within a year (not shown).
4. *Inventory Assets*—the value of unsold products purchased for resale.
5. *Undeposited Funds* or *Payments to Deposit*—the money customers have paid you that has not yet cleared the bank.
6. *Fixed Assets*—vehicles, equipment, furniture, buildings, and other large purchases.

Liabilities

7. *Accounts Payable*—the money you owe vendors (viewed on accrual basis).

8. *Credit Cards*—the total balances on your credit cards.

9. *Other Current Liabilities*—sales tax, payroll tax, and other debts likely to be paid within a year.

10. *Long-term Liabilities*—loans and other debts to be repaid over more than one year.

Equity

11. *Opening Balance Equity*—a temporary category used to set up accounts in QuickBooks Online. The balance should be transferred to Retained Earnings upon completion so that it equals zero.

12. *Retained Earnings*—undistributed revenue, calculated automatically by QuickBooks Online based on accumulated net income over time, with adjustments for owner equity.

13. *Net Income*—the grand total from the bottom of a Profit and Loss Statement run for the same date range.

FIGURE 7-13: *The Balance Sheet report*

Statement of Cash Flows

The *Statement of Cash Flows* report provides information about a business's receipts and payments during a given period. In addition, it provides information about investing and financing activities, such as purchasing equipment or borrowing. The *Statement of Cash Flows* shows the detail of how you spent the cash shown on the company's *Balance Sheet*.

It also explains the mystery of why you see more profit on your *P&L* than you have money in your bank account.

HANDS-ON PRACTICE

STEP 1. Click on **Reports** in the *Left Navigation Bar*.

STEP 2. Click on **Statement of Cash Flows** in the *Business Overview* section.

STEP 3. Set the *Report Period* to **This Year-to-Date**.

STEP 4. On the report shown in Figure 7-14, you can see that although there was a net income of $1,642.46, there was a net increase in cash of $4063.52, even higher.

Many financial transactions occurred this year outside normal business activity:

▸ Invoices in Accounts Receivable haven't been paid yet.

▸ Cash is tied up in inventory.

▸ Money in Accounts Payable is already allocated to paying bills.

- Money is owed to pay the credit card balance.
- Money is owed for to the Board of Equalization for Sales Tax.
- $4,000 is owed on a loan.
- $13,495 was spent to buy a truck.
- The company took out a $25,000 loan, incurring a liability but adding cash to the company.

Bankers look closely at this report to determine if your business is able to generate a positive cash flow, or if your business requires additional capital to satisfy its cash needs.

Craig's Design and Landscaping Services
Statement of Cash Flows

	TOTAL
▼ OPERATING ACTIVITIES	
Net Income	1,642.46
▼ Adjustments to reconcile Net Income to Net Cash provid…	
Accounts Receivable (A/R)	-5,281.52
Inventory Asset	-596.25
Accounts Payable (A/P)	1,602.67
Mastercard	157.72
Arizona Dept. of Revenue Payable	0.00
Board of Equalization Payable	370.94
Loan Payable	4,000.00
Total Adjustments to reconcile Net Income to Net Cash…	253.56
Net cash provided by operating activities	$1,896.02
▼ INVESTING ACTIVITIES	
Truck:Original Cost	-13,495.00
Net cash provided by investing activities	$ -13,495.00
▼ FINANCING ACTIVITIES	
Notes Payable	25,000.00
Opening Balance Equity	-9,337.50
Net cash provided by financing activities	$15,662.50
NET CASH INCREASE FOR PERIOD	$4,063.52
CASH AT END OF PERIOD	$4,063.52

FIGURE 7-14: *Statement of Cash Flows report*

General Ledger

The ***General Ledger*** report shows you all the activity in all your accounts during a specific period.

HANDS-ON PRACTICE

STEP 1.   Click on **Reports** in the *Left Navigation Bar.*

STEP 2. Click on **General Ledger** in the *For My Accountant* section near the bottom (see Figure 7-15).

STEP 3. Change the date range to **This Year**, then click **Run Report**.

The General Ledger can be a very long report. Every transaction appears at least twice, once in the account(s) being debited and again in the account(s) being credited behind the scenes. Every active account is included: even if it had no activity, it will still show a Beginning Balance.

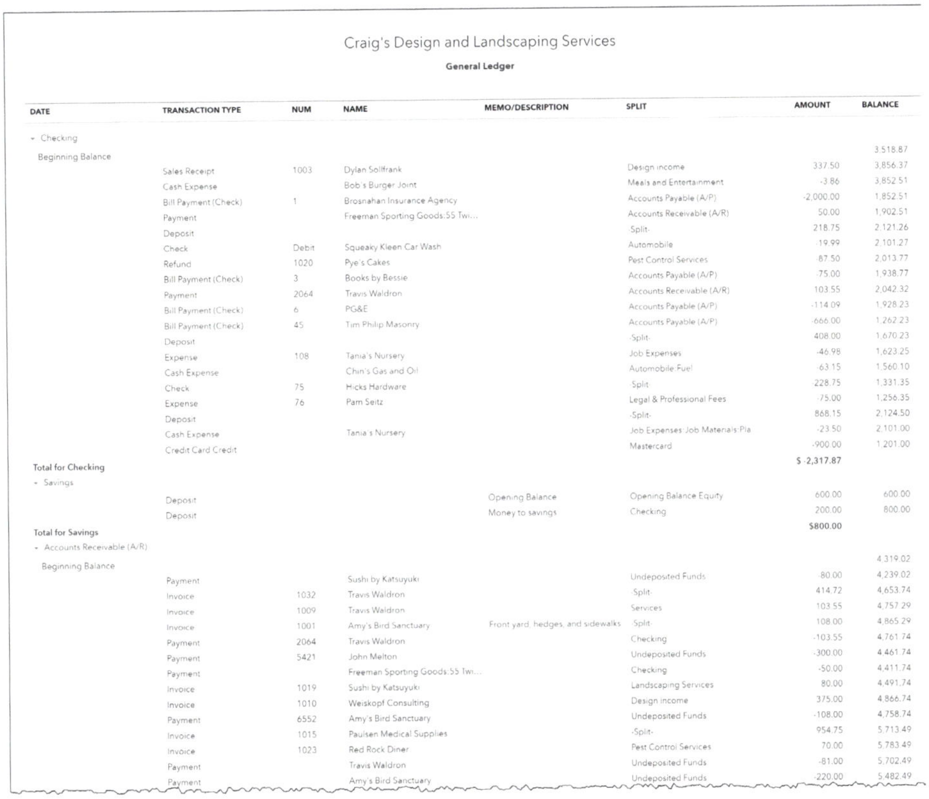
Craig's Design and Landscaping Services

General Ledger

DATE	TRANSACTION TYPE	NUM	NAME	MEMO/DESCRIPTION	SPLIT	AMOUNT	BALANCE
▾ Checking							
Beginning Balance							3,518.87
	Sales Receipt	1003	Dylan Sollfrank		Design income	337.50	3,856.37
	Cash Expense		Bob's Burger Joint		Meals and Entertainment	-3.86	3,852.51
	Bill Payment (Check)	1	Brosnahan Insurance Agency		Accounts Payable (A/P)	-2,000.00	1,852.51
	Payment		Freeman Sporting Goods:55 Twi...		Accounts Receivable (A/R)	50.00	1,902.51
	Deposit				-Split-	218.75	2,121.26
	Check	Debit	Squeaky Kleen Car Wash		Automobile	-19.99	2,101.27
	Refund	1020	Pye's Cakes		Pest Control Services	-87.50	2,013.77
	Bill Payment (Check)	3	Books by Bessie		Accounts Payable (A/P)	-75.00	1,938.77
	Payment	2064	Travis Waldron		Accounts Receivable (A/R)	103.55	2,042.32
	Bill Payment (Check)	6	PG&E		Accounts Payable (A/P)	-114.09	1,928.23
	Bill Payment (Check)	45	Tim Philip Masonry		Accounts Payable (A/P)	-666.00	1,262.23
	Deposit				-Split-	408.00	1,670.23
	Expense	108	Tania's Nursery		Job Expenses	-46.98	1,623.25
	Cash Expense		Chin's Gas and Oil		Automobile:Fuel	-63.15	1,560.10
	Check	75	Hicks Hardware		-Split-	-228.75	1,331.35
	Expense	76	Pam Seitz		Legal & Professional Fees	-75.00	1,256.35
	Deposit				-Split-	868.15	2,124.50
	Cash Expense		Tania's Nursery		Job Expenses:Job Materials:Pla	-23.50	2,101.00
	Credit Card Credit				Mastercard	-900.00	1,201.00
Total for Checking						**$ -2,317.87**	
▾ Savings							
	Deposit			Opening Balance	Opening Balance Equity	600.00	600.00
	Deposit			Money to savings	Checking	200.00	800.00
Total for Savings						**$800.00**	
▾ Accounts Receivable (A/R)							
Beginning Balance							4,319.02
	Payment		Sushi by Katsuyuki		Undeposited Funds	-80.00	4,239.02
	Invoice	1032	Travis Waldron		-Split-	414.72	4,653.74
	Invoice	1009	Travis Waldron		Services	103.55	4,757.29
	Invoice	1001	Amy's Bird Sanctuary	Front yard, hedges, and sidewalks	-Split-	108.00	4,865.29
	Payment	2064	Travis Waldron		Checking	-103.55	4,761.74
	Payment	5421	John Melton		Undeposited Funds	-300.00	4,461.74
	Payment		Freeman Sporting Goods:55 Twi...		Checking	-50.00	4,411.74
	Invoice	1019	Sushi by Katsuyuki		Landscaping Services	80.00	4,491.74
	Invoice	1010	Weiskopf Consulting		Design income	375.00	4,866.74
	Payment	6552	Amy's Bird Sanctuary		Undeposited Funds	-108.00	4,758.74
	Invoice	1015	Paulsen Medical Supplies		-Split-	954.75	5,713.49
	Invoice	1023	Red Rock Diner		Pest Control Services	70.00	5,783.49
	Payment		Travis Waldron		Undeposited Funds	-81.00	5,702.49
	Payment		Amy's Bird Sanctuary		Undeposited Funds	-220.00	5,482.49

FIGURE 7-15: *Upper portion of General Ledger report (your screen will vary)*

Trial Balance

The ***Trial Balance*** report shows the balance of each of the accounts as of a certain date, in a Debit and Credit format. Your accountant will usually prepare this report at the end of each fiscal year.

The *Debit* column always equals the *Credit* column, because in double-entry accounting, every transaction debits one account and credits another (the money goes from one category to another category). For more information, refer back to page 5.

HANDS-ON PRACTICE

STEP 1. Click on **Reports** in the *Left Navigation Bar.*

STEP 2. Click on **Trial Balance** in the *For My Accountant* section near the bottom (see Figure 7-16). The default *Report Period* is **This Month-to-Date**.

STEP 3. Drill into any amount to see the transaction history within that date range.

Craig's Design and Landscaping Services
Trial Balance

	DEBIT	CREDIT
Checking	1,201.00	
Savings	800.00	
Accounts Receivable (A/R)	5,281.52	
Inventory Asset	596.25	
Undeposited Funds	2,062.52	
Truck:Original Cost	13,495.00	
Accounts Payable (A/P)		1,602.67
Mastercard		157.72
Arizona Dept. of Revenue Payable		0.00
Board of Equalization Payable		370.94
Loan Payable		4,000.00
Notes Payable		25,000.00
Opening Balance Equity	9,337.50	
Design income		2,250.00
Discounts given	89.50	
Landscaping Services		1,477.50
Landscaping Services:Job Materials:Fountai…		2,246.50
Landscaping Services:Job Materials:Plants a…		2,351.97
Landscaping Services:Job Materials:Sprinkle…		138.00
Landscaping Services:Labor:Installation		250.00
Landscaping Services:Labor:Maintenance an…		50.00
Pest Control Services		110.00
Sales of Product Income		912.75
Services		503.55
Cost of Goods Sold	405.00	
Advertising	74.86	
Automobile	113.96	
Automobile:Fuel	349.41	
Equipment Rental	112.00	
Insurance	241.23	
Job Expenses	155.07	
Job Expenses:Job Materials:Decks and Patios	234.04	
Job Expenses:Job Materials:Plants and Soil	353.12	
Job Expenses:Job Materials:Sprinklers and …	215.66	
Legal & Professional Fees	75.00	
Legal & Professional Fees:Accounting	640.00	
Legal & Professional Fees:Bookkeeper	55.00	
Legal & Professional Fees:Lawyer	400.00	
Maintenance and Repair	185.00	
Maintenance and Repair:Equipment Repairs	755.00	
Meals and Entertainment	28.49	
Office Expenses	18.08	
Rent or Lease	900.00	
Utilities:Gas and Electric	200.53	
Utilities:Telephone	130.86	
Miscellaneous	2,916.00	
TOTAL	$41,421.60	$41,421.60

FIGURE 7-16: *Trial Balance Report—Balance of each account as of a specific date*

BUSINESS MANAGEMENT REPORTS

In the following exercises, you will use QuickBooks Online to create several different reports that help you manage your business.

QuickReports

QuickReports can quickly give you detailed transactions about a *Chart of Accounts* category or an item on the *Product and Services list*, without going into the *Reports Center*.

HANDS-ON PRACTICE

STEP 1. Click on **Chart of Accounts** in the *Accounting* section of the *Left Navigation Bar*.

STEP 2. Scroll down to the **Inventory Asset** account.

STEP 3. Click the **drop-down arrow** in the *Action* column and select **Run Report** (see Figure 7-17).

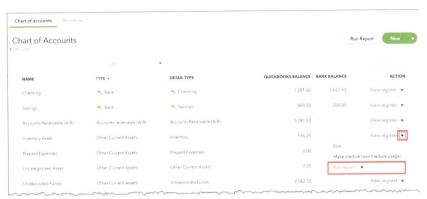

FIGURE 7-17: *Run a QuickReport of the Inventory Asset account*

STEP 4. QuickBooks Online displays all transactions involving the **Inventory Asset** account (see Figure 7-18). You'll see inventory added through bills, checks, and expenses, then removed through invoices and sales receipts. Look here for starting inventory entries and adjustments as well.

Craig's Design and Landscaping Services

Account QuickReport

Since

DATE	TRANSACTION TYPE	NUM	NAME	MEMO/DESCRIPTION	ACCOUNT	CLR	AMOUNT	BALANCE
▾ Inventory Asset								
07/06/2021	Check	75	Hicks Hardware	Fountain Pump	Inventory Asset		30.00	30.00
07/06/2021	Inventory Qty Adjust	START		Opening inventory for Rock Fou...	Inventory Asset			30.00
07/06/2021	Check	75	Hicks Hardware	Sprinkler Heads	Inventory Asset		11.25	41.25
07/06/2021	Check	75	Hicks Hardware	Rock Fountain	Inventory Asset		125.00	166.25
07/06/2021	Invoice	1035	Mark Cho	Sprinkler Pipes	Inventory Asset		-10.00	156.25
07/06/2021	Invoice	1035	Mark Cho	Rock Fountain	Inventory Asset		-125.00	31.25
07/06/2021	Invoice	1036	Freeman Sporting Goods:0969 ...	Fountain Pump	Inventory Asset		-10.00	21.25
07/06/2021	Invoice	1036	Freeman Sporting Goods:0969 ...	Rock Fountain	Inventory Asset		-125.00	-103.75
07/06/2021	Invoice	1037	Sonnenschein Family Store	Fountain Pump	Inventory Asset		-10.00	-113.75
07/06/2021	Invoice	1037	Sonnenschein Family Store	Rock Fountain	Inventory Asset		-125.00	-238.75
07/06/2021	Bill		Norton Lumber and Building Ma...	Rock Fountain	Inventory Asset		125.00	-113.75
07/06/2021	Bill		Norton Lumber and Building Ma...	Fountain Pump	Inventory Asset		80.00	-33.75
07/06/2021	Inventory Qty Adjust	START		Opening inventory for Pump	Inventory Asset		160.00	126.25
07/06/2021	Inventory Qty Adjust	START		Opening inventory for Pump	Inventory Asset			126.25
07/06/2021	Inventory Qty Adjust	START		Opening inventory for Sprinkler ...	Inventory Asset		7.50	133.75
07/06/2021	Inventory Qty Adjust	START		Opening inventory for Sprinkler ...	Inventory Asset			133.75
07/06/2021	Inventory Qty Adjust	START		Opening inventory for Sprinkler ...	Inventory Asset		25.00	158.75
07/06/2021	Inventory Qty Adjust	START		Opening inventory for Sprinkler ...	Inventory Asset			158.75
07/06/2021	Inventory Qty Adjust	START		Opening inventory for Rock Fou...	Inventory Asset		375.00	533.75
07/06/2021	Check	75	Hicks Hardware	Sprinkler Pipes	Inventory Asset		62.50	596.25
Total for Inventory Asset							**$596.25**	
TOTAL							**$596.25**	

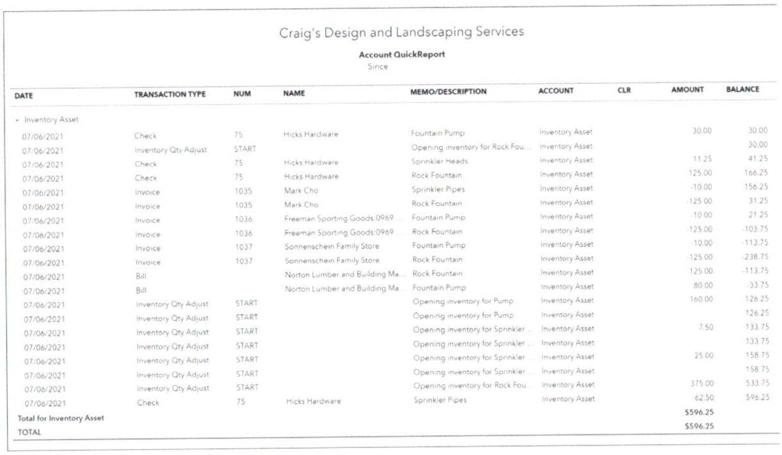

FIGURE 7-18: *A QuickReport of Inventory Asset transactions in the last 90 days*

Note that the QuickReport shows the activity **Since 90 Days Ago**, but you can change the date range and click the **Run Report** button again as needed.

Customer Contact List

The ***Customer Contact List*** is a listing of your customers' phone numbers, email addresses, point of contact, and street addresses. To create this report, follow these steps:

HANDS-ON PRACTICE

STEP 1. Click on **Reports** in the *Left Navigation Bar.*

STEP 2. Click on **Customer Contact List** in the *Sales and Customers* section.

STEP 3. If you don't need both the *Billing Address* and the *Shipping Address*, click on the **Customize** button in the upper right. Click on the blue **Change Columns** link, then **uncheck** *Shipping Address.*

STEP 4. Click **Run Report**. Your report will now look like Figure 7-19.

Craig's Design and Landscaping Services

Customer Contact List

CUSTOMER	PHONE NUMBERS	EMAIL	FULL NAME	BILLING ADDRESS
Amy's Bird Sanctuary	Phone: (650) 555-3311	Birds@Intuit.com	Amy Lauterbach	4581 Finch St. Bayshore CA 94326
Bill's Windsurf Shop	Phone: (415) 444-6538	Surf@Intuit.com	Bill Lucchini	12 Ocean Dr. Half Moon Bay CA 94213
Cool Cars	Phone: (415) 555-9933	Cool_Cars@intuit.com	Grace Pariente	65 Ocean Dr. Half Moon Bay CA 94213
Diego Rodriguez	Phone: (650) 555-4477	Diego@Rodriguez.com	Diego Rodriguez	321 Channing Palo Alto CA 94303
Dukes Basketball Camp	Phone: (520) 420-5638	Dukes_bball@intuit.com	Peter Dukes	25 Court St. Tucson AZ 85719
Dylan Sollfrank			Dylan Sollfrank	
Freeman Sporting Goods	Phone: (650) 555-0987 Fax: (520) 555-7894 Mobile: (973) 555-8849	Sporting_goods@intuit.com	Kirby Freeman	370 Easy St. Middlefield CA 94482
Freeman Sporting Goods:0969 O...	Phone: (415) 555-9933 Fax: (520) 555-7894 Mobile: (973) 555-8849	Sporting_goods@intuit.com	Sasha Tillou	370 Easy St. Middlefield CA 94482
Freeman Sporting Goods:55 Twin ...	Phone: (650) 555-0987 Fax: (520) 555-7894 Mobile: (973) 555-8849	Sporting_goods@intuit.com	Amelia	370 Easy St. Middlefield CA 94482
Geeta Kalapatapu	Phone: (650) 555-0022	Geeta@Kalapatapu.com	Geeta Kalapatapu	1987 Main St. Middlefield CA 94303
Gevelber Photography	Phone: (415) 222-4345	Photography@intuit.com	Lisa Gevelber	1045 Main St. Half Moon Bay CA 94213
Jeff's Jalopies	Phone: (650) 555-8989	Jalopies@intuit.com	Jeff Chin	12 Willow Rd. Menlo Park CA 94305
John Melton	Phone: (650) 555-5879	John@Melton.com	John Melton	85 Pine St. Menlo Park CA 94304
Kate Whelan	Phone: (650) 554-8822	Kate@Whelan.com	Kate Whelan	45 First St. Menlo Park CA 94304 USA
Kookies by Kathy	Phone: (650) 555-7896	qbwebsamplecompany@yahoo....	Kathy Kuplis	789 Sugar Lane Middlefield CA 94303
Mark Cho	Phone: (650) 554-1479	Mark@Cho.com	Mark Cho	36 Willow Rd

FIGURE 7-19: *Customer Contact List report, with Shipping Address hidden*

Vendor Contact List

The ***Vendor Contact List*** is a listing of your vendors along with their contact information. To create this report, follow these steps:

HANDS-ON PRACTICE

STEP 1. Click on **Reports** in the *Left Navigation Bar.*

STEP 2. Click on **Vendor Contact List** in the *Expenses and Vendors* section (see Figure 7-20).

Craig's Design and Landscaping Services

Vendor Contact List

VENDOR	PHONE NUMBERS	EMAIL	FULL NAME	ADDRESS	ACCOUNT #
Bob's Burger Joint					
Books by Bessie	Phone: (650) 555-7745	Books@Intuit.com	Bessie Williams	15 Main St. Palo Alto CA 94303	1345
Brosnahan Insurance Agency	Phone: (650) 555-9912 Fax: (555) 123-4567 Mobile: (650) 555-9874		Nick Brosnahan	P.O. Box 5 Middlefield CA 94482	7653412
Cal Telephone	Phone: (650) 555-1616			10 Main St. Palo Alto CA 94303	
Chin's Gas and Oil					
Cigna Health Care	Phone: (520) 555-9874				123456789
Computers by Jenni	Phone: (650) 555-8721 Fax: (650) 999-2663 Mobile: (650) 111-5648	Msfixit@Intuit.com	Jenni Winslow	1515 Main St. Middlefield CA 94482	
Diego's Road Warrior Bodyshop					
EDD					
Ellis Equipment Rental	Phone: (650) 555-3333 Mobile: (650) 445-3333	Rental@intuit.com	Ms. Julie I. Ellis	45896 Main St. Middlefield CA 94303 USA	39765
Fidelity					
Hall Properties	Phone: (973) 555-3827 Mobile: (973) 888-6222		Melanie Hall	P.O.Box 357 South Orange NJ 07079	55642
Hicks Hardware	Phone: (650) 554-1973 Mobile: (650) 445-6666		Geoff Hicks	42 Main St. Middlefield CA 94303	556223
Lee Advertising	Phone: (650) 554-4622		Mrs. Laurel J. Lee	53 Main St. Middlefield CA 94303	776543

FIGURE 7-20: *Vendor Contact List report*

Product/Service List

The ***Product/Service List*** is a listing of the products you sell and services you provide, including their price, cost, and quantity on hand (for inventory). To create this report, follow these steps:

HANDS-ON PRACTICE

Craig wants to see a list of his products and services, but he also wants to make sure sales and purchases are hitting the correct accounts on the General Ledger.

STEP 1. Click on **Reports** in the *Left Navigation Bar.*

STEP 2. Click on **Product/Service List** in the *Sales and Customers* section (see Figure 7-21).

Sort ▾ Add notes

Craig's Design and Landscaping Services

Product/Service List

PRODUCT/SERVICE	TYPE	DESCRIPTION	PRICE	COST	QTY ON HAND
Design:Design	Service	Custom Design	75.00		
Design:Fountains:Concrete	Service	Concrete for fountain installation	0.00		
Design:Fountains:Pump	Inventory	Fountain Pump	15.00	10.00	25.00
Design:Fountains:Rock Fountain	Inventory	Rock Fountain	275.00	125.00	2.00
Design:Lighting	Service	Garden Lighting	0.00		
Design:Rocks	Service	Garden Rocks			
Design:Services	Service				
Landscaping:Gardening	Service	Weekly Gardening Service	0.00		
Landscaping:Hours	Service				
Landscaping:Installation	Service	Installation of landscape design	50.00		
Landscaping:Maintenance & Repair	Service	Maintenance & Repair	0.00		
Landscaping:Sod	Service	Sod			
Landscaping:Soil	Service	2 cubic ft. bag	10.00	6.50	
Landscaping:Sprinklers:Sprinkler ...	Inventory	Sprinkler Heads	2.00	0.75	25.00
Landscaping:Sprinklers:Sprinkler ...	Inventory	Sprinkler Pipes	4.00	2.50	31.00
Landscaping:Trimming	Service	Tree and Shrub Trimming	35.00		
Pest Control:Pest Control	Service	Pest Control Services	35.00		
Refunds & Allowances	Service	Income due to refunds or allowa...			

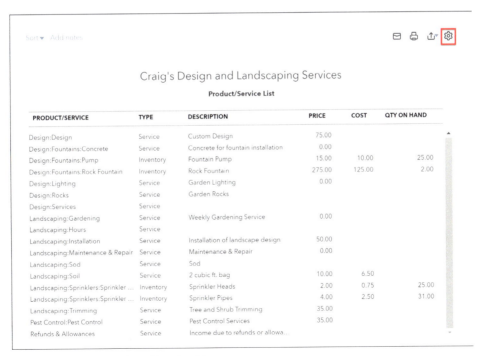

FIGURE 7-21: *Product/Service List report*

STEP 3. Click on the **Grid Gear** just above the report on the right.

STEP 4. Click on the blue **Show More** link.

STEP 5. Add checkmarks before **Income Account** and **Expense Account**, as shown in Figure 7-22. Reviewing these columns is an excellent way to check the behind-the-scenes accounting setup.

Note that there are many different useful fields on this list.

STEP 6. Click the blue **Reorder Columns** link at the bottom.

FIGURE 7-22: *Add columns to the report*

STEP 7. Use the 9-dot waffles on the left to drag **Income Account** and **Expense Account** below *Description*, as shown in Figure 7-23.

STEP 8. Click **Run Report**.

STEP 9. Increase the size of the **Income Account** column by dragging the fine line between the *Income Account* and *Expense Account* header to the right until you can see more of the account names.

You may decide to make the other columns wider and narrower as needed.

STEP 10. Your report should look like Figure 7-24.

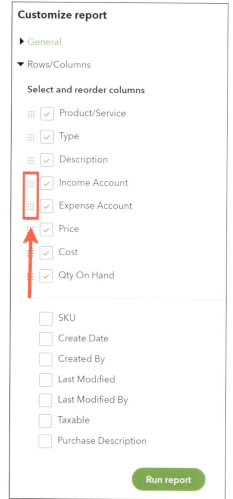

FIGURE 7-23: *Reorder columns using the waffles*

PRODUCT/SERVICE	TYPE	DESCRIPTION	INCOME ACCOUNT	EXPENSE ACCOUNT	PRICE	COST	QTY ON HAND
			Craig's Design and Landscaping Services				
			Product/Service List				
Design:Design	Service	Custom Design	Design income		75.00		
Design:Fountains:Concrete	Service	Concrete for fountain installation	Landscaping Services:Job Materials:Fountains an...		0.00		
Design:Fountains:Pump	Inventory	Fountain Pump	Sales of Product Income	Cost of Goods Sold	15.00	10.00	25.00
Design:Fountains:Rock Fountain	Inventory	Rock Fountain	Sales of Product Income	Cost of Goods Sold	275.00	125.00	2.00
Design:Lighting	Service	Garden Lighting	Landscaping Services:Job Materials:Fountains an...		0.00		
Design:Rocks	Service	Garden Rocks	Landscaping Services:Job Materials:Fountains an...				
Design:Services	Service		Services				
Landscaping:Gardening	Service	Weekly Gardening Service	Landscaping Services		0.00		
Landscaping:Hours	Service		Services				
Landscaping:Installation	Service	Installation of landscape design	Landscaping Services:Labor:Installation		50.00		
Landscaping:Maintenance & Repair	Service	Maintenance & Repair	Landscaping Services:Labor:Maintenance and Re...		0.00		
Landscaping:Sod	Service	Sod	Landscaping Services:Job Materials:Plants and Soil				
Landscaping:Soil	Service	2 cubic ft. bag	Landscaping Services:Job Materials:Plants and Soil	Job Expenses:Job Materials:Pla...	10.00	6.50	
Landscaping:Sprinklers:Sprinkler ...	Inventory	Sprinkler Heads	Sales of Product Income	Cost of Goods Sold	2.00	0.75	25.00
Landscaping:Sprinklers:Sprinkler ...	Inventory	Sprinkler Pipes	Sales of Product Income	Cost of Goods Sold	4.00	2.50	31.00
Landscaping:Trimming	Service	Tree and Shrub Trimming	Landscaping Services		35.00		
Pest Control:Pest Control	Service	Pest Control Services	Pest Control Services		35.00		
Refunds & Allowances	Service	Income due to refunds or allowa...	Other Income				

FIGURE 7-24: *The Product/Service List with Income and Expense Accounts*

The Business Snapshot

One of the best ways to quickly get information from QuickBooks Online Plus and Advanced is by viewing it graphically. There are quick charts on your Dashboard, as we saw on page 14, but the Business Snapshot provides additional interactive visual views.

The *My Income* and *My Expenses* charts display your income and expenses with interactive pie charts.

The **Previous Year Income Comparison** and the **Previous Year Expense Comparison** allow you to compare this year's income and expenses to last year (because these are sample companies, there is no previous year history to be viewed).

At the bottom, **Who Owes Me** and **Whom I Owe** provide interactive glimpses into your Accounts Receivable and Accounts Payable.

> **IMPORTANT!**
>
> QuickBooks Online creates charts based on products and services sold using sales forms (sales receipts and invoices). Any income entered directly into the general ledger through deposits and journal entries will not be included.

HANDS-ON PRACTICE

STEP 1. Click on **Reports** in the *Left Navigation Bar*.

STEP 2. Click on **Business Snapshot** in the *Business Overview* section (see Figure 7-25).

STEP 3. Change the *Date drop-down* in *My Income* to **Last Month** (see Figure 7-26).

STEP 4. Change the *Date drop-down* in *Previous Year Income Comparison* to **Monthly**. You will now see columns for income broken down by month. Once this file is more than a year old, you will also see blue graphs for the last year's sales income.

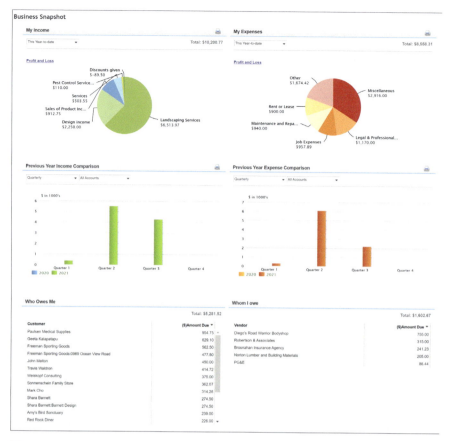

Figure 7-25: *Business Snapshot*

STEP 5. Click on the green **Landscaping Services** pie slice to see a *Transaction Report* for all sales in that category, including subcategories.

STEP 6. Click your browser's **Back Button** to return to the Business Snapshot.

Tag Reports

The **Tags Center** under the *Gear* provides running totals of your most popular tags at a glance. Many popular reports also use tags as a filter.

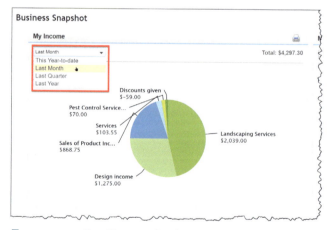

Figure 7-26: *Change the dates on any chart*

Because the Craig's Landscaping sample file doesn't have Tags applied by default, we cannot demonstrate these reports now, but you will run them in Imagine Photography's *Apply Your Knowledge* exercise at the end of the chapter.

The Tags Center

At the top of the *Tags Center* are two boxes, one for *Money In* and one for *Money Out*, as shown in Figure 7-27. The colored bars display the tags in descending order. Click on the *Date* and *Type* drop-down arrows to change the time period and the Tag Group displayed.

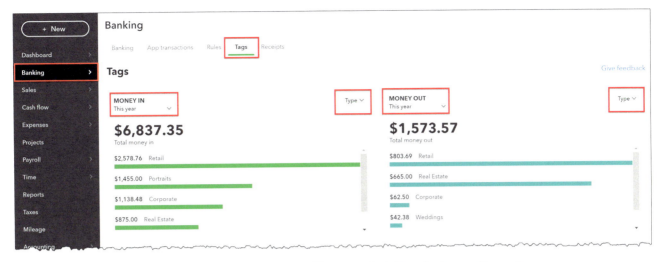

FIGURE 7-27: *The Tags Center displaying Imagine Photography's Tags in descending order*

Click on a bar to drill in to a *Transactions by Tag* list. From here you can adjust your *Filters* from the funnel or dismiss them by clicking the **X** in each of the labels across the top. Click on any transaction to view and edit it.

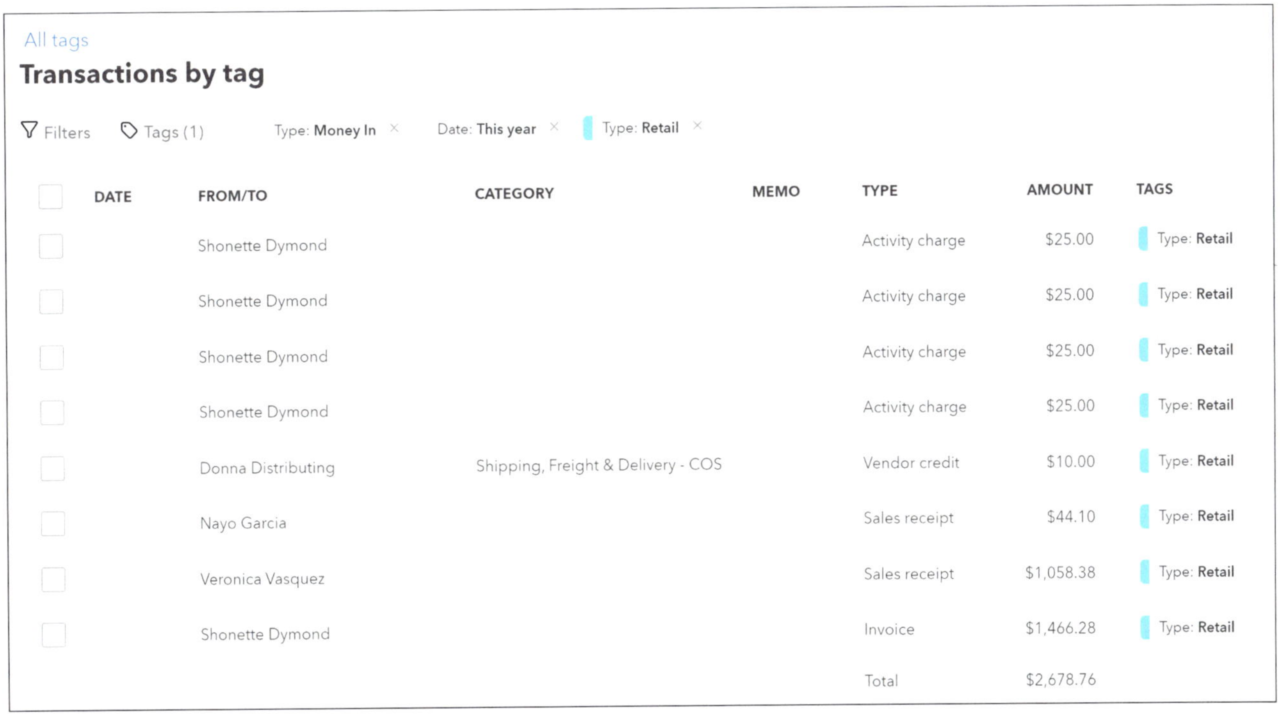

FIGURE 7-28: *The Transactions by Tag list*

Using Tags in Reports

There are two reports in the *Reports Center* that incorporate tags: **The Profit and Loss by Tag Group** report, and the **Transaction List by Tag Group** report (see Figure 7-29).

In addition, some reports can be customized by tag.

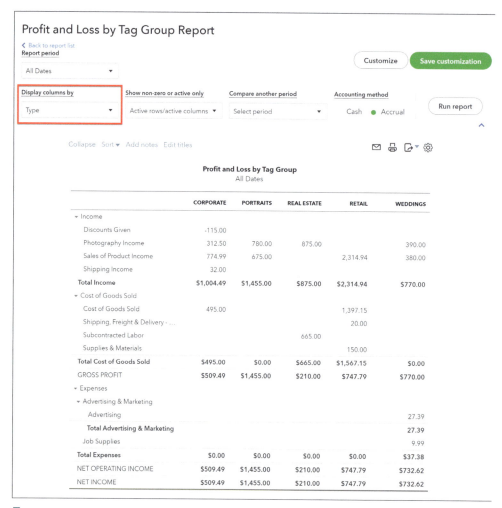

FIGURE 7-29: *Imagine Photography's Profit and Loss Statement using a Tag Group for columns*

ACCOUNTS RECEIVABLE AND ACCOUNTS PAYABLE REPORTS

There are several reports that you can use to keep track of the money that your customers owe you (**Accounts Receivable**) and the money that you owe to your vendors (**Accounts Payable**). We discussed the *Accounts Receivable Aging Summary* on page 140 and the *Accounts Payable Aging Summary* on page 185.

Collections Report

The **Collections Report** shows each customer's outstanding invoices along with their telephone number. Use this list to reach out to customers who are behind on payments.

HANDS-ON PRACTICE

STEP 1. Click on **Reports** in the *Left Navigation Bar*.

STEP 2. Click on **Collections Report** in the *Who Owes You* section (see Figure 7-30). The default *Report Period* is **Today**.

Craig's Design and Landscaping Services

Collections Report

As of

DATE	TRANSACTION TYPE	NUM	DUE DATE	PAST DUE	AMOUNT	OPEN BALANCE
▾ Amy's Bird Sanctuary (650) 555-3311						
	Invoice	1021		18	459.00	239.00
Total for Amy's Bird Sanctuary					**$459.00**	**$239.00**
▾ Bill's Windsurf Shop (415) 444-6538						
	Invoice	1027		44	85.00	85.00
Total for Bill's Windsurf Shop					**$85.00**	**$85.00**
▾ Freeman Sporting Goods:55 Twin Lane (650) 555-0987						
	Invoice	1028		44	81.00	81.00
	Invoice	1005		5	54.00	4.00
Total for Freeman Sporting Goods:55 Twin Lane					**$135.00**	**$85.00**
▾ Jeff's Jalopies (650) 555-8989						
	Invoice	1022		18	81.00	81.00
Total for Jeff's Jalopies					**$81.00**	**$81.00**
▾ John Melton						

FIGURE 7-30: *The top half of the Collections Report for Accounts Receivable*

Invoices and Received Payments Report

Use the ***Invoices and Received Payments*** report to see the details of each customer's payments using Accounts Receivable.

The report is organized by **Payment**, listing all the associated invoices and credit memos.

HANDS-ON PRACTICE

STEP 1. Click on **Reports** in the *Left Navigation Bar.*

STEP 2. Click on **Invoices and Received Payments** in the *Who Owes You* section (see Figure 7-31). The default *Report Period* is **This Year-to-Date**.

Invoices and Received Payments

DATE	TRANSACTION TYPE	MEMO/DESCRIPTION	NUM	AMOUNT
▾ Amy's Bird Sanctuary				
	Payment		6552	108.00
	Invoice	Front yard, hedges, and sidewalks	1001	108.00
	Payment			105.00
	Invoice		1025	205.00
	Payment			0.00
	Invoice		1025	205.00
	Credit Memo		1026	-100.00
	Payment			220.00
	Invoice		1021	459.00
▾ Bill's Windsurf Shop				
	Payment		1053	175.00
	Invoice		1002	175.00
▾ Cool Cars				
	Payment		1886	694.00
	Invoice		1004	2,369.52
	Payment			1,675.52
	Invoice		1004	2,369.52
▾ Dukes Basketball Camp				
	Payment			460.40
	Invoice		1029	460.40

FIGURE 7-31: *The Invoices and Received Payments report*

Deposit Detail Report

The ***Deposit Detail*** report is quite valuable to see what sales transactions were included in each deposit from Undeposited Funds.

The *Deposit Amount* is a positive number, and each *line item* in the deposit is a negative number.

HANDS-ON PRACTICE

STEP 1. Click on **Reports** in the *Left Navigation Bar.*

STEP 2. Click on **Deposit Detail** in the *Sales and Customers* section.

STEP 3. Change the *Report Period* to **All Dates**, then click **Run Report** (see Figure 7-32).

Craig's Design and Landscaping Services

Deposit Detail
All Dates

DATE	TRANSACTION TYPE	NUM	CUSTOMER	VENDOR	MEMO/DESCRIPTION	CLR	AMOUNT
▾ Checking							
02/20/2021	Deposit				Opening Balance	R	5,000.00
							5,000.00
04/11/2021	Payment	1053	Bill's Windsurf Shop				175.00
			Bill's Windsurf Shop				-175.00
06/11/2021	Payment	5664	Freeman Sporting Goods:55 Twi...				86.40
			Freeman Sporting Goods:55 Twi...				-86.40
06/11/2021	Sales Receipt		Kate Whelan				225.00
			Kate Whelan		Custom Design		225.00
06/13/2021	Payment		Amy's Bird Sanctuary		Amy claims the pest control did ...		105.00
			Amy's Bird Sanctuary				-105.00
06/29/2021	Payment	1886	Cool Cars				694.00
			Cool Cars				-694.00
07/01/2021	Sales Receipt	10264	Dylan Sollfrank				337.50
			Dylan Sollfrank		Custom Design		337.50
07/04/2021	Payment		Freeman Sporting Goods:55 Twi...				50.00
			Freeman Sporting Goods:55 Twi...				-50.00
07/04/2021	Payment	2064	Travis Waldron				103.55
			Travis Waldron				-103.55
07/04/2021	Deposit						218.75
			Diego Rodriguez				-140.00
			Pye's Cakes				-78.75
07/05/2021	Deposit						408.00
		6552	Amy's Bird Sanctuary				-108.00
		5421	John Melton				-300.00
07/06/2021	Deposit						868.15
			Freeman Sporting Goods:0969 ...				-226.75
			Dukes Basketball Camp				-460.40
			Sushi by Katsuyuki				-80.00
			Travis Waldron				-81.00
			Amy's Bird Sanctuary				-220.00
					Money to savings		200.00
▾ Savings							
07/02/2021	Deposit				Opening Balance	R	600.00
							600.00

FIGURE 7-32: *Deposit Detail report*

Vendor Balance Detail Report

The ***Vendor Balance Detail*** report is similar to the *Collections Report* and the *Customer Balance Detail* reports, but it shows transactions that use Accounts Payable, displaying open bills with their balances.

Craig's Design and Landscaping Services

Vendor Balance Detail
All Dates

DATE	TRANSACTION TYPE	NUM	DUE DATE	AMOUNT	OPEN BALANCE	BALANCE
▾ Brosnahan Insurance Agency						
	Bill			241.23	241.23	241.23
Total for Brosnahan Insurance Agency				**$241.23**	**$241.23**	
▾ Diego's Road Warrior Bodyshop						
	Bill			755.00	755.00	755.00
Total for Diego's Road Warrior Bodyshop				**$755.00**	**$755.00**	
▾ Norton Lumber and Building Materials						
	Bill			205.00	205.00	205.00
Total for Norton Lumber and Building Materials				**$205.00**	**$205.00**	
▾ PG&E						
	Bill			86.44	86.44	86.44
Total for PG&E				**$86.44**	**$86.44**	
▾ Robertson & Associates						
	Bill			315.00	315.00	315.00
Total for Robertson & Associates				**$315.00**	**$315.00**	
TOTAL				**$1,602.67**	**$1,602.67**	

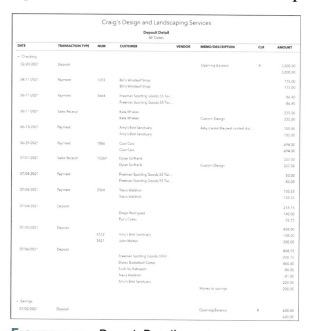

FIGURE 7-33: *Vendor Balance Detail report*

HANDS-ON PRACTICE

STEP 1. Click on **Reports** in the *Left Navigation Bar.*

STEP 2. Click on **Vendor Balance Detail** in the *What You Owe* section (see Figure 7-33). The default *Report Period* is **All Dates**.

CREATING SALES REPORTS

In this section, you'll learn how to create reports that will help you analyze your company's sales.

Transaction List by Customer Report

Create a **Transaction List by Customer** report to view all the invoices, payments, credit memos, sales receipts, and billable expenses for every customer during a specific date range.

HANDS-ON PRACTICE

> **STEP 1.** Click on **Reports** in the *Left Navigation Bar*.
>
> **STEP 2.** Click on **Transaction List by Customer** in the *Sales and Customers* section.
>
> **STEP 3.** Change the *Report Period* to **All Dates**, then click **Run Report** (see Figure 7-34).

Craig's Design and Landscaping Services
Transaction List by Customer
All Dates

DATE	TRANSACTION TYPE	NUM	POSTING	MEMO/DESCRIPTION	ACCOUNT	AMOUNT
Amy's Bird Sanctuary						
	Invoice	1025	Yes		Accounts Receivable (A/R)	205.00
	Payment		Yes	Amy claims the pest control did ...	Checking	105.00
	Invoice	1021	Yes		Accounts Receivable (A/R)	459.00
	Credit Memo	1026	Yes		Accounts Receivable (A/R)	-100.00
	Payment		Yes	Created by QB Online to link cre...		0.00
	Invoice	1001	Yes	Front yard, hedges, and sidewalks	Accounts Receivable (A/R)	108.00
	Time Charge		No	Custom Design	Accounts Receivable (A/R)	375.00
	Payment	6552	Yes		Undeposited Funds	108.00
	Payment		Yes		Undeposited Funds	220.00
Total for Amy's Bird Sanctuary						**$1,480.00**
Bill's Windsurf Shop						
	Invoice	1002	Yes		Accounts Receivable (A/R)	175.00
	Payment	1053	Yes		Checking	175.00
	Invoice	1027	Yes		Accounts Receivable (A/R)	85.00
Total for Bill's Windsurf Shop						**$435.00**
Cool Cars						
	Invoice	1004	Yes		Accounts Receivable (A/R)	2,369.52
	Payment	1886	Yes		Checking	694.00
	Payment		Yes		Undeposited Funds	1,675.52
Total for Cool Cars						**$4,739.04**
Diego Rodriguez						
	Sales Receipt	1014	Yes		Undeposited Funds	140.00
Total for Diego Rodriguez						**$140.00**
Dukes Basketball Camp						

FIGURE 7-34: *The top of the Transaction List by Customer report*

Income by Customer Summary Report

The *Income by Customer Summary* report shows the **Net Income** for each of your customers over a given date range. This report displays the total income and expenses related to the customer, showing the profit earned.

If you are not using job costing, you can run the *Sales by Customer Summary* report instead, which just displays total income by customer.

HANDS-ON PRACTICE

> **STEP 1.** Click on **Reports** in the *Left Navigation Bar*.

STEP 2. Click on **Income by Customer Summary** in the *Sales and Customers* section. The default *Report Period* is **This Year-to-Date** (see Figure 7-35).

Sales by Product/Service Summary Report

The *Sales by Product/Service Summary* report shows how much you have sold of each item over a given date range, by both quantity, amount, % of sales, and average price.

If you have Inventory products, you will also see columns for COGS (Cost of Goods Sold), Gross Margin (Amount—COGS), and Gross Margin % (COGS/Amount).

HANDS-ON PRACTICE

FIGURE 7-35: *Income by Customer Summary report*

STEP 1. Click on **Reports** in the *Left Navigation Bar*.

STEP 2. Click on **Sales by Product/Service Summary** in the *Sales and Customers* section.

STEP 3. Change the *Report Period* to **All Dates**, then click **Run Report** (see Figure 7-36).

	QUANTITY	AMOUNT	% OF SALES	AVG PRICE	COGS	GROSS MARGIN	GROSS MARGIN %
▼ Design							
Design	30.00	2,250.00	21.89 %	75.00			
▼ Fountains							
Concrete	10.00	122.50	1.19 %	12.25			
Pump	4.00	72.75	0.71 %	18.1875	20.00	52.75	72.51 %
Rock Fountain	9.00	2,475.00	24.08 %	275.00	375.00	2,100.00	84.85 %
Total Fountains		2,670.25	25.98 %		395.00		
Lighting	3.00	45.00	0.44 %	15.00			
Rocks	25.00	384.00	3.74 %	15.36			
Services	8.00	503.55	4.90 %	62.94375			
Total Design		5,852.80	56.93 %		395.00		
▼ Landscaping							
Gardening	56.50	1,447.50	14.08 %	25.619469			
Installation	5.00	250.00	2.43 %	50.00			
Maintenance & Repair	1.00	50.00	0.49 %	50.00			
Sod	90.00	2,231.25	21.70 %	24.7916667			
Soil	20.00	200.00	1.95 %	10.00			
▼ Sprinklers							
Sprinkler Heads	25.00	50.00	0.49 %	2.00			
Sprinkler Pipes	37.00	148.00	1.44 %	4.00	10.00	138.00	93.24 %
Total Sprinklers		198.00	1.93 %		10.00		
Trimming	2.00	30.00	0.29 %	15.00			
Total Landscaping		4,406.75	42.87 %		10.00		
▼ Pest Control							
Pest Control	5.00	110.00	1.07 %	22.00			
Total Pest Control		110.00	1.07 %				
Not Specified	-1,397.50	-89.50	-0.87 %	0.0640429			
TOTAL		$10,280.05	100.00 %		$405.00		

FIGURE 7-36: *Sales by Product/Service Summary report*

CUSTOMIZING REPORTS

To refine your reports to show specific information, you can **Customize** (i.e., modify) any existing report. Some customization can be done right from the report itself. Additional filters and tools can be applied when you click the **Customize** button above any report.

All reports allow at least some modification and filtering, although the options will vary. Summary reports generally have different choices than detail reports.

For the examples below, we will demonstrate using a Profit and Loss report.

The Report Header

There are number of modifications you can make right at the top of the report, as shown in Figure 7-37.

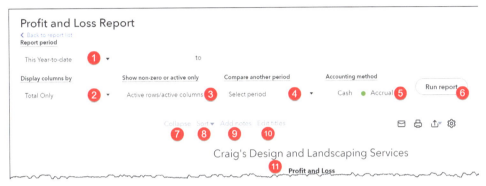

FIGURE 7-37: *Customize Reports right from the Header*

1. *Report Period*—We've already seen that you can easily modify report dates from the Report Period drop-down field. Familiarize yourself with over 30 built-in date ranges on the drop-down list. Note that you may need to scroll up to find **All Dates**, or you can type the letter **a** in the *Report Period* box to quickly find **All Dates**. If you don't see the period you need, choose **Custom** and manually enter the date range. Don't forget the date shortcuts we learned on page 21!

2. *Display Columns By*—Many reports can be split into columns for comparison. A date range can be split into days, weeks, months, quarters, and years. Summary reports can be split into columns by classes, customers, vendors, employees, products, and tags. Note that if these lists are long, your report may become unwieldy.

3. *Show Non-zero or Active Only*—**Active** rows and columns appear when there were transactions during the date range, and will show zeros if there were equal debits and credits to the category. **All** will display rows and columns even if there was no activity; unused accounts will show blanks. **Non-zero** rows and columns will only appear if there is a balance in the account.

4. *Compare With Another Period*—Compare the selected date range with previous periods, including $ change and % change columns if desired. You can also apply % of income, expense, row, and column for complex analysis.

5. *Accounting Method*—Toggle the basis of the report from Cash to Accrual.

6. *Run Report*—Always click this button to apply new settings.

7. *Collapse/Expand*—Show and hide subcategories.

8. *Sort*—Some reports can be rearranged by totals or alphabetically.

9. *Add Notes*—Add a footer to a report with additional information. This information is stored if you use **Save Customization** to memorize the report (see page 330).

10. *Edit Titles*—This feature allows you to rename your groupings to match your industry terms, or to make reports easier to understand.

11. *Editable Labels*—Click on the report header to edit the company name and report title.

> **TIP:**
>
> Use these options in different combinations to get creative with your reports. Here are two examples of common ways of manipulating the *Profit and Loss* report that we are unable demonstrate in the sample company without more than one year of history:
>
> ▸ Modify a **Profit and Loss** report for **All Dates** with columns by **Year**. This is an especially useful way to scan for trends, and spot anomalies. For example, if you change how you categorize particular transactions, this report will help you spot inconsistencies.
>
> ▸ Run a **Profit and Loss** report using the *Report Period* **This Month-to-Date**, and in *Compare Another Period*, select **Previous Year (PY)**. This will show you how the company is doing this month compared to last year at the same time.

The Customize Button

The **Customize** button contains many of the same modifications as the report header, but there are many more powerful options, as shown in Figure 7-38.

The *Customize Report* box will include different sections depending upon the report being modified. For example, a *Profit and Loss* report does not allow you to choose columns for the report, while a *Product/Service List* report does.

1. *Number Format*—Design how the numbers display on the report. You can reduce numbers to multiples of 1000, hide amounts of 0.00, show dollar amounts without cents, and choose from several formats for negative numbers.

2. *Filters*—This powerful option allows you to filter a report on one or more parameters. Narrow the contents of the report so that you can analyze specific areas of your business. You can filter or choose specific accounts, dates, names, or items to include in the report.

    For example, you can filter a Profit and Loss report for just one customer for job costing.

    A creative use would be to pick **Unspecified** on any filter to find only empty entries.

3. *Header/Footer*—You can include or omit information at the top or bottom of the report.

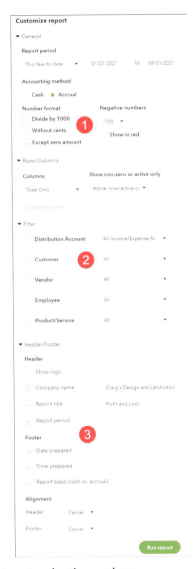

FIGURE 7-38: *Report customization options*

HANDS-ON PRACTICE

Craig's Landscaping wants a report of all transactions that include **Design services** that you have sold, grouped and totaled by customer. The report should only display the date, type of transaction, transaction number, service provided, and amount. Finally, the report should be titled *Design Services*.

Begin by creating a **Transaction Detail** report and then modify it to display the specific information required.

STEP 1.   From the *Reports Center*, scroll down to the *For My Accountant* section and select **Transaction Detail by Account**.

STEP 2.   Change the *Report Period* to **All Dates**.

STEP 3.   Change the *Group By* drop-down to **Customer**, then click **Run Report**.

STEP 4.   This report will now show all transactions this year, subtotaled by customer (see Figure 7-39).

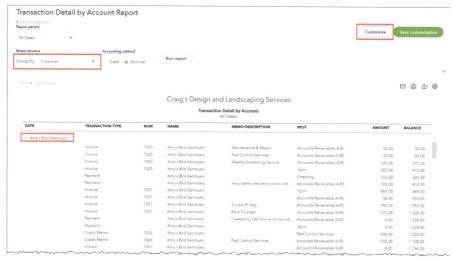

FIGURE 7-39: *Upper portion of Transaction Detail by Account report totaled by Customer*

For Craig's purposes, there are several problems with this report:

- The report shows different columns than we want to display.
- The report shows all transactions, not just the Design services performed for customers.
- The report title is not descriptive.

Let's modify the report to correct the four problems listed above.

STEP 5. Click the **Customize** button in the upper right.

STEP 6. Click the tiny blue **Change Columns** link.

Notice that several fields at the top of the list have check marks (see Figure 7-40), while the ones below do not. The check marks indicate which columns show on the report.

STEP 7. Deselect **Name, Memo/Description, Split,** and **Balance**.

STEP 8. Select **Product/Service** on the bottom list.

STEP 9. Use the 9-dot waffle to move **Product/Service** after **Num**.

STEP 10. Scroll down and click on **Filter** to display the filter list.

STEP 11. To include only design services, select the **Product/Service** drop-down arrow and check **Design** (see Figure 7-41). Selecting the main service category will select all of its subcategories as well.

The *Product/Service filter* jumps to the top of the list, and shows a checkmark.

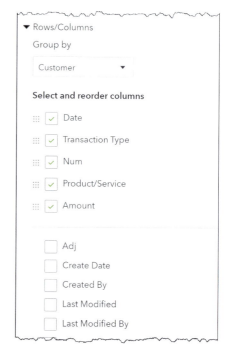

FIGURE 7-40: *Add, remove, and rearrange columns*

REPORTS | 329

STEP 12. Scroll down and click **Header/Footer** at the bottom of the *Customize Report* window.

STEP 13. To modify the title of the report so that it accurately describes the content of the report, enter **Design Services Performed** in the *Report Title* field as shown in Figure 7-42.

STEP 14. Turn off **Time Prepared**.

STEP 15. Click **Run Report**. You will now see the *Design Services Performed* report with the settings you just selected (see Figure 7-43).

Notice the **Filters** you applied to the report in the upper left corner. You can click the **X** to reset the filter without going back into *Customize*.

STEP 16. Leave this report open to use in the next exercise.

FIGURE 7-41: *Filter for Design services*

FIGURE 7-42: *Change the Report Title*

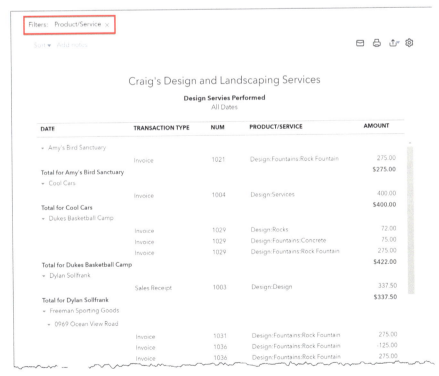

FIGURE 7-43: *Customized report with Filters shown*

Saving Reports

After you have modified a report, you can use **Save Customization** to memorize the formatting and filtering so that you don't have to perform all of the modification steps the next time you want to view the report.

> **NOTE:**
>
> Saving a report does not memorize the data on the report, only the format, dates, and filtering.

If you enter a specific custom date range (e.g., January 1 to June 30), QuickBooks Online will use those dates the next time you bring up the report. However, if you select a *relative* date range in the *Report Period* field (e.g., Last Year, Since 90 Days Ago, or Today) before memorizing a report, QuickBooks Online will use the relative dates the next time you open the report.

For example, if you save a report with the *Report Period* field set to **This Month-to-Date**, that report will always use the first day of the current month as the start date and today as the end date.

HANDS-ON PRACTICE

STEP 17. With the *Design Services Performed* report displayed, click the green **Save Customization** button at the top right of the window.

STEP 18. In the *Custom Report Name* field, confirm the name of this report displays the new name (see Figure 7-44).

STEP 19. You could use *Add This Report To a Group* to organize your Custom reports into groups. This allows you to run or email several reports together in a batch.

In the *Share With* box, you would choose **All** to make the report available to all users and accountants who log into the file. Because this is a sample company with no other users, we will leave it on **None**.

Do not select *Share Reports With Community*. If checked, this feature would share your report template (though not your data) with the greater QuickBooks Online user community.

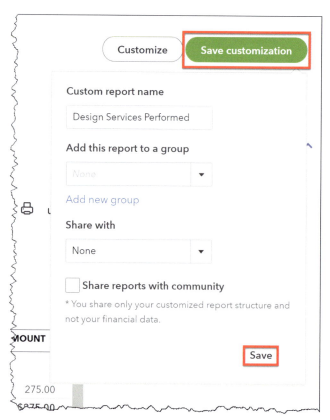

FIGURE 7-44: *Save Customization window*

STEP 20. Click **Save**.

Viewing Custom Reports

The next time you want to open this report follow these steps:

HANDS-ON PRACTICE

STEP 1.   From the *Report Center*, click on the **Custom Reports** tab at the top of the window.

STEP 2.   Run the report you just memorized by **clicking its name**. Scroll up to the top and click **Back to Report List** to return to this window.

FIGURE 7-45: *Saved custom report in the Reports Center*

We will continue using this custom report in the next exercise.

Emailing Customized Reports on a Schedule

QuickBooks Online allows you to automatically email reports on a schedule. You can email a single report, or group them together and set a schedule for an entire group.

You may want to use this feature to print a series of monthly reports for your files (e.g., monthly *Profit and Loss* and *Balance Sheet* reports).

HANDS-ON PRACTICE

STEP 3.   Click the word **Edit** on the right under *Action*.

STEP 4.   Set the *Set Email Schedule* slider to **On**.

STEP 5.   Apply the *Set Recurrence* options to monthly as shown in Figure 7-46. By setting the **Day** to the **15**th, you know you'll finish your reconciliations before the reports are sent.

STEP 6.   Enter **your email address** in the *Email Information*.

You can enter additional email addresses by separating them with a comma. There is also a **CC** option.

STEP 7.   You could further customize the subject line and message in the email. We will leave the defaults.

STEP 8.   Check **Attach the Report as an Excel File**. Some owners and board members prefer to be able to further manipulate the data.

STEP 9.   Click **Save and Close**.

FIGURE 7-46: *Email reports automatically on a schedule*

PRINTING REPORTS

Every report in QuickBooks Online is printable. When you print reports, QuickBooks Online allows you to specify the orientation (landscape or portrait) and page-break characteristics for the reports.

HANDS-ON PRACTICE

STEP 1. Create a **Profit & Loss by Customer** report dated **All Dates** (see page 307 for instructions). Click **Run Report**.

STEP 2. To print the report, scroll all the way to the far right of the report. Click the **Printer** at the top of the report as shown in Figure 7-47.

STEP 3. The *Print, Email, or Save as PDF* window displays (see Figure 7-48).

STEP 4. Select **Landscape** in the *Orientation* drop-down. The report now fits on two pages.

FIGURE 7-47: Click the Printer to print the report

The *Portrait* setting makes the print appear straight up across the 8½-inch dimension of the page, while the *Landscape* setting makes the print appear sideways across the 11-inch dimension of the page.

STEP 5. Confirm that the **Smart Page Breaks** setting is selected. This keeps items in the same group together to make multi-page reports easier to read.

STEP 6. Confirm that the **Repeat Page Header** setting is selected. This repeats the column headers at the top of each page.

STEP 7. Click the green **Print** button.

Note that you can also email the report or save it as a PDF right from this window.

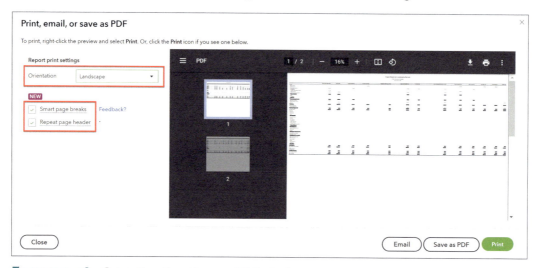

FIGURE 7-48: Print, Email, or Save as PDF window

STEP 8. The report opens in a new tab using the browser's printing tools. Click the **Printer** in the upper right corner.

STEP 9. A print dialog box opens, like the one shown in Figure 7-49. Note that your window will vary depending on what browser and type of printer you are using.

STEP 10. Choose your printer in the *Destination* box. If you don't have a printer, use **Save as PDF** instead.

STEP 11. Click the **More Settings** link to see additional printer options. We will not change any of these defaults, but sometimes they are helpful.

STEP 12. If everything looks right, click **Print** to print the report.

STEP 13. When you are done, close the **extra browser tab** containing the report to go back to QuickBooks Online.

STEP 14. Click **Close** to leave the print window.

> **TIP:**
>
> Sometimes the **Print Using System Dialog** option gives better results than using the browser's printing tools. If your results are not satisfactory, try this option instead.

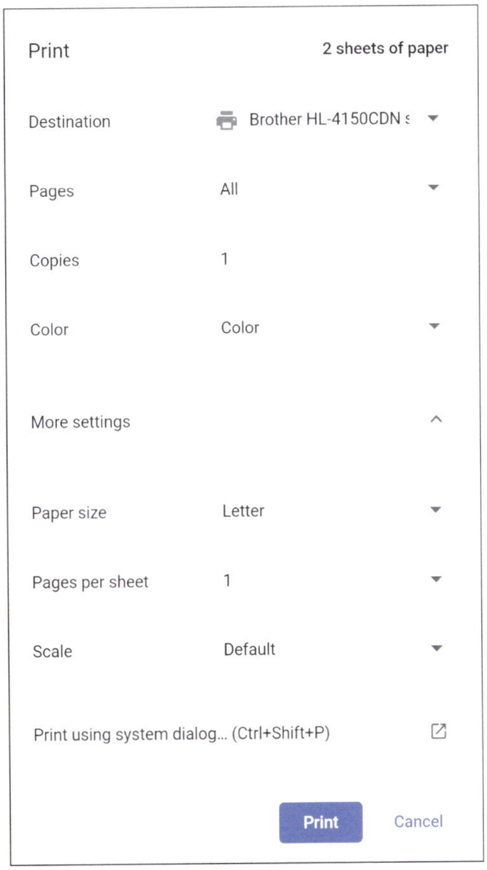

FIGURE 7-49: *The Print dialog box*

EXPORTING REPORTS TO SPREADSHEETS

When you need to modify reports in ways that QuickBooks Online does not allow (e.g., changing the name of columns, or removing rows and columns you don't want), you will need to export the report to a spreadsheet program like Microsoft Excel. Users of QuickBooks Online Advanced can also export to Google Sheets.

HANDS-ON PRACTICE

- **STEP 1.** From the *Report Center*, open the **Sales by Customer Detail** report in the *Sales and Customers* section.
- **STEP 2.** Change the *Report Period* to **All Dates**, then click **Run Report**.
- **STEP 3.** Drop down the **Export** icon and choose **Export to Excel** (see Figure 7-50).

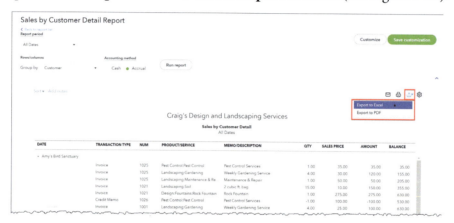

FIGURE 7-50: *Click the Export button in the upper right to Export to Excel*

- **STEP 4.** In the *Save As* dialog box, choose a *File Name* and location. We will leave this on the defaults. Click **Save**.
- **STEP 5.** The file is downloaded to your computer. Most browsers display the download at the bottom of the browser window, and export to a **Downloads** folder. Your computer may vary (see Figure 7-51).

FIGURE 7-51: *Open the downloaded Excel file*

> **TIP**
>
> Use this drop-down arrow for additional actions including *Show in Folder* to open the file location. Choose *Always Open Files of This Type* to skip this step in the future.

Step 6. Click on the **downloaded file** to open it. The Excel spreadsheet opens (see Figure 7-52).

Step 7. Depending on your security settings, you may need to click **Enable Editing** in the yellow bar at the top in order to update and modify the spreadsheet.

You are welcome to use **Save As** to move the Excel report to a new location and give it a descriptive name.

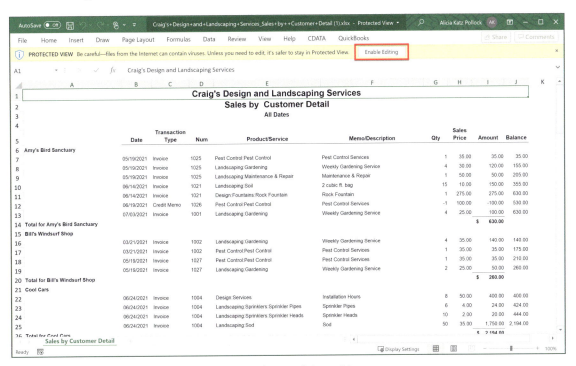

Figure 7-52: The report is now in an Excel spreadsheet. Your screen may vary.

REVIEW QUESTIONS

Comprehension Questions

1. Explain what you can do to see more detail about a Summary report.
2. Name an example of how the Statement of Cash Flows report is valuable.
3. How can you hide the sub-accounts on the Profit & Loss report?
4. Explain how using Filters helps you get the reports you want.
5. Explain how saving customized reports help you save time.

Multiple Choice

Choose the best answer(s) for each of the following:

1. What are the two major types of reports in QuickBooks Online?
    a. Register and List.
    b. Monthly and Annual.
    c. Accounting and Business Management.
    d. Balance Sheet and Profit & Loss.

2. Use the Customize button on any report to:
    a. Add or delete columns or apply filters to a report.
    b. Change the width of columns on the report.
    c. Print the report on blank paper.
    d. Memorize the report for future use.

3. You cannot create a QuickReport for:
    a. The Chart of Accounts.
    b. Products.
    c. Services.
    d. Customers.

4. To create a report that lists each of your vendors along with their address and telephone information:
    a. Display the Vendor Contact List.
    b. Open the *Search* window and do a search for vendors and the corresponding address and phone numbers.
    c. Customize the Vendor Center.
    d. You must create a *Customized Report* to see this information.

5. In order to analyze the profitability of your company, you should:
    a. Only do an analysis if the company is profitable.
    b. Create a *Profit & Loss* report.
    c. Review all detailed transaction reports.
    d. Create a *Balance Sheet* report.

6. Which statement is false? You may analyze your income and expenses for a given period:
    a. By class.
    b. By customer.
    c. By customer location.
    d. For the whole business.

7. Which report shows monies owed to your company by customers?
    a. The Balance Sheet report.
    b. The Collections Report.
    c. The Accounts Payable Aging report.
    d. The Customer Contact List report.

8. In order to modify the header and footer of your report:
    a. Click the **Customize** button and then click the **Filters** tab.
    b. Click the **Edit Titles** link.
    c. Click the **Header/Footer** button.
    d. Click the **Customize** button and then scroll down to the **Header/Footer** section.

9. Creating report groups allows you to:
    a. Rearrange the Report Center.
    b. Organize the Custom Reports list into groups of related reports.
    c. Share reports with others in your company.
    d. Group reports by date.

10. The Profit & Loss report shows which of the following:
    a. Assets, Liabilities, and Equity accounts.
    b. Checks written for the period.
    c. Income, Cost of Goods Sold, Expenses, Other Income, and Other Expenses.
    d. Accounts Receivable increases for the period.

11. If the Profit & Loss by Class report has a Not Specified column:
    a. There is an error in the filters on the report.
    b. You must refresh the report.
    c. You should eliminate the column using the *Customized* window.
    d. Some of the transactions for the period were not assigned to a class.

12. You can export Reports to:
    a. Microsoft Excel.
    b. Microsoft Word.
    c. Other Accounting Software.
    d. You cannot export reports.

13. Which is a feature of the **Filters** tab on the Customize window?
    a. Filters allow you select the columns on a report so that you can analyze specific areas of your business.
    b. Filters allow you to change how reports total and subtotal.
    c. Filters allow you to choose specific accounts, names, or products/services to include on a report.
    d. Filters allow you to modify the date range on most reports.

14. To modify which columns are displayed on a report, click **Customize** and then go to:
    a. The Header/Footer section.
    b. The Change Columns link in the Rows/Columns section.
    c. The Filter section.
    d. The General section.

15. The **Print Dialog Box** feature does not:
    a. Allow you to print to a PDF.
    b. Keep groups together on one page.

c. Look the same on every computer.
d. Repeat row or column headings on multiple pages.

Completion Statements

1. The _____ _____ is a report of your items along with description, price, cost, and quantity on hand.

2. To modify the contents of a report, you can _____ it to include certain accounts, names, columns, or transaction types.

3. A _____ _____ report shows the balances in all the Chart of Accounts categories as debits and credits as of a specific date.

4. If you're looking for a transaction and you don't know which register to look in, or if you want to find more than just a single transaction, you can use the _____ command.

5. The _____ _____ is a report that shows your financial position, as defined by the balances in each of your asset, liabilities, and equity accounts on a given date.

REPORTS—APPLY YOUR KNOWLEDGE

> **Log into your Imagine Photography class file at qbo.intuit.com.**

To submit these exercises for grading, ask your instructor if you should print out each report, or save them as PDFs to upload electronically.

> **IMPORTANT!**
>
> If you find any errors on these reports after your instructor grades them, that indicates that you made a mistake during the earlier exercises. Be sure to go back and fix those errors, so that your data is accurate.

1. Run the **Profit and Loss** report for **All Dates** twice, once **Cash-based** and once **Accrual-based**.
    a. Why is the *Net Income* negative on the *Cash-based* report? Enter this answer in the footer of the Cash-based P&L by clicking **Add Notes**. Print or save as PDF.
    b. Why is the *Net Income* positive in the *Accrual-based* report? Enter this answer in the footer of the Accrual-based P&L by clicking **Edit Notes**. Print or save as PDF.
    c. Notice that the Cash-based report includes a new category, **Unapplied Cash Payment Income**. This is because the invoice for Jaime Madeira's bounced check was dated the first of the month, but the bounced check was drafted from the checking account the day before, according to the Banking Feed. We will leave these dates in place as an illustration, but the fix would be to change the date of the invoice to match the date the money was withdrawn from the checking account.

2. Print or save a **Profit and Loss by Class** report for **All Dates, Accrual-based**.

3. Print or save the **Balance Sheet** report for **All Dates, Accrual-based**.

4. Print or save the **Statement of Cash Flows** report for **All Dates**.

5. Print or save a **QuickReport** from the *Chart of Accounts* for **Payments to Deposit**, for **All Dates**.

6. Print or save an **Income by Customer Summary** for **All Dates, Accrual-based**.

7. Print or save a **Sales by Product/Service Summary** report for **All Dates, Cash-based**.

8. Print or save a **Check Detail** report for **All Dates**.

9. Print or save a **Profit and Loss by Tag Group** report for **All Dates, Accrual-based**. Change *Display Columns By* to **Type**.

10. Create a **Sales by Customer Detail** report for **All Dates**.
    a. Run the report as **Accrual-based**.
    b. Filter the report to only display transactions from your *Sales Rep* **MM**.
    c. Change the *Report Title* to **Mario Mabilia's Sales**.
    d. Print or save the report as a PDF.
    e. **Save the Customization**.
    f. Use the email schedule to send *Quarterly* by setting *Repeats* to **Monthly**, *Every* **3** *Months*, *On* **Day 1**ˢᵗ. End the schedule after **4** occurrences.
    g. Send it *To* **your email address**.
    h. Check **Attach the Report as an Excel File**.

11. Save or print an **Invoices and Received Payments** report for **This Year**.
    a. Customize the report to **hide the Memo/Description** field, and **add the Payment Method** column after the **Transaction Type**, as shown in Figure 7-53.
    b. **Save the Customization**. Name the memorized report **Customer Payments This Year**.

DATE	TRANSACTION TYPE	PAYMENT METHOD	NUM	AMOUNT
▾ Liz Kildal				
	Payment	Credit Card		806.99
	Invoice		1008	1,138.48
	Payment			
	Invoice		1008	1,138.48
	Credit Memo		1010	-62.50
▾ Lynda Fulton				
	Payment	Check	5309	1,455.00
	Invoice		1004	1,455.00
▾ Madeira Builders				
	Payment	Check	90210	875.00
▾ Barnett Residence				
	Invoice		1006	500.00
▾ Devoe Residence				
	Invoice		1007	375.00

FIGURE 7-53: *Customize your report to look like this*

12. Run the **Business Snapshot**. Print or save the **My Income Chart**.

13. Answer the following questions about Imagine Photography based on these reports:
    a. _____ Which store location makes the most Gross Profit, San Jose or Walnut Creek?
    b. _____ How much Sales Tax does Imagine Photography owe the California Department of Tax and Fee Administration?
    c. _____ Looking at the Statement of Cash Flows, if the Net Income was negative, how come there is a Net Cash Increase For Period?
    d. _____ Which customer provided the highest Net Income?
    e. _____ Which Product or Service was the most popular (Quantity sold)?
    f. _____ Which Product or Service made the most money (% of Sales)?
    g. _____ What type of photography (Tag Type) had the highest Net Income?
    h. _____ How much revenue did Mario Mabilia make for the company?
    i. _____ According to the Business Snapshot, what percentage of Imagine Photography's revenue decreased because of Discounts Given?

CHAPTER 8

CASE STUDY: YINYANG GRAPHIC DESIGN

DESCRIPTION OF COMPANY

MaryBeth Yang has decided to follow her dream and start her own business. She developed a well-thought-out business plan for a graphic design business with an online store. She took her accumulated savings and started YinYang Graphic Design.

MaryBeth lives in Seattle, WA, a metropolitan city with a growing economy and many potential clients. She decided to offer web and print graphics services, including logo creation and website design. She will also offer consulting services to help clients focus their branding towards target markets.

In addition to working with clients, she will have an online store selling gift items printed with her artwork. To do this, she utilizes an online service that oversees all production, inventory, and shipping.

To help her new start-up, she selected QuickBooks Online Plus software to help manage the business. She has organized her company as a single-member Limited Liability Company (LLC) filing taxes as a Sole Proprietor, and has no employees. She has leased 600 square feet of office space.

MaryBeth is interested in analyzing her business by comparing her e-commerce sales to her consulting services, and tracking what industries her clients are in.

GOALS

Using a brand new QuickBooks Online Plus file, YinYang Graphic Design, you will perform the following:

- Set up a new file.
- Record initial start-up costs.
- Record a month of business transactions, including purchases, sales, deposits, Accounts Receivable and Accounts Payable.

Revenue and expense transactions will be recorded into one of the three classes that YYGD uses to track performance. At the end of the month, you will reconcile the bank statement and then produce financial statements and sales analysis reports, including a report of business performance by class.

CREATE THE COMPANY FILE

Your Instructor will send you an email message with a link to create your account.

1. Make sure you are logged out of QuickBooks Online completely.
2. Accept the invitation by clicking on the button in the email.

3. Log in as using the same information you used in the *Apply Your Knowledge* homework assignments. Click **Next**.

4. When it asks, *"What's your business name?"* enter the company name using this format **[Your name]'s YinYang Graphic Design**. Be sure to use your full name so that your instructor can easily identify your file on their class list.

5. Go through the next setup questions. Note that this wizard is subject to change and your options may not exactly match these instructions.
   a. *How have you been managing your finances?* Choose **Nothing, I'm Just Getting Started**.
   b. *What's your industry?* choose **Graphic Design Services**.
   c. *What kind of business is this?* click the **Sole Proprietor** button.
   d. *How does your business make money?* click both **Provides Services** and **Sells Products.**
   e. *What's your main role at the business?* select **Bookkeeper or Accountant**.
   f. *Who works at this business?* select **Contractors** and **We Plan to Hire in the Future**.
   g. *What apps do you already use?* choose **Skip For Now**.
   h. *Link your accounts and see everything in one place,* click **Skip For Now**.
   i. For *What would you like to do in QuickBooks?* or *What is everything you want to set up?* click **all the boxes**.
   j. *Ready for a free trial of QuickBooks Online Payroll?* select **No, I Don't Want to Add Payroll**.
   k. *Ready to Dive In?* Click **Let's Go**. Take the quick tour or close the window to dismiss the guides.

6. Turn to *Setting up the Chart of Accounts* on page 33. Confirm that your default Chart of Accounts matches the book, or follow the steps to replace it with the correct list.

OVERVIEW

1. If necessary, Purge the Chart of Accounts and import the replacement.
2. Set up the Account and Settings.
3. Turn on Sales Tax for Washington state.
4. Set up the Chart of Accounts.
5. Set up the Classes and Tags lists.
6. Add the Products & Services.
7. Set up the Custom Form Style.
8. Enter the business transactions. You will add all vendors and customers on the fly.
9. Import the Banking Feed.
10. Reconcile the bank account.
11. Prepare the reports.
12. Complete the analysis questions.

YINYANG GRAPHIC DESIGN CASE STUDY

1. Account and Settings

1. Set up the following **Account and Settings: Company** settings:

COMPANY SETTINGS	
LOGO	Yinyanglogo.jpg
COMPANY NAME	[Your Name]'s YinYang Graphic Design
LEGAL NAME	YinYang Graphic Design, LLC
EIN	12-3456788
INCOME TAX FORM	Sole Proprietor (Form 1040)
INDUSTRY	Graphic Design Services
COMPANY EMAIL	[Your email address]
CUSTOMER-FACING E-MAIL	info@yinyanggraphicdesign.com
COMPANY PHONE	+1 (206) 555-1212
WEBSITE	http://www.yinyanggraphicdesign.com
ADDRESS	400 Broad St, Seattle WA 98109

TABLE 8-1: *Company Settings*

2. Set up the following **Account and Settings: Advanced** settings as shown in Table 8-2:

ADVANCED SETTINGS	
FIRST MONTH OF THE FISCAL YEAR	January
FIRST MONTH OF INCOME TAX YEAR	Same as fiscal year
ACCOUNTING METHOD	Accrual
CLOSE THE BOOKS	Off
ENABLE ACCOUNT NUMBERS	Off
TRACK CLASSES	On
WARN ME WHEN A TRANSACTION ISN'T ASSIGNED A CLASS	Yes
TRACK LOCATIONS	Off
PRE-FILL FORMS WITH PREVIOUSLY ENTERED CONTENT	On
AUTOMATICALLY APPLY CREDITS	Off
AUTOMATICALLY INVOICE UNBILLED ACTIVITY	Off
AUTOMATICALLY APPLY BILL PAYMENTS	Off
PROJECTS	On
CUSTOMER LABEL	Clients
SIGN ME OUT IF INACTIVE FOR	3 Hours

TABLE 8-2: *Advanced Settings*

3. Turn on the following **Account and Settings: Time** settings as shown in Table 8-3:

TIME SETTINGS	
FIRST DAY OF WORK WEEK	Sunday
SHOW SERVICE FIELD	On
ALLOW TIME TO BE BILLABLE	On
SHOW BILLING RATE TO USERS ENTERING TIME	Off

TABLE 8-3: *Time Settings*

4. Turn on the following **Account and Settings: Sales** settings as shown in Table 8-4:

SALES SETTINGS	
PREFERRED INVOICE TERMS	Due on Receipt
PREFERRED DELIVERY METHOD	None
SHIPPING	Off
CUSTOM TRANSACTION NUMBERS	Off
SERVICE DATE	On
DISCOUNT	On
DEPOSIT	Off
ACCEPT TIPS	Off
TAGS	On
SHOW PRODUCT/SERVICE COLUMN ON FORMS	On
SHOW SKU COLUMN	Off
PRICE RULES	Off
TRACK QUANTITY AND PRICE/RATE	On
TRACK INVENTORY QUANTITY ON HAND	On
LATE FEES	Off
PROGRESS INVOICING	On (Update your invoice template)
STATEMENTS	On

TABLE 8-4: *Sales Settings*

5. Set up **Account and Settings > Expenses** with the preferences in Table 8-5:

EXPENSES SETTINGS	
SHOW ITEMS TABLE	On
SHOW TAGS FIELD ON EXPENSE AND PURCHASE FORMS	On
TRACK EXPENSE AND ITEMS BY CLIENT	On
MAKE EXPENSES AND ITEMS BILLABLE	On
MARKUP WITH A DEFAULT RATE OF	On, 100%
TRACK BILLABLE EXPENSES AND ITEMS AS INCOME, IN A SINGLE ACCOUNT	On
CHARGE SALES TAX	Off
DEFAULT BILL PAYMENT TERMS	Net 30
USE PURCHASE ORDERS	On

TABLE 8-5: *Expense Settings*

2. Sales Tax

6. Turn on **Sales Tax**. You will only collect tax for **WA** customers. File sales taxes **Monthly**.

3. Chart of Accounts

7. Set up your **Chart of Accounts** using Table 8-6. Add, edit, or inactivate these categories.

	CHANGES TO MAKE TO THE CHART OF ACCOUNTS			
ACTION	ACCOUNT NAME	ACCOUNT TYPE	SAVE ACCOUNT UNDER	TAX FORM SECTION OR *EDIT TO MAKE
Add	National Bank Checking (0042)	Banks	Bank Accounts	Checking
Add	National Bank Savings (4236)	Banks	Bank Accounts	Savings
Add	National Bank Visa (1818)	Credit Cards	Credit Cards	Credit Card
Add	Design Income	Income	Income	Service/Fee Income
Add	Marketing	Expenses	Advertising & Marketing	Advertising/Promotional
Edit	Sales: *Rename to **Consulting Income**	Income	Income	*Change to **Service/Fee Income**
Inactivate	Utilities:Heating & Cooling	Expenses		*Not needed
Inactivate	Utilities:Water & Sewer	Expenses		*Not needed
Inactivate	Supplies:Supplies & materials	Expenses		*Not needed

TABLE 8-6: *Additional customization for the Chart of Accounts*

4. Classes and Tags

8. Set up your **Classes List**.
    a. Set up classes for the two revenue streams used by YYGD—**Design** and **Products**.
    b. Set up a third class for **Overhead**.

9. Set up your **Tag Group**.
    a. Create a **Tag Group** called **Industry**. Choose any color you'd like.
    b. Create tags in the Industry group for **Clothing**, **Spa**, **Service**, and **Other Retail**.

5. Products and Services

10. Set up your **Products and Services List**. Create the items shown in Table 8-7. Leave any other fields blank or accept the defaults if not shown in the table.
    a. For all **Inventory products**, use the following parameters:

FIELD	SETTINGS
Initial Quantity on Hand	0
As of Date	January 1 of the current year
Reorder Point	5
Inventory Asset Account	Inventory Asset
Purchasing Information	Copy sales description
Expense Account	Cost of Goods Sold:Supplies & Materials
Preferred Vendor	Nile Online (add on the fly the first time)

TYPE	ITEM NAME	CATEGORY	CLASS	DESCRIPTION	SALES PRICE/ RATE	ACCOUNT	TAX CODE	COST
Service	Logo Design	Services (add on the fly)	Design	Logo Design	50	Design Income	Nontaxable	
Service	Consulting	Services	Design	Consulting	60	Consulting Income	Nontaxable	
Service	Web Design	Services	Design	Web Design	50	Design Income	Taxable—Web Design	
Inventory	T-Shirts	Items (add on the fly)	Products	Art Tees	24	Sales of Product Income	General Clothing	10
Inventory	Caps	Items	Products	Baseball Hats	24	Sales of Product Income	Taxable—Hats (informal)	12
Inventory	Mugs	Items	Products	Coffee Mugs	18	Sales of Product Income	Taxable—based on location only	9
Inventory	Tote Bags	Items	Products	Art Totes	20	Sales of Product Income	Taxable—based on location only	9
Bundle	Distributor Items			Products Sold	*Display bundle components: T-Shirts, 1. Caps, 1. Mugs, 1. Tote Bags, 1.			

TABLE 8-7: *Products and Services List*

6. Custom Form Styles

11. Edit the **Custom Form Styles**. Make the changes shown in Table 8-8. If an option is skipped, leave the default.

	ELEMENT	STYLE
DESIGN TAB	Edit Template	**Progress Invoicing Optimized Template**
	Rename Template	**YYGD Invoices**
	Make logo edits	Size = **Large**, Placement = **Center**
CONTENT TAB, TOP SECTION	Phone	Turn on, **(206) 555-1212**
	Address	Hide **Country**
CONTENT TAB, MIDDLE SECTION	Columns	Turn off **Date**
	Show More Activity Options	Turn on **Show progress on line items**.
CONTENT TAB, BOTTOM SECTION	Estimate Summary	Turn on
	Message to Customer on Invoices	**Thank you for your business!** Size = **12pt**.
	Add Footer Text	**Graphic Design With Meaning** Size = **12pt**.

TABLE 8-8: *Use this data to edit the Progress Invoicing form style.*

7. Business Transactions

Use the previous month for all dates. For example, if it is currently September and the Date column says 1, use the date August 1. If the previous month happens to be February, use Feb 28 for all end-of-month transactions.

Create all Vendors and Customers on the fly without entering details.

Date	Business Transaction	Transaction Details
1	Deposited owner investment from MaryBeth Yang to provide cash for operations.	Transaction type: **Bank Deposit** Deposit to: **National Bank Checking (0042)** Received From: **MaryBeth Yang** (add as employee) From Account: **Owner Investments** Description: **Deposit Owners Investment** Payment Method: **Check** Ref No.: **7031968** Amount: **$85,000.00** Class: **Overhead**
1	Paid rent plus refundable deposit to Orr Realty.	Transaction type: **Check** Payee: **Orr Realty** (add as vendor) Bank Account: **National Bank Checking (0042)** Check#: **1001** Line 1 Category: **Rent** Description: **First Month's Rent** Amount: **$1250** Class: **Overhead** Line 2 Category: **Security Deposits** Description: *Security Deposit* Amount: **$1250** Class: **Overhead** Total Check: **$2,500.00**
2	Received bill from Nile Online for website merchandise.	Transaction type: **Bill** Vendor: **Nile Online** Terms: **Net 30** Tags: **Clothing** In *Item Details* section (click to open): Product/Service: **T-Shirts**, Quantity **100** Product/Service: **Caps**, Quantity **75** Product/Service: **Mugs**, Quantity **75** Product/Service: **Tote Bags**, Quantity **50** Amount: **$3025.00** Class (all lines): **Products**
2	Received bill from Mitchell Office Supply.	Transaction type: **Bill** Vendor: **Mitchell Office Supply** (add as vendor) Terms: **Net 30** Line 1 Category: **Furniture & Fixtures** Line 1 Description: **Desks, chairs, filing cabinets** Line 1 Amount: **$2,825.00** Line 2 Category: **Long-term office equipment** Line 2 Description: **High-volume copier** Line 2 Amount: **$2,600.00** Class (both lines): **Overhead** Total: **$5,425.00**

CASE STUDY: YINYANG GRAPHIC DESIGN | 349

Date	Business Transaction	Transaction Details
3	Received bill from Mitchell Office Supply. *Delete the automatically prepopulated rows when you create this second bill.*	Transaction type: **Bill** Vendor: **Mitchell Office Supply** Terms: **Net 30** Category: **Office Expenses:Office Supplies** Description: **Paper, pens, folders, supplies** Amount: **$632.00** Class: **Overhead**
3	Entered Credit Card Charge to Kilsheimer Design for design tools.	Transaction type: **Expense** Vendor: **Kilsheimer Design** (add as vendor) Payment Account: **National Bank Visa (1818)** Category: **Office Expenses:Small Tools and Equipment** Description: **Graphic design equipment** Amount: **$499.00** Class: **Design**
4	Issued check to Tameko Insurance for liability insurance premium.	Transaction type: **Check** Payee: **Tameko Insurance** (add as vendor) Bank Account: **National Bank Checking (0042)** Check No.: **1002** Category: **Insurance:Liability Insurance** Total: **$250.00** Class: **Overhead**
8	Prepared invoice for consulting with LaTanya's Beauty Salon.	Transaction type: **Invoice** Client: **LaTanya's Beauty Salon** (add as client) Terms: **Due on Receipt** Tags: **Spa** Service Date: **the 8th of this month** Product/Service: **Consulting** Description: **Marketing consultation** Qty: **6 (@ $60.00/hr)** Amount: **$360.00** Class: **Design**
14	Prepared invoice for logo creation and web design work for Shelia's Boutique.	Transaction type: **Invoice** Client: **Shelia's Boutique** (add as client) Terms: **Due on Receipt** Tags: **Clothing** Line 1 - Service Date: **the 4th of this month** Line 1 - Product/Service: **Logo Design (3 @ $50.00/hour)** Line 2 - Service Date: **the 12th of this month** Line 2 - Product/Service: **Web Design (10 @ $50.00/hour)** Class (both lines): **Design** Total: **$650.00**
15	Received payment from LaTanya's Beauty Salon.	Transaction type: **Receive Payment** Client: **LaTanya's Beauty Salon** Payment Method: **Check** Reference No: **9864** Deposit to: **Payments to Deposit** Amount: **$360.00** Apply to: **Invoice # 1001**

Date	Business Transaction	Transaction Details
16	Recorded receipt for first two weeks of sales from online store.	Transaction type: **Sales Receipt** Client: **Nile Online Sales** (add as client) Tags: **Clothing** Payment Method: **Direct Deposit** (add on the fly) Deposit To: **Payments to Deposit** Product/Service: **Distributor Items** Qty: **T-Shirts, Qty 15** **Caps, Qty 13** **Mugs, Qty 12** **Tote Bags, Qty 0** Class: **Products** (all lines) Sales Tax: **Based on Location, $91.02** Total: **$979.02**
16	Deposited Online Sales minus listing fees.	Transaction type: **Bank Deposit** Deposit to: **National Bank Checking (0042)** Tags: **Clothing** Payments to Deposit: **Nile Online Sales** Add Funds to this Deposit: Received From: **Nile Online Sales** Account: **Advertising & Marketing:Listing Fees** Amount: **-97.90** (enter as negative amount) Class: **Products** Total Deposit Amount: **$881.12**
17	Received bill from Megia Printing, Inc. for printing of business cards and flyers.	Transaction type: **Bill** Vendor: **Megia Printing, Inc.** (add as vendor) Terms: **Net 30** Category: **Advertising & Marketing:Marketing** Description: **Flyers and business cards** Amount: **$320.00** Class: **Design**
22	Received bill from Caleb Productions. Caleb Productions is an LLC, and you are paying them more than $600. When you create them as a new Vendor, add this information: **Caleb Jackson** Display as: **Caleb Productions, LLC** **123 Central Square, Seattle WA 98106** Business ID No: **46-1234567** **Track Payments for 1099**	Transaction type: **Bill** Vendor: **Caleb Productions, LLC** (add as vendor) Terms: **Net 30** Bill No: **8248** Tags: **Clothing** Category: **Contract Labor** Description: **Fees for product designs** Amount: **$1,500.00** Billable: **No** Customer: **Nile Online Sales** Class: **Products**

Date	Business Transaction	Transaction Details
24	Prepared invoice for Bello Kane Clothing Design for web design services.	Transaction type: **Invoice** Client: **Bello Kane Clothing Design** (add as vendor) Terms: **Due on Receipt** Tags: **Clothing** Service Date: **the 28th of this month** Product/Service: **Web Design (145 @ $50/hr)** Description: **Shopping Cart** Total: **$7,250.00** Class: **Design**
26	Received check from Bello Kane Clothing Design.	Transaction type: **Receive Payment** Client: **Bello Kane Clothing Design** Payment Method: **Check** Reference No: **1079** Deposit To: **Payments to Deposit** Amount: **$3,625.00** Apply to: **Invoice #1004** (partial payment)
28	Received payment from Shelia's Boutique by credit card.	Transaction type: **Receive Payment** Client: **Shelia's Boutique** Payment Method: **Credit Card** Deposit To: **Payments to Deposit** Amount: **$650.00** Apply to: **Invoice #1002**
28	Deposited Shelia's Boutique credit card payment. National Bank deducts a 2.75% merchant service fee. Don't forget you can use the amount field as a calculator, and that the fee is negative. Try calculating **650*-.0275** in the *Amount* box.	Transaction type: **Bank Deposit** Deposit to: **National Bank Checking (0042)** Tags: **Clothing** Payments to Deposit: **Shelia's Boutique** *Add Funds to this Deposit:* Received From: **National Bank** (add as vendor) Account: **Office Expenses:Merchant Account Fees** Amount: **-17.88** (enter as negative amount) Class: **Design** Total Deposit Amount: **$632.12**
29	Prepared invoice for Lannister Stark Industries.	Transaction type: **Invoice** Client: **Lannister Stark Industries** (add as client) Terms: **Net 30** Tags: **Service** Product/Service: **Consulting (15 @ $60/hr)** Description: **Brochure and ad** Product/Service: **Web Design (57 @ $50.00/hr)** Description: **Website setup** Class (all lines): **Design** Total: **$3,750.00**
29	Received bill from Seattle Light & Power for utilities.	Transaction type: **Bill** Vendor: **Seattle Light & Power** (add as vendor) Terms: **Net 30** Bill No: **7599** Category: **Utilities:Electricity** Description: **Electric bill** Amount: **$501.00** Class: **Overhead**

Date	Business Transaction	Transaction Details
29	Received bill from Western Bell for telephone.	Transaction type: **Bill** Vendor: **Western Bell** (add as vendor) Terms: **Net 30** Bill No: **2332** Category: **Utilities:Phone Service** Description: **Telephone bill** Amount: **$288.00** Class: **Overhead**
30	Recorded receipt for two weeks of sales from online store.	Transaction type: **Sales Receipt** Client: **Nile Online Sales** Tags: **Clothing** Payment Method: **Direct Deposit** Deposit To: **Payments to Deposit** Product/Service: **Distributor Items** Qty: **T-Shirts, Qty 35** **Caps, Qty 32** **Mugs, Qty 28** **Tote Bags, Qty 3** Class (on all lines): **Products** Sales Tax: **Based on Location, $222.63** Total: **$2394.63**
30	Received check from Bello Kane Clothing Design.	Transaction type: **Receive Payment** Client: **Bello Kane Clothing Design** Payment Method: **ACH** (add on the fly) Deposit To: **Payments to Deposit** Amount: **$3,625.00** Apply to: **Invoice #1004**
30	Received ACH payment from Lannister Stark Industries.	Transaction type: **Receive Payment** Client: **Lannister Stark Industries** Payment Method: **ACH** Deposit To: **Payments to Deposit** Amount: **$1,875** Apply to: **Invoice #1005** (partial payment)
30	Deposited two **checks** held in the Payments to Deposit account to National Bank.	Transaction type: **Bank Deposit** Deposit to: **National Bank Checking (0042)** Payments to Deposit: **Checks from Bello Kane, LaTanya's Boutique** Total Deposit Amount: **$3,985.00**
30	Deposited two **ACH payments** held in the Payments to Deposit account to National Bank.	Transaction type: **Bank Deposit** Deposit to: **National Bank Checking (0042)** Payments to Deposit: **ACH payments from Bello Kane, Lannister Stark Industries** Total Deposit Amount: **$5,500.00**
30	Deposited Online Sales minus listing fees.	Transaction type: **Bank Deposit** Deposit to: **National Bank Checking (0042)** Tags: **Clothing** Payments to Deposit: **Nile Online Sales** *Add Funds to this Deposit:* Received From: **Nile Online Sales** Account: **Advertising & Marketing:Listing Fees** Amount: **-239.46** (enter negative amount) Class: **Products** Total Deposit Amount: **$2155.17**

Date	Business Transaction	Transaction Details
Last	Paid all bills in a batch by check. Select **Print Later**.	Select **Pay Bills**, and then pay the following bills by check from **National Bank Checking (0042)** (to be printed later): Mitchell Office Supply Nile Online Mitchell Office Supply Megia Printing, Inc. Caleb Productions, LLC Seattle Light & Power Western Bell Total payments: **$11,691.00**
Last	Print all checks on **Standard checks**. Use setup defaults (no need for test print).	Starting Check No.: **1003** On first page print: **3 checks** Print on blank paper or save to PDF.
Last	Enter Credit Card Charge to Community Computing for computer repairs.	Transaction type: **Expense** Payee: **Community Computing** (add as vendor) Payment Account: **National Bank Visa (1818)** Category: **Repairs & Maintenance** Description: **Replace hard drive** Amount: **$147.00** Class: **Design**

8. Import the Banking Feed

Because we can't connect a live bank account to YinYang Graphic Design, we will create and import a .csv data file. Save **YinYangGraphicDesign.xls** to your computer from your textbook files.

1. Create a bank file to upload.
    a. In Excel (or Google Sheets), open the **YinYangBankingImport.xls** file from the textbook's Classroom Files.
    b. Click on **File** and choose **Save As**.
    c. Change the *File type* to **.csv** as shown in Figure 8-1, then **Save** the new file.
    d. **Close** Excel.

FIGURE 8-1: *Save the Excel spreadsheet as csv for import*

2. Upload transactions into the Banking Center downloaded from your bank.
    a. In the *Banking Center*, click the **Upload Transactions** button.
    b. **Browse** to select your **YinYangBankingImport.csv** file, then click **Continue**.
    c. In the *QuickBooks Account* field, choose **National Bank Checking (0042)**, then click **Continue**.

d. Set the *What's the Date Format Used in Your File?* to **MM/dd/yyyy**. Click **Continue**.
e. **Check** the *box* to the left of *Date* to select all transactions.
f. Review the transactions, then click **Continue** again.
g. In the box that says *17 Transactions Will Be Imported. Do You Want To Continue?* Click **Yes**.
h. In the next window, click **Done**.

3. Accept all the Banking matches.

4. Categorize the two **Rockstar Parking** charges.
   a. When you add a new Vendor/Customer, just name it **Parking** so that you can also use it for all parking lots.
   b. *Categorize* both as **Vehicle Expenses:Parking & Tolls** with the *Class* of **Design**.
   c. In the **$4.85** transaction, enter **Shelia's Boutique** as the *Client/Project*, and enter the *Tag* **Clothing**.
   d. In the **$11.42** transaction, enter **Lannister Stark Industries** as the *Client/Project*. Use the *Tag* **Service**.
   e. If QBO asks *Is Rockstar Parking always Parking and Tolls?* turn **Off** the *Auto-add* option so that you can assign customers to each transaction, then click **Create Rule**.

5. Create a **Rule** called **Vision Wireless** to split the charge.
   a. Add **Vision Wireless** as new vendor on the fly.
   b. Split the charge **80% Utilities:Phone Service, 20% Owner Distributions**.
   c. Use the *Class* **Overhead** on both splits.
   d. **Auto-add** the transaction.

6. Verify that all transactions have been matched or added before moving on to the next step.

9. Reconcile the Checking Account

1. Reconcile the checking account to the statement in Figure 8-2. Note that your dates may vary.
   a. Create a Bank Deposit into **National Bank Checking (0042)** *Received From* **National Bank** into the *Account* **Interest Earned** for the amount shown on the statement, with the *Class* **Overhead**. Enter the *Date* as the **last date of the previous month**.
   b. Enter an Expense to **National Bank** for **General Business Expenses:Bank Fees & Service Charges**, also to **Overhead**, on the **last day of the previous month**.
   c. Mark the **Interest** and **Service Charges** as cleared. Verify the *Difference* is **$0.00** before finishing the reconciliation.
   d. Note that the six bill payment checks written at the end of the month have not cleared yet, so uncheck these rows.

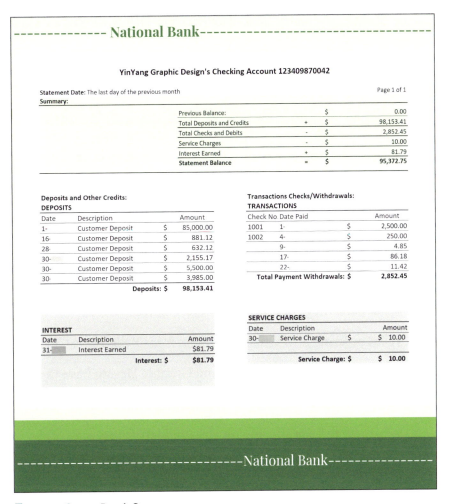

FIGURE 8-2: Bank Statement

10. Prepare the Reports
Print or save PDFs of the following reports:

1. Product/Service List
2. Reconciliation Report
3. Balance Sheet for All Dates, Accrual-based
4. Profit and Loss for All Dates, Accrual-based
5. Profit and Loss for All Dates, Cash-based
6. Profit and Loss by Class for All Dates, Accrual Based
7. Profit and Loss by Tag Group, Display columns by the Industry group, All Dates, Accrual-Based
8. Statement of Cash Flows for All Dates
9. Accounts Receivable Aging Summary for Today
10. Sales by Product/Service Summary for All Dates

11. Profit and Loss by Client for All Dates, filtered for Specified clients, displaying a % of Row comparison

12. Sales Tax Liability Report, All Dates, Cash-based

11. Complete the Analysis Questions
Use the completed reports to answer the following questions.

1. _____ What is the net income or net loss for this year on an accrual basis?

2. _____ What are the total Expenses on an accrual basis?

3. _____ What is the amount of Total Product Sales?

4. _____ What is the amount of rent paid?

5. _____ What is the net cash increase for the period?

6. _____ What percentage of total sales were T-Shirts?

7. _____ What percentage of Gross Profit was from Bello Kane Clothing Design?

8. _____ In which Industry does YingYang Graphic Design have the most net income?

9. _____ How much does YinYang Graphic Design have in total liabilities as of today?

10. _____ What was the Net Income for the Products Class?

11. _____ What was the total amount of Uncleared checks and payments from the bank reconciliation?

12. Explain the difference in the Net Income between the Accrual and Cash-based Profit and Loss Statements.

CHAPTER 9

PROJECTS AND JOB COSTING

TOPICS

In this chapter, you will learn about the following topics:

▸ Creating and Using Estimates (page 358)

▸ Using Progress Invoicing (page 361)

▸ Creating Purchase Orders from Estimates (page 365)

▸ Tracking Estimates (page 366)

▸ Taking Customer Deposits on Work to Be Performed (page 368)

▸ Managing Vendor Deposits (page 373)

▸ Passing Through Billable Expenses (page 376)

▸ Using Two-Sided Items (page 381)

▸ Entering Time on a Project (page 384)

▸ Using the Projects Center (page 387)

▸ Running Job Costing Reports (page 395)

▸ Additional Job Costing Features (page 397)

OPEN THIS FILE:

Open the *Craig's Landscaping sample company* using the bookmark you created on page 8, or go to http://qbo.intuit.com/redir/testdrive.

Some companies are project-oriented, meaning their customer jobs occur over time and incur dedicated costs. They may invoice at milestones, or all at once. They may get reimbursed for time and materials, or just charge a flat rate. Construction, law firms, and creative arts are all examples of businesses that use project management and *job costing* in their bookkeeping.

In this chapter, we'll look at how to use QuickBooks Online's tools to track the income and expenses related to complex customer jobs.

We will also explore QBO's **Projects Center** to manage multi-stage projects, pass through billable expenses, and analyze profitability.

357

> **IMPORTANT:**
>
> Because the Craig's Landscaping sample file resets itself between sessions, we will practice QuickBooks Online's project and job costing features throughout the lessons, then build a complete project from start to finish in the *Apply Your Knowledge* exercise at the end of the chapter.

CREATING AND USING ESTIMATES

Estimates allow you to track bids for your services or products, recording a proposal to give to the customer. Estimates do not post to the General Ledger since the bid may never become an actual project. In fact, you can prepare more than one estimate for the same job if a customer is not sure exactly what they want to order.

When a bid is accepted and you perform the work, an invoice can be created right from the estimate so that you don't have to enter the information twice. If the customer never accepts the estimate, mark the status as *Rejected*. Your list of estimates should always reflect current and pending jobs.

Sometimes you invoice for an entire estimate all at one time, but QuickBooks Online also provides a *Progress Invoicing* feature that allows you to generate several partial invoices as each stage of a project is completed. The original estimate is used to track progress towards each milestone until the invoice is paid in full.

Entering an estimate in QuickBooks Online is similar to entering an invoice, because you fill out all of the customer and product or service information the same way. The big difference is that because estimates are non-posting, they do not affect any of your financial reports.

You can create a new **Estimate** from any of several menus, whichever is most convenient:

- The *+New* button.
- While looking at a *Customer Record*.
- From the *Get Things Done* tab on the *Dashboard*.
- While looking at a customer's *Project*.

> **TIP:**
>
> You can save an estimate as an **Unscheduled Recurring Transaction** to use it as a template for future projects. This is useful for either frequent or complex jobs.

HANDS-ON PRACTICE

To create an **Estimate**, follow these steps:

STEP 1. Open the **Shara Barnett:Barnett Design sub-customer's** transaction list.

STEP 2. Click on the green **New Transaction button** and select **Estimate** (see Figure 9-1).

STEP 3. Enter an *Expiration Date* that is **one month from now**.

Estimates typically have an expiration date in case costs change, and to create a sense of urgency for the customer.

STEP 4. Enter **Design** in the *Product/Service* field and press **Tab**.

STEP 5. Type **Custom Design for back yard** in the *Description* field.

STEP 6. Update the *Qty* to **5** and press **Tab**.

STEP 7. Click **Save and Close** to record the estimate.

FIGURE 9-1: *Create a new Estimate*

> **NOTE:**
>
> You can design your printed and emailed estimates by creating or modifying a **Custom Form Style** in the same way you customize your invoices.

Creating Invoices from Estimates

When an estimate is approved or accepted by a customer, you can convert the information from the estimate into an *Invoice*. This eliminates the need to manually re-enter the detail.

There are several convenient ways to do this:

- Viewing an estimate on a customer's transaction list and clicking **Create Invoice** in the *Action* column.
- Starting a new invoice from scratch, and adding the open estimate from the *drawer* that appears on the right.
- Opening a saved estimate and clicking the **Create Invoice** button.

HANDS-ON PRACTICE

To turn Barnett Design's **Estimate** into an **Invoice**, follow these steps:

STEP 1. Click on the *Magnifying Glass* in the upper right corner, and select **the estimate you just created**.

STEP 2. Click the **Create Invoice** button at the top right (see Figure 9-2).

QuickBooks Online transfers the information from the estimate onto the invoice.

FIGURE 9-2: *Open a saved estimate to convert it to an invoice*

STEP 3. Change the *Quantity* column for the **Design** service from **5** to **4** (see Figure 9-3) and then press **Tab**.

The estimate was for 5 hours of design work, but Craig actually completed the work in 4 hours, so you're making this change to reflect the actual charge.

STEP 4. Click **Save and Close** to record the invoice.

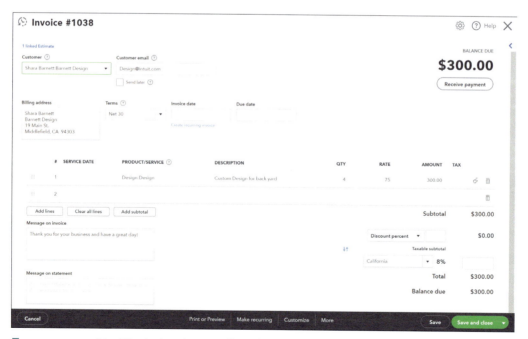

FIGURE 9-3: *Modify the invoice to reflect the actual charges*

When you look at the Barnett Designs transaction list, you can see that the estimate is now **Closed**, meaning that it has been invoiced in full (see Figure 9-4).

FIGURE 9-4: *The estimate on the transaction list is marked Closed*

Using Progress Invoicing

Progress Invoicing allows you to charge your customers a portion of the total estimate at each stage of a project. QuickBooks Online tracks how much of the estimate has been invoiced, and how much remains.

When you use progress invoicing, you have the flexibility to send the customers several invoices reflecting your company's policies. For example,

- Some projects require multiple payments by activity. A customer may start with an upfront payment for design and initial materials, make a second payment for installation, and send a final payment for cleanup and disposal.

- You may choose to invoice for milestone percentages throughout the project. For example, a 25% payment to schedule the job, 50% partway through, and the remaining 25% upon completion.

HANDS-ON PRACTICE

To create a **Progress Invoice** from an **Estimate**, first modify your preferences. Follow these steps:

- **STEP 1.** Click on the *Gear* in the upper right corner and then choose **Account and Settings**.
- **STEP 2.** Select the **Sales tab** and scroll down to *Progress Invoicing*. Turn the slider to **On** (see Figure 9-5).

FIGURE 9-5: *Turn on Progress Invoicing in Account and Settings*

STEP 3. An alert appears asking you to *Update Your Invoice Template*, as shown in Figure 9-6. Click **Update**, click **Save**, and then click **Done** to close the *Account and Settings* window.

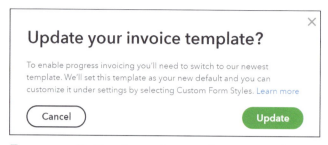

FIGURE 9-6: *Turning on Progress Invoicing updates your form styles*

STEP 4. To create a new **Estimate**, click on the **+New** button at the top of the *Left Navigation Bar* and select **Estimate**.

STEP 5. Enter **Sushi by Katsuyuki** in the *Customer* field.

STEP 6. Use an **Expiration Date** one month from now.

STEP 7. Enter the products and services on the *Estimate* form, as shown in Figure 9-7.

STEP 8. Apply **California** *Sales Tax*.

STEP 9. Click **Save and Close** to record the estimate.

FIGURE 9-7: *Create a new Estimate*

STEP 10. Katsuyuki reviewed the estimate and emailed you immediately to accept the bid as they want to get started on the project right away. Go to the *Customers Center* and click on the **first blue box** in the *Money Bar*. You'll see the open estimate for Sushi by Katsuyuki (see Figure 9-8).

FIGURE 9-8: Open Estimates in the Customers Center

STEP 11. Click the blue **Start Invoice** link on the right in the *Action* column. QuickBooks Online brings up the *Add to Invoice* drawer listing all open estimates for that customer (see Figure 9-9).

> **NOTE:**
>
> When you work with a customer on a prospective project, you may need to create several estimates showing different alternatives for the job. If you do, QuickBooks Online will show each of the open estimates in the *Add to Invoice* drawer.

FIGURE 9-9: Open estimates appear in a drawer

STEP 12. Click the blue **Add** link in the drawer.

STEP 13. An alert appears, asking you *How Much Do You Want To Invoice?*, as shown in Figure 9-10. Choose **Custom Amount for Each Line**. This option allows you invoice for specific line items, and leave the rest until later.

FIGURE 9-10: *Choose to invoice for percentages or line items*

> **NOTE:**
>
> As you can see in Figure 9-10, you can create an invoice for the entire estimate (i.e., no Progress Invoicing), a flat percentage of all lines, or specific line items. Select the option that applies to your situation.

STEP 14. Click **Copy to Invoice**. QuickBooks Online transfers the information from the estimate onto the invoice.

STEP 15. Craig charges upfront for the initial design work. Click in the first line for *Design*. Change the *Amount* to **1000** and press **Tab**.

STEP 16. Craig requires a 50% prepayment for materials. On line 2 for *Concrete*, change *Amount* to **Percent**, and enter **50**. Press **Tab**.

STEP 17. Repeat this step to invoice 50% for the rest of the materials on lines 3-5. Craig will not invoice for *Installation* until it's time to break ground.

STEP 18. Compare your estimate to Figure 9-11. When it matches, click **Save and Close**.

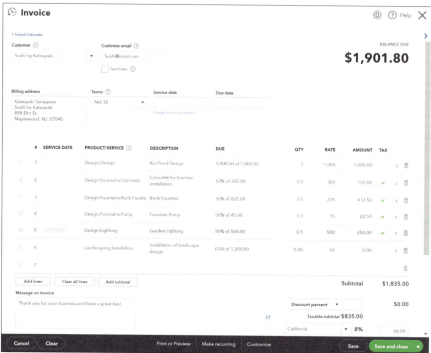

FIGURE 9-11: *Create a Progress Invoice based on the Estimate*

Creating Purchase Orders from Estimates

QuickBooks Online Plus and Advanced allow you to create a purchase order for inventory and other two-sided products and services that appear on estimates.

Purchase Orders (**POs**) are non-posting transactions that keep track of vendor purchases which have not yet arrived or been billed. POs can be emailed to vendors, although QBO does not place the actual order on your behalf. Purchase orders can later be converted into bills once the products arrive and the vendor sends you their invoice.

HANDS-ON PRACTICE

Craig needs to order the fountains and pumps for the Katsuyuki project. Follow these steps:

STEP 1. Open the *Sushi by Katsuyuki estimate* you previously created.

STEP 2. Drop down the **arrow** on the right of the *Create Invoice* button. Click **Copy to Purchase Order**, as shown in Figure 9-12.

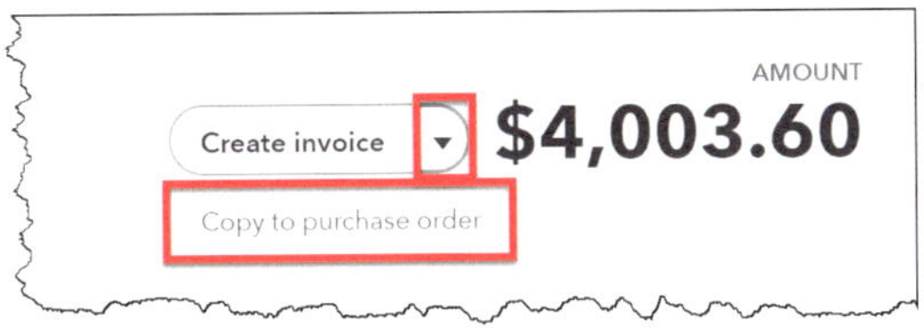

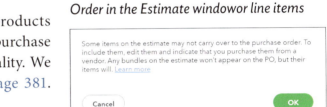

FIGURE 9-12: *Select Copy to Purchase Order in the Estimate window or line items*

STEP 3. An alert appears indicating that products and services must be available for purchase to take full advantage this functionality. We will explore *two-sided items* on page 381. Click **OK**.

FIGURE 9-13: *Products and services must be two-sided*

STEP 4. QuickBooks Online displays a new *Purchase Order* as shown in Figure 9-14. Add **Tim Philip Masonry** as the *Vendor*, and add **Sushi by Katsuyuki** as the *Customer* for both rows. Click **Save and Close**.

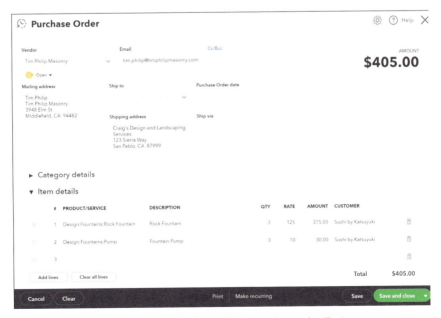

FIGURE 9-14: *A Purchase Order with items from the Estimate*

> **NOTE:**
>
> If a *Preferred Vendor* is set up on the item(s) selected, the purchase order will be made out to that vendor. If not, choose the correct vendor from the list.

Tracking Estimates

Estimates can be monitored from the Customer Center, from within the estimates themselves, and by running reports.

Viewing Estimate Progress

STEP 1. Open up the Sushi by Katsuyuki estimate again, shown in Figure 9-15. The *Status* in the upper left corner has been updated to **Accepted**. The *Design* line item has been fully invoiced, so it is marked **Closed**. Lines 2-5 all show that half has been invoiced and half is remaining. When you scroll down to the totals, there's a summary of the original estimate, how much has been invoiced, and how much still remains open.

If you want to view or open the original invoice, click the **1 Linked Invoice** link in the upper right corner.

STEP 2. Click **Save and Close.**

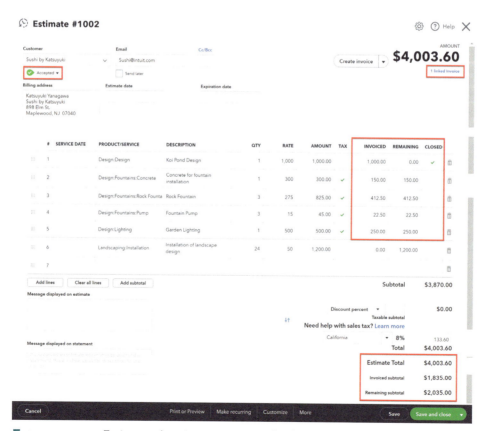

FIGURE 9-15: *Estimate showing progress on the Sushi by Katsuyuki project*

Running Estimate Reports

In addition to the *Estimates* list in the *Sales Centers*, and the progress tracked in the estimates themselves, QuickBooks Online also provides reports that help you manage your proposals.

Estimates by Customer Report

To see a list of estimates for all your jobs, create an *Estimates by Customer* report.

HANDS-ON PRACTICE

- **STEP 1.** Click on **Reports** in the *Left Navigation Bar*, and scroll down to *Sales and Customers*. Run the **Estimates by Customer** report.

- **STEP 2.** Change the *Report Period* to **All Dates**, and click **Run Report.**

- **STEP 3.** Most of the estimates display an *Estimate Status* of **Closed** along with an *Invoice #*, showing that they have been invoiced in full to the customer. Sushi by Katsuyuki displays as **Accepted**, showing that it is current.

    If you wish to only see current estimates, use the **Customize** button and *Filter* the report by *Estimate Status* to only show **Pending and Accepted** estimates.

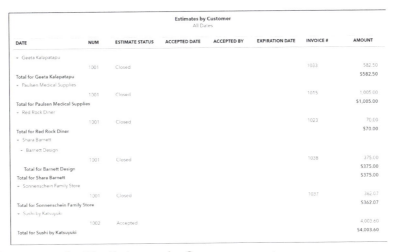

FIGURE 9-16: *The Estimates by Customer report—your screen may vary*

The Estimates & Progress Invoicing Summary by Customer Report

Use the *Estimates & Progress Invoicing Summary by Customer* report to track your progress invoicing. This report shows the amount of the original estimate, the amount invoiced, the percentage invoiced, and the balance remaining.

HANDS-ON PRACTICE

To create the *Estimates & Progress Invoicing Summary by Customer* report, follow these steps:

- **STEP 1.** From the *Reports* window, scroll down to the *Sales and Customers* section, then click on the **Estimates & Progress Invoicing Summary by Customer** report.

STEP 2. Change the *Report Period* to **This Month**.

STEP 3. The report in Figure 9-17 appears. Note that Sushi by Katsuyuki is 47.42% invoiced.

			Estimates & Progress Invoicing Summary by Customer				
DATE	NUM	STATUS	AMOUNT	BALANCE	INVOICED AMOUNT	% INVOICED	REMAINING AMOUNT
▼ Shara Barnett:Barnett Design							
	1001	Closed	375.00	375.00	375.00	100.00%	0.00
Total for Shara Barnett:Barnett Design			$375.00	$375.00	$375.00		$0.00
▼ Sushi by Katsuyuki							
	1002	Accepted	4,003.60	3,870.00	1835.00	47.42%	2035.00
Total for Sushi by Katsuyuki			$4,003.60	$3,870.00	$1,835.00		$2,035.00
Total			$4,378.60	$4,245.00	$2,210.00		$2,035.00

FIGURE 9-17: *The Estimates & Progress Invoicing Summary by Customer report—Your screen may vary*

> **TIP:**
>
> Remember to manually update all estimates that a customer does not accept or complete. To do this, open unused estimates and change the status to **Rejected**. If an estimate was not fully invoiced but the project is complete, update the status to **Closed**.

TAKING CUSTOMER DEPOSITS ON WORK TO BE PERFORMED

Many companies take **Customer Deposits** when a bid is accepted, both to confirm the customer's commitment, and so they have the resources they need to start the job.

When accepting this money as a retainer, it's not yet considered income. Instead, it's booked as Other Current Liabilities on your Balance Sheet because it's *unearned revenue*. If the job is cancelled, you must refund the money (unless you asked for a non-refundable deposit).

When the project's total invoice is reduced by the pre-payment, the **Customer Deposit** debits the liability account on your Balance Sheet, while the total revenue is recognized on your *Profit and Loss Statement* as income.

Setting Up Prepayments and Deposits

There are two steps involved to set up **deposits on work to be performed**. These only need to be done once. The first is to set up the **Liability** account on the Balance Sheet for unearned revenue. The second is to create a **Service** that moves money in and out of the liability account using the sales forms.

> **IMPORTANT!**
>
> In new QBO subscriptions, there may already be a customer deposits liability account called **Customer Prepayments**. If you have this category in your Chart of Accounts, you can skip the steps to create the Other Current Liabilities account in Figure 9-18 and use the existing **Customer Prepayments** category in the *Income Account* field when you create the *Service* in Figure 9-19.

PROJECTS AND JOB COSTING | 369

HANDS-ON PRACTICE

STEP 1. From the *Left Navigation Bar,* click on **Accounting** to open the **Chart of Accounts**.

STEP 2. Click on the **New** button.

STEP 3. Click the **Liabilities** circle at the top, then in *Save Account Under* choose **Other Current Liabilities**. Enter the same option in *Tax Form Section* as well (see Figure 9-18).

STEP 4. In the *Account Name* field, enter **Customer Prepayments**. Type **Down payments from customers for future goods and services** in the *Description* field.

STEP 5. Click **Save**.

STEP 6. Open the **Products and Services** list under *Sales* in the *Left Navigation Bar.*

STEP 7. Click the **New** button.

STEP 8. On the *Product/Service Information* screen, choose **Service**.

STEP 9. Fill in the *Product/Service Information* window to match Figure 9-19 below. Enter **Customer Prepayment** in the *Name* field, and in the *Description* box type **Deposit for work to be performed**.

STEP 10. Leave the *Sales Price/Rate* empty since the price will vary. Enter **Customer Prepayments** in the *Income Account* field.

By entering the liability account in the field that typically points to income, when you use this service the money will post to your *Balance Sheet* instead of your *Profit and Loss Statement.*

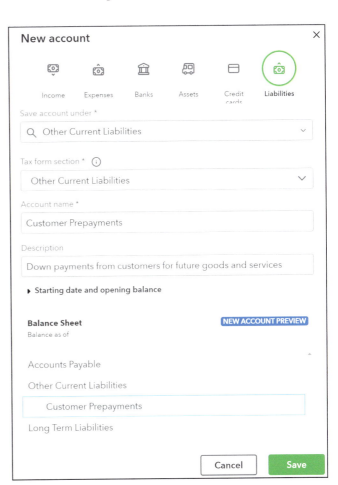

FIGURE 9-18: *Add an Other Current Liabilities category to the Chart of Accounts*

STEP 11. Click **Edit Sales Tax**, scroll down to the bottom, and select **Nontaxable**. Click **Done**.

STEP 12. Click **Save and Close**.

Receiving the Customer Prepayment

Now you're ready to take **Deposits on work to be performed**.

If you have already received the retainer payment, create a sales receipt. If the customer has yet to pay, create an invoice.

HANDS-ON PRACTICE

Geeta Kalapatapu is planning a large landscaping remodel in a few months. To hold time on his schedule, Craig asks for an $800 refundable prepayment. Geeta pays by credit card.

STEP 1. From the **+New** button, choose **Sales Receipt**.

STEP 2. Select **Geeta Kalapatapu** from the *Customer* drop down list.

STEP 3. Click **MasterCard** as the *Payment Method*. Make sure the *Deposit To* field says **Undeposited Funds** (it may be called **Payments to Deposit**).

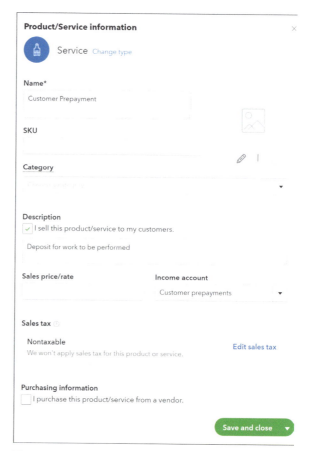

FIGURE 9-19: *Creating a Service for Customer Prepayments*

DID YOU KNOW?

If you already see line items when you create a brand new transaction, QuickBooks Online's autofill automations are turned on. QBO is helping you save time by repeating your most recent transaction for that same customer or vendor. If the entry is not the intended product or service, click the **Trashcan** on the far right of the row to remove the line item(s). If this behavior creates more work than it saves time, or if it is causing inaccuracies, turn off the Automations as we saw on *page 44*.

STEP 4. In the *Product/Service* field, enter **Customer Prepayment**.

STEP 5. In the *Description*, enter **Deposit for landscaping remodel**.

STEP 6. Enter a *Quantity* of **1**, and **800** in the *Rate* field.

STEP 7. Confirm your *Sales Receipt* matches Figure 9-20, then click **Save and Close**.

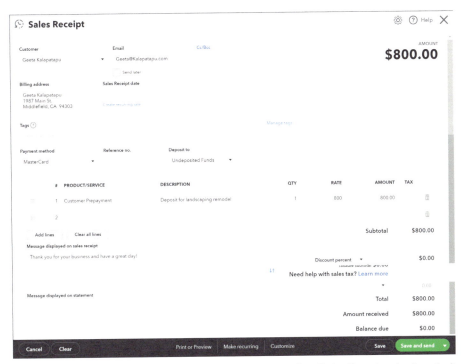

FIGURE 9-20: *Receive the Customer Deposit with a Sales Receipt (or Invoice)*

STEP 8. To see the **Customer Prepayments Liability**, run a *Balance Sheet* from the *Reports Center*. Notice the **Customer Prepayments** in *Other Current Liabilities*, shown in Figure 9-21.

The customer deposit is held on the *Balance Sheet* as a liability because the income hasn't been earned yet. If the job falls through, Craig would refund the customer. When we invoice the customer for the project in the next step, the deposit will become income.

Total Credit Cards	$157.72
▾ Other Current Liabilities	
Arizona Dept. of Revenue Payable	0.00
Board of Equalization Payable	370.94
Customer prepayments	800.00
Loan Payable	4,000.00
Total Other Current Liabilities	$5,170.94
Total Current Liabilities	$6,931.33
▾ Long-Term Liabilities	
Notes Payable	25,000.00
Total Long-Term Liabilities	$25,000.00
Total Liabilities	$31,931.33
▾ Equity	
Opening Balance Equity	-9,337.50
Retained Earnings	
Net Income	1,642.46
Total Equity	$ -7,695.04
TOTAL LIABILITIES AND EQUITY	$24,236.29

FIGURE 9-21: *The bottom of the Balance Sheet showing the Customer Prepayments Liability*

Applying the Deposit to the Customer's Invoice

When it's time to invoice the customer, include the same Customer Prepayment item, but this time subtract the dollar amount, leaving the remaining balance to be paid.

HANDS-ON PRACTICE

STEP 1. Create a new **Invoice** for Geeta Kalapatapu as shown in Figure 9-22. In the *Product/Service* box, enter **Design**. Change the *Rate* to **2000** and press **Tab**.

STEP 2. On the second line, add the item **Customer Prepayment**.

STEP 3. Enter **-1** in the *Quantity* field.

STEP 4. **Tab** over to the *Rate* field and enter **800**, then press **Tab** again.

STEP 5. The initial customer deposit is subtracted from the Design on the invoice, leaving a $1,200.00 *Balance Due*.

STEP 6. **Save and Close** the invoice.

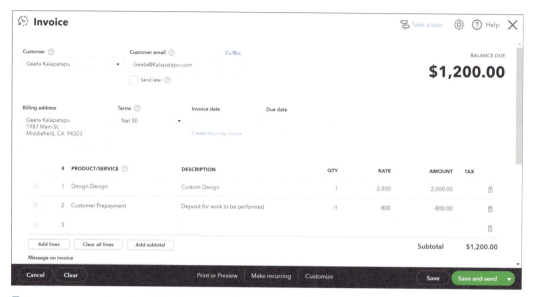

FIGURE 9-22: *Invoice with Customer Prepayment deducted*

THE ACCOUNTING BEHIND THE SCENES:

The **Design** service on the invoice credits the **Design Income** account for the full amount of the sale. The prepaid **Customer Prepayment** debits the **Customer Prepayments liability**. The remainder of new charges debit **Accounts Receivable** for collection.

The debit to the **Customer Prepayments liability** zeroes out the credit created by the initial **Sales Receipt**.

STEP 7. **Run** the *Balance Sheet* again. **Customer Prepayments** is now **$0**.

STEP 8. **QuickZoom** on the **$0 total** to look at the Customer Prepayments Transaction Report.

The $800 deposit held on the *Balance Sheet* has been debited to zero out the previous balance (see Figure 9-23).

DATE	TRANSACTION TYPE	NUM	NAME	MEMO/DESCRIPTION	ACCOUNT	SPLIT	AMOUNT	BALANCE
▼ Customer prepayments								
	Sales Receipt	1038	Geeta Kalapatapu	Deposit for landscaping remodel	Customer prepayments	Undeposited Funds	800.00	800.00
	Invoice	1039	Geeta Kalapatapu	Deposit for work to be performed	Customer prepayments	Accounts Receivable (A/R)	-800.00	0.00
Total for Customer prepayments							$0.00	

FIGURE 9-23: *Customer Prepayments Liability activity*

DID YOU KNOW?

It's important to keep an eye on remaining customer deposits, since QuickBooks Online doesn't automate the workflow. One way to do this is to periodically reconcile the Customer Prepayments liability account to $0. Check off each prepaid deposit and its associated reduction to confirm it was fully applied to the job. This way, completed deposits will show as *reconciled* in the liability's register, and pending deposits will show as *unreconciled*.

Then create the report shown in Figure 9-23. QuickZoom into the **Customer Prepayments** total. Change the *Group By* drop-down to **Customer** and click **Run Report**. Then you'll be able to see all your Deposits grouped by customer. Unused deposits will show a balance, and fully-applied deposits will show as $0.00. Add a **Filter** so that the *Cleared* status only shows *Uncleared* transactions. Then the report will only show unapplied Customer Prepayments. Save the customized report for future use!

MANAGING VENDOR DEPOSITS

Sometimes suppliers require you to give them a *deposit* before they will provide you with services or products. To do this, create a **Check** or **Expense** for the vendor and enter **Accounts Payable** as the *Category*. This creates a credit in QuickBooks Online for the vendor that you can use to discount the bill when it arrives.

HANDS-ON PRACTICE

Craig's Landscaping is going to rent a jackhammer from Ellis Equipment Rental to dig out the existing concrete patio behind Kate Whelan's house. Ellis asks for a $200 security deposit, which will be deducted from the bill when it comes time to pay.

STEP 1. Open **Ellis Equipment Rental's** Vendor record. Select **Check** from the *New Transaction* button.

STEP 2. Enter the rest of the expense as shown in Figure 9-24.

Notice that the *Category* account is coded to **Accounts Payable (A/P)**. You ONLY code checks to A/P when you are sending deposit money to a vendor prior to receiving the bill.

STEP 3. Click **Save and Close**.

FIGURE 9-24: *Coding a vendor deposit check to Accounts Payable*

After closing the expense, notice that Ellis Equipment Rental's balance is -**$200.00**. The negative balance indicates that you have a credit.

Later, when the bill is received, enter it in full as you would any other bill. Apply the deposit using a payment by following the procedures outlined in Chapter 4 in the *Applying Vendor Credits* section, then pay the remainder of the balance.

Vendor Refunds When You Used Accounts Payable

If you **overpaid a Vendor Deposit** using the method above because the amount of your prepayment turns out to be more than the bill, your Accounts Payable account will continue to have a negative (debit) balance for that vendor. When the vendor returns the balance, you will apply the refund check from the vendor to this credit balance in Accounts Payable.

To record a refund from a vendor that you prepaid using the expense in Figure 9-24, follow the steps below. Enter the bill from the vendor just like you would any other bill. Use the *Bank Deposits* window to record your refund from the vendor, then apply the credit to both.

HANDS-ON PRACTICE

In our example, Craig's Landscaping already paid Ellis Equipment Rental a $200.00 deposit to rent the jackhammer, in advance of receiving their bill. When Ellis sent the bill, it was only $185.00. Since the deposit was more than the bill, the vendor returned the remainder with a $15.00 refund check.

STEP 1. Open a new *Bill* from Ellis Equipment Rental and fill it in as shown in Figure 9-25. Use **today's date**, **Job Expenses:Equipment Rental** as the *Category*, **Jackhammer** in the *Description* field, **185** as the *Amount*, and enter **Kate Whelan** in the *Customer* field.

STEP 2. Change the green button to **Save and Close** to record the bill.

STEP 3. Select **Bank Deposit** from the *+New* button (see Figure 9-26).

STEP 4. Leave **Checking** selected in the *Account* field. Use **today's date**.

STEP 5. Scroll down to *Add Funds to This Deposit*. Enter **Ellis Equipment Rental** in the *Received From* field.

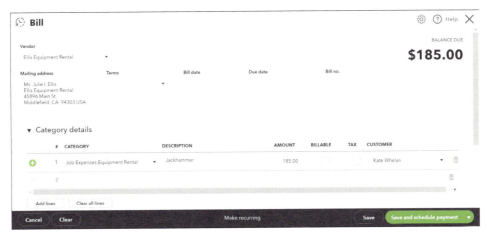

FIGURE 9-25: *Enter the Bill received from Ellis Equipment Rental*

STEP 6. The *Account* is **Accounts Payable (A/P)** because refunds are always coded back to their original category, which in this case was the prepaid deposit.

Note that this is the ONLY circumstance where you would enter **Accounts Payable** in the *Account* field. If the refund had been for services provided or for products, you would enter the actual categories used in the original bill or expense.

STEP 7. Enter in the remaining data as shown in Figure 9-26.

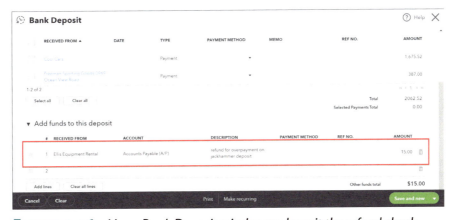

FIGURE 9-26: *Use a Bank Deposit window to deposit the refund check*

STEP 8. Click **Save and Close** in the green button at the bottom of the window.

After you have recorded the deposit in Figure 9-26, create a *Bill Payment* for Ellis Equipment Rental to apply both the $200.00 prepayment and the $15 refund check to the *Bill* (i.e. use the $200.00 prepayment check and the $15 refund to pay the $185 bill). Even if Ellis's Vendor Record already showed a $0 balance, the Accounts Payable reports will not be correct until you complete this step.

STEP 9. Find the $185 bill on Ellis's transaction list. Select **Mark As Paid** from the drop-down arrow on the far right.

STEP 10. Edit the *Bank/Credit Account* field to come from **Checking**, even though no money will be paid.

STEP 11. Verify *today's date* in the *Payment Date* field.

STEP 12. Place **checkmarks** on both rows in the *Outstanding Transactions* grid (the $185.00 **Bill** and the $15 **Deposit**), as well as the $200 **Expense** in the *Credits* grid as shown in Figure 9-27.

Although this window seems to show two bills for Ellis Rentals, one of the lines is actually the refund check you recorded using the *Bank Deposits* window back in Figure 9-26.

STEP 13. The *Amount* of the transaction nets to **$0.00**.

STEP 14. Click **Save and Close**.

FIGURE 9-27: *Pay Bill window applying $200 deposit and $15 check to the $185.00 bill*

While this type of workflow is rare, this advanced technique demonstrates that you can use forms creatively in unusual circumstances.

PASSING THROUGH BILLABLE EXPENSES

Assigning expenses to customers or projects allows you to track all the related costs using a technique called *job costing*. Taking it a step further, QuickBooks Online even allows you to invoice customers so that you can get reimbursed for those costs. On expense transactions, using the **Billable** checkbox indicates that the expense should be passed through to the customer on their next invoice. We already looked at how to set these options on page 152, and how to mark expenses as *Billable to Customers* on page 161.

Bills, **checks**, **expenses**, and **timesheets** all allow customers and billable status to be assigned to products and services, or directly to expense and cost of goods sold accounts. Billable expenses are also generated by **delayed charges** and **delayed credits** (see page 224).

Most companies track these reimbursements in QuickBooks Online's default **Billable Expenses Income** account. It's also possible to use multiple accounts, categorizing each reimbursement right back into the original expense account to offset the cost incurred on behalf of a customer.

If you're using *Markup*, that margin will go to its own **Markup Income** account.

To see a list of expenses waiting to be invoiced to customers, click on the blue **Unbilled Activity** box on the *Money Bars* in either the *All Sales Center* or the *Customers Center* (see Figure 9-28). You can drill in further by clicking on the blue # **Unbilled Activity** links to see the actual charges.

FIGURE 9-28: *Unbilled Activity*

The Billable Expense Workflow

HANDS-ON PRACTICE

STEP 1. Follow the instructions starting on page 152 to confirm your *Bills and Expenses* settings, and to turn on **Markup**.

STEP 2. Click **Expense** on the **+New** button of the *Left Navigation Bar*.

STEP 3. Enter the expense to **Ellis Equipment Rental** shown in Figure 9-29. Mark it as **Billable** to **Amy's Bird Sanctuary**. The **Markup** should fill in automatically, although it can be edited.

STEP 4. Click **Save and Close** to record the charge.

FIGURE 9-29: *Record a reimbursable expense*

The next time you create an invoice for Amy's Bird Sanctuary, pass the cost through to the invoice. If you're looking at the *Unbilled Activity* list, you can click **Start Invoice**. You can also start an invoice by any other method, and then pull the unbilled activity into the form:

STEP 5. Click on **Invoice** on the **+New** button on the *Left Navigation Bar,* or alternatively from the **New Transaction** button when looking at Amy's *Customer Record.*

STEP 6. Enter **Amy's Bird Sanctuary** in the *Customer* field. Once the name is entered, the drawer opens up to prompt you to select the expenses that you designated as **Billable** (see Figure 9-30).

FIGURE 9-30: *The Add to Invoice window with Billable Time and Expense*

STEP 7. Click **Add All** to move all the expenses onto the invoice.

You could also click the blue **Add** links to just choose individual transactions.

STEP 8. The two billable charges are added to the invoice (see Figure 9-31). The **Design** *Product/Service* was inherited from a non-posting estimate, so it is specified in order to be processed for the first time. The **Equipment Rental** on line 2 was passed through from the original posted expense, so its *Product/Service* field is blank.

The markup appears on its own line, and is not shown to the customer. The *Custom Form Styles Activity defaults* give you the option of displaying markup if the customer requires that transparency (see page 81).

Figure 9-31: *An invoice with Billable costs*

Step 9. To see what the invoice will look like when you print it, click **Print or Preview** (see Figure 9-32). Notice that the markup has been included in the Equipment Rental.

Step 10. When you are finished reviewing, **Close** the *Print Preview* window, and click **Save and Close** to record the invoice.

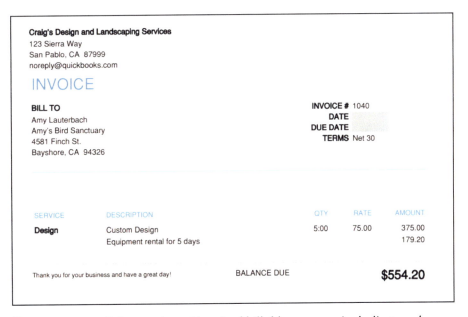

Figure 9-32: *Print preview of invoiced billable expenses including markup*

Step 11. To see the pass-through expenses, run a **Profit and Loss** report. Set the *Report Period* to **Today** to focus on the transactions entered in this exercise (see Figure 9-33, your screen will vary).

The **Equipment Rental** line shows the actual expense to Ellis Equipment Rental, the **Billable Expense Income** account shows the reimbursement from Amy's Bird Sanctuary, and the markup is split out into a separate **Markup** account.

Craig's Design and Landscaping Services

Profit and Loss

	TOTAL
Income	
Billable Expense Income	112.00
Design income	2,375.00
Markup	67.20
Total Income	**$2,554.20**
GROSS PROFIT	**$2,554.20**
Expenses	
Equipment Rental	112.00
Total Expenses	**$112.00**
NET OPERATING INCOME	**$2,442.20**
NET INCOME	**$2,442.20**

FIGURE 9-33: *Billable Expenses on the Profit and Loss report—your screen will vary*

THE ACCOUNTING BEHIND THE SCENES:

When you recorded the expense in Figure 9-29, the **Equipment Rental Expense** account increased (was debited). When you recorded the invoice in Figure 9-31, the **Billable Expense Income** account was then increased (credited). The two amounts cancel each other out. The **Net Income** therefore only includes the **Markup**.

Troubleshooting Billable Expenses

Do not perform these steps now. They are for reference only.

If you find you have unbilled time or costs that you will not pass on to a customer, you don't have to edit each expense transaction individually to remove the *Billable* checkmarks. Instead, there are two ways you can remove them.

The first is to pass all the unbilled activity through to an invoice, save the invoice, and then void it. You would need to do this for each customer.

The second is a "back door" link that's not on the menu (this will not work in Craig's Landscaping, but it will in real QBO companies). In a new Chrome browser tab, go to qbo.intuit.com/app/managebillableexpense. Enter the **Date** before which you want to clear all the Billable checkboxes, and click **Save** (see Figure 9-34). All the ***Billable*** checkmarks will be removed.

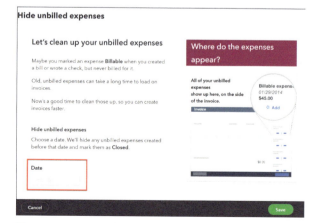

FIGURE 9-34: *The Hide Unbilled Expenses window*

USING TWO-SIDED ITEMS

QuickBooks Online allows you to use the same items on both expense forms (e.g., *expenses*, *checks* and *bills*) and sales forms (e.g., *invoices* and *sales receipts*). When you use **Products and Services** to track both expenses and revenue, you can generate reports showing the profitability of each item.

> **NOTE:**
>
> A **Two-Sided Product or Service** is an item used on all customer and vendor forms. It is commonly called "two-sided" because the item setup screen includes both sales information using an Income account, and purchase information using an Expense account.

Possible uses of *two-sided items* include:

- **Reimbursable Expenses:** When you use the Billable Expenses workflow, using two-sided items on the expense transactions as well as the sales forms provides added detail to your reports. For example, you can run reports on categories of products and services.

- **Retail Item Profitability:** If you buy and sell merchandise, use two-sided items to both buy and sell the products. You'll be able to see your profit margin on each inventory item.

- **Custom-Ordered Products**: If you sell custom-ordered products you might want to create two-sided Non-inventory Products to track both the purchase and the sale of each item. Doing so will show you which of the sales were profitable, and by how much.

- **Subcontracted Labor**: If you hire subcontractors, use two-sided services to track both the expense and the revenue for the work they perform. That way, you can find out which subcontracted services are profitable, and by how much.

Tracking Custom Orders

If you sell custom-ordered items that you don't hold in inventory, you can use the **two-sided items** function to track the revenue and costs for each sale. We introduced Non-inventory products created for pass-through sales on page 60.

You can create one generic product for each category of specialty item. You do not need to create a new product for every sale.

The procedure is the same as *Billable Expenses* workflow, except that instead of using the *Category Details* grid at the top to record directly to a Cost of Goods Sold account, you'll use the *Item Details* grid at the bottom to purchase the item for resale.

Figure 9-35: *An expense using a Two-sided Non-inventory Product for a custom order*

> **THE ACCOUNTING BEHIND THE SCENES:**
>
> When you use a **two-sided product** on expense forms, QuickBooks Online increases (debits) the product's **Expense account** field. When you use a two-sided item on sales forms, QuickBooks Online increases (credits) the product's **Income account**.

Using Services to Track Subcontracted Labor

If you hire subcontractors, you may want to create a *two-sided service* for each subcontracted service. This will allow you to create reports showing the profitability of your subcontracted services, and pass subcontractor costs through to invoices.

HANDS-ON PRACTICE

Craig sometimes performs pest control during his landscaping projects, but he brings in an exterminator instead of spraying the chemicals himself.

In this example, we'll update the *Pest Control* service to make it **two-sided**, create a bill to pay the subcontractor, and pass the expense through to the customer for reimbursement.

STEP 1. Open the *Products and Services list* and click **Edit** on the right of the **Pest Control** service. This will open the *Product/Service Information* screen for this item (see Figure 9-36).

STEP 2. Scroll down to the *Purchasing Information* section at the bottom. Add a **checkmark** in the box entitled *I Purchase This Product/Service From a Vendor*.

As we've seen before, when this box is clicked, QuickBooks Online opens the *Purchase* side of the item, revealing fields for entering the *Description on Purchase Forms, Cost, Expense Account,* and *Preferred Vendor*.

STEP 3. Copy **Pest Control Services** from the *Description* above and paste it into the *Description on Purchase Forms* box.

STEP 4. Add **20** to the *Cost* field, and in the *Expense Account*, assign it to **Cost of Goods Sold**.

This subcontracted service is considered Cost of Goods Sold (or Cost of Sales) and not an Expense because it is a direct cost—you are reselling the service.

STEP 5. Enter **Tania's Nursery** in the *Preferred Vendor* field.

STEP 6. Click **Save and Close** to close the *Pest Control* service.

FIGURE 9-36: *A two-sided Service for tracking subcontracted labor*

When Craig enters a bill, writes a check, or enters credit charges for an exterminator, use the **Pest Control** service to record the expense.

STEP 7.   If *Markup* is not already turned on from the *Billable Expenses* exercise in the previous section, follow the instructions starting on page 152 to turn on **Markup with a default rate of 60%**.

STEP 8.   Select **Bill** from the *+New* button.

STEP 9.   Enter a bill for **Tania's Nursery** as shown in Figure 9-37.

STEP 10.   Enter **Pest Control** in the *Product/Service* field in the *Item Details* grid at the bottom of the form, instead of in the *Category Details* at the top. You may need to click on **Item Details** if the grid is collapsed.

STEP 11.   Type **Ant extermination** in the *Description* field.

STEP 12.   Add a checkmark in the **Billable** box, and change the *Markup %* to **60**. The *Sales Amt* will auto-calculate to **32.00**. Assign the service to the *Customer* **Cool Cars**.

STEP 13.   Change the green button to **Save and Close** to record the bill.

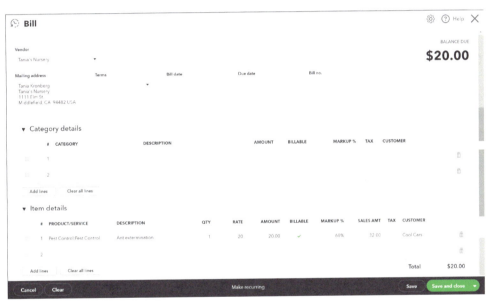

FIGURE 9-37: *Enter a Bill for subcontracted services*

The next time you create an invoice for Cool Cars, you'll pass the expense on to them.

STEP 14.   Select **Invoice** on the **+New** button in the *Left Navigation Bar*.

STEP 15.   Enter **Cool Cars** in the *Customer* field.

STEP 16.   The *Ant extermination Billable Expense* displays in the *Add to Invoice* drawer. Click **Add All**.

STEP 17.   Add a new line for **Gardening** services, with a *Qty* of **2** and a *Rate* of **25**.

STEP 18.   When your invoice matches Figure 9-38, click the **Save** button to record the invoice without closing it.

STEP 19.   Click on the blue **1 Linked Billable Charge** in the upper left corner, and then on **Billable Expense**. The window in Figure 9-39 opens.

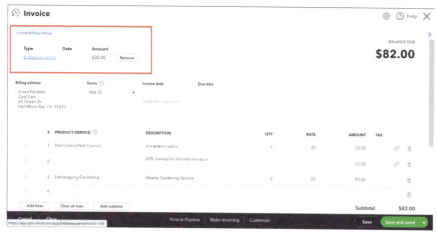
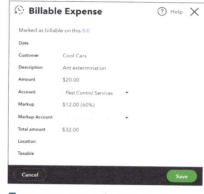

FIGURE 9-38: The Invoice with the subcontracted service passed through

FIGURE 9-39: The Billable Expense for the subcontracted service

This transaction was created by QuickBooks Online automatically when you checked *Billable* on the bill. If you wanted to see the original Tania's Nursery transaction, you could click the blue **Marked as Billable on this Bill** link at the top.

STEP 20. Click **Save**.

ANOTHER WAY:

If you want to track subcontractors' time yourself, you can fill in QuickBooks Online's **timesheets** for each contractor, just as you do with your employees. You can then pass the time information straight through to the invoice instead waiting for the contractor's bill. *Timesheets* are covered in the next section, and in the *Payroll* chapter.

ENTERING TIME ON A PROJECT

When you enter timesheet information into QuickBooks Online that includes a customer or job name, you can pass the time through to the customer's invoice. This example shows how to ***pass billable hours on timesheets through to invoices***.

The time tracking feature in QuickBooks Online is quite simple on the surface, but very powerful for streamlining businesses that pay hourly employees through QuickBooks Online Payroll, or for businesses that provide time-based services to customers.

Timesheets allows you to track how much time each employee, owner, partner, or subcontractor spends working on each job. In addition, you can track which service the person performs and to which class the time should apply. Then, once you record timesheet information, you can use it to calculate paychecks and create invoices for the billable time.

PROJECTS AND JOB COSTING | 385

> **IMPORTANT!**
>
> If you are using **QuickBooks Time**, an optional feature that allows employees and contractors to enter their timecards using their phone app, you may see different time entry screens than the Craig's Landscaping sample company. The *Apply Your Knowledge* exercise uses the new alternative time entry system.

Timesheets come in two styles, **Single Time Activity** and **Weekly Timesheets** (see Figure 9-40). Both allow you to pass timesheet information through to payroll. When you mark time activities as **Billable**, QuickBooks Online also allows you to transfer the time information onto the next invoice for that customer using the **Billable Rate**.

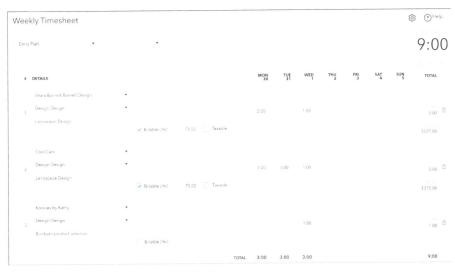

FIGURE 9-40: *A Sample Weekly Timesheet*

HANDS-ON PRACTICE

Craig wants to start tracking time on specific tasks in order to pass accurate labor charges onto a customer's invoice.

STEP 1. From the *+New* button select **Single Time Activity,** as shown in Figure 9-41.

STEP 2. Fill out the *Time Activity* as shown in Figure 9-42.

FIGURE 9-41: *Open a Single Time Activity*

STEP 3. In the *Name* field select **Tania's Nursery**. In the *Customer* field, enter **Cool Cars**. The *Service* is **Pest Control**.

STEP 4. The *Billable (/hr)* box is imported from the *Vendor Details*, entered when the vendor was set up. If you want to specify a different rate to charge the customer, change it here or on the invoice itself.

STEP 5.   Put a **checkmark** in *Enter Start and End Times*. Choose **4:15 PM** for the *Start Time* and **5:00 PM** for the *End Time*. There is an additional box to record unpaid breaks.

Alternately, you could leave this option off, and type **0:45** into the *Time* field to record the total minutes worked without saving the timeclock entries.

STEP 6.   In the *Description*, type **Set mousetraps around garage**.

STEP 7.   The *Summary* at the bottom calculates the charge to the customer. Change the green button to **Save and Close**.

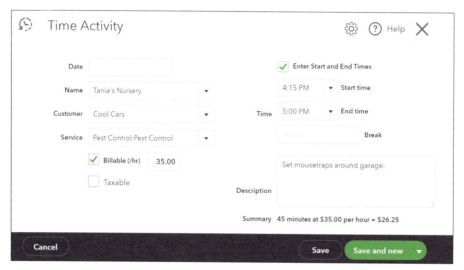

FIGURE 9-42: *A Single Time Activity entry for a subcontractor*

STEP 8.   Create a new **Invoice** for **Cool Cars**, using the same techniques from earlier in the chapter. Add the billable time, so that the invoice matches Figure 9-43. Note the *1 Linked Time Charge* link in the upper left if you want to see the *Billable Expense* and original timesheet.

STEP 9.   Click **Save and Close**.

FIGURE 9-43: *Invoice with billable time passed through*

USING THE PROJECTS CENTER

At the beginning of this course, we discussed how creating **sub-customers** allows you to track and report on work you do for a customer in multiple locations or for distinct jobs (see page 108).

QuickBooks Online's **Projects Center**, found in QBO's Plus and Advanced versions, takes this concept a step further. The Projects Center provides a dashboard for jobs, bringing together income and expense transactions in a one-stop shop.

By converting sub-customers to projects, you gain management insight. As a job progresses, the Projects Center provides graphs, a status overview, transaction lists, and reports.

We will introduce the Projects Center here, and then build a project from scratch in the *Apply Your Knowledge* exercise at the end of the chapter.

Creating a Project

Turn on **Projects** in the *Account and Settings* under the *Advanced* section, as shown in Figure 9-44. It is already on by default in the Craig's Landscaping sample company, so we do not need to do this now.

FIGURE 9-44: *Turn on the Projects Center in Advanced Account and Settings*

Projects is found in the *Left Navigation Bar*. The first time you visit the Projects Center, you'll see the screen shown in Figure 9-45.

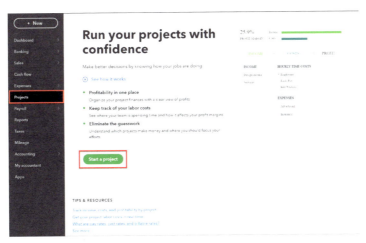

FIGURE 9-45: *The first time you visit Projects*

HANDS-ON PRACTICE

Craig's Landscaping is installing a koi pond for the outdoor dining area at the Sushi by Katsuyuki restaurant. Craig would like to track all the income and expenses for the project all together in one place.

STEP 1. Click the green **Start a Project** button.

STEP 2. In the *Project Name* field, enter **Koi Pond** (see Figure 9-46).

STEP 3. Choose **Sushi by Katsuyuki** from the *Customer* list.

STEP 4. In the *Start Date* field, enter **the first day of this month** (remember, you can type the letter **M** as a shortcut (see page 21 to learn more).

STEP 5. In the *End Date* field, enter **the last day of this month** (type the shortcut **H**).

STEP 6. You can update the *Project Status* as needed. We will leave it on the default.

STEP 7. In the *Notes*, enter **Install a 20' koi pond with a water element**.

STEP 8. Click **Save**.

STEP 9. A *Your Project at a Glance* guided tour appears. Take the tour by clicking **Next** through the steps, or dismiss it by clicking the **X** in the upper right corner. You can take this project tour again later by clicking the blue link on the right side of the project.

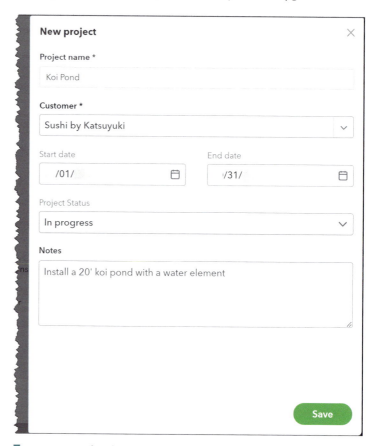

FIGURE 9-46: *Create your first Project*

The *Project Overview* shown in Figure 9-47 has four tabs offering a variety of ways of looking at your job, and several project management tools.

1. The *Overview* contains columns for your *Income*, *Costs*, and *Profit*. As you create invoices, bills, expenses, and timesheets, these will populate with the details.

2. *Transactions* brings together all the job-related transactions in one list, without having to take the time to search or run reports. Instead of having to view all estimates, invoices, and payments in the Customer Record, then find job-related expense transactions under their Vendors, this list brings them all together in one place for easy access.

3. *Time Activity* summarizes labor activity imported from QuickBooks Online's timesheets or the QuickBooks Time app. It can be grouped by employee or by service provided. Labor costs are calculated using the **Hourly Cost Rate** calculator and do not affect actual payroll.

4. The *Project Reports* include customized and filtered reports for *Project Profitability*, *Time Cost by Employee or Vendor*, and *Unbilled Time and Expenses*.

5. An *Attachments* area gives you a place to upload contracts and other documentation.

6. If you need to change the *Project Name* or update the *Notes*, click the **Edit** button.

7. Click the green **Add to Project** button to create new income and expense transactions, all from this one central location.

8. As new transactions are created, the *Profit Margin* provides at-a-glance statistics about the job.

9. Click the links and buttons in the upper left to visit the project's Customer Record, change its status, view the notes, or click the star to pin the job to the top of the Projects Center.

10. Switching between Hourly Costs and Payroll Expenses offers two different views of the job costing. The *Hourly Costs* view includes fully burdened labor costs using the **Hourly Cost Rate calculator**. The *Payroll Expenses* option only considers labor costs that have been allocated through Payroll.

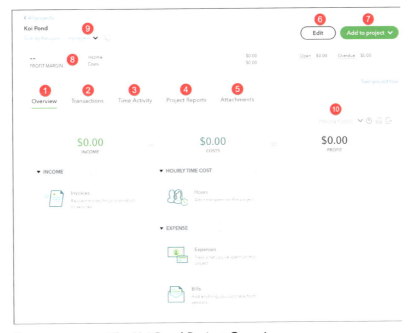

FIGURE 9-47: *The Koi Pond Project Overview*

To return to the *Projects Center*, either click on **Projects** in the *Left Navigation Bar*, or use the tiny blue **<All Projects** link in the upper left corner. If a *Some Hourly Cost Rates Are Missing* alert appears, dismiss it. This window, shown in Figure 9-48, provides an overview of all active projects.

1. The *Project/Customer List* shows all your projects, including dynamic income and cost graphs, a time summary, and a list of *Actions* you can take.

2. Use the *Filters* to limit the list by project status or customer.

3. Use the green button to start a *New Project*.

4. Add *Hourly Cost Rates* for employees to calculate labor costs for each project.

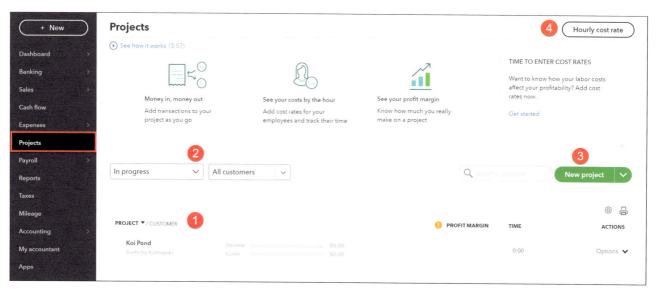

FIGURE 9-48: *Figure 9-48 The Projects Center*

Adding Transactions

Any income and expense transactions created from the *+New* button or from within a Customer Record will appear in the Projects Center when they are assigned to a Project using the *Customer/Project field*. Many business owners find it more efficient to use the Projects Center as their central hub to create invoices and take payments, enter expenses and time, and pay bills, because the job costing happens automatically.

Click on the **Koi Pond project** to open it. The **Add to Project** button in the upper right corner allows you to create any job-related form, and pre-populates it with the project name (see Figure 9-49). As you create new transactions, the project dashboard updates instantly.

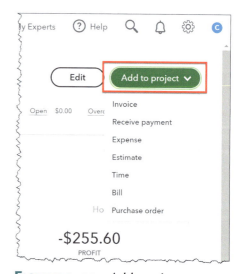

FIGURE 9-49: *Add any income or expense transactio n from one button*

Labor Costing

Tracking labor is essential to job costing. On page 386, we created a *Single Time Activity* and passed the cost through to a customer. We will also look at timesheets in the Payroll chapter. But even if you don't invoice for time and materials, or run payroll inside QuickBooks Online, you may still want to include labor in your job costing reports so that you can analyze the true expense of the work your company performs. Time equals money!

In some businesses, owners and partners do not receive paychecks, but they still need to track their time activity, record the labor costs to specific jobs, and even pass the time through to their customers' invoices.

> **DID YOU KNOW?**
>
> Business owners who are sole proprietors frequently take a "draw" (a check, expense, or transfer coded to the **Owner Draws** equity account) instead of getting paid through payroll.

The *Hourly Cost Rate* button shown in Figure 9-48 above allows you to incorporate fully-burdened labor costs without impacting payroll or the general ledger. These calculations analyze profitability by including not just an employee's wages, but insurance, taxes, and overhead as well.

Filling in a timecard sends the total hours to the Hourly Cost Rate calculator for reporting purposes, but doesn't create actual cost transactions. The hours on a timecard do flow through to QuickBooks Payroll, which is based solely on the employee's hourly wage. Traditionally, some companies have micro-managed payroll costs by manually assigning them to sub-customers and classes through journal entries, but QBO's timesheets do that work for you.

HANDS-ON PRACTICE

STEP 1. Click the blue <**All Projects** link in the upper left corner to return to the *Projects Center*.

STEP 2. Click the **Hourly Cost Rate** button in the upper right.

STEP 3. Click **Add** next to *Emily Platt*, then click on the **Calculator** to open the *Hourly Cost Rate Calculator* shown in Figure 9-50.

STEP 4. Enter **15** in the *Wages (/hr)* field and press **Tab**. It will expand to **$15.00**, and the *Employer taxes (/hr)* will auto-calculate.

STEP 5. Add the *Additional Employer Taxes (/hr)*, the *Workers' Compensation (/hr)*, and the *Overhead (/hr)* shown in Figure 9-50. Note that you would need to calculate these numbers for each employee.

Overhead refers to additional time and expense related to administration on behalf of that employee, allowing you to capture additional management costs and allocate it to customer projects.

STEP 6. The *Total Hourly Cost Rate* for Emily comes out to **$21.30**. Click **Add**, then click the blue **Save** link.

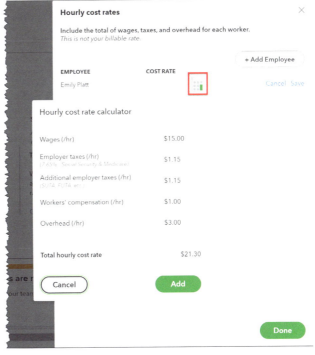

FIGURE 9-50: *Add Hourly Cost Rates for each employee*

> ### DID YOU KNOW?
> While Emily's wages are $15/hr, workers cost more than just their paychecks. The Hourly Cost Rate Calculator helps company owners understand the true cost of doing business.

STEP 7. Repeat these steps for *John Johnson*, who also gets paid **$15** and has the **same administrative costs**.

STEP 8. Click **Done**.

STEP 9. Click on the **Koi Pond** project to open it.

STEP 10. Click on the green **Add to Project** button, then choose **Time**.

STEP 11. A *Time Activity* window appears. Fill it in as shown in Figure 9-51. Click **Save and New**.

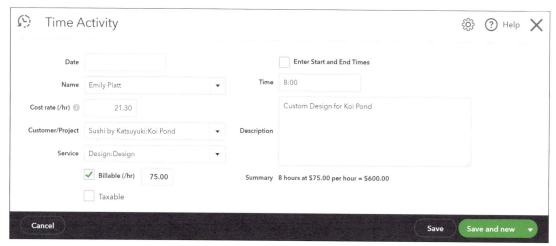

FIGURE 9-51: *Fill in Emily's time card for the koi pond design*

STEP 12. Create a second *Time Activity* for John Johnson, who dug out the pond, as shown in Figure 9-52. Click **Save and Close**.

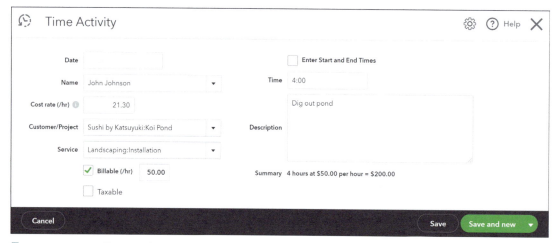

FIGURE 9-52: *Enter John's time for digging out the pond*

When you return to the *Koi Pond Project*, you'll see Hourly Time Costs for Emily and John (see Figure 9-53). You can also see the costs represented by the green bar at the top. Note that this is fully burdened labor costing for the project, is not related to actual payroll expenses, and will not show up on your Profit and Loss Statement.

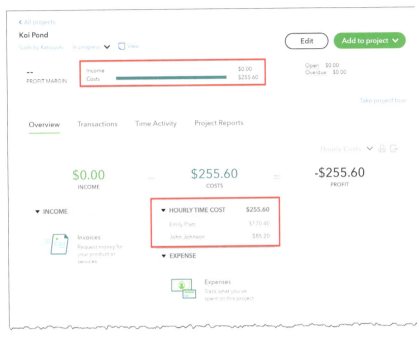

Figure 9-53: *Labor costs for the koi pond project (so far)*

Step 13. Click on the **Time Activity** tab in the middle of the window (see Figure 9-54). Click on the **triangles** to expand the date range and each employee.

This shows you the time cost and labor breakdown for each employee or vendor on the project.

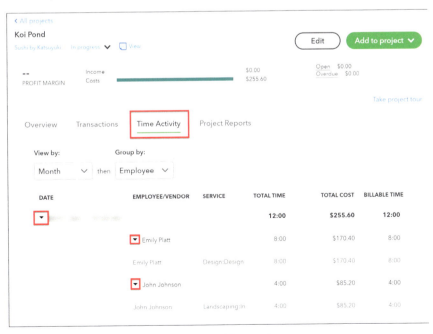

Figure 9-54: *Time activity grouped by worker*

STEP 14. Change the *Group By* drop-down to **Service**. Expand the **triangles** to see the details by service type.

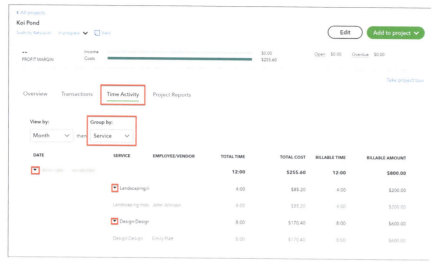

FIGURE 9-55: *Time activity grouped by Service performed*

Creating Project Reports

When you click on the **Project Reports** tab, three reports are available. They are similar to the reports we'll look at in the next section, but they have been customized and filtered for just this one customer and job.

- **Project Profitability** is a Profit and Loss by Customer report, customized to only show this one project.

- **Time Cost by Employee or Vendor** lists all time activity for the project, grouped by worker.

- **Unbilled Time and Expenses** lists billable expenses for this project that have not yet been passed through to a customer invoice.

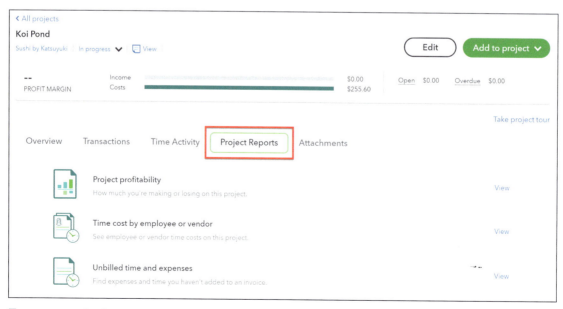

FIGURE 9-56: *Project reports are pre-filtered*

RUNNING JOB COSTING REPORTS

Customer Profitability

There are several reports that help you summarize and track customer-related activity and profitability. We already looked at two of them earlier in the *Reports* chapter:

- **Profit and Loss by Customer**, page 307
- **Income by Customer Summary**, page 324

Unbilled Charges Report

Create an *Unbilled Charges* report to view all of the billable expenses and delayed charges that you haven't passed through to invoices.

HANDS-ON PRACTICE

STEP 1. Select the *Reports* menu, scroll down to *Who Owes You*, and then choose **Unbilled Charges**. Review the report in Figure 9-57, then click **Back To Report List** in the upper left corner.

DATE	TRANSACTION TYPE	NUM	POSTING	MEMO/DESCRIPTION	AMOUNT	BALANCE
▼ Amy's Bird Sanctuary						
	Time Charge		No	Custom Design	375.00	375.00
Total for Amy's Bird Sanctuary					$375.00	
▼ Sushi by Katsuyuki						
▼ Koi Pond						
	Time Charge		No	Custom Design for Koi Pond	600.00	600.00
	Time Charge		No	Dig out pond	200.00	800.00
Total for Koi Pond					$800.00	
Total for Sushi by Katsuyuki					$800.00	
▼ Video Games by Dan						
	Charge	1	No	Installation of landscape design	300.00	300.00
	Charge	1	No	Weekly Gardening Service	75.00	375.00
Total for Video Games by Dan					$375.00	
TOTAL					$1,550.00	

Craig's Design and Landscaping Services
Unbilled Charges
All Dates

FIGURE 9-57: *The Unbilled Charges report—your screen may vary*

Unbilled Time Report

Create an *Unbilled Time* report to view all of the billable timesheet entries that you haven't passed yet through to invoices.

HANDS-ON PRACTICE

STEP 1. Go to *Reports* in the *Left Navigation Bar*, scroll down to *Who Owes You*, and then click on **Unbilled Time**. Review the report in Figure 9-58, then click **Back To Report List** in the upper left corner.

ACTIVITY DATE	POSTING	EMPLOYEE	MEMO/DESCRIPTION	RATE	DURATION	AMOUNT	BALANCE
▼ Amy's Bird Sanctuary							
	No	John Johnson	Custom Design	75.00	5:00	375.00	375.00
Total for Amy's Bird Sanctuary					5:00	$375.00	
▼ Sushi by Katsuyuki							
▼ Koi Pond							
	No	John Johnson	Dig out pond	50.00	4:00	200.00	200.00
	No	Emily Platt	Custom Design for Koi Pond	75.00	8:00	600.00	800.00
Total for Koi Pond					12:00	$800.00	
Total for Sushi by Katsuyuki					12:00	$800.00	

Craig's Design and Landscaping Services
Unbilled Time
Activity: All Dates

FIGURE 9-58: The Unbilled Time report—your screen may vary

Time Activities by Employee Detail Report

The *Time Activities by Employee Detail* report shows how many hours employees spent on each customer or project.

HANDS-ON PRACTICE

To create the *Time Activities by Employee Detail* report, follow these steps:

STEP 1. From the *Reports Center*, scroll down to *Employees*, and then choose **Time Activities by Employee Detail**.

STEP 2. Change the *Time Activities Date* field to **All Dates**, then click **Run Report** (see Figure 9-59).

Craig's Design and Landscaping Services
Time Activities by Employee Detail
Activity: All Dates

ACTIVITY DATE	CUSTOMER	PRODUCT/SERVICE	MEMO/DESCRIPTION	RATES	DURATION	BILLABLE	AMOUNT
▼ Emily Platt							
	Mark Cho	Landscaping:Hours	Designed Garden. Poured Concr...		4:45	No	
	Rondonuwu Fruit and Vegi	Design:Lighting	Garden Lighting	15.00	3:00	Yes	45.00
	Rondonuwu Fruit and Vegi	Landscaping:Trimming	Tree and Shrub Trimming	15.00	2:00	Yes	30.00
	Sushi by Katsuyuki:Koi Pond	Design:Design	Custom Design for Koi Pond	75.00	8:00	Yes	600.00
Total for Emily Platt					17:45		$675.00
▼ John Johnson							
	Amy's Bird Sanctuary	Design:Design	Custom Design	75.00	5:00	Yes	375.00
	Amy's Bird Sanctuary	Landscaping:Hours	Gardening		4:00	No	
	Sushi by Katsuyuki:Koi Pond	Landscaping:Installation	Dig out pond	50.00	4:00	Yes	200.00
Total for John Johnson					13:00		$575.00

FIGURE 9-59: The Time Activities by Employee Detail report—your screen may vary

STEP 3. Update the *Group By* drop-down box to **Customer**, then click **Run Report**. The report is regrouped by customer or project, as shown in Figure 9-60.

ACTIVITY DATE	EMPLOYEE	PRODUCT/SERVICE	MEMO/DESCRIPTION	RATES	DURATION	BILLABLE	AMOUNT
▼ Amy's Bird Sanctuary							
	John Johnson	Design:Design	Custom Design	75.00	5:00	Yes	375.00
	John Johnson	Landscaping:Hours	Gardening		4:00	No	
Total for Amy's Bird Sanctuary					9:00		$375.00
▼ Mark Cho							
	Emily Platt	Landscaping:Hours	Designed Garden. Poured Concr...		4:45	No	
Total for Mark Cho					4:45		
▼ Rondonuwu Fruit and Vegi							
	Emily Platt	Design:Lighting	Garden Lighting	15.00	3:00	Yes	45.00
	Emily Platt	Landscaping:Trimming	Tree and Shrub Trimming	15.00	2:00	Yes	30.00
Total for Rondonuwu Fruit and Vegi					5:00		$75.00
▼ Sushi by Katsuyuki							
▼ Koi Pond							
	Emily Platt	Design:Design	Custom Design for Koi Pond	75.00	8:00	Yes	600.00
	John Johnson	Landscaping:Installation	Dig out pond	50.00	4:00	Yes	200.00
Total for Koi Pond					12:00		$800.00
Total for Sushi by Katsuyuki					12:00		$800.00

FIGURE 9-60: *Time Activities by Employee grouped by customer project—your screen may vary*

Estimate vs. Actuals

There is no report in QuickBooks Online for comparing your estimates to your actual expenses. An alternative is to create a **Budget** for the project using QBO Plus or Advanced, using the **Budget** tool found under the *Gear*.

You can create multiple budgets for your entire company, a specific customer project, or for each class. Planning a project budget allows you to assess the scope of a job before you begin, prepare for how much income you expect to receive and when, and allocate how much you will spend on materials, time, and overhead expenses over time.

QBO's *Budget vs Actual* reports let you know when you are above and below your targets, both by amount and percentage.

ADDITIONAL JOB COSTING FEATURES

Tracking Vehicle Mileage

If the business's name is on a vehicle's title, all the loan, fuel, and maintenance costs can be categorized as business deductions. Vehicles owned by the owner or employees instead require that trips taken on behalf of the business be tracked and reimbursed by the mile.

> **IMPORTANT!**
>
> Only trips between clients count as business mileage. Traveling between home and office is considered a commute and is not tax deductible.

QuickBooks Online has a **Mileage Center** to help you track mileage for tax deductions. It can be activated for all Company Admin and Primary Admin users (see page 84).

Mileage can be manually entered into QBO, but if you log into the QuickBooks Online smartphone app, you can set up your device to automatically record your trips. Then all you have to do is categorize whether each trip is business or personal, and specify the business purpose.

Every year, QBO will automatically update the current mileage allowance dictated by the IRS. As a result, the rates you see may vary from those shown in these exercises.

> **NOTE:**
>
> You cannot use **Mileage Tracking** to include mileage costs on paychecks, invoices, or bills for reimbursement. Pass-through expenses for travel must be created manually.

HANDS-ON PRACTICE

STEP 1. Click on **Mileage** (or **Trips**) in the *Left Navigation Bar*. The window shown in Figure 9-61 appears the first time you activate it. Click **Add a Trip Manually**.

STEP 2. Click **Manage Vehicles** in the center of the screen. In the drawer that opens, click the green **Add Vehicle** button (see Figure 9-62).

STEP 3. Type **Ford F150** in the *Vehicle Make and Model* box. Enter **2021** as the *Vehicle Year*.

STEP 4. The *Ownership Status* is **You Own This Vehicle**.

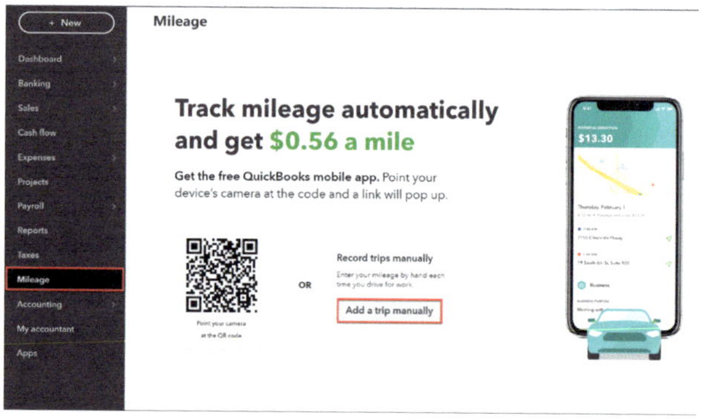

FIGURE 9-61: *The Mileage Center the first time you activate it—your rate will vary*

STEP 5. In the *Date You Bought the Vehicle* box, enter **January 1 of this year**. Use the same date for *Date Placed In Service*.

STEP 6. Turn on **Set as Primary Vehicle**. The *Mileage Dashboard* will display the primary vehicle's data, although additional vehicles can also be tracked.

STEP 7. In the *Tax Info* section, we will enter mileage **By Recording Odometer Readings**.

The second option allows you to simply enter a grand total for the year.

STEP 8. Click **Save**.

STEP 9. You will see the new Ford F150 on the list. Click the **X** in the upper right corner of the *Manage Vehicles* window to close it.

STEP 10. To add a trip, click the green **Add Trip** button. The *Add Trip* window opens as shown in Figure 9-63.

STEP 11. *Trip Date*, *Distance*, and selecting *Business vs. Personal* are required. Trips marked as **Personal** will be excluded from mileage calculations, but are needed for complete records.

Enter **today's date**, **42** in the *Distance* field, and **Meeting with Client** in the *Business Purpose*.

> **TIP:**
>
> Although you will not do this now, note that you can also enter the addresses of the *Start Point* and *End Point*. QBO will autofill addresses as you type. An alert popup will ask you if you want to *Use Auto Calculated Distance*.
>
> When you use the mobile app to track mileage, the *Start Point* and *End Point* addresses will populate automatically based on your phone's GPS. You only need to specify whether the trip was **Business** or **Personal**, and complete the **Business Purpose** field.

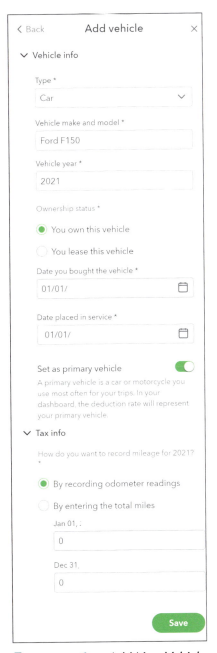

FIGURE 9-62: Add New Vehicle to Vehicle List

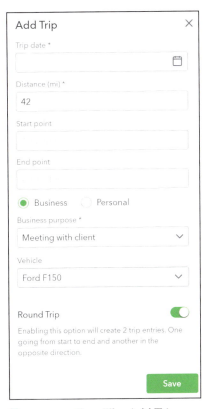

FIGURE 9-63: The Add Trip window

STEP 12. Turn on the **Round Trip** slider.

STEP 13. Click **Save** to complete your mileage entry.

The *Mileage Center* shown in Figure 9-64 now displays statistics for Business trips this year (personal trips are ignored). You can see the *Potential Deduction, Business Miles* compared to *Total Miles driven*, and a graph of your mileage across the year.

Trips are grouped on tabs for *Unreviewed, Business, Personal,* and *All. Filters* above the list hone in on specific vehicles or trip types.

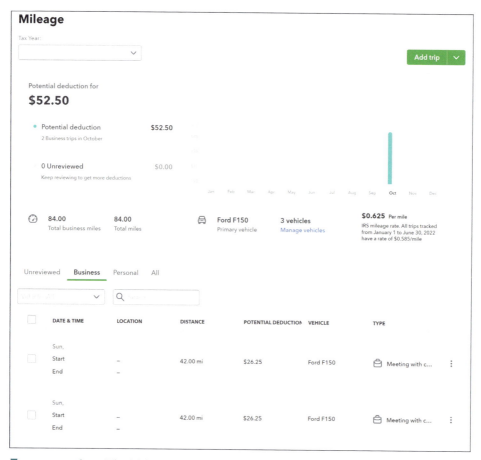

FIGURE 9-64: *The Mileage Center's Business tab after your first trip has been entered—your screen will vary*

STEP 14. Export your trip log by clicking the drop-down arrow on the green *Add Trip* button and choosing **Download Trips**. Open the csv file in your favorite spreadsheet software and save it as documentation for compliance or taxes.

	A	B	C	D	E	F	G	H	I	J
1	Date	Type	Trip Purpo	Vehicle	Start Addr	End Addre	Distance	Deduction	Logging	Method
2		BUSINESS	Cool Cars	Ford F150			42	23.52	Manual	
3		BUSINESS	Cool Cars	Ford F150			42	23.52	Manual	
4										

FIGURE 9-65: *Download the trip log to csv—your deduction will vary*

Applying Price Rules

Price Rules allow you to define custom pricing for different customers, products, and time periods. Use Price Rules on invoices or sales receipts to create drop-downs in the *Rate* field to choose from applicable price options.

Price rules are completely flexible, allowing you to:

▸ Charge different price tiers for retail, wholesale, manufacturing, students, seniors, or friends & family.

▸ Apply discounts to specific products.

▸ Put products on sale for a limited time.

HANDS-ON PRACTICE

Craig's Landscaping charges different rates to commercial and residential customers. In addition, they are having an anniversary sale, and are discounting all Rock Fountains by 10% for two weeks.

STEP 1. Turn on Price Rules by clicking on the *Gear* and then **Account and Settings**. On the left side, click **Sales**.

STEP 2. Click the *Products and Services* section, then turn the slider to **On** for *Turn on Price Rules* (see Figure 9-66).

STEP 3. Click **Save**, then **Done**.

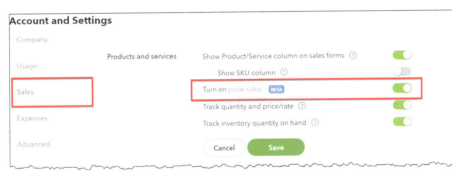

FIGURE 9-66: *Turn on Price Rules in Account and Settings*

STEP 4. The next step is to identify which customers receive the discount. Craig's Landscaping gives residential customers a 5% discount. To create a **Residential** *Customer Type*, go to the *Customers Center* and click the **Customer Types** button (see Figure 9-67).

FIGURE 9-67: *The Customer Types button in the Customer Center*

Step 5. Click the green **New Customer Type** button in the upper right corner.

Step 6. Enter **Residential** in the *New Customer Type* box. Click **Save**.

Step 7. Repeat steps 5 and 6 to add a second customer type, **Commercial**.

Step 8. Your *Customer Types* list should look like Figure 9-68.

FIGURE 9-68: *The Customer Types list*

Step 9. Go back to the *Customers Center* using the blue **Customers** link in the upper left. The next step is to assign the new **Residential** customer type to the people on the list. Place a **checkmark** in the boxes to the left of **Diego Rodriguez** and **Dylan Solfrank**.

The best practice would be to now assign Customer Types to all of the customers, but for the sake of this exercise we will just do the first few.

Note that you can also assign default Customer Types when you create a new customer.

Step 10. Click the **Batch Actions** button, then choose **Select Customer Type**, as shown in Figure 9-69.

Step 11. In the next window, pick **Residential**, then click **Apply**.

Step 12. Open up the *Price Rules* by going to the *Gear*, selecting **All Lists**, then clicking **Price Rules**. The first time you use it, you'll see a *Boost Sales And Keep Your Best Customers Happy* message. Click **Create a Rule**. The window in Figure 9-70 opens.

Step 13. Name the rule **Residential Discount.**

Step 14. In the *Customer* field, select **Residential**. Note that you can specify one Customer Type, apply the discount to all customers, or even apply the rule to individual customers.

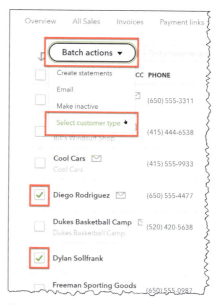

FIGURE 9-69: *Batch assign Customer Types*

The list at the bottom limits itself to **Diego Rodriguez** and **Dylan Solfrank.**

Step 15. In the *Products and Services* field, leave the default, **All Products and Services**. Note that you can specify products or services, individual products, or item categories.

Step 16. Click on the **Products and Services** tab to the right of the *Customers* tab. As you change the parameters at the top, the prices will adjust automatically below, and you can manually override them.

Step 17. In the *Price Adjustment Method*, choose **Percentage**. Other options include adjusting the price by a specific dollar amount, and setting custom prices for each item.

Step 18. The name of the next box, *Percentage* or *Fixed Amount*, changes according to your choice in the previous step. We will leave it on the default, **Decrease by**, but notice you can also use Price Rules to increase prices as well.

For example, we could have chosen to charge Commercial customers more, instead of charging Residential customers less.

Step 19. In the next box, enter **5**.

Step 20. You also have the option of *Rounding* the price to the nearest round number, or declare an amount of cents that helps the staff identify sale items by sight. We will leave it on the default, **No Rounding**.

Step 21. When your screen looks like Figure 9-70, click the green **Apply Rule** button.

Step 22. Change the green button at the bottom to **Save and New** to save this rule and begin a new one.

Figure 9-70: *Price Rule window with a 5% discount for all Residential customers*

Step 23. Next, we'll discount all Rock Fountains by 10% for two weeks. Enter the *Rule Name* to **Fountain Anniversary Sale**.

Step 24. Set the *Customer* field to **All Customers**.

Step 25. Update the *Percentage* to **Decrease by 10**.

Step 26. Enter **today's date** in the *Start Date* field, and select an *End Date* **two weeks from now**.

Step 27. Change the *Products and Services* field to **Select Individually**, then click the **+Add Product or Service** button below.

Step 28. Chose **Rock Fountain** in the *Products* field.

Step 29. Verify that your screen looks like Figure 9-71, then click **Apply Rule**.

Step 30. Change the green button to **Save and Close**.

Step 31. To apply the **Residential Discount** Price Rule, create a new **Sales Receipt** for **Dylan Solfrank**.

Figure 9-71: *Price Rule window with one item on sale for two weeks*

Step 32. Enter **Cash** for the *Payment Method*, and make sure the *Deposit To* field says **Undeposited Funds** (or **Payments to Deposit**).

Step 33. Add a bag of **Soil** to the receipt, as shown in Figure 9-72.

Step 34. The *Rate* field has a new drop-down arrow. In it, you'll see all the eligible Price Rules that you can apply to the sale. Choose **Residential Discount**. Dylan will now pay **$9.50** instead of $10.

Step 35. Update the green button to **Save and New**.

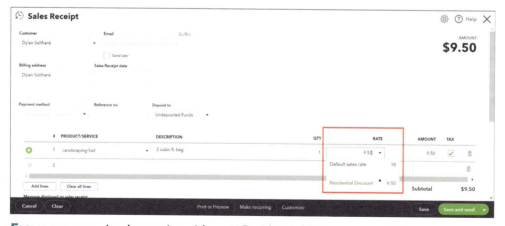

Figure 9-72: *A sales receipt with a 5% Residential Discount applied*

Step 36. Create a new sales receipt for **Cool Cars** with **today's date**.

Step 37. Enter **American Express** for the *Payment Method*, and make sure the *Deposit To* field says **Undeposited Funds** (or **Payments to Deposit**).

Step 38. Add a **Rock Fountain** to the *Product/Service* grid.

Step 39. In the *Rate* box, notice that the price defaulted to the **Fountain Anniversary Sale**. Note that the *Residential Discount* price rule also applies, so it can be selected as an alternative.

Step 40. When your sales receipt looks like Figure 9-73, click **Save and Close**.

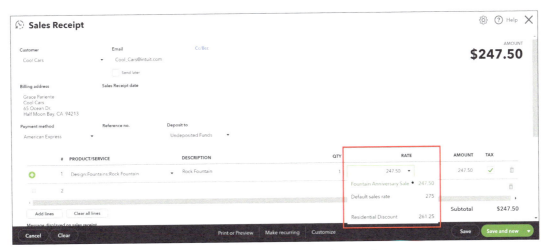

FIGURE 9-73: *A sales receipt with a product temporarily on sale*

REVIEW QUESTIONS

Comprehension Questions

1. Explain the primary difference between an *Estimate* and an *Invoice*, and describe what *Estimates* help you do.

2. Explain what Progress Invoicing allows you to do in QuickBooks Online.

3. How do you pass through billable expenses to customers?

4. What is a two-sided *Item* and under what circumstances should you use one?

5. Why is a Customer Prepayment considered a Liability instead of Income?

6. What is the benefit of using QuickBooks Online's Projects Center?

Multiple Choice
Select the best answer(s) for each of the following:

1. Creating an Invoice from an Estimate:
    a. Has no effect on the financial statements.
    b. Eliminates the need to manually enter *Estimate* details on the *Invoice*.
    c. Can affect the P&L because creating an *Estimate* itself affects the P&L.
    d. Can take up to several hours because some Estimates are very complex.

2. Which statement is false?
    a. Progress invoicing allows you to charge your customers a portion of the total estimate for each stage of the job.
    b. QuickBooks Online can track how much of the *Estimate* has been invoiced, and how much remains to be invoiced.

c. Progress Invoicing can create an *Invoice* for the entire *Estimate*, but only after the *Estimate* is closed.
d. Progress Invoicing allows you to create an *Invoice* for some *Estimate* items.

3. If you do not have enough stock on hand to fill orders, you can:
   a. Create a *Purchase Order* from an *Estimate* using QuickBooks Online Plus or Advanced.
   b. Send the Customer an order delay receipt.
   c. Replace the order with another item the customer did not ask for.
   d. Both b and c.

4. In QuickBooks Online you are allowed to pass through billable expenses to customers:
   a. Only if you paid by credit card.
   b. If you used a bill, check, or expense and assigned the customer or project to the expense.
   c. If you used a bill, check, or expense, assigned the customer or project, and marked the expense as *Billable*.
   d. None of the above.

5. In an invoice, you can automatically add markup to pass-through expenses. This income appears in:
   a. The Sales Income on a Profit and Loss Report.
   b. Markup Income on a Profit and Loss Report
   c. The Cost of Goods section of a Profit and Loss Report.
   d. None of the above.

6. Two-sided items can be used for:
   a. Reimbursable expenses.
   b. Custom order parts.
   c. Subcontracted labor.
   d. All of the above.

7. To see a detailed listing of all the billable expenses that you have not passed through to invoices:
   a. Create an *Unbilled Charges* report.
   b. Create an *Unbilled Time* report.
   c. Create an *Unbilled Costs by Project* report.
   d. None of the above.

8. The Mileage Center allows you to:
   a. Track vehicle mileage and run reports to assist with tax preparation.
   b. Reimburse your employees for mileage on their paycheck, a bill or a check.
   c. Pass through mileage to customer invoices.
   d. All of the above.

9. The Hourly Cost Rate calculator:
   a. Flows through to payroll.
   b. Calculates fully-burdened labor costs.
   c. Allows you to view time reports by employee or service.
   d. Both b and c.

10. Price Rules can be set to adjust by:
    a. Percentage.
    b. Fixed amount.
    c. Custom price per item.
    d. All of the above.

Completion Statements

1. The _____ _____ brings income and expenses together for one customer job. In QuickBooks Online, you can create multi-stage _____ Invoices from Estimates.

2. The _____ checkmark specifies that an expense should be passed through to a customer's next invoice.

3. A Product or Service used on both expenses and sales forms is commonly called a(n) _____-_____ _____.

4. A(n) _____ is used to enter time by employees or vendors.

PROJECTS AND JOB COSTING—APPLY YOUR KNOWLEDGE

> Log into your **Imagine Photography** class file at qbo.intuit.com.

Veronica Vasquez is shooting a commercial and creating a marketing campaign for her consulting company. She asks Ernest to do a photo shoot for headshots. He sends her an estimate and she pays 50% up front.

1. Go to **Account and Settings** to update the job costing settings for Imagine Photography:
    a. In the *Sales* section, turn on **Progress Invoicing**. If QuickBooks Online asks you to *Update Your Invoice Template?* click **Update**.
    b. In the *Expenses* section, turn on **Make Expenses and Items Billable**. Turn on **Markup** and set the *default rate* to **50%**.
    c. In the *Advanced* section, confirm that **Projects** is turned on.

2. Create a new **Project**:
    a. *Project Name:* **Marketing Photos**
    b. *Customer:* **Veronica Vasquez**
    c. *Start Date:* **Today**
    d. *End Date:* **The last day of next month**
    e. *Notes:* **Headshots and photos for commercial**

3. Use the information in Table 9-1 to create an Estimate for the photo shoot. Use the defaults for any fields not specified.

INFORMATION	DATA
CUSTOMER	Veronica Vasquez:Marketing Photos
ESTIMATE DATE	Today
EXPIRATION DATE	Two weeks from today
SALES REP	KR
TAGS	Corporate
SERVICE DATE (BOTH LINE ITEMS)	The last day of this month
1 -PRODUCT/SERVICE	Indoor Session
QTY	3
2 -PRODUCT/SERVICE	Retouching
QTY	2
CLASS (BOTH LINES)	San Jose
ESTIMATE TOTAL	$1065

Table 9-1 *The Marketing Photos Estimate information*

4. Save the Estimate, then turn it into an Invoice for 50% of the project ($532.50).

5. Create an **Estimates & Progress Invoicing Summary by Customer Report** for **All Dates**. Print the report or save it to PDF for your instructor.

6. Ernest wants to see how much his time is going to affect the profit on the job, even though it's built into the project price and he isn't going to charge Veronica.

   In the **Hourly Cost Rate calculator**, add these rates for Ernest:

INFORMATION (/HR)	DATA
WAGES	25
EMPLOYER TAXES	1.91 (default)
ADDITIONAL EMPLOYER TAXES	1.91
WORKERS' COMPENSATION	.75
OVERHEAD	1.00
TOTAL HOURLY COST RATE	30.57

Table 9-2: *Ernest Withers' labor costs*

7. Add two time entries dated the last day of this month, for the **Indoor Session** and **Retouching** services and quantities on the original estimate in Table 9-1.

NOTE:

If your **Imagine Photography company** says **Time Entry** instead of *Single Time Activity* and *Weekly Timesheet*, it is using the **QuickBooks Time** interface, QBO Payroll's time tracking app. Follow these directions to use the updated tools:

a. Click on **Check Out Pricing**.

b. Scroll to the bottom of the window and click **Use Basic Time Tracking (included in your current plan)**.

c. Go back to the **Marketing Photos Project**.

d. On the **Add to Project** button, choose **Time**, then click on **Withers, Ernest**.

e. Click on the *Date* Range, change it to **Custom**, then click on **the last day of this month** in the calendar.

f. In the *Duration* field, enter **3**, then click **Add Work Details**.

g. In *Customer/Project* click on **Veronica Vasquez**, then choose **Marketing Photos**, in the *Service* choose **Photography:Indoor Session**, for the *Class* enter **San Jose**, and in the *Notes* type **Headshots and stills**. Click **Done**.

h. Click **Add** to repeat these steps to add **2 hours of Photography:Retouching**.

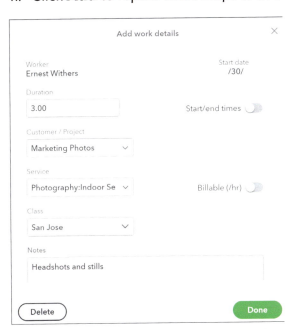

FIGURE 9-74: *Enter time using the new interface*

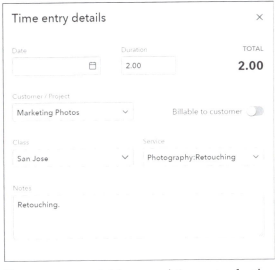

FIGURE 9-75: *Add a second time entry for the Retouching*

Veronica Vasquez decides to have Imagine Photography also produce the commercial. Ernest needs to buy a green screen background, and subcontract out to Gandhi Video, LLC for the videography. He needs Veronica to make a deposit so that he can buy the fabric and pre-pay Esther Gandhi. Ernest will pass on the cost of the green screen and the videographer to Veronica for reimbursement on her next invoice.

8. Create a new **Customer Prepayment** service item in *Products and Services* with an *Income Account* that points to the **Customer Prepayments** account in **Other Current Liabilities**. Save it in the **Admin** *Category*, with the *Class* **San Jose**. The Service is **Nontaxable**.

9. Using the **+New** button, create a **Sales Receipt** for the **Marketing Photos** project. Veronica is paying by **Credit Card** for a **Customer Prepayment** for $500. The *Tag* is **Corporate** and the *Class* is **San Jose**.

10. Create a new **Two-sided Non-inventory Product** to use for Custom Background orders as shown in Table 9-3.

FIELD	DATA
PRODUCT TYPE	Non-inventory
NAME	Custom Background
CATEGORY	Products
CLASS	Walnut Creek
DESCRIPTION	Custom Background
SALES PRICE/RATE	Leave blank
INCOME ACCOUNT	Sales of Product Income
SALES TAX	Taxable – standard rate
I PURCHASE THIS PRODUCT/SERVICE	Checked
DESCRIPTION ON PURCHASE FORMS	Custom Background
COST	Leave blank
EXPENSE ACCOUNT	Cost of Goods Sold: Supplies and Materials
PREFERRED VENDOR	Ogaga Photo Supply

TABLE 9-3 *Create a two-sided Non-inventory custom product*

11. From inside the **Marketing Photos** project, click on **Add to Project** and create the following **Expense** in Table 9-4. If any products or services autofill when you select **Ogaga Photo Supply**, click the **Trashcan** to remove them.

FIELD	DATA
PAYEE	Ogaga Photo Supply
PAYMENT ACCOUNT	Business Visa (5678)
PAYMENT DATE	Today
TAGS	Corporate
IN THE ITEM DETAILS GRID:	
PRODUCT/SERVICE	Custom Background
DESCRIPTION	10x10 green screen
QTY	1

FIELD	DATA
RATE	125
BILLABLE	Yes
MARKUP	50
CUSTOMER/PROJECT	Veronica Vasquez:Marketing Photos
CLASS	Walnut Creek
EXPENSE TOTAL	$125.00

TABLE 9-4 *Create an Expense to buy the green screen*

12. From inside the **Marketing Photos** project, click on **Add to Project** and create the following **Bill** in Table 9-5.

FIELD	DATA
VENDOR	Gandhi Video, LLC
TERMS	Due on Receipt
BILL DATE	Today
TAGS	Corporate
IN THE ITEM DETAILS GRID:	
PRODUCT/SERVICE	Videographer
DESCRIPTION	Commercial
QTY	5
RATE	150
BILLABLE	Yes
MARKUP	50
CUSTOMER/PROJECT	Veronica Vasquez:Marketing Photos
CLASS	San Jose
EXPENSE TOTAL	$750.00

TABLE 9-5 *Create a bill for the subcontracted videographer*

13. From the *Project Reports* inside the *Marketing Photos project*, run an **Unbilled Time and Expenses** report. Print the report or save it to PDF for your instructor.

14. Ernest is ready to finish invoicing Veronica for the Marketing Photos project.
    a. From the *Transactions* tab in the *Marketing Photos project*, find the row with the **Estimate**. Click the blue **Create Invoice** link in the *Action* column to convert the remaining estimate to an invoice.
    b. In the *How Much Do You Want To Invoice?* pop-up window, choose **Remaining Total of All Lines**.
    c. Click **Add All** to include the green screen and commercial reimbursements on the invoice.

d. On *row 7*, add **Customer Prepayment** to the *Product/Service* field. Change the *Qty* to **-1** and the *Rate* to **500** so that the *Amount* subtracts $500 from the invoice total. Add the class **San Jose**.
e. The invoice total will total **$1,345.00**. Print the invoice or save it as a PDF for your instructor.
f. Click **Print or Preview** and print or save a copy of the customer's invoice.

15. In the *Project Reports* tab, run a **Time Cost by Employee or Vendor** report. Print or save it as PDF.

16. Run a **Project Profitability** report. Print or save it as PDF.

17. In the *Project Dashboard*, toggle between the *Hourly Costs* view and the *Payroll Expenses* view using the drop-down shown in Figure 9-47. Answer the following questions:
    a. In Hourly Cost mode, what was the total **Profit** on the project?
    b. In Hourly Cost mode, what was the **Profit Margin** on the project?
    c. In Payroll Expenses mode, what was the total **Profit** on the project?
    d. In Payroll Expenses mode, what was the **Profit Margin** on the project?
    e. What is the difference between these two calculations?

CHAPTER 10

INVENTORY

TOPICS

In this chapter, you will learn about the following topics:

- Tracking Inventory with QuickBooks Online (page 415)
- Setting up Inventory Products (page 417)
- Calculating FIFO Inventory (page 417)
- Using Purchase Orders (page 418)
- Selling Inventory Products (page 423)
- Handling Inventory Issues (page 425)
- Adjusting Inventory (page 427)
- Inventory Reports (page 429)

> **OPEN THIS FILE:**
>
> Open the *Craig's Landscaping sample company* using the bookmark you created on page 8, or go to http://qbo.intuit.com/redir/testdrive.

We have already touched on *Inventory products* several times throughout this book.
In this chapter, you will learn additional tools to understand and manage your **Products** and **Inventory** in QuickBooks Online.
Inventory management is available in QuickBooks Online Plus and Advanced.

DO YOU REALLY NEED TO TRACK INVENTORY?

It is critical to think through your company's reporting needs before implementing inventory tracking. New users sometimes try to use **Inventory** to track products they don't really need to analyze in detail.

- *What is your sales volume?* You must enter every purchase and sale for each inventory product. That might not seem like too much work at first, but if you have dozens of products or high-volume sales each day, you might overwhelm your bookkeeping system with detailed transactions.

▸ *Can you monitor stock just by looking?* If all your products for resale fit on a few shelves and you can see when you need to reorder at a glance, it may not be worth the effort to track inventory in your financial software.

▸ *Do you use a Point-of-Sale system or e-Commerce solution?* If your inventory is tracked through your POS system or your website shopping cart, maintaining a parallel count in QuickBooks Online is redundant. If you can get sufficient stock and sales reports in your third-party system, consider a simplified workflow with Non-inventory products using QuickBooks Online Essentials instead of Plus. You may also be able to create daily, weekly, or monthly sales summaries instead of importing every transaction.

Every company has different inventory requirements. As you read through this chapter, determine whether QBO's Inventory feature will be overkill, insufficient for your company's complicated workflow, or exactly perfect for your needs.

MANAGING INVENTORY

Products designated as **Inventory** are physical items that you buy and sell, allowing you to see at-a-glance how many of each item you have on hand, and when you are running low and need to reorder.

QuickBooks Online takes care of the accounting for you when you use sales and expense forms to record your product-related income and purchases.

Most companies that track inventory use Accrual-based accounting because purchases in one period commonly aren't sold until some time in the future (see *Accounting Basis: Cash or Accrual?* on page 6).

Table 10-1 shows an overview of the accounting behind the scenes for different business transactions that involve inventory.

BUSINESS TRANSACTION	ACCOUNTING ENTRY	COMMENTS
ORDERING INVENTORY WITH PURCHASE ORDERS	Non-posting entry used to record **Purchase Orders**.	You do not have to use **Purchase Orders** to track pending deliveries, but they allow you to track products you have on order.
RECEIVING INVENTORY WITH A BILL	Increase (debit) **Inventory**, increase (credit) **Accounts Payable**. Increases inventory quantities for each item received.	Use this transaction when you receive inventory accompanied by an invoice from the vendor.
PAYING A BILL FOR PREVIOUSLY RECEIVED INVENTORY PRODUCTS	Decrease (debit) **Accounts Payable**, decrease (credit) **Checking** or increase (credit) **Credit Card Liability**.	No change to inventory.

BUSINESS TRANSACTION	ACCOUNTING ENTRY	COMMENTS
BUYING INVENTORY USING CREDIT CARD EXPENSES AND CHECKS	Increase (debit) **Inventory,** increase (credit) **Credit Card Liability** or decrease (credit) **Checking**. Increases inventory quantities for each item received.	Use the **Item Details** grid at the bottom of these forms to purchase inventory items.
SELLING INVENTORY USING SALES RECEIPTS AND INVOICES	Decrease (credit) **Inventory,** increase (debit) **Cost of Goods Sold**. Decreases inventory quantities for each item sold.	The Product/Services grid calculates the original cost of the item and transfers the value from **Inventory Asset** to **Cost of Goods Sold**.

TABLE 10-1 *Summary of Inventory transactions*

QuickBooks Online's inventory tools are sufficient for small businesses with simple needs. If a company's workflow involves additional inventory requirements including sales orders, pick lists, barcoding, bin numbers, assemblies, and/or multi-channel e-commerce, you will need a third-party app integration that synchronizes sales and stock. There are many solutions to choose from at apps.com.

Tracking Inventory with QuickBooks Online

Inventory is defined as goods that are purchased from a vendor that will be resold at a future date. When you use **Inventory Products** to track inventory, QuickBooks Online handles all the accounting for you automatically, depending upon how you set them up in the *Products and Services List*. For example, a retailer buys goods and holds them as an **Inventory Asset** until they sell the merchandise to customers. When the inventory is sold, it is removed from the **Inventory Asset** account and expensed to **Cost of Goods Sold**, typically in a **Supplies & Materials** sub-account. This enables the sale to be properly matched to its cost in the correct accounting period.

QuickBooks Online keeps a perpetual inventory, meaning that every purchase and every sale of inventory immediately updates all your account balances and reports.

When QuickBooks Online Plus or Advanced calculates the cost of inventory, it uses the **FIFO** ("First In, First Out") method. If you need Average Cost or LIFO ("Last In, First Out") inventory tracking, you will need to use QuickBooks Desktop Premier or Enterprise, or a third-party Inventory app that integrates with QBO.

KEY TERMS:

Perpetual inventory in QuickBooks Online keeps a continuous record of increases, decreases, and balance on hand of inventory items.

FIFO method calculates the cost of every sale based on the actual purchase price of the oldest item in stock. QuickBooks Online calculates the value of inventory using this method.

You must always use the *Item Details* grid at the bottom of every purchase transaction that involves inventory. Figure 10-1 illustrates entering an **Expense** using **Item Details.**

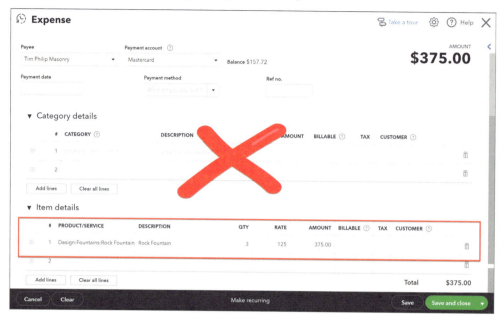

FIGURE 10-1: *The Items Details grid is used for inventory purchases*

It is crucial that you do not let inventory quantities fall below zero before you sell them. Because QuickBooks Online relies on FIFO calculations using the actual purchase cost of each item, sales forms that include products with 0 quantity have $0 in Inventory Assets, and therefore will result in inaccurate reports.

To help you avoid overselling your stock, invoices and sales receipts show a **Qty On Hand** popup in the *Qty* field as you sell inventory products.

IMPORTANT!

To avoid negative inventory, always make sure the date of your expense or bill purchasing a product is before the invoice or sales receipt selling those same items.

Activating the Inventory Function

The first step in using QuickBooks Online for inventory is to activate **Inventory** in your *Account and Settings*.

We looked at turning on Inventory features in the *Configuring the Sales Settings* section on page 97.

After you activate the **Inventory** function, the *Products and Services List* displays **Inventory Stock Status** with alerts for items that are low on stock or out of stock, as shown in Figure 10-2.

The first time you create an **inventory product**, QuickBooks Online automatically creates two accounts in your Chart of Accounts: An **Other Current Assets** account called **Inventory Asset,** and a **Cost of Goods Sold** account. QuickBooks Online uses these two important accounts to track inventory (see Table 10-2). The Inventory Asset account stores the value of your inventory on your Balance Sheet until you sell it. The Cost of Goods Sold account records the original cost of the inventory on your Profit and Loss Statement after it has been sold.

INVENTORY | 417

FIGURE 10-2: The Products and Services list with Inventory turned on

ACCOUNTS FOR TRACKING INVENTORY	
INVENTORY ASSET	A special Other Current Assets account on the Balance Sheet that tracks the cost of each inventory item purchased. This account increases (by the actual purchase cost) when inventory is purchased, and decreases (by the purchase cost of the oldest of that item in stock) when inventory products are sold.
COST OF GOODS SOLD	Cost of Goods Sold (COGS) represents the price you paid for the goods you sold. COGS is subtracted from total income on the *Profit and Loss Report* to show Gross Profit. Each time you sell an inventory item, QuickBooks Online automatically increases Cost of Goods Sold by the FIFO cost of the oldest of that item stock.

TABLE 10-2 *Two accounts that track inventory*

Many companies will further break Cost of Goods Sold into several sub-accounts:

- **Supplies & Materials**, containing the cost of products purchased for resale. If you include this category, be sure to use it as the *Expense account* when you create your Inventory Product list.
- **Shipping, Freight & Delivery**, tracking the cost to have products delivered to the store or warehouse.
- **Vendor Discounts**, if the supplier gives you discount terms (see page 234).

SETTING UP INVENTORY PRODUCTS

Inventory items are managed on the *Products and Services list* in the *Sales Center*.

In order to keep your inventory system working smoothly, it is critical that you use **Two-sided Inventory Products** on all transactions involving inventory.

We learned how to set up Inventory Products in Chapter 2. We also created Bundles to group related products together.

CALCULATING FIFO INVENTORY

When you enter an inventory product on a purchase form like a bill, QuickBooks Online increases (debits) the **Inventory Asset** account for the *actual* cost of the purchase.

When you enter an inventory item on a sales form like an invoice, in addition to recording income and Accounts Receivable, QuickBooks Online moves the money from **Asset** to **Expense** by increasing (debiting) **Cost of Goods Sold (COGS)** and decreasing (crediting) the **Inventory Asset** account for the cost of the oldest of that product still in stock.

This is called **FIFO inventory**, meaning "First In, First Out." The oldest item in stock is the cost basis for the next sale. Each time you sell inventory products, the original cost per unit is multiplied by the number of units sold. Then this amount is deducted from the **Inventory Asset** account and added to the **Cost of Goods Sold** account.

Table 10-3 shows how QuickBooks Online calculates the FIFO cost of inventory items as it moves sales from Inventory Asset to COGS.

ACTIVITY	SITUATION/TRANSACTION	CALCULATION	INVENTORY & COGS
1	You have ten garden gnomes. Each originally costs $5.00.	10 units x $5.00 per unit = $50.00 total cost	Inventory Asset = $50.00
2	You buy ten more garden gnomes at $6.00 each.	10 units x $6.00 per unit = $60.00 total cost	Inventory Asset = $110.00
3	You sell five gnomes.	5 units x $5.00 per unit = $25.00 total cost.	Inventory Asset = $85.00 COGS = $25.00
4	You sell ten more gnomes.	5 units x $5.00 per unit = $25.00 cost 5 units x $6.00 per unit = $30.00 cost $25 + $30 = $55 total cost	Inventory Asset = $30.00 COGS = $80.00

TABLE 10-3 *QuickBooks Online calculates the FIFO cost of inventory items*

BUYING AND SELLING INVENTORY PRODUCTS

Cash-based transactions including checks, credit card expenses, and sales receipts are valid ways to record inventory activity. We have already explored those transactions while buying and selling inventory products in Chapters 3, 4, 5, and 9.

Rather than repeat those instructions, we will only step through the Accrual-based accounts payable and receivable inventory cycle to illustrate the accounting behind the scenes.

Using Purchase Orders

Use **Purchase Orders** to track items you have on order. When you use purchase orders, you will be able to create reports that show pending deliveries.

Purchase orders are non-posting. They do not affect the *P&L* or *Balance Sheet*.

Creating a Purchase Order

Create a **Purchase Order** to order inventory, filling out each item and quantity.

> **NOTE:**
>
> Since **Purchase Orders** are non-posting, QuickBooks Online does not include them in the *Pay Bills* windows.

HANDS-ON PRACTICE

STEP 1. Create a **Purchase Order** from the *+New* menu. Alternately, if you are looking at a Vendor Record, you can also click the **New Transaction** button. This displays a *Purchase Order* window (see Figure 10-3).

STEP 2. Select **Tim Philip Masonry** from the *Vendor* drop-down list or type the name into the *Vendor* field.

STEP 3. Enter **today's date** in the *Purchase Order Date* field (if not displayed already).

STEP 4. Leave the default *Mailing Address* and *Shipping Address*.

By default, QuickBooks Online enters your company's address in the *Shipping Address*. If you want the order drop shipped directly to one of your customers, select the customer from the drop-down list of the *Ship To* field.

STEP 5. Scroll down to the *Item Details* grid. Notice that the *Category Details* may be collapsed, since purchase orders are typically used for products.

STEP 6. If you see **Design:Fountains:Rock Fountain** in the *Product/Service* field, QuickBooks Online's autofill automations are turned on, and QBO is helping you save time by repeating your most recent purchase. In this case, this is saving us a few steps, but if it was not the product you intended to order, you could click the **Trashcan** on the far right of the row.

STEP 7. Update the *Qty* to **5**.

STEP 8. Add a second row to order **Pumps**, also with a *Qty* of **5**, as shown in Figure 10-3.

The Customer column gives you the opportunity to associate your purchases with a particular customer or project. Since you are purchasing inventory, you do not know the customer information, so do not enter anything in this field.

STEP 9. Click **Save and Close**.

FIGURE 10-3: *Create a Purchase Order*

Receiving Shipments Against Purchase Orders

When you created a purchase order and the inventory arrives, convert the purchase order into a bill. If you receive a partial shipment, you can create multiple bills. Follow these steps:

HANDS-ON PRACTICE

STEP 10. Open the **Tim Philip Masonry** *Vendor Record*.

STEP 11. In the *Action* column on the right of the top purchase order, click the drop-down arrow to select **Copy to Bill**.

STEP 12. The *Item Details* grid populates with the content of the purchase order. There is a blue **1 Linked Purchase Order** link in the upper left corner if you want to view the original order.

In the *drawer* on the right, we see that we already had one PO open with Tim Philips Masonry already. Click the **blue** > to hide the drawer—we will not include it in this shipment.

STEP 13. When the delivery arrived, it only had three of the five rock fountains and pumps in the box. Change both *Qty* fields to **3**.

STEP 14. Change the green button to **Save and Close**.

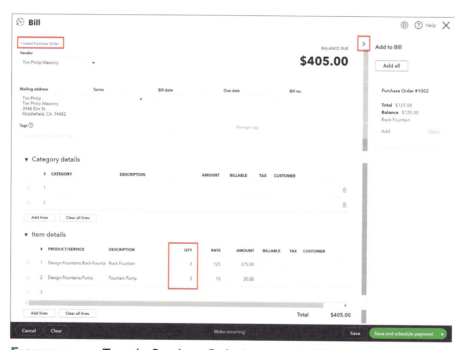

FIGURE 10-4: *Turn the Purchase Order into a partial Bill*

Monitoring Purchase Order Status

View the purchase order to check its status, change it, or cancel it.

HANDS-ON PRACTICE

STEP 1. Open the Purchase Order again by clicking on it (see Figure 10-5).

STEP 2. Review the quantity of each item in the *Received* column. You can see that Craig's Landscaping has received **3 Rock Fountains** and **3 Pumps**. Because 5 of each were ordered, the PO status is still **Open**, as indicated in the upper left corner.

STEP 3. After reviewing the purchase order, click **Save and Close**.

> ### DID YOU KNOW?
>
> If you know you will not receive the remaining backordered items on a purchase order, you can close specific line items or close the whole order. To close any line of the order, click in the *Closed* column and add a **checkmark**. To close the whole PO and cancel the rest of the order, update the **Open** *Purchase Order Status* at the top of the form and change it to **Closed**.

FIGURE 10-5: *Open a purchase order to view its status*

Running Open Purchase Order Reports

HANDS-ON PRACTICE

STEP 1. From the *Reports Center*, scroll down to *Expenses and Vendors*, and then choose the **Open Purchase Order List**.

This report lists all open purchase orders grouped by vendor (see Figure 10-6). It includes the original *Amount* of the PO, and the *Open Balance* shows how much is yet to be received.

STEP 2. Since you only partially received Purchase Order 1005, it is still open. A previously created Purchase Order 1002 is also open for 1 Rock Fountain. You can click on the links to both purchase orders to open and see their details. When you're done reviewing the report, click the blue **<Back to Report List** link in the upper left to return to the *Reports Center*.

	Craig's Design and Landscaping Services				
	Open Purchase Order List by Vendor				
	All Dates				
DATE	NUM	MEMO/DESCRIPTION	SHIP VIA	AMOUNT	OPEN BALANCE
▾ Tim Philip Masonry					
	1002			125.00	125.00
	1005			675.00	270.00
Total for Tim Philip Masonry				$800.00	$395.00
TOTAL				$800.00	$395.00

FIGURE 10-6: *The Open Purchase Orders Report*

STEP 3. Scroll down to the *Expenses and Vendors* section again, and open the **Open Purchase Order Detail** report. Update the *Report Period* to **All Dates**. This report is grouped by product, and includes information about cost accounts, quantities, and amounts for products received and backordered.

FIGURE 10-7: *Open Purchase Orders Detail Report*

Receiving the Rest of the Shipment

Two days later, three more rock fountains and two pumps arrive from Tim Philip Masonry. You will receive them into inventory and convert the PO into a bill.

STEP 1. Return to **Tim Philip Masonry's** *Vendor Record*.

STEP 2. Use the **New Transaction** button to create a new **Bill**.

STEP 3. Change the *Bill Date* to **the day after tomorrow** (the easiest way to do this is to click in the *Bill Date* field and tap the + key on your keyboard twice).

STEP 4. Scroll down to the *Item Details* grid. Two rows autofilled for Rock Fountains and Pumps because of the automation that repeats the previous bill. Click the **Trashcans** next to each row to remove them.

TIP:

If you process a lot of bills and purchase orders, you won't want to constantly delete old items from new transactions. In that case, turn **Off** the *Pre-fill Forms with Previously Entered Content* automation setting, as we discussed on page 198.

STEP 5. In the drawer on the right, there are two open purchase orders for this vendor. Click **Add All** (see Figure 10-8).

STEP 6. Set the *Terms* to **Net 30**.

STEP 7. Enter **2042** in the *Bill No.* field (see Figure 10-9), from the vendor's packing slip or invoice number that accompanied the shipment.

STEP 8. All the remaining items arrived, but because of supply chain issues, the price for the products increased. Change the *Rate* for all of the Rock Fountains to **175** and update the pump to **20**, as shown in Figure 10-9.

STEP 9. Click **Save and Close** to record the bill with the new prices.

FIGURE 10-8: Add open POs to a new Bill to receive the products into inventory

FIGURE 10-9: Create a Bill for the remainder of the PO

THE ACCOUNTING BEHIND THE SCENES:

When you record a **Bill** for **Inventory Products**, QuickBooks Online increases (credits) **Accounts Payable** for the total cost of the items. It also increases (debits) **Inventory Asset** for the same amount.

TRANSACTION TYPE	NUM	NAME	MEMO/DESCRIPTION	ACCOUNT	DEBIT	CREDIT
Bill	2042	Tim Philip Masonry		Accounts Payable (A/P)		$565.00
			Rock Fountain	Inventory Asset	$175.00	
			Rock Fountain	Inventory Asset	$350.00	
			Fountain Pump	Inventory Asset	$40.00	
					$565.00	$565.00

Selling Inventory Products

When you sell inventory, always use an *Invoice* or a *Sales Receipt* to record the sale. In the same way, be sure to use Credit Memos or Refund Receipts for credits and returns. This ensures that QuickBooks

Online updates your inventory counts and your financial reports at the same time. We explored these transactions in Chapters 3 and 5.

Using any other form to enter transactions involving inventory, such as journal entries or deposits, will cause discrepancies between your assets, income, COGS, and inventory quantities.

HANDS-ON PRACTICE

Weiskopf Consulting decides to gift their biggest clients with Rock Fountains. They order seven Rock Fountains and Pumps.

STEP 1. Enter the *Invoice* as shown in Figure 10-10, recording a sale of **seven Rock Fountains** and **Pumps** to **Weiskopf Consulting**. Be sure to set the *Sales Tax* to **California (8%)**. Verify that the date is set to **the day after tomorrow**.

Note that when you click in the *Qty* field, QBO will let you know how many of that item are in stock so that you don't sell more than you have.

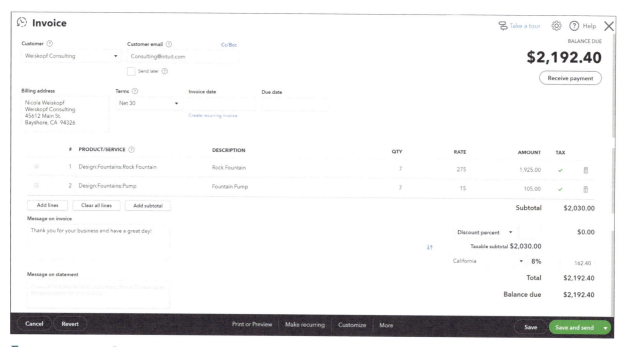

FIGURE 10-10: *Create an invoice to sell Inventory Products*

STEP 2. Click the black **Save** button at the bottom of the *Invoice* to save it without closing it.

STEP 3. To see how this invoice affects the *General Ledger*, click the **More** button at the bottom of the *Invoice* and then choose **Transaction Journal**.

In this transaction journal, there are four different FIFO Inventory-to-COGS transfers for the cost of the Rock Fountain, because the seven fountains were brought into inventory through four different separate transactions. Two were already in stock at $125 each. The first three you ordered were delivered at $125 each. When the remaining order arrived, you were charged $175 each ($350).

TRANSACTION TYPE	NUM	NAME	MEMO/DESCRIPTION	ACCOUNT	DEBIT	CREDIT
Invoice	1038	Weiskopf Consulting		Accounts Receivable (A/R)	$2,192.40	
			Rock Fountain	Sales of Product Income		$1,925.00
			Rock Fountain	Inventory Asset		$125.00
			Rock Fountain	Cost of Goods Sold 1 @ $125	$125.00	
			Rock Fountain	Inventory Asset		$125.00
			Rock Fountain	Cost of Goods Sold 1 @ $125	$125.00	
			Rock Fountain	Inventory Asset		$375.00
			Rock Fountain	Cost of Goods Sold 3 @ $125	$375.00	
			Rock Fountain	Inventory Asset		$350.00
			Rock Fountain	Cost of Goods Sold 2 @ $175	$350.00	
			Fountain Pump	Sales of Product Income		$105.00
			Fountain Pump	Inventory Asset		$70.00
			Fountain Pump	Cost of Goods Sold	$70.00	
				Board of Equalization Payable		$162.40
					$3,237.40	$3,237.40
					$3,237.40	$3,237.40

FIGURE 10-11: The Transaction Journal for the Inventory sale

THE ACCOUNTING BEHIND THE SCENES:

When you sell an **Inventory Product**, QuickBooks Online increases (credits) the **Income** account defined for the product sold using an *Invoice* or *Sales Receipt* form. The cost of each stock involved in the sale purchase reduces (credits) **Inventory Asset** and increases (debits) **Cost of Goods Sold**.

HANDLING INVENTORY ISSUES

Managing inventory is complex. On occasion, what arrives in your warehouse doesn't match what you ordered.

Vendor Refunds for Inventory Items

We explored the workflow for receiving a refund from a vendor for returned inventory products in Chapter 5.

Handling Overshipments

If your vendor ships more than you ordered on a purchase order, you have three choices.

1. You could refuse the extra shipment and send it back to the vendor without recording anything in QuickBooks Online.

2. You could receive the extra shipment into inventory and keep it (and pay for it).

3. You could receive the extra shipment into inventory, and then send it back and record a bill credit in QuickBooks Online.

> *Do not perform these steps now. They are for reference only:*

If you keep the overshipment (and pay for it).

1. Override the number in the *Qty* column on the *Bill* so that it exceeds the quantity on your purchase order. This increases the **Inventory Asset** and **Accounts Payable** accounts for the total amount of the shipment, including the overshipment.

2. When the bill arrives from the vendor, pay the amount actually due. Unless you edit the purchase order, it will not match the bill. This may be important later when you look at purchase orders and actual costs, so consider whether you should update your purchase order to match the actual costs, or leave it as is so that you have an accurate history of events.

If you send the overshipment back after receiving it into Inventory.

1. Override the number in the *Qty* column on the *Bill* so that it exceeds the quantity on your purchase order. This increases the Inventory Asset and Accounts Payable accounts for the total amount of the shipment, including the overshipment. However, you do not plan to actually pay the vendor for this "overshipment." Instead, you will return the extra items, and ask the vendor to credit your account.

2. If you return the excess items for credit, create a **Vendor Credit** for the vendor. On the Vendor Credit, enter the quantity returned and the cost for each item.

    If you return the items and receive a refund from the vendor, record a **Vendor Refund** instead.

Handling Vendor Overcharges

If you have a discrepancy between your purchase order and the vendor's bill, there are several ways to handle it. If the vendor overcharged you, the vendor might agree to revise the bill and send you a new one. In this case, wait for the new bill before recording anything in QuickBooks Online.

On the other hand, you might decide to pay the incorrect bill and have the vendor adjust the next bill. In that case, use the *Category Details* grid on the bill in QuickBooks Online to track the error.

For example, you discover that Tim Philips Masonry overcharged you by $10.00. You add an extra row to the most recent bill, directly to Cost of Goods Sold, as shown in Figure 10-12.

Depending upon the vendor's action, do one of the following:

- If the vendor refunds your money, add the refund directly into your next deposit. Code the deposit to the **Cost of Goods Sold** account.

- If the vendor sends you a credit memo, enter a **Vendor Credit**. Categorize the bill credit to the **Cost of Goods Sold** account.

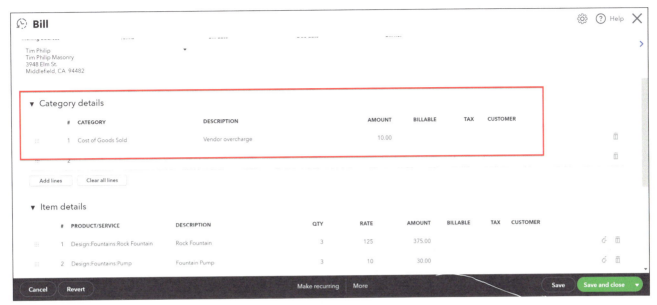

FIGURE 10-12: Record a vendor overcharge in the Category Details grid

> **IMPORTANT:**
>
> Always use the same account when you record the overcharge and the refund or credit. In the example above, the *Category* of the bill for Tim Philip Masonry increases **Cost of Goods Sold** by $10.00, so the deposit or credit from the vendor should also reduce **Cost of Goods Sold** by the same amount.

ADJUSTING INVENTORY

QuickBooks Online automatically updates inventory each time you purchase or sell inventory items. However, it may be necessary to manually adjust inventory after a physical count, or in case of an increase or decrease in the value of your inventory on hand. For example, you might decrease the value of your inventory if it has lost value due to new trends.

Using QuickBooks Online's Inventory Quantity Adjustment form moves the FIFO value of the inventory between the Inventory Asset account and a Cost of Goods Sold account of your choice.

> **DID YOU KNOW?**
>
> Although these adjustment entries can be made to an expense account (decrease in inventory) or an income account (increase in inventory), offsetting inventory variances to a separate Cost of Goods Sold account (for either inventory increases or decreases) more accurately reflects the recording of shrinkage, damage, theft and loss.

Adjusting the Quantity of Inventory on Hand

HANDS-ON PRACTICE

Craig did a manual inventory count in the stock room, and realized some of the Sprinkler Heads and Sprinkler Pipes were missing. He asks you to update the inventory counts in QuickBooks Online.

STEP 1. Go to the *Chart of Accounts*. Click the **New** button and create a new **Expenses** account saved under **Cost of Goods Sold** (see Figure 10-13). *The Tax Form Section* is **Supplies & Materials – COGS**, and the *Account Name* is **Inventory Shrinkage**. In the *Description* field type **Inventory damage, loss, theft**. Click **Save**.

STEP 2. Click the **+New** button, then select **Inventory Qty Adjustment** in the right column. QuickBooks Online displays the window shown in Figure 10-14.

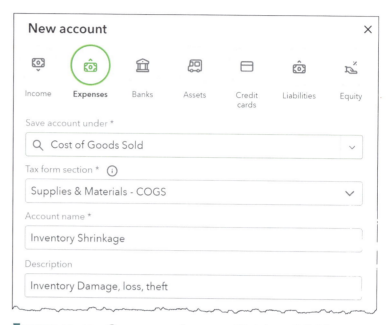

FIGURE 10-13: *Create a new Inventory Shrinkage COGS account*

STEP 3. Use **today's date** in the *Adjustment Date* field.

STEP 4. Choose your new **Inventory Shrinkage** category for the *Inventory Adjustment Account*.

STEP 5. Leave *1* in the *Reference No.* field. You can create your own numbering system if you wish.

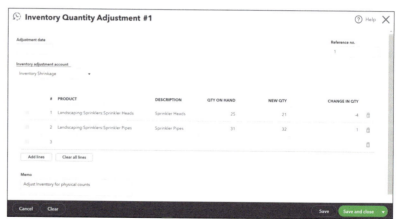

FIGURE 10-14: *The Inventory Quantity Adjustment window*

STEP 6. Enter **Sprinkler Heads** in the *Product* field.

STEP 7. Enter **21** in the *New Qty* box and press **Tab**. The *Change in Qty* recalculates to **-4**.

STEP 8. On the second line, enter **Sprinkler Pipes** in the *Product* field, and update the *New Qty* to **32**. The *Change in Qty* field updates to **1**.

STEP 9. Enter **Adjust Inventory for physical counts** in the *Memo* field.

STEP 10. Compare your screen to Figure 10-14. To save the adjustment, click **Save and Close**.

THE ACCOUNTING BEHIND THE SCENES:

Inventory value adjustments always affect your *Inventory Asset* account. If the **Total Value of Adjustment is a positive number**, the **Inventory** account increases (debits) by that amount and the **Adjustment** account decreases (credits). If the **Total Value of Adjustment is a negative number**, the debits and the credits are reversed.

TRANSACTION TYPE	MEMO/DESCRIPTION	ACCOUNT	DEBIT	CREDIT	PRODUCT/SERVICE
Inventory Qty Adjust	Adjust Inventory for physical cou...	Inventory Shrinkage			Landscaping:Sprinklers:Sprinkler He...
	Adjust Inventory for physical cou...	Inventory Asset			Landscaping:Sprinklers:Sprinkler He...
	Adjust Inventory for physical cou...	Inventory Asset		$3.00	Landscaping:Sprinklers:Sprinkler He...
	Adjust Inventory for physical cou...	Inventory Shrinkage	$3.00		Landscaping:Sprinklers:Sprinkler Pip...
	Adjust Inventory for physical cou...	Inventory Asset			Landscaping:Sprinklers:Sprinkler Pip...
	Adjust Inventory for physical cou...	Inventory Asset	$2.50		Landscaping:Sprinklers:Sprinkler Pip...
	Adjust Inventory for physical cou...	Inventory Shrinkage		$2.50	Landscaping:Sprinklers:Sprinkler Pip...

Adjusting the Value of Inventory

Sometimes the value of your stock changes. Products may become obsolete and lose value. Or an item becomes rare or sought-after, and its value goes up. QuickBooks Online does not have the ability to easily modify the cost of the stock to represent a new valuation.

In most cases, you would not revalue your inventory anyway. Because QBO calculates FIFO inventory, your actual cost would transfer from Inventory Asset to COGS, no matter whether you lost money on the sale, or gained a windfall.

If your company needs this ability, that's a sign your inventory is more complex than QBO's features, and you may need to subscribe to a third-party inventory app.

In order to adjust the value of your inventory asset to reflect current market value, the steps would be to

1. Zero out the inventory quantity for the product using the steps above using a **Cost of Goods Adjustment** account

2. Create a bill to repurchase the stock at the new price.

3. Create a journal entry that debits Accounts Payable to the vendor and credits the same Cost of Goods Adjustment account.

4. Use the journal entry as a vendor credit to pay the bill.

The balance in the Cost of Goods Adjustment category now compensates for the gain or loss in value of the Inventory Asset account.

INVENTORY REPORTS

QuickBooks Online provides several reports for inventory analysis, all of which are customizable just like other reports. In the *Reports* chapter, we looked at several reports that included products:

- The *Product/Service List* on page 315.
- The *Sales by Product/Service Summary Report* on page 324.
- *Inventory Asset QuickReports* on page 313.

The reports in this chapter are specific to inventory management.

Inventory Product QuickReport

The *Product/Service QuickReport* is useful for seeing all transactions involving a specific product, including initial setup, purchases, sales, and adjustments.

HANDS-ON PRACTICE

STEP 1. Open the **Products and Services Center** from *Sales* on the *Left Navigation Bar*.

STEP 2. Scroll down to the **Sprinkler Heads** and click the drop-down arrow on the far right in the *Action* column. Choose **Run Report**.

STEP 3. Set the *Report Period* date to **All Dates**. The *QuickReport* for Sprinkler Heads displays (see Figure 10-15).

DATE	TRANSACTION TYPE	NUM	NAME	MEMO/DESCRIPTION	QTY	RATE	AMOUNT	BALANCE
▼ Inventory Asset								
	Check	75	Hicks Hardware	Sprinkler Heads	15.00	0.75	11.25	11.25
	Inventory Qty Adjust	START		Opening inventory for Sprinkler...	10.00	0.75	7.50	18.75
	Inventory Qty Adjust	START		Opening inventory for Sprinkler...	10.00			18.75
	Inventory Qty Adjust	1		Adjust Inventory for physical cou...	-4.00	0.75	-3.00	15.75
	Inventory Qty Adjust	1		Adjust Inventory for physical cou...	-4.00			15.75
Total for Inventory Asset							$15.75	
▼ Opening Balance Equity								
	Inventory Qty Adjust	START		Opening inventory for Sprinkler...	-10.00	0.75	7.50	7.50
Total for Opening Balance Equity							$7.50	
▼ Landscaping Services								
▼ Job Materials								
▼ Sprinklers and Drip Systems								
	Invoice	1012	Shara Barnett:Barnett Design	Sprinkler Heads	-15.00	2.00	30.00	30.00
Total for Sprinklers and Drip Systems							$30.00	
Total for Job Materials							$30.00	
Total for Landscaping Services							$30.00	
▼ Sales of Product Income								
	Invoice	1004	Cool Cars	Sprinkler Heads	-10.00	2.00	20.00	20.00
Total for Sales of Product Income							$20.00	
▼ Inventory Shrinkage								
	Inventory Qty Adjust	1		Adjust Inventory for physical cou...	4.00	0.75	3.00	3.00
Total for Inventory Shrinkage							$3.00	

FIGURE 10-15: *An Inventory Product QuickReport*

Purchases by Product/Service Detail Report

The *Purchases by Product/Service Detail Report* is useful for reviewing the purchases of inventory products, including the quantity and price.

HANDS-ON PRACTICE

STEP 1. Open the **Reports Center** on the *Left Navigation Bar*. Scroll down to the *Expenses and Vendors* section, and choose **Purchases by Product/Service Detail**.

STEP 2. Change the *Report Period* to **All Dates**. The report displays.

STEP 3. Modify this report further by clicking the **Customize** button.

INVENTORY | 431

STEP 4. To remove the opening inventory adjustments, click the **Filter** option. In the drop-down next to *Transaction Type*, add checkmarks in front of **Credit Card Expense, Check, Bill, Credit Card Credits**, and **Vendor Credit**, as shown in Figure 10-16.

STEP 5. Click **Run Report** (see Figure 10-17).

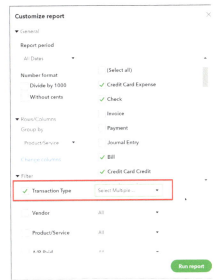

FIGURE 10-16: *Customize the report to see purchase transactions*

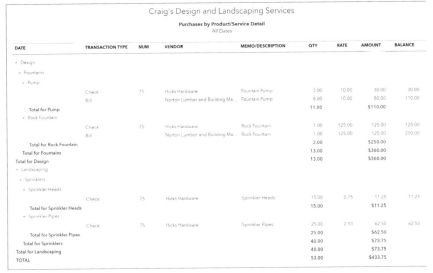

FIGURE 10-17: *Purchases by Product Report—your screen may vary*

STEP 6. To view purchases by vendor, scroll up to the *Group By* field at the top of the report and change the drop-down to **Vendor**, then click **Run Report**. The report updates to group purchases by payee as shown in Figure 10-18.

FIGURE 10-18: *Purchases grouped by Vendor—your screen may vary*

Inventory Stock Status Report

While there is no official inventory stock report, you can get creative with QuickBooks Online's interface to generate a stock status report.

HANDS-ON PRACTICE

Step 1. Go to the **Products and Services Center** from *Sales* on the *Left Navigation Bar*.

Step 2. Using the *Grid Gear* on the right just above the grid, click **Show More**, and turn on all the fields, as shown in Figure 10-19.

Step 3. Click on the *Filter* and change the *Type* to **Inventory**. Notice that there is also an option to filter by *Stock Status* for products that are **Low Stock** or **Out of Stock**. Click **Apply**.

Step 4. The list automatically updates to reflect your changes. The columns also resize themselves, although you may wish to adjust them further.

Figure 10-19: *Turn on all the fields, then filter by Inventory products*

Step 5. Click on the **Printer** just above the grid on the right. A printer-friendly report opens in a new tab, as shown in Figure 10-20. You will want to change the page orientation to **Landscape**.

Figure 10-20: *An inventory stock list generated from the Products and Services interface*

Physical Inventory Worksheet

Physical inventory counts must be performed at least annually, but should be done monthly or quarterly as needed. There is a **Physical Inventory Worksheet** report you can print with a list of products and expected quantities. Bring it to the stockroom to verify current quantity counts, then use the worksheet to make your *Inventory Qty Adjustment* (see page 428).

HANDS-ON PRACTICE

Step 1. Click on the **Physical Inventory Worksheet** in the *Reports Center* under *Sales and Customers* (see Figure 10-21).

	Craig's Design and Landscaping Services				
	Physical Inventory Worksheet				
PRODUCT	DESCRIPTION	QTY ON HAND	REORDER POINT	QTY ON PO	PHYSICAL COUNT
Design:Fountains:Pump	Fountain Pump	25.00			
Design:Fountains:Rock Fountain	Rock Fountain	2.00			
Landscaping:Sprinklers:Sprinkler ...	Sprinkler Heads	21.00			
Landscaping:Sprinklers:Sprinkler ...	Sprinkler Pipes	32.00			

FIGURE 10-21: *The Physical Inventory Worksheet—your report may vary*

Inventory Valuation Summary

The *Inventory Valuation Summary Report* gives you information about the value of your inventory items on a certain date. This report shows each product in inventory, the quantity on hand, the asset value, and the average cost of each item.

HANDS-ON PRACTICE

STEP 1. Click the **Inventory Valuation Summary** report in the *Reports Center* under *Sales and Customers* (see Figure 10-22).

		Craig's Design and Landscaping Services			
		Inventory Valuation Summary			
		As of			
		SKU	QTY	ASSET VALUE	CALC. AVG
▼ Design					
▼ Fountains					
Pump		P461-17	25.00	250.00	10.00
Rock Fountain		R154-88	2.00	250.00	125.00
Total Fountains				500.00	
Total Design				500.00	
▼ Landscaping					
▼ Sprinklers					
Sprinkler Heads		S867-56	21.00	15.75	0.75
Sprinkler Pipes		S867-62	32.00	80.00	2.50
Total Sprinklers				95.75	
Total Landscaping				95.75	
TOTAL				$595.75	

FIGURE 10-22: *Inventory Valuation Summary report—your report may vary*

> **NOTE:**
>
> All inventory reports have an option to **Show Non-Zero** or **Active Only** items. Select your desired view from the drop-down at the top of the report.

Inventory Valuation Detail Report

The *Inventory Valuation Detail Report* breaks out each inventory item into a list of its transactions. This report shows each product, the type of transaction affecting inventory, the vendor name, quantity, rate, FIFO cost, quantity on hand, and total asset value.

HANDS-ON PRACTICE

STEP 1. Click the **Inventory Valuation Detail** report in the *Reports Center* under *Sales and Customers* (see Figure 10-23). Change the *Report Period* to **All Dates** and click **Run Report**.

Craig's Design and Landscaping Services
Inventory Valuation Detail
All Dates

DATE	TRANSACTION TYPE	NUM	NAME	QTY	RATE	FIFO COST	QTY ON HAND	ASSET VALUE
▼ Design								
▼ Fountains								
▼ Pump								
	Inventory Qty Adjust	START		16.00	10.00	160.00	16.00	160.00
	Check	75	Hicks Hardware	3.00	10.00	30.00	19.00	190.00
	Bill		Norton Lumber and Building Ma…	8.00	10.00	80.00	27.00	270.00
	Invoice	1036	Freeman Sporting Goods:0969 …	-1.00	10.00	-10.00	26.00	260.00
	Invoice	1037	Sonnenschein Family Store	-1.00	10.00	-10.00	25.00	250.00
Total for Pump				25.00		$250.00	25.00	$250.00
▼ Rock Fountain								
	Inventory Qty Adjust	START		3.00	125.00	375.00	3.00	375.00
	Check	75	Hicks Hardware	1.00	125.00	125.00	4.00	500.00
	Invoice	1035	Mark Cho	-1.00	125.00	-125.00	3.00	375.00
	Bill		Norton Lumber and Building Ma…	1.00	125.00	125.00	4.00	500.00
	Invoice	1036	Freeman Sporting Goods:0969 …	-1.00	125.00	-125.00	3.00	375.00
	Invoice	1037	Sonnenschein Family Store	-1.00	125.00	-125.00	2.00	250.00
Total for Rock Fountain				2.00		$250.00	2.00	$250.00
Total for Fountains				27.00		$500.00	27.00	$500.00
Total for Design				27.00		$500.00	27.00	$500.00

FIGURE 10-23: *Inventory Valuation Detail report—your report may vary*

Profit and Loss Report by Product/Service

Another way to customize a Profit and Loss Statement is to include columns by Product/Service. This allows you to see the Net Income for each item bought and sold.

Note that if your Products & Services List is very long, this report may be unwieldy.

HANDS-ON PRACTICE

STEP 1. Click the **Profit and Loss** report in the *Reports Center* under *Business Overview*.

STEP 2. Change the *Display Columns By* field to **Products/Services**.

STEP 3. Under *Show Non-Zero or Active Only*, change both *Show Rows* and *Show Columns* to **Non-zero**.

STEP 4. Click the **Customize** button, and then the **Filter**. Under *Product/Service*, select **Specified**.

STEP 5. Click **Run Report** (see Figure 10-24).

	DESIGN	DESIGN	FOUNTAINS	CONCRETE	PUMP	ROCK FOUNTAIN	TOTAL FOUNTAINS	LIGHTING	ROCKS	SERVICES	TOTAL DESIGN
▾ Income											
Design Income		2,250.00									2,250.00
▾ Landscaping Services											
▾ Job Materials											
Fountains and Garden Li...				122.50	45.00	1,650.00	1,817.50	45.00	384.00		2,246.50
Plants and Soil											
Sprinklers and Drip Syste...											
Total Job Materials				122.50	45.00	1,650.00	1,817.50	45.00	384.00		2,246.50
▾ Labor											
Installation											
Maintenance and Repair											
Total Labor											
Total Landscaping Services				122.50	45.00	1,650.00	1,817.50	45.00	384.00		2,246.50
Pest Control Services											
Sales of Product Income					27.75	825.00	852.75				852.75
Services										503.55	503.55
Total Income	$0.00	$2,250.00	$0.00	$122.50	$72.75	$2,475.00	$2,670.25	$45.00	$384.00	$503.55	$5,852.80
▾ Cost of Goods Sold											
Cost of Goods Sold					20.00	375.00	395.00				395.00
Total Cost of Goods Sold	$0.00	$0.00	$0.00	$0.00	$20.00	$375.00	$395.00	$0.00	$0.00	$0.00	$395.00
GROSS PROFIT	$0.00	$2,250.00	$0.00	$122.50	$52.75	$2,100.00	$2,275.25	$45.00	$384.00	$503.55	$5,457.80
Expenses											
Total Expenses							$0.00				$0.00
NET OPERATING INCOME	$0.00	$2,250.00	$0.00	$122.50	$52.75	$2,100.00	$2,275.25	$45.00	$384.00	$503.55	$5,457.80
NET INCOME	$0.00	$2,250.00	$0.00	$122.50	$52.75	$2,100.00	$2,275.25	$45.00	$384.00	$503.55	$5,457.80

FIGURE 10-24: *Profit and Loss Report with columns for Products—your report may vary*

REVIEW QUESTIONS

Comprehension Questions

1. Why must Inventory be tracked on an Accrual basis instead of a Cash basis?
2. What accounts will QuickBooks Online automatically create when you first create an Inventory Product in the Products and Services list?
3. Describe the purpose of the Inventory Asset and Cost of Goods Sold accounts in QuickBooks Online.
4. Describe the purpose of using Purchase Orders in QuickBooks Online.

Multiple Choice

Select the best answer for each of the following:

1. Which Product or Service type should be selected when adding a new item that you buy and/or sell but don't keep track of in inventory?
   a. Service.
   b. Inventory.
   c. Non-inventory.
   d. Bundle.
2. QuickBooks Online tracks inventory using which of these methods?
   a. First In, First Out.
   b. Last In, First Out.
   c. Average Cost.
   d. All of the above.

3. If your vendor ships more than you ordered on a purchase order (an overshipment), which of the following actions would not be appropriate?
    a. You could refuse the extra shipment and send it back to the vendor without recording anything in QuickBooks Online.
    b. You could receive the extra shipment using an *Inventory Qty Adjustment* transaction.
    c. You could update the bill to receive the extra shipment into Inventory and keep it (and pay for it).
    d. You could update the bill to receive the extra shipment into Inventory, and then send it back and record a Vendor Credit or Vendor Refund in QuickBooks Online.

4. When you sell a product, how does QBO calculate the cost to move from Inventory Asset to Cost of Goods?
    a. It averages the prices you paid for all your stock.
    b. It uses the price you paid for the newest items in stock.
    c. It uses the price you paid for the oldest items in stock.
    d. It uses the price the customer is paying.

5. To activate QuickBooks Online's Inventory:
    a. Turn it on in the Dashboard.
    b. Turn it on in Account and Settings > Advanced.
    c. Turn it on in the Products and Services Center.
    d. Turn it on in Account and Settings > Sales.

6. The Inventory Asset account:
    a. Tracks open purchase orders of inventory items.
    b. Decreases when inventory is purchased.
    c. Increases when inventory is sold.
    d. Increases when inventory is purchased.

7. In QuickBooks Online, Inventory can do all of the following except:
    a. Provide reports on the status of each item in inventory including how many are on hand and how many are on order.
    b. Use the Average Cost method of determining inventory cost.
    c. Calculate gross profit on inventory sold.
    d. Track the open purchase orders for every inventory item.

8. Which of the following statements is false regarding Purchase Orders (POs)?
    a. POs are held as non-posting account until you receive the product(s) ordered by creating a bill.
    b. POs that include inventory items are posted to the inventory account at the end of each month.
    c. You can list your open purchase orders at any time.
    d. You may close a purchase order in part or in full at any time.

9. To display the window used to record inventory adjustments in QuickBooks Online:
    a. Select the *Gear* and then choose *Inventory Qty Adjustment*.
    b. No adjustments should ever be made. QuickBooks Online automatically adjusts inventory each time you purchase or sell inventory items.

c. Select the *+New* button and then choose *Inventory Qty Adjustment*.
d. Go to *Account and Settings>Sales* and then choose *Inventory Qty Adjustment*.

10. Which of the following is NOT a report available through QuickBooks Online?
    a. Goods-In-Process Inventory by Item.
    b. Physical Inventory Worksheet.
    c. Inventory Valuation Summary.
    d. Product QuickReport.

11. Which of the following statements is not true regarding the recording of receipts of inventory items?
    a. How you record inventory received depends on how you pay for the items.
    b. You can record a bill from a purchase order even before you receive *all* the items ordered.
    c. You can purchase components and assemble them into a new product.
    d. You cannot enter the receipt of inventory items before entering the bill from the vendor.

12. When entering a bill for the purchase of inventory products, which grid of the Bills window should you use?
    a. Item Details.
    b. Category Details.
    c. Either of the above.
    d. None of the above.

13. Before setting up your inventory, it is a good idea to think about what products you will track as Inventory because:
    a. It is necessary to separately track *every* product you sell as an Inventory Product.
    b. You could use Non-inventory Products if you do not need detailed reports and inventory status information about certain products you sell.
    c. It is better to use Inventory Products rather than Non-inventory Products when you sell custom items.
    d. Your accountant needs the detail information on Inventory Products to be able to close your books for the year.

14. QuickBooks Online's Inventory tools are found in this subscription level:
    a. Essentials
    b. Plus
    c. Advanced.
    d. Both b and c.

15. When processing a vendor overcharge, what do you NOT want to do?
    a. Wait for a new bill from the vendor before recording the bill in QuickBooks Online, if the vendor agrees to revise the bill and send you a new one.
    b. Use the *Category Details* tab on the bill to track the error, if you decide to pay the overcharge and have the vendor adjust the next bill.
    c. Use two separate accounts when recording the overcharge and the refund or credit, to keep the transactions from becoming confusing.
    d. Contact the vendor to discuss the overage on the bill.

Completion Statements

1. QBO's inventory values are based on FIFO, which stands for _____ _____ _____ _____.
2. In order to easily determine which products you have on order, use _____ _____ when you buy inventory.
3. QuickBooks Online keeps a(n) _____ inventory, meaning that every purchase and every sale of inventory immediately updates all of your reports.
4. To update inventory quantities, use the _____ _____ _____ tool.
5. The _____ _____ _____ _____ account category tracks the total cost for all products sold to customers.

INVENTORY—APPLY YOUR KNOWLEDGE

> Log into your **Imagine Photography** class file at qbo.intuit.com.

1. Create three new Inventory Products in the *Products and Services List* with the following data. Remember that you can duplicate an item and update it with the necessary changes.

FIELD	ITEM 1	ITEM 2	ITEM 3
ITEM TYPE	Inventory	Inventory	Inventory
ITEM NAME	Frame 8.5x11 Black	Frame 8.5x11 Bronze	Frame 8.5x11 Gray
SKU	F811BL	F811BR	F811GR
CATEGORY	Products	Products	Products
CLASS	Walnut Creek	Walnut Creek	Walnut Creek
INITIAL QUANTITY ON HAND	0	0	0
AS OF DATE	January 1 of this year	January 1 of this year	January 1 of this year
REORDER POINT	25	25	25
INVENTORY ASSET ACCOUNT	Inventory Asset	Inventory Asset	Inventory Asset
DESCRIPTION	Picture Frame—8.5x11in Black	Picture Frame—8.5x11in Bronze	Picture Frame—8.5x11in Gray
SALES PRICE/RATE	$37.99	$35.99	$34.99
INCOME ACCOUNT	Sales of Product Income	Sales of Product Income	Sales of Product Income
SALES TAX	Taxable – Standard Rate	Taxable – Standard Rate	Taxable – Standard Rate
DESCRIPTION ON PURCHASE FORMS	Picture Frame—8.5x11in Black	Picture Frame—8x11 Bronze	Picture Frame—8x11 Gray

FIELD	ITEM 1	ITEM 2	ITEM 3
COST	$19.99	$18.99	$18.49
EXPENSE ACCOUNT	Cost of Goods Sold:Supplies & Materials	Cost of Goods Sold:Supplies & Materials	Cost of Goods Sold:Supplies & Materials
PREFERRED VENDOR	Ogaga Photo Supply	Ogaga Photo Supply	Ogaga Photo Supply

TABLE 10-4 *Data for a new Inventory Part*

2. Create a **Purchase Order** to **Ogaga Photo Supply** dated the **first day of this month.** Use the *Retail* Tag. Leave the *Ship To* drop-down field at the top blank so that the default shipping address is Imagine Photography's store address. Purchase **50** of **each of the three frames** above (Black, Bronze, and Gray) using the **Walnut Creek** *Class*. The total PO amount is **$2,873.50**. Print the Purchase Order on blank paper or save it as a PDF for your instructor.

3. A partial shipment arrives one week later. Copy the *Purchase Order* to a **Bill** dated **the 8th of the month**. The *Bill No.* on the packing slip and invoice is **3883**. In the box are **25 Frame 8x11 Black**, **25 Frame 8x11 Bronze**, and **50 Frame 8x11 Gray**. The total bill amount is **$1,899.00**.

4. The next day, Satterley Wedding Planners buys 50 frames to use as client gifts. Create a **Sales Receipt** dated **the 9th of the month** to **Satterley Wedding Planners** (no sub-customer).
   a. The *Sales Rep* is **MM** and the *Tag* is **Retail**.
   b. The *Payment Method* is **Credit Card**, and the *Deposit To* field is **Payments to Deposit**.
   c. Add these *Products*: **20 Frame 8x11 Black, 20 Frame 8x11 Bronze**, and **10 Frame 8x11 Gray**. Use the **Walnut Creek** *Class*.
   d. The *Sales Tax* should calculate to **$171.52**. The total sales receipt amount is **$2,001.02**.

5. More of the order from Ogaga Photo Supply arrives three days later. Copy the *Purchase Order* to a **Bill** dated **on the 11th of the month**. The *Bill No.* on the packing slip and invoice is **3994**.
   a. In the box are **15 Frame 8x11 Black** and **15 Frame 8x11 Bronze**.
   b. The price on both frames has gone up to **21.99**.
   c. The invoice includes an additional **$35** delivery charge. In the *Category Details* grid, add **Shipping, Freight & Delivery – COS**. In the *Description*, enter **Shipping charges on Bills 3883 and 3994**. Add the *Class* **Walnut Creek**.
   d. The total bill amount is **$694.70**.

6. Ogaga Photo Supply lets you know that they won't be getting any more of the frames you ordered. Edit the Purchase Order and mark the *Black and Bronze frames* as **Closed**. Change the *Purchase Order Status* in the upper left corner to **Closed**.

7. Create a **Sales Receipt** to **Nayo Garcia** on the **15th of the month**, for **10 Bronze Frames**. Use the *Tag* **Retail**, *Sales Rep* **MM** and the **Walnut Creek** *Class*. She pays with **Check** number **5353**. The *Sales Tax* autocalculates to **$36.89**. The total sale is **$396.79**.

8. The next day, Nayo returns. Two of the Bronze frames had cracked glass. You give her two more frames out of inventory to replace the broken items.

a. Enter an *Inventory Qty Adjustment* dated **the 16th of the month**.
b. The *Inventory Adjustment account* defaults to **Inventory Shrinkage**.
c. In the *Product* field enter **Frame 8x11 Bronze**, and update the *New Qty* field to **8**. The *Change in Qty* will populate automatically with **-2**. Confirm the **Walnut Creek** *Class*.
d. In the *Memo* box, enter **Exchange 2 broken frames for Nayo Garcia**.

9. Run a **QuickReport** from the *Products and Services List* for the **Frame 8x11 Bronze** with the *Dates* set to *All*. Save or print the report.
    a. Why does the Sales Receipt for Nayo Garcia split her 10 Bronze frames into two lines of 5 and 5 with different prices?

10. Run a **Sales by Product/Service Summary** for **This Month,** on an **Accrual** basis.
    a. Which frame had the highest **Quantity** sales?
    b. Which frame had the highest **Gross Margin %**?

11. Create an **Inventory Stock Status Report** by modifying the *Products and Services List.*
    a. View the *Products and Services List.*
    b. Turn on **all fields**.
    c. **Filter** the list for the *Type* of **Inventory** only.
    d. Save or print the report in **Landscape** so that the data fits on one page.
    e. What three items need to be **reordered**? How can you tell?

12. Create an **Inventory Valuation Summary** for **All Dates**:
    a. Which product has the highest **Asset Value**?
    b. Which product is the least valuable per item (**Lowest Calculated Average**)?

CHAPTER 11

ADJUSTMENTS AND YEAR-END PROCEDURES

TOPICS

In this chapter, you will learn about the following topics:

- Making Journal Entries (page 441)
- Zero-Dollar Checks and Sales Receipts (page 444)
- Tracking Depreciation of Fixed Assets (page 448)
- Processing 1099s (page 451)
- Managing Equity (page 456)
- Closing the Accounting Period (page 460)
- Closing Equity Accounts at the End of the Fiscal Year (page 461)
- Setting the Closing Date (page 463)

> **OPEN THIS FILE:**
>
> Open the *Craig's Landscaping sample company* using the bookmark you created on page 8, or go to http://qbo.intuit.com/redir/testdrive.

This chapter covers various ways to make **Adjustments** as well as process **end of year tasks**. Topics include how to use **Journal Entries** and **Zero-Dollar Checks** to adjust balances and close the year. You will also learn how to use the **Closing Date** in QuickBooks Online.

CREATING ADJUSTMENTS

Making Journal Entries

Journal Entries are transactions that adjust the balance of two or more accounts. They give you control over the accounting behind the scenes. We introduced journal entries earlier on page 206.

Journal entries are used to make adjustments in QuickBooks Online, allowing you to:

- Recategorize a transaction from one class to another.
- Recategorize a transaction from one account to another.
- Record non-cash expenses, such as depreciation.

- Close the Owner Draws and Investments accounts into Owners Equity
- Enter adjustments requested by a tax professional.

However, never use a journal entry if there is a QuickBooks Online form that serves the same purpose. Journal entries contain limited data, provide no context, and can be challenging to understand later.

Journal entries always balance. The total of the *Debit* column must match the total of the *Credit* column. In fact, every time you move to the next line QBO will automatically enter the remaining amount needed to make your JE balance, but you can simply override this amount as you build the transaction.

When accountants create journal entries, QBO for Accountants (QBOA) has an *Is Adjusting Journal Entry* checkbox to indicate that they created the JE to correct an error in the data.

DID YOU KNOW?

If you are using **QuickBooks Online for Accountants (QBOA)**, there's a feature in the *Accountant Tools* briefcase called **Reclassify Transactions**. This tool will allow you to fix incorrect account categories and classes in batches, instead of editing them individually or patching them with JEs as in the example below. This feature is preferable whenever possible, so that when you look up a transaction, you see what it was really for, and bad habits and mistakes aren't repeated in the future.

Regular users may be able to use this magical tool by using the URL **https://app.qbo.intuit.com/app/reclassify-transaction**. Replace everything after "app/" in your QBO's web address with "reclassify-transaction," and see if the tool is available to you.

HANDS-ON PRACTICE

When looking at a Profit and Loss Detail Report, you discover that the expenses to Bob's Burger Joint should have been Owner Draws, because the owner was eating lunch by themselves. Instead of editing and correcting the transactions, you decide to make an adjusting journal entry.

STEP 1. Select the *+New* button and then choose **Journal Entry**, as shown in Figure 11-1.

Those using QuickBooks Online for Accountants can also click the *Accountant Tools* briefcase and select **Journal Entries**.

STEP 2. Enter **today's date** in the *Journal Date* field and then press **Tab** (see Figure 11-3).

STEP 3. Enter **your intials-1** in the *Journal No.* field. The very first time you enter a journal entry, enter whatever identification number you'd like in the *Journal No.* field. After that, QuickBooks Online will increment the number.

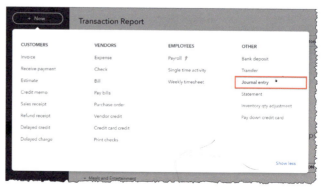

FIGURE 11-1: *Choose Journal Entry from the +New button*

> **TIP:**
>
> It's a common practice to include your initials when numbering journal entries. This helps identify at-a-glance if the adjusting entry was created by the accountant, bookkeeper, or business owner.

STEP 4. Because we're working in the Craig's Landscaping sample file, there are no existing owner equity accounts, so we need to create one. In the *Account* field in row 1, create a new **Owner Draws** equity account on the fly, as shown in Figure 11-2. **Save and close** the new equity account to return to the journal entry.

STEP 5. In the *Debits* field, enter **28.49**. In the *Description* column, type **Recategorize meals**.

STEP 6. In the *Name* field, choose **Bob's Burger Joint**.

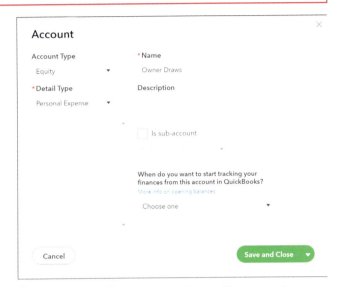

FIGURE 11-2: *Create a new Owner Draws equity account*

STEP 7. In the *Account* field in row 2, choose **Meals and Entertainment**.

STEP 8. In the *Credits* field, verify **28.49** is entered. In the *Description* column, type **Recategorize meals** if it did not autofill. In the *Name* field, choose **Bob's Burger Joint**.

> **NOTE:**
>
> Your JE may make sense at the time, but it can be hard to remember its purpose in the future. Good accounting practice suggests that you write a detailed *Description* in each line of the journal entry. This annotation will be very helpful if you are ever audited or if you have to research the reasons for the adjustment.

STEP 9. When your journal entry matches Figure 11-3, click **Save and Close.**

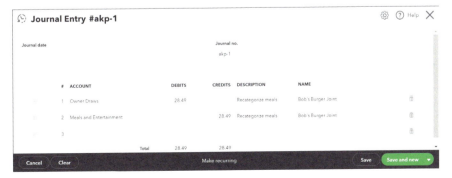

FIGURE 11-3: *Create a Journal Entry to recategorize Meals to Owner Draws*

Zero-Dollar Checks and Sales Receipts

Zero-Dollar Checks and *Zero-Dollar Sales Receipts* are an advanced technique you can use instead of journal entries to make adjustments that involve products and services, job costing, or vendors.

For example, if you use products and services to track the details of your expenses, you may need to enter adjustments to the items as well as the accounts to which the items are assigned. However, the *Journal Entry* window in QuickBooks Online has no provision for including products or services as part of the journal entry.

To solve the problem, use a transaction (such as a *Check*) that has an *Item Details* grid. The check will be a "Zero-Dollar Check" in that it will have an equal amount of debits and credits, so no actual bank account activity is involved.

Let's look at two examples of zero-dollar checks, one for adjusting product values, and another for bartering.

> **KEY TERM**
>
> Some people create a holding bank account called **Clearing Account** and use it as the source for zero-dollar checks, Daily Sales Receipts, and other in-and-out transactions. This keeps the operating checking account from getting cluttered with $0 transactions that did not really touch the bank.

Adjusting Expense Accounts Associated with Items

When you purchase products for resale, their Cost of Goods may not be the only relevant expense in determining your profit. You may have paid for shipping, import duties, and sales tax. You may have incurred additional costs associated with the item, repackaged the products, or performed a repair. The sum of all these costs is called **Landed Costs**.

You can use a Zero-Dollar Check to include a variety of fully-burdened costs in your Inventory Asset and Cost of Goods calculations.

HANDS-ON PRACTICE

Craig needs to repair two of the rock fountains before reselling them. He spends $25 on parts and concrete for each one, but instead of leaving the materials cost in Cost of Goods, he wants to add the materials used to the inventory value of the fountains.

In this $0 check, you'll subtract the cost of the parts from Cost of Goods Sold, remove the fountains from Inventory Asset, and then create a new Rock Fountain Refurbished product as a combined Inventory Asset (see Figure 11-6).

Now when Craig sells the refurbished fountains, the automatic adjustment from Inventory Asset to Cost of Goods Sold will include the full cost of the Rock Fountains and the materials used for repair.

STEP 1. Select **Check** from the *+New* menu.

STEP 2. In the *Payee* field, add **Inventory Adjustment** as a new **Vendor** on the fly. You can use this payee for similar transactions in the future.

STEP 3. In the *Bank Account* field, create a new Bank account called **Clearing Account**, as shown in Figure 11-4.

STEP 4. Back in the check, enter **today's date** and keep the default *Check No.* **1**.

STEP 5. In the *Category Details* grid, enter the Category **Cost of Goods Sold**. Enter **Material to repair fountains** in the *Description* field. Tab to *Amount* and enter **-$50** (be sure it's negative).

STEP 6. Click on the triangle next to *Item Details* if it is collapsed.

STEP 7. Enter **Rock Fountain** as the *Product/Service*, with a *Quantity* of **-2** (make sure it's negative), and **$125** in the *Rate* field.

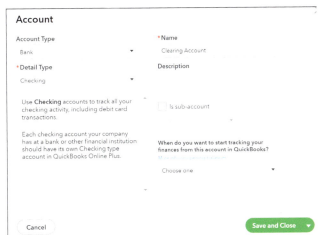

FIGURE 11-4: *Create a Clearing Account to store zero-dollar transactions*

STEP 8. On line 2 in the *Item Details* grid, enter **Rock Fountain Refurbished**. Create a new **Inventory** product on the fly to using the information in Table 11-1 to match Figure 11-5.

Because QuickBooks Online calculates Inventory Asset and Cost of Goods Sold based on FIFO, the repaired fountains must be moved out of inventory and changed to Refurbished products. Without moving this inventory quantity and valuation adjustment to a new product, there would be no way to properly identify when these two specific fountains were sold.

NAME	ROCK FOUNTAIN REFURBISHED
CATEGORY	Design:Fountains
INITIAL QUANTITY ON HAND	0
AS OF DATE	The first day of this month
REORDER POINT	0
INVENTORY ASSET ACCOUNT	Inventory Asset
SALES DESCRIPTION	Rock Fountain Refurbished
SALES PRICE	250 (price is slightly less than new)
INCOME ACCOUNT	Sales of Product Income
SALES TAX	Taxable – Standard Rate
PURCHASE DESCRIPTION	Rock Fountain Refurbished
COST	150 (the original cost plus the concrete)
EXPENSE ACCOUNT	Cost of Goods Sold
PREFERRED VENDOR	None

TABLE 11-1 *Create a new inventory product*

Step 9. Enter a *Qty* of **2** (positive), and the new cost of **$150** ($125 plus $25 in materials).

Step 10. When your check equals **$0** and matches Figure 11-6, **Save and Close** the check.

Figure 11-6: *A Zero-Dollar Check for Inventory Value Adjustments*

Figure 11-5: *Create a Refurbished Inventory product on the fly*

THE ACCOUNTING BEHIND THE SCENES

This $0 check decreases (credits) **Inventory Asset** and **Cost of Goods Sold** for the broken product and repair materials. The new inventory product increases (debits) the **Inventory Asset** account for the combined amount.

TRANSACTION TYPE	NUM	NAME	MEMO/DESCRIPTION	ACCOUNT	DEBIT	CREDIT
Check	1	Inventory Adjustment		Checking	$0.00	
			Rock Fountain	Inventory Asset		$250.00
			Rock Fountain Refurbished	Inventory Asset	$300.00	
			Material to repair fountain	Cost of Goods Sold		$50.00
					$300.00	$300.00
					$300.00	$300.00

Bartering

In this scenario, Craig's Landscaping is buying two more Rock Fountains from Tim Philip Masonry. Instead of paying for them, though, Craig is going to **Barter** for two hours of Design work.

Bartering trades are still business revenue and costs; the IRS requires that such transactions be properly entered into the company's books. While no money is changing hands, Craig's Landscaping is still making a purchase, and is still selling a service. The barter's income and expense wash out on the Profit and Loss report with a $0 net.

HANDS-ON PRACTICE

To see your reports reflect the full job-related activity even though there is no exchange of money, use a **Zero-Dollar Check**:

STEP 1. Select **Check** from the *+New* button.

STEP 2. Enter **Tim Philip Masonry** as the *Payee*.

STEP 3. Use **Clearing Account** as the bank account, as shown in Figure 11-7.

STEP 4. Leave the default *Payment Date* and *Check No.*.

STEP 5. In the *Category* field, enter **Design Income**. In the *Description*, type **Bartered 2 Fountains for 3.5 hours of Design work**. In the **Amount** field, enter **-250** (make sure the amount is negative).

By including a negative line item using an income category on a check normally used to record expenses, we are in effect increasing the income.

STEP 6. On the *Items Details* grid (you may need to delete any items that auto-filled), enter **Rock Fountain**, and a *Qty* of **2**. When you press **Tab**, the *Amount* will update to **250**.

The total *Check* amount nets to zero.

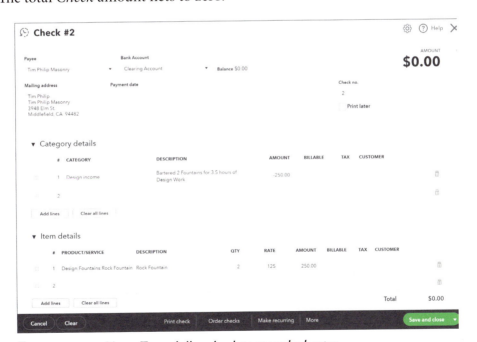

FIGURE 11-7: *Use a Zero-dollar check to record a barter*

STEP 7. To review the adjustment made to the General Ledger, **Save and Close** the zero-dollar check but open it again immediately from the *Search* magnifying glass. Click on the **More** button in the black bar at the bottom of the screen, and then choose **Transaction Journal**. QuickBooks Online displays the report shown in Figure 11-8 below.

TRANSACTION TYPE	NUM	NAME	MEMO/DESCRIPTION	ACCOUNT	DEBIT	CREDIT
Check	2	Tim Philip Masonry		Checking	$0.00	
			Rock Fountain	Inventory Asset	$250.00	
			Bartered 2 Fountains for 3.5 Hou...	Design income		$250.00
					$250.00	$250.00
					$250.00	$250.00

Craig's Design and Landscaping Services — Journal — All Dates

FIGURE 11-8: *Transaction Journal from the Zero Dollar Check*

Inventory Asset is debited, increasing its value, and **Design Income** is credited for the same amount, increasing revenue. Once the fountains have sold and their bartered expense becomes Cost of Goods Sold, the *Profit and Loss Statement* will contain a net of $0.

In addition to the examples above, zero-dollar checks are very useful for adjustments involving any combination of categories and items.

Similarly, you can use zero-dollar sales receipts to adjust items that affect income and payment method clearing accounts. These are commonly used to enter **Daily Sales Z-Tapes** from Point-of-Sale (POS) systems.

IMPORTANT!

If you use a regular checking account instead of a clearing account for zero-dollar transactions, be sure to mark these $0 transactions as cleared when you reconcile the bank account.

TRACKING DEPRECIATION OF FIXED ASSETS

When you incur large purchases of equipment, furniture, buildings, computers, and vehicles that have useful lives of more than one year and a value of over $2500, add them to your General Ledger as **Fixed Assets**.

Periodically record the **depreciation** of the assets as an operating expense. Depreciation spreads the value of the fixed asset evenly over time, so companies don't record unusually large expenses all in one year. Depreciation expense adjustments are typically made at the end of the year, and can be entered monthly for the highest level of accuracy.

Check with your accountant if you need help deciding which purchases should be added to a fixed asset account, and how often they should be depreciated.

Setting Up the Fixed Asset Accounts

To track your asset values, create a separate fixed asset account for each grouping of assets you want to track. Common categories include **Furniture and Fixtures**, **Machinery and Equipment**, **Vehicles**, **Land**, **Buildings**, and **Computer Equipment**.

An **Accumulated Depreciation** account is also created as a *contra account* to track the total depreciation of these assets. This account reduces their value on the Balance Sheet until it reaches $0.00.

> ### KEY TERM:
>
> A **Contra Account** is an account that carries a balance that is opposite from the normal balance for that account type. For example, an asset that carries a credit balance is a Contra Asset account since assets normally carry a debit balance. Also, an income account that carries a debit balance (like sales discounts) is a contra income account since income accounts normally carry a credit balance.

Fixed Assets	
Accumulated Depreciation	-24,000.00
Computer Equipment	11,000.00
Furniture & Fixtures	3,000.00
Machinery & Equipment	17,000.00
Total Fixed Assets	**$7,000.00**

FIGURE 11-9: *Fixed Assets and Accumulated Depreciation Accounts*

> ### THE ACCOUNTING BEHIND THE SCENES
>
> As you purchase fixed assets, categorize the purchases to the appropriate **Fixed Asset** account. This increases (debits) the **fixed asset** account and decreases (credits) the **checking** account (or increases/credits the **loan or credit card liability**) you use to pay for it.
>
> When you record depreciation, the entry increases (debits) the **Depreciation Expense** account and increases (credits) the **Accumulated Depreciation** asset account.

Calculating and Recording Depreciation

Using Control Accounts and Net Book Value

An alternative method of managing Fixed Assets allows you to track the value and accumulated depreciation of each individual asset. To do this, you would set up each Fixed Asset using three accounts: a *Control* account with two *Sub-accounts* for the *Original Cost* and its *Accumulated Depreciation*.

The method tracks each individual asset separately, instead of grouping similar assets together.

Using control accounts allows you to see the **Net Book Value** of each Fixed Asset on the **Balance Sheet** in the *Total* for the asset, as shown in Figure 11-13.

Trailer	Fixed Assets	Machinery & Equipment
Depreciation	Fixed Assets	Accumulated Depreciation
Original cost	Fixed Assets	Machinery & Equipment

FIGURE 11-10: *An alternative Fixed Asset setup with control accounts*

> ### KEY TERM:
>
> **Net Book Value (NBV)** is the book value of your Fixed Asset at any point in time. Calculate NBV by subtracting the amount of use of the asset (accumulated depreciation) from the original purchase price to determine the value of the remaining useful life. As you can see in Figure 11-13, the original cost of a Truck is $13,495. The accumulated depreciation to date is $224.92. Therefore, the Net Book Value of the Truck Fixed Asset is $13,270.08.

Calculating and Recording Depreciation Manually

There are different ways to calculate and enter depreciation. The most common is to enter depreciation annually with a Journal Entry, using the straight-line method. Be sure to talk to your accountant to get a depreciation schedule for each fixed asset.

Alternatively, you can record depreciation monthly instead of annually. Determine the total annual depreciation, divide that amount by 12, and then record the depreciation expense automatically by scheduling a monthly **Recurring Journal Entry** (see Figure 11-12).

HANDS-ON PRACTICE

Craig wants to record the depreciation for his truck monthly instead of annually. His accountant is using straight-line depreciation over five years, meaning that the expense is divided up equally over 60 months.

STEP 1.   Create a **Journal Entry** to match Figure 11-11. Use **the last day of the previous month** for the *Journal Date*, and include **your initials** in the *Journal No.* field. Debit **Depreciation (Other Expense)** for **$224.92**. In the *Description* enter **Monthly Truck Depreciation**. Credit **Truck:Depreciation** for the same amount, with the same *Description*.

STEP 2.   **Save** the journal entry using the black **Save** button in the toolbar at the bottom (don't close it).

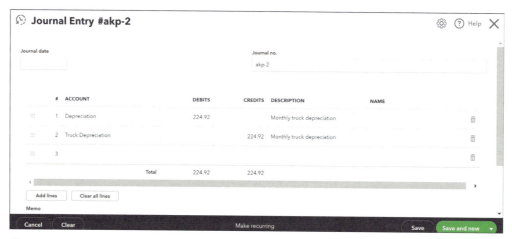

FIGURE 11-11: *Monthly Depreciation Journal Entry for the Vehicle*

STEP 3.   Click **Make Recurring**. Call the *Template Name* **Monthly Truck Depreciation** and **Schedule** the transaction **Monthly** on the **Last** day of every **1** month. No *Start Date* is needed, since the scheduled transaction will trigger automatically on the last day of this month.

We already entered one of the monthly depreciation entries over five years, so *End* the recurring journal entry after **59** occurrences.

STEP 4. Click **Save Template** to close the *Recurring Journal Entry* window.

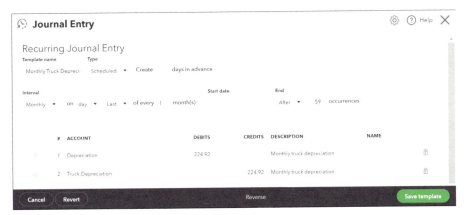

FIGURE 11-12: *A recurring scheduled journal entry for monthly depreciation*

STEP 5. Run a **Balance Sheet** report. Scroll down to the *Truck Fixed Asset control account*. Now you can see the Original Cost, Accumulated Depreciation, and Net Book Value of the truck.

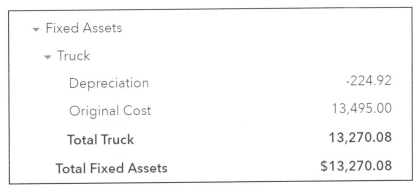

FIGURE 11-13: *Fixed Assets with Cost, Accumulated Depreciation, and Net Book Value*

PROCESSING 1099S

At the end of each year, you must prepare and send each of your eligible vendors a Form 1099-NEC or 1099-MISC. 1099 forms must be sent to your non-employee contractors, and also to the IRS along with a 1096 summary form. All 1099 forms must be submitted by the last day of January.

Form 1099-NEC is used to report **Non-employee Compensation** for payments made to vendors and subcontractors who performed business-related services for your company. Typically, "services" includes direct labor, legal and professional services, consulting, marketing, repairs, commissions, and other work performed by independent contractors.

Form 1099-MISC is used to report payments for rent, legal proceeds, royalties, prizes and awards, and other miscellaneous income.

1099 forms are sent to vendors under these circumstances:

- The vendor is a Sole Proprietor, Partnership, or LLC, but not a Corporation.
- You paid them over $600 in the calendar year.
- You paid them by cash, check, online bill pay, ACH, or direct deposit (all transactions affecting your checking account). It is not necessary to send 1099s for payments made by credit card or PayPal, as all merchant services providers send their own 1099K forms to qualifying vendors.
- They provided services or labor, not products or materials. If a payment to a vendor included materials, be sure to break those out into a separate category.

Before preparing 1099 forms, you should have a clear understanding of which vendors should receive them, as well as what types of payments are eligible for reporting on Form 1099. For current IRS instructions on this topic, please visit https://www.irs.gov/pub/irs-pdf/i1099mec.pdf.

When set up properly, QuickBooks Online automatically tracks the details of your payments to 1099 vendors. At the end of the year when you send 1099s, QuickBooks Online looks at the expense accounts you specify for subcontracted services and tallies them by vendor.

In January, you'll review your 1099-related payments by creating a **1099 Transaction Detail** report. After verifying that the report includes the all eligible vendors and covers the correct accounts, you can use QBO's 1099 wizard to print 1099s directly onto preprinted 1099 forms or file them electronically.

> **NOTE:**
>
> QuickBooks Online is only capable of preparing 1099-NEC and 1099-MISC forms. If you need to prepare other types of 1099s (e.g., 1099-INT or 1099-DIV), you will need to do so outside of QuickBooks Online.
>
> The 1099 wizard is only available between November and February.

Documenting Vendor Eligibility

Every time you hire a new service provider, have them fill in a **W-9 Form**. This will save you time chasing down documentation each January to confirm eligibility.

Vendors are required by law to provide you with this information and it is best to collect this data when you first engage the vendor. Require the vendor to complete a W-9 Form before they begin services so that their information is on file. You can download W-9 forms in a PDF version from the IRS at https://www.irs.gov/pub/irs-pdf/fw9.pdf. The IRS may reject the 1099s you submit if the taxpayer ID or address is incorrect.

FIGURE 11-14: *Invite a contractor to fill in their W-9 form electronically*

Once you have their form, add their information to QuickBooks Online by editing their vendor record. In the *Vendor Information* window, there is a field for their *Business ID No.*. Be sure to check off **Track Payments for 1099**.

QBO has an automation to make this document collection easier. To use this feature, visit the **Contractors Center** under *Payroll* in the *Left Navigation Bar*.

Click the **Add a Contractor** button on the right. Fill in the form (see Figure 11-14), which will send them an email asking them to fill out their W-9 form electronically. The integration invites the contractor to create a free **QuickBooks Online Self Employed** company file to store all their W-9 requests from all their clients in one place.

The Print/E-file 1099 Forms Wizard

QuickBooks Online uses the **1099 Wizard** to help create accurate 1099-NEC and 1099-Misc forms. Available between November and February of each year, the wizard will allow users to go through five steps to process these forms:

1. Confirm your company info.
2. Set up account mapping for the categories you use.
3. Review and update 1099 contractor info.
4. Filter eligible contractors.
5. File the forms electronically, or print 1099 and 1096 forms.

As of 2020, the IRS removed Box 7 from the earlier version of the 1099-MISC form and gave it its own form, the 1099-NEC (Non-Employee Compensation). You may need to submit both forms.

> **IMPORTANT!**
>
> Because the QuickBooks Online 1099 Wizard can only be activated between November and February of each year, and does not work with the Craig's Landscaping sample company, you will not be able to try out the feature right now. When it's time to process your forms, follow these steps:

Part 1: Confirm Your Company Information

Step 1. From the *Contractors Center*, choose **Prepare 1099s**, then click **Let's Get Started**.

Step 2. The first window will ask you to *Review Your Company Info* and confirm your company's registered name, address, phone number, and Tax ID, as shown in Figure 11-15. Click **Next**.

Part 2: 1099 Account Mapping

The next step is to map the QuickBooks Online accounts you use to track 1099 vendor payments.

FIGURE 11-15: *Review your company info*

It's important to be thorough when choosing accounts to appear on a 1099-NEC form. Common expense accounts include (but are not limited to) Cost of Labor, Contract Labor, Subcontractors, Advertising and Marketing, Legal and Professional Fees, Accounting, Consulting, Repairs and Maintenance, Continuing Education, and sometimes Prepaid Expenses.

Be thorough and select all the categories for outside services that might possibly apply, even if you didn't meet the thresholds this year. You're better off selecting more than you need than forgetting one and having to refile again later.

STEP 3. In the *Categorize Payments to Contractors* window, check **Non-employee Compensation (most common), Box 1 1099-NEC** form (see Figure 11-16). Use the drop-down arrow to open the list and choose all the possible expense and labor categories that you may potentially have used with your subcontractors through the year.

> **NOTE:**
>
> When products and services are used to track purchases, each one is linked to an expense or cost of sales category in the Chart of Accounts. Therefore, if you use Service items to track payments to 1099 vendors, make sure the correct accounts are used when the item is set up, and that they are mapped to the proper box in the 1099 Wizard.

STEP 4. If you pay rent to an independent landlord, repeat this step to choose your rent accounts for **Rents, Box 1** of the **1099-Misc** form.

STEP 5. If you made payments for Direct Sales commissions, Royalties, Medical Payments, lawsuit settlements paid to your lawyer, Fishing activity, and other relevant contractor expenses, select the appropriate boxes under *Other Payment Types*. If you're uncertain which box to map an account to, talk with your accountant or QuickBooks Online ProAdvisor.

STEP 6. Click **Next**.

FIGURE 11-16: *The Map vendor payment accounts window—your screen will vary*

Part 3: Editing 1099 Information in Vendor Records

In this next step, verify your 1099 Vendors. You can edit each 1099 vendor to confirm or update that you have their complete name, address, and identification number (e.g., social security number or federal employer identification number).

STEP 7. QuickBooks Online displays the *Review Your Contractors' Info* window showing the vendors you had marked for 1099s (see Figure 11-17). Review the *Contractor Name* column to verify that all vendors eligible for 1099s are displayed.

Step 8. Edit any incorrect vendor information or add in missing information. Even though these forms will be emailed to the contractors, the correct street address is also required for e-filing with the IRS. Click **Next**.

Part 4: Filtering Eligible Contractors

The next window will show a list of your vendors who have qualified to receive a 1099-NEC or MISC after being filtered for entity type, service provided, payment threshold, and payment method (see Figure 11-18). Confirm the list for accuracy.

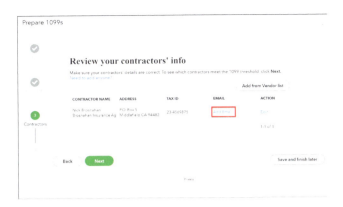

FIGURE 11-17: *Review your contractors for missing information*

Step 9. Use the *1099 Contractors That Meet Threshold* drop-down to confirm and modify vendors included or excluded according to the payment method used (credit card, debit card, PayPal, and gift card payments are excluded).

Step 10. Choose *1099 Contractors Below Threshold* to compare this list with contractors who did not meet the 1099 requirements.

Step 11. Choose *Contractors Not Marked for 1099s* to look for LLCs and Sole Proprietors who were not marked as eligible but should have been.

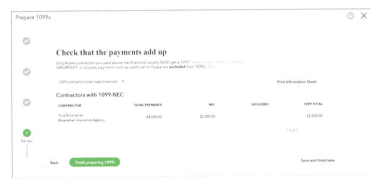

FIGURE 11-18: *Review the list of eligible vendors*

Click on a contractor name to add their W9 information.

Step 12. If a contractor is missing, click the **Back** button to go back to the account mapping and double-check your choices. When you're ready, click **Finish Preparing 1099s**.

Part 5: Submitting Your 1099 Forms

You may submit your forms to the IRS and your contractors either by printing them out yourself on pre-printed forms, or by filing them electronically. In this age, it doesn't make sense not to e-file except in special circumstances.

Step 13. After January 1, you can send your contractors digital and paper copies of their 1099 forms, and e-file with the IRS. Alternatively, you can order a 1099 print kit with paper forms to fill out and send (see Figure 11-19).

Step 14. In the E-File window, review your information to confirm you have all the correct contractors and payment totals. Click **Continue** through the rest of the payment options. Be sure to print out the reports for your own records.

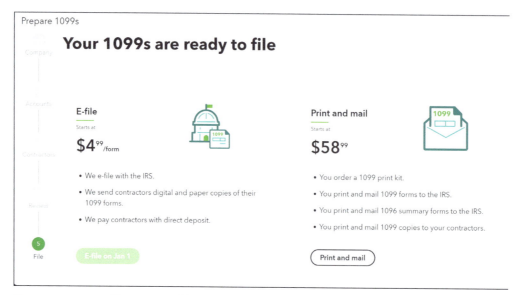

FIGURE 11-19: Choose to e-file or print your 1099 forms in January

FIGURE 11-20: e-File your 1099s

The cost to e-file your 1099s is only a few dollars apiece, with volume discounts. Intuit's E-file Service will send 1099-NEC and 1099-MISC forms to your contractors both by email and snail-mail, as well as submit to the IRS.

Some state filings are also supported, although not all. You may also have to file manually with your state.

MANAGING EQUITY

Equity refers to the valuation of a company attributed to its owners, partners, or shareholders. Equity is the money contributed to start up a company, the cumulative earnings of the business, and money withdrawn by the owners, partners, or shareholders. This activity is tracked in the *Equity* section of the *Balance Sheet*.

Different terminology is used for **Sole Proprietorships**, **LLCs**, **Partnerships**, and **S-Corps**, although the general workflow is the same for each.

Equity for Sole Proprietorships

Sole Proprietorships have the following accounts in the Equity section of the Chart of Accounts (see Figure 11-21): **Owner Draws**, **Owner Investments**, and **Owner's Equity**.

> **TIP:**
>
> Because a Sole Proprietor and their company are one and the same, you might rename **Retained Earnings**, QuickBooks Online's default account, to **Owner Equity**.

FIGURE 11-21: *Sample Equity Section—Sole Proprietorships*

Throughout the year, as owners or partners put money into and take money out of the business, you will add transactions that increase and decrease the appropriate equity accounts.

An **Owner Investments** account is used whenever the owner deposits money into the company or pays for business expenses with personal funds. The **Owner Draws** account is used whenever the owner "pays" themselves, or uses the company checking account or credit card for personal expenses.

Note that although "Owner Draws" is the common terminology, your QuickBooks Online subscription may call the default account *Owner's Pay and Personal Expenses*. You may leave the default name or update it.

> **NOTE:**
>
> If the owner considers their money in and out to be a loan and expects repayment, instead create accounts for **Other Current Asset** (if the company is loaning money to the owner) or **Other Current Liability** (if the owner is loaning money to the company).

To record an owner's investments in the company, create a *Bank Deposit* transaction to your Checking account and enter **Owner Investments** in the *Account* field (see Figure 11-22).

To record owner's withdrawals from the company, create an expense, check, or transfer. Use **Owner Draws** as the destination account (see Figure 11-23).

Owner Draws can be used to record any transaction made from company funds for personal use, such as a personal expense paid for on the company's credit card. Instead of using the actual *Payee*, use the owner's name so that you don't clutter the business's vendor list. This also consolidates all personal expenses in one place. The actual vendor name will still be referenced in the Bank Detail associated with each transaction (see Figure 11-24).

FIGURE 11-22: Record Owner Investments in the Bank Deposit window

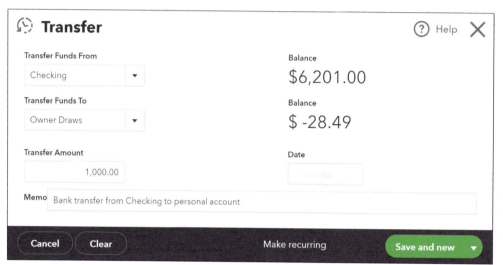

FIGURE 11-23: An Owner Draw by bank transfer

FIGURE 11-24: A personal expense paid by debit card

ADJUSTMENTS AND YEAR-END PROCEDURES | 459

> **IMPORTANT!**
>
> It's important to keep business and personal finances separate, and not **commingle** funds. Commingling makes it look like the owner is drawing additional money out of the company, or treating the business as a personal resource. The IRS calls this "piercing the corporate veil" and it's a red flag for an audit.
>
> Suggest that the business owner instead "pays" themselves every month with a reasonable lump sum. To do this, write a monthly check or make a bank transfer to their personal account, categorized as an Owner Draw. They will then appropriately pay for all personal expenses using their personal bank account or credit card, and keep these charges out of QuickBooks Online entirely.

Equity for LLCs and Partnerships

LLCs and *Partnerships* work much like Sole Proprietors, except that you need parallel accounts for each **Member** or **Partner**.

In these entities, sometimes the terms **Contributions** and **Distributions** are used instead of Investments and Draws. This is largely personal preference, or may be determined by the tax forms used (see Figure 11-25).

Although this list of accounts has a **Retained Earnings** account, it may be divided between the partners at the end of each year to keep it from accumulating a balance (see page 462). If this procedure is used, call the Investment accounts **Partner Equity** instead, as shown in Figure 11-25.

Opening Balance Equity	Equity	Opening Balance Equity
Partner 1 Draw	Equity	Partner Distributions
Partner 1 Equity	Equity	Partner's Equity
Partner 2 Draw	Equity	Partner Distributions
Partner 2 Equity	Equity	Partner's Equity
Retained Earnings	Equity	Retained Earnings

FIGURE 11-25: *Sample Equity section—Partnerships*

Equity for S-Corps

The terminology is different for equity in S-Corps. Create **Shareholder Contributions** and **Shareholder Distributions** accounts for each owner (see Figure 11-26).

FIGURE 11-26: *Shareholder Equity Accounts*

CLOSING THE BOOKS

Closing the Accounting Period

The following is a list of actions you should take at the end of each accounting period. Perform these steps as often as you close your company's books. Many companies close yearly, while some close monthly or quarterly. No matter when you close, these steps are to help you create proper reports that incorporate year-end transactions. These entries may include non-cash entries such as depreciation, prepaid expense allocations, and adjustments to equity to properly reflect the closing of the year.

At the end of the year (or month or quarter), consider doing some or all of the following:

1. **Reconcile** cash, credit card, and loan accounts with the period-end statements.

2. Enter **depreciation** entries.

3. If your business has **inventory**, perform a physical inventory count, then enter an **Inventory Qty Adjustment** transaction in QuickBooks Online. See the *Inventory* chapter for more information about adjusting inventory.

4. Confirm income and expenses were categorized properly, and move them as needed. If you are using QuickBooks Online for Accountants, use **Reclassify Transactions** in the *Accountant Tools* to change their *account, location,* and/or *class*. If not, edit each transaction manually or make adjusting journal entries.

5. If you are on the **accrual** basis of accounting and using unearned revenue workflows such as customer prepayments, prepare journal entries to adjust expenses and revenues. Ask your accountant for help with these entries.

6. Close your **equity** accounts. If your business is a partnership, enter a journal entry to **distribute net income** for the year to each of the partner's capital accounts. If your business is a sole proprietorship, enter a journal entry closing Owner Draws and Owner Investments into Owner Equity. See the sections below for more information.

7. Run **reports** for the year and verify their accuracy. Enter adjusting entries as necessary and rerun the reports.

8. Print or create a PDF and file the following reports as of your closing date: *General Ledger, Balance Sheet Standard, Statement of Cash Flows, Trial Balance, Inventory Valuation Summary,* and *Profit and Loss Standard* for the year.

9. If possible, **back up** and export your data file using **Online Backup and Restore** in QBO Advanced, or a third-party app like Rewind.com. The year-end backup should be permanent and stored in a safe place.

10. Set the **closing date** to the last day of the period and use a closing date password to prevent transactions in the closed period from being changed. See page 463 for details on setting the closing date.

Closing Equity Accounts at the End of the Fiscal Year

Step 6 above refers to closing Equity. At the end of each year, accounting principles dictate that you must enter an adjusting entry to transfer net income or loss into the **Retained Earnings** (or **Owners Equity**) account. This entry is known as the *closing entry*.

Closing Retained Earnings

QuickBooks Online automatically closes **Retained Earnings** for you. **You do not need to make this closing entry.** When you create a *Balance Sheet,* QuickBooks Online calculates the balance in Retained Earnings by adding together the total net income for all prior years. At the end of your company's fiscal year, QuickBooks Online automatically transfers the net income into Retained Earnings.

On the left side of the example in Table 11-2, notice that the *Balance Sheet* for 12/31/2024 shows net income for the year is $100,000.00. The right side shows the same *Balance Sheet*, but for the next day (January 1, 2025). Since January is in a new fiscal year, last year's net income has been automatically transferred to the Retained Earnings account.

EQUITY ON DEC 31, 2024		EQUITY ON JAN 1, 2025	
Opening Balance Equity	0.00	Opening Balance Equity	0.00
Preferred Stock	50,000.00	Preferred Stock	50,000.00
Common Stock	75,000.00	Common Stock	75,000.00
Retained Earnings	100,000.00	Retained Earnings	200,000.00
Net Income	100,000.00	Net Income	0.00
Total Equity	325,000.00	Total Equity	325,000.00

TABLE 11-2 *Example of QuickBooks Online's automatic closing entry*

Closing Sole Proprietorship Draw and Investment Accounts

On the first day of each fiscal year, create a **Journal Entry** to zero out the **Owner Draws** and **Owner Investments** accounts from the previous year, and close them into **Owner Equity (Retained Earnings)**.

To find the amounts for this journal entry, create a *Trial Balance Report* for the end of the year. Use the balance in the Owner Draws account for a journal entry to close the account. For example, if the Trial Balance shows a **debit** balance of $1,004.95 in *Owner Draws*, enter **$1,004.95** in the **credit** column on the *Owner Draws* line of this journal entry. Then enter the same figure as a **debit** to the *Owner Equity* account to make the entry balance (see Figure 11-27).

FIGURE 11-27: *Journal Entry to close Owner Draws*

Follow the same procedure to zero out **Owner Investments** as well.

The **Owner Equity** account now shows the amount of the owner's money contributed, minus the amount paid out, plus the year's profits (or minus its losses), cumulative over the life of the company.

Reconcile the Owner Draws and Owner Investments accounts to $0 on January 1 so that you have a visual confirmation that the closing entries have been created.

Closing Entries for LLCs and Partnerships

To close the **Partner Draws** and **Investments** accounts into each partner's **Equity** account, use journal entries like the one shown in Figure 11-28. Use the same process explained above to get the numbers from the year-end *Trial Balance*.

Repeat the process for each Member or Partner's accounts.

FIGURE 11-28: *Create journal entries to close Partners' Draws and Investments accounts into their Equity*

Distributing Net Income to Owners and Partners

For LLCs and Partnerships, on the first day of each fiscal year you'll zero out the balance in **Retained Earnings** and **distribute the net income** to the partners. To do this, use a journal entry to distribute the company's profits into each of the partner's profit accounts.

After making all year-end closing entries as listed on page 460, create a *Profit and Loss Report* for the fiscal year. Use the **Net Income** figure at the bottom of the *Profit and Loss Report* to create the *Journal Entry* in Figure 11-29. In this example, assume net income for the year is $50,000 and that there are two equal partners in the business.

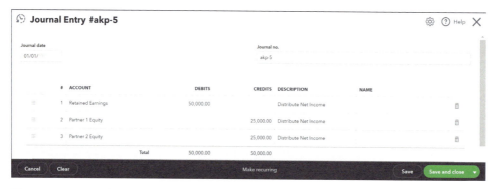

FIGURE 11-29: *Use a journal entry to distribute partners' profits*

The journal entry in Figure 11-29 debits **Retained Earnings** because QuickBooks Online automatically closes net income into Retained Earnings each year.

This technique may also be used for Sole Proprietors, since their taxable income flows through to their Schedule C and there are no Retained Earnings.

Again, note that the journal entry is dated **January 1**. The December 31 *Balance Sheet* shows **undistributed** net income for the year. If the journal entry were made on December 31, it would zero out the account, and you would never be able to see a proper year-end *Balance Sheet*. Therefore, using January 1 for this closing entry preserves the December 31 before-closing *Balance Sheet* and starts the new fiscal year fresh.

Considerations for S-Corps

With *S-Corps*, **Shareholder Contributions** and **Distributions** are closed into **Retained Earnings** as part of the cumulative profit (or loss) of the company. That way you can see how much net profit the company earned including the owner's personal financial activity.

#	ACCOUNT	DEBITS	CREDITS	DESCRIPTION	NAME	CLASS
1	Shareholder Contributions	11,000.00		To close Shareholder Contributions to RE		Overhead
2	Shareholder Distributions		4,105.10	To close Shareholder Distributions to RE		Overhead
3	Retained Earnings		6,894.90	To close Shareholder Contributions and Distributions to RE		Overhead
	Total	11,000.00	11,000.00			

FIGURE 11-30: *Close Shareholder Contributions and Distributions to Retained Earnings*

SETTING THE CLOSING DATE

It's important that your QuickBooks Online file always matches your tax returns and historic reports.

QuickBooks Online allows a Company Administrator to set a closing date that effectively locks the file so that no one can make changes to transactions dated on or before a specified date.

At the very least, you should lock the file at the end of each fiscal year after taxes are filed so that it always matches the tax returns.

You may also choose to lock the file monthly, after you perform bank reconciliations and adjusting entries for the month. For example, in February you can close the books through January 31. If management makes decisions based on **printed** financial information dated January 31, any changes to QuickBooks Online information dated before that date will cause the reports in QBO to disagree with the previously printed reports. Also, many companies submit financial information to third parties (e.g., banks or shareholders) during their tax year on a monthly or quarterly basis.

The *Closing Date* specifies that all transactions dated on or before that date are "locked." QuickBooks Online either warns against or prohibits additions, changes, or deletions to these transactions. Unless a *Closing Date Password* is set, anyone can simply ignore the warning window. You can require all users, including the bookkeeper, to enter a password before they make changes.

HANDS-ON PRACTICE

To set or modify the closing date and closing date password, follow these steps:

STEP 1. Select **Account and Settings** from the *Gear*. Go to the *Advanced* tab and click the **Pencil** next to the *Accounting section*.

STEP 2. Change the *Close the Books* slider to **On** (see Figure 11-31).

STEP 3. Enter **12/31 of this year** in the *Closing Date* field.

STEP 4. Drop down the *Allow Changes After Viewing a Warning* box and select **Allow Changes After Viewing a Warning and Entering Password**.

STEP 5. Enter **Abc1234$** in the *Password* and *Confirm Password* fields. In a real file, you will want to create a stronger password.

STEP 6. Click **Save**, then **Done**.

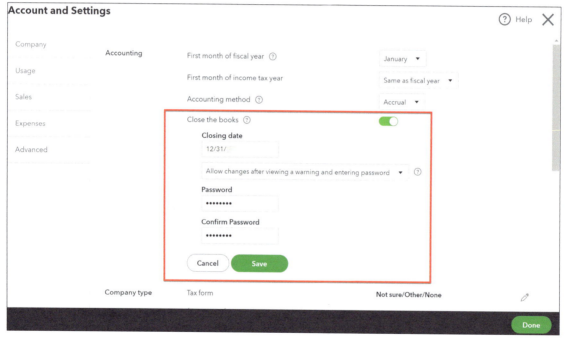

FIGURE 11-31: *Set the Closing Date and Password*

STEP 7. Create a transaction of any type dated today. When you try to save the transaction, you will see the message in Figure 11-32. Enter **Abc1234$** and click **Yes**. QuickBooks Online now requires all users to enter this password when attempting to add, change, or delete transactions dated on or before the closing date.

FIGURE 11-32: *The Closing Date warning message*

REVIEW QUESTIONS

Comprehension Questions

1. Why would you not want to make changes to transactions in QuickBooks Online that are dated in a closed accounting period?

2. How would you set up QuickBooks Online to automatically enter a depreciation journal entry each month?

3. Explain how QuickBooks Online automatically closes the year. What effect does it have on your income and expense accounts?

4. Which vendors should receive a 1099-NEC or 1099-MISC in January?

5. What are zero-dollar checks? Give an example of a situation when one would be useful.

Multiple Choice
Select the best answer for each of the following:

1. Which of the following tasks does QuickBooks Online perform automatically at year-end?
    a. Creates adjusting journal entries to the income and expense accounts that can be viewed in the *General Ledger* report.
    b. Identifies expenses that are too high in comparison with prior years.
    c. Adjusts the balance in the *Retained Earnings* account to include the net income or loss for the year.
    d. Automatically backs up the data file.

2. Entering a date in the Closing Date field accomplishes which of the following:
    a. Determines which date QuickBooks Online will use to automatically close the year.
    b. Determines which date QuickBooks Online closes your file.
    c. Locks the data file so that no unauthorized users can add, change, or delete transactions dated on or before the *Closing Date*.
    d. Prepares a closing entry on that date.

3. Which is NOT true about zero-dollar checks?
    a. No money goes in or out of the checking account.
    b. They are better than journal entries because you can capture all the detail about the transaction.
    c. You can send the check to the supplier.
    d. They can be used to affect both the Chart of Accounts and Products and Services list.

4. To make an adjustment to items as well as their associated accounts, create a:
    a. Journal Entry.
    b. Fixed Asset.
    c. Zero-Dollar Check.
    d. Recurring Transaction.

5. At the end of the year, you should perform the following:
   a. Enter depreciation entries.
   b. Perform a physical inventory.
   c. If your business is a partnership, enter a journal entry to distribute net income for the year to each of the partner's capital accounts. If your business is a sole proprietorship, enter a journal entry closing Owner Draws and Owner Investments into Owner's Equity.
   d. All of the above.

6. To track payments to a 1099 vendor and print 1099 forms accurately, you must complete all of the following, EXCEPT:
   a. Send all potentially eligible contractors a W-9 form.
   b. Set up Account and Settings to track accounts linked to 1099-related services.
   c. Select that the vendor is eligible for a 1099 on the Vendor Information card.
   d. Enter the vendor's EIN or SSN and address on the Vendor Information card.

7. The IRS may reject the 1099s you submit if:
   a. The phone number for the 1099 vendor is incorrect.
   b. The email address for the 1099 vendor is incorrect.
   c. The taxpayer ID is incorrect.
   d. The vendor did not fill out a W-9 Form.

8. Which is NOT true about setting a Closing Date?
   a. It is required for all QuickBooks Online files.
   b. You can require a password.
   c. You can opt for a warning message instead of a password.
   d. A Closing Date can only be set by an Administrator or Accountant user.

9. When you depreciate a Fixed Asset, you should categorize the entry to:
   a. A Depreciation Income account.
   b. A Depreciation Other Expense account.
   c. A Depreciation Fixed Asset contra account.
   d. Both b and c.

10. Which of the following is not true about 1099s?
    a. You need to send a W-9 to every vendor in your *Vendor List* that provides professional services to your company.
    b. You only need to submit 1099 forms to vendors who received more than $600.
    c. The 1099 Wizard helps you prepare 1099-MISC, 1099-NEC, 1099-INT, and 1099-DIV forms.
    d. You will not include payments made to contractors by credit card.

11. Which of the following is an example of a fixed asset?
    a. A $5000 high-speed copier.
    b. A $1200 laptop computer.
    c. A box of paper.
    d. All of the above.

12. Which of the following is false?
    a. Journal entries allow you to reallocate funds from one class to another.
    b. You can use journal entries to move funds from one account category to another.
    c. Journal entries can be used to transfer sales from one product or service to another one.
    d. When creating a journal entry, the debits and credits are required to balance.

Completion Statements

1. Create a _____ _____ to recategorize funds when there is no other form that will perform the same function.

2. Use Form 1099-NEC to report payments made to vendors who performed business-related _____ for your company.

3. At the end of the fiscal year, QuickBooks Online automatically calculates the balance of _____ _____ by adding together the total net income for all prior years.

4. QuickBooks Online allows you to set a(n) _____ _____ that effectively locks the file so that no changes can be made to the file on or before a certain date.

5. _____ spreads significant expenditures across several years instead of deducting the purchase all in one year.

ADJUSTMENTS AND YEAR-END PROCEDURES—APPLY YOUR KNOWLEDGE

*Log into your **Imagine Photography** class file at qbo.intuit.com.*

1. Run a **Profit and Loss by Class** report for **All Dates**. In the *Not Specified* column, there are totals for *Discounts Given* and *Shipping Income* that both belong under Walnut Creek, but the forms didn't have a field for *Class*.
    a. Create a **Journal Entry** with a *Journal Date* of **12/31 of this year** and *Journal No.* **your initials-2**. Enter the information in Table 11-3 below.
    b. Run the report again to confirm that both entries are under Walnut Creek.

ROW	ACCOUNT	DEBIT	CREDIT	DESCRIPTION	CLASS
1	Discounts Given	115		Reclassify to Walnut Creek	Walnut Creek
2	Discounts Given		115	Reclassify to Walnut Creek	(leave blank)
3	Shipping Income	32		Reclassify to Walnut Creek	(leave blank)
4	Shipping Income		32	Reclassify to Walnut Creek	Walnut Creek

TABLE 11-3 *Create a Journal Entry to reclassify Not Specified Classes*

2. Enter the annual depreciation for the Cargo Van.
    a. Create a **Journal Entry** dated **12/31 of this year**, *Journal No.* **your intials-3**. Enter the information in Table 11-4 below.

b. Run a **Balance Sheet** report for **All Dates**. Confirm that the net book value for *Total Cargo Van* is **$24,000**.

ROW	ACCOUNT	DEBIT	CREDIT	DESCRIPTION	CLASS
1	Depreciation	6000		Annual Depreciation for Cargo Van	Overhead
2	Cargo Van: Depreciation		6000	Annual Depreciation for Cargo Van	Overhead

TABLE 11-4 *Create a Journal Entry to depreciate the cargo van*

3. Make the depreciation Journal Entry from the previous step **Recurring**. Name the template **Annual Cargo Van Depreciation**. Schedule it to be automatically entered **Yearly** on the **Last day of December**. Set the *Start Date* to **12/31 of next year.** *End* the recurring journal entry **After 4 occurrences**.

4. Create a **Journal** report for **All Dates** (the Journal Report is in the *For My Accountant* section of the Reports Center). **Customize** the report to *Filter* it to only show the *Transaction Type* **Journal Entry**. **Print** the report or save it as a PDF.

5. Imagine Photography needs to repair a camera before reselling it. They spent $75 on non-inventory parts, and an additional $30 on shipping. Instead of leaving the materials cost in Cost of Goods, they want to add the parts and shipping to the inventory value of the camera. That way, when Imagine sells the refurbished camera, the automatic adjustment from Inventory Asset to Cost of Goods Sold will include the true cost of the camera and the parts used for repair. Create a zero-dollar check to subtract the parts and shipping from Cost of Goods Sold, remove the camera from Inventory Asset, and then create a new refurbished camera product that combines all costs.
    a. Create a new **Check**. Add a new *Payee* (*Vendor*) on the fly called **Inventory Adjustment**. You can use this payee for similar transactions in the future.
    b. Create a new **Bank** account on the fly with the *Detail Type* **Checking**. Name it **Clearing Account**.
    c. The *Payment Date* is **today**. The *Check No.* is **ADJ 1**. The *Tag* is **Retail**.
    d. In the *Category Details* grid, enter the *Category* **Cost of Goods Sold:Supplies & Materials**. Enter **Parts to repair camera** in the *Description* field. Tab to *Amount* and enter **-$75** (be sure it's negative). The *Class* is **Walnut Creek**.
    e. On line 2, add **Cost of Goods Sold:Shipping, Freight & Delivery – COS**. In the *Description*, enter **Overnight shipping**. Tab to *Amount* and enter **-$30** (be sure it's negative). The *Class* is **Walnut Creek**.
    f. In the *Item Details* grid, enter **Camera SR32** as the item with a *Quantity* of **-1** (make sure it's negative), and **$450** in the *Rate* field. Add the *Class* **Walnut Creek**.
    g. On the next line, create a new **Inventory Product** on the fly using the information in Table 11-5.
    h. The *Quantity* is **1** (positive), with a new total cost of **$555**. The cost of refurbished camera is now the cost of the camera plus shipping and the parts used in the repair. The sales price of the item is slightly less than the new camera.

i. The check total should be **$0**. **Save and Close** the check, then **open it again**.
j. From the *More* button in the black bar at the bottom, create a **Transaction Journal** showing the debits and credits to Inventory Asset and Cost of Goods Sold. **Save or print** the report.

FIELD	DATA
ITEM TYPE	Inventory
PRODUCT NAME	Camera SR32 Refurbished
SKU	None
CATEGORY	Products
CLASS	Walnut Creek
INITIAL QUANTITY ON HAND	0
AS OF DATE	January 1 of this year
REORDER POINT	0
INVENTORY ASSET ACCOUNT	Inventory Asset
DESCRIPTION	Camera SR32 Refurbished
SALES PRICE/RATE	650
INCOME ACCOUNT	Sales of Product Income
SALES TAX	Taxable—Standard Rate
DESCRIPTION ON PURCHASE FORMS	Camera SR32 Refurbished
COST	555
EXPENSE ACCOUNT	Cost of Goods Sold:Supplies & Materials
PREFERRED VENDOR	None

TABLE 11-5 *Create a new refurbished camera to bring into inventory*

6. Set a **Closing Date** for the file. Use **December 31 of last year**. Leave the default of **Allow changes after viewing a warning** (we don't want to accidentally lock students out of this file by using a password!).

CHAPTER 12

ADVANCED COMPANY SETUP

TOPICS

In this chapter, you will learn about the following topics:

- Migrating an Existing QuickBooks Desktop file to QuickBooks Online (page 471)
- Starting a New QuickBooks Online File From Scratch for an Existing Company (page 472)

In the beginning of this book, we learned how to set up a QuickBooks Online (QBO) subscription from scratch for a new company. But existing companies who have decided to convert from QuickBooks Desktop (QBDT) or another accounting system will already have existing data with a history that may go back years.

In this chapter, we will pick up where we left off in Chapter 2 and use a 12-Step setup process to address the considerations involved with migrating an existing company from any accounting system to QuickBooks Online.

MIGRATING AN EXISTING QUICKBOOKS DESKTOP FILE TO QUICKBOOKS ONLINE

If a company wishes to migrate to QBO from QuickBooks Desktop, their first consideration is whether their data is clean. If their reports are accurate and their lists are current, then they are a good candidate to import their existing QBDT file into QuickBooks Online. But if their reports aren't right, there are stray transactions, and their lists are full of old products and customers they haven't seen in years, they should consider a fresh start.

If they do decide to convert an existing file from QuickBooks Desktop to QBO, there are built-in tools in QuickBooks Desktop to export the company's file, as shown in Figure 12-1.

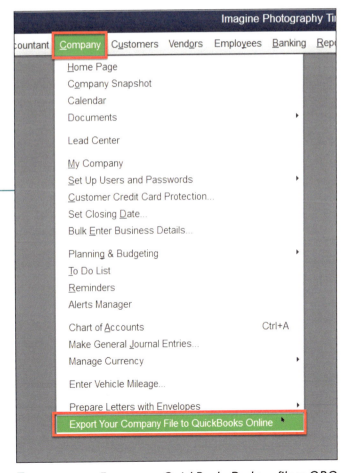

FIGURE 12-1: *Export your QuickBooks Desktop file to QBO*

471

After the data is imported, there are a few more steps in order to get up and running:

First, compare the **Balance Sheet** and **Profit and Loss Statement** in both files. Be sure to run each report for **All Dates** on an **Accrual** basis to capture the entire history. The reports should be identical, with the exception of Inventory Assets and Cost of Goods Sold, since Desktop uses Average Cost and Online uses FIFO. If there are differences, determine if you can make an adjusting entry or if you need to fix an error in QuickBooks Desktop and import the data again.

The next step is to **re-reconcile all bank accounts and credit cards**. The reconciliation status for each transaction migrates, but the reconciliation history must be reestablished. Simply repeat the most recent reconciliation, and you will be brought up to date. Note that if your Reconcile screen includes old unreconciled transactions, the historical data was not accurate and this must be addressed.

Last, connect your bank accounts to the new Banking Feed. If transactions are imported that are already in the registers, they won't show as matches and should be **Excluded**.

Some features do not import. Do a thorough analysis of your entire setup to look for other features that need to be recreated. For example, budgets and custom reports may not convert.

STARTING A NEW QUICKBOOKS ONLINE FILE FROM SCRATCH FOR AN EXISTING COMPANY

If the business decides to start a new QuickBooks company subscription from scratch without bringing over old data, you'll need to enter historic data summaries, enough that the reports are accurate as of the file start date but without replicating the problems in the old system.

This fresh start means that the opening balances on all the accounts need to match the previous accounting system and most recent tax reports. Systematically rebuilding the data creates an uncluttered, clean, current, and accurate financial record. The steps are shown in Table 12-1.

THE 12-STEP SETUP CHECKLIST

1. Choose the start date (page 473).
2. Create the company subscription and customize the settings (page 473).
3. Create the Chart of Accounts and company Lists (page 474).
4. Enter opening balances for most Balance Sheet accounts (page 474).
5. Enter outstanding transactions as of the start date (page 479).
6. If needed, enter your year-to-date income and expenses (page 481).
7. Adjust Sales Tax Payable (page 481).
8. Adjust Inventory to match physical counts and set up Fixed Assets (page 482).
9. Set up Payroll Lists and year-to-date (YTD) payroll information (page 483).
10. Verify that the Trial Balance report matches your previous trial balance (page 483).

11. Close the Opening Balance Equity account into Retained Earnings (page 483).
12. Set the Closing Date and backup your company file (page 484).

TABLE 12-1 *The 12-Step Setup Checklist*

Companies interested in year-over-year comparisons will also go one step further and enter additional Trial Balance journal entries for previous fiscal years. This allows for useful trend reporting across the company history, but adds significant complexity to the setup process because each year requires adjusting journal entries to calculate the financial evolution instead of simply duplicating previous reports.

Step 1: Choosing a Start Date

Before you create your company file, choose a *start date*. Your start date is the day before you start using QuickBooks Online to track your daily transactions. You will need complete information for your opening balances as of this date. If you file taxes on a calendar-year basis, the best start date for most companies is December 31. If you file taxes on a fiscal year, choose the last day of your fiscal year as your start date.

Do not use January 1 (or the first day of your fiscal year) for your start date, because doing so would cause the opening balances to affect your first year's *Profit and Loss Report*. This could affect your taxes and distort the picture of the company's financial history.

If you are starting a new business, your start date is the day you formed the company.

In order for your records to be complete and accurate, you will need to enter all of the transactions (checks, invoices, deposits, etc.) between your start date and the day you perform the QuickBooks Online setup. For example, if you begin setting up the QuickBooks Online company file on January 5 with a start date of December 31, you will need to enter all the business activity from January 1 through January 5.

Because of this, your start date has a big impact on how much work you will do during setup. If you do not want to go back to the end of last year, choose a more recent date, such as the end of last quarter or the end of last month.

> **TIP:**
>
> During the setup process, QuickBooks Online's **Banking Feed** can speed up historic data entry. By creating **Rules**, you can import routine expenses automatically, instead of manually creating each one (see page 270). This can save hours of time with high-volume companies and when creating a new file late in the year.

Step 2: Create the Company Subscription and Customize the Settings

New QuickBooks Online files are created by subscribing at quickbooks.intuit.com. If you are a member of Intuit's ProAdvisor Program, you can manage multiple client files, and receive a discount on subscriptions.

At the end of Chapter 1, we created your company file for Imagine Photography. During the file setup process, the wizard walked you through questions about the company.

In Chapter 2 we customized the **Account and Settings** starting on page 38 so that *Craig's Landscaping* and *Imagine Photography* were ready to do business. We also explored additional settings throughout the book as we discussed the use of each QBO feature.

Step 3: Setting Up the Chart of Accounts and Other Lists

The **Chart of Accounts** (COA) is one of the most important lists in QuickBooks Online. It is a list of all the accounts in the General Ledger. We set up the COA in Chapter 2 on page 45. If you are not sure how to design your Chart of Accounts, ask your accountant or QuickBooks ProAdvisor for help.

At this point in the 12-Step Setup process, you would also enter additional lists, such as **Products and Services**, **Customers**, and **Vendors**. These records can be entered manually, or imported from existing lists in Excel or .csv formats, as we saw on page 36.

We created the Products and Services List on page 56. Please refer to page 104 and page 157 for more information on adding customers and vendors.

Step 4: Entering Opening Balances

After you've set up your Chart of Accounts, you're ready to enter your opening balances so that your new file matches your previous reports and tax records. To set up your opening balances, you will need to gather several documents prepared as of your start date.

Gathering Your Information

The following is a list of items needed to complete your setup. Collect this information before you begin.

1. **Trial Balance**: Ask your accountant to provide you with a trial balance for your start date. If your start date is the end of your fiscal year, ask your accountant for an "after-closing" trial balance. The term "after-closing" means "after all of the income and expenses have been closed into Retained Earnings."

This report will be used at the end of the process to confirm that all of your setup steps were performed correctly.

If a trial balance is not available, use an after-closing *Balance Sheet* and a year-to-date *Profit and Loss Statement* as of your start date. Table 12-2 shows a sample after-closing trial balance on the start date of 12/31.

SAMPLE NEW COMPANY		
TRIAL BALANCE, DECEMBER 31		
	DEBIT	**CREDIT**
Checking	$17,959.60	
Money Market	14,100.00	
Savings	500.00	
Accounts Receivable	1,253.41	
Inventory	7,158.67	
Furniture and Equipment	13,250.00	
Fixed Assets:Accumulated Depreciation		$1,500.00
Accounts Payable		142.00
Business Visa		3,450.00

SAMPLE NEW COMPANY

TRIAL BALANCE, DECEMBER 31

	DEBIT	CREDIT
Payroll Liabilities:Payroll Taxes		368.00
Sales Tax Payable		141.79
Line of Credit		6,700.00
Truck Loan		12,000.00
Common Stock		10,000.00
Retained Earnings		19,919.89
TOTAL	$54,221.68	$54,221.68

TABLE 12-2 *Sample Trial Balance as of a December 31 start date*

2. **Bank Statements** (for all bank accounts): For each bank account and credit card, you will need the most recent statement prior to your start date. For example, if your start date is 12/31, you will need the 12/31 statements for all of your accounts.

   You will use the Bank Statements to confirm your bank and credit card balances after setting up the Banking Feed.

3. **Outstanding Checks and Deposits**: You'll need a list of all of your checks and deposits that have not cleared the bank as of the bank statement dated on or prior to your start date.

OUTSTANDING DEPOSITS ON 12/31		
Date	Description	Amount
12/30	Customer Prepayment	$3,000.00

OUTSTANDING CHECKS ON 12/31			
Check No.	Date Paid	Payee	Amount
324	12/26	National Bank	$1000.00

TABLE 12-3 *Outstanding deposits and checks on the start date*

4. **Unpaid Bills**: List each vendor bill by date of the bill, amount due, and what items or expenses you purchased on the bill (see Table 12-4).

BILL NUMBER	BILL DATE	VENDOR	AMT. DUE	ACCOUNT/ITEM	JOB	CLASS	TERMS
2342	12/21	Gandhi Video, LLC	$142.00	Subcontractors Expense	Nayo Garcia (Not Billable)	San Jose	Net 30

TABLE 12-4 *Unpaid bills as of the company's start date*

5. **Open Invoices**: List each customer invoice including the date of the invoice, amount due, and the items sold on the invoice (see Table 12-5).

INV #	INVOICE DATE	CUSTOMER	CLASS	TERMS	ITEM	QTY	AMT DUE
3947	12/18	Nayo Garcia	San Jose	Net 30	Camera 8.25% Sales Tax Total	1	$695.99 $57.42 $753.41
4003	12/21	Liz Kildal: Branch Opening	San Jose	Net 30	Photographer $125/hr Total	4	$500.00 $500.00

TABLE 12-5 *Open Invoices on Imagine Photography's start date*

6. **Employee list and W-4 information for each employee**: Gather complete name, address, social security number, and withholding information for each employee. All payroll setup instructions are covered in the "Payroll Setup" chapter beginning on page 487.

> **NOTE:**
>
> The next three payroll-related lists are necessary only if your start date is in the middle of a calendar year and you want to track payroll details with QuickBooks Online.
>
> If your start date is 12/31, skip these lists unless you want to use QuickBooks Online to create payroll reports (Form 940, Form 941, or W-2s) for the previous year. Instead, enter the opening balances for unpaid payroll liabilities as shown later in this section.

7. **Payroll Liabilities**: List the amount due for each of your payroll liabilities as of your start date. For example, list the amounts due for federal withholding tax, social security (employer), social security (employee), and any other payroll liabilities.

8. **Year-to-Date Payroll Detail by Employee**: If your start date is not 12/31 and you want QuickBooks Online to track your payroll, you will need gross earnings, withholdings, employer taxes, and any other deductions for each employee so far this year. For the most detail, this list should include each employee's earnings for each month this year.

9. **Year-to-Date Payroll Tax Payments**: If your start date is not 12/31, list each payroll tax payment made during the year.

10. **Physical Inventory by Inventory product**: List the quantity and cost for each product in inventory (see Table 12-6).

PHYSICAL INVENTORY ON 12/31		
ITEM	QTY. ON HAND	VALUE
Camera	10	$4,500.00
Case	25	1,125.00
Frame	25	53.75
Lenses	8	1,479.92

TABLE 12-6 *Physical inventory on hand as of the company's start date*

> **TIP:**
>
> If you don't have actual counts and costs for your inventory, you'll need to estimate. However, the accuracy of your reports will be compromised if you don't have accurate setup numbers. If possible, we strongly recommend conducting a physical inventory as of your QuickBooks Online start date.

Understanding Opening Balance Equity

The **Opening Balance Equity account** is created automatically by QuickBooks Online as the "holding tank" for your starting balances as you set up your new file. As you enter the existing balances for your assets and liabilities as of the start date of your file, offset the amounts to **Opening Balance Equity**.

Then, after you have entered all of the opening balances, "close" Opening Balance Equity by moving the total to **Retained Earnings** (or **Owner's Equity**). Finish by reconciling OBE to $0.

After the set up process is complete, the Opening Balance Equity account must always maintain a zero balance.

> **TIP:**
>
> By using the **Opening Balance Equity** account during setup, you will be able to quickly access the detail of your setup transactions by looking at the **Opening Balance Equity register**.

Opening Balances for Accounts

To enter opening balances, you can either edit the account category or create a **Journal Entry**.

A journal entry is the preferred method because it allows you to set up the Opening Balances for several accounts at once. With this method, the starting balance on your first reconciliation will be zero, with the *Opening Balance Journal Entry* waiting in the Reconciliation window to be checked off.

> **IMPORTANT!**
>
> Do not enter opening balances for bank accounts and credit cards. When you connect each financial institution to QBO and begin to download transactions, an Opening Balance Equity entry will be created for you. Note that these automatic entries are pre-reconciled, and usually need to be edited to compensate for outstanding checks and other open transactions.

Directly Editing the Account

QuickBooks Online allows you to directly enter opening balances for some of your Balance Sheet accounts, as shown in Figure 12-2. When you use these fields, QBO will automatically create the correct type of transaction and offset the debits and credits for you.

Do not use this method to enter the opening balances for *Accounts Receivable, Undeposited Funds, Accounts Payable, Sales Tax Payable,* and *Opening Balance Equity.* Those will be created as a result of the other setup steps in this chapter.

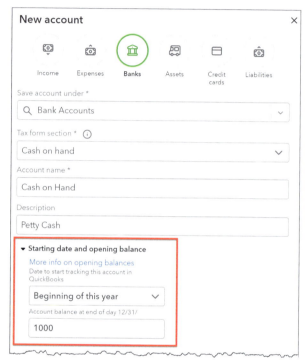

FIGURE 12-2: Enter an opening balance in the Account details window

---

ACCOUNTING BEHIND THE SCENES:

When you enter an opening balance from within an account info window, a transaction posts to **Opening Balance Equity**. The **Debit** or **Credit** will depend on the type of account.

TRANSACTION TYPE	MEMO/DESCRIPTION	ACCOUNT	DEBIT	CREDIT
Deposit	Opening Balance	Cash on hand	$1,000.00	
		Opening Balance Equity		$1,000.00
			$1,000.00	$1,000.00

Recording Opening Balances Using a Journal Entry

You can use a journal entry to record some, but not all, of your opening balances. This is the easiest way to set up the opening balances on assets and liabilities including loans, lines of credit, fixed asset values, and accumulated depreciation.

Do not include the following accounts in the journal entry: Accounts Receivable, Accounts Payable, Inventory Asset, Sales Tax Payable, and Retained Earnings, as these opening balances will be created later in the 12-Step setup. For example, you'll exclude Accounts Receivable and Accounts Payable because recreating open *Invoices* and *Bills* will populate the balances in these accounts.

Because total debits always equal total credits, the total of the debit column and the total of the credit column must be equal, or you will not be able to save the journal entry. As you create the journal entry, QuickBooks Online automatically calculates the amount required to make these entries balance as you add each new line. To override the amount, simply type the correct number in the correct column and keep going. On the last line of this journal entry, categorize the final amount to the **Opening Balance Equity** account, as shown in Figure 12-3. This amount may be a debit or a credit, depending on the other figures in the entry.

Although the **Trial Balance** report didn't show any balance in Opening Balance Equity, this account is used during setup as a placeholder. At the end of the setup process, you'll transfer the balance from this account into Retained Earnings, as shown later in the setup steps.

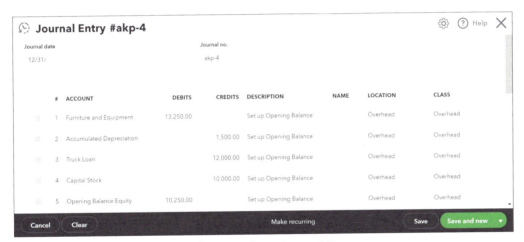

FIGURE 12-3: *Enter opening balances using a Journal Entry*

Step 5: Entering Open Transactions

When you set up your company file, it is important that you enter all open **Invoices**, **Credit Memos**, **Bills**, and **Vendor Credits** separately. Also enter remaining quantities on open Purchase Orders and Estimates. QuickBooks Online needs the details of the transactions, such as the date, terms, and customer or vendor information, to prepare accurate aging reports (e.g., *Unpaid Bills Detail* and *A/R Aging Summary*).

When you receive money against one of your prior year invoices or pay a prior year bill, you will match the receipts and payments to their actual invoices and bills.

Enter Outstanding Checks and Deposits

To help with the first bank reconciliations, you need all the outstanding checks and deposits in QuickBooks Online so that you can match them with your bank statement as they clear after the start date. If you don't enter the individual transactions, you won't see them in the QuickBooks Online bank reconciliation window. In addition, if a transaction never clears the bank, you won't know the transaction is missing without going back to your old records.

For each of your bank accounts and credit cards, enter all uncleared transactions in the account register. Enter each outstanding check and deposit with the date the check was written or the deposit made.

You can post each transaction with the account category **Opening Balance Equity**. It is not necessary to code these entries to their actual income or expense, because your first Profit and Loss Statement begins after the date of these transactions.

FIGURE 12-4: Enter outstanding checks to Opening Balance Equity

> **IMPORTANT!**
>
> After you enter your outstanding checks and deposits and connect your bank account to the Banking Feed, look at the bank account register(s). You'll see an already-reconciled Opening Balance Equity transaction that was automatically created by QuickBooks Online when you connected the bank. It doesn't include the open transactions, so you will need to update the amount to compensate for the pending bank transactions you just created.

Enter Open Bills (Accounts Payable)

Enter your **Unpaid Bills** and **Vendor Credits** as of the start date. By entering the actual individual bills, you can preserve detailed job costing and class tracking data if needed. Use the original date of the bill (or credit) along with all of the details (terms, vendor, items, etc.) of the bill.

Enter Open Invoices (Accounts Receivable)

Enter all open **Invoices** and **Credit Memos** as of the start date. Enter each one with its original date and details (terms, customer, products & services, etc.).

Enter Open Purchase Orders

If you have open **Purchase Orders**, enter them individually, just as you did with bills, vendor credits, invoices, and credit memos. Enter each purchase order with its original date and all of its details. If you have partially received items on the purchase order, enter only the quantities yet to be received from the vendor as of the start date of your file.

Enter Open Estimates

If you have open **Estimates**, enter them individually, just as you did with the other accounts receivable transactions. Enter each estimate with its original date and all of its details. If you have already progress-invoiced a portion of the estimate, enter only the remaining amount to be invoiced as of the file start date.

Step 6: Entering Year-to-Date Income and Expenses

Income and Expense accounts are totaled at the end of the fiscal year as the Net Profit (or Loss) and then combined with Retained Earnings (see page 461). Later in the 12-Step process you will see the Income and Expense accounts zeroed out and their balances combined with Retained Earnings on the first day of your fiscal year.

However, when your company file has a start date that is *not* the end of the fiscal year, the year-to-date amounts for the Income and Expense accounts will need to be entered so that they match the *Profit and Loss Statement* from the previous accounting system. This may involve calculating and adjusting for the difference between the P&L category totals and the totals from your outstanding invoices and bills. Enter these compensating entries in a journal entry (see Figure 12-5).

All the income amounts should be entered into the **Credits** column. All the expense amounts should be entered into the **Debits** column. Use your **Opening Balance Equity** account to record your net income (or loss).

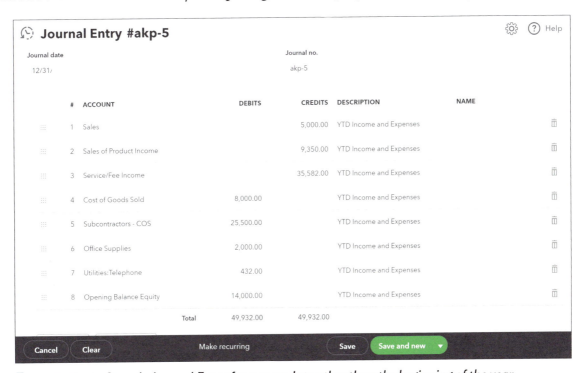

FIGURE 12-5: *Sample Journal Entry for a start date other than the beginning of the year*

Step 7: Adjusting Sales Tax Payable

To enter the opening balance for ***Sales Tax Payable***, begin by looking at the *Sales Tax Center* to view the activity. Notice the total for the open invoices you just entered. This is your **uncollected** tax. The tax on sales receipts and closed invoices has already been **collected**, but you are not entering those transactions into QBO. Since the total Sales Tax Liability is usually accrual-based, it is a combination of the **collected** tax and the **uncollected** tax. You will need to subtract the current balance in the account (the **uncollected** tax) from the amount shown on the trial balance from your accountant (or your 12/31 sales tax return) to arrive at the unpaid **collected** tax.

Total Tax Due	= Collected Tax + Uncollected Tax
Collected Tax	= Amounts on closed invoices and sales receipts, but not yet paid
Uncollected Tax	= Tax on Open Invoices
. . . therefore . . .	
Adjustment Amount	= Total Tax Due—Uncollected Tax

EQUATION 12-1 *Calculating the amount of your sales tax adjustment*

For example, you know from the trial balance that the Total Sales Tax Due is $141.79. The Uncollected Tax on Invoice #3947 was $57.42. By subtracting the Uncollected Sales Tax ($57.42) from the Total Tax Due ($141.79), you can calculate the Collected Tax, $84.37.

Create a journal entry dated 12/31 with a **sales tax adjustment** for the collected tax amount, as shown in Figure 12-6. If you pay sales tax to more than one sales tax agency, you will need to split the credits into a separate line for each agency.

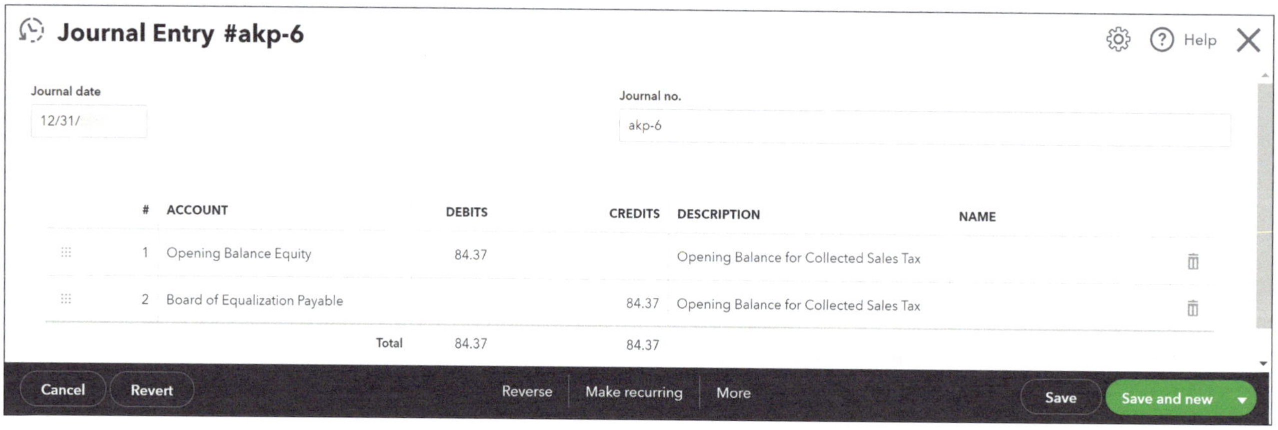

FIGURE 12-6: *A Sales Tax Adjustment*

Step 8: Adjusting Inventory and Setting Up Fixed Assets

Adjust Inventory

If you have inventory, you will need to create an ***inventory adjustment*** to enter the actual quantity and value on hand as of your start date. This is done *after* you enter your outstanding checks, bills and invoices, so that the actual inventory count and costs will be accurate even if some of the pending transactions include inventory items.

Open the *Products and Services List* to view the current stock status of each inventory item. Then use an **Inventory Qty Adjustment** to update the quantity on hand of each item so that inventory agrees with the physical inventory counts.

After inventory counts have been corrected, confirm that the **Inventory Asset** and **Cost of Goods Sold:Supplies & Materials** accounts agree with the company's trial balance as of your start date. If they do not, adjust both accounts against Opening Balance Equity.

Add Fixed Assets

Follow the instructions on page 448 to set up the company's Fixed Assets, unless you entered their values in the journal entry in Step 4 above.

Step 9: Set Up Payroll with YTD Payroll Information

Setting up payroll in QuickBooks Online is a lengthy and involved process. Refer to the "Payroll Setup" chapter beginning on page 487 for a step-by-step walkthrough.

Step 10: Verifying Your Trial Balance

The last step before completing the set-up process is to confirm that the account balances in QuickBooks Online match your accountant's Trial Balance.

Run a Trial Balance report for the company start date. Be sure to match the reporting basis for Cash or Accrual.

Your **Trial Balance** may look slightly different from your accountant's report because of the balances in the income and expense accounts as well as in **Opening Balance Equity**. The income and expense accounts have balances because you just entered the **Open Invoices** and **Unpaid Bills** for the prior year.

If you see other differences in the numbers, review your work to discover anything you might have missed, or discuss the situation with the accountant.

If you have to make any further adjusting entries to force the two reports to match, create a journal entry. Calculate the differences for each account category, and offset the remainder to Opening Balance Equity.

Step 11: Closing Opening Balance Equity

Once you have verified your Trial Balance report to your accountant's report, use a **Journal Entry** to transfer (close) the starting balances in **Opening Balance Equity (OBE)** into **Retained Earnings**.

Retained Earnings is the account that automatically tracks the cumulative undistributed income over the course of a company's history. All the opening balances represent the assets and liabilities of the company to date (i.e., the money in the bank, tied up in inventory and fixed assets, and owed on debts).

At the end of the setup process, we move the total of **Opening Balance Equity** into **Retained Earnings** so that you have this total as of the start date. Look at the Opening Balance Equity register or a Balance Sheet to find the balance, and create a journal entry debiting and crediting the amount correctly to zero out OBE.

Since Opening Balance Equity is only used for the file setup process, its balance will remain at zero in the future. If you see a balance here later, look for transaction errors.

FIGURE 12-7: *Journal Entry to close Opening Balance Equity into Retained Earnings*

Step 12: Setting the Closing Date

Now that you have entered all of your opening balances in the file, set the closing date to the file's start date. For details on setting the **Closing Date** and the **Closing Date password**, see page 463.

REVIEW QUESTIONS

Comprehension Questions

1. What information should you gather before setting up a QuickBooks Online file?
2. Explain how the Opening Balance Equity account is used when you set up a new bank account in the Chart of Accounts.
3. Explain how you would adjust your inventory to agree with the Trial Balance from the accountant.
4. Explain the importance of entering your outstanding checks as of the Start Date into the Checking account.
5. Why is it important to enter all unpaid Invoices and Bills?

Multiple Choice

Select the best answer(s) for each of the following:

1. Your company has decided to begin using QuickBooks Online in January at the beginning of the calendar year, which is also the fiscal year. The best start date for your company file setup is:
   a. January 1.
   b. The date when you first start entering data in QuickBooks Online.
   c. December 31 of the prior year.
   d. There is no best start date, you can use whatever date is convenient.

2. The best way to set up A/R and A/P balances in QuickBooks Online is to:
   a. Enter the total amount of A/R and A/P on a *Journal Entry* dated on your start date.
   b. Enter the balance of each account by editing the accounts in the *Chart of Accounts*.
   c. Use a special account called A/R Setup (or A/P Setup) to record the opening balances.
   d. Enter a separate invoice for each open invoice and enter a separate bill for each unpaid bill.

3. Setting up a company file does not include:
   a. Obtaining a business license.
   b. Selecting the appropriate chart of accounts for your type of business.
   c. Adding accounts to the chart of accounts.
   d. Entering invoices.

4. To ensure the accuracy of the information entered during setup, it is important to:
   a. Know your Retained Earnings.
   b. Verify that your *Trial Balance* matches the one provided by your accountant.
   c. Start at the beginning of the fiscal period.
   d. Know everything there is to know about accounting.

5. Close Opening Balance Equity into Retained Earnings by:
   a. Starting to enter new daily transactions.
   b. Creating a journal entry.
   c. Setting the Closing Date. QuickBooks Online will then make the entry for you.
   d. Wait until the first day of the next fiscal year, and QBO will make the entry for you.

6. When verifying your setup, create a Balance Sheet and verify that Retained Earnings matches the Trial Balance from the accountant. If your start date is 12/31, what date should you use on this Balance Sheet?
   a. Always use the Start Date.
   b. December 31.
   c. January 1.
   d. December 30.

7. To set up the opening balance in your Sales Tax Payable account, wait until after you've entered your open invoices. Then adjust the Sales Tax Payable account for the additional sales tax due. Why is this adjustment necessary?
   a. Because Opening Balance Equity is not involved.
   b. Because the total amount in Sales Tax Payable is the sum of the *uncollected* sales tax (from the open invoices) plus the *collected* sales tax. Since you already entered the open invoices, the Sales Tax Payable account only has the *uncollected* sales tax and you have to add in the *collected* sales tax by adjusting the account balance.
   c. Because there is no other way to set up the opening balance in Sales Tax Payable.
   d. All of the above.

8. If you have an open invoice for an inventory item on your start date, to properly set up your inventory balances (Quantity and Value):
   a. Use a Journal Entry to debit Inventory Asset for the total value of the inventory.
   b. Use an Inventory Quantity Adjustment transaction *after* you enter in your opening invoices and bills.
   c. Use an Inventory Quantity Adjustment transaction *before* you enter in your opening invoices and bills.
   d. Use the *Opening Balance* field in the *Edit Account* window.

Completion Statements

1. At the end of your setup, close the _____ _____ _____ account into Retained Earnings.

2. You can use a(n) _____ _____ to record multiple accounts' opening balances at one time.

3. The account balances on your _____ _____ from your previous books and your QuickBooks Online file should match at the end of your file setup.

CHAPTER 13

PAYROLL SETUP

TOPICS

In this chapter, you will learn about the following topics:

- Intuit's Payroll Subscriptions (page 488)
- Getting Help With Payroll (page 488)
- Checklist for Setting Up Payroll (page 489)
- The Accounting Behind the Scenes (page 489)
- Payroll Accounts (page 490)
- Payroll Items (page 491)
- The Payroll Setup Wizard (page 493)
- Setting Up a Payroll Subscription (page 493)
- Adding Employees (page 495)
- Developing Company Pay Policies (page 498)
- Specifying Benefit Deductions and Contributions (page 502)
- Customizing the Payroll Settings (page 504)
- The Payroll Overview (page 515)

> **OPEN THIS FILE:**
>
> Because we cannot set up payroll in the Craig's Landscaping sample file, we will set up payroll using **Imagine Photography** from the *Apply Your Knowledge* exercise at the end of the chapter. Your student subscription comes with a free 30-day trial of QuickBooks Online Payroll. Note that you must finish these exercises within 30 days or pay for the subscription to continue.

In this chapter, you will learn how to set up QuickBooks Online to track your **Payroll**. In order to use QuickBooks Online to track payroll, you must properly set up your **Payroll subscription**, **policies**, **employees**, and if necessary, *year-to-date payroll history*.

There are several advantages to subscribing to Intuit's automated payroll subscriptions:

- Payroll integrates with the QuickBooks Time app.

- The Workforce website at workforce.intuit.com provides employees with electronic paystubs and a self-service portal. The guided payroll setup includes the option to invite employees to enter their own personal information, W4 tax withholding details, and direct deposit bank information.

- Running payroll right inside QuickBooks Online creates a seamless business management solution.

If you plan to utilize an outside payroll service, you will still need to set up the Chart of Accounts to correctly record your payroll transactions. Most third-party payroll services will import data into QuickBooks Online, but some may require you to manually enter payroll journal entries yourself.

> **IMPORTANT!**
>
> Intuit frequently enhances their Payroll options, and there will be changes since the publication of this book. These instructions will not exactly match your interface, but you will be able to look around and find the related content.

INTUIT'S PAYROLL SUBSCRIPTIONS

You have three subscription choices for using QuickBooks Online to track payroll: **Core**, **Premium**, and **Elite**. For detailed information on the differences between these subscription options, go to https://quickbooks.intuit.com/payroll/pricing/.

- **Core** provides full-service payroll including direct deposit, taxes paid for you, 1099 e-filing, and Auto Payroll.

- **Premium** also includes same-day direct deposit, QuickBooks Time for time tracking, and an expert to review your setup.

- **Elite** features tax penalty protection, enhanced time tracking, an HR portal, and setup is done for you.

GETTING HELP WITH PAYROLL

Running payroll for a company is not a simple task. Not only do you have to learn how to set up the software correctly, but every state and every industry has its own set of requirements.

It's a good idea to get help when setting up a company's payroll. Consult with a ProAdvisor, talk to your accountant, and be sure to take advantage of the support that comes with your paid QuickBooks Payroll subscription.

Some companies enroll in the Elite program for a few months until they have confidence that payroll is running properly, and then downgrade to Premium or Core.

When you do need assistance, use QuickBooks Online's help, or look for a popup in the lower right corner like the one in Figure 13-1. There are several variations for this alert, but it consistently appears in the same location on the *Payroll Overview* tab.

FIGURE 13-1: *Getting help from QuickBooks Payroll support*

CHECKLIST FOR SETTING UP PAYROLL

Like the setup of your company file, the proper setup of your **Payroll** is the most important factor in getting it to work well for you. Use the checklist in Table 13-1 as a guide.

PAYROLL SETUP CHECKLIST

1. **Gather information** about each of your employees, including their name, address, social security number, and W-4 information.
2. **Subscribe** to QuickBooks Online Payroll.
3. Using the **Payroll Setup Wizard**, create company policies, add employees, and assign employee defaults.
4. If setting up mid-year, **enter the year-to-date history** for each employee and all liability payments.
5. **Edit Payroll Items** to modify the way they map to the Chart of Accounts.
6. **Verify** all Payroll settings and employee setup.

TABLE 13-1 *Payroll Setup Checklist*

> **NOTE:**
>
> Each of your employees must complete **IRS Form W-4** upon hire. The IRS requires employees to provide you with their name, address, social security number, and withholding information on this form. The Internal Revenue service has many payroll forms available online at **www.irs.gov.** For form W-4, enter **W4** in *Search* field. Note that the W-4 form was updated in 2020; be sure not to give employees older versions of the form.

THE ACCOUNTING BEHIND THE SCENES

Before you begin setting up Payroll, it's important to understand the accounting behind the scenes. QuickBooks Online automatically makes all the accounting entries when you process paychecks and payroll liability payments.

Payroll Items are used by the system to track the compensation, additions, deductions, and employer-paid expenses listed on the employee's paycheck. These items include wages, commissions, tips, benefits, taxes, dues, retirement plans, garnishments, reimbursements, and other less common types.

Payroll Items are connected to the Chart of Accounts so that as paychecks are created, the accounting behind the scenes is handled automatically. This way, QuickBooks Online tracks the detail it needs to calculate paychecks, look up taxes in the tax table, prepare detailed reports, submit your payroll tax forms, and create the appropriate entries in the General Ledger.

Payroll Tax Tables

Payroll Tax Tables include the tax rates necessary to calculate an employee's paycheck. One of the benefits of a QuickBooks Online Payroll service subscription is that your Federal tax tables always stay up to date automatically. You may have to customize your State tables annually.

QuickBooks Online Payroll automatically calculates the amounts of taxes that are withheld from an employee's check (e.g., Federal and State income tax) as well as the amounts of taxes the company must pay on behalf of the employee (e.g., Federal and State unemployment tax). The Payroll Tax Tables also include data that updates the forms that are filed directly from QuickBooks Online (i.e., 940, 941, and W-2).

Payroll Accounts

When you perform your first Payroll run, QuickBooks Online automatically creates all its liability and expense account categories in your Chart of Accounts. You can later customize this list if needed, so that they appear on your *Balance Sheet* and *Profit and Loss* reports the way your company stakeholders would like to see them. If you are not sure which accounts you should include, ask your accountant.

If you are using a third-party payroll provider, you can also create these accounts manually.

Liability Accounts

Payroll Liability accounts gather deductions from paychecks that are passed through to other agencies, like taxes and employee contributions including retirement and health insurance. A sample setup appears in Figure 13-2—yours will not match.

☐	Payroll Liabilities	Other Current Liabilities	Other Current Liabilities
☐	Federal Taxes (941/944)	Other Current Liabilities	Other Current Liabilities
☐	Federal Unemployment (940)	Other Current Liabilities	Other Current Liabilities
☐	Fidelity	Other Current Liabilities	Payroll Clearing
☐	OR Employment Taxes	Other Current Liabilities	Other Current Liabilities
☐	OR Income Tax	Other Current Liabilities	Other Current Liabilities
☐	OR Statewide Transit Taxes	Other Current Liabilities	Other Current Liabilities
☐	OR Transit Taxes	Other Current Liabilities	Other Current Liabilities
☐	Payroll Adjustment	Other Current Liabilities	Other Current Liabilities
☐	Regence BC/BS Dental	Other Current Liabilities	Other Current Liabilities
☐	Regence BC/BS Dental Pre-Tax	Other Current Liabilities	Other Current Liabilities
☐	Regence BC/BS Medical	Other Current Liabilities	Other Current Liabilities

FIGURE 13-2: *Sample Payroll Liability Accounts—your screen will not match*

Expense Accounts for Payroll

Payroll Expense accounts show the costs the company incurs on behalf of employee wages, benefits, and fees. A sample setup appears in Figure 13-3—yours will not exactly match.

Payroll Items

QBO uses **Payroll Items** to map paychecks to appropriate payroll accounts. This is important because many taxes and benefits include employee contributions that are matched by the company.

Payroll Expenses	Expenses	Payroll Expenses
Company Contributions	Expenses	Payroll Expenses
Health Insurance	Expenses	Payroll Expenses
Retirement	Expenses	Payroll Expenses
Payroll Fees	Expenses	Payroll Expenses
Taxes	Expenses	Taxes Paid
Wages	Expenses	Payroll Expenses

FIGURE 13-3: Sample Payroll Expense Accounts—your screen will not match

Earnings:

Earnings items track regular wages, overtime, sick leave, and vacation pay. For example, if you pay an employee for 32 regular hours and 8 hours of vacation, you'll use a regular pay item and a vacation pay item, with the corresponding number of hours for each.

There are several types of Earnings:

- **Salary Wage** items are used to track payments of gross wages to employees who are paid a fixed annual amount regardless of actual hours worked, divided evenly across the number of pay periods in the year. Since these items represent company expenses, they increase (debit) an expense account, usually Wages or Officer's Compensation.

- **Hourly Wage** items are used to track payments to employees who are paid for actual hours worked. Just like the Salary items, these items increase (debit) an expense account, usually Wages or Officer's Compensation.

- **Commission** items are used to track wages based on sales. For example, you would create a Sales Rep report and calculate the commission based on the information in the report, then enter the calculated amount in the employee's next paycheck. Commission items increase (debit) an expense account, usually Wages or Commissions.

- **Bonus** items are used to track employee performance incentives or end-of-year holiday bonuses. You can decide whether the company grosses up the bonus to pay the tax so that the employees receive a specific dollar amount, or whether taxes will be taken out of the bonus, reducing the total. Bonus items increase (debit) an expense account, usually Wages or Bonuses.

> **NOTE:**
>
> QuickBooks Online automatically accumulates sick and vacation hours, but it does not record a liability for this unpaid expense in the General Ledger. If you want to accrue expenses and liabilities for unpaid sick and vacation time, you'll need to make an adjustment using a journal entry.

Additions, Deductions, and Contributions:

Addition items are used to track amounts added to paychecks beyond gross wages. For example, you might set up an Addition item to track tips or employee expense reimbursements. Additions increase (debit) an expense account. Some Addition items can be added before or after taxes are calculated.

Deduction items are used to track deductions from paychecks. Create separate deduction items for each deduction you use on paychecks. Since deductions are withheld from paychecks, they increase (credit) a liability account, accumulating a balance due to the agency or vendor to whom the deductions are paid. Different Deduction items are calculated before or after taxes.

Company Contribution items are used to track additional business expenses as a result of payroll, such as the company match for employees' retirement plan deductions. Some are State and Federally-mandated company matches. Others are benefits that companies include as employee incentives. A company contribution is not paid to the employee, but to a vendor on behalf of an employee. Company contributions are calculated at the time of payroll and held in a liability account until the vendor is paid. Since this represents an additional company expense, the item increases (debits) an expense account and increases (credits) a liability account.

> **DID YOU KNOW?**
>
> It is common to see the abbreviations **EE** and **ER** when working with payroll. EE refers to the employ**EE**'s portion and ER refers to the employ**ER**'s portion of the Payroll Items.

Federal Tax Items:

These are used to track Federal taxes that are withheld from paychecks or are paid by the employer:

Employee Taxes are Federal Tax items withheld from paychecks: **Federal Withholding**, **Social Security Employee**, and **Medicare Employee**. These items are associated with a liability account and with the vendor to whom the tax is paid.

Company Taxes are Federal Tax items paid by the business: **Federal Unemployment**, **Social Security Company**, and **Medicare Company**. They increase (debit) an expense account, usually **Payroll Taxes**, and increase (credit) a liability account.

State Tax Items:

State Tax items are used to track state taxes that are withheld from paychecks or paid by the employer. Each state has different taxes, so depending on your state, you might have **State Withholding, State Disability**, and/or **State Unemployment Tax** items.

State Withholding taxes are paid by the employees by reducing their paychecks. These items are held in a liability account until paid to the vendor, usually the State Department of Revenue or Taxation.

State Disability taxes are usually employee taxes, but this varies by state.

State Unemployment taxes are usually company taxes, but this also varies by state.

Local Tax items are used to track other county or city taxes that are withheld from paychecks or paid by the employer. Each locality has different taxes, so check with your state for which local taxes apply to payroll. If your local tax is not directly supported by QuickBooks Online, you'll need to set up a user-defined tax to track it.

THE PAYROLL SETUP WIZARD

The *Payroll Setup Wizard* is a set of screens that step you through starting a QuickBooks Online Payroll subscription. Using this guided tour is optional, but if you are starting from scratch (as shown here), you will find it helpful.

> **IMPORTANT!**
>
> We will start the *Payroll Setup Wizard* but leave partway, so that you can get to know each section as they appear in the Payroll Center. If you stick with the wizard, these specific steps may be in a different order, but you will be able to find each area and enter the required information.

SETTING UP A PAYROLL SUBSCRIPTION

HANDS-ON PRACTICE

STEP 1. Log into your **Imagine Photography** practice file used in the *Apply Your Knowledge* exercises at the end of each chapter. Because we can't set up payroll in the Craig's Landscaping sample file, we will create a 30-day free trial subscription and use it for practice.

STEP 2. From the *Payroll Center* on the *Employees* tab, click the green **Get Started** button, as shown in Figure 13-4.

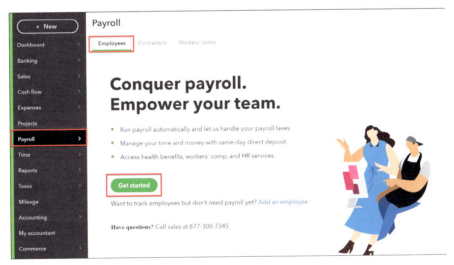

FIGURE 13-4: *The Payroll Center*

STEP 3. QuickBooks Online displays the *QuickBooks Online Payroll Setup* window shown in Figure 13-5. Under the column for **Core**, click **Try Now**.

STEP 4. On the next window that appears, click **Get Started**.

STEP 5. In the *Getting Started* wizard, answer the questions:

a. *Have you paid employees in [this year]?* Click **No**, then **Next**.
b. *When is your next payday?* Choose **the Friday after two weeks from today**, then click **Next**.
c. *What's the primary work location?* Confirm your company's **Business Name** and **Address**, then click **Next**.
d. *Who's your payroll contact?* This can be the business owner, bookkeeper, or an employee, whichever is appropriate for your situation. Here, change the *First Name* and *Last Name* to **your name**. Click **Next**.

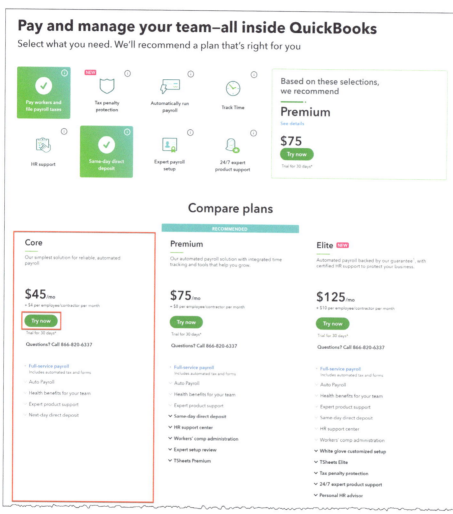

FIGURE 13-5: *Compare QuickBooks Payroll plans*

> **IMPORTANT!**
>
> If you were setting up payroll in the middle of the year for an existing company, you would answer **Yes** to the question *Have you paid employees in [this year]?*. During the setup process, QuickBooks Online Payroll would lead you through a set of screens where you would recreate each employee's payroll history summary for the current year, cross-referencing your monthly and quarterly totals with your tax payments made this year-to-date. However, our example assumes that you're setting up payroll at the beginning of the year.

PAYROLL SETUP | 495

ADDING EMPLOYEES

While we could add our next employee through the Payroll Setup Wizard's guided tour, it's more important to understand how the Payroll Center works. We will continue our payroll setup process through the *Employees Center* instead.

HANDS-ON PRACTICE

STEP 1. So that we can get to know QuickBooks Online's Payroll interface, click the **X** in the corner to **Cancel** out of the *Payroll Setup Wizard*.

STEP 2. Click on **Payroll** in the *Left Navigation Bar* and then go to the **Employees** tab. This takes you to the screen shown in Figure 13-6.

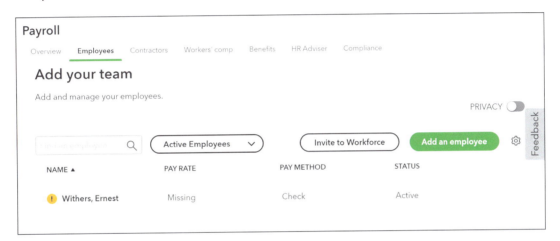

FIGURE 13-6: *The Employees Center—your screen may vary*

Employee Self-setup Through QuickBooks Workforce

If your employees have filled in their new hire paperwork and you have a W-4 form, you can enter their personal details manually. You also have the option of inviting them to submit their W-4 form, set up their direct deposit, view their paystubs, and receive their annual W-2 forms through an online portal at workforce.intuit.com called **QuickBooks Workforce**.

Workforce is an employee portal where your team can view their pay stubs, enter their personal information, and even set up their own direct deposit.

STEP 3. Because we added the store owner as an employee earlier, we will set continue his payroll setup first. Click on **Ernest Withers**.

STEP 4. In the *Edit Employee* screen shown in Figure 13-7, click the **slider** for *Employee Self-setup*.

STEP 5. Change the *First Name* to **Ernest** and the *Last name* to **Withers**, as shown in Figure 13-8. Enter **your email address** so that you can see the email message employees would receive. Click **Send Email**.

FIGURE 13-7: *Invite employees to Workforce*

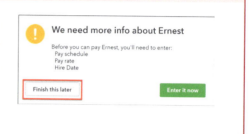

FIGURE 13-8: *Send employees an invitation to set up their payroll*

DID YOU KNOW?

The minimum information needed to add an employee is their name and email address, but QBO can't process the employee's payroll until you also enter their pay schedule, pay rate, and hire date. If you don't use the *Employee Self-setup* tool, QBO will remind you that it doesn't have enough information to actually pay them.

Setting Up Employees

You will need to enter the **employee information** for every person who your company will send a **W-2 Form** at year end for taxes. We will manually enter the information for the next employee, Kaydee Roppa.

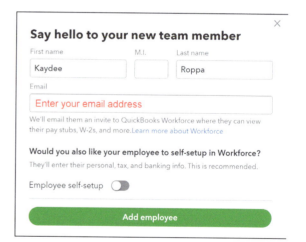

FIGURE 13-9: *Entering Kaydee Roppa's name and email*

HANDS-ON PRACTICE

STEP 1. Click the blue **Employee List** link in the upper left of Ernest's screen.

STEP 2. Click the green **Add An Employee** button.

STEP 3. Enter Kaydee Roppa as shown in Figure 13-9. Enter your email address.

STEP 4. Turn off the Employee self-setup invitation slider. Click Add Employee to continue.

NOTE:

QuickBooks Online uses the **employee name** fields (first name, middle initial, and last name) to distinguish between employees. If two employees have the same name, or an employee also has a vendor or customer account, add a **middle initial** to distinguish between them.

STEP 5. In Kaydee's *Personal Info* section, click the blue **Edit** link (seen in Figure 13-7).

STEP 6. Fill in the information in based on Kaydee's W-4 form and other employment documents (see Table 13-2).

STEP 7. Click **Save**.

BIRTH DATE	04/20/2001
ADDRESS	2501 Golden Rain Rd, Apt 11
CITY OR TOWN	Walnut Creek
STATE	CA
ZIP CODE	94595
SOCIAL SECURITY NUMBER	503-28-1026
GENDER	Non-binary/Other
MOBILE PHONE NUMBER	503-761-1677

TABLE 13-2 *Personal information from W-4 and other documents*

Entering Tax Withholding Information

The next step is to enter the employee's **Federal and State Tax Withholdings**. This information comes from the employee's **W-4 form**. Using QuickBooks Payroll's Workforce integration to have the employee enter their own information saves time and assures accuracy. If you need a blank W-4 form for the employee, there is a direct link inside the *Add Withholdings* window.

HANDS-ON PRACTICE

STEP 8. In the *Tax Withholding* box, click the blue **Edit** link.

STEP 9. A *When Did You Hire Kaydee?* alert appears. Click **2020 or later**.

FIGURE 13-10: *Kaydee Roppa's W-4 Federal and State tax withholdings*

STEP 10. In the *Federal Withholding* section, drop-down *Filing Status (Step 1c)* and select **Single or Married Filing Separately**. Kaydee has no *Dependents* or *Other Adjustments*.

STEP 11. Scroll down to *State Withholding*. Under *CA State Taxes*, choose the *Filing Status* **Single or Married (with Two or More Incomes)**.

STEP 12. Kaydee has no *Tax Exemptions*. Click **Save**.

STEP 13. Confirm Kaydee's *Tax Withholding* as shown in Figure 13-10.

Setting Up Direct Deposit

Setting up **Direct Deposit** is the easiest way to pay employees. In fact, Workforce even allows you to view the status of pending payroll deposits processing for full transparency.

HANDS-ON PRACTICE

Step 14. In the *Payment Method* box, click the blue **Start** link.

Step 15. Drop down the *Payment Method* field and change it to **Direct Deposit**, which opens the screen shown in Figure 13-11. Note that you have the ability to split a paycheck into two bank accounts, or deposit part directly into the bank and pay the rest by check.

Step 16. At the moment, we don't have Kaydee's bank account information, so for now we will change it back to **Paper Check**. Click **Save**.

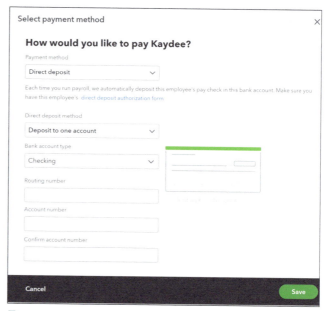

Figure 13-11: Set up Direct Deposit

DEVELOPING COMPANY PAY POLICIES

A company's **payroll schedules**, **compensation**, and **time off policies** are defined as you add employees. This way you can create new pay types as you need them, and assign employees to existing types as you add them.

The next section provides Kaydee's employment details, including creating your first *Pay Schedule*.

Step 17. In the *Employment Details* box, click the blue **Start** link to enter Kaydee's job-related information.

Step 18. Her *Status* is **Active**. Note that if an employee separates from the company, there are both temporary and permanent options.

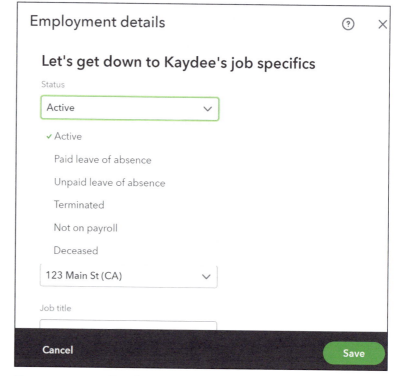

Figure 13-12: Employee Status Options

Step 19. In the *Hire Date* field, enter **the date two months before today**. Confirm the *Work Location* contains **123 Main St (CA)**.

Step 20. We will leave *Job Title*, *Employee ID*, and *Workers' Comp Class* blank.

Creating Pay Schedules

You can run payroll on one or more pay schedules: weekly, every other week (bi-weekly), twice a month (semi-monthly), or monthly. Employees can be grouped into different schedules. For example, hourly employees can be paid weekly, while salaried employees can be paid monthly.

After you create your first pay schedule, you can add employees to it, and select it as the default for all new employees. The *Pay Schedules* list can be viewed again later while editing any employee's settings.

STEP 21. While still in the Employment Details screen, click on the *Pay Schedule* box and click **+Add Pay Schedule**. QuickBooks Online displays the *Pay Schedule* window. Complete the schedule shown in Figure 13-13.
   a. The *Pay Frequency* is **Every Other Week**. This will result in 26 pay periods a year, with some months having three paydays.
   b. The *Next Payday* will be **the Friday after two weeks from today.**
   c. The *End of Next Pay Period* will be **the Friday before.**
   d. The *Pay Schedule Name* is **Every Other Friday**.
   e. Make sure there is a **checkmark** in front of *Use This Pay Schedule For Employees You Add After This One*. This sets the default for all employees created after this one, and it can be unchecked for employees with alternative pay periods.
   f. Look at the *Upcoming Pay Periods* to confirm that the pay periods will run as expected.

STEP 22. Compare your screen to Figure 13-13. The dates will be different, but the pattern will be similar. Click **Save** to close the Pay Schedule window.

STEP 23. Click **Save** to close the *Employment Details*.

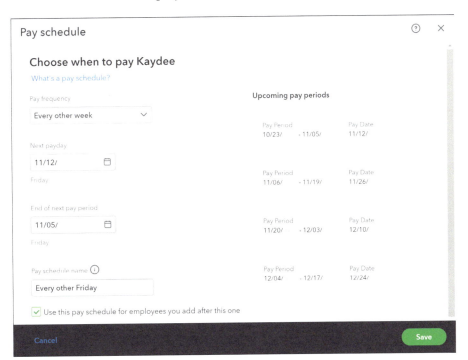

FIGURE 13-13: *Create a Pay Schedule for Every Other Friday—your dates will vary*

DID YOU KNOW?

If a pay date falls on a national bank holiday, QuickBooks Online Payroll will automatically backdate payroll to the day before. For example, if payroll falls on January 1, it will be paid out on December 31. Be sure to plan ahead!

Defining Pay Types

In the next section, you will set up compensation including salary and hourly wages, and additional pay types such as bonuses, commissions, and paid time off policies.

HANDS-ON PRACTICE

Step 24. In the *Pay Types* box, click the blue **Start** link.

Step 25. In the *Set Employee Type* section, the first drop-down field allows you select *Hourly*, *Salary*, or *Commission Only*. Select **Hourly**.

Step 26. In the *Rate Per Hour* box, enter Kaydee's hourly wage, **17**.

Step 27. QuickBooks Online gives you the option of setting *Default Hours*. If you are not using a time-clock or time sheets to calculate hours worked, use *Hours Per Day* and *Days Per Week* to set the defaults for the employee. The hours can be manually adjusted each pay period as needed.

Enter **8** *Hours Per Day* and **5** *Days Per Week*.

DID YOU KNOW?

Entering *Default Hours* allows you to run **Auto Payroll**, QuickBooks Online's option to just let Payroll run automatically without being initiated by a user or bookkeeper.

Step 28. Notice the blue **+Add Pay Type** link. If your employees sometimes receive pay at an alternative rate, you could activate additional *Pay Types* with multiple **Hourly** rates as demonstrated in Figure 13-14 (do not do this now).

Step 29. Scroll down and check off additional *Common Pay Types* for **Overtime Pay**, **Holiday Pay**, **Bonus**, and **Commission** (see Figure 13-15).

Figure 13-14: *Adding additional hourly pay rates (we will not do this now)*

Figure 13-15: *Check off additional pay types*

Assigning Paid Time Off Policies

If you pay employees for time off, the next step is to set up **Paid Time Off (PTO)**, **Vacation Pay**, and **Sick Pay**.

The options to calculate sick and vacation time are flexible to comply with state requirements. You can set a limit for the maximum sick or vacation time earned at any time, not just by the calendar year.

Choose sick and vacation time settings to match your company policies. You can choose *Beginning of year* if your policy is to give each employee a set number of hours per year. If employees earn sick or vacation time for each pay period, then choose *Every paycheck*. You can also choose to accrue sick and vacation time based on the number of hours worked or just once per year. Select the appropriate option from the *Accrual period* drop-down list.

HANDS-ON PRACTICE

Imagine Photography offers its employees two weeks of vacation time and 40 hours of sick leave per year. Vacation pay is accrued on the anniversary date of their hire, so that they can use the time throughout the year.

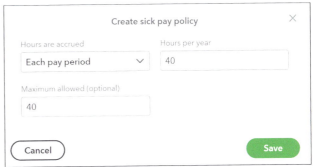

FIGURE 13-16: Create the Sick Pay policy

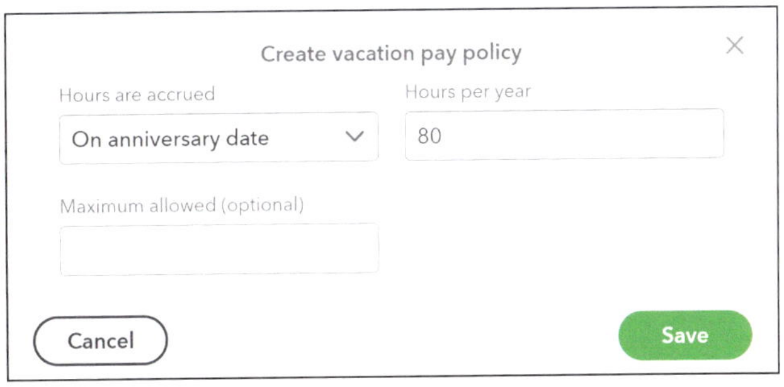

FIGURE 13-17: Create the Vacation Pay policy

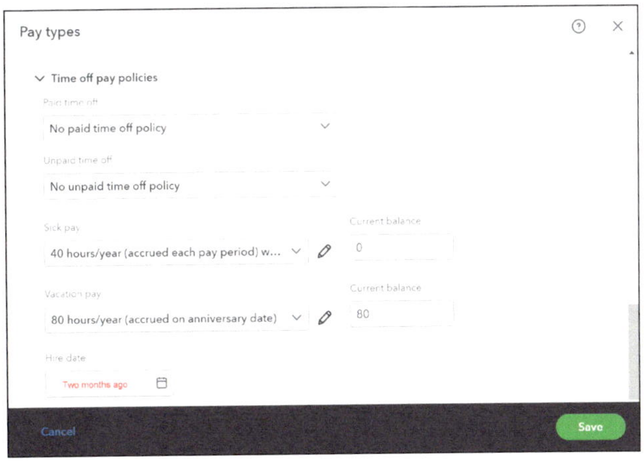

STEP 1. Scroll down to the *Time Off Pay Policies* section.

STEP 2. In the *Sick Pay* drop-down, select **Add New Sick Pay Policy**. Imagine Photography's sick pay is accrued by pay period, with a maximum cap of 40 hours. Leave the *Description* blank. When your screen matches Figure 13-16, click **Save**.

STEP 3. In the *Vacation Pay* box, select **Add New Vacation Pay Policy**. Vacation pay is accrued **On Anniversary Date** at **80** *Hours Per Year*. There is no maximum. When your results match Figure 13-17, click **Save** to continue.

STEP 4. Update the *Current Balance* for *Vacation Pay* to **80** hours so that Kaydee's vacation pay is available to her. Your screen should match Figure 13-18.

FIGURE 13-18: Time off Pay Policies for Sick and Vacation Pay

Additional Compensation and Pay Types

Many employees are also subject to a variety of *reimbursements* and *compensation*. These can be assigned to employees on an as-needed basis.

Some simply provide the option to add additional pay to a paycheck. Others can also include a default recurring amount.

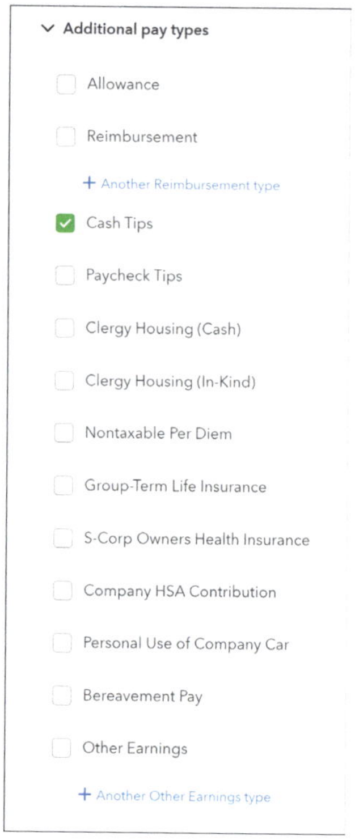

HANDS-ON PRACTICE

At Imagine Photography's retail store, customers frequently leave money in a tip jar that is distributed between all employees during that shift. While the employees receive the cash immediately instead of through their paychecks, the amount must still be reported through payroll so that the appropriate taxes are calculated and withheld.

- **STEP 5.** Scroll down to the *Additional Pay Types* section. Expand it if necessary.
- **STEP 6.** Place a **checkmark** in front of *Cash Tips*, as shown in Figure 13-19.
- **STEP 7.** Click **Save** to close the *Pay Types* screen.

FIGURE 13-19: *Additional pay types*

SPECIFYING BENEFIT DEDUCTIONS & CONTRIBUTIONS

In the next section, you will set up the *benefits* you offer (health insurance, dental insurance, retirement plans, etc.), and any other *deductions* that affect the employees' gross income, like *garnishments* or loan repayments.

If your company provides benefits, there are three options for allocating the costs between the company and the employee:

1. The company could pay the entire expense.
2. The company and employee could share the expense.
3. The employee could pay the entire expense.

> **NOTE:**
>
> If your company pays the entire expense, payroll is usually not involved. However, there are certain circumstances when you would need to adjust the W-2s to include the benefits. Check with your tax professional.

If the costs are shared between the company and the employees, or if the employees pay for the entire cost via payroll deductions, use a **Deduction** to calculate the portions.

Health Insurance

QuickBooks Online Payroll provides options for **Health Insurance benefits** including medical, dental, and vision coverage. All three can be deducted pre-tax or after taxes. In addition, there are also options for Flexible Spending accounts and HSA plans.

HANDS-ON PRACTICE

Imagine Photography splits their health insurance costs 50/50 with employees, deducting the expense after taxes are calculated.

STEP 8. Continue editing Kaydee's employee setup by scrolling down to her *Deductions & Contributions* box, and click the blue **Start** link.

STEP 9. In the *Deductions/Contributions* section, click **+Add Deduction/Contribution**.

STEP 10. In the *Deduction/Contribution Type* drop-down, choose **Health Insurance**.

STEP 11. In the next *Type* box, choose **Medical Insurance**.

STEP 12. In the *Description (appears on paycheck)* box, enter how you would like the benefit to appear on the check stub. Type **Medical Insurance**.

STEP 13. The *Employee Deduction* is *Calculated As* a **Flat Amount** at **$150.00** *Per Paycheck*.

STEP 14. Because Imagine Photography does not have a pre-tax Cafeteria plan, make sure to select the **Taxable Insurance Premium** option.

STEP 15. In the *Company Contribution* section, duplicate the Employee Deductions, a **Flat Amount** of **$150.00**. Note that while QBO Payroll will track these company contributions, it is still up to the company to pay the provider directly.

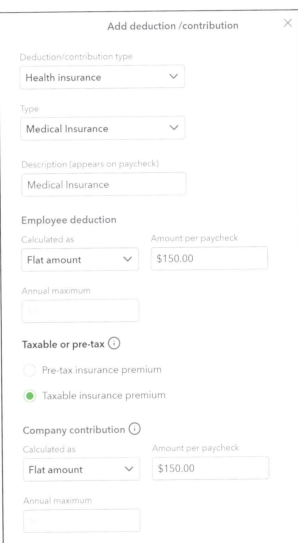

FIGURE 13-20: *Health Insurance benefits*

STEP 16. When your screen looks like Figure 13-20, click **Save**.

STEP 17. If you also had Vision or Dental insurance as a benefit, you would repeat the steps for additional Health Insurance deductions. We will not do this now.

Retirement Plans

If you have a **401(k)** or other **Retirement plan**, you can track the employer contributions and the employee contributions (salary deferral) to the plan. Employee contributions such as a 401(k) are excluded from taxable earnings when calculating federal withholding.

HANDS-ON PRACTICE

STEP 18. In the *Deductions/Contributions* section, click **+Add Deduction/Contribution**.

STEP 19. In the *Deduction/Contribution Type* drop-down, choose **Retirement Plans**.

STEP 20. In the *Type* box, select the type of retirement plan offered. Imagine Photography provides a **401(k)**.

STEP 21. In the *Description (appears on paycheck)* box, enter how you would like the benefit to appear on the check stub. Type **401k**.

STEP 22. The *Employee Deduction* is *Calculated As* a **Percent of Gross Pay** at **3.00%** *Percent Per Paycheck*.

STEP 23. In the *Company Contribution* section, duplicate the Employee Deduction, a **Percent of Gross Pay** of **3.00%**. Note that while QBO Payroll will track these company contributions, it is still up to the company to pay the provider directly.

STEP 24. When your screen looks like Figure 13-21, click **Save**.

STEP 25. Click **Done** to complete the deductions and contributions.

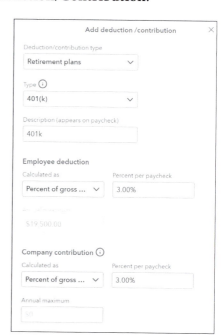

FIGURE 13-21: *Adding the 401(k) retirement benefit*

CUSTOMIZING THE PAYROLL SETTINGS

Not all of Payroll's settings are found in the *Payroll Center*. You also need to go into the *Payroll Settings* under the *Gear* to make sure your setup is complete. It's crucial to set up Payroll Taxes properly, whether you do it as a step in the Payroll Setup Wizard or directly in the *Payroll Settings*.

In the Payroll Settings, you'll see options for Federal, State, and Local tax preferences, as well as your QuickBooks Online Payroll preferences, as shown in Figure 13-23.

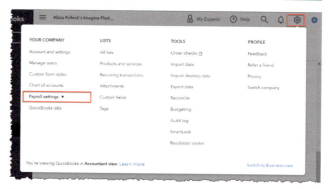

FIGURE 13-22: *Click on the Gear for Payroll Settings*

PAYROLL SETUP | 505

FIGURE 13-23: *Payroll Settings—your screen will vary*

General Tax Info

This screen is filled in automatically based on your company information. Make sure it matches the information submitted when the company filed for its Employer Identification Number (EIN). Confirm it for accuracy.

HANDS-ON PRACTICE

STEP 1. Click on the **Gear** and then **Payroll Settings**, as shown in Figure 13-22.

STEP 2. Click on the **Pencil** next to *General Tax*. The *General Tax Info* window opens (see Figure 13-24).

STEP 3. The *Company Legal Name* should be the same as the company name registered with the IRS.

STEP 4. Make sure the *Company Legal Address* is correct.

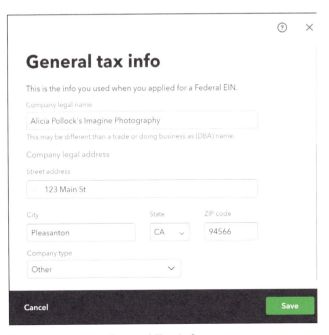

FIGURE 13-24: *General Tax Info*

STEP 5.   If you are a Sole Proprietor or 501c3, make sure the *Company Type* reflects that designation. Otherwise, leave it on **Other**.

STEP 6.   Click **Save**.

Scheduling Federal Tax Payments

This window sets up your *Federal tax filing requirements*.

HANDS-ON PRACTICE

STEP 1.   Click on the **Pencil** next to *Federal Tax*. The *Federal Tax Info* window opens (see Figure 13-25).

STEP 2.   In the *EIN* field, enter **11-1234567**.

STEP 3.   In the *Which Payroll Tax Form Do You File With the IRS?* field, choose **Form 941 each quarter (most common)**.

STEP 4.   In the *How Often Do You File and Pay Your Taxes?* box, select **Monthly**. Depending on the size of your payroll, you may be required to file more often.

STEP 5.   Click **Save**.

Sometimes alerts such as Figure 13-26 appear to confirm that you've selected the proper settings. If you see such warnings while setting up your Payroll, be sure to confirm your settings with your accountant.

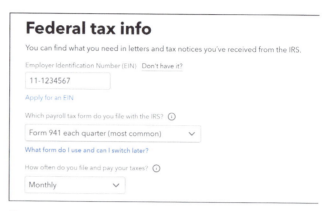

FIGURE 13-25: *Federal Tax Info*

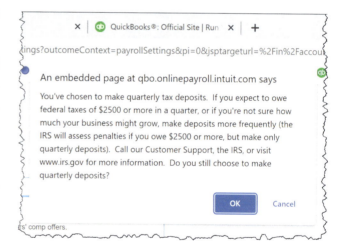

FIGURE 13-26: *An alert to confirm you've chosen the proper setting*

Scheduling State Tax Payments

The next section helps you schedule your **State tax payments** and specify your company's rates. Your **State Withholding** tax setup will vary according to your state's requirements.

Some tax rates are assigned to your company by your state's Department of Revenue according to the company's industry, size, age, claims history, and other factors. Be sure to review your **State Unemployment Tax** rate and other local tax rates at the beginning of each year and manually update them when necessary.

HANDS-ON PRACTICE

Continue setting up Imagine Photography's California rates and filing schedule by following these steps:

PAYROLL SETUP | 507

STEP 6. Click on the **Pencil** next to *California Tax*. The *California Tax Information* window opens (see Figure 13-27).

STEP 7. In the *Withholding Employer Account Number* field, enter **123-4567-9**.

STEP 8. In the *How Often Do You Pay Your Taxes?* field, choose **Monthly**.

STEP 9. For the *Unemployment Insurance (UI) Rate*, enter **3.4**. You should receive your rate from your state's Department of Revenue.

STEP 10. In the *Employment Training Tax Rate* field, choose **0.1%**. Be sure to locate the correct rate from your state's Department of Revenue.

STEP 11. When your screen looks like Figure 13-27, click **Save**.

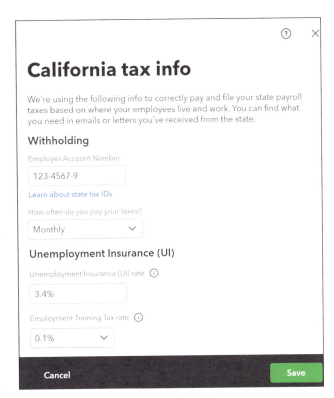

FIGURE 13-27: *Set up CA State Taxes*

STEP 12. Click on the **Pencil** next to *California Tax* again. Notice in Figure 13-28 that the window has changed. Your State Unemployment Insurance rates may change annually. Every year, be sure to **Edit** these settings as your company and its track record grows.

STEP 13. Click **Save** to close the window and return to *Payroll Settings*.

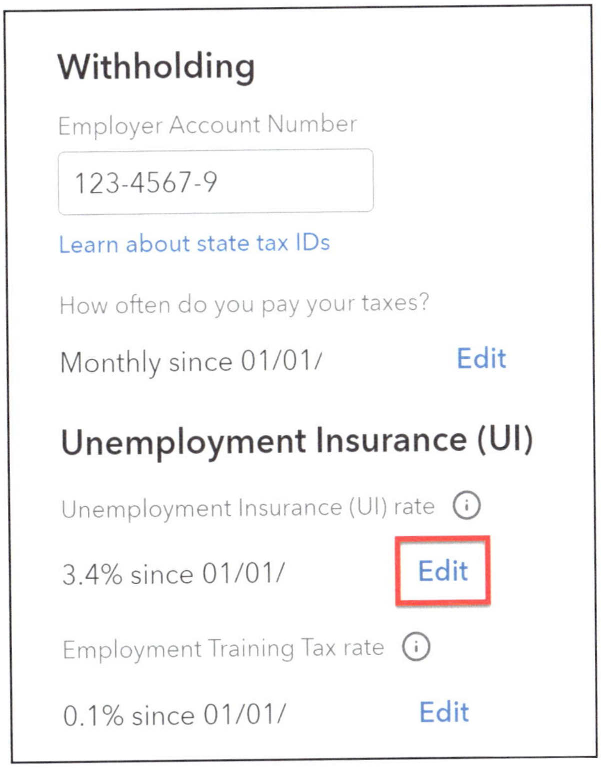

Setting Up Auto Payroll

QuickBooks Online Payroll has a time-saving feature for companies whose payroll runs are identical every time. **Auto Payroll** becomes available after your first payroll run, and will repeat your most recent paychecks automatically according to the schedule you choose.

You can specify a particular payroll schedule or individual employees for automation. For example, you can use Auto Payroll for your salaried employees and run payroll manually for hourly employees.

You will receive a notification a few days prior to the scheduled date to confirm that you want Auto Payroll to proceed, allowing you to modify an employee's hours as necessary.

FIGURE 13-28: *Adjust your state's rates annually*

Automating Tax Payments and Forms

Because QuickBooks Online Payroll is full-service, it will even pay and file your federal and state payroll taxes, including year-end filings. This is a good idea because missing a payment deadline has consequences including fines. All tax forms are archived so you can view and print them for your own records.

HANDS-ON PRACTICE

Confirm that QuickBooks Online will file your payroll taxes for you by following these steps:

STEP 14. Click on the **Pencil** next to *Taxes and Forms* (see Figure 13-29).

STEP 15. Make sure there's a **checkmark** in front of **Automate Taxes and Forms**. You may see a warning box that there are additional setup steps before QuickBooks Online Payroll can submit your forms. You will find these tasks on the *Payroll Overview* screen on page 515.

STEP 16. Click **Save** to return to the *Payroll Settings* list.

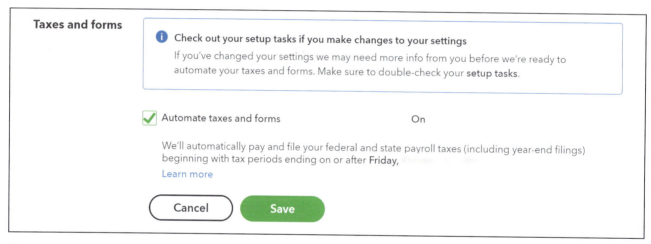

FIGURE 13-29: *Automate your taxes and form filings*

Designating a Third-Party Preparer

Even though QuickBooks Online Payroll is full-service, there may be times when you will want your accountant to communicate with the IRS on your behalf. Some companies also pay their accountant or bookkeeper to do their payroll and taxes for them. When this is the case, authorize these representatives in QuickBooks Online Payroll.

While we will not do this now, you would add contact information for third-party preparers by clicking on the **Pencil** next to *Federal Form Preferences* (see Figure 13-30). When you select **Yes** on each option, fields become available to add this information to your payroll forms.

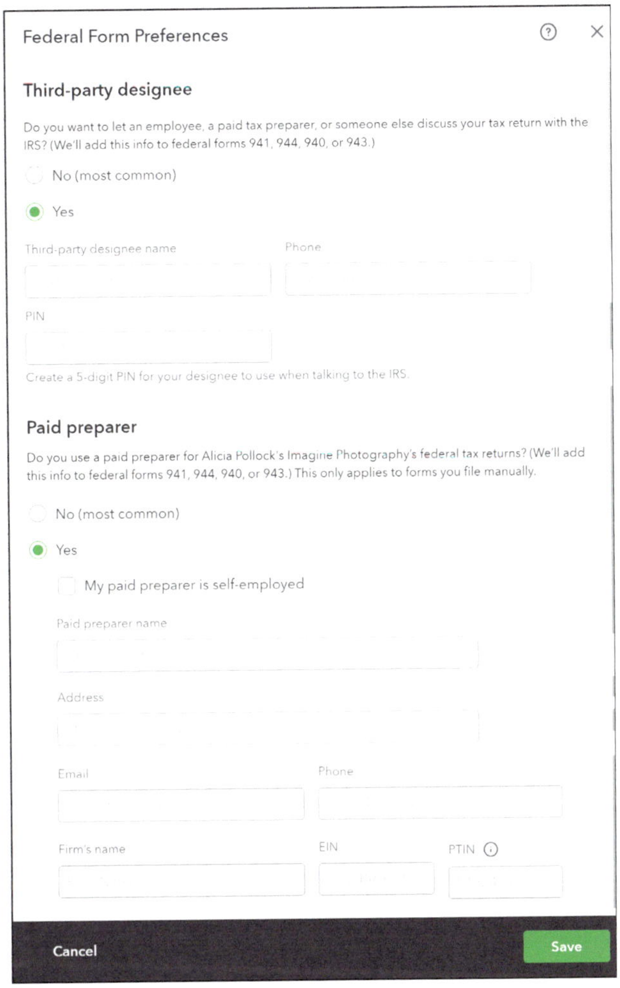

FIGURE 13-30: *Designate a tax preparer*

Activating Email Notifications

QuickBooks Online Payroll will send you email reminders when it's time to run payroll and submit taxes. The notifications are sent to the email address specified for the company in *Account and Settings* (see *page 38*), as well as all *Accountant Users* associated with the subscription.

While we will not do this now, you can turn on and off two of the payday notifications and tax payment reminders by clicking on the **Pencil** next to *Email Notifications* (see Figure 13-31).

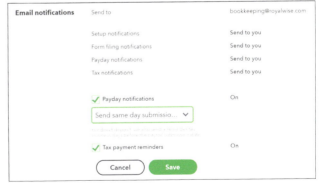

FIGURE 13-31: *Turn on email notifications*

You can **uncheck** these options, or specify that you would like *Payday Notifications* to arrive the day before it's time to submit payroll or on the day itself.

Employee Workforce Profile Management

As we saw earlier, Workforce is the portal where employees can log in to view their pay stubs. You can also give them the authorization for self-service to update their own personal and tax information as their life changes. When an employee moves, gets married or divorced, or has a child, they don't need to visit HR and fill in forms—they can simply log in and edit their W-4 information (see Figure 13-32).

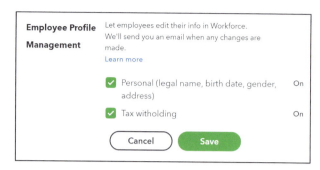

FIGURE 13-32: *Workforce portal settings*

Authorizing Shared Data

Intuit, the company who makes QuickBooks Online, also owns TurboTax, the software millions of people use to pay their taxes every year. By authorizing this connection, you can make it easy for your employees to connect their Workforce portal to their TurboTax.

This connection is turned **On** by default. While we will not do this now, if you would like to turn it **Off**, you would click the **Pencil** next to *Allow Employees to Import W-2 Data Into TurboTax*, uncheck the box, and click **Save**.

In addition, Intuit also has an agreement with Equifax to provide employment and income verification using their The Work Number® program. Lenders typically ask for this information when your employees apply for loans, credit, or public aid. The service is only accessed by credentialed and approved lenders and government agencies when your employee requests verification. The service is governed by the Fair Credit Reporting Act (FCRA) in accordance with federal law.

While we will not do this now, if you would like to turn the service **Off**, you would click the **Pencil** next to *Include Automated Income and Employment Verification Service Powered by The Work Number from Equifax*, uncheck the box, and click **Save** (see Figure 13-33).

FIGURE 13-33: *Allow Shared Data with Intuit Partners*

Connecting Bank Accounts

While some companies still print paper checks to hand out to employees or send in the mail, most companies now pay their employees by direct deposit. By authorizing the bank to withdraw money from your checking account and distribute it directly to employees, you save hours of time and effort.

In addition, one of the benefits of connecting your bank account to QuickBooks Online Payroll

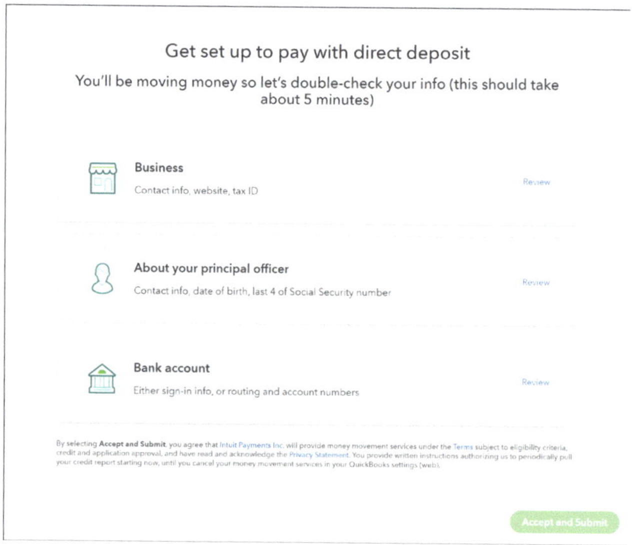

FIGURE 13-34: *Enter your banking information*

is that it will pay your taxes on your behalf, without you having to print and mail forms, write checks, or pay through the agency's website.

As with the Banking Feed, connecting your checking account is completely secure, utilizing the same encryption used by financial institutions for online banking.

When you click the **Pencil** next to *Bank Accounts*, you can authorize your payroll funding source. While we will not do this now, you would fill in your *Business* information, your *Principal Officer's* contact information, and the *Bank Account* routing and account numbers (see Figure 13-34).

Check Printing Options

In addition to direct deposit, you have the option to print checks, or just paystubs.

Checks can be printed on QuickBooks-compatible check paper, either voucher-style or standard 3-up.

HANDS-ON PRACTICE

Even though Imagine Photography wants to pay all its employees by direct deposit, you don't yet have their bank information. For the time being, you will print out your paychecks using these settings.

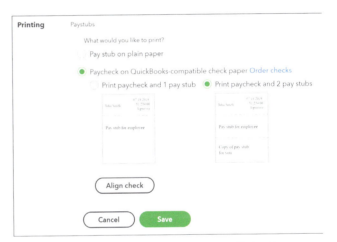

STEP 17. Click on the **Pencil** next to *Printing* (see Figure 13-35).

STEP 18. Click the **Circle** next to *Paycheck on QuickBooks-compatible Check Paper*.

STEP 19. Click the **Circle** next to *Print Paycheck and 2 Pay Stubs*.

FIGURE 13-35: *Print settings for payroll checks*

STEP 20. Click **Align Check** to set up your browser to print on your check stock. Be sure to use the same web browser that you will use when it's time to print the payroll checks.

a. While we will not do this now, you would first click **Print Alignment Form**. This will print a sample check on blank paper.

b. You would then hold up the sample check up to a light together with a blank sheet of check stock. In the boxes, enter the letter and number closest to the *Pay to the Order of* and *$*, as shown in Figure 13-36.

c. Confirm the alignment by clicking **Print Sample Check**, and hold it up to the light with your check stock. If the alignment is not perfect, repeat these steps.

d. When you're done, click **Save** to return to the *Printing Settings*.

FIGURE 13-36: *Print a sample to test the payroll check alignment*

STEP 21. Click **Save** to return to the *Payroll Settings* list.

Editing Payroll Account Mapping

QuickBooks Online Payroll will create its own liability and expense categories in the Chart of Accounts when you run your first payroll. Most of the time it is not necessary to adjust the default accounts, but some companies require more specific mapping. If needed, you can update them in *Payroll Settings* in the *Accounting* section at the bottom of the screen.

If you are converting to QBO from QuickBooks Desktop, or switching to QBO Payroll from another provider, you may already have existing Payroll liability and expense categories. It is essential to edit the *Accounting Preferences* to map to your existing accounts, or else QBO will create a second set that you will then need to merge.

In addition, if you modify any payroll accounts in the Chart of Accounts, be sure to go to these preferences and update them, or else QBO will recreate the original accounts on the next payroll run.

HANDS-ON PRACTICE

STEP 22. To modify Payroll's liability and expense category defaults, click on the **Pencil** next to *Accounting*.

STEP 23. The *Bank Account* is missing because we did not connect the checking account earlier. Click the **Pencil** next to *Paycheck and Payroll Tax Payments*.

STEP 24. In the *Bank Account* drop-down, choose **Business Checking (1025)**, as shown in Figure 13-37. Click **Save**.

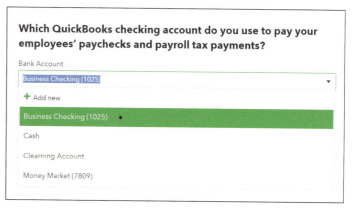

FIGURE 13-37: *Select which bank account you will use for payroll and tax payments*

Adding a Wage Expense

By default, all payroll wages are mapped to one expense account, *Payroll Expenses:Wages*. The colon indicates that *Payroll Expenses* is the header account, and *Wages* is a sub-account.

QuickBooks Online Payroll is flexible enough to distribute wages and salaries to multiple accounts, either by employee or by compensation type. For example, Commissions and Bonuses can have their own expense accounts.

HANDS-ON PRACTICE

Because Imagine Photography is taxed as an S-Corporation, the IRS requires them to report compensation of officers separately from the rest of the employees. To do this, create an additional *Wage* account called **Officer's Salary**.

STEP 25. Click the **Pencil** next to *Wage Expenses*.

STEP 26. Click the **circle** in front of *Each Employee's Wages Are Posted To Their Own Expense Account* (see Figure 13-38). In Kaydee Roppa's box, choose **Payroll Expenses:Wages**.

STEP 27. For Ernest Withers, add a new category with the *account name* **Officer's Salary**. Use the *Account Type* **Expenses,** the *Detail Type* or *Tax Form Section* **Payroll Wage Expenses**, and make it a *Sub-account of/Save Account Under* **Payroll Expenses**.

STEP 28. Click **Save** to close the *Wages* window.

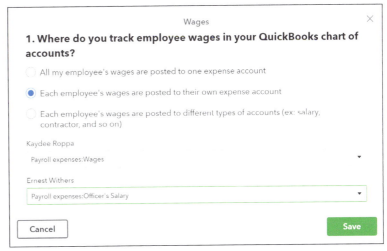

FIGURE 13-38: *Specify the expense account for each employee's wages*

Class Tracking

Subscribers to QBO Plus and Advanced frequently use **Classes** to label transactions for job costing. QBO Payroll has the ability to assign classes to payroll as well.

HANDS-ON PRACTICE

Kaydee works out of the San Jose location, and the owner, Ernest oversees the entire operation.

STEP 29. Click the **Pencil** next to *Class Tracking*.

STEP 30. Select **I Use Different Classes for Different Employees**, as shown in Figure 13-39.

STEP 31. Assign *Kaydee Roppa* to **San Jose.**

STEP 32. Assign *Ernest Withers* to **Overhead**.

STEP 33. Click **Save**.

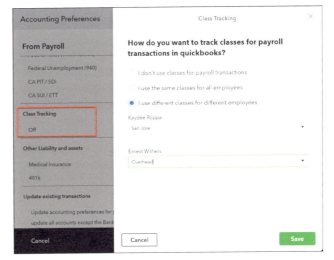

FIGURE 13-39: *Class Tracking for Payroll*

Understanding Payroll Expenses vs. Liabilities

When you look at the rest of the *Accounting Preferences* list shown in Figure 13-40, you'll notice that Retirement and Health Insurance show up in two places.

- The *Company Contribution Expenses* at the top are the business's out-of-pocket expenses.
- The *Other Liabilities and Assets* at the bottom are the corresponding **Payroll Liability** accounts that collect the employee payroll deductions until the payments are made to the appropriate agencies.

When payroll is run, the employee and company contributions are calculated according to the flat rates or percentages specified during setup. The employee portion is deducted from their net pay, and the company contribution is allocated to its expense account. The combined total becomes the payroll liability.

When the business pays the health insurance bill or remits payment to the retirement plan, it is categorized to the liability account, zeroing it out.

The same holds true for the *Employer Tax Expenses* and the *Tax Liabilities*. The Federal and State liability accounts collect the employee deductions and the employer contribution expenses.

When QuickBooks Online Payroll remits tax payments to the IRS and your state, it will categorize the payments to the proper liability account.

> **IMPORTANT!**
>
> If you make changes to the list after you've begun running payroll, use the **Update Existing Transactions?** option to update historical payroll transactions as well.

STEP 34. When you are done exploring this list, click **Done** to return to the *Payroll Settings*, and then click **Done** again to exit back to your *Dashboard*.

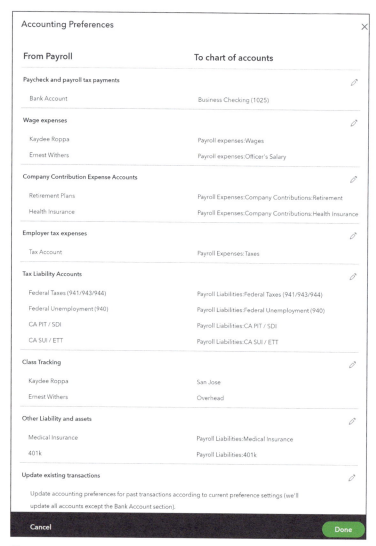

FIGURE 13-40: *Accounting Preferences map to your payroll liability and expense accounts*

THE PAYROLL OVERVIEW

Always keep an eye on the **Payroll Overview** tab, shown in Figure 13-41. This dashboard communicates with you if there are issues you need to address, alerts you when it's time to run payroll or pay taxes, and makes sure you're taking advantage of all the features. It's also where you will find the link to Payroll Support.

HANDS-ON PRACTICE

Although we've set up our Payroll, there are still a few outstanding tasks that we must complete, both for compliance with State and Federal regulations, and so that QuickBooks Online Payroll has all the information it needs to run paychecks and remit taxes.

STEP 35. Click on the **Overview** tab in the *Payroll Center*.

STEP 36. Workers' Comp is required in most states. Click the **Start** button next to *Add a Workers' Comp Policy*. Depending on your situation, you have several options:
  a. If you do not have Workers' Comp insurance, click **Request a Quote**. This initiates an inquiry with one of Intuit's partners to find a policy that suits your needs and your budget. If you want your QBO to be a one-stop shop, this is a great benefit.
  b. If you already have Workers' Compensation insurance already, click **I'm Already Covered**. This returns you to the *Overview*. Click this now.

STEP 37. Click the **Start** button next to *Explore 401(k) Retirement Plans*. Depending on your situation, you have several options:
  a. If you do not have an employee retirement plan, click **Find my plan**. Just like with Workers' Comp, this initiates an inquiry with one of Intuit's partners to find a policy that's a best-fit for your needs.
  b. If you already have a retirement plan already, click **I'm Already Covered**. This returns you to the *Overview*. Click this now.

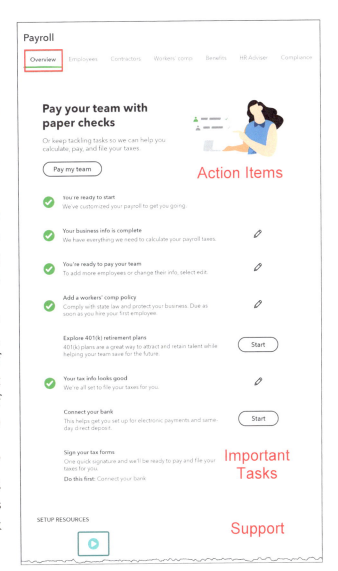

FIGURE 13-41: *The Payroll Overview Center—your screen will vary*

STEP 38. Because this is a practice file, we will not *Connect Your Bank*.

STEP 39. The last step, *Sign Your Tax Forms*, is extremely important, but we can't do it because we haven't connected a bank account. In order to file your taxes, the IRS and your state's Department of Revenue need the company officer to sign authorization forms. Be sure to fill in these forms. Some states allow you to submit them electronically, while others require you to fax them.

> **IMPORTANT!**
>
> Be sure to follow up and make sure these authorization forms have been received and accepted by the government agencies. If the process isn't smooth, not only will you have to print out your payroll tax forms and mail a check, but you may be penalized for late payments.

REVIEW QUESTIONS

Comprehension Questions

1. What are Company Contributions?
2. Explain why some payroll costs are *liabilities* while others are *expenses*.
3. How do you know what payroll withholdings to use for each employee?

Multiple Choice
Select the best answer(s) for each of the following:

1. An easy and convenient way to process payroll in QuickBooks Online for employees on different payroll schedules would be to:
   a. Move all employees onto a single schedule.
   b. Use the *Payroll Schedule* function.
   c. Outsource payroll.
   d. Convert some employees to independent contractors.

2. Which of the following payroll periods is not an option in QuickBooks Online?
   a. Every week.
   b. Every other week.
   c. Twice a month.
   d. Quarterly.

3. Which Payroll Item cannot be created in the Payroll Setup Wizard?
   a. Commissions.
   b. Bonuses.
   c. Medical Insurance Deductions.
   d. You can create all items above during the Payroll Setup Wizard.

4. Which is not an option when setting the accrual period for sick and vacation time?
    a. At Beginning of Year.
    b. Every Month.
    c. Each Pay Period.
    d. Per Hour Worked.

5. The Payroll Setup Wizard will not allow you to:
    a. Create multiple wages for the same employee.
    b. Set up deduction and withholding items.
    c. Set the pay rate for an employee.
    d. Add two employees with exactly the same name.

6. You enter the Federal ID for your company:
    a. In the Payroll Settings under the *Gear*.
    b. In the Payroll Setup Wizard.
    c. In QBO's *Account and Settings*.
    d. A and C above.

7. Use a **Payroll Deduction** item to track medical insurance costs when:
    a. The employees pay part (or all) of the cost.
    b. Costs exceed $100 per month for the employee.
    c. The employer pays the total cost.
    d. You do not track medical insurance costs as a Payroll Deduction item.

8. Which of the following would QuickBooks Online exclude from taxable earnings when calculating federal withholding?
    a. Vacation salary.
    b. Sick leave salary.
    c. Overtime earnings.
    d. Employee contributions to a 401(k).

9. Why are there two **Health Insurance** and two **Retirement** categories in the **Accounting Preferences**?
    a. Different tax rates apply to employee and employer portions.
    b. You use separate accounts because you must write separate checks for employee and employer portions.
    c. QuickBooks Online manages the employee and employer portions separately.
    d. You maintain separate ledger accounts for the two portions of each tax.

10. Which of the following is not a feature of QuickBooks Online Core Payroll?
    a. Calculates gross pay by hours worked or salaries.
    b. Prints paychecks on standard checks or pays by Direct Deposit.
    c. Support agents set up payroll for you and guarantee accuracy.
    d. Calculates and electronically remits federal payroll tax liabilities.

11. QuickBooks Online uses Payroll Items to:
    a. Accumulate payroll liabilities.

b. Track each different kind of compensation.
c. Define the relationship between items you put on paychecks and the Chart of Accounts.
d. All of the above.

12. If you no longer want an employee to show in the Employees Center:
    a. Stop paying the employee.
    b. Deselect the employee for payments.
    c. Change their employment Status.
    d. Remove all wage items from the employee's record.

13. Which is not true about Auto Payroll?
    a. It takes payroll out of your control.
    b. It repeats the previous payroll on a set schedule.
    c. You can set default hours for each employee.
    d. It notifies you a few days before so that you can confirm.

14. Sick leave, vacation leave, and PTO are:
    a. Standardized for all businesses in the US.
    b. Optional for all businesses in the US.
    c. Only accrued by the number of hours worked.
    d. Completely flexible according to your company's policies.

Completion Statements

1. The three QuickBooks Online Payroll subscription levels are _____, _____, and _____.
2. To refine the names of the Payroll Liability and Expense accounts, click on _____ _____ under the Gear.
3. QuickBooks Online uses _____ items to track amounts withheld from gross or net pay of employees. Since these represent amounts withheld, these items usually credit a(n) _____ account.
4. _____ is the online portal where employees can fill in their W-4 form and view their payroll stubs.

PAYROLL SETUP—APPLY YOUR KNOWLEDGE

> Log into your **Imagine Photography** class file at qbo.intuit.com.

1. Follow the steps in the chapter to set up Imagine Photography's payroll subscription, company settings, and first employee, **Kaydee Roppa**. You may follow the steps in the book or use the Payroll Setup Wizard, as long as you make sure you have entered all the information.
2. Complete Ernest Withers' Employee Record as shown in Table 13 3, without using the *Workforce Employee Self-setup*. If a setting is not specified, keep the defaults. As the owner of an S-Corp,

Ernest does not track his *Time Off* or use any other *Additional Pay Types* (he takes an occasional Owner Draw instead). He is eligible to have his medical insurance deducted as a **fringe benefit**.

FIELD	DATA
FIRST NAME	Ernest
LAST NAME	Withers
EMAIL	Your email address
BIRTH DATE	07/04/1968
ADDRESS	42 Comistas Ct, Walnut Creek, CA 94598
SOCIAL SECURITY NUMBER	321-12-1345
GENDER	Male
HIRE DATE	01/01/2020
FEDERAL WITHHOLDING FILING STATUS (2020 OR LATER)	Married Filing Jointly (or Qualifying Widower)
STATE WITHHOLDING	Single or Married (with two or more incomes)
HOW OFTEN DO YOU PAY ERNEST?	Add a new *Pay Schedule* with the *Pay Frequency* **Every Month**. The *Next Payday* is **the first day of next month**, and the *End of the Next Pay Period* is **the last day of this month**. Name the schedule **First of the Month**. **Uncheck** *Use this pay schedule for employees you add after this one.*
PAY TYPE	Salary
PAY FREQUENCY	Per Year
SALARY	$75,000.00
DEFAULT HOURS	Ernest works **8** hours per day and **5** days per week
ADDITIONAL PAY TYPES	S-Corp Owners Health Insurance, Recurring Amount **$500.00**
DEDUCTIONS AND CONTRIBUTIONS	401K, Employee Deduction **3%**, Company Contribution **3%**

TABLE 13-3 *Fill in owner Ernest Withers' payroll information*

3. Manually set up a third employee with the following information:

FIELD	DATA	
FIRST NAME	Mario	
LAST NAME	Mabilia	
EMAIL	Your email address	☐
BIRTH DATE	06/07/1996	☐
HIRE DATE	11/29/2020	☐
ADDRESS	98 Cashew Blossom Dr, San Jose CA 95125	☐
SS NO.	567-89-2345	☐
GENDER	Male	☐
MOBILE PHONE NUMBER	925-987-2345	☐
FEDERAL WITHHOLDING FILING STATUS (2020 OR LATER)	Single or Married Filing Separately	☐
STATE WITHHOLDING	Single or Married (with two or more incomes)	☐
PAYMENT METHOD	Paper check	☐
PAY SCHEDULE	Every other Friday	☐
PAY TYPE	Hourly	☐
RATE PER HOUR	$25.00	☐
DEFAULT HOURS	8 Hours Per Day, 5 Days Per Week	☐
COMMON PAY TYPES	Overtime Pay, Holiday Pay, Bonus, Commission	☐
SICK PAY	40 hours/year (accrued each pay period), Current Balance 23.5	☐
VACATION PAY	80 hours/year (accrued on anniversary date), Current Balance 36	☐
DEDUCTIONS AND CONTRIBUTIONS	Medical Insurance	☐
EMPLOYEE DEDUCTION	Flat Amount, $150.00	☐
COMPANY CONTRIBUTION	Flat Amount, $150.00	☐
DEDUCTIONS AND CONTRIBUTIONS	401K	☐
EMPLOYEE DEDUCTION	Percent of Gross Pay, 5.00% (he contributes extra)	☐
COMPANY CONTRIBUTION	Percent of Gross Pay, 3.00% (company max)	☐
GARNISHMENT	Child/Spousal Support	☐
DESCRIPTION (APPEARS ON PAYCHECK)	Child Support	☐
AMOUNT REQUESTED	$250	☐
MAXIMUM PERCENT OF DISPOSABLE INCOME	25.00%	☐

TABLE 13-4 *New Employee setup information*

4. In the *Payroll Settings* under the *Gear*, click the **Pencil** next to *Taxes and Forms*. **Uncheck** *Automate Taxes and Forms*. Select **I'll Pay and File the Right Agencies Through Their Website or By Mail**.

   Because this is a practice file, we do not want to use QuickBooks Online Payroll's tools to accidentally submit forms to the IRS and the State of California.

   If an alert appears like the one shown in Figure 13-42, make a note of the date the change will go into effect. You will adjust the dates of your time sheets and payroll run in the next chapter to ensure it is after this date. In this example, the service will be turned off on February 1, so you will create time sheets and run payroll in February. Click **Yes**.

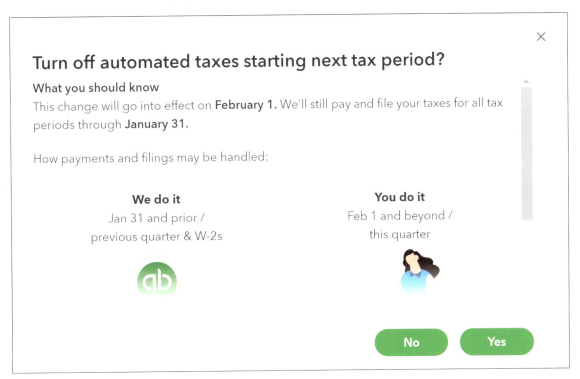

   FIGURE 13-42: *Turning off Automated Taxes—make note of the "You Do It" date.*

5. Click the **Pencil** next to *Accounting* at the bottom of the *Payroll Settings*. Set Mario Mabilia's *Class* to **Walnut Creek**.

6. In the *Payroll* section of the *Reports Center*, run an **Employee Details** report. Click the **Share** button in the upper right corner to create a **Printer Friendly** version. Save it as a PDF by clicking the blue **Print** link in the top center, then choosing **Save as PDF** in the Destination box.

CHAPTER 14

PAYROLL PROCESSING

TOPICS

In this chapter, you will learn about the following topics:

- Using the Payroll Center (page 523)
- Time Sheets (page 525)
- Payroll Processing Checklists (page 528)
- Paying Employees (page 529)
- Correcting Errors (page 537)
- Paying Taxes and Liabilities (page 545)
- Running Payroll Reports (page 548)
- Managing Employees (page 551)

OPEN THIS FILE:

Because we cannot set up payroll in the Craig's Landscaping sample file, we will run payroll using **Imagine Photography** from the *Apply Your Knowledge* exercises at the end of each chapter.

Before proceeding with this chapter, be sure to complete Chapter 13: Payroll Setup including the Apply Your Knowledge exercise at the end.

In this chapter, you'll learn to process your payroll smoothly using QuickBooks Online Core Payroll. You will create paychecks, see how payroll taxes are calculated automatically, and learn how to process payroll taxes and liability payments.

USING THE PAYROLL CENTER

The **Payroll Center** is found by clicking **Payroll** in the *Left Navigation Bar*. It has several tabs across the top. These will vary with the level of your payroll subscription, but typically include *Overview*, *Employees*, *Contractors*, *Workers' Comp*, *Benefits*, *HR Advisor*, and *Compliance*. You can use these tabs to pay employees and contractors, purchase insurance and benefit through Intuit partners, and learn about complex payroll topics.

The *Overview* tab contains alerts and action items to make sure your payroll and taxes are up-to-date. We used the *Overview* list to complete our payroll setup in the previous chapter.

One of the perks of your QuickBooks Online Payroll subscription is that you can also use it to pay 1099 contractors. We explored the *Contractors Center* in Chapter 4.

The Employees Center

The **Employees** tab, shown in Figure 14-1, is your main dashboard for managing payroll. It displays a list of all employees, which you can filter to view *Active*, *Inactive*, and *All Employees*.

Here you will also find notifications about current legislation affecting payroll, compliance issues, and other educational alerts. You can click the **X** in the corner of each to dismiss the box after you have reviewed its contents.

The **Grid Gear** on the right just above the *Employees List* allows you to customize the view by adding or removing columns.

Click the green **Run Payroll** button when it's time to create paychecks.

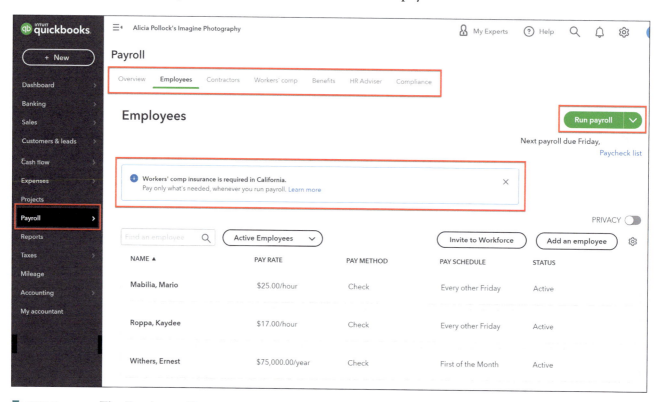

FIGURE 14-1: *The Employees Center—your screen will vary*

The employees are listed in this center, and can be filtered to view *Active Employees*, *Inactive Employees*, and *All Employees*. By clicking on each employee, you can view and edit their *Profile*, view their *Paycheck List*, view *Documents* such as the employee's W-4 form and add *Notes* about the employee (see Figure 14-2).

Before processing payroll each pay period, it is a good idea to open the *Paycheck List* and review the latest payroll activity for each employee. Doing so will help reduce payroll processing errors like creating duplicate checks or processing payroll checks with incorrect data.

FIGURE 14-2: *View an employee's Profile and Paycheck List after your first payroll run*

TIME SHEETS

Built-in Time Sheets

Timesheets are available in all versions of QuickBooks Online, from Simple Start to Advanced. As we saw in *Entering Time on a Project* in Chapter 9, employees can enter their time on Weekly Timesheets or using Single Time Activities. Note that your version of QuickBooks Online may only give you one option, ***Time Entry***, which is similar to Single Time Activity (instructions for this option are found on page 409).

A ***Single Time Activity*** is the time spent by a single person performing a single service on a single date. For example, an attorney might enter an activity on the timesheet to record a phone conversation that she will bill to one of her clients.

A ***Weekly Timesheet*** is a record of several activities performed during a one-week period by a single employee, owner, or subcontractor. Each activity or task is recorded on a separate line of the timesheet horizontally, and each day's hours are tracked vertically.

When an employee or subcontractor performs a service for a customer, you can include the customer or project name in the time activity, and mark each time activity as *Billable* if you wish to pass that charge through to the customer's next invoice.

Timesheets populate employee hours for payroll. Be sure to record all of the time for each employee, including non-billable hours like sick leave, PTO, and administrative time.

Timesheets also populate reports in the *Projects Center*. They are non-posting and do not affect the Balance Sheet.

> **DID YOU KNOW?**
>
> You can create free user accounts for employees to enter their own time directly into QuickBooks Online. When you go to *Manage Users*, choose the *Time Tracking Only* user type.

HANDS-ON PRACTICE

On Monday, Mario retouched wedding photos from two photo shoots over the weekend, then worked in the store the rest of the day. On Tuesday, Wednesday, and Friday he staffed the counter all day. He was out sick on Thursday.

To enter these time activities, follow these steps:

- **STEP 1.** Click on the **+New** button, and then choose **Weekly Timesheet** (see Figure 14-3).

    Note that if your version only shows **Time Entry**, you will have to create each of the following time activities individually instead of all in one form.

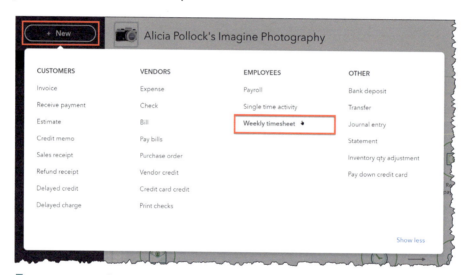

FIGURE 14-3: *Create a new Weekly Timesheet*

- **STEP 2.** Enter **Mario Mabilia** in the *Whose Time Are Your Tracking?* field at the top.

- **STEP 3.** Click the **Date Range** drop-down and choose **the first full pay period AFTER AND NOT INCLUDING the date** mentioned when you turned off *Automated Taxes* in Step 4 of Chapter 13's *Apply Your Knowledge* exercise on page 521.

- **STEP 4.** Mario only works during weekdays. Click the **Grid Gear** just above the grid on the right. Turn off **Sat** and **Sun**.

- **STEP 5.** Enter each activity in Table 14-1 on a separate line in the weekly timesheet (or create four individual time entries).

ROW	CUSTOMER OR PROJECT	SERVICE WORKED ON	DESCRIPTION	PAY ITEM	CLASS	BILLABLE (/HR)	MON	TUE	WED	THU	FRI
1	Gregg and Andrew David	Retouching	Select and edit wedding photos	Regular Pay	San Jose	Yes (195, Not Taxable)	3				
2	Robyn and Brad Tarnow	Retouching	Select and edit family photos	Regular Pay	San Jose	Yes (195, Not Taxable)	3				
3		Hours	Store	Regular Pay	Walnut Creek	No	2	8	8		8
4		Hours	Out sick	Sick Pay	Walnut Creek	No				8	

TABLE 14-1 *Create Mario Mabilia's timesheet using this data*

STEP 6. If you'd like to print your timesheet, click on the **Printer** icon on the top right of the grid (see Figure 14-4). You can also export the data to Excel.

FIGURE 14-4: *Print out your timesheet using the Printer icon in the timesheet*

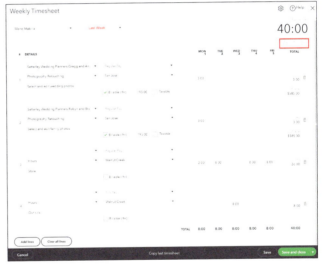

FIGURE 14-5: *Mario Mabilia's weekly timesheet separated into tasks*

STEP 7. When your screen matches Figure 14-5, click **Save and Close** to record the timesheet.

Using QuickBooks Time

If you are subscribed to QuickBooks Online Payroll Premium or Elite, you gain access to QuickBooks Time for your company. This third-party app is fully integrated into QuickBooks Online, synchronizing employees, contractors, services, classes, and more.

Using QuickBooks Time is more accurate than filling in timesheets, because the data is real-time, instead of estimated (see Figure 14-6).

Employees can clock in and clock out through a web browser, an onsite kiosk, or even on their cellphones. They can start and stop a timer, assign tasks to customer projects, and make their time billable.

QuickBooks Time allows employees to log their own PTO. At the Elite level, Time will even geofence your employees to ensure they don't clock in until they're onsite.

Managers approve all hours, which then flow through to payroll automatically.

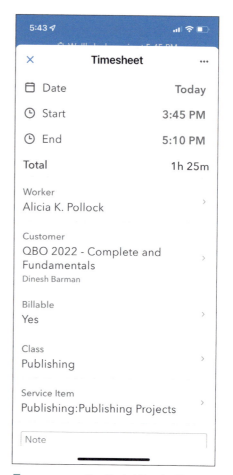

FIGURE 14-6: *QuickBooks Time on a cellphone*

PAYROLL PROCESSING CHECKLISTS

To keep your payroll running smoothly and to minimize errors, you should complete the following steps at these intervals:

Every Payday

- Visit the Payroll Overview center for notifications and action items.
- Review the previous payroll activity.
- Verify hours worked and time off.
- Create and review paychecks.
- Print paychecks and pay stubs (if necessary).

Every Tax Deposit Due Date (monthly or semi-weekly)

- Create and review liability payments.
- Submit liability payments and forms.

Every Quarter (after the end of the quarter)

- Verify the accuracy of all payroll transactions for the previous quarter.
- Create Payroll reports for the previous quarter and year-to-date.
- Create Payroll tax returns (Federal Form 941 and state quarterly returns).

Every January

- Verify the accuracy of all payroll transactions for the entire previous year.
- Submit Payroll reports for the previous quarter and year-to-date.
- Create Payroll tax returns (Federal Form 941, 940, and state yearly returns).
- Send W2s and W3.
- Submit 1099s if you paid independent contractors.
- Update State taxes for the following year if they have changed.

PAYING EMPLOYEES

In the previous chapter and *Apply Your Knowledge* exercise, you set up payroll for Imagine Photography. Once the payroll setup is complete, you are ready to process payroll checks.

Creating Paychecks

You can initiate payroll from the *Overview* tab or the *Employees* tab in the *Payroll Center*.

HANDS-ON PRACTICE

STEP 1. Start a payroll run from the *Employees* tab of the *Payroll Center* by clicking the green Run Payroll button.

STEP 2. Because we set up two Payroll Schedules, you will start by selecting which employees to pay. Select **Every Other Friday** as shown in Figure 14-7, then click **Continue**.

STEP 3. The *Run Payroll: Every Other Friday* window opens (see Figure 14-9). Leave the default **Business Checking (1025)** in the *Pay From* field.

STEP 4. The two date fields in this window are very important. The *Pay Period* indicates the date range of compensation included on the paychecks, and the *Pay Date* sets the date of the actual paycheck. Make sure you always verify these dates.

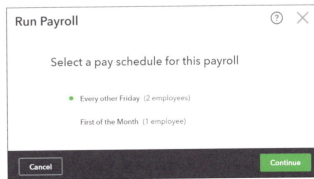

FIGURE 14-7: *Choose which payroll schedule to run*

Set the *Pay Period* to the **previous two week period**. Be sure to pick the date range that includes the timesheet you created for Mario Mabilia on page 526. You'll know you picked the right one when the *Regular Pay Hrs* and *Sick Pay Hrs* populate, although the exact amounts may vary depending on when you complete these exercises.

> **IMPORTANT:**
>
> The check date on paychecks determines when the payroll expenses show on all reports. For example, if you pay Employees on the 16th of the month for wages earned during the first half of the month, the reports will show the expenses for that payroll on the 16th.

STEP 5. Click the blue **Customize Table** link on the right. Uncheck **Memo** to hide the column. Click away from the popup to close it.

STEP 6. Because we only filled in one weekly timesheet for Mario, we only see one week's worth of time. Change his *Regular Pay Hrs* box to 72, to include his previous week of work.

STEP 7. An alert may appear, because we are entering hours directly into the grid instead of using a timesheet to allocate the hours to services or jobs. If you get the alert shown in Figure 14-8, click **Keep These Hours**.

STEP 8. Kaydee Roppa did not complete a timesheet, but during setup we entered *Default Hours*. 80 appears in the *Regular Pay Hrs* box.

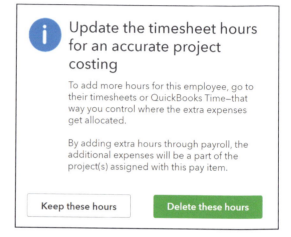

FIGURE 14-8: *An alert that the hours did not come from a timesheet*

STEP 9. Because Kaydee's role includes selling and scheduling photo shoots for Ernest, she also earns a commission. Enter **200** in her *Commission* box.

STEP 10. Kaydee also reports that she took home **$96** from the tip jar while working the register during this time period. Add this amount to the *Cash Tips* box.

STEP 11. Confirm that your paychecks match Figure 14-9.

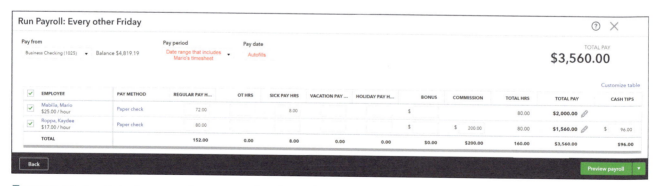

FIGURE 14-9: *Enter hours and compensation for each employee during that pay period*

STEP 12. To view the *Paycheck Detail* including taxes, deductions, and contributions, click the **Pencil** next to Kaydee's *$1,560.00 Total Pay* (see Figure 14-10).

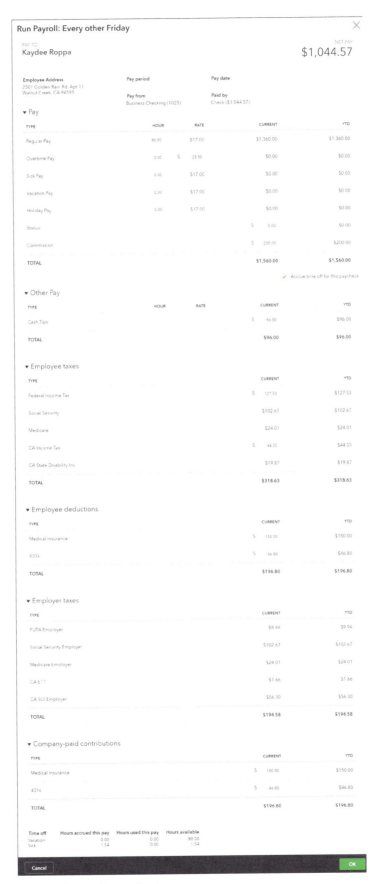

FIGURE 14-10: Preview Kaydee Roppa's paycheck—your screen may vary

Open each of the triangles next to *Employee Taxes*, *Employee Deductions*, *Employer Taxes*, and *Company-paid Contributions*. This allows you to view all the automatic deductions that QuickBooks Online has calculated for the payroll liabilities based on the tax tables and employee settings entered in the *Payroll Setup* chapter. Also note the *Time Off* accruals at the bottom.

> **NOTE:**
>
> The tax withholdings shown in Figure 14-10 may be different than what you see on your screen. Withholdings are automatically calculated using current tax tables.

Step 13. Click **OK** to close Kaydee's paycheck details and return to the *Run Payroll: Every Other Friday* window. To continue, click **Preview Payroll**.

Step 14. The *Review and Submit* window appears (see Figure 14-11). At the top, you can see the total payroll cost including employer contributions. Only the *Net Pay* will be deducted from the checking account through paychecks. The *Employee* and *Employer* subtotals are liabilities and company expenses that will be paid later.

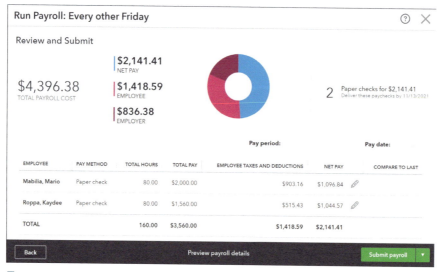

Figure 14-11: *Review and Submit is a preview of total payroll—your screen may vary*

> **DID YOU KNOW?**
>
> Many companies create a second checking account to save the payroll tax liability and employer expense portions of each payroll run until it's time to remit payment. This helps ensure cash flow so that the business is not caught short when it's time to pay.
>
> The built-in QuickBooks Checking account is a great solution for this, since it is designed to integrate with QuickBooks Payroll and QuickBooks Payments merchant services. It pays 1.75% APY interest on the money in its Envelopes, sub-accounts used to earmark funds for the future.

STEP 15. Click **Preview Payroll Details** in the black bar at the bottom of the window. A *Payroll Details Report* opens in a new window (see Figure 14-12). Verify that your report matches (Net and taxes may vary), then close the window.

Payroll Details Report

Mario Mabilia — Net $1,096.84 — Pay date:

PAY	HRS	AMT	DEDUCTIONS	AMT	EMPLOYEE-PAID TAXES	AMT	EMPLOYER-PAID TAXES	AMT
Regular Pay	72	$1,800.00	Medical Insurance	$150.00	Federal Income Tax	$162.42	FUTA Employer	$12.00
Overtime Pay	0	$0.00	401k	$100.00	Social Security	$124.00	Social Security Employer	$124.00
Sick Pay	8	$200.00	Child Support	$250.00	Medicare	$29.00	Medicare Employer	$29.00
Vacation Pay	0	$0.00			CA Income Tax	$63.74	CA ETT	$2.00
Holiday Pay	0	$0.00			CA State Disability Ins	$24.00	CA SUI Employer	$68.00
Bonus	0	$0.00						
		$2,000.00						

Kaydee Roppa — Net $1,044.57 — Pay date:

PAY	HRS	AMT	DEDUCTIONS	AMT	EMPLOYEE-PAID TAXES	AMT	EMPLOYER-PAID TAXES	AMT
Regular Pay	80	$1,360.00	Medical Insurance	$150.00	Federal Income Tax	$127.53	FUTA Employer	$9.94
Overtime Pay	0	$0.00	401k	$46.80	Social Security	$102.67	Social Security Employer	$102.67
Sick Pay	0	$0.00			Medicare	$24.01	Medicare Employer	$24.01
Vacation Pay	0	$0.00			CA Income Tax	$44.55	CA ETT	$1.66
Holiday Pay	0	$0.00			CA State Disability Ins	$19.87	CA SUI Employer	$56.30
Bonus	0	$0.00						
Commission	0	$200.00						
		$1,560.00						

TOTAL

Net $2,141.41

PAY	HRS	AMT	DEDUCTIONS	AMT	EMPLOYEE-PAID TAXES	AMT	EMPLOYER-PAID TAXES	AMT
Regular Pay	152	$3,160.00	Medical Insurance	$300.00	Federal Income Tax	$289.95	FUTA Employer	$21.94
Overtime Pay	0	$0.00	401k	$146.80	Social Security	$226.67	Social Security Employer	$226.67
Sick Pay	8	$200.00	Child Support	$250.00	Medicare	$53.01	Medicare Employer	$53.01
Vacation Pay	0	$0.00			CA Income Tax	$108.29	CA ETT	$3.66
Holiday Pay	0	$0.00			CA State Disability Ins	$43.87	CA SUI Employer	$124.30
Bonus	0	$0.00						
Commission	0	$200.00						

GRAND TOTAL

Net $2,141.41		160	$3,560.00		$696.80		$721.79	$429.58

FIGURE 14-12: *The Payroll Details report*

STEP 16. Back in the *Review and Submit* window, click **Submit Payroll**. The *Payroll Is Done!* window opens (see Figure 14-13). This window will vary depending on whether your employees are paid by check, direct deposit, or both. Because both Mario and Kaydee receive printed checks, the window contains a *Print Paychecks* button.

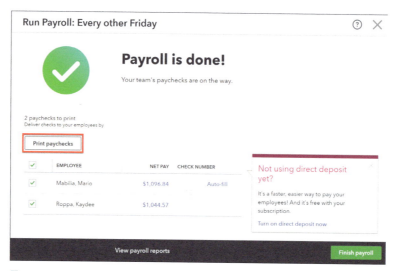

FIGURE 14-13: *The Payroll is Done window*

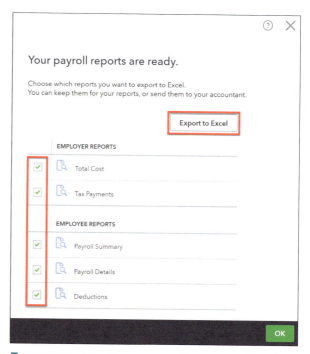

FIGURE 14-14: *Export payroll reports to Excel*

STEP 17. Click **View Payroll Reports** in the black bar at the bottom of the window. From here you can export five different Employer and Employee reports to Excel: *Total Cost, Tax Payments, Payroll Summary, Payroll Details,* and *Deductions* (see Figure 14-14). We will not do this now.

STEP 18. Click **OK** to close the payroll reports. If an additional confirmation window appears, click the **X** in the upper right to cancel it.

Printing Paychecks

Paychecks can be printed on QuickBooks Online-compatible *voucher* check stock. It's best to use voucher checks for payroll because QuickBooks Online prints the paystub information including used and available sick and vacation time. You may keep the bottom stub for your own records.

We customized the paycheck print settings on page 511.

Encourage your employees to sign up for Direct Deposit if possible. Because the service is free with your payroll subscription, it eliminates the time and cost of manually printing and delivering checks.

HANDS-ON PRACTICE

STEP 1. Click the **Print Paychecks** button, as shown in Figure 14-13. The checks will appear in a new browser window to be downloaded or printed. Note that there is no check number because it is part of the pre-printed check.

STEP 2. Click the **Printer** in the upper right corner of window (see Figure 14-15).

STEP 3. Choose **your printer** from the *Destination* drop-down as shown in Figure 14-16 (note that if you are using a browser other than Chrome, your print window will vary). Click **Print**.

> **NOTE:**
>
> For this exercise you'll print on blank paper instead of real checks. When you're printing on real checks, make sure to load the checks into the printer correctly.
>
> Every printer prints differently: front or back, bottom or top, first or last page. Experiment on blank paper until you are familiar with your printer's paper path.

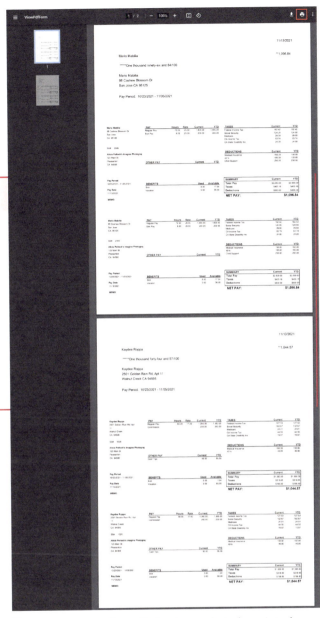

FIGURE 14-15: *Payroll checks ready to be printed—your amounts may vary*

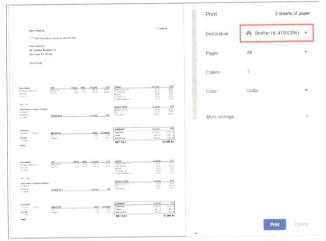

FIGURE 14-16: *Print out your paychecks on voucher stock*

STEP 4. **Close** the *browser tab* with the payroll checks.

STEP 5. Back in the *Payroll Is Done!* window, enter the *Check Numbers* that match your printed paychecks. Enter **1004** for Mario and **1005** for Kaydee.

STEP 6. Click the **Finish Payroll** button. If an alert pops up asking you to *Set Up Taxes Now*, click **I'll Do It Later**.

Printing Pay Stubs

Paystubs are the same as paychecks, but are not printed on check stock. When you pay employees by **Direct Deposit**, there is no need to print paychecks. Instead, you can print **Pay Stubs** on blank paper to distribute to your employees.

> **NOTE:**
>
> If you did not print earlier from the *Payroll Is Done!* window, these steps also allow you to print your paychecks after-the-fact.

HANDS-ON PRACTICE

STEP 1. Click on the **Overview** tab, and then click the **View Paycheck List** link (see Figure 14-17).

STEP 2. Click in the boxes to the left of the checks or paystubs you wish to print as shown in Figure 14-18, then click **Print**. From here the instructions are the same as printing paychecks.

STEP 3. **Close** the browser tab with the check stubs when done.

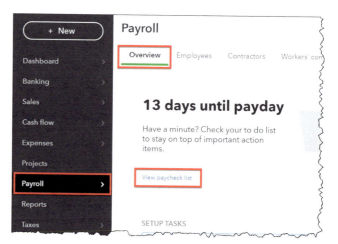

FIGURE 14-17: *Click View Paycheck List to print checks or paystubs*

FIGURE 14-18: *Select the paychecks you wish to print*

Supplemental Payroll Runs

There will be times when you need to pay employees outside of payroll. For example, you might pay a Sales Rep a straight Commission without wages. At the end of the year you may give your employees a holiday bonus, or need to pay the owner fringe benefits, like their S-Corp Owners Health Insurance.

To run these supplemental paychecks, click the **drop-down arrow** next to the *Run Payroll* button (see Figure 14-19).

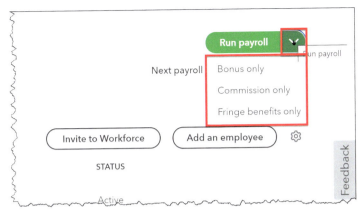

FIGURE 14-19: *Supplemental payroll is found under the Run Payroll drop-down*

> **KEY TERM:**
>
> **Fringe Benefits** are incentives and compensation packages that companies offer employees in addition to their pay in order to foster a positive work environment. These include health insurance and retirement, but can also include perks such as gym memberships, tuition reimbursement, child care, or workplace catering. Some are deducted from paychecks, while others are offered for free. Some fringe benefits are considered taxable income and therefore are included when running payroll.

CORRECTING ERRORS

It is possible to edit, void, or delete paychecks, but it's best to avoid changing any except the most recent.

If you need to correct past paychecks that have already been processed or deposited, you will need to contact Payroll Support and submit a correction. If the employee has other paychecks dated after this check, changes you make may invalidate the tax calculations on newer checks.

Editing Paychecks

Editing paychecks should only be done while you are processing payroll, before checks have been printed or Direct Deposit funds have been drawn. If the *Status* column on the *Paycheck List* indicates that payroll has already been processed, you will need to contact Payroll Support to perform the correction.

While it is possible to edit paychecks in QuickBooks Online even after they've been printed, this should only be done if you haven't sent the paycheck to the employee. If the check has already been printed, you will need to update the check number, then create a blank placeholder check with the missing check number in order to maintain a complete activity record and check numbering sequence.

HANDS-ON PRACTICE

Kaydee reminds you that she worked an extra two hours of overtime on one of the photo shoots with Ernest over the weekend. Since she hasn't cashed her paycheck yet, you can edit and replace it.

STEP 1.   From the *Employees Center*, click on **Kaydee Roppa**.

Step 2. Click on the **Paycheck List** tab.

Step 3. Click on the paycheck to view it.

Step 4. Click the **Make Adjustment** button on the top right of the screen and select **Edit** (see Figure 14-20).

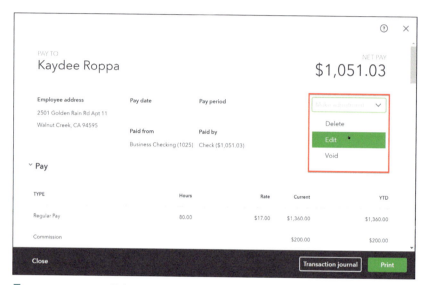

Figure 14-20: *Editing, Deleting, and Voiding a paycheck*

Step 5. Note that the *Hours* boxes can be edited. Under the collapsed sections, some of the current taxes and contributions are also editable (see Figure 14-21). Be sure to consult your accountant before manually changing these totals.

Step 6. Add **2** hours of *Overtime Pay* and update the *Check Number* to **1006** (see Figure 14-21).

Step 7. Click **OK** to save the changes and return to the *Paycheck List*.

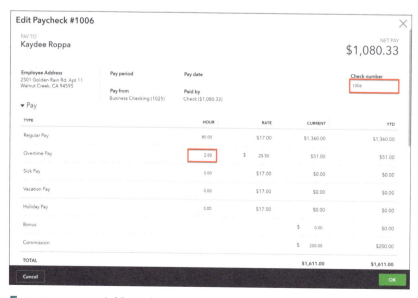

Figure 14-21: *Add two hours of overtime and update the check number. Amounts may vary*

STEP 8.   Because check 1005 is now missing from the register, we will create a new check as a placeholder. From the **+New** button, create a **Check** from the **Business Checking (1025)** account with the **same date** as the payroll run, numbered **1005**, made out to **Kaydee Roppa**. Categorize it to the *Wages* account. In the *Description* field add **Incorrect Paycheck—replaced with 1006**. Enter the *Amount* of **1044.57**, the original net pay. Add **Walnut Creek** in the *Class*. When your check matches Figure 14-22, **Save and Close** it.

FIGURE 14-22: *Void a placeholder check to maintain your check numbering sequence*

STEP 9.   Using the **Search** magnifying glass in the upper right corner of the window, reopen the check you just created.

STEP 10. Click the **More** button to **Void** the new check you just created, and confirm the warning alert that appears. This converts the check into a placeholder with the same check number and information as the missing check, maintaining your check numbering. The **Void** notation flags this check as unusual.

The paychecks and voided placeholder appear in the checking register, as shown in Figure 14-23.

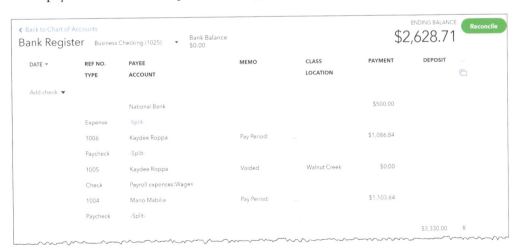

FIGURE 14-23: *Paychecks in the checking register*

Voiding or Deleting Paychecks

These actions should only be taken on the most recent paycheck for this employee.

The only time you should **Delete** a paycheck is when you created it in error, and it hasn't been processed or printed. If you need to make changes to a paycheck that you have already printed, it's best to **Void** the check in order to maintain your check numbering sequence.

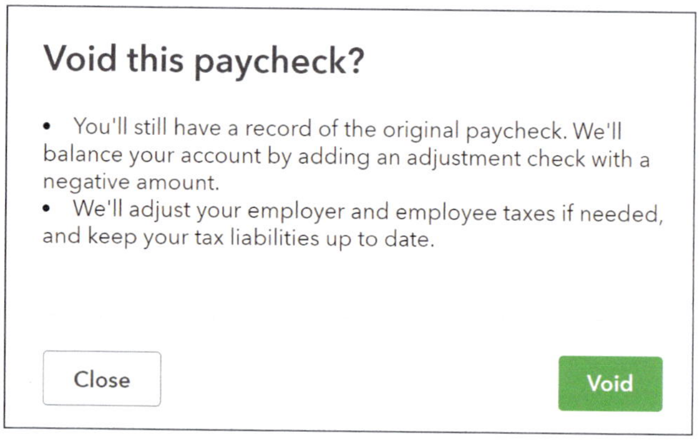

Paychecks can be voided by clicking **Void** in the *Make Adjustment* drop-down, as we saw in Figure 14-20, or depending on what screen you're on, from the black bar at the bottom of the check. The alert message may let you know that your upcoming tax liabilities will be adjusted to compensate.

FIGURE 14-24: *An alert before voiding a paycheck*

Replacing Lost or Stolen Checks

When a paycheck is lost, you can't just void the original transaction and create a new one. If the paycheck to be replaced was not the most recent paycheck for that employee, QuickBooks Online would not be able to recreate the check exactly as the original, because the year-to-date information is calculated by taking all paychecks (regardless of their date) and adding their amounts together.

To avoid this problem, reprint the original paycheck using a new check number, and void a dummy check as a placeholder for the lost paycheck.

Be sure to put a Stop Payment on the missing check with the bank, in case the employee later finds the original and tries to cash it.

> *Do not perform these steps now. They are for reference only.*

1. Find the check in the *Paycheck List* or in the *Checking* account register, then click to open it. Update the *Check Number* to the new check number.

2. Add a *Memo* at the bottom of the check that says **Reprinted on [current date]**.

3. Click **OK** to save your change.

4. Reprint the original check with the new check number.

5. Create a voided placeholder check, just as we did earlier in Figure 14-22 when we edited Kaydee's paycheck. Use the same date, payee, amount, and check number as the original lost check. Categorize it to the **Wages** account. In the *Description* field add **Lost paycheck—replaced with [new check number]**.

6. After saving the placeholder check, **Void** it.

PAYING TAXES AND LIABILITIES

The Payroll Tax Center

The **Payroll Tax Center** is found under **Taxes** in the *Left Navigation Bar*. This is where you go to make your payments, as well as view past payments, archived forms, and future accruing taxes (see Figure 14-25).

There is also a tab here for *1099 Filings*, although you will only be able to use the tool from November through January.

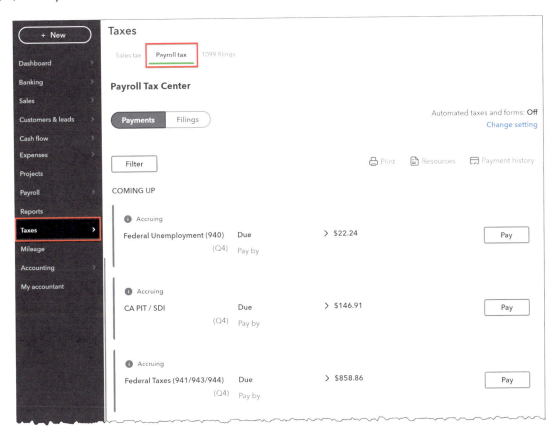

FIGURE 14-25: *The Payroll Tax Center—your screen will vary*

The *Payments* tab lists your upcoming and overdue taxes. The *Filings* tab contains the archive of past forms for easy access.

QuickBooks Online Payroll encourages you to e-file your payments directly with the IRS and your state. When you file electronically, you can manually initiate the payment or automate the process to file for you so that you never miss a deadline.

To correctly pay your payroll liabilities, always follow the prompts in the Payroll Tax Center. If filing electronically through QuickBooks Online Payroll is not possible for some reason, and you instead pay online through the agency website or send checks in the mail, you will still initiate the process and mark the transaction as Paid through the Payroll Tax Center.

Do not manually create checks or categorize the payments through the Banking Feed, because neither action affects the Payroll calculations. As a result, your reports will be incorrect and those liability payments won't be included on tax forms 940 or 941.

Payroll Compliance

Payroll Liabilities are the money collected from employees through payroll deductions and owed to various government and local agencies on their behalf. They are not company expenses because they are pass-throughs from the employees.

Paying your payroll liabilities correctly is a critical part of maintaining accurate payroll information in QuickBooks Online.

The IRS *Publication 15, Circular E, Employer's Tax Guide,* specifies the rules for when your payroll taxes must be paid. Depending on the size of your payroll, most businesses will be either a **Monthly** depositor or a **Semi-weekly** depositor. Monthly depositors are required to pay all Payroll Liabilities by the 15th of the month following the payroll date. Semi-weekly depositors are required to pay all Payroll Liabilities by the Wednesday after the payroll date if the payroll date is Wednesday, Thursday, or Friday, and are required to pay all Payroll Liabilities by the Friday after the payroll date if the run falls on a Saturday through Tuesday.

Very few businesses qualify to make deposits quarterly, as total payroll liabilities for the quarter must be less than $2,500.

THE ACCOUNTING BEHIND THE SCENES:

You must use **QuickBooks Online Payroll** to record liability payments. Payroll Liability payments decrease (debit) the Payroll Liability accounts and decrease (credit) your payment method.

Paying Taxes

When it's time to make your semi-weekly, monthly, quarterly, or annual payroll tax payments, QuickBooks Online Payroll alerts you through notifications on your Dashboard and Payroll Overview screens. Clicking on the alerts brings you directly to the Payroll Tax Center.

In our sample file, taxes are accruing based on Imagine Photography's recent paychecks, but it's not time to pay them yet. After the period ends, the screen will change to indicate which taxes are ready to be paid. You will have an opportunity to *Review* the forms for accuracy, and then either create the electronic payment, or use the *Pay* button to indicate that you made the payment by check or on the agency's website.

HANDS-ON PRACTICE

Even though it may not be time to make these payments yet, let's walk through the process to show how it works.

STEP 1. Click on **Taxes** in the *Left Navigation Bar*, then choose **Payroll Tax**. A list of upcoming payments appears.

STEP 2. Click **Show All** at the bottom of the list to see all the accruing taxes. Find **CA SUI/ETT** on the list, and click the **Pay** button on the far right. A warning message may appear if it's not actually time to make the payment. In real life, you would click **No, I'll Wait**. For this exercise, choose **Yes, Continue**.

STEP 3. In Figure 14-26 we can see the *Liability Period, Due Date,* and the list of Liabilities that will be included in this payment. Confirm that the *Bank Account* is the correct checking account. Your dates will vary.

Step 4. You can set your *Payment Date* to be the **Earliest** date available (today) or the **Latest** date (the day it's due). If you select **Other**, you'll be able to use the calendar to suggest the date of your choice.

If you are making a payment manually by sending a check instead of using QuickBooks Online Payroll's e-filing system, enter the *Check Number* at the bottom. There is also a field for entering *Notes* that you want to remember.

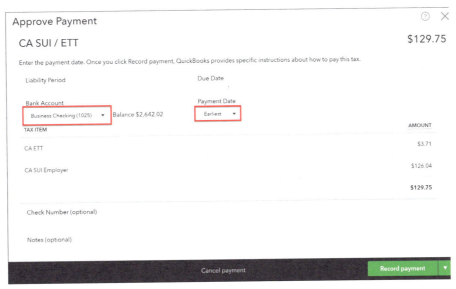

Figure 14-26: *Making a State Payroll Tax payment*

Step 5. Click the **Record Payment** button. Note that the drop-down arrow in this button includes the option to print a copy of the filing. QuickBooks Online will also archive a copy of the payment for easy access.

Step 6. A *Payment Confirmation* alert appears, as shown in Figure 14-27. Review the information to confirm it is correct. Because we have indicated that we are paying the tax manually, the instructions include information for paying by check. If we had e-filed the payment, the message in this box would relate to that method.

Click **View and Print Form**.

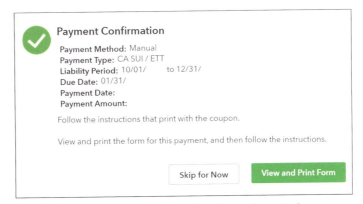

Figure 14-27: *The Payment Confirmation window*

STEP 7. Next you would print out the payment voucher shown in Figure 14-28 and mail it with your printed check. **Close** this window when you are done.

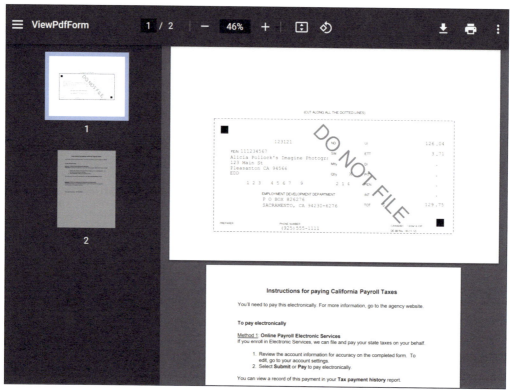

FIGURE 14-28: *Print out the State Tax payment voucher if you are paying by check*

At the end of the year, you will be able to submit **Annual Payroll Forms** including Form 941, Form 940, and W-2s right from the *Payroll Center*.

Be sure to process your monthly and quarterly tax payments prior to sending your annual forms and payments. The 941 will use these payments for its *Deposits Made* calculation. The 940 form computes your Federal Unemployment Tax based on the 940 contributions, your State Unemployment liabilities, and payments made throughout the year (if applicable). All of the payroll tax forms calculate automatically using the information on paychecks and Payroll Liability payments.

At the end of the year, not only will you be able to quickly and simply e-file all this documentation, but QuickBooks Online Payroll will also send W2s to your employees through the mail as well as digitally in their Workforce portal.

Tax Payment Errors

If you find an error in the amount that QuickBooks Online suggests you owe, it could be for several reasons. For example, if your state unemployment rate changed in this period and you didn't update it in the *Payroll Settings*, the amount due may still be calculating at the old rate. In this case, the Payroll Item needs to be corrected, and QBO will create a **Liability Adjustment** to correct the period in question.

Another reason **Pay Liabilities** accruals may appear wrong is that prior payments were not created through the *Payroll Tax Center*, or were dated incorrectly. In this case, the payments may need to be created properly, and the incorrect transactions voided.

Finally, you could check each paycheck to see if one created the error. When you find the erroneous paycheck or paychecks, modify the Payroll Items on the paycheck. Of course, if you've already printed the paycheck, you should never make adjustments affecting net pay. Instead, contact Payroll Support, or make an adjustment on the next check for the affected employees.

If you need to edit an existing liability payment, you can delete it and recreate it as shown in Figure 14-29. However, make sure you only do this if you haven't yet submitted the payment to the tax agency. If you already made the payment, call Payroll Support to fix the error. You will then need to file an amendment with the government agency.

Paying Deduction Liabilities

When you look at your Balance Sheet, you are able to see your current Payroll Liabilities, as shown in Figure 14-30.

Every time you run payroll, these amounts will increase. When you use the Payroll Tax Center to make a liability payment, these amounts will decrease.

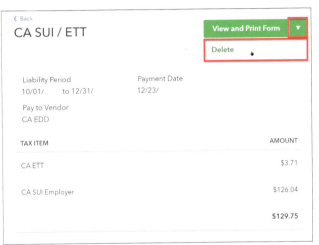

FIGURE 14-29: *Deleting an incorrect tax liability payment*

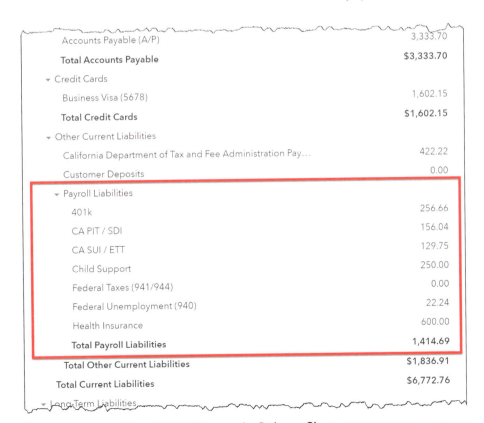

FIGURE 14-30: *Payroll Liabilities on the Balance Sheet—your screen may vary*

Liability payments for Health Insurance, Worker's Comp, and Child Support are not part of the QuickBooks Online Payroll workflow. When you make payments to vendors for child support garnishments and health insurance, be sure to categorize them to the proper liability account.

- Health insurance costs, depending on your situation, may need to be split between the liability (the *Employee* portion deducted from paychecks) and the Insurance Expense (the *Employer* portion paid by the company). QBO Payroll takes care of this for you behind the scenes.

- Child support garnishments are deducted from the employee's paycheck and held as a liability. The payment must be made directly to the appropriate agency. When you make the payment to the vendor, categorize it to the Child Support Payroll Liabilities account.

> **TIP:**
>
> It's a best practice to reconcile these accounts on a monthly, quarterly, or annual basis, just as you would a bank account. By reconciling to liability account to zero and matching the accruals to each payment, you ensure that liability and expense payments are being categorized correctly, and that you have remitted the same amounts that you have collected.

Viewing Payroll Tax History and Resources

The **Payroll Tax Center**, found by clicking on **Taxes** in the *Left Navigation Bar* and then on **Payroll Tax**, contains more than just accruing payroll taxes. It is also a wealth of resources you need to stay in compliance.

The **Resources** button (shown on the right in Figure 14-25) contains different links when you toggle between the *Payments* button and the *Filings* button. Both contain links to:
   a. Upload tax notices you receive from the IRS or your state, so that you can share them with Intuit to get issues resolved.
   b. Year-end procedures and compliance resources.
   c. Direct links to edit your Payroll Settings.
   d. Links to forms to register your business with the IRS, and for your employees to fill out upon hire.

HANDS-ON PRACTICE

STEP 8. Go to the *Payroll Tax Center* if you are not there already. Click on the **Payments** button, then click on the **Resources** button on the right. There are shortcuts here for:
   a. Your archived tax payment history.
   b. Your tax liability reports.
   c. Recording the history of tax payments made before your first payroll run in QBO.

STEP 9. Click on **Tax Payment History**. The window in Figure 14-31 opens. Click on the **CA SUI/ETT** payment to view it. From there you can also *View and Print* the voucher or *Delete* the payment altogether.

STEP 10. Click the blue **<Back** link in the upper left corner to return to the *Payroll Tax Payments* screen.

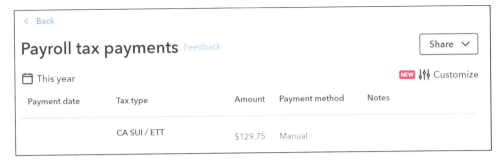

FIGURE 14-31: *View Payroll Tax payments made—your screen may vary*

STEP 11. To see archived forms, return to the *Payroll Tax Center* and click on the **Filings** tab. This window will list upcoming form filings with due dates. You can also access your archived forms, grouped by type.

STEP 12. Click on the **Resources** button again to open the screen in Figure 14-32. This list is mostly the same as before, with a few new options specific to submitting forms:
   a. Annual, monthly, and quarterly forms to send to employees and government agencies, such as your employees' W2 forms.
   b. Archived forms and filings.
   c. A place to order paper forms if you are processing manually.

STEP 13. Click on **Archived Forms and Filings** to view your history. There is nothing there because we have not actually filed anything yet. Click **<Back to Payroll Tax Center**, then click on the **Payments** button.

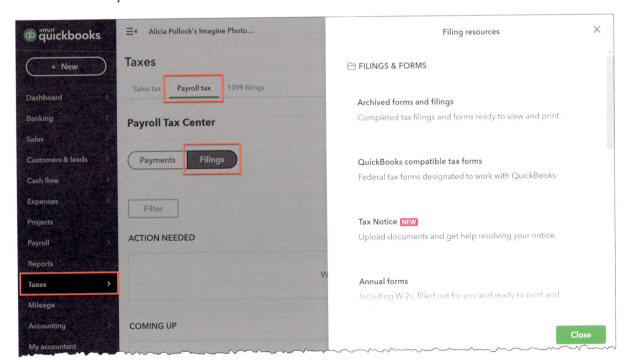

FIGURE 14-32: *The Payroll Tax Filings Resources Center*

RUNNING PAYROLL REPORTS

The *Reports Center* has an entire section for payroll reports. If you are using an outside payroll company instead of QuickBooks Online Payroll, you will only see a few related to employees. After you have subscribed to QBO Payroll, this section expands to include a variety of reports about payroll, taxes, retirement plans, PTO, and more.

We will highlight a few key reports, but you should explore the rest of the reports to discover which ones are most important to your company. Remember that many reports can be further customized and saved for payroll analysis.

Payroll Details Report

We already viewed the *Payroll Details* report while running payroll. This report listing all the employees' pay, deductions, and taxes for a single payroll run is also available in the *Reports Center*.

Payroll Summary Report

The *Payroll Summary* report shows the detail of each employee's earnings, taxes, and net pay.

HANDS-ON PRACTICE

STEP 1. Click on **Reports** in the *Left Navigation Bar*. Scroll down to the *Payroll* section, and then choose **Payroll Summary** (see Figure 14-33).

STEP 2. The date range defaults to the **Last Pay Date**, but you could extend it to see a longer timeframe.

FIGURE 14-33: *Payroll Summary report—amounts may vary*

STEP 3. The *Payroll Summary* report shows columns for deductions and contributions. You can filter this report by employee or hide columns by clicking the **Customize** button at the top right of the report as shown in Figure 14-34.

We will not make any changes at this time. Click **Cancel** to return to the report.

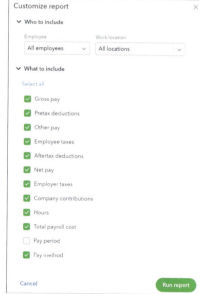

FIGURE 14-34: *Customize the Payroll Summary*

Payroll Tax Liability Report

The *Payroll Tax Liability* report is used to track the status of your payroll liabilities by Payroll Item.

HANDS-ON PRACTICE

Step 1. Click on **Reports** in the *Left Navigation Bar*. Scroll down to the *Payroll* section, and then choose **Payroll Tax Liability** (see Figure 14-35).

Step 2. The report defaults to the **Last Pay Date**. Change the date range to **This Quarter** and click **Apply.**

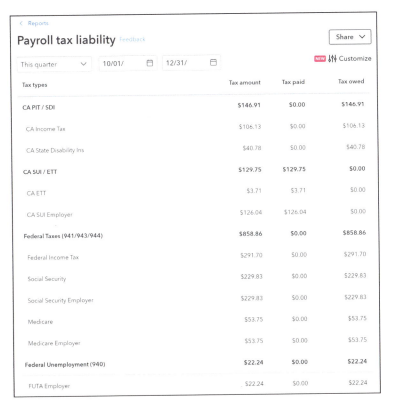

Figure 14-35: *Payroll Tax Liability Report—your report may vary*

Figure 14-36: *Total Payroll Cost report—your report may vary*

Total Payroll Cost Report

The *Total Payroll Cost* report is used to track net pay, company contributions, and employer taxes, showing the complete cost to the company on behalf of employees. This report does not include payments for liabilities deducted from gross wages.

HANDS-ON PRACTICE

Step 1. Click on **Reports** in the *Left Navigation Bar*. Scroll down to the *Payroll* section, and then choose **Total Payroll Cost** (see Figure 14-36).

Step 2. Change the date range to **This Quarter** and click **Apply.**

Vacation and Sick Leave Report

The *Vacation and Sick Leave* report lets you know how much Paid Time Off employees have accrued and used for your Sick Pay and Vacation Leave policies.

HANDS-ON PRACTICE

STEP 1. Click on **Reports** in the *Left Navigation Bar.* Scroll down to the *Payroll* section, and then choose **Vacation and Sick Leave** (see Figure 14-37).

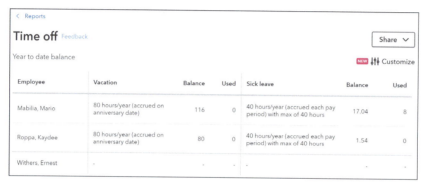

FIGURE 14-37: *Vacation and Sick Leave Report*

Sales Rep Commissions

This report is not built into QBO, but if you pay *commissions* to your employees, you can create a custom report to view your sales grouped by Sales Rep to help calculate the commissions due.

In order to have this information available, be sure to create a **Custom Field** for Sales Reps as demonstrated on page 70, and include the information on all invoices and sales receipts.

If the report basis is set to **Accrual**, it will show sales recorded on invoices even if the customer has not paid the invoice. If you want to show only sales for which the company has received payment, change the basis to **Cash** on this report.

HANDS-ON PRACTICE

STEP 1. Select **Reports** in the *Left Navigation Bar*, then scroll down to *Sales and Customers*, and run the **Sales by Customer Detail** report (see Figure 14-38).

STEP 2. Change the *Report Period* to **Last Month**.

STEP 3. Change the *Group By* to **Sales Rep**.

STEP 4. Choose **Cash** as the *Accounting Method.* Click **Run Report**.

STEP 5. Change the columns shown by clicking on the **Grid Gear** at the top of the report. Check **Customer** and uncheck **Memo/Description**.

STEP 6. Click on the title of the report and change it to **Sales Rep Commissions**.

STEP 7. Your report will now look like Figure 14-38, although the transactions listed will vary. Click **Save Customization** to save the report to use it again next month.

PAYROLL PROCESSING | 551

FIGURE 14-38: *Sales Rep Commissions Report—your report will vary*

> **NOTE:**
>
> These instructions demonstrate how to make a Sales Rep report that you can memorize and use every month. Depending on when you created the sales transactions in Chapters 5 and 10, your list will vary.

MANAGING EMPLOYEES

Terminating Employees

When you release or terminate an employee, edit the employee's *Employment Details*. Update the **Status** field with their reason for leaving and the date on which the employee separated from the company (see Figure 14-39). You have the option to show released employees in the *Employee List*.

HANDS-ON PRACTICE

Kaydee Roppa is offered another job and decides to leave Imagine Photography. Ernest needs to remove her from payroll.

FIGURE 14-39: *Terminating an employee*

STEP 1. Open the *Employees Center* by clicking on **Payroll** in the *Left Navigation Bar*, then clicking on the **Employees** tab.

STEP 2. Click on **Kaydee Roppa**.

STEP 3. Click the **Edit** link in the *Employment Details* section.

STEP 4. Change the *Status* to **Terminated** (see Figure 14-39). Notice that there are many reasons for releasing employees including a paid or unpaid leave of absence, no longer on payroll, and deceased.

STEP 5. In the *Termination Date* field, enter **today's date**.

STEP 6. **Uncheck** the *Show in Employee Lists Only* option so that her employee record will continue to appear in relevant lists and reports.

STEP 7. Click **Save**. Click back to the *Employee List*. Kaydee no longer appears.

Reactivating Employees

If an employee returns to work, reactivate their employee record instead of starting a fresh account.

HANDS-ON PRACTICE

After just a week away, Kaydee realizes that she made a mistake and would like to return to Imagine Photography. Ernest is willing to rehire her.

STEP 8. While in the *Employees Center*, click the *Active Employees* button and change it to **Inactive Employees** (see Figure 14-40).

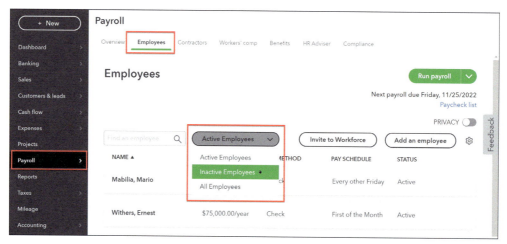

FIGURE 14-40: *Show inactive employees*

STEP 9. Click on **Roppa, Kaydee**, then on the **Edit** link in the *Employment Details* section.

STEP 10. Update her *Status* to **Active**. You could update her *Hire Date* or leave the original date in place, according to your company policies. Click **Save** to close the window.

STEP 11. Click the blue **Employee List** link in the upper left corner to return to the *Employees Center*.

REVIEW QUESTIONS

Comprehension Questions

1. What type of check (standard 3-up or voucher) is the best choice for printing paychecks? Why?
2. What are some of the benefits of using QuickBooks Time instead of QBO's built-in timesheets?
3. Should you ever delete a paycheck that was printed and given to the employee? Why or why not?
4. Why should all Federal and State Tax payments be made from within the Payroll Tax Center?

Multiple Choice
Select the best answer(s) for each of the following:

1. To properly affect Payroll liabilities, which workflow should you use to pay the Payroll taxes?
   a. Checks
   b. Bills
   c. Run Payroll
   d. Payroll Tax Center

2. Voucher style checks, when used for processing payroll, may contain:
   a. Earnings and tax withholdings.
   b. Company taxes.
   c. Federal filing status.
   d. All of the above.

3. The Payroll Tax Liability report identifies:
   a. Liability payments made during the payment period.
   b. Tax Liability amounts by Payroll Item.
   c. Liabilities for Employee deductions only.
   d. Liabilities for employer taxes only.

4. Which statement is true?
   a. You can print pay stubs at any time.
   b. Pay stubs can be printed using Standard 3-Up checks.
   c. If you find an error in a past paycheck, you should delete and recreate the paycheck to ensure accuracy.
   d. You cannot void a paycheck.

5. To begin processing your payroll:
   a. Select Checks from +New button.
   b. In the *Payroll Taxes Center*, click the Run Payroll button.
   c. View an employee and then click Pay Now.
   d. In the *Employees Center*, click the Run Payroll button.

6. QuickBooks Online automatically calculates paychecks using information from the following sources except:
   a. Amounts on all previous paychecks.
   b. The employee's timesheet.
   c. The employee's tax settings in the employee record.
   d. The employee's expense report.

7. With a QuickBooks Online Core Payroll subscription, which forms cannot be submitted directly from QuickBooks Online?
   a. State Payroll Tax forms.
   b. 940.

    c. W2.
    d. All of the above can be submitted through QuickBooks Online Core payroll subscription.

8. Which of these is not true about Auto Payroll?
    a. It's not available until after your first payroll run.
    b. There is no way to edit each run.
    c. It uses an employee's Default Hours as the basis.
    d. You can use it for some employees but not others.

9. The Payroll Summary Report shows:
    a. The detail of each employee's earnings only.
    b. The YTD employee's earnings by Class.
    c. The employee's personal profile information.
    d. The detail of each employee's hours, earnings, taxes, and net pay.

10. If the Pay Liabilities window shows incorrect tax amounts due, the problem could be caused by:
    a. Incorrect user entry of current state payroll tax rates.
    b. Writing Checks to pay taxes.
    c. Users overriding calculated taxes.
    d. Any of the above.

11. To have data from timesheets affect an employee's paychecks:
    a. Use the Weekly Timesheet.
    b. Use the Single Time Activity.
    c. Use QuickBooks Time.
    d. Any of the above.

12. Which report breaks down all employees' pay, deductions, and taxes for a single payroll run?
    a. Total Payroll Cost report.
    b. Payroll Tax Liability report.
    c. Payroll Details report.
    d. Payroll Summary report.

13. How do you pay a salaried employee for vacation time?
    a. Vacation time is not available for salaried employees.
    b. Use a Vacation payroll item and enter the hours in the *Vacation Pay* column.
    c. Enter vacation time in the employee's record.
    d. Enter vacation hours on the pay stub.

14. When employees are on Direct Deposit, how can they see their paystubs?
    a. They can't.
    b. They can log in to Workforce.
    c. You can print out their paystubs on plain paper.
    d. Both b and c.

Completion Statements

1. To job-cost wages, employees should submit their hours using _____.

2. The pay employees receive as a percentage of their sales is called a _____.

3. The feature that allows you to repeat the previous payroll run is called _____ _____.

4. When you pay state and federal payroll taxes, the payment credits your _____.

5. When you release an employee, edit the employee record and change the Status to _____.

PAYROLL PROCESSING—APPLY YOUR KNOWLEDGE

> Log into your **Imagine Photography** class file at qbo.intuit.com.
>
> **Before proceeding with this chapter, be sure to complete Chapter 13: Payroll Setup including the Apply Your Knowledge exercise at the end.**

1. Follow the steps in the chapter to complete your first payroll run for **Kaydee Roppa** and **Mario Mabilia**. Print out the **Payroll Summary Report**.

2. Run a **First of the Month** payroll for **Ernest Withers**. It should automatically enter the **first day of next month** for a *Total Pay* of **$6,250**. Assign *Check Number* **1007**.

3. Run a **Total Payroll Cost** report with a **Custom Date Range for the month including both of the two payroll runs**. **Print** or **Save** the report.

4. Create a **Weekly Timesheet** for **Mario Mabilia** dated the **week following the timesheet you created for Mario in Chapter 14**, using the hours in Table 14-2.

ROW	CUSTOMER OR PROJECT	SERVICE WORKED ON	DESCRIPTION	PAY ITEM	CLASS	BILLABLE (/HR)	MON	TUE	WED	THU	FRI
1	Madeira Builders: Barnett Residence	Retouching	Photo Retouching Services	Regular Pay	San Jose	Yes (not Taxable)	3				
2	Madeira Builders: Devoe Residence	Retouching	Photo Retouching Services	Regular Pay	San Jose	Yes (not Taxable)		5			
3		Hours	Manage Store	Regular Pay	Walnut Creek	No			8	8	8
4	Veronica Vasquez: Marketing Photos	Retouching	Photo Retouching Services	Regular Pay	San Jose	Yes (not Taxable)					4
5		Hours	Took time off	Vacation Pay	San Jose	No					4

TABLE 14-2 *Mario Mabilia's hours*

5. Process paychecks for using the **Every other Friday** *pay schedule* for Kaydee Roppa and Mario Mabilia for the **date range following the one used in the chapter**. Leave the default *Pay Date*. Each employee should display **80** *Total Hrs*. For **Kaydee**, include a **$100** *Commission* and **$40** in *Cash Tips*. The *Total Pay* will equal **$3,460.00**. Print both paychecks on blank paper. Use voucher checks for the format of the printed checks. Assign *Check Number* **1008** to Mario and **1009** to Kaydee.

6. Run a **Payroll Details Report** for the **Last Pay Date** in **Portrait** orientation. **Print or Save as PDF.**

7. Pay the most recent **Upcoming CA PIT/SDI tax**, even though it's not due yet (for the sake of the exercise—don't pay early in real life). Choose the *Payment Date* **Latest**. Assign *Check Number* **1010**. **View and Print Form.**

8. Print or save a **Payroll Tax Liability** report for **This Year**. This report includes the CA payment you just made, as well as the state tax payment from the chapter.

9. Answer the following questions using your payroll reports:
   a. What is the **Net Pay** for the Kaydee and Mario's **second payroll run**? What does this figure represent?
   b. What is the **Total Payroll Cost** for the Kaydee and Mario's payroll run? What does this figure represent?

c. In the **Payroll Tax Liability** report for this year, how much **Federal Tax (941/943/944)** is owed?
d. Mario's Total Payroll Cost is much higher than Kaydee's, but his paycheck was almost the same. Why?
e. Some of Mario's time includes doing photo retouching, and this time is Billable to customers. What is the total cost of the Unbilled Activity waiting to be invoiced to the customers? Where can you go to look for this information?

CHAPTER 15

CAPSTONE PROJECT: YINYANG GRAPHIC DESIGN

OUR STORY CONTINUES...

MaryBeth Yang's graphic design and marketing company has been an instant success. By leveraging a few YouTube influencers, her retail e-commerce website has gone viral.

She has also become a sought-after consultant by other local boutiques who want to leverage her know-how to tap into the mind (and pockets) of Millennials. She gives weekly lunch-and-learn marketing trainings at businesses around town, where she also sells samples of her merchandise.

To keep up with demand, she has hired a full-time employee, Hartley McGill, for project management. She also hired a 1099 contractor, Ingrid Swick, to help create the graphics and videos for her clients' marketing campaigns.

MaryBeth loves her QuickBooks Online subscription to help not only manage her business operations, but also fulfill her fiduciary responsibilities from an accounting, tax and compliance perspective.

Using QuickBooks Online and the company you created in Chapter 8, you will set up a project with job costing, manage inventory, record a barter, and run payroll. At the end, you will answer several questions about the finances for YinYang Graphic Design.

> **Open this File**:
> Open the YinYang Graphic Design company you created in Chapter 8. If you have not completed that case study, you will need to do so before continuing with this exercise.

INSTRUCTIONS

1. Set up Payroll.
2. Create a Project.
3. Set up a Contractor.
4. Set up Mileage.
5. Set up Price Rules.
6. Enter business transactions.
7. Prepare reports.
8. Complete analysis questions.

> **IMPORTANT!**
>
> Because you are a student and have never entered billing information, you will not get charged for the Payroll subscription, but the Payroll features will stop working after the trial period unless you pay! Be sure to complete this chapter within 30 days.

YINYANG GRAPHIC DESIGN CAPSTONE PROJECT

1. Set Up Payroll

STEP 1. **Turn on Payroll** in the YinYang Graphic Design Student Trial subscription. Be sure to scroll down to the bottom of the page and choose the **Core** plan with a **free 30-day trial**.

STEP 2. You have not paid employees yet this year.

STEP 3. Your next *payday* is **the 1st of next month**.

STEP 4. The *Primary Work Location* is **400 Broad St, Seattle WA 98109**.

STEP 5. Enter **your name and email address** as the *Payroll Contact*. Leave the default phone number.

STEP 6. MaryBeth will not receive a paycheck because she is the owner of an LLC. She will be paid using Owner Draws instead. As a result, you can skip setting up her employee profile.

STEP 7. Set up MaryBeth's new employee, Hartley McGill, along with the Payroll Items for YinYang Graphic Design. **Uncheck** the option to *Self-setup in Workforce*.

Instead, use the information in the tables below to create Hartley's employee record as well as YinYang Graphic Design's company payroll policies.

Table 15-1 contains *Hartley's personal information*, and Table 15-2 contains *YinYang Graphic Designs' payroll policies and employee benefits*.

The information will not be entered sequentially since it depends on whether you use the Payroll Setup Wizard or enter the information manually. You will need to look in both tables for the required data.

Note that Intuit may change the location or the wording of some of the settings.

If a field is not mentioned, leave the defaults.

There are check boxes in each table to help you keep track of the information you have entered.

INFORMATION ABOUT HARTLEY MCGILL		
FIELD	**PERSONAL INFO**	**COMPLETED**
FIRST NAME	**Hartley**	☐
M.I.	**J**	☐
LAST NAME	**McGill**	☐
EMAIL	**Your email address**	☐
EMPLOYEE SELF-SETUP THROUGH WORKFORCE	**Uncheck.** You will fill in the information manually.	☐
BIRTH DATE	**12/07/1980**	☐
STREET ADDRESS	**1420 24th Ave, Seattle, WA 98122**	☐
SOCIAL SECURITY NUMBER	**123-45-9876**	☐
GENDER	**Non-binary/Other**	☐
MOBILE PHONE NUMBER	**206-402-2044**	☐
FEDERAL FILING STATUS	**Single or Married Filing Separately** (leave all other defaults)	☐
PAYMENT METHOD	**Paper Check**	☐
HIRE DATE	**The first day of this month**	☐
HOW MUCH DO YOU PAY HARTLEY?	Hourly—**$25** per hour	☐
DEFAULT HOURS	**8** hours per day, and **5** days per week	☐
OCCUPATIONAL CODE	**27-1024**	☐

TABLE 15-1 *Hartley McGill's personal employee information*

INFORMATION ABOUT YINYANG DESIGNS' PAYROLL POLICIES AND BENEFITS		
FIELD	SETTINGS	COMPLETED
PAY FREQUENCY	**Twice a Month**	☐
NEXT PAYDAY	**The first of next month**	☐
END OF THE FIRST PAY PERIOD	**The last day of the current month**	☐
SECOND PAY PERIOD OF THE MONTH	**The 16th of next month**	☐
END OF THE SECOND PAY PERIOD	**The 15th of the next month**	☐
PAY SCHEDULE NAME	**1st and 16th** (**Check** *Use This Pay Schedule For Employees You Add After This One*)	☐
COMMON PAY TYPES	**Overtime Pay**, **Holiday Pay**, **Bonus**	☐
PAID TIME OFF	Hours are accrued: **Each Pay Period** Hours Per Year: **40** Maximum allowed: **80**	☐
DEDUCTION—RETIREMENT PLANS	Type: **Simple IRA** Description on Paycheck: **Retirement IRA** Calculated as: Percent of Gross Pay, **3%** Company Contribution Calculated as: Percent of Gross Pay, **3%**	☐
DEDUCTION—HEALTH SAVINGS ACCOUNT HSA PLANS	Deduction/Contribution Type: **HSA Plans** Type: **Pretax HSA** Description on Paycheck: **Health Savings Account, Pretax** Calculated as: **Flat Amount** Amount Per Paycheck: **$175**	☐
WORKER'S COMP	Effective Date: **The first day of the current quarter** (January, April, July or October) Class: **4904** Subclass: **00** Composite Rate: **.19%** Payroll Deduction: **.08%** Nature of work: **Clerical**	☐

TABLE 15-2 *Company Payroll Policies*

STEP 8. Update the **Payroll Settings** under the *Gear* to add tax information for YinYang Graphic Design. Use the information State and Federal Tax info in Table 15-3. If a field isn't mentioned, leave the defaults.

TAX INFORMATION FOR YINYANG GRAPHIC DESIGN		
FIELD	TAX NOTES	COMPLETED
FEDERAL TAX: EMPLOYER IDENTIFICATION NUMBER (EIN)	12-3456788	☐
PAYROLL TAX FORM FILED WITH THE IRS	**Form 941 Each Quarter** (Most Common)	☐
HOW OFTEN DO YOU FILE AND PAY YOUR TAXES?	**Monthly**	☐
WASHINGTON STATE TAX INFO	WA ESD Number: Leave blank WA SUI rate: **6%** WA Employment Administrative Fund Rate: **0.03%** WA Paid Family and Medical Leave Premium ER Rates: **Employee: .7322%, Employer: .2678%**	☐
AUTO PAYROLL	**No**	☐
TAXES AND FORM AUTOMATION	Turn **Off**. Choose **I'll initiate payments and filings using QuickBooks**.	☐
ACCOUNTING PREFERENCES: BANK ACCOUNT	**National Bank Checking (0042)**	☐
ACCOUNTING PREFERENCES: CLASS TRACKING	All employees are tracked as **Overhead**	☐

TABLE 15-3 *Company state and federal tax info*

2. Set Up a Project

MaryBeth has begun giving monthly Lunch-and-Learn workshops to Seattle small business owners to help them learn about target marketing. At these events, she also sells samples of her merchandise.

MaryBeth would like to know whether these workshops are profitable or not, including the overhead costs to produce the events. In order to gain insight into these job costs, she decides to turn her next event at Shelia's Boutique into a Project, allowing her to bring all the revenue and costs together. You will assign business transactions and payroll timecards to this Customer/Project.

STEP 1. Start a new **Project**.

STEP 2. Call it **Marketing Lunch-and-Learn**. Assign it to the *Client* **Shelia's Boutique**.

STEP 3. Use **the first day of next month** as the *Start Date*. Use **the 22nd of next month** as the *End Date*.

STEP 4. In the *Notes*, enter **Teach Shelia's Boutique clients about target marketing based on their ideal customer avatar**.

STEP 5. In the **Hourly Cost Rate** calculator on the main *Projects Center* dashboard, set MaryBeth's *Cost Rate* to **$20** of *Overhead (/hr)*.

3. Add a Contractor

MaryBeth has begun using a local intern for small graphic design jobs. Add Ingrid Swick to QuickBooks Online through the **Contractors** tab in the *Payroll Center*.

- **Step 1.** Go to the **Contractors Center**. Click the **Add a Contractor** button.
- **Step 2.** Enter the name **Ingrid Swick**. **Uncheck** the option to email the Contractor. Leave the email address blank.
- **Step 3.** In Ingrid Swick's *Personal Details*, click **Add**.
- **Step 4.** Files taxes as an **Individual**
   a. Add Ingrid's *First* and *Last* name.
   b. Enter her *Social Security Number*, **765-43-2123**.
   c. Enter **your email address** so that you can see what she would receive.
   d. Add her *Address*: **4540 8th Ave NE, Seattle, WA 98105**.

4. Set Up Mileage

MaryBeth occasionally drives to clients. Set up *Mileage* to track trips she takes driving her **2018 Ford Focus**. She *bought the vehicle* on **July 4, 2018** and *placed it in service* when she started the company on **January 1 of this year**.

She will record her mileage for this year by **Recording Odometer Readings**.

5. Set Up Price Rules

When MaryBeth speaks at the lunch-and-learns, she plans on offering a **10% discount** for new clients as an incentive if people schedule a consultation within one week.

- **Step 1.** Turn on **Price Rules** in *Account and Settings > Sales > Products and Services*.
- **Step 2.** Create a *Client Type* called **L&L** in the Clients Center.
- **Step 3.** Apply a *Price Rule* called **L&L Clients** that gives all **Lunch-and-Learn (L&L)** clients a **10% decrease** off **All Services**. Leave all other defaults.

6. Enter Business Transactions

Next month

Dates are important in this exercise, and are relative to today's date. YinYang's transactions will start next month to make sure our payroll transactions are outside QBO Payroll's automatic filing dates.

For example, if it is currently October and the Date column says 1, use the date November 1. When instructions say "the following month," use December.

If next month happens to be February, use Feb 28 for all end-of-month transactions.

DATE NEXT MONTH	BUSINESS TRANSACTION	TRANSACTION DETAILS
1	Pay rent to Orr Realty.	Transaction type: **Check** Payee: **Orr Realty** Bank Account: **National Bank Checking (0042)** Check#: **1009** Category: **Rent** Description: **Rent** Amount: **$1250** Class: **Overhead** (Delete any other lines that may autofill on the transaction)
1	Receive bill from Nile Online for website merchandise.	Transaction type: **Bill** Vendor: **Nile Online** Terms: **Net 30** Bill No.: **5687** Tags: **Clothing** In the *Item Details* grid: Product/Service: **T-Shirts, 200** Product/Service: **Caps, 105** Product/Service: **Mugs, 75** Product/Service: **Tote Bags, 50** Amount: **$4,385.00** Class (all lines): **Products**
2	MaryBeth orders special products for the Lunch-and-Learn event. Issue purchase order to Nile Online to order custom-branded merchandise.	Transaction type: **Purchase Order** Vendor: **Nile Online** Tags: **Clothing** In the *Item Details* grid: Product/Service: **T-Shirts, Qty 5** Product/Service: **Tote Bags, Qty 5** Client/Project: **Shelia's Boutique:Marketing Lunch-and-Learn** Class (all lines): **Products** Amount: **$95.00**
4	Issue check to Tameko Insurance for liability insurance premium.	Transaction type: **Check** Payee: **Tameko Insurance** Bank Account: **National Bank Checking (0042)** Check No.: **1010** Category: **Insurance:Liability Insurance** Description: **General Liability Insurance** Total: **$250.00** Class: **Overhead**

DATE NEXT MONTH	BUSINESS TRANSACTION	TRANSACTION DETAILS
6	Use the Contractors Center to pay the contractor for design work for Shelia's Boutique event advertising. Be sure to choose **Create Expense** under the *drop-down arrow on Ingrid's row,* not the *Pay Contractors* button since we are not using Payroll to process their payment.	Transaction type: **Create Expense** Payee: **Ingrid Swick** Payment Account: **National Bank Checking (0042)** Payment Method: **ACH** Tags: **Service** Category: **Contract Labor** Description: **Ads for Lunch-and-Learn** Amount: **$100.00** Client/Project: **Shelia's Boutique:Marketing Lunch-and-Learn** Class: **Design**
FIRST WEEK	Enter a weekly timesheet for Hartley McGill's hours the first days of next month. Hartley works Monday through Friday for 8 hours each day. Your exact days and dates will vary—*only enter hours M-F during next month.* If the beginning of the date range was during the current month, leave those days blank.	Transaction type: **Weekly timesheet** Name: **Hartley McGill** Week of: **The date range including the first of next month** *Line 1:* Client or Project: **Leave Blank** Service Item: **Hours** Pay Item: **Regular Pay** Class: **Overhead** Billable: **Not Billable** Enter 8 hours on weekdays starting with the **1st of the month**.

DATE NEXT MONTH	BUSINESS TRANSACTION	TRANSACTION DETAILS
8	Copy PO to a Bill, then add additional costs for custom order received from Nile Online for Shelia's Boutique merchandise.	Transaction type: **Copy PO to Bill** (*this will bring over the 5 T-Shirts and 5 Tote Bags. If additional items appear because of the automation, delete them*). Vendor: **Nile Online** Bill No.: **1000097** Tags: **Clothing** Line 1—Category: **Cost of Goods Sold:Supplies & Materials—COGS** Line 1—Description: **Custom design fee** Line 1—Amount: **$40.00** Line 1—Customer/Project: **Shelia's Boutique:Marketing Lunch-and-Learn** Line 1—Class: **Products** Line 2—Category: **Cost of Goods Sold:Shipping** Line 2—Description: **Rush shipping** Line 2—Amount: **$10.00** Line 2—Customer/Project: **Shelia's Boutique:Marketing Lunch-and-Learn** Line 2—Class: **Products** Total: **$145.00**
10	Use the Sales Tax Center to record a payment made through the State's website for unpaid sales tax.	Transaction type: **Sales Tax Payment (View Tax Return)** Account: **National Bank Visa (1818)** Tax amount: **$313.65**

DATE NEXT MONTH	BUSINESS TRANSACTION	TRANSACTION DETAILS
SECOND WEEK	Enter a weekly timesheet for Hartley McGill's hours the second week of next month. Hartley helped MaryBeth with the logistics for the upcoming event at Shelia's Boutique, and MaryBeth wants to see that in the job costing reports. Your exact days and dates will vary.	Transaction type: **Weekly timesheet** Name: **Hartley McGill** Week of: **The second week of next month** *Line 1:* Client or Project: **Leave Blank** Service Item: **Hours** Pay Item: **Regular Pay** Class: **Overhead** Billable: **Not Billable** Mon: **8 hours** Tue: **8 hours** Wed: **8 hours** Thu: **6 hours** Fri: **6 hours** *Line 2:* Client or Project: **Shelia's Boutique:Marketing Lunch and Learn** Service Item: **Consulting** Pay Item: **Regular Pay** Class: **Overhead** Billable: **Not Billable** Thu: **2 hours** Fri: **2 hours**
THIRD WEEK	Enter a weekly timesheet for Hartley McGill's hours the third week of next month. Hartley works Monday through Friday for 8 hours each day. Your exact days and dates will vary.	Transaction type: **Weekly timesheet** Name: **Hartley McGill** Week of: **The third week of next month** *Line 1:* Client or Project: **Leave Blank** Service Item: **Hours** Pay Item: **Regular Pay** Class: **Overhead** Billable: **Not Billable** Enter **8** hours on all weekdays.

DATE NEXT MONTH	BUSINESS TRANSACTION	TRANSACTION DETAILS
15	Pay employee for time worked during payroll period the 1st through 15th.	Transaction Type: **Run Payroll** Bank Account: **National Bank Checking (0042)** Pay Period: **1st through 15th of next month** Pay Date: **16th** *(if you get an error message because the date is in the past, change the date to today's real date and dismiss all alerts)* Hartley McGill: **80 or 88 hours** (will vary depending on your dates) Check No: **1011** *If prompted to set up or pay taxes, dismiss the alert.*
16	Record receipt for first two weeks of sales from online store.	Transaction type: **Sales Receipt** Client: **Nile Online Sales** Tags: **Clothing** Payment Method: **Direct Deposit** Deposit To: **Payments to Deposit** Product/Service: **Distributor Items** Qty: **T-Shirts, 50** **Caps, 42** **Mugs, 24** **Tote Bags, 15** Class: **Products** (all lines) Sales Tax: **Based on Location, $301.35** Total: **$3,241.35**
16	Deposit Online Sales minus listing fees.	Transaction type: **Bank Deposit** Deposit to: **National Bank Checking (0042)** Tags: **Clothing** Payments to Deposit: **Nile Online Sales** (Client) Add Funds to this Deposit: Received From: **Nile Online Sales** (Client) Account: **Advertising & Marketing:Listing Fees** Amount: **-97.24 (enter as negative amount)** Class: **Products** Total Deposit Amount: **$3144.11**

DATE NEXT MONTH	BUSINESS TRANSACTION	TRANSACTION DETAILS
18	Receive bill from Megia Printing, Inc. for printing handouts for Lunch-and-Learns. One third of them will be distributed at the Shelia's Boutique event. The rest will be saved for future events.	Transaction type: **Bill** Vendor: **Megia Printing, Inc.** Terms: **Net 30** Bill No.: **8869** Tags: **Clothing** (the workshop audience is clothing boutiques) Line 1—Category: **Advertising & Marketing:Marketing** Line 1—Description: **Handouts for Shelia's workshop** Line 1—Amount: **$50.00** Line 1—Client/Project: **Shelia's Boutique:Marketing Lunch and Learn** Line 1—Class: **Design** Line 2—Category: **Advertising & Marketing:Marketing** Line 2—Description: **Handouts for Lunch-and-Learn workshops** Line 2—Amount: **$100.00** Line 2—Client/Project: **None** Line 2—Class: **Design** Total: **$150.00**
21	Receive ACH payment from Lannister Stark Industries.	Transaction type: **Receive Payment** Client: **Lannister Stark Industries** Payment Method: **Credit Card** Deposit To: **Payments to Deposit** Amount: **$1,875** Apply to: **Invoice #1005** (closes invoice)

DATE NEXT MONTH	BUSINESS TRANSACTION	TRANSACTION DETAILS
22	Today's the day! MaryBeth holds her free workshop at Shelia's Boutique. 10 business owners from neighborhood shops attend. She sells most of the customized event t-shirts and tote bags she brought with her.	Transaction type: **Sales Receipt** Client: **Shelia's Boutique:Marketing Lunch and Learn** Tags: **Clothing** Payment Method: **Credit Card** Deposit To: **Payments to Deposit** Line 1—Service Date: **the 22nd of next month** Line 1—Product: **T-shirts (4 @ $24.00)** Line 2—Service Date: **the 22nd of next month** Line 2—Product: **Tote Bags (4 @ $20.00)** Class: **Products** (on both lines) Sales tax: **$18.04** (automatically added) Total: **$194.04** Message Displayed on Statement: **Shelia's Boutique Luncheon Sales**

DATE NEXT MONTH	BUSINESS TRANSACTION	TRANSACTION DETAILS
22	Barter one T-shirt and Tote Bag for clothes from Shelia's Boutique. The barter exchange was agreed on using the retail value of the products and clothing ($44), but it is recorded using the actual inventory cost of the items. The outfit is not work-related, so the Category is Owner Draws, to show the exchange was for a personal item. We are using an Expense instead of a Check so that we can use **Barter** as the Payment Method. Because we normally use an Expense to increase inventory, a negative Quantity decreases the inventory.	Transaction type: **Expense** Client: **Shelia's Boutique:Marketing Lunch and Learn** Payment Account: **Cash** Payment Method: **Barter** (add on the fly) Tags: **Clothing** *In the Category Details grid:* Line 1—Category: **Owner Draws** Line 1—Description: **Bartered merchandise for personal outfit** Line 1—Amount: **$19.00** Line 1—Client/Project: **Shelia's Boutique:Marketing Lunch and Learn** Line 1—Class: **Products** *In the Item Details grid:* Line 1—Product/Service: **T-shirts** Line 1—Description: **Bartered merchandise for personal outfit** Line 1—Qty: **-1** (negative, removes the item from inventory) Line 1—Amount: **$10.00** (the cost of the item) Line 1—Client/Project: **Shelia's Boutique:Marketing Lunch and Learn** Line 1—Class: **Products** Line 2—Product/Service: **Tote Bags** Line 2—Description: **Bartered merchandise for personal outfit** Line 1—Qty: **-1** (negative, removes the item from inventory) Line 2—Amount: **$9.00** (the cost of the item) Line 2—Client/Project: **Shelia's Boutique:Marketing Lunch and Learn** Line 2—Class: **Products** Total: **$0.00**

DATE NEXT MONTH	BUSINESS TRANSACTION	TRANSACTION DETAILS
22	MaryBeth gives Shelia a Mug as a thank you gift. Remove the mug from inventory.	Transaction type: **Inventory Qty Adjustment** Inventory Adjustment Account: **Advertising & Marketing:Marketing** Product: **Mugs** New Qty: **85** Change in Qty: **-1** Class: **Products** Memo: **Mug given as promotional item**
22	Add a trip to the Mileage Tracker.	Transaction type: **Add Trip** Distance: **8** Business Purpose: **Meeting with Client** Vehicle: **2018 Ford Focus** Round Trip: **Yes**
22	Create a Single Time Activity for MaryBeth to track the time she put into planning the Lunch-and-Learn and the event itself.	Transaction type: **Single Time Activity** Name: **MaryBeth Yang** Cost Rate (/hr): **20** Client: **Shelia's Boutique:Marketing Lunch and Learn** Service Item: **Consulting** Billable: **Not Billable** Class: **Overhead** Time: **6:00** Description: **Prep and talk at Shelia's Boutique**
23	Deposit credit card sales minus 3% merchant service fees.	Transaction type: **Bank Deposit** Deposit to: **National Bank Checking (0042)** Payments to Deposit: **Lannister Stark** and **Shelia's Boutique** *Add Funds to This Deposit:* Received From: **National Bank** Account: **Office Expenses:Merchant Account Fees** Amount: **-62.07 (enter as negative amount)** Class: **Overhead** Total Deposit Amount: **$2,006.97**

DATE NEXT MONTH	BUSINESS TRANSACTION	TRANSACTION DETAILS
FOURTH WEEK	Enter a weekly timesheet for Hartley McGill's hours the fourth week of the month. Hartley works Monday through Friday for 8 hours each day. Your exact days and dates will vary.	Transaction type: **Weekly timesheet** Name: **Hartley McGill** Week of: The fourth week of next month *Line 1:* Client or Project: **Leave Blank** Service Item: **Hours** Pay Item: **Regular Pay** Class: **Overhead** Billable: **Not Billable** Mon: **8 hours** Tue: **8 hours** Wed: **4 hours** Thu: **8 hours** Fri: **8 hours** *Line 2:* Client or Project: **Leave Blank** Service Item: **Hours** Description: **Out sick** Pay Item: **Paid Time Off** Class: **Overhead** Billable: **Not Billable** Wed: **4 hours**
24	Shelia was inspired by your presentation, and wants to go all-in on an eCommerce shopping cart for her boutique starting immediately. MaryBeth creates a new Project for the Online Shopping Cart and sends her an estimate for the project.	Project Center: **Shelia's Boutique: Online Shopping Cart** (create a new *Project* for Shelia's Boutique with a *Start Date* of **this date**) Transaction type: **Estimate** Expiration Date: **the 24th of the following month** Tags: **Clothing** Service Date: **leave blank** Product/Service: **Web Design** Description: **E-commerce website to sell store inventory online** Qty: **75** Rate: **$50** Class: **Design** Sales tax: **none** Total: **$3750.00**

DATE NEXT MONTH	BUSINESS TRANSACTION	TRANSACTION DETAILS
25	Shelia accepts the estimate. Create a progress invoice for one quarter (25%) of the project.	Transaction type: **Invoice** Client: **Shelia's Boutique: Online Shopping Cart** Progress Invoice: **25% ($937.50)** Tags: **Clothing** Service Date: **the 26th of next month** Product/Service: **Web Design** Due: **25% of 3750.00** Class: **Design** Total: **$937.50**
25	Shelia pays the invoice by credit card.	Transaction type: **Receive Payment** Client: **Shelia's Boutique: Online Shopping Cart** Payment Method: **Credit Card** Deposit To: **Payments to Deposit** Amount Received: **$937.50**

DATE NEXT MONTH	BUSINESS TRANSACTION	TRANSACTION DETAILS
26	Provide consultation to an attendee of the Lunch-and-Learn, with a 10% discount using a Price Rule. Jesse is excited and wants to get started. He gives you a $200 deposit for you to put together a proposal and reserve time on your schedule.	Transaction type: **Sales Receipt** Client: **Jesse Salsbury** (add new client, including +Details with the following information) • Company: **Salsbury Hill, Ltd.** • Display Name As: **Jesse Salsbury** • Additional Info tab at bottom: Client Type—**L&L** Tags: **Service** Payment Method: **Credit Card** Deposit To: **Payments to Deposit** Line 1—Service Date: **the 26th of next month** Line 1—Product/Service: **Consulting** Line 1—Description: **Follow up from Shelia's Boutique Lunch-and-Learn** Line 1—Rate: **54** (automatically applies Lunch-and-Learn 10% discount) Line 1—Class: **Design** Line 2—Product/Service: **Client Deposit** (create on the fly with the following information) • Type: **Service** • Category: **Services** • Class: **Design** • Description: **Client deposit on work to be performed** • Income Account: **Customer Prepayments** • Sales Tax: Nontaxable Line 2—Service Date: **leave blank** Line 2—Rate: **200** Line 2—Class: **Design** Sales tax: **Taxable** (Webdesign is a taxable service, but not in Seattle) Total: **$254.00** Message Displayed on Statement: **Shelia's Boutique Luncheon Client**

DATE NEXT MONTH	BUSINESS TRANSACTION	TRANSACTION DETAILS
26	Create an Estimate for work to start the following month.	Transaction type: **Estimate** Client: **Jesse Salsbury** Expiration Date: **the 26th of the following month** Tags: **Service** Line 1—Service Date: **the 5th of the following month** Line 1—Product/Service: **Logo Design** Line 1—Qty: **3** Line 1—Rate: **$45** (automatically applies Lunch-and-Learn 10% discount) Line 1—Class: **Design** Line 2—Service Date: **the 15th of the following month** Line 2—Product/Service: **Web Design** Line 2—Qty: **20** Line 2—Rate: **$45** (automatically applies Lunch-and-Learn 10% discount) Line 2—Class: **Design** Sales tax: **Taxable** (Webdesign is a taxable service, but not in Seattle) Total: **$1035.00**
27	Deposit Jesse and Shelia's credit card payments minus 3% merchant service fees.	Transaction type: **Bank Deposit** Deposit to: **National Bank Checking (0042)** Tags: **None** Payments to Deposit: **Jesse Salsbury, Shelia's Boutique** *Add Funds to This Deposit:* Received From: **National Bank** Account: **Merchant Account Fees** Amount:—**32.77 (enter as negative amount)** Class: **Design** Total Deposit Amount: **$1158.73**

DATE NEXT MONTH	BUSINESS TRANSACTION	TRANSACTION DETAILS
28	Jesse accepts the estimate. Create a progress invoice for just the Logo Design portion of the project. Deduct $135 of the Client Deposit for the prepayment.	Transaction type: **Invoice** Client: **Jesse Salsbury** Tags: **Service** Line 1—Service Date: **the 5th of the following month** Line 1—Product/Service: **Logo Design** Line 1—Due: **135.00 of 135.00** Line 2—Product/Service: **Web Design** Line 2—Qty: **0** Line 3—Product/Service: **Client Deposit** Line 3—Qty: **-1** (negative) Line 3—Amount: **135** Class: **Design** (on all lines) Total: **$0.00**
29	Receive bill from Seattle Light & Power for utilities.	Transaction type: **Bill** Vendor: **Seattle Light & Power** Terms: **Net 30** Bill No: **9753** Category: **Utilities:Electricity** Description: **Electric bill** Amount: **$147.00** Class: **Overhead**
29	Receive bill from Western Bell for telephone.	Transaction type: **Bill** Vendor: **Western Bell** Terms: **Net 30** Bill No: **2332** Category: **Utilities:Phone Service** Description: **Telephone bill** Amount: **$288.00** Class: **Overhead**
30	Pay all bills in a batch by credit card.	Select **Pay Bills**, and then pay all the bills using the **National Bank Visa (1818)**: Nile Online (two bills) Megia Printing, Inc. Seattle Light & Power Western Bell Total payments: **$5,115.00**

DATE NEXT MONTH	BUSINESS TRANSACTION	TRANSACTION DETAILS
LAST	Pay the Credit Card Bill in full.	Transaction type: **Pay Down Credit Card** Which Credit Card Did You Pay?: **National Bank Visa (1818)** Payee: **National Bank** How Much Did you Pay?: **$6074.65** What Did You Use to Make This Payment?: **National Bank Checking (0042)**
LAST WEEK	Enter a weekly timesheet for Hartley McGill's hours the last week of the month. Hartley works Monday through Friday for 8 hours each day. Your exact days and dates will vary.	Transaction type: **Weekly timesheet** Name: **Hartley McGill** Week of: **The last week of next month** *Line 1:* Client: **Leave Blank** Service Item: **Hours** Payroll Item: **Regular Pay** Class: **Overhead** Billable: **Not Billable** Enter **8** hours on all weekdays. *If the end of the week contains dates during the following month, it's OK to fill them in.*
LAST	Run payroll for period from the 16th through the end of the month.	Transaction type: **Run Payroll** Bank Account: **National Bank Checking (0042)** Pay Period: **16th through last** Pay Date: **1st of the following month** Hartley McGill: **Regular Pay hours will vary, 4 hrs PTO** Starting Check No: **1012**

DATE NEXT MONTH	BUSINESS TRANSACTION	TRANSACTION DETAILS
LAST	Record receipt for last two weeks of sales from online store.	Transaction type: **Sales Receipt** Client: **Nile Online Sales** Tags: **Clothing** Payment Method: **Direct Deposit** Deposit To: **Payments to Deposit** Product/Service: **Distributor Items** Qty: 　T-Shirts, **Qty 65** 　Caps, **Qty 47** 　Mugs, **Qty 26** 　Tote Bags, **Qty 19** Class: **Products** (all lines) Sales Tax: **Based on Location, $362.44** Total: **$3898.44**
LAST	Record an Owner Draw to MaryBeth as her "pay" for the month. She is making an online banking transfer to a personal checking account outside of QuickBooks Online.	Transaction type: **Expense** Payee: **MaryBeth Yang** (Employee) Bank Account: **National Bank Checking (0042)** Payment Method: **Direct Deposit** Category: **Owner Draws** Description: **Owner pay** Total: **$2000.00** Class: **Overhead**
LAST	After talking to her CPA, MaryBeth realizes that she's doing better than expected, and doesn't need the entire Owner Investment she put in the bank to start the company. She writes herself a check to pull the money back out of the company and reinvest it personally.	Transaction type: **Check** Payee: **MaryBeth Yang** Bank Account: **National Bank Checking (0042)** Check No.: **1013** Category: **Owner Draws** Description: **Didn't need as much startup capital as expected** Total: **$60,000.00** Class: **Overhead**

The following month
Enter the upcoming transactions in the table below for the following month to wrap up the month-end.

DATE THE FOLLOWING MONTH	BUSINESS TRANSACTION	TRANSACTION DETAILS
1	Deposit Online Sales minus listing fees.	Transaction type: **Bank Deposit** Deposit to: **National Bank Checking (0042)** Tags: **Clothing** Payments to Deposit: **Nile Online Sales** Add Funds to This Deposit: Received From: **Nile Online Sales (Client)** Account: **Advertising & Marketing:Listing Fees** Amount: **-116.95 (enter negative amount)** Class: **Products** Total Deposit Amount: **$3,781.49**
1	Pay rent to Orr Realty.	Transaction type: **Check** Payee: **Orr Realty** Bank Account: **National Bank Checking (0042)** Check#: **1014** Line 1 Category: **Rent** Description: **Rent** Amount: **$1250** Class: **Overhead**
1	Transfer money to Savings account.	Transaction type: **Transfer** Transfer Funds From: **National Bank Checking (0042)** Transfer Funds To: **National Bank Savings (4236)** Transfer Amount: **$500**
4	Issue check to Tameko Insurance for liability insurance premium.	Transaction type: **Check** Payee: **Tameko Insurance** Bank Account: **National Bank Checking (0042)** Check No.: **1015** Category: **Insurance:Liability Insurance** Description: **General Liability Insurance** Total: **$250.00** Class: **Overhead**

DATE THE FOLLOWING MONTH	BUSINESS TRANSACTION	TRANSACTION DETAILS
5	Pay the Federal Taxes (941/944) Payroll Liabilities that are due *(your dates and amounts may vary due to tax tables)* Accept all warning messages	Transaction type: **Payroll Federal Taxes (941/944) Liability Payment** Bank Account: **National Bank Checking (0042)** Date: **Latest (your date will vary)** Amount: **Will vary** View and Print Form: **Save PDF**
6	Use the Contractors Center to pay contractor for design work for the Salsbury logo and preliminary work on the Shelia's Boutique website.	Transaction type: **Create Expense** Payee: **Ingrid Swick** Payment Account: **National Bank Checking (0042)** Payment Method: **ACH** Tags: **Clothing** Line 1—Category: **Contract Labor** Line 1—Description: **Logo design** Line 1—Amount: **$75.00** Line 1—Customer/Project: **Jesse Salsbury** Line 2—Category: **Contract Labor** Line 2—Description: **Web design—preliminary sketches** Line 2—Amount: **$450.00** Line 2—Customer/Project: **Shelia's Boutique:Online Shopping Cart** Class: **Design** (both lines) Total: **$525.00**

DATE THE FOLLOWING MONTH	BUSINESS TRANSACTION	TRANSACTION DETAILS
6	Record Health Insurance payment made by logging into medical plan website.	Transaction type: **Expense** Payee: **Green Cross Green Shield** (add new vendor on the fly) Payment Account: **National Bank Checking (0042)** Payment Method: **ACH** Line 1—Category: **Payroll Liabilities:Health Savings Account, Pretax** Line 1—Description: **EE Contribution** Line 1—Amount: $**175** Line 2—Category: **Employee Benefits:Health Insurance & Accident Plans** Line 2—Description: **ER Contribution** Line 2—Amount: $**175** Class: **Overhead** (both lines) Total Amount: $**350.00**

7. Prepare Reports

1. Prepare the following reports and graphs:
   a. Employee Details report
   b. Total Payroll Cost report—use a date range that includes both paychecks
   c. Project Profitability for Shelia's Boutique Marketing Lunch and Learn Report, Accrual basis
   d. Profit and Loss report for All Dates, filtered for all Shelia's Boutique including both Projects
   e. Estimates & Progress Invoicing Summary by Customer, All Dates
   f. Inventory Valuation Summary, All Dates
   g. In the Contractors Center, View All Contractor Payments, use a date range that includes all four payments. Save as PDF.
   h. Sales Tax Liability report, All Dates
   i. Profit and Loss by Class, All Dates, Accrual basis
   j. Profit and Loss by Industry (Tag Group), All Dates, Accrual basis

8. Analysis Questions

Use the completed reports and company file to answer the following questions.

1. In the Employee Details report, why does Retirement IRA 3.0% show up as both a Deduction and a Contribution?

2. Using the Total Payroll Cost report, how much more does Payroll cost the company beyond the amount paid as wages?

3. Looking at the Shelia's Boutique Marketing Lunch and Learn Project Profitability Report, did the event make money?

4. Looking at the P&L filtered for all Shelia's Boutique activity, was the event worth it even though it lost money?

5. Looking at the Estimates and Progress Invoicing Summary, how much remains on all Estimates that has not been invoiced yet? Is this figure represented in standard financial reports?

6. Looking at the Inventory Valuation Summary, which product has the least Asset Value? Which product has the least Quantity in stock?

7. Looking at the Contractor Payments, how many contractors will need to receive 1099s in January?

8. Looking at the Sales Tax Liability report, are most of YinYang Graphic Designs' sales taxable?

9. Looking at the P&L by Class, is YinYang making more money off of Design services or Product sales?

10. Looking at the P&L by Tag, what Industry is YinYang Designs' most active niche?

11. Looking at the Mileage Center in QuickBooks Online, how much is the potential Mileage Deduction total for the year?

ANSWER KEY FOR END OF CHAPTER QUESTIONS

This section shows the answers to the questions at the end of each chapter.

Chapter 1: Introducing QuickBooks Online

Comprehension Questions:

1. The QuickBooks Online sample company, Craig's Design and Landscaping, is the QBO "sandbox" file where you can experiment because it resets itself each time. This book's practice file, Imagine Photography, is the file students will build from scratch for real-world experience.

2. QuickBooks Desktop is the software-based version of QuickBooks Online, where the application is downloaded and installed, and files are saved on your computer. QuickBooks Online is cloud-based and can be accessed on any computer, PC or Mac. The versions of QuickBooks Online include Simple Start, Essentials, Plus, Advanced, and Accountant.

3. The Dashboard is the landing page that displays the most common QuickBooks Online tasks. It is divided into Get Things Done, with shortcuts that make the sequence of workflow easier to understand. The Business Overview tab displays interactive charts to monitor the health of your company.

4. Transactions are created by filling out familiar-looking forms such as invoices, bills, and checks. As you fill out forms, you choose from lists such as the Customers Center, the Products and Services list, and the Accounts list. When you finish filling out a form, QuickBooks Online automatically records the accounting entries behind the scenes. By using sales forms (e.g. Invoices, Sales Receipts and Credit Memos) QuickBooks Online populates sales reports, and provides additional fields that are not available in the Accounts Receivable register.

5. Accounting's primary concern is the accurate recording and categorizing of transactions so that you can produce reports that accurately portray the financial health of your organization. Put another way, accounting's focus is on whether your organization is succeeding and how well it is succeeding. The purpose of accounting is to serve management, investors, creditors, and government agencies. Accounting reports allow any of these groups to assess the financial position of the organization relative to its debts (liabilities), its capabilities to satisfy those debts and continue operations (assets), and the difference between them (net worth or equity).

Multiple Choice:

1. c
2. c
3. b
4. d
5. d

Completion Statements:

1. forms, accounting
2. back up
3. Dashboard
4. Products and Services
5. Chart of Accounts

Chapter 2: Customizing QuickBooks Online

Comprehension Questions:

1. Account and Settings are used to make global changes to the features and functionality of the data file. Not only does it populate the file with the company's contact information, but this is where you turn on and off features in the software.

2. The Chart of Accounts categories define the company's General Ledger. The accounts populate many of QuickBooks Online's reports including the Profit and Loss Statement and the Balance Sheet.

3. The Products and Services List are the items that a company buys and sells. The Products and Services list items appear on every sales form, and in some cases, in the expense transactions as well. Using Products and Services allows the business to analyze their most popular sales items with the best profit margin.

4. In QuickBooks Online, classes give you a way to label your transactions. You can use QuickBooks Online classes to separate your income and expenses by line of business, department, location, profit centers, or any other meaningful breakdown of your business.

    For example, a dentist might classify all income and expenses as relating to either the dentistry or hygiene department. A law firm formed as a partnership might classify all income and expenses according to which partner generated the business. If you use classes, you'll be able to create separate reports for each class of the business. Therefore, the dentist could create separate Profit & Loss reports for the dentistry and hygiene departments, and the law firm could create separate reports for each partner.

5. QuickBooks Online calculates sales tax automatically based on the eligibility of the customer and the products or services purchased. QBO will calculate the tax rate according to each state's rules, whether the sale is taxable based on the customer's billing and shipping address, or based on the

business's location. It's important that you use the Sales Tax Center to report payments, otherwise they may be recorded as an expense instead of debiting the liability.

6. Custom Fields allow you to track additional information about a transaction. Each file has up to three fields that can be used for Sales Reps, PO numbers, or anything the business would like.

Multiple Choice:

1. d
2. a
3. c
4. c
5. b
6. d
7. d
8. d
9. a
10. d
11. d
12. b
13. c
14. d
15. d

Completion Statements:

1. Account and Settings
2. Products and Services
3. Custom Fields
4. Date-driven
5. Two-sided

Apply Your Knowledge:
The completed Product and Services List:

NAME ▲	TYPE	SALES DESCRIPTION	SALES PRICE	COST	TAXABLE	QTY ON HAND	REORDER POINT
Deluxe Shoot	Bundle	Deluxe Photo Shoot					
Hours	Service						
Photography							
Indoor Session	Service	Indoor Studio Session	225				
Outdoor Session	Service	Outdoor Photo Session	195				
Retouching	Service	Photo retouching services	195				
Standard Package	Non-inventory	Standard Package of Photos from Session	155		✓		
Videographer	Service	Photography Income	125	75			
Products							
Camera SR32	Inventory	Supra Digital Camera SR32	695	450	✓	5	2
Case	Inventory	Camera and Lens High Impact Case	79.99	45	✓	5	2
Frame 5x7 Metal	Inventory	Picture Frame - 5x7in Metal	10	2.15	✓	5	2
Frame 6x8 Wood	Inventory	Picture Frame - 6x8in Wood	15	5	✓	5	2
Lens	Inventory	Supra Zoom Lens	184.99	100	✓	5	2
Photo Paper	Non-inventory	Standard Photo Paper, Glossy, 8.5"x11", Pa...	25	15	✓		
Sales	Service						
Supra Package	Bundle	Supra Camera Package					

FIGURE O-1: The completed Products and Services list

The sample Custom Form:

Alicia Pollock's Imagine Photography

(925) 555-1111
info@imaginephoto.biz

INVOICE

BILL TO	SHIP TO	SHIP DATE	01/03/2015	INVOICE	12345
Smith Co.	John Smith	SHIP VIA	FedEx	DATE	01/12/2016
123 Main Street	20637 Palm Drive	TRACKING#	12345678	TERMS	Net 30
City, CA 12345	City, CA 12345			DUE DATE	02/12/2016

SALES REP	PO NUMBER
Custom-1	Custom-2

ACCOUNT SUMMARY

01/12/2016	Balance Forward	$100.00
	Payments and credits between 01/12/2016 and 12/01/2016	-$50.00
	New charges (details below)	$665.00
	Total Amount Due	$715.00

DATE		DESCRIPTION	QTY	RATE	AMOUNT
12/01/2016	Item name	Description of the item	2	$225.00	$450.00
01/12/2016	Item name	Description of the item	1	$225.00	$225.00

Satisfaction guaranteed! Come back within 30 days for a store credit.

SUBTOTAL	$675.00
TAX	$101.25
SHIPPING	$3.50
TOTAL	$779.75
TOTAL OF NEW CHARGES	$779.75
BALANCE DUE	**$776.25**

Give It Your Best Shot!
Page 1 of 1

FIGURE O-2: *The sample Custom Form*

Chapter 3: The Sales Process

Comprehension Questions:

1. When customers pay at the time of the sale either by check or by credit card, create a Sales Receipt transaction.

2. Undeposited Funds may also be called Payments to Deposit. Each sale increases the balance in the Undeposited Funds account. Later, when you make a Bank Deposit, you'll group all of the funds from several sales into one deposit in the bank. This will decrease your Undeposited Funds account. It is best to use Undeposited Funds when recording receipts because you can then group the receipts together by payment method and date when you record the deposit, so that the register matches the bank statement. If you post each Sales Receipt and Payment directly to a bank account, QuickBooks Online will record a separate increase in cash for each customer receipt/payment. As a result, bank reconciliatons will be more difficult since QuickBooks Online deposits won't match the bank statement.

3. When you enter a payment amount, QuickBooks Online looks at all of the open Invoices for that customer. If it finds an amount due on an open Invoice that is the exact amount of the payment, it matches the payment with that Invoice. If there is no such match, it applies the payment to the oldest Invoice first and continues applying to the next oldest until the payment is completely applied. This auto application of payments may result in incorrect partially paid Invoices.

4. It's important to keep a record of the business documents behind the income and expenses in your business. This "paper trail" is necessary to demonstrate IRS compliance. You can attach Word and Excel documents, PDFs, and images to almost all transactions.

Multiple Choice:

1. d
2. a
3. b
4. d
5. d
6. c
7. d
8. a
9. a
10. b
11. c
12. c
13. b
14. b
15. c

Completion Statements:

1. Add New
2. bank, Undeposited Funds
3. calculating
4. Accounts Receivable
5. QuickBooks Payments

Chapter 4: Managing Expenses

Comprehension Questions:

1. If you want to track the expenses for each customer (i.e., track job costs), you'll need to link each expense with the customer or project to which it applies. When you record an expense transaction, use the **Customer** column to associate each expense account or item with the customer or sub-customer for whom it applies.

2. The steps in tracking A/P in QuickBooks Online are:
   a. When you receive a bill from a vendor, enter it into QuickBooks Online using the *Bill* window. Recording a bill allows QuickBooks Online to track the amount you owe to the vendor along with the detail of what you purchased.
   b. Pay the bill using the *Pay Bills* window.
   c. If you want to make a partial payment on a bill, enter only the amount you want to pay in the *Payment* column. If you pay less than the full amount due, QuickBooks Online will track the remaining amount due for that bill in Accounts Payable. The next time you go to the *Pay Bills* window, the partially paid bills will show with the remaining amount due.
   d. When a vendor credits your account, record that transaction in the *Vendor Credit* window and apply it as a payment against one of your unpaid bills.

3. Credit vendors use the A/P process, creating bills and making payments. Cash vendor transactions are recorded upon payment with Checks and Expenses.

4. To track your charges and payments on your company credit card, set up a separate credit card liability account in the Chart of Accounts for each card. Use the Credit Card type when creating each account. Then enter each charge individually using the Expense window. To pay the credit card bill, use Pay Down Credit Card and code the payment from correct checking account to the appropriate credit card liability account.

5. Treat Petty Cash as a checking account. Move money into Petty Cash either with Transfers, or by keeping back cash from a Bank Deposit. Record each expense individually. Make sure to keep receipts for all expenses paid in cash. If possible, use the Receipt Center to attach pictures of the receipts to each expense transaction.

Multiple Choice:

1. d
2. d
3. d
4. a
5. b
6. d
7. c
8. c
9. b
10. c
11. a
12. b
13. a
14. d
15. b

Completion Statements:

1. Vendors Center
2. Credit
3. Liability
4. customer
5. Contractors Center

Chapter 5: Advanced Transactions

Comprehension Questions:

1. Refunds are money given back to customers who return merchandise or who have unused services after these items have been paid for. Refunds should be given in the same type as the payment. If a customer paid with a check, he or she should be issued a refund check. If a customer paid by credit card, the refund should be issued to the same credit card.

2. Credit memos can be used in three different ways:
   a. To record a return of merchandise from a customer.
   b. To record a credit-on-account for services.
   c. As a correction technique to clean up Accounts Receivable on an accrual basis.

3. Invoice and Bill Payments cannot be saved as recurring, because there is no way to determine which invoice or bill to pay down.

4. Making your payment through the Sales Tax Center gives you an opportunity to adjust your payments to match your state's Department of Revenue calculations. It also ensures that your payment relieves the liability on the balance sheet so that you don't accidentally record it as an expense.

5. You can create pricing tiers for different types of customers, apply them to specific products or services, and create a set of sales prices.

Multiple Choice:

1. a
2. d
3. b
4. d
5. d
6. d
7. b
8. a
9. c
10. a
11. c
12. d
13. a
14. c
15. d

Completion Statements:

1. Cash, check, credit card
2. Credit Memos
3. Write off
4. Late Fees
5. Statement

Chapter 6: Banking & Reconciliation

Comprehension Questions:

1. QuickBooks Online calculates the Beginning Balance field by adding and subtracting all previously cleared transactions. The resulting calculation is shown in the Reconcile window. The amount in the Beginning Balance field will differ from your bank statement if a user deleted or changed one or more reconciled transactions. The balance will also differ if the user removes the checkmark from one or more reconciled transactions in the bank account register.

2. You don't want to change transactions dated in a closed accounting period because doing so would change financial information after you have already issued financial statements and/or filed tax returns.

3. When using the Banking Feeds, QuickBooks Online imports your transactions, matches and verifies existing transactions, and allows you to quickly categorize expenses that are not already in your file.

Multiple Choice:

1. d
2. a
3. d
4. c
5. b
6. b
7. d
8. a
9. d
10. d
11. b
12. c
13. c
14. d
15. a

Completion Statements:

1. reconciled
2. Rules
3. For Review
4. Receipts
5. encryption

Chapter 7: Reports

Comprehension Questions:

1. You can drill into see the detail behind totals on reports. As your cursor moves over numbers on a report, it will turn into a pointer finger, and the total will appear as a link. When you click the number, a Transaction Detail by Account report that shows the details of each transaction in the account that you zoomed in on.

2. The Statement of Cash Flows shows all the money coming in and out of the company, not just from sales and expenses, but also including inventory purchases, prepaid expenses, loan payments, and other financial transactions. It serves as a bridge between the Profit and Loss Statement and the Balance Sheet. It helps explain why profit can be high, while having less money in the checking account.

3. To hide subaccounts on the Profit & Loss report (or any summary report), click **Collapse** at the top of the report. The button changes to Expand when you want to see the detail again.

4. Use the **Filters** tab in the Customize window to narrow the contents of reports so that you can analyze specific areas of your business. On the **Filters** tab, you can (select) specific accounts, dates, names, or products/services to include in the report.

5. After designing a report, you can save the customizations so you won't have to go through all of the modification steps the next time you want to view the report.

Multiple Choice:

1. c
2. a
3. d
4. a
5. b
6. c
7. b
8. d
9. b
10. c
11. d
12. a
13. c
14. b
15. c

Completion Statements:

1. Product/Service List
2. filter
3. Trial Balance
4. Search
5. Balance Sheet

Chapter 8: YinYang Graphic Design Business Scenario

Answers to the YinYang Analysis reports are available in the Instructor's Manual for this book.

Chapter 9: Projects and Job Costing

Comprehension Questions

1. The big difference is that Estimates do not post to the general ledger, and therefore they do not affect any of your financial reports. They do help you track your future sales and they do help you track how your actual revenues and costs compare with what was estimated. Estimates do not record any financial information themselves because they represent quotes that may or may not be accepted by the customer.

2. Progress Invoicing allows you to charge your Customers a portion of the total Estimate for each stage of the project. QuickBooks Online can track how much of the Estimate has been invoiced, and how much remains to be invoiced. You can create a progress invoice based on a percentage or by selecting line items.

3. When you create an invoice for the customer, you can pass through the billable cost to the invoice using the drawer on the right where pass-through expenses are displayed. Select the appropriate charges to be included in the invoice.

4. QuickBooks Online allows you to use the same Item on expense forms (e.g., checks and bills) and sales forms (e.g., invoices and sales receipts). When you use Products and Services to track both expenses and revenue, you can generate reports showing the profitability of each. Possible uses of two-sided Items include Reimbursable Expenses, Custom Ordered Parts, Subcontracted Labor, and Cost of Goods Sold.

5. Customer deposits are prepayments or retainers for work to be performed in the future. Since the service hasn't been provided yet, the money received is not income. It is held on the Balance Sheet as Other Current Liabilities until the work is performed, or the deposit is refunded. The funds become income when the Invoice is created..

6. The Projects Center organizes QBO by customer job, bringing income and expense transactions together in one dashboard. It provides status charts, a unified transaction list, time costs, and reports filtered specifically for the project.

Multiple Choice

1. b
2. c
3. a
4. c
5. b
6. d
7. a
8. a
9. d
10. d

Completion Statements

1. Projects Center
2. Progress
3. Billable
4. Two-sided item
5. Timesheet

Chapter 10: Inventory

Comprehension Questions

1. The lifecycle of inventory activity typically takes place over time. Products are ordered, received, held, and later sold. Vendors frequently provide billing terms..

2. The first time you create an Inventory Product in the Products and Services List, QuickBooks Online automatically creates two accounts in your **Chart of Accounts**: An *Other Current Asset* account called **Inventory Asset** and a *Cost of Goods Sold* account called **Cost of Goods Sold**.

3. QuickBooks Online uses these two important accounts to track inventory. The **Inventory Asset** account holds the value of your inventory until you sell it. The **Cost of Goods Sold** account records the cost of the inventory when you sell it.

4. If you use purchase orders, you'll be able to create reports that show what is on order and when it is due to arrive from your supplier. In addition, you can create a list of open purchase orders. Purchase orders do not post to the **Chart of Accounts**..

Multiple Choice

1. c
2. a
3. b
4. c
5. d
6. d
7. b
8. b
9. c
10. a
11. c
12. a
13. b
14. d
15. c

Completion Statements

1. First In, First Out
2. purchase orders
3. perpetual
4. Inventory Qty Adjustment
5. Cost of Goods Sold

Chapter 11: Adjustments and Year-End Procedures

Comprehension Questions

1. When you change or delete a transaction, QuickBooks Online immediately updates the General Ledger with your change, regardless of the date of the transaction. Therefore, if you make changes to transactions in a closed accounting period, your QuickBooks Online financial statements will change for that period, causing discrepancies between your QuickBooks Online reports and your tax return.

2. If you want QuickBooks Online to automatically enter the depreciation journal entry each month, create a journal entry to record one month of depreciation, and then memorize it and schedule it to automatically enter each month.

3. At the end of each fiscal year, QuickBooks Online automatically "closes" the net income into Retained Earnings. QuickBooks Online does not show this entry, but when you run a Balance Sheet, QuickBooks Online calculates the balance in Retained Earnings by adding together the total net income for all prior years. For Sole Proprietorships, LLCs, Partnerships, or other business structures that don't use Retained Earnings, additional journal entries may be required.

4. Vendors who are Sole Proprietors, LLCs, or LLPs receive 1099s when they provide more than $600 in services, directly paid for through transactions from the checking account such as checks and ACH payments. Exclude payments made by debit card, credit card, and PayPal. Be sure to send each vendor a W-9 form so that you know whether to send them a 1099 each year.

5. Zero-dollar checks are a creative way of using QuickBooks Online to move funds from one account to another. They are a substitute for journal entries, especially when more information is required, such as affecting products and services or job costing

Multiple Choice

1. c
2. c
3. c
4. c
5. d
6. b
7. c
8. a
9. d
10. c
11. a
12. c

Completion Statements

1. Journal entry
2. services
3. Retained Earnings
4. closing date
5. Depreciation

Chapter 12: Advanced Company Setup

Comprehension Questions:

1. You should have each of the following before setting up a QuickBooks Online file:
   a. Trial Balance
   b. Bank Statement for all bank accounts
   c. Outstanding Checks and Deposits
   d. Unpaid Bills
   e. Open Invoices

f. Employee List and W-4 information for each employee
  g. Payroll Tax Liabilities
  h. Year-to-Date Payroll Detail for Employee
  i. Year-to-Date Payroll Tax Payments
  j. Physical Inventory by Inventory Product

2. As you enter opening balances in your QuickBooks Online accounts, an offsetting transaction is entered into an automatically-created account calling Opening Balance Equity.

   This transaction is recorded differently depending on which method you use for the opening balance. If you enter the opening balance by entering a value in the Opening Balance field in the Account window, a Journal entry is created to add the amount to Opening Balance Equity. If you enter the opening balance through a journal entry, the transaction should be offset to Opening Balance Equity.

   Opening Balance Equity is closed into Retained Earnings or Owners Equity at the end of setting up the company file.

3. To adjust Inventory to agree with the Trial Balance from the accountant, first make sure that all outstanding checks, bills, and invoices have been entered. Then run inventory reports to compare quantities. Use an Inventory Qty Adjustment to create accurate inventory counts as of the start date. Last, compare the Inventory Asset and Cost of Goods Sold to the Trial Balance. If there is a difference, use a journal entry to adjust both to Opening Balance Equity, or discuss the issue with your accountant.

4. It is important to enter all outstanding checks and deposits as of your start date so that your first bank reconciliation goes smoothly. You need all of the checks and deposits to show in QuickBooks Online so that you can match them with your first bank statement after the start date. If you don't enter the individual transactions, you won't see them in the QuickBooks Online reconciliation window. Also, if a transaction never clears the bank, you won't know which transaction it was without going to your old records.

5. When it's time for customers to pay, it's important to have the history of their activity to pay against, as well as to be able to run Accounts Receivable reports. Bills are important so that you can plan ahead to pay your vendors and know what you owe through Accounts Receivable.

Multiple Choice:

1. c
2. d
3. a
4. b
5. b

6. c
7. b
8. b

Completion Statements:

1. Opening Balance Equity
2. Journal Entry
3. Trial Balance

Chapter 13: Payroll Setup

Comprehension Questions

1. Company Contributions are the employer's portion of tax and benefits associated with payroll. Some are State and Federally-mandated company matches. Others are benefits companies include as employee incentives. Company contributions are expenses instead of liabilities because they are not deducted from employee paychecks.

2. Employees contribute some of their gross pay for taxes and benefits, which are then paid out to State, Federal, and other agencies. These are liabilities, because the business takes them from the paycheck and holds them until it's time to make the monthly, quarterly, or annual payment. Other costs, like company contributions, are operating costs of the business, such as company taxes, the company portion of benefits, and the wages themselves. These are expenses because they are not deducted from employee paychecks.

3. When a new employee is hired, they fill in a W-4 form with their personal information, social security number, filing status, and desired withholdings. This information can also be gathered electronically through QuickBooks Online Payroll's Workforce integration.

Multiple Choice

1. b
2. d
3. d
4. b
5. d
6. d
7. a
8. d
9. c
10. c
11. d
12. c
13. a
14. d

Completion Statements

1. Core, Premium, and Elite
2. Payroll Settings
3. deduction, liability
4. Workforce

Chapter 14: Payroll Processing

Comprehension Questions

1. Voucher checks are the best choice because QuickBooks Online prints the payroll summary information on the voucher portion of the checks. The check voucher will include the current period information as well as year-to-date information for the employee. Other types can be used, but Paystubs would need to be printed separately.

2. QuickBooks Time is an external app that integrates with QuickBooks Online to extend timesheet abilities. Employees can track their time from their computers or their cell phones by clocking in and clocking out. Time entries can include customer projects, services, classes, and billable expenses.

3. No. The only time you should delete a paycheck is when you created it in error, and you haven't printed the check. Otherwise, you should void the paycheck so you can keep a record of it.

4. When you use the Tax Center, all payments are applied directly to the liabilities. If you simply write a check or pull in the payment through the Banking Feed, you are likely to accidentally categorize the payment as a tax expense.

Multiple Choice

1. d
2. a
3. b
4. a
5. d
6. d
7. d
8. b
9. d
10. d
11. d
12. c
13. b
14. d

Completion Statements

1. timesheets
2. Commission
3. Auto Payroll
4. Liabilities
5. Terminated

Chapter 15: YinYang Graphic Design Business Scenarios

Answers to the questions at the end of the YinYang problems are available in the Instructor's Manual for this book.

CERTIPORT MAPPING

*A****fter completing this course***, you should be prepared to pass the QuickBooks Online Certified User exam at Certiport.com.

The exam objectives map to topics and sections starting on these pages:

1		QUICKBOOKS ONLINE ADMINISTRATION	
1.1		**Set up QuickBooks Online**	**Chapters 1 & 2**
	1.1.1	Recognize features and benefits of QuickBooks Online Plus	1, 2, 3, 12
	1.1.2	Describe licensing requirements for setting up an entity in QuickBooks Online	1, 2, 3, 12
	1.1.3	Describe the process of migrating a company to QuickBooks Online	32, 35, 471
	1.1.4	Describe the access of each default user role	83
1.2		**Manage QuickBooks Online settings for a company**	**Chapter 2**
	1.2.1	Identify the company information that you can and can't edit	39
	1.2.2	Recognize the benefits of the Close the Books feature	199, 286, 460, 463
	1.2.3	Compare and contrast the cash and accrual accounting methods	6, 42, 155, 220, 299
	1.2.4	Identify the purposes of project tracking, class tracking, and locations	71, 72, 102, 108, 161, 162, 177, 305, 306, 357
	1.2.5	Describe how to activate project tracking, class tracking, and locations	43, 44, 71, 72, 387
	1.2.6	Identify the tasks performed by automation	44, 123, 135, 174, 198, 208, 209, 223, 234
1.3		**Manage lists**	**Chapters 2, 3, and 4**
	1.3.1	Identify the lists that you can import	34, 36, 38, 46, 92, 143
	1.3.2	Identify the content of various lists	17, 25, 45, 67, 70
	1.3.3	Identify the appropriate lists for different purposes	24, 25, 66, 70
	1.3.4	Identify when and how to add, edit, delete, and merge list items	45, 57, 66, 70, 104, 157
	1.3.5	Manage the Chart of Accounts	34, 45, 448, 457, 459
1.4		**Manage recurring transactions**	**Chapter 5**
	1.4.1	Describe reasons for making transactions recurring	123, 203, 242, 256
	1.4.2	Define types of recurrence	203
	1.4.3	Describe how to implement recurring transactions	19, 204
1.5		**Manage journal entries**	**Chapter 5**
	1.5.1	Identify the information required for journal entries	206, 241, 449, 461
	1.5.2	Describe how to implement journal entries	23, 206, 207, 461–463

1.6		**Connect QuickBooks Online to apps**	**Chapter 2**
	1.6.1	Identify the purpose of apps	2, 38, 52, 62, 135
	1.6.2	Identify where to get apps	2, 137
	1.6.3	Identify the risks and benefits of extending functionality through apps	2, 137, 414
2		**SALES AND MONEY IN**	
	2.1	**Set up customers**	**Chapter 3**
	2.1.1	Identify the importance of the Display Name field	105, 106, 111, 144, 157, 161
	2.1.2	Differentiate between billing and shipping addresses	77, 112, 144
	2.1.3	Define and describe the use of customer payment terms	67
	2.1.4	Identify taxable and non-taxable customers	76, 77, 106
	2.1.5	Define and describe the correct use of sub-customers	108, 144, 307
	2.2	**Set up products and services**	**Chapter 2**
	2.2.1	Describe and differentiate between products and services	57, 58
	2.2.2	Identify the information required to set up products or services	56, 92, 99
	2.2.3	Describe reasons for setting up products or services	27, 50
	2.2.4	Contrast inventory products and non-inventory products	60, 61, 62, 415
	2.3	**Manage sales settings**	**Chapter 3**
	2.3.1	Customize sales forms	82
	2.3.2	Customize email message forms	81
	2.3.3	Describe the purpose of activating customer discounts	98, 119, 401
	2.3.4	Describe the QuickBooks Payments feature and how it differs from traditional payments	69, 82, 88, 123, 124, 125, 135, 203
	2.4	**Record basic money-in transactions**	**Chapters 3 & 5**
	2.4.1	Describe the money-in transaction workflow	101, 103
	2.4.2	Record and manage invoices and sales receipts	102, 111, 115
	2.4.3	Receive, record, and manage payments, undeposited funds, and deposits	122, 123, 128, 129
	2.4.4	Record credit memos and refund receipts	207, 211
3		**VENDORS AND MONEY OUT**	
	3.1	**Manage vendor records**	**Chapter 4**
	3.1.1	Describe how to identify existing customers as vendors	106, 157
	3.1.2	Describe when and how to merge vendor accounts	161
	3.1.3	Describe how to add or change vendor payment terms	159
	3.1.4	Describe how and why to identify vendors as 1099 contractors	159, 183, 451, 452
	3.2	**Manage expense settings**	**Chapter 4**
	3.2.1	Describe how and why to activate expense tracking by customer	152, 263
	3.2.2	Describe when and how to make expenses and items billable	152, 263
	3.2.3	Describe how to identify unbilled billable expenses	19
	3.3	**Record and manage basic money-out transactions**	**Chapters 4 & 5**
	3.3.1	Describe the money-out transaction workflow	156

3.3.2	Identify types of money-out transactions	156
3.3.3	Compare and describe the appropriate use of checks and bill payments	178
3.3.4	Describe the effects of recording bills, checks, and credit card transactions	163, 168, 176
3.3.5	Differentiate between expense transactions and bank feed transactions	260
3.3.6	Describe how to record check, credit card, and debit card expense transactions	163, 168, 176
3.3.7	Describe the use and effects of vendor credits and refunds	186, 232, 234, 236
3.3.8	Describe why and how to void, delete, and edit money-out transactions and the impact thereof	182, 200, 201, 220, 286, 537, 538
4	**BANK ACCOUNTS, TRANSACTION RULES, AND RECEIPTS**	
4.1	*Implement financial account connections*	*Chapter 6*
4.1.1	Identify the types of financial accounts QuickBooks Online can connect to	258, 259
4.1.2	Describe the benefits of connecting QuickBooks Online to accounts	258, 260
4.2	*Manage bank feeds*	*Chapter 6*
4.2.1	Process bank feed transactions	260, 269
4.2.2	Define and describe the use of bank rules	270
4.3	*Manage receipts*	*Chapter 6*
4.3.1	Identify methods of uploading receipts	273
4.3.2	Describe how to record transactions from uploaded receipts	274
5	**BASIC REPORTS AND VIEWS**	
5.1	*Describe the content and purpose of reports*	*Chapters 3, 4 & 7*
5.1.1	Describe the content and purpose of financial reports	299, 313
5.1.2	Describe the content and purpose of money-in reports	138, 140, 321, 324
5.1.3	Describe the content and purpose of money-out reports	185, 187
5.2	*Customize and deliver standard reports*	*Chapter 7*
5.2.1	Customize standard reports	325, 327
5.2.2	Identify report delivery formats	331, 335
5.3	*Access other reports and views*	*Chapters 1, 3, 4, 5*
5.3.1	Describe the content of the Audit Log	202
5.3.2	Describe the content and functionality of the dashboards	14, 15, 103, 203

TABLE 0-1: *Certiport Exam Objective Mapping*

INDEX

Symbols
+New button 22
1099s 158, 541. *See Vendors*

A
Account and Settings 38
  Account Numbers 46
  Advanced Settings 41, 46
  Automation 174, 198, 370, 419
  Class Tracking 43
  Closing Date 463
  Expenses 152
  Inventory 416
  Products and Services 99
  Progress Invoicing 361
  Sales 97, 198
Accounting 3
  Accrual Basis 6, 299, 414
  Cash Basis 6, 299
  Closed Period 199, 286, 460
  Current Period 285
  Double-Entry 5, 311
Accounting Behind the Scenes xix, 5–6, 23, 29, 65, 75, 101–104, 114, 127, 129, 133, 164, 171, 174, 176, 189, 208, 215, 223–234, 242–243, 247, 256, 380, 414, 423, 425, 429, 441, 446, 449, 489, 542
Accounts
  Assets 3–4, 6, 46, 308, 448
  Bank 46
  Billable Expenses 152, 161, 376
  Clearing Accounts 444, 448
  Contra Account 119, 232
  Cost of Goods Sold 29, 60–61, 381–382, 416, 429, 444
  Equity 4, 46, 309
  Expenses 46, 481
  Income 46, 103, 481
  Inventory Asset 63, 429
  Liabilities 3–4, 6, 46, 239, 308, 338
  Opening Balances 477
  Other Current Assets 102, 416, 513
  Other Current Liabilities 368
  Reconciling 276

Sales of Product Income 61
Undeposited Funds 113
Accounts Payable 44, 155, 162
  A/P Aging Summary 185
  Bill Payments 44
  Bills 163
  Electronic Payments 172
  Entering Bills 163–167
  Mark as Paid 168
  Paying Bills 168
  Schedule Payments Online 172
  Vendor Credits 44, 185, 232, 426
Accounts Receivable 44, 101, 103
  Applying Payments to Invoices 126
  A/R Aging Summary 140
  Bounced checks 214
  Customer Deposits 368
  Customer Statements 118, 226
  Invoice History 139
  Invoices 97, 102, 115
  Payment Reminders 228
  Unearned Revenue 368
Attachments 120, 159, 167, 273
Audit Log 19, 202
Autofill 21, 370, 419

B
Backing Up 12, 38, 460
Bad Debts 220
Bank Deposits 104, 128, 130, 213
  Cash Back 131
  Credit Cards 135
  Deposit Slips 133
  Troubleshooting 137
  Vendor Refunds 374
Bank Statements 475. *See Reconciling*
Banking Feed 113, 129–130, 172, 256–257, 473
  Accountant View 257
  Bank Detail 261
  Bank Downloads 260, 274
  Batch Actions 265
  Business View 257

Connect Accounts 258
Credit Card Payments 269
Deposits 272
Excluded 269
Find Match 267
Match 260
Opening Balance Entry 480
Paired to Another Transaction 264
Products and Services 273
Rules 263, 270, 473
Split 266
Suggestions 262
Transfers 255
Uncategorized 263
Web Connect 274
Bartering 446, 572
Bid (Customer Bid) 102
Billable Expenses 376, 378, 395, 525
    Accounting Behind the Scenes of Pass-Throughs 380
    NSF Fees 218
    Time Passed Through to Invoices 384–385
Bills. *See Accounts Payable*
Budget 397
Business Type
    LLC 460
    Partnership 459
    S-Corps 459
    Sole Proprietors 391, 457

C

Cash on Hand. *See Petty Cash*
Centers 17
    Contractors 183, 453
    Customers 13, 17–19, 104
    Employees 524, 551
    Invoicing 18, 138
    Receipts 273–274
    Reports 300–301
    Sales 17
    Vendors 154–155
Certification xxiii, 603
Chart of Accounts 4, 25, 27, 45–47, 54, 92, 166, 345, 474. *See Accounts:Chart of Accounts*
    Account Numbers 25, 43, 46
    Account Types 46
    Adding Accounts 46, 172
    Inactivating Accounts 51
    Include Inactive 54
    Make Active 55
    Merging Accounts 52
    Modifying 48
    Reordering the Account List 55

    Subaccounts 49
Checks
    Bounced Checks 214, 238
    Check Numbers 113, 180
    Paying Bills 178
    Print Later 177–178
    Printing 178, 182
    Stop Payment 286
    Voiding 239
    Writing Checks 176
    Zero-dollar 444
Chrome 7
    Bookmarks 8
    Incognito window 7, 10
    Multiple Tabs 9
    Person Profiles 10
    QBO URL 7
    Refresh tabs 9
Classes 43, 71, 176, 397
    Not Specified 305
    Payroll, 513
Closing the Books 42, 199, 460, 463
Closing the Year
    Distributing Net Income to Partners 462
Cloud computing 2
Commissions 550
Company ID 21
Contra Account 449. *See Accounts*
Contractors Center 183. *See Vendors*
Credit Cards 172
    Entering Charges You Make 172
    Paying the Credit Card Bill 174, 236
    Reconciling Credit Card Accounts 287
Credit Memos 44, 207–208, 222
    Automatically Apply Credits 210, 223
Current Ratio 308
Custom Fields 70, 550
Custom Form Styles 19, 98
    Estimates 359
    Locations 78
Custom Orders 381
Customers
    Customers Center 17, 104
    Inactivating 109
    Job Costing 109
    Merging 110
    Notes 106
    Prepayments and Deposits 368
    Projects 108
    Setting up Customers 104
    Sub-customers 108
    Unearned Revenue 368

D

Dashboard. *See Interface; See Interface*
   Privacy button 15
Data Files
   Logging Out 12
   Opening Company Files 11
   Switching Company Files 12
Delayed Charges 224, 377, 395
Delayed Credits 224
Deposits. *See Bank Deposits*
Depreciation 448, 449–450
   Control Accounts 449
   Net Book Value 240, 449–451
Description 113
Discounts 81, 98, 114, 118, 127
Drawer 116, 359, 363, 378

E

Employees. *See Payroll*
Equity
   Contributions 459
   Distributing Net Income 461–463
   Distributions 459
   Owner Draws 391, 457
   Owner Equity 456, 477
   Owner Investments 457
   Retained Earnings 457, 459, 477, 483
Estimates 101, 358
   Creating Estimates 358
   Creating Invoices from Estimates 359
   Creating Purchase Orders from Estimates 365
   Estimates by Customer report 367
   Estimates & Progress Invoicing Summary by Customer Report 367
Exporting Data 334

F

Feedback 21
Fiscal Year 42
Fixed Assets 448–451
Forms 97
   +New button 22
   Custom Transaction Numbers 98
   Customizing 78
   Discounts 98
   Entering Data on Forms 22
   Expense 153
   Preferred Delivery Method 98
   Service Date 98
   Subtotals 118

G

Gear 20
General Ledger 4, 102, 358, 490
Grid Gear. *See Interface*

H

Help - Getting Help 29, 488, 515
Hourly Cost Rate 389

I

Interface 13
   +New button 13
   Business Overview 14
   Centers 17
   Customize 19
   Dashboard 14
   Gear 13, 20
   Get Things Done 14
   Grid Gear 54, 56, 110, 145, 154, 160, 191–192, 260, 316
   Hamburger 17
   Left Navigation Bar 13, 17
   Money Bar 18, 138
   More Button 19, 57, 133, 200–202, 286
   Print or Preview 19
   Revert 19
   Save 19
   Tabs 13
   Top bar 13
Inventory 100, 413, 482
   Account and Settings 416
   Adjusting Inventory 427
   Cost of Goods Sold 29, 64–65, 416–417, 427
   FIFO 64, 304, 415, 418
   Inventory Asset 29, 65, 416–417, 444, 513
   Inventory Products 62, 415, 417
   Inventory Qty Adjustment 63
   Landed Costs 444
   Perpetual Inventory 415
   Products and Services List 62, 417
   Purchase Orders 418
   Reports 429
   Revaluation 429
   Setup 413, 476
   Worth Tracking? 413
Invoices. *See Accounts Receivable*
   Applying Payments to Invoices. *See Receiving Payments*
   Invoicing for Billable Expenses 378
   Progress Invoicing 361
Invoicing Center 18, 138

J

Job Costing 109, 161, 164, 307, 357, 376, 444
    Labor Costing 390
    Reports 395
Journal Entries 206, 241, 304, 391, 441, 450, 483
    Adjusting Entry 442
    Opening Balances 477, 478

L

Language 106
Late Fees 231
Lists 67
    Center-based 25
    Importing 36
    Menu-based 25
    Merging 52
Loans 239
    Loan Payments 242
Locations 43, 71, 176
Logging in 10
    Switching Accounts 11

M

Make Deposits. *See Bank Deposits*
Make Recurring. *See Recurring Transactions*
Manage Users 83-84, 526
Markup 152, 377
Melio Bill Pay 172. *See Accounts Payable*
Memo 123, 177. *See Description*
Merchant Services. *See QuickBooks Payments*
Mileage 397
Mobile App 273
Money Bar. *See Interface*
More Button. *See Interface*

N

New Business - Start Date for 473
Non-Posting Entries 101-102, 156, 418, 525
Non-Profit Organizations 71
Notes 159

O

Opening Balance Equity 51, 477-481, 483
    Banking Feed 480
Opening Balances
    Account Opening Balances 477
    Directly Entering 478
    Entering with Journal Entry 478
Overshipments 425

P

Pass-through Expenses. *See Billable Expenses*
Payee 173
Payment methods 69
Payment Reminders 197, 228-229, 249
Payment Settings 125
Payments to Deposit 569, 573, 577, 581. *see Undeposited Funds*
PayPal 123, 135
Payroll 184, 488
    Adding Employees 495-498
    Auto Payroll 500, 507
    Chart of Accounts 490-491
    Connecting Bank Accounts 510
    Creating Paychecks 529
    Default Hours 500, 530
    Direct Deposit 495, 534, 536
    Editing Paychecks 537
    EE and ER 492
    E-filing 541, 546
    Email notifications 509
    Employees Center 524, 551
    Expenses vs. Liabilities 513
    Liabilities 541, 548
    Net Pay 532
    Paying Taxes 542
    Payroll Center 523
    Payroll Details Report 548
    Payroll Forms 489, 508, 544
    Payroll Schedule 529
    Payroll Summary Report 548
    Printing Paychecks 534
    Printing Paystubs 536
    Processing Checklist 528
    Reactivating Employees 552
    Replacing Paychecks 540
    Reports 533-534
    Setup 489, 493
    Shared Data 510
    Subscriptions 488, 523
    Supplemental Pay 536
    Support 537
    Tax Center 541, 544-547
    Tax Tables 490
    Terminating Employees 551
    Third-party Preparers 508
    Total Payroll Cost 549
    Viewing Payment History 548
    Viewing Tax Forms 548
    Voiding Paychecks 540
    W-2 476, 490, 495, 496, 544
    W-4 476, 489, 497, 524

Workforce 488, 495, 510, 543, 560
Payroll Items 490–491
   Accounting Behind the Scenes 489
   Benefits 536
   Bonuses 491, 500, 512
   Child Support 546
   Class Tracking 513
   Commissions 491, 550
   Company Contributions 492
   Deductions 492
   Employee Reimbursements 492
   Federal Taxes 492
   Federal Withholding 476, 492, 497, 504
   Fringe Benefits 519, 536–537
   Garnishments 546
   Hourly Wage Items 491
   Liabilities 490
   Local Taxes 492
   Medical Insurance 546
   Medicare 492
   Officer's Compensation 513
   Paid Time Off (PTO) 491, 532, 550
   Retirement Plans 504, 515
   Salary Items 491
   Sick Pay 501, 550
   Social Security Tax 492
   State Taxes 492, 506
   Tips 492
   Vacation Pay 491, 501
   Workers' Compensation 546
Petty Cash 133, 153, 182
Point-of-Sale (POS) systems 448
Preferences. *See Account and Settings*
Price Rules 57, 99, 401–404
Primary Administrator 463
Print Later. *See Checks*
ProAdvisors 43, 87, 299, 488
   ProAdvisor Program 12, 29, 123
Products and Services 27, 56
   Bundle 58, 65
   Categories 57, 59
   Importing 36, 57
   Inventory 58, 62, 413, 417
   Item Details 416
   Item Types 57
   Non-inventory 58, 60–61
   Preferred Vendor 60, 64
   Products and Services List 56, 417
   Sales Tax 67
   Service 58, 221
   Subcontracted Services 59
   Two-sided 59– 62, 165, 365, 381–382

Progress Invoicing 81, 102, 358. *See Invoices*
Projects Center 102, 357, 387
Purchase Orders 164, 365, 418
   Closing/Canceling 421
   Creating Purchase Orders 418
   Overshipments 425
   Receiving against Purchase Orders 420
   Status 420

Q

QBOA. *See QuickBooks Products*
Quick Add 112
QuickBooks Checking 532
QuickBooks Online Versions 83
   Accountant View vs. Business View xxiv, 17, 257
   Accountants 3, 11, 87, 203, 221, 306, 460
   Advanced 13, 45, 59, 62, 70, 84–85, 161, 218, 334, 365, 387, 397, 413, 460
   All QBO Versions 2, 525
   Essentials 183, 414
   Mobile 183
   Plus 59, 62, 161, 218, 365, 387, 397, 413
   Self Employed 453
QuickBooks Payments Merchant Services 69, 82, 85, 123, 135, 203, 213–214, 532
QuickBooks Products
   Desktop xix, 1, 12, 415
   Enterprise 415
   QuickBooks Online 1
   Subscriptions 2
QuickBooks Solutions Provider 123
QuickBooks Time 385, 389, 409, 488, 528
QuickFill 116
QuickMath 136

R

Receipt Capture 273
Receiving Payments 103, 125
   Partial Payments 125
   Payment By ACH 123
   Payment by Check 122
   Payment By Credit Card 123
   Payment Reminders 228–230
Reclassify Transactions 306, 442, 460
Reconciling
   Balance Sheet accounts 373
   Bank Accounts 276, 448
   Correcting Errors 285
   Finding Reconciliation Errors 283
Recurring Transactions 197, 203, 242, 256, 358
   Templates 203
Refunds 212–213, 236

Customer Refunds 211
Product Refunds 237
Refunding Credit Cards 212
Vendor Refunds 236, 264
Registers 26
Filtering 296
Reorder Point 63
Reports
1099 Transaction Detail Report 452
Accounting 299, 301
Accounts Payable 185
Accounts Payable Aging Summary 185
Accrual Basis 299
A/R Aging Reports 320, 479
A/R Aging Summary 140
A/R Collections Report 320
Balance Sheet 4, 29, 63, 118, 155, 242, 276, 308, 368, 545
Bills and Applied Payments 186
Business Management 299
Business Snapshot 317
Cash Basis 299
Collapsed Reports 49
Column Widths 308
Customer Contact List 314
Customize Button 326
Customizing Reports 325
Deposit Detail Report 322
Detail Reports 299
Emailing 331
Estimates by Customer 367
Estimates & Progress Invoicing Summary by Customer 367
Estimate vs. Actuals 397
Exporting Reports to a Spreadsheet 334
Filtering 325
General Ledger 310
Income by Customer Summary 323
Inventory Stock Status 431
Inventory Valuation Detail 434
Inventory Valuation Summary 433
Invoices and Received Payments 321
Journal 133
% of Income column 304
Open Invoices 121
Payroll Details Report 533, 548
Payroll Summary Report 548
Payroll Tax Liability 548
Physical Inventory Worksheet 432
Printing 332
Products and Services 50
Product/Service List 315
Product/Service QuickReport 430
Profit and Loss 15, 49, 119, 233, 394
Profit and Loss by Class 71, 305
Profit and Loss by Customer 162, 307, 394–395
Profit and Loss by Job 109
Profit and Loss by Product/Service 434
Profit and Loss by Tag Group 319
Profit & Loss 4, 118, 301
Purchases by Product/Service Detail 430
QuickReports 27, 51, 313, 430
Repeat Page Headers 332
Sales by Customer Detail Report 550
Sales by Customer Summary Report 323
Sales by Product/Service Summary 324
Saving Customizations 330
Smart Page Breaks 332
Statement of Cash Flows 309
Summary Reports 299
Time Activities by Employee Detail 396
Time Off 550
Total Payroll Cost 549
Transaction Detail by Account 327
Transaction Journal 424
Transaction List by Customer 323
Transaction List by Tag Group 319
Transaction List by Vendor 187
Trial Balance 311, 474, 483
Unbilled Charges 395
Unbilled Time 395
Vendor Balance Detail 187, 322
Vendor Contact List 314
Reports Center 300
Retained Earnings. *See Equity*
Rules. *See Banking Feed*

S

Sales 100
Sales Center 18
Sales Receipts 97, 101, 111
Sales Reps 70, 491, 536, 550
Sales Tax 76
Agencies 73
Calculating 76
Collecting Sales Tax 73
Defaults 76
Exempt 73, 76, 107
Nontaxable products 59
Paying Sales Tax 244
Sales Tax Liability 103
Special Tax Categories 61
Standard Rates 64
Search 20, 22, 296
Filter a Register 296

Setup 35
    12-Step Setup Process 471
    Accounts Payable Opening Balance 475, 480
    Accounts Receivable Opening Balance 476, 480
    Bank Statement for Setup Balance 475
    Closing Opening Balance Equity to Retained Earnings 483
    Entering Purchase Orders 480
    Estimates 480
    Fixed Assets 483
    Income and Expenses 481
    Inventory 476, 482
    Inventory Opening Balance 479
    Opening Balances 474
    Outstanding Checks and Deposits 475, 479
    Payroll 476, 483
    Payroll Liabilities Opening Balances 476
    Payroll Taxes 476
    Retained Earnings Opening Balance 479
    Sales Tax Opening Balance 479, 481
    Setting the Closing Date 484
    Start Date 473
    Trial Balance on Start Date 474
    Users and Passwords 84
Shipping 98
Shipping Address 105
Shortcuts
    Calculators 22
    Currency 22
    Dates 21
    Keyboard Commands 21
    Search 22
SKU Number 99
Square 123, 135
Subcontractors 59, 382, 384
Support 21, 29

T
Tags 72, 318
Templates. *See Recurring Transactions*
Terms 67, 116, 185
    Discount 232
Third-party Apps 2, 38, 52, 137, 414–415, 429, 460, 528
Timesheets 384, 525
Time Tracking
    Invoicing for Time 384
    Labor Costing 390
    Reports 395
    Single Time Activity 385, 525
    Subcontractors 384
    Tracking an Owner's Time 390
    Weekly Timesheets 385, 525

Tips 99
Transaction Journal 19
Transactions
    Copying 199
    Deleting 19, 200
    Editing 199
    Voiding 19
Transfers 182, 255, 264, 306
Troubleshooting 284
TurboTax 52

U
Undeposited Funds 101, 113, 129, 237
User Types
    Accountant Users 98
    Company Admin 397
    Primary Admin 397
    Time Tracking Only 526
Users and Passwords 83–87

V
Vendors 157
    1099s 183, 451, 454
    Account Numbers 158
    Adding New 157
    Also Customers 106
    Contractors 183
    Contractors Center 453
    Deposits 373
    Discounts 232
    Inactivating 159, 161
    Merging 161
    Overcharges 426
    Refunds 131, 236, 264
    Vendor Credits 185, 232, 234, 426
    Vendors Center 157
    W-9 452
Vendors Center 154
Voiding Transactions 200
    Bill Payments 201
    Checks 286
    Invoices 220

W
W-9s. *See Vendors*

Z
Zero-Dollar Transactions
    Checks 444
    Sales Receipts 444, 448